the perfect
acco

So next time that you are eating out, ask for and enjoy a jug of fresh water - a healthy and high quality alternative to expensive bottled water. It is the perfect accompaniment to any meal.

The Water Services Association is the trade association for the major water service companies in England and Wales

Illustrator: Jo Goodberry

Egon Ronay's Guides
Richbell House
77 St John Street
London EC1M 4AN

Managing Director **Christopher Lewis**
Editorial Director **Erica Brown**
Managing Editor **Angela Nicholson**
Editor **Nigel Edmund-Jones**

Leading Guides Ltd
Part of the Richbell NewMedia Ltd Group of Companies

Designed and typeset in Great Britain by Victorily Design for Bookman Projects Ltd.
Printed in Italy.

First published 1997 by Bookman Projects Ltd.
Floor 22
1 Canada Square
Canary Wharf
London E14 5AP

Establishments are independently researched or inspected. Inspections are anonymous and carried out by Egon Ronay's Guides team of professional inspectors. They may reveal their identities at hotels in order to check all the rooms and other facilities. The Guide is independent in its editorial selection and does not accept advertising, payment or hospitality from listed establishments.

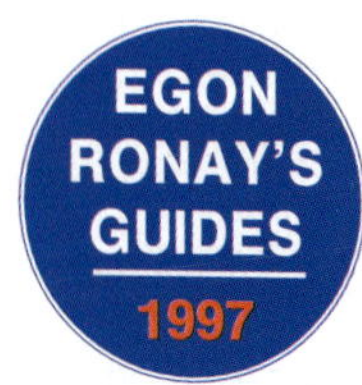

Egon Ronay's Guides Family Awards

This year's award winners are presented here. Full details of the recipients can be found on the pages indicated.

12 Merton Hotel
St Saviour
Family Hotel of the Year

14 Great House
Lavenham
Family Restaurant of the Year

16 National Trust
Tea Rooms
Young Customer Care Award

18 White Hart
Crowborough
Family Pub of the Year

Full Contents: Page 4

1997 AWARDS

CONTENTS

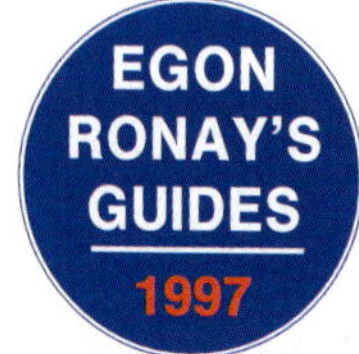
EGON
RONAY'S
GUIDES
1997

Introduction

by Nigel Edmund-Jones

Welcome to the 7th edition of our guide for families on the move. It recommends hotels, restaurants, pubs, inns and budget eating places that provide good facilities and good food for families with children of all ages. Entries in *...and Children Come Too* are collated from research for our *Hotels & Restaurants*, *Pubs & Inns* and *Bistros, Bars & Cafés* 1997 Guides.

Our Henry the Duck Awards highlight the best overall places for families (with both young and not-so-young children) throughout the country. New Ducks are awarded this year to the *Alton Towers Hotel*, the *Old Bell* in Malmesbury, *South Sands Hotel* in Salcombe, *Victoria Hotel* in Sidmouth, the *Trearddur Bay Hotel* on the Isle of Anglesey and to *Harry Ramsden's* new outlet in Cardiff Docks. See page 10 for all this year's award winners and map.

Are we going mad?

In a letter to *The Sunday Times* last year, a reader wrote: *'It isn't only in schools that children need controlling – it seems their noisy presence is polluting a lot of good hotels and restaurants, with the acquiescence of seemingly badly trained or helpless staff'*. The writer continues: *'Are hoteliers and restaurateurs going mad, or am I? There are surely enough suitable places for small children to eat without including first-class hotel cocktail bars, or quality restaurants at night? A proper training programme is required to ensure staff know how to deal with what is simply a management problem – keeping noisy or intrusive children and their parents where they won't disturb others'*.

Are there really enough places where children are treated as welcome customers? Egon Ronay's Guides have always respected the rights of owners to run their establishments as they seem fit, but there has been a wave of indignation from parents who have felt excluded or treated as second-class customers, in a manner that would probably never exist in most European countries where they have a tradition of eating out *en famille*. However, it is evident that the problem, more often than not, lies with the parents and not necessarily with the children. Hopefully, if the parents are kept happy then their attitude will be reflected in their children's behaviour. Nevertheless, hoteliers and restaurateurs (as well as parents) have to know where to draw the line.

Who needs kids?

Readers should note that, in the course of our research, many establishments listed in *Egon Ronay's Visa Guide 1997 Hotels & Restaurants* have stated a wish *not* to be included in the Guide as they are either 'busy enough already' or do not want to actively promote themselves to families (although they do cater for them). Thus, while many readers may think they have found a delightful family retreat and written to tell us about it, it may not be listed in this year's Guide because of the proprietor's specific wishes.

1997 Award Winners

The Merton Hotel in St Saviour, Jersey has undergone a transformation between the 1996 and 1997 seasons, so its choice as our 1997 Family Hotel of the Year (see page 12) seems entirely appropriate – the best has got even better! Half a million pounds has been invested in developing the public reception areas and various dining facilities, which now include 'Jersey Joe's' 50s' diner – an ideal, informal venue for families. The amazing 'Aquadome' water centre is probably well known to those visitors who have already visited Jersey, but readers who choose to holiday at The Merton will have it right on their doorstep as well as 'Dantés' night club, the 'games zone' for kids and the 'Star Room' cabaret room. Jersey's fair climate and its sandy beaches are major attractions and there are always lots of interesting things to do on the island, so why not make The Merton your base for a family holiday?

Our 1997 Family Restaurant of the Year Award (see page 14) is not such an obvious choice. Over the last few years we have chosen restaurants that go out of their way to attract a family audience, however, this year we have chosen *The Great House* in Lavenham for slightly different reasons. Here, you won't find any fancy children's menu but you will find the right attitude towards dining *en famille* and the sort of environment in which dining out with children can be a pleasure. It's an ideal, friendly place in which to celebrate a family anniversary or to simply enjoy Sunday lunch. Probably the best way to enjoy the Great House is to stay overnight as the restaurant's location and its bedroom suites make The Great House an ideal destination for a family weekend away. We hope that you enjoy our recommendation – we're sure that Régis and Martine Crepis will make you feel as comfortable as you would be at home. Their Continental attitude towards dining out with children is echoed at Raymond Blanc's new restaurant, *Le Petit Blanc* in Oxford, where the menu reads: 'children of all ages are not just accepted, they are welcome and we have created a special menu for them'; if only more restaurateurs would feel the same way.

Our Young Customer Care Award (see page 16) recognises the part the *National Trust Tea Rooms* play in setting standards that many tea rooms around the country could do well to emulate. They set minimum standards for young children in all their NT-run properties (not always matched by concession-run outlets); these now include the provision of high-chairs, bottle-warming, child-sized portions of adult dishes as well as a children's menu with special plates, bowls and beakers provided, along with colouring sheets with crayons. A jug of water is always willingly offered – as it should be everywhere, which is certainly not always the case. 'Trusty the Hedgehog' is the children's theme character throughout and he is entrusted with ensuring that every child enjoys his or her trip to a National Trust property.

Finally, this year's Family Pub of the Year Award (see page 18) is of the all-singing, all-dancing kind. *The White Hart* at Crowborough in East Sussex is a perfect example of individual pub enterprise, where Carl and Judith Martin have turned around the fortunes of a previously unsuccessful pub by changing a white elephant into a cash cow! They have thought of almost every conceivable entertainment feature to make sure that families are not only welcome but keep coming back; from the indoor and outdoor play areas through to picnic boxes, sugar-free drinks and the Wibbly Wobbly Farmyard mini-zoo, there is plenty to enjoy at this family pub *par excellence*. *The White Hart* and all the other pubs in this Guide will also be found in *Egon Ronay's 'Old Speckled Hen' Guide 1997 Pubs & Inns.*

Buyer beware

It is a hard job trying to write a Guide for every family requirement – readers may want to find a holiday hotel destination, to find an overnight stop en route to it, to find the ideal restaurant for a birthday celebration or just to find a simple pit-stop while shopping with Granny. A guide such as this can never *guarantee* that a hotel has enough cots or high-chairs (particularly at breakfast time) to satisfy all the families staying; neither can it guarantee that a pub's quoted 'family room' (where children are not permitted in the bar) has not been let out for a private function. Our inspectors regularly witness such occurrences but often give the establishments the benefit of the doubt after discussing the matter with the management. We urge our readers *always* to book in advance and to enquire whether private functions (weddings, funerals and so on) might change the character of your chosen establishment during a proposed visit.

Chain hotels & lodges

We have not included the vast majority of group-owned hotels in this Guide as they are generally well promoted and covered in thorough detail in our *Hotels & Restaurants* Guide. In particular, we recommend Granada's group of (former Forte) Posthouse hotels (Tel 0800 404040 for central reservations) for their good-value weekend packages and family bedrooms; however, since the takeover of Forte by Granada prices have risen and they do vary considerably across the country. Real value will be found in the big group's lodges: Travelodges (including former Granada Lodges, Tel 0800 850950), Whitbread's Travel Inns (Tel 01582 414341), Campanile hotels (Tel 0181-569 6969) and the relative newcomer, Holiday Inn Express; all these group hotels offer exceptional value for money for families and most are in convenient locations with easy access to the motorway network. If you're heading for Scotland you should look up the entry in the Guide for *Annandale Lodge* (Tel 0800 741174), an exceptional, modern lodge with stunning lake and country views, by the M74 J16 Blue Boar motorway service area in Johnstonebridge (30 miles north of Carlisle) – most unusual.

Broadly speaking

Egon Ronay's Guides' quest for excellence is on-going and continues throughout the year; we stand by our independent assessments and value our freedom from commercial compromise. However, we are also extremely grateful for the support of our sponsors: Visa, The Water Services Association and Morland 'Old Speckled Hen'.

We also value the contributions from readers who return the Readers' Comments pages from all our Guides; their input is invaluable and we urge readers to continue sending us their experiences, both good and bad. Please remember that if you find it necessary to complain then your best chance of satisfaction will come from discussion with the management of the establishment at the time.

We hope that readers who are looking for something a little different from undistinguished motorway service stations, catering-pack pubs, sanitised chain restaurants and tired holiday hotels will find our 7th guide for families, *...and Children Come Too*, an invaluable Guide.

How To Use This Guide

Order of Entries

London appears first and is in alphabetical order by establishment name. Listings outside London are in alphabetical order by location within divisions of England, Scotland, Wales and Channel Islands (including the Isle of Man). Readers wishing to visit Northern Ireland should consult *Egon Ronay's Jameson Guide 1997 Ireland*. See the contents page for specific division page numbers and the index for those of individual entries. Gazetteer entries contain references to the map section at the rear of the Guide (before the index). Map 13 E2, for example, refers to map square E2 on page 13 of the maps. Use this section to help select establishments in areas that you wish to visit.

Types of Establishments

Categories such as **H** (Hotel), **B** (Budget Hotel, mainly in London), **HR** (Hotel with recommended Restaurant), **RR** (Restaurant with Rooms), **R** (Restaurant), **I** (Inn with recommended Restaurant, **I** (Inn), **P** (Pub), **JaB** (Just a Bite) are printed within the header for each establishment. If a hotel features in *Egon Ronay's Visa Guide 1997 Hotels & Restaurants* then it is given the % grading from that Guide; several private house hotels, more modest London hotels (**B**) and country inns (**I**, many of which include 'hotel' in their title but are of a more modest nature than that title might imply) also feature in both Guides but are not given a grading as their range of public rooms is limited; nevertheless, good facilities for families are offered in all establishments.

Hotels

Prices given are high season rates and are accurate at the time of research but may well have changed by the middle of 1997. We urge readers to ask about weekend break prices as many hotels that fill up with business people during the week offer reduced prices at weekends; family facilities may also be extended at weekends and during school holidays. The price quoted in the header for each hotel entry is for a double room (occupied by two adults) with private en suite facilities and two cooked breakfasts; children's beds and cots may well attract an extra charge. The percentage shown is an individual rating arrived at after careful testing, inspection and calculation according to Egon Ronay's Guides' unique grading system. *The size of a hotel and the prices charged are not considered in the grading.*

Please note: *only* in those hotels that feature a separate entry for their restaurant do we specifically recommend the food for adults; children's meals are considered separately and, where information has been provided, details are given. Where a hotel's brochure says 'Egon Ronay listed' this does *not* automatically include the restaurant; there are many hotels in the UK where the food continues to disappoint but where the overnight accommodation is perfectly acceptable. Children may be easily satisfied with homely offerings such as fish fingers and baked beans but once they are safely tucked up in bed their parents have a right to expect higher standards.

Pubs

We include establishments where our team of professional inspectors recommend the good-quality *bar food* (not restaurant food). Reference may also be made to the pub's restaurant (see below), but our specific recommendation in this guide is for bar food and facilities for families, both inside and outside. Typical dishes, valid at the time of research, are usually listed. We indicate when bar food is served and also any times when food is not available. Times of restaurant meals may differ and are listed separately only when there is one menu served throughout or when we *do* recommend the pub restaurant food.

Where a pub offers B&B accommodation suitable for families we give the relevant statistics at the end of that establishment's story. The price quoted is for a double room with en suite facilities and two cooked breakfasts. If residents cannot check in at any time during the day then we print the appropriate check-in times; if it's advisable to arrange a check-in time (say, out of pub hours) when booking, we print *check-in by arrangement*. Please note that where bar food times are not given for B&B pubs we do not recommend the bar food in that particular establishment.

Many of the shorter pub entries are recommended for their atmosphere only – with no bar food or accommodation statistics – are recommended as interesting places for a drink (perhaps an ideal summer pub) rather than for their bar food or accommodation. Invariably these pubs offer outdoor areas where children can let off steam, and are thus a useful family 'pit-stop' or fresh-air destination venue.

Restaurants

Wherever possible we have given an indication of a restaurant's attitude towards children; some obviously attract families like bees to a honey pot, others may have a menu, room layout and staff attitude that offer more subtle attractions. Prices given in the header are for two people and include a *three-course meal for two including one of the least expensive bottles of wine, coffee, service and VAT*. Set-price menu prices quoted often do not include service, usually exclude wine and may not necessarily comprise three courses. Where two prices are given thus – £14.50/£17.75 – it indicates that there is a 2- or 3-course option; prices given this – £17.95 & £24.95 – indicates that there are two different set-price menus. Many restaurants and hotel dining-rooms now offer *only* a set-price menu, although this will usually include a choice. Vegetarians should always inform the establishment of their requirements when booking. Facilities such as the provision of high-chairs and children's cutlery have been listed where known. *We urge readers to confirm facilities that they require for their children when booking.*

Credit Cards

We list credit cards currently accepted by each establishment. If it is vital to your visit that an establishment takes a particular credit card then we suggest that you always confirm this information at the time of booking; credit card facilities sometimes change after we have gone to press.

Symbols

 **'Henry the Duck' award for outstanding family facilities**

 **signifies an establishment which will happily provide a jug of fresh water**

1997 Duck Awards

London

Chicago Pizza Pie Factory **W1**
Deals **W6**
Gourmet Pizza Company **SW19**
PJ's Grill **WC2**
Planet Hollywood **W1**
Smollensky's Balloon Bar & Restaurant **W1**
Smollensky's on the Strand **WC2**

England

Alfriston (E Sussex) **Toucans Restaurant**
Alton (Staffs) **Alton Towers Hotel**
Ashby St Ledgers (Northants) **Olde Coach House Inn**
Bassenthwaite (Cumbria) **Armathwaite Hall**
Batcombe (Somerset) **Batcombe Inn**
Bath (NE Somerset) **Bath Spa Hotel**
Blackpool (Lancashire) **Pembroke Hotel**
Borrowdale (Cumbria) **Stakis Keswick Lodore Hotel**
Bournemouth (Dorset) **Chine Hotel**
Bournemouth (Dorset) **De Vere Royal Bath**
Bournemouth (Dorset) **Swallow Highcliff**
Bradford-on-Avon (Wilts) **Woolley Grange**
Brightling (E Sussex) **Jack Fuller's**
Brighton (E Sussex) **Dig In The Ribs**
Brighton (E Sussex) **Dove Hotel**
Bristol **Café Première**
Bristol **Browns**
Cambridge (Cambs) **Browns**
Camelford (Cornwall) **Lanteglos Hotel**
Carlisle (Cumbria) **The Grapevine**
Carlyon Bay (Cornwall) **Carlyon Bay Hotel**
Chale (Isle of Wight) **Clarendon Hotel & Wight Mouse Inn**
Chester (Cheshire) **Francs**
Eastbourne (E Sussex) **De Vere Grand**
Evesham (Hereford & Worcs) **Evesham Hotel**
Felbrigg (Norfolk) **Felbrigg Park**
Great Bircham (Norfolk) **Windmill Tea Room**
Harrogate (N Yorks) **Bettys**
Higham (Kent) **The Knowle**
Hythe (Kent) **Hythe Imperial**
Ilkley (Bradford) **Bettys**
Kilnsey (N Yorks) **Kilnsey Park Garden Room**
Kingscote (Glos) **Hunters Hall**
Kington (Hereford & Worcs) **Penrhos Court**
Lavenham (Suffolk) **Great House**
Leeds **Salvo's**
Linwood (Hants) **High Corner Inn**
Louth (Lincolnshire) **Mr Chips**
Lytham St Annes (Lancashire) **Dalmeny Hotel**
Malmesbury (Wilts) **Old Bell**
Manchester **Harry Ramsden's**
Marlborough (Wilts) **Polly Tea Rooms**
Mawgan Porth (Cornwall) **Bedruthan Steps Hotel**
Mullion (Cornwall) **Polurrian Hotel**
Northallerton (N Yorks) **Bettys**
Norton (Shropshire) **Hundred House Hotel**
Norwich (Norfolk) **Norwich Sport Village**
Odiham (Hants) **Blubeckers**
Oxford (Oxfordshire) **Browns**
Poole (Dorset) **Sandbanks Hotel**
Porth (Cornwall) **Trevelgue Hotel**
Richmond (Surrey) **The Refectory**
Salcombe (Devon) **South Sands Hotel**
Saunton (Devon) **Saunton Sands Hotel**
Shanklin (Isle of Wight) **Hambledon Hotel**
Shepperton (Surrey) **Blubeckers Eating House**
Sidmouth (Devon) **Victoria Hotel**
Skipton (N Yorks) **Randell's Hotel**
Slough (Berkshire) **Spaggo's**
Snettisham (Norfolk) **Rose & Crown**
South Holmwood (Surrey) **Gourmet Pizza Company**
St Martin's (Scilly Isles) **St Martin's Hotel**
Stretton (Leicestershire) **Ram Jam Inn**
Studland Bay (Dorset) **Knoll House Hotel**
Swanton Morley (Norfolk) **Darby's**
Swindon (Wilts) **Blunsdon House**
Tetbury (Glos) **Calcot Manor**
Thurlestone (Devon) **Thurlestone Hotel**
Torquay (Devon) **Palace Hotel**
Ullswater (Cumbria) **Old Church Hotel**
Wantage (Oxfordshire) **Vale & Downland Museum**
Weston (Devon) **The Otter**
Whitby (N Yorks) **Magpie Café**
Whitby (N Yorks) **Trenchers**
Willerby (East Riding of Yorks) **Grange Park Hotel**
Woolacombe (Devon) **Woolacombe Bay**
York (N Yorks) **Taylors**

Scotland

Aviemore (Highland) **Stakis Coylumbridge**
Banchory (Aberdeenshire) **Raemoir House**
Crieff (Perth & Kinross) **Crieff Hydro**
Drumnadrochit (Highland) **Polmaily House**
Largs (North Ayrshire) **Nardini's**
Peebles (Scottish Borders) **Peebles Hotel Hydro**
Ratho (City of Edinburgh) **Bridge Inn**

Wales

Abersoch (Gwynedd) **Porth Tocyn Hotel**
Bodfari (Denbighshire) **Dinorben Arms**
Cardiff **Harry Ramsden's**
Holyhead (Isle of Anglesey) **Trearddur Bay Hotel**
Llanarmon Dyffryn Ceiriog (Wrexham) **West Arms Hotel**
Machynlleth (Powys) **Centre for Alternative Technology**

Channel Islands

St Brelade's Bay (Jersey) **St Brelade's Bay Hotel**
St Peter's Village (Jersey) **Star & Tipsy Toad Brewery**
St Saviour (Jersey) **Merton Hotel**

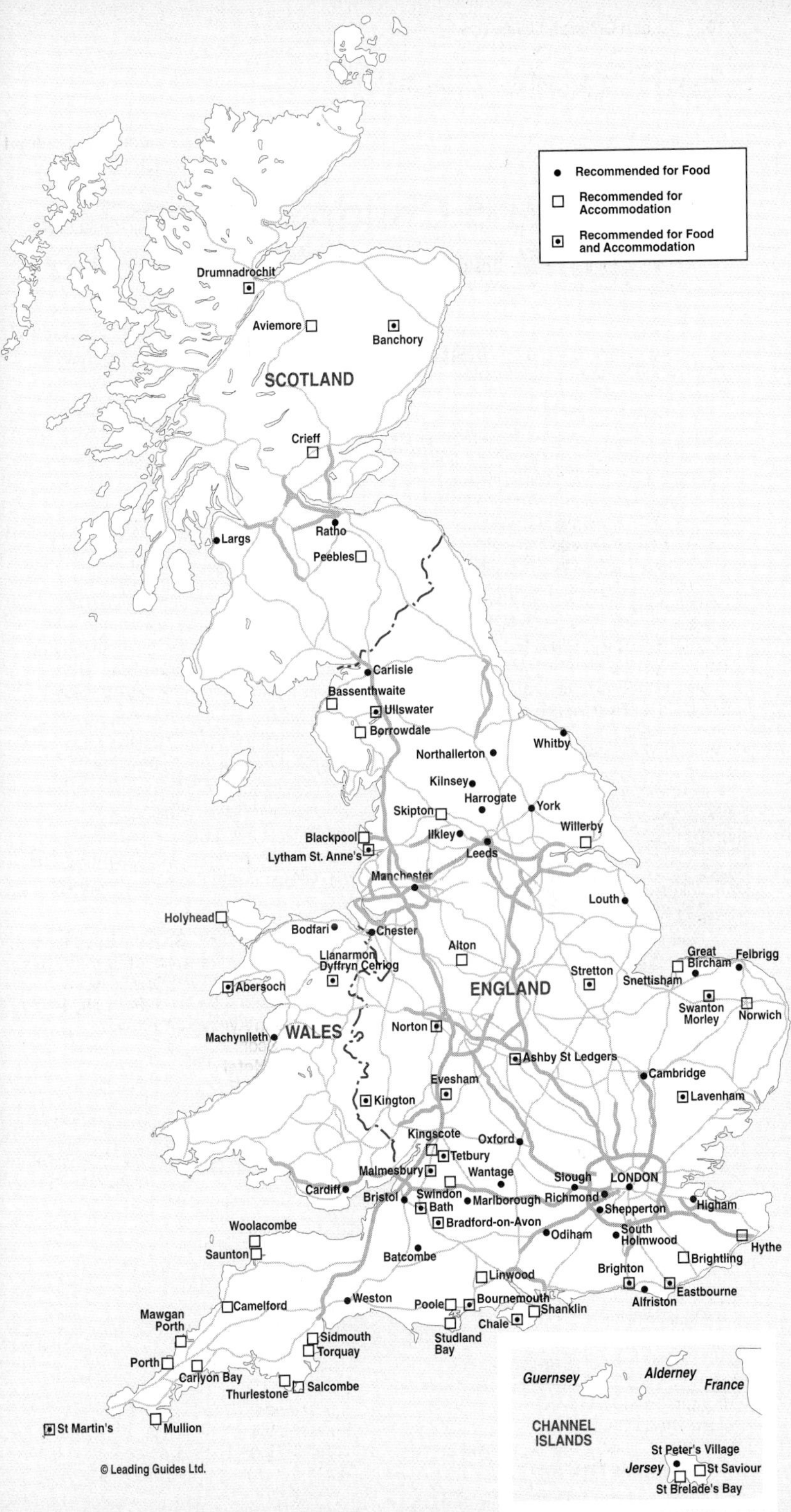

Recommended for Food
Recommended for Accommodation
Recommended for Food and Accommodation
SCOTLAND
Drumnadrochit
Aviemore
Banchory
Crieff
Ratho
Largs
Peebles
Carlisle
Bassenthwaite
Ullswater
Borrowdale
Whitby
Northallerton
Kilnsey
Harrogate
York
Skipton
Blackpool
Ilkley
Willerby
Lytham St. Anne's
Leeds
Manchester
Louth
Holyhead
Bodfari
Chester
Alton
Llanarmon Dyffryn Ceiriog
Great Bircham
Felbrigg
Stretton
Snettisham
Abersoch
ENGLAND
Swanton Morley
Norwich
Norton
WALES
Machynlleth
Ashby St Ledgers
Cambridge
Evesham
Kington
Lavenham
Kingscote
Oxford
Tetbury
Malmesbury
Wantage
Slough
LONDON
Cardiff
Bristol
Swindon
Marlborough
Richmond
Higham
Bath
Shepperton
Bradford-on-Avon
Woolacombe
Odiham
South Holmwood
Hythe
Saunton
Batcombe
Brightling
Linwood
Brighton
Eastbourne
Alfriston
Weston
Camelford
Poole
Bournemouth
Shanklin
Mawgan Porth
Chale
Studland Bay
Sidmouth
Torquay
Porth
Carlyon Bay
Guernsey
Alderney
France
Thurlestone
Salcombe
St Martin's
Mullion
CHANNEL ISLANDS
St Peter's Village
Jersey
St Saviour
St Brelade's Bay
© Leading Guides Ltd.

... and Children Come Too Family Hotel of the Year 1997

Merton Hotel

St Saviour, Jersey, Channel Islands

The most family-friendly hotel in Jersey's Seymour Hotel Group offers all the ingredients for a successful holiday *en famille*. Situated on the edge of St Helier, five minutes from the centre of town, its amazing, all-weather Aquadome water leisure centre is the major attraction. Here, there's a vast outdoor swimming pool and supervised indoor pools with slides of all sizes, cascade pools, water cannon and children's boats plus a toddler's pool, play pen and changing facilities. Among the 304 bedrooms are nearly 60 family rooms with an extra bed or bunk beds. Parents with babies and toddlers (and grandparents) will appreciate the lifts to all floors, the playroom with its own toilet and changing facilities and the fully supervised evening creche facilities (for 1-3s). Children's entertainers in the Neptune Club will keep 3-12s busy from 6.30-9.30pm. Teenagers head for the games room where there are pool tables and electronic games machines. Adults are offered squash, tennis, evening floor shows, dancing and a late-night bar, with baby-sitting and baby-listening both arranged. Jersey's east coast beaches are a short drive away and one of the island's most attractive parks – Howard Davis Park – is just a short stroll from the hotel. Informal eating places with child-friendly waiters attending children's mealtimes, dozens of high-chairs, room fridges, guests' launderette and full travel arrangements from the mainland are all typical of the attention paid to detail. Seasonal opening.

Awards

Past Winners

1996	**Hythe Imperial** Hythe, Kent
1994	**Trevelgue Hotel** Porth, Cornwall
1993	**Crieff Hydro** Crieff, Scotland
1992	**Woolley Grange** Bradford-on-Avon, Wiltshire
1991	**Saunton Sands** Saunton, Devon
1990	**Knoll House** Studland Bay, Dorset

Egon Ronay's Guides

Congratulate the

Family Hotel of the Year 1997

The Merton Hotel

... and Children Come Too
Family Restaurant of the Year 1997

The Great House
Lavenham, Suffolk

A little corner of France nestling in medieval England is an apt description of this lovely old restaurant with rooms. But where do families fit in to what might appear to be a rather adult affair? Régis and Martine Crepis have two children of their own and understand the needs of families well: 'we welcome guests of all ages, including children of course, and will make a determined effort to look after your every wish' – no hollow claim. Three high-chairs are provided (as is a room upstairs for nursing or changing baby); there's no special children's menu, but you only have to ask and suitable (proper) food will be produced, even at high-tea times if required – nothing seems too much trouble. The variety of menus covers snack lunches, good-value fixed-price menus, Saturday night à la carte and family Sunday lunch. In summer the restaurant comes into its own as there is a York stone-paved dining terrace and a walled garden with swings and a slide. Martine tries to keep youngsters involved during service and can produce crayons, little toys and books to keep them occupied. Upstairs are four delightful bedroom suites, one of which will accommodate a family of five; all have two double beds and a seating area; a cot and baby-listening are available. Lavenham has 300 picturesque timber-framed listed buildings and is arguably England's finest medieval town – an ideal destination for a family weekend away.

Awards

Past Winners

1996	**Spaggo's** Slough, Berkshire	1992	**Blubeckers** Odiham, Hampshire
1994	**Browns** Oxford & Cambridge	1991	**Toucans** Alfriston, East Sussex
1993	**Smollensky's On The Strand & Smollensky's Balloon** London	1990	**Bettys** Harrogate, North Yorkshire

Egon Ronay's Guides

Congratulate the

Family Restaurant of the Year 1997

The Great House

... and Children Come Too
Young Customer Care Award 1997

National Trust Tea Rooms

Throughout the UK

When it comes to catering for the requirements of families with young children, the National Trust certainly knows what it takes and have many years' experience under their belt. Their popular refreshment destinations are dotted across the country (see list opposite) and provide the ideal environment in which to enjoy an informal meal *en famille*. With both the young and the young-at-heart in mind there is always much to satisfy the palates of both the no-toothed and the sweet-toothed! Home baking is a theme that runs through all their catering operations and is undoubtedly the main attraction: excellent tea breads, scones (or unusual soft white yeast buns – 'splits' – in Cornwall) and tempting cakes are always on offer alongside good home-made soups and puddings. Youngsters with a vegetarian diet will always find something tasty on the menu and children's menus are always offered with either small portions of daily specials or the more ubiquitous offerings alongside the likes of gingerbread men, chocolate crispies and junior sandwiches. There are high-chairs, bibs, baby food, bottle-warming and baby-changing facilities in the National Trust-operated locations, and easy parking usually helps further lighten the load for parents. For those who are forever young (but may have arthritic hands) large-handled cutlery is provided; disabled toilet facilities are at almost every location. Lovely garden walks and interesting tours of the properties make a visit to any of our recommended National Trust tea rooms a delight for families. Note: some properties require an entrance fee for admission to the grounds; the majority of properties are closed in winter but some tea rooms open for reduced hours during this period.

Awards

National Trust Tea Rooms

Anglesey Abbey
Lode (Cambridgeshire)

Blickling Hall
Blickling (Norfolk)

Corfe Castle Tea Rooms
Corfe Castle (Dorset)

Edgcumbe Arms at Cotehele Quay
St Dominick (Cornwall)

Felbrigg Park
Felbrigg (Norfolk)

Lanhydrock House
Lanhydrock (Cornwall)

National Trust Tea Rooms
York (North Yorkshire)

Nunnington Hall
Nunnington (North Yorkshire)

Petworth House
Petworth (West Sussex)

Sail Loft Restaurant
St Michael's Mount (Cornwall)

Trelissick Garden Restaurant
Feock (Cornwall)

... and Children Come Too Family Pub of the Year 1997

The White Hart

Crowborough, East Sussex

Two years ago, the run-down White Hart – a large, mock-Tudor pub with a twin-gabled facade on the top of Crowborough Hill – was in a sorry state, but Carl and Judith Martin spotted the pub's potential as an independently-run family pub. So they started work on providing every conceivable family facility, from an indoor play area, complete with kitchen playhouse, video, chalkboards, multiplication tables and books, to a well-equipped outdoor play area (with bouncy castle, wooden fort, climbing rope, sandpit and baby swing) in the large garden. There is now much to satisfy the demands of today's parents: good bar food, and particularly good ales for the adults, along with baby food, a children's menu (including picnic boxes), vegetarian dishes, sugar-free drinks, high-chairs and a baby-changing area in the disabled toilet. The Wibbly Wobbly Farmyard mini zoo houses a menagerie of pygmy goats, rabbits, ducks, chickens, guinea-pigs and a pot-bellied pig. Dad, however, may be more interested in the Old Hen served at the bar! Summer barbecues and special holiday events are all geared towards entertaining the whole family.

Awards

Past Winners	
1996	**Olde Coach House** Ashby St Ledgers, Northamptonshire
1995	**Batcombe Inn** Batcombe, Somerset

THIS PIECE O
OPENS THE D
THE BEST HO

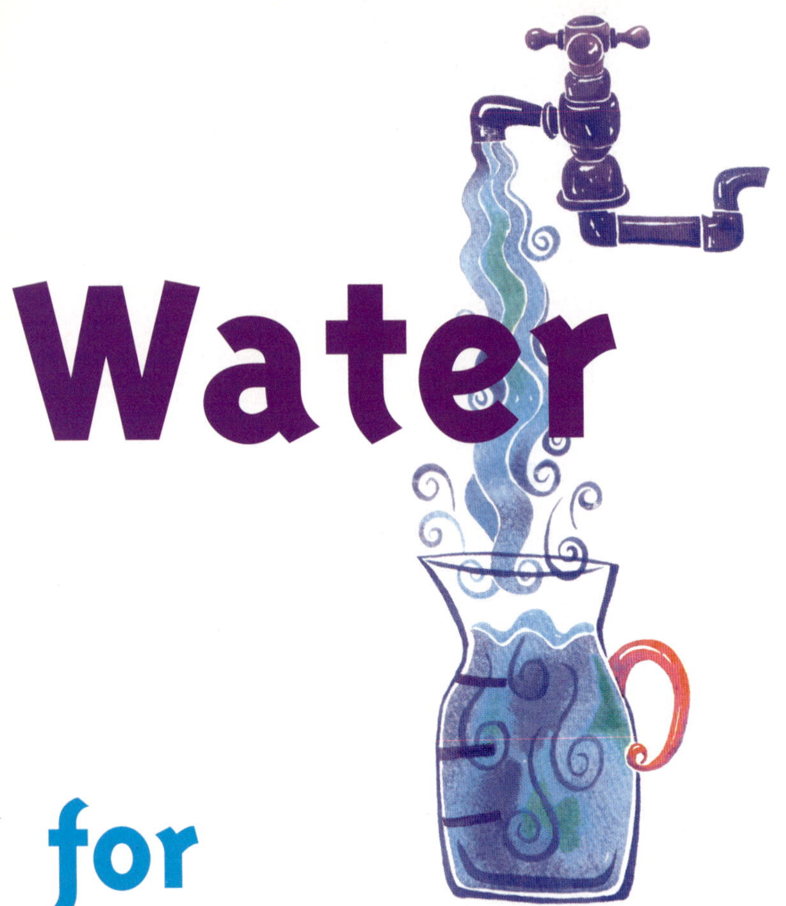

Water for Life

We enjoy very high quality drinking water in this country. It is the best it has ever been and is probably equal to the best in the world. Billions of pounds have been spent by the water industry to ensure that this is so.

Certainly nowhere in the world is quality monitored and results published so comprehensively. Last year 99.5 per cent of more than three million samples met all the British and European standards required of them. Of those that did not, none posed even a remote threat to health. These standards are set with very wide safety margins.

British water passes the taste test. A recent Gallup survey of people returning from abroad found two-thirds saying tap water is better in Britain. Only one in ten are happy to drink water from Spanish taps, for example, yet over two-thirds of us enjoy at least one glass of tap water every day and are satisfied, taste-wise.

But are we drinking enough? A normal adult eliminates around two and a half litres of water every day through perspiration and waste matter and needs to replace this fluid to keep the body in balance.

On top of the water obtained from food, nutritionists recommend at least two pints of water, plus other refreshments - more when it's hot, while exercising or during illness.

Increasing your intake of tap water may be the health and beauty boost your body needs - keeping your skin clear and fresh and your body in tip top condition.

For a free leaflet outlining the health and beauty benefits of water, introduced by Olympic athlete Sally Gunnell, telephone 0114 273 7331 or write to:-

Water for Life

WSA Publications

St Peter's House

Hartshead

Sheffield S1 1EU

THE ELUSIVE ALE AT LAST IN VIEW

(and thought of the heady pleasures that await spurs them on).

On finding The Coveted Ale.

Happy thought.~ "Our exhausting foxtrot through the fields, those daring leaps over thorny hedges, that close encounter with an Alsatian… all worthwhile. What a pint! See that colour, as rich as autumn leaves. Now savour that unique smoothness, the subtle blend of flavours."

"Our dogged pursuit of perfection has been amply rewarded in – of all places – The Farmer's Arms!"

BREWED BY MORLAND OF ABINGDON. EST'D. 1711.

WHEREVER

BE SURE T

THE BEST P

VISA

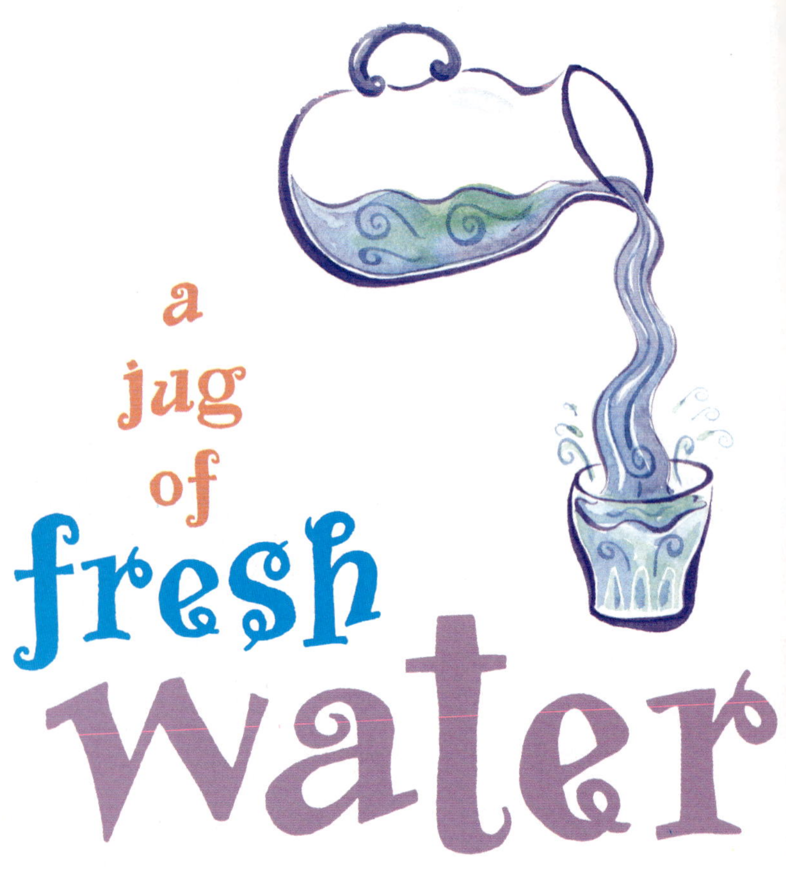

For a source of fresh drinking water with the highest standards of quality and good taste, look no further than the tap.

Served chilled, tap water is a refreshing and re-vitalising drink. It is perfect for drinking at home, at work, and also when eating out.

Our drinking water is world class. To ensure it is the best, tap water is quality tested and analysed millions of times each year. Over 50 stringent standards relating to health, taste and appearance must be met so that every glass of tap water is of the highest quality.

the perfect accompaniment to any meal

So next time that you are eating out, ask for and enjoy a jug of fresh water - a healthy and high quality alternative to expensive bottled water. It is the perfect accompaniment to any meal.

The Water Services Association is the trade association for the major water service companies in England and Wales

Illustrator: Jo Goodberry

FOUND! THE ALE THAT MAKETH THE MEAL.

London

NW9 Abeno £30

Tel 0181-205 1131 **Fax 0181-201 3022** Map 16 A1 
399 Edgware Road Colindale NW9 0JJ

A visit to Yaohan Plaza Japanese shopping complex, which is situated alongside the A5 well north of Staples Corner, would be incomplete without looking in on this splendid, family-friendly, simply decorated and spotless restaurant on the first floor. It's owned and run by Jonathan Brown and his charming Japanese wife who, together, offer the simplest of menus based on okonomi-yaki, which is a cross between pizza and omelette. Diners sit at hibachi tables and the okonomi-yaki are prepared before them. Ranging from £3.95 to £13.80 they are the perfect light meal made more substantial by the addition of noodles (£3.20) and a number of appetisers or side dishes (from £1.25). Dishes, many of which might be unfamiliar, are fully explained with further help always at hand from the extremely pleasant staff. Some of the dishes are especially designed for children and there are high-chairs for the very young. ***Seats*** *58. L 12-3 D 6-11 (all day Sat, Sun & Bank Hols 12-11). Closed L Mon & Tue, all 25 Dec. Set L £7.80, £10.80 & £15.80. MasterCard,* ***VISA***

N1 Anna's Place £50

Tel 0171-249 9379 Map 16 D2 R
90 Mildmay Park Newington Green N1 4PR

Every neighbourhood should have a restaurant like this! Don't expect designer elegance and hushed tones – it's much more intimate, with some 20 years' of life behind it and a genuinely warm welcome from the amiably eccentric Swedish-born Anna Hegarty and her daughter. In fact, all the staff are terrific. Use the restaurant for an intimate candle-lit dinner, a lively gathering, a lazy lunch in the patio garden, or just pop in for a plate of gravlax or herrings, or a speciality such as beef Strindberg (diced marinated beef in a mustard sauce with pickled cucumber) or roast pheasant stuffed with bacon, chicken and cashew nuts in a game sauce served with potato and parsnip gratin. Super ice creams and sorbets to finish, though trencherpersons will delight in waffles and blueberries. Fairly-priced wines on a sensible list. ***Seats*** *42. Parties 12. L 12.15-2.15 D 7.15-10.30 (Fri & Sat 7-11). Closed Sun, Mon, Easter, Aug, Christmas & New Year. No credit cards.*

W1 Arisugawa £60

Tel 0171-636 8913 **Fax 0171-323 4237** Map 18 D2 
27 Percy Street W1P 9FF

A smart and formal basement restaurant with a stylish modern decor and an extensive menu of beautifully prepared and presented Japanese food. Familiar dishes sit alongside some more unusual dishes including those that could be considered an acquired taste. Dishes with *natto* (fermented soya bean) fall into the latter category, their extremely slimy nature considered off-putting by some. The set meals include a vegetarian option and it's far better to explore the carte, which offers dishes such as salted cuttlefish, spinach with bonito flakes, diced fried pork on a skewer and a lengthy list of sushi. Teppan cuisine is offered in the ground-floor room, traditional Japanese in the basement. ***Seats*** *120. Parties 15. Private Room 30. L 12.30-2.30 D 6-10. Closed L Sat, all Sun & Bank Holidays. Set L from £7 Set D from £25. Amex, Diners, MasterCard,* ***VISA***

JaB is short for 'Just a Bite'. The majority of these establishments are also recommended in our *Bistros, Bars & Cafés* Guide which features establishments where one may eat well for less than £15 per head.

SW11 B Square £60

Tel 0171-924 2288 **Fax 0171-924 6450** Map 17 B5 R
8 Battersea Square SW11 3RA

Square by name it may be but the decor and the food are definitely hip. The palest pink textured walls set off flying saucer-style circular steel lamps. Other striking features include a boat-shaped bar and a dining area split into several levels each guarded by very stylish knob-ended iron balustrades arranged like waves. The daily-changing menu offers a choice of one, two, or three courses. Look out for the £3 lunch (one simple course till 5pm) in the bar. The short, imaginative selection offers the likes of a saffron risotto (rather too *al dente* on our most recent visit), salt cod brandade with a dandelion and parsley dressing or warm chorizo with new potatoes and a red onion salad to begin, followed by seared salmon with spinach on a generous bed of Puy lentils, coq au vin with mash, mushrooms and lardons or pan-fried calf's liver with bubble and squeak and onions. Finish with a slice of very rich bitter chocolate tart with clotted cream, rum and coconut cheesecake or poached pears with red wine, crème fraiche and almond biscuits. There's a short but well-chosen wine list featuring a good choice of wines by the glass. ***Seats** 100. Parties 40. Private Room 40. Meals 12-11 (Sun till 10). Closed 4 days Christmas & 4 days Easter. Set menus from £9. Amex, Diners, MasterCard,* ***VISA***

EC2 Barbican Centre, Waterside Restaurant

Tel 0171-638 4141 Map 20 B1 
Barbican Centre EC2Y 8DS

The Waterside Restaurant offers counter-service food, attractively displayed and presented, and dispensed by friendly, helpful staff. Dishes – listed on a blackboard menu – might include baked salmon with couscous (£6.50), haddock and crab meat cakes (£5.95) plus a good selection of salads – often including roast vegetables with mozzarella (£5.35) and chicken with fresh herbs (£5.95). The focal point is the dessert counter, strategically placed in the centre to draw your eye to some tempting offerings. The dining-room extends to an agreeable terrace in the summer.
An addition this year is the Balcony Café on level 2, serving lighter dishes, such as chicken livers with cream, sage and sherry sauce (£3.85) plus freshly cooked pasta and pizzas (pasta with pesto and broccoli £2.95/£3.85). Choose parking levels 2 or 3 for easy access to the restaurants. ***Seats** 180. **Open** 12-3 & 5-8 (Balcony Bar 9am-8pm – Sun & Bank Holidays from 11.30. **Closed** 25 Dec. Amex, MasterCard,* ***VISA***

SE3 Bardon Lodge 56% £84

Tel 0181-853 4051 **Fax 0181-858 7387** Map 17 D5 
15 Stratheden Road Blackheath SE3 7TH

Just off the A2 and conveniently close to the A102(M), the hotel, which has easy access on to Blackheath Common, also offers cosy, homely comforts. Rooms are neatly maintained and all are double-glazed. There's also a quite separate annexe across on another road; here there's only limited service and guests have to return to the main building for the bar and breakfast. ***Rooms** 60. Garden. Amex, MasterCard,* ***VISA***

SW3 Basil Street Hotel 71% £210

Tel 0171-581 3311 **Fax 0171-581 3693** Map 19 C4 
Basil Street Knightsbridge SW3 1AH

There's a timeless quality to this very traditional and very English hotel, which enjoys a relatively quiet location off Sloane Street and behind Brompton Road. Its proximity to the stores and shopping of Knightsbridge makes it ideal for ladies, who can enjoy the peace and seclusion of their very own Parrot Club (no gentlemen allowed). The public rooms have an elegant and restrained country house feel and the bedrooms, all of good size and many with a sitting-area, have a delightful old-fashioned appeal. Children under 16 may share their parents' room free. Old-fashioned standards of courteous and obliging service include shoe cleaning, servicing of rooms in the evenings and 24hr room service. 24hr NCP car park within 100yds. ***Rooms** 93. Amex, Diners, MasterCard,* ***VISA***

W1 Benihana £75

Tel 0171-494 2525 **Fax 0171-494 1456** Map 18 D3 R
37 Sackville Street Piccadilly W1X 2DQ

London's third and latest Benihana opened in the autumn of 1995 in the former Italian Trade Centre on the corner of Sackville Street and Piccadilly. Picture windows look on to the striking, spacious interior, whose 10,000 sq ft include a feature bar, sushi counter and a series of walkways linking the various levels. The tried and tested Benihana formula is continued here, with diners sitting at semi-circular tables watching the knife-flailing chefs chopping and slicing and dicing and flipping and grilling on the hibachi grill. Apart from the hibachi complete meals (main dish, onion soup, prawns, vegetables, rice, salad, dessert and tea) there's an à la carte hibachi section, with Japanese hot and cold starters, and ice creams/sundaes/sorbets to finish. The lunch menu offers tempura, sushi, sashimi, bento box hibachi set meals (from £21.75) and a few international dishes. Short wine list, long cocktail card. Baby-changing facilities are provided within the separate disabled toilet. No price reductions for children. ***Seats*** *180. Parties 10. Private Room 10. L 12-3 D 6-11 (Fri & Sat till 12). Closed L Mon, 25 Dec. Set L from £12. Amex, Diners, MasterCard,* ***VISA***
Also at:
SW3 Benihana Chelsea 77 Kings Road SW3 4NX Tel 0171-376 7799 Map 19 C5
Closed 25 Dec
NW3 Benihana Swiss Cottage 100 Avenue Road Swiss Cottage NW3 3HF
Tel 0171-586 9508 Map 16 B3

We welcome bona fide complaints and recommendations on the tear-out pages at the back of the Guide for Readers' Comments. They are followed up by our professional team.

W1 Bentinck House Hotel £82

Tel 0171-935 9141 **Fax 0171-224 5903** Map 18 C2 B
20 Bentinck Street W1M 5RL

A small bed-and-breakfast hotel in a central yet quiet location north of Oxford Street. Bedrooms are quite large and comfortable. ***Rooms*** *20. Amex, Diners, MasterCard,* ***VISA***

SW3 Big Easy

Tel 0171-352 4071 **Fax 0171-352 0844** Map 19 B6 JaB
332 Kings Road Chelsea SW3 5UR

Describing itself as a corner of America in the heart of London – its general motto being 'dig in and get messy' – Big Easy is relaxed and friendly, and prides itself on being a family-orientated restaurant. An air of cheerful eccentricity extends to the enormous menu, which offers dishes as diverse as baby back pork ribs (£7.95/£9.95), a ½lb hamburger with fries, pickles and coleslaw (£5.95) and crab claws with honey mustard sauce (£9.95). Good-value soups and salads. Kids eat free – one per adult – all day every day. A bar offers traditional cocktails plus a colourful range of 'frozen' margaritas (from £4.45 per glass, £14.95 per pitcher). 'Kids eat free' menu (one child per adult, additional servings at £2.95), served all-day every day. Crayons, badges, colouring paper and a lucky dip bag are all part of the service. ***Seats*** *130.* ***Open*** *12-12 (Fri & Sat till 12.30), Bar 12-11 (Sun till 10.30).* ***Closed*** *25 & 26 Dec. Amex, MasterCard,* ***VISA***

SW3 Blair House Hotel £105

Tel 0171-581 2323 **Fax 0171-823 7752** Map 19 C5 
34 Draycott Place SW3 2SA

Neat bed-and-breakfast hotel in a smart location close to Sloane Square with quieter bedrooms at the back. Lift to all rooms. ***Rooms*** *16. Amex, Diners, MasterCard,* ***VISA***

NW11 Bloom's £40

Tel & Fax 0181-455 3033 Map 16 B1 R
130 Golders Green Road NW11

Little has changed at what is now the only Bloom's, since the original East End branch has closed. Chopped liver (£2.90), tzimmas (£1.90) and gedempte meatballs (£6.90) are perennial favourites, but nothing beats the superb salt beef. Service from suitably sardonic staff is so quick you can order course by course if you wish. Children's helpings and take-away service available. ***Seats*** *70.* ***Open*** *10-9.30 (Fri till 3, 2 in winter).* ***Closed*** *D Fri, all Sat & Jewish Holidays. Amex, Diners, MasterCard,* ***VISA***

WC1 The Bonnington in Bloomsbury 62% £108

Tel 0171-242 2828 **Fax 0171-831 9170** Map 16 C3 H
92 Southampton Row Bloomsbury WC1B 4BH

In the same family ownership since 1911, this hotel is conveniently located for the British Museum and the shops of Oxford Street. Spacious public rooms include a comfortable pine-clad bar, and the airy Waterfall restaurant/breakfast room, complete with a waterfall. Comfortable, modestly furnished bedrooms are all en suite, with tub and overhead shower. Under-14s share parents' room free. Four rooms are equipped for disabled guests. Air-conditioned facilities for up to 250 conference delegates. ***Rooms*** *215. Amex, Diners, MasterCard,* ***VISA***

SW18 Brady's

Tel 0181-877 9599 Map 17 B5 JaB
513 Old York Road Wandsworth SW18 1TF

Constantly busy in the evening, this bustling little restaurant offers fresh fish from Grimsby and Cornwall simply prepared to preserve all the natural flavours. The menu is written on a blackboard, so dishes change with availability, but starters could include potted shrimps (£2.75), half a pint of prawns (£2.75) or cod's roe paté (£2.95); main courses might be whole plaice (£5.35), Dover sole (£5.95) or skate (£5.55) – either grilled or battered, and served with good chips and various flavoured mayonnaises. There are generally some interesting specials, maybe swordfish or crab cakes. Treacle tart and apple crumble are popular desserts (£1.85). ***Seats*** *38.* ***Open*** *D only 7-10.45 plus L Sat & during the winter (please enquire).* ***Closed*** *Sun & some Bank Holidays. No credit cards.*
Also at:
696 Fulham Road SW6 Tel 0171-736 3938 Map 17 B5

> We endeavour to be as up-to-date as possible, but inevitably some changes to data and key personnel may occur at restaurants and hotels after the Guide goes to press. Prices should also be taken as indications rather than firm quotes.

SW3 La Brasserie £65

Tel 0171-581 3089 Map 19 B5 R
272 Brompton Road Knightsbridge SW3 3AW

Authentic French brasserie, almost opposite the Michelin building at Brompton Cross, with long opening hours and unpretentious French cooking. The day starts quietly, as the locals enjoy breakfast with the papers (ham and eggs with excellent frites £6.20). The choice soon expands to include the main menu, which is available from 10am to closing time. Soups (onion £3.75), escargots (£6.50), salads (niçoise £6.80) for a quick snack; boeuf bourguignon (£9.50), grilled sole with new potatoes (£14.90) or confit of duck (£11.40) for something more substantial. Good simple desserts. Half portions for children. ***Seats*** *135.* ***Open*** *8am-midnight (Sun 9am-11.30pm).* ***Closed*** *25 Dec. Amex, Diners, MasterCard,* ***VISA***

WC1 British Museum, Milburns Restaurant

Tel 0171-580 9212 Fax 0171-580 9215 Map 18 D2 JaB
British Museum Great Russell Street Bloomsbury WC1

Professionally run self-service café and restaurant on the ground floor of the British Museum. Drinks, sandwiches (from £2.20), cakes and pastries and a cold buffet are available all day, while a comprehensive lunchtime menu is served in the restaurant between 11.30 and 3.30. John Mcgeever provides some excellent dishes. All the food displayed is freshly made and beautifully presented. Afternoon teas (£4.95) are served from 2.30pm. Queues, although fast-moving, can be long after 12.30. No smoking throughout. ***Seats*** *Restaurant 160, Café 90.* ***Open*** *10-4.30 (Sun 2.30-5.30).* ***Closed*** *25, 26 Dec & 1 Jan. MasterCard,* ***VISA***

W1 Brown's Hotel

Tel 0171-493 6020 Fax 0171-493 9381 Map 18 D3 JaB
Albermarle Street Mayfair W1A 4SW

Afternoon tea, served in the comfortable panelled lounge, is a long-standing tradition here: finger sandwiches, brown bread and butter with preserves, hot toasted scones with clotted cream, home-made cakes and pastries, and a comprehensive choice of leaf teas. This treat will set you back £16. No denim allowed. No smoking. ***Seats*** *80.* ***Open*** *3-6. Amex, Diners, MasterCard,* ***VISA***

SE1 Butlers Wharf Chop-house

Tel 0171-403 3403 Fax 0171-403 3414 Map 17 D4 JaB
Butlers Wharf Building 36e Shad Thames SE1 2YE

Near Tower Bridge and just across the river from some of London's main tourist attractions, the impressive Butlers Wharf complex offers a wide variety of different Conran-owned eating venues. For those seeking a light meal the bar menu here offers a carefully prepared selection and an impressive river terrace. Soups such as leek and potato (£2.95) or curried smoked haddock (£4) or perhaps a bacon and tomato sandwich (£4.95) provide tasty snacks; fish and chips with tartare sauce (£9.50), chicken breast with mushrooms and mash (£8.50) or the chophouse mixed grill (£9.50) something more substantial. Sticky toffee pudding (£4.25) and Cambridge burnt cream (£4.50) are among offerings to tempt the sweet-toothed. On Saturday and Sunday from 12 till 3 there's a 2-or 3-course brunch at £13.50 or £15.75 with a drink (maybe a pint of Theakston's Best) included. A 12½% service charge is added to all bills. ***Seats*** *115 (+ 45 bar & 80 outside).* ***Open*** *12-3 & 6-11 (bar brunches only Sat & Sun).* ***Closed*** *D Sun. Amex, Diners, MasterCard,* ***VISA***

W8 Café Flo

Tel 0171-727 8142 Fax 0171-243 2935 Map 18 A3 
127 Kensington Church Street W8 7LP

A French brasserie chain, in the same ownership as *La Coupole* in Paris. The French atmosphere is accentuated by traditional posters and accordion music. The carte offers simple bistro classics: fish soup (£3.95), home-made terrines (£4.20) or onion tart (£3.50); steaks (from £10.25) and coq au vin (£8.95). These are backed up by blackboard specials, perhaps tomato and fennel soup (£2.95), lemon sole meunière (£9) or a lamb casserole with roasted garlic (£9). Standard desserts include crème brulée (£3.25), profiteroles with chocolate (£3.95) and various ices (£3.50). ***Seats*** *80.* ***Open*** *9am-11.30pm (Sun till 11pm). Amex, MasterCard,* ***VISA***

Also at:

334 Upper Street Islington Green N1 Tel 0171-226 7916 Map 16 D3
Open 9am-11.30pm (Sat & Sun from 8.30am, Sun till 11pm)

205 Haverstock Hill NW3 Tel 0171-435 6744 Map 16 B2
Open 10am-11.30pm (Sun till 11pm)

676 Fulham Road SW6 Tel 0171-371 9673 Map 17 B5
Open 9am-11.30pm (Sun till 11pm)
13 Thayer Street W1 Tel 0171-935 5023 Map 18 C2
Open 9am-11.30pm (Sun till 11pm)
26 Chiswick High Road W4 Tel 0181-995 3804 Map 17 A4
Open 10am-11.30pm
51 St Martin's Lane WC2 Tel 0171-836 8289 Map 21 B3
Open 10am-11.30pm (Sun till 11pm)
149 Kew Road Richmond Tel 0181-940 8298 Map 15 E2
Open 12-4 (Sat & Sun from 10am, Sun till 4.30) & 6-11.30 (Sun 7-10.30)

SW7 Café Lazeez

Tel 0171-581 9993 **Fax 0171-581 8200** Map 19 B5 JaB
93 Old Brompton Road South Kensington SW7 3LD

Close to Christie's South Kensington auction rooms, Café Lazeez provides good Indian cooking, mixing the traditional with interesting modern influences. The café menu (a shorter version of the main à la carte) offers the likes of pakoras (vegetarian, chicken or shrimp £4.95), shami kebabs (£5.45) or an Indian version of Welsh rarebit (£3.75). Main courses vary from a simple chicken jalfrezi (£6.65) to the 'house feast' of marinated meats, cooked in the tandoor (£12.85). There is a good-value two-course lunch menu from Mon-Fri (£7.50) offering a few dishes taken from the carte. Outside tables in good weather. Live music Wed, Fri & Sat in the piano bar. ***Seats*** *110 (+20 outside).* ***Open*** *11am-1am (Sun till 10.30pm), café menu till 7pm. Amex, Diners, MasterCard,* ***VISA***

N1 Casale Franco £60

Tel 0171-226 8994 **Fax 0171-359 5569** Map 16 C3 R
134 Upper Street Islington N1 1PQ

Sharing a cul-de-sac with a Citroën garage, the restaurant with its authentic rustic decor and courtyard tables captures more than a hint of Italy. The food, too, is quite authentic - a mix between a traditional trattoria and pizzeria. Chargrilled fish and meat and huge pizzas are the specialities. Arrive early or expect to queue. ***Seats*** *140. Parties 25. Private Room 35. L Fri-Sun 12.30-2.30 D 6.30-11.30 (Sun till 11pm). Closed L Tue-Thu, all Mon, 1 week end Aug & 1 week Christmas. MasterCard,* ***VISA***

SW11 The Castle

Tel 0171-228 8181 **Fax 0171-924 5887** Map 17 B5 P
115 Battersea High Street SW11 3JR

Tucked away in 'Battersea Village', a little off the beaten track, with a simple frontage almost consumed by ivy. Inside is a successful combination of bare boards and rugs and an eclectic mix of furniture plus a large open fire. Three rooms are all served by one bar and include a separate dining area, an open-plan main bar room and a high-ceilinged conservatory to the rear, opening on to a paved garden edged with plants. Food is taken seriously and the weekly-changing blackboard menu offers the likes of a freshly-made soup, roast leeks with egg and caper vinaigrette, corned beef hash, pumpkin and ricotta lasagne with salad, cod in beer batter with chips and tartare sauce, roast lamb with caponata, and poached salmon with ginger butter. Calvados-stewed plums with custard, grilled banana with chocolate sauce or cheeses from Neal's Yard Dairy to finish. The Sunday menu is simpler but still offers a good choice. An espresso coffee machine is another little touch that distinguishes the Castle from so many of London's more mundane pubs. Friendly staff serve well-kept Young's ales and around a dozen wines by the glass. *Open 11-11 (Sun 12-10.30).* ***Bar Food*** *12-3, 7-10 (no food Sun eve).* ***Beer*** *Young's. Paved garden, outdoor eating, occasional summer weekend barbecue. Amex, MasterCard,* ***VISA***

A jug of fresh water!

SE1 The Chapter House Restaurant

Tel 0171-378 6446 Map 20 C3 JaB
Southwark Cathedral Montague Close SE1 9DA

A church has stood on this site since Anglo-Saxon times, and makes an unusual setting for a branch of Pizza Express. But here it is, maintaining their usual high standards. The menu progresses from a basic margherita (£3.50) through marinara – anchovies, garlic, olives, tomato (£4.90) – to the unusual King Edward – with a potato base, four cheeses and tomato (£4.50). Extra topping items are charged at 80p each. A few salads are also offered: salade niçoise with baked dough balls £6. In fine weather ten tables are set out on an enclosed terrace. Pizza Express has branches throughout the country, which are too numerous to list. ***Seats** 100. **Open** 11.30-4. **Closed** Sat, Sun, Bank Holidays & 1 week Christmas. Amex, Diners, MasterCard, **VISA***

E2 Cherry Orchard

Tel 0181-980 6678 Map 16 D3 JaB
241 Globe Road Bethnal Green E2

This charming vegetarian café is affiliated to the London Buddhist Centre and run by a group of five Buddhist women. There is an excellent range of teas and a selection of home-made cakes to accompany them (sugar-free and dairy-free available). For those with a savoury preference there are salads, houmus with pitta bread (£1.75), chili bean pie (£3.65), Neapolitan stuffed peppers (£3.75) or Thai-style tofu and vegetables with coconut sauce and brown rice (£3.55) or perhaps an interesting home-made coleslaw with huso dressing (small £1.60, large £2.20). Unlicensed. £1 corkage. No smoking except at the seven outside tables. The Museum of Childhood is in Cambridge Heath Road nearby. ***Seats** 55 (+ outside). **Open** 11-7 (Mon 11-3). **Closed** Sat, Sun, Bank Holidays & 1 week Christmas. MasterCard, **VISA***

W1 Chicago Pizza Pie Factory

Tel 0171-629 2669 **Fax 0171-491 2821** Map 18 C2 JaB
17 Hanover Square off Oxford Street W1R 9AJ

Tucked away in the north-western corner of Hanover Square with a glossy red facade is one of London's original American pizza restaurants. Opened in 1977, it still attracts the crowds and nightly buzzes with noise and activity. Sited in a large basement, it is decorated with wall-to-wall posters of and from Chicago. Thin-crust pizzas (£6.25) are available but it's the deep-pan pizzas (£9.50) that are the mainstay of what's on offer. A good choice is 'everything and the pan' (£11.50) which has peperoni, sausage, mushrooms, onion, green peppers, tomato, oregano and cheese. Hamburgers, chicken sandwich, salads and stuffed mushrooms are among the other offerings, along with carrot cake and home-made cheesecake for afters. Our Henry the Duck symbol is awarded for 'Sunday Funday' when an entertainment programme is offered for 3- to 12-year-olds and accompanying parents (booking advisable). Face-painting, party-games and 'absolutely no computer games' is the order of the day in The Boardroom or Bar from noon to 5pm, while a children's menu (£7) offers pizza with mushrooms or ham or 'London's best' cheeseburger and fries with bottomless Coke (or Diet Coke) and 'build your own dessert' from the ice cream trolley. Watch out for the Wicked Witch of Chicago who makes regular appearances in the restaurant; children's entertainer Smarty Arty appears at 1pm,2pm and 3pm. Children are given a button badge and balloon with which to go home. Ten high-chairs, booster seats and nappy-changing facilities are all provided, as are crayons and paper for drawings to be entered into the CPPF Annual Art Show. Bookings are taken from 12-4.30 and two hours are allocated to each table booking during this time. No-smoking. ***Seats** 250. **Open** 11.45am-11.30pm (Sun 12-10.30). **Closed** 25 & 26 Dec. Amex, MasterCard, **VISA***

SW7 The Chicago Rib Shack

Tel 0171- 581 5595 Map 19 C4 JaB
1 Raphael Street Knightsbridge Green SW7

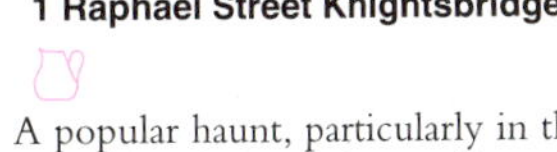

A popular haunt, particularly in the evening, when you may have to wait 15 minutes to be seated. Lunchtimes offer a similar menu to dinner, but at slightly lower prices. The dishes are supplemented by a few lighter dishes such as salads and sandwiches (Italian salad £6.45, barbecued pork sandwich £7.75). Dishes are straightforward and include rack of barbecued ribs (£7.95 half, £10.45 full), vegetable chili (£6.45), 14oz rib steak (£14.95) and barbecued salmon (£10.95), but most come fully garnished with coleslaw and buttered corn. Simple desserts include banana split (£4.75), Ben & Jerry's ice cream (£2.95) and the ever-popular mud pie (£4.75). Very much a family restaurant, with bibs (even for adults), fifteen high-chairs, booster seats, colouring menu, crayons and balloons provided; the background music is usually loud enough to cover any kid's scream of delight as they tuck into a messy rack of ribs. A children's menu offers child-size rack, burger, barbecue chicken or nuggets, plus soft drink and mud pie or ice cream for *£5.95.* Fold-down table in the Ladies for nappy-changing. Happy hour 5.30-7.30. Valet parking service in the evenings and Sat/Sun lunchtimes. ***Seats*** *220.* ***Open*** *12-11.45 (Sun till 11). Amex, MasterCard,* ***VISA***

A jug of fresh water!

W1 Chuen Cheng Ku £35

Tel 0171-437 1398 **Fax 0171-434 0533** Map 21 A2 
17 Wardour Street Soho W1V 3HD

Huge and long-popular Chinese restaurant in the heart of Chinatown, stretching through the block back to Rupert Street and up a couple of floors. Best value here are the dim sum (priced between £1.75 and £3.50), available between 11am and 5.45pm daily. Customers have to match photographs on the menus with the tasty morsels which are wheeled around on trolleys by smiling waitresses. It is easy to take too much from one vendor, not realising several more are bringing up the rear. The à la carte menu is extensive, and there are set menus from £19 for 2. ***Seats*** *450.* ***Open*** *11am-11.45pm (Sun till 11).* ***Closed*** *24 & 25 Dec. Amex, Diners, MasterCard,* ***VISA***

SW6 Ciao

Tel 0171-381 6137 **Fax 0171-386 0378** Map 17 B5 
222 Munster Road Fulham SW6 6AY

Popular sister restaurant to *Gavin's* in Putney. Lunch offers chicken, ham and apricot terrine (£3.60), layered salmon crepe with crème fraiche (£3.50) or home-made soup (£2.50) for a snack; roasted cod with horseradish crust and olive oil mash (£6.90), lamb's liver with bacon and onion gravy (£5.40) or varieties of their own pastas – perhaps fettuccine with basil, artichokes and sun-dried tomatoes (£5.70) for something bigger. An enlarged menu is brought in at 5pm, also bringing an increase in some prices. Sunday lunch 3-course set menu £9.50. Children's helpings available. ***Seats*** *80.* ***Open*** *12-11 (Sun till 10.30).* ***Closed*** *L Bank Holidays, all 25, 26 Dec, 1 Jan & Sun prior to Bank Holidays. Amex, Diners, MasterCard,* ***VISA***

NW3 Clive Hotel 60% £73

Tel 0171-586 2233 **Fax 0171-586 1659** Map 16 C3 
Primrose Hill Road NW3 3NA

Modern hotel close to Primrose Hill Park, with modestly furnished bedrooms which have the usual modern amenities. Children up to 12 stay free in their parents' room. Small free car park. Versatile conference facilities for up to 350. ***Rooms*** *96. Amex, Diners, MasterCard,* ***VISA***

SW3 Cliveden Town House £260

Tel 0171-730 6466 **Fax 0171-730 0236** Map 19 C4
26 Cadogan Gardens SW3 2RP

Reflecting the standards of *Cliveden* at Taplow (see entry), our 1996 Hotel of the Year, this is a town house hotel *par excellence*, comprising a pair of redbrick Victorian houses overlooking a garden square. Ground-floor areas with antiques, period furniture, fine paintings and objets d'art include a reception hall, a no-smoking drawing-room (venue for morning coffee and afternoon tea) with an open fireplace, magnificent floral display and a magnum of champagne (free to guests!), and a small library where breakfast is served if you don't want to eat it in your room. Bedrooms range from standard, superior and de luxe to junior and full suites. Most are air-conditioned, all are sumptuously and thoughtfully furnished (note the real bed linen, guests who prefer duvets need just ask), each providing a drinks tray, private fax and modem line, voice mail, satellite TV, stereo video and CD player – CDs and videos are available from a library. Striking bathrooms, with large overhead power shower, offer fine toiletries, own-design striped bathrobes (even a small version for children) and slippers, and, of course, there's a nightly turn-down service with a bed mat indicating the day of the week! Butler service, under the direction of experienced GM Michael Holiday, is exemplary and the choice from the room service menu (there's no restaurant) substantial. Children welcome (some rooms interconnect), charged at £25 per night (cots/extra beds/high-chairs supplied). Street parking. ***Rooms*** *25. Amex, Diners, MasterCard,* ***VISA***

SW1 Collin House £52

Tel & Fax 0171-730 8031 Map 19 C5 B
104 Ebury Street SW1W 9QD

A modest bed-and-breakfast hotel close to Victoria coach and railway stations run with pride by Dafydd and Beryl Thomas. Most of the quite comfortable bedrooms have their own private shower and toilet, but there are no TVs or phones. A hearty cooked breakfast is served between 7.30 and 9 which should stand you in good stead till at least lunchtime. No dogs. ***Rooms*** *13. Closed 2 weeks Christmas. No credit cards.*

Any person using our name to obtain free hospitality is a fraud. Proprietors, please inform the police and us.

W9 Colonnade Hotel 63% £90

Tel 0171-286 1052 **Fax 0171-286 1057** Map 18 A2 H
2 Warrington Crescent Maida Vale W9 1ER

In the heart of residential Little Venice, the Victorian Grade-II listed building stands across from Warwick Avenue Underground station. Owned and personally run for almost half a century by the Richards family, the hotel maintains an attractive, homely and friendly environment, helped along by Mouse, the cat. First-floor rooms are the biggest, but all are of quite good size and are kept in good decorative order with smart bathrooms. A good number are now air-conditioned. ***Rooms*** *48. Amex, Diners, MasterCard,* ***VISA***

W2 Columbia Hotel £65

Tel 0171-402 0021 **Fax 0171-706 4691** Map 18 B3 B
95 Lancaster Gate W2 3NS

Overlooking Kensington Gardens, the hotel is a splendid 'white wedding cake' of classic Victorian architecture with elegantly proportioned public rooms. Modestly furnished bedrooms vary in size but all have hairdryer, TV, mini-safe and direct-dial phones as well as en suite facilities; some enjoy great park views. There are four-bedded rooms and interconnecting rooms which are ideal for families; one room is adapted for disabled guests. No room service. Small free car park. The Windsor suite has a maximum capacity of 200 for theatre-style conferences. ***Rooms*** *103. Amex, MasterCard,* ***VISA***

W1 Concorde Hotel £90

Tel 0171-402 6169 **Fax 0171-724 1184** Map 18 C2 **B**

50 Great Cumberland Place Marble Arch W1H 7FD

Just north of Marble Arch and next door to the *Bryanston Court Hotel* under the same ownership, the Concorde offers neat, practical accommodation, each room with private bath or shower, TV, direct-dial phone and a hairdryer. Breakfast is served in bright, cheerful surroundings from 7.30 to 10am. Furnished apartments also available. ***Rooms*** *27. Closed 1 week Christmas. Amex, Diners, MasterCard,* **VISA**

Our inspectors *never* book in the name of Egon Ronay's Guides. They disclose their identity only if they are considering an establishment for inclusion in the next edition of the Guide.

W8 Costa's Fish Restaurant

Tel 0171-727 4310 Map 18 A3 **JaB**

18 Hillgate Street Notting Hill Gate W8 7SR

Behind the take-away fish and chip shop there's a licensed restaurant serving cod, plaice, haddock, skate and lemon sole in normal or big helpings (cod £4.70/£8.40, lemon sole £5.90/£9.90). A few simple desserts, such as baklava or ice cream, are available. ***Seats*** *46.* ***Open*** *12-2.30 & 5.30-10.30.* ***Closed*** *Sun, Mon, Bank Holidays & 3 weeks in July. No credit cards.*

W8 Costa's Grill £25

Tel 0171-229 3794 Map 18 A3 **R**

14 Hillgate Street Notting Hill Gate W8 7FR

This two-roomed restaurant has long been popular for its friendly service, reliable cooking and excellent value for money: the owners boast that few prices have changed for five years. Begin with houmus and pitta bread (£1.50), possibly the best in London! Follow with a house speciality – garlic sausages (£4.50), lamb on the spit (£5) or nephra (lamb's kidneys cooked with wine and onions £4.50). The whole place brings back memories of Greek holidays past. Costa's Fish Restaurant is almost next door. ***Seats*** *50 (+20 outside).* ***Open*** *12-2.30 & 5-10.30.* ***Closed*** *Sun, Bank Holidays, last 3 weeks Aug & 1st week Sep. No credit cards.*

If we recommend meals in a hotel a *separate* entry is usually made for its restaurant. Pub and inn entries include bar food details where recommended.

W4 Coyote Café

Tel 0181-742 8545 **Fax 0181-742 8498** Map 17 A5 **JaB**

2 Fauconberg Road Chiswick W4

Bright and airy Tex-Mex restaurant, offering freshly prepared food, way above the run-of -the-mill standard often encountered. Popular dishes include hickory BBQ chicken wings (£3.50), spicy crab and salmon fishcakes (£5.95) and the house taco salad (£4.50) as starters; Santa Fe chicken (£7.95), chargrilled chili burger with ranchero potatoes (£7.95) and chicken fajita (£6.75) – which is produced on a sizzling griddle accompanied by soft tortillas, tomato salsa and excellent guacamole. Margaritas are a speciality, produced ice-cold from a machine on the bar. ***Seats*** *45 (+36 outside).* ***Open*** *11-11 (Sun 11-3 & 5-10.30).* ***Closed*** *2 days Christmas. Amex, Diners, MasterCard,* **VISA**

W1 Cranks

Tel 0171-437 9431 **Fax 0171-287 1270** Map 18 D3 JaB
8 Marshall Street Soho W1 1LP

A long-established small chain of restaurants still offering consistently enjoyable vegetarian and vegan foods. Snacks could include fruit or cheese scones, croissants, Danish pastries (70-95p), a choice of soups with roll and butter (£2.45) and cakes – maybe carrot cake (£1.15) or cherry and sherry clafoutis (£1.95). More substantial dishes vary on a daily basis, but will include the likes of vegetable paella (£4.95), a filo parcel filled with leeks and curd cheese (£3.95) and penne with cream and sun-dried tomato sauce (£4.50). Dutch apple pie (£2.20) and strawberry brulée (£1.95) will appeal to the sweet-toothed. A short selection of alcoholic beverages is available at all branches except Adelaide Street. All are no-smoking restaurants. ***Seats*** *114.* ***Open*** *8-8 (Wed-Fri till 9, Sat 9-9).* ***Closed*** *Sun & Bank Holidays.*
Amex, MasterCard, ***VISA***

Also at:

9 Tottenham Street W1 Tel 0171-631 3912 Map 18 D2
23 Barrett Street W1 Tel 0171-495 1340 Map 18 C2
Unit 11 8 Adelaide St WC2 Tel 0171-836 0660 Map 21 B3
Open Sunday 12-6
17 Great Newport Street WC2 Tel 0171-836 5226 Map 21 B2
1 The Market Covent Garden WC2 Tel 0171-379 6508 Map 21 B2
Open Sunday 10-8

W2 Craven Gardens Hotel £66

Tel 0171-262 3167 **Fax 0171-262 2083** Map 18 B3 B
16 Leinster Terrace W2 3ES

Comfortable bed-and-breakfast hotel in a residential street just off Bayswater Road, handy for Hyde Park and the West End. Refurbished bedrooms now all offer TV, tea/coffee-making facilities, direct-dial phone and en suite bathrooms. Children under 7 can stay free in parents' room. No room service. No dogs. ***Rooms*** *43. Amex, Diners, MasterCard,* ***VISA***

SW15 Dan Dan £50

Tel & Fax 0181-780 1953 Map 17 B5 R
333 Putney Bridge Road Putney SW15 2PG

Simply furnished modern Japanese restaurant with friendly, helpful staff who provide a selection of well-prepared traditional dishes including yakitori, sushi, sashimi and tonkatsu. For the more adventurous there's squid with natto and pan-fried beef liver with sweet miso paste, otherwise the choice includes pork dumplings, tempura and a selection of good-value set meals. High-chairs are provided. ***Seats*** *60. Parties 20. Private Room 24. L 12-2.30 D 6.30-10. Closed L Sat & Sun, all Mon, Bank Holidays & 1 week Oct. Set L £6/£10.50 Set D from £17/£25. Amex, MasterCard,* ***VISA***

W6 Deals

Tel 0181-563 1001 **Fax 0181-748 2266** Map 17 B4 JaB
Bradmore House Queen Caroline St Hammersmith Broadway W6 9YD

The original Georgian facade of Bradmore House (complete with sweeping stone staircase) belies the modernity of the newest branch of Deals behind it. The main, first-floor restaurant (up the steps) offers an eclectic, jokey menu which trawls the globe for inspiration (the Thai dishes are becoming increasingly popular); begin with Tong's Yum Soup (Thai hot and sour soup £3.25), spring rolls, sesame prawn toast, Balls Bros (spicy veal croquettes with mustard sauce £3.95) or taramasalata with crudités (£3.25) as a starter; Oriental salads (£6.50/£7.50), Deals' spare ribs (£10.50), Jamaican jerk chicken (£7.25), chef Tong's Thai curries (£6.95-£9.50 including vegetarian) or beefburgers (from £5.95) are among the 30-odd main courses. Sundays - for when our Henry the Duck award is given - see a magician and face painter on hand to entertain the youngsters from 1-3pm. Kids' Deals (for under-

12s) are always on the menu and offer Dealsburger (£4.25) and fishyfingers (£3.95) with fries, baked beans and 'all the ketchup you can handle' plus baby pork banger with mashed potato (£3.95); children's helping of ice cream £1.25, unless they can handle chocolate mud ('dark, deadly and Dealicious' £3.50) or hot sticky toffee pudding (£3.25). No great gastronomic heights are achieved - but none are seemingly seeked! On the ground floor, the Coca Cola Deals Café is aimed more at the fast-food and take-away market with a shorter menu (noodles or rice with chicken or vegetables around £4.75, salads in summer, steak sandwich, hot dogs, burgers) and early morning breakfasts (from around £3.50, £1 for a waffle: served 10am-noon Mon-Fri, 9.30am-noon at weekends). Afternoon tea is served all year. Six high-chairs and four booster seast are provided in the restaurant and there's a baby-changing unit in the separate, disabled loo. Deals is within the Hammersmith Broadway Centre, thus convenient for shows at the Apollo Hammersmith and Riverside Studios; NCP car parking is available on the south side of the Broadway Centre. ***Seats** Restaurant 105 Café 50. **Open** Restaurant 12-3, 5-11 Mon-Fri (to 11.30, 12-11 Fri, Sat 12.11.30, 12-10 Sun (Restaurant). Café 10am-8pm (9.30am-8pm Sat & Sun, to 11 in summer all week). Closed 3 days Christmas. Amex, Diners, MasterCard,* ***VISA***

Also at:

Deals Chelsea Harbour SW10 Tel 0171-376 3232 Map 19 B6

Deals Soho 14 Fouberts Place off Regent Street W1 Tel 0171-287 1001 Map 18 D3

SW5 La Delizia

Tel 0171-373 6085 Map 19 A5 JaB

246 Old Brompton Road Earls Court SW5

Excellent pizzas with various toppings on fine crisp bases (£4.90-£5.90) are the stock-in-trade of this modern pizzeria. Garlic bread pizza (£3) and delicious tomato bread pizza (£3.50) are on offer as well as some pasta dishes. Also at Chelsea Manor Street and Chelsea Farmer's Market, where there are seats outside. Minimum charge £7. ***Seats** 50. **Open** 12-11.30. **Closed** 25, 26 Dec & 1 Jan. No credit cards.*

W1 The Dorchester, The Promenade

Tel 0171-629 8888 Fax 0171-409 0114 Map 18 C3 JaB

53 Park Lane W1A 2HJ

Light meals are served in the comfort of the Promenade for both lunch and dinner, but for many years it has been renowned for its fine afternoon teas. The set version gives the best value, with a selection of finger sandwiches, scones with clotted cream and jam plus French pastries (£17.50, £23.50 with a glass of champagne). New this year is a feast of a High Tea, definitely aimed at grown-ups: a glass of champagne with finger sandwiches and scrambled eggs with smoked salmon to begin, then a choice of bacon and onion tart with crispy aubergines or chicken livers with spinach leaves and marinated wild mushrooms; the whole finished with pastries and tea or coffee. Booking for afternoon tea advisable. ***Seats** 100. **Open** for tea 3-6. Amex, Diners, MasterCard,* ***VISA***

W1 Dragon Inn £30

Tel 0171-494 0870 Map 21 A2 

12 Gerrard Street Soho W1V 7LJ

A window full of hanging roast meats catches the eye and whets the appetite at this very popular restaurant offering Peking and Cantonese dishes. A good range of dim sum is available between 11 and 5 (priced from £1.50 to £3.30); this includes standards such as spring rolls and sesame prawn toasts plus the likes of stewed tripes and chicken feet in black bean sauce for the more adventurous. Set menus, starting at £8, offer good value, and include one for vegetarians. A 10% service charge is added to bills. ***Seats** 200. **Open** 12-11.45 (Fri & Sat till 12). Amex, MasterCard,* ***VISA***

SW3 Ed's Easy Diner

Tel 0171-352 1952 **Fax 0171-431 3829** Map 19 B6 JaB
362 Kings Road Chelsea SW3 5UZ

One of four busy American-themed diners with tall bar stools round a curved counter. Mini-juke-boxes are placed at regular intervals along the bar (5p per play). The excellent hamburgers (from £3.95) are the main attraction, but additions this year include an extra selection of chicken dishes – including chicken baja, grilled breast with Emmental cheese and barbecue sauce (£4.50); and a chicken burger with mayonnaise and lettuce (£3.95). Chips (£1.55) and onion rings (£1.95) are charged separately. Also on the menu are hot dogs, salads, breakfast items and cakes. Milk shakes are the favourite drinks. Service always comes with a smile and often with a good line in back chat. No bookings. ***Seats** 32. **Open** 11.30-11.30 (Fri till midnight, Sat/Sun 9am-midnight). MasterCard,* ***VISA***

Also at:

16 Hampstead High Street NW3 Tel 0171-431 1958 Map 16 B2
12 Moor Street Soho W1 Tel 0171-439 1955 Map 21 A5
Unit S5 Brent Cross Shopping Centre NW4 Tel 0181-202 0999 Map 16 A1
Open 10am-8pm (Sat till 6, Sun 11-5)

SW7 Eden Plaza £73

Tel 0171-370 6111 **Fax 0171-370 0932** Map 19 B5 B
68-69 Queen's Gate SW7 5JT

A different name perhaps (it was called the Periquito Queen's Gate) but little else has changed at this colourfully decorated hotel close to the museums. Though compact, the bedrooms are attractive. ***Rooms** 61. Amex, Diners, MasterCard,* ***VISA***

Always ring ahead and inform establishments of your exact requirements when travelling with children. Unannounced can, sadly, still mean unwelcome.

SW1 Elizabeth Hotel £70

Tel 0171-828 6812 Map 19 D5 B
37 Eccleston Square SW1V 1PB

Convenient for the coach and railway stations, this neatly-maintained bed-and-breakfast hotel overlooks a garden square. Bedrooms are modestly furnished; all have tea- and coffee-making facilities and the majority have a TV and en suite facilities. The house's historical connections are well documented in the impressive collection of old prints and photographs that decorate the walls of the public rooms. Local, covered, car parking at very competitive rates (by arrangement). No dogs. ***Rooms** 40. No credit cards.*

SW15 Enoteca Turi £45

Tel 0181-785 4449 Map 17 B5 
28 Putney High Street SW15 1SQ

A relaxed, informal Italian restaurant immediately south of Putney Bridge. The cooking is modern with a menu based on regional dishes, each with a suggested accompanying wine from an outstanding selection of Italian vintages (these all have detailed tasting notes). Typical of the starters (all dishes change regularly) are fresh grilled squid with oyster mushrooms with a spicy dressing of fresh chili and ginger, crispy duck with white bean purée and radicchio, and artichoke heart filled with garlic, pecorino and mint. Main courses show the same levels of innovation: grilled breast of chicken marinated with chili, rosemary and garlic served with honeyed vegetables; roast breast of duck coated with thyme and black pepper and accompanied by a dry Marsala sauce. ***Seats** 40. Private Room 45. L 12.30-2.30 D 7-11. Closed L Sat, all Sun & 1 week Christmas. Set L £6.90/£9.50. Amex, Diners, MasterCard,* ***VISA***

E8 Faulkners

Tel 0171-254 6152 Map 16 D3 JaB
424/426 Kingsland Road Hackney E8 4AA

It's mainly take-away at this excellent fish and chip restaurant set in a parade of shops, but the eating area can be busy too. Groundnut oil is used to fry generous portions of fresh fish – traditional favourites like cod fillet (£6), plaice fillets (£6), haddock on the bone (£6.50), and rock salmon (£5.50), to halibut and Dover sole at £9.50. French fish soup (£1.70), jellied eels (£1.90), and rollmops (£1.15) are among the starters. A good-value children's menu (£3) offers either fried scampi or chicken nuggets, plus an ice cream or cola. Short wine list (or you can bring your own – corkage £2). ***Seats*** *60.* ***Open*** *12-2 & 5-10 (Sat 11.30-10 Sun 12-9).* ***Closed*** *Bank Holiday Mon & 2 weeks Christmas. No credit cards.*

SW1 Fifth Floor Café at Harvey Nichols

Tel 0171-235 5250 Fax 0171-235 5020 Map 19 C4 JaB
Harvey Nichols Knightsbridge SW1X 7RJ

Sandwiched between the tempting food hall and the main restaurant and bar, this café holds its own admirably on Harvey Nichols' fifth floor. Baby spinach salad with gruyère, avocado, bacon and croutons (£7.95), mussels with leeks, saffron and crème fraiche (£8.25) and wonton-wrapped prawns with chili jam (£5.25) are all light options, while more substantial dishes might include pan-fried duck breast with fried aubergine, pinto beans and thyme jus (£10.50) and roast rump of lamb in a grain mustard and parsley crust with braised cabbage and boulangère potatoes. Home-made cakes are included in the popular Fifth Floor Tea (£10.50), but may be ordered individually (£2.95). Bookings are only accepted for dinner, when there's live music. The Mother & Baby room (in the Ladies' powder room) is also situated on the fifth floor (next to the express lift) – so you're ideally placed for any kind of emergency! However, note that the café is a rather adult affair and no high-chairs are provided. The basement restaurant is now **Foundation**, where Mediterranean, seafood and yakitori menus are served. ***Seats*** *110 (+20 outside).* ***Open*** *10am-10.30pm (Sun 12-6).* ***Closed*** *D Sun & Bank Holidays. Amex, Diners, MasterCard,* ***VISA***

WC2 Food for Thought

Tel 0171-836 9072 Fax 0171 379 1249 Map 21 B2 JaB
31 Neal Street Covent Garden WC2H 9PA

This friendly self-service restaurant set on two floors is in an 18th-century building. Imaginative and varied vegetarian cooking is on offer for breakfast, followed by an all-day menu which changes every day. A spring visit included sweetcorn chowder (£1.90), a satay stir-fry (£2.70) and a cauliflower and dill quiche (£2) among its offerings, plus a good selection of scones, flapjacks and desserts. Excellent wholemeal bread. Dishes for vegans always available. In summer a few tables are set outside. No bookings and no smoking. ***Seats*** *50.* ***Open*** *9.30-8.45 (Sun 10.30-3.45).* ***Closed*** *Easter Sunday & 1 week Christmas. No credit cards.*

NW3 Forte Posthouse Hampstead 65% £121

Tel 0171-794 8121 Fax 0171-435 5586 Map 16 B2 H
215 Haverstock Hill NW3 4RB

A tall, modern hotel block a short stroll from the centre of Hampstead. Top-floor bedrooms offer splendid views; 30 Executive rooms are equipped with various extras, including mini-bars and stereo in the bathrooms. Half the bedrooms are designated non-smoking. Children up to 14 stay free in parents' room. Ample free parking. Brasserie with outdoor seating. ***Rooms*** *140. Amex, Diners, MasterCard,* ***VISA***

W1 Fortnum & Mason – St James's Restaurant

Tel 0171-734 8040 **Fax 0171-437 3278** Map 18 D3 JaB
181 Piccadilly W1A 1ER

The fourth-floor St James's restaurant is very handy if you're viewing pictures at the Royal Academy! Booking is essential, and the buzz of people and music from the grand piano lends the magnificent room just the right atmosphere. A wide selection of dishes is available for tea, though the set deals are best value (from £10.50, or £15 including a glass of champagne) with delicious sandwiches, scones with clotted cream, a pastry and tea. The restaurant is also open for lunch, offering dishes such as potato and bacon gratin (£4.25), lobster bisque (£3.25) venison terrine (£4.95), rare beef salad (£9.95), calf's liver and bacon with mash and onion gravy (£11.95) or chicken and mushroom pie (£8.95). Both the Fountain Restaurant on the lower ground floor (open – via a separate entrance – until 11pm for dinner) and the Patio restaurant (the best for families) on the mezzanine (9.30-5.30) offer tempting dishes for breakfast and lunch, including Fortnum's Welsh rarebit (£5.95), filled croissants and mozzarella salad (£7.75). The famous Fortnum & Mason Tea is available in both – but lacking the pzazz of the fourth floor. A mother's changing room, with full facilities, is situated on the second floor of the store. ***Seats*** *140.* ***Open*** *7.30am-11pm.* ***Closed*** *Sun, Bank Holidays, 25, 26 & 31 Dec & 1 Jan. Amex, Diners, MasterCard,* ***VISA***

W1 Four Seasons Hotel, The Lounge

Tel 0171-499 0888 **Fax 0171-493 1895** Map 19 C4 JaB
Hamilton Place Park Lane Mayfair W1A AZ

A relaxing feel to this hotel lounge with its comfortable sofas, panelled walls, leafy plants and a view over the rear gardens. Breakfasts – both Continental (£13) and English (£16.95)– are served until noon. Light meals, from club sandwiches (£7.90) to Oriental duck and mango salad with figs and kumquats (£13.75) and mixed smoked fish on warm blinis with caviar sour cream (£11) are available from 9am right through to midnight, and a short hot selection including roast lamb on toasted tomato bread with tapénade (£10.50) and hamburger with salad (£9.75) added at lunchtime and after 6pm. Traditional afternoon teas (from £12) present crumpets, scones, cakes and delicious sandwiches plus a vast selection of tea blends. Two high-chairs are provided; children's portions and a separate children's menu offer all-day sustenance for hungry beaks; they'll enjoy the milk shakes (fresh seasonal berries with vanilla ice cream £5.50) and are generally taken good care of. Nursing mums can use the excellent Ladies Room. ***Seats*** *60.* ***Open*** *9am-1am. Amex, Diners, MasterCard,* ***VISA***

We do not accept free meals or hospitality
– our inspectors pay their own bills.

N16 The Fox Reformed

Tel 0171-254 5975 Map 16 D2 JaB
176 Stoke Newington Church Street N16 OJL

There is a short printed menu of snacks and main dishes, but the blackboard specials are the real draw at this simple brasserie. Starters on offer might be Italian fennel salami with new potato and apple salad (£3.75) or smoked haddock with mustard and tarragon cream. Follow with a baked foil parcel of salmon with vegetables and herb butter (£8.25) or maybe potato gnocchi with Provençal sauce and salad (£6.25). Puds such as crème brulée (£2.95) or ices and sorbets (£2.75) complete the picture. Starters and desserts are available as light snacks all day and the main courses are on offer from 12 to 2.30 and 6.30 to 10.30. A delightful garden is open for alfresco dining in fine weather. ***Seats*** *40 (+20 outside).* ***Open*** *12-10.30.* ***Closed*** *25 & 26 Dec. Amex, MasterCard,* ***VISA***

N16 Francesca £45

Tel 0171-275 8781 Map 16 D2 R
226 Stoke Newington High Street N16 7HU

Francesca will be remembered by many as ***Le Soir***; few other changes are apparent, and the ownership remains the same. The food is a mixture of Continental and Oriental cuisine, so starters might include sautéed duck liver in a bed of salad; oyster mushroom salad, with garlic and white wine sauce (both £2.95) or grilled scallops in Pernod butter with parmesan (£3.25). Follow with breast of chicken with port sauce (£6.95), tuna steak with salsa verde (£7.55) or sirloin steak marinated in garlic (£9.50) – all main courses come with salad or vegetables. For those with room there are simple puds like banana mango fool, sticky date pudding or bread-and-butter pudding (all £ 2.55). A set-price menu offers three courses for (£9.95), with five choices at each stage. Booking is advisable, and essential on Friday and Saturday. ***Seats*** *46.* ***Open*** *6pm-midnight, also for lunch bookings during Dec.* ***Closed*** *Mon & 25-27 Dec. MasterCard,* **VISA**

N1 Frederick's £75

Tel 0171-359 2888 **Fax 0171-359 5173** Map 16 D3 R
Camden Passage Islington N1 8EG

Newly refurbished, new chef (Andrew Jeffs, formerly with Nico Ladenis) and new ideas, though happily owner Louis Segal is still around after almost 30 years in the business. His son Nick is also hands-on and you can now sit at the bar for a bite (perhaps a salade niçoise with garlic-roasted crayfish tails) and wash it down with a fairly-priced glass of champagne or a good choice of wines by the glass. The dining-area overlooks a pretty patio garden (where you can eat alfresco in fine weather), the perfect spot for some very competent cooking: a brochette of salmon teriyaki with spicy cabbage or chicken and foie gras sausage with spinach and truffle jus to start; breaded escalope of veal with garlic, lettuce and spicy tomato sauce or smoked haddock and asparagus risotto with poached egg as main courses. Several classic desserts might include creamy rice pudding, chocolate tart or tarte tatin with cinnamon ice cream. Service is first-class, the wine list terrific - many wines are personally selected from French vineyards by Louis himself. Note the fixed-price business lunch, early dinner menu and Saturday lunch kids menu. ***Seats*** *130. Parties 20. Private Room 30. L 12-2.30 D 6-11.30. Closed Sun & Bank Holidays. Set L £12 (2 courses) & £13.50 (Sat, 3 courses). Set D £12 (6pm-7pm). Amex, Diners, MasterCard,* **VISA**

SW1 The Garden Restaurant

Tel & Fax 0171-730 2001 Map 19 C5 
General Trading Company 144 Sloane Street SW1X 9B2

Very useful for the Sloane Square shopping area, in the premises until recently occupied by The Café de Blank, the restaurant is little changed apart from now being open only during shop hours. Reached through the shop, it serves a range of breakfasts from 9.30 till noon with a choice of croissants, brioches and breads, freshly squeezed orange juice and unlimited cafetière coffee, or toast with scrambled eggs, grilled tomatoes and mushrooms (£3.95), full English breakfast (£4.95), or perhaps a special of sausages with French toast and maple syrup (£4.25). An all-day menu offers home-made cakes and pastries, and a number of savoury dishes such as soup, smoked salmon or mixed salad. Lunch (12-3) is à la carte, with the likes of spinach and bacon soup (£3.50), an excellent country paté with cornichons and walnut bread (£5.95) and specials from the blackboard such as smoked Cheddar, avocado and tomato tart or warm salad of chicken livers, bacon and mushrooms (both £6.75). Desserts are typified by pecan pie and kiwi fruit and raspberry meringue roulade (both £3.50). For weary shoppers afternoon teas with home-made cakes provide a pleasant pause. Additional tables in the garden in summer. No-smoking room. ***Seats*** *52 (+34 outside).* ***Open*** *9.30-6 (Wed till 7).* ***Closed*** *Sun, some Bank Holidays & 1 week Christmas. Amex, MasterCard,* **VISA**

W6 The Gate Vegetarian Restaurant

Tel 0181-748 6932 **Fax 0181-563 1719** Map 17 B4 **JaB**
51 Queen Caroline Street Hammersmith W6

Located in a former artist's studio in Hammersmith, this agreeable restaurant tries hard to bring vegetarian cooking within the folds of modern European cookery and for the most part succeeds – so there's little in the way of nut cutlets! The monthly-changing menu could include wild mushrooms sautéed with garlic and white wine then grilled with fresh tomatoes and cheese, home-made ravioli stuffed with oyster mushrooms in a pesto sauce (both £3.90) or fresh asparagus with grilled polenta and truffle oil (£4.50) as starters. The main courses are just as interesting: possibly an Indian thali platter, with chick pea curry, lemon okra, vegetable pakora and smoked aubergine pilau rice (£7.50); a tortilla filled with black bean chili, served with grilled vegetables and guacamole (£7.50) or ricotta and spinach dumplings with two sauces (£8.50). A few excellent fruit desserts. Organic and New World wines available. Over half the menu is suitable for vegans. ***Seats** 50 (+25 outside in private courtyard). **Open** 12-3 & 6-10.45. **Closed** L Sat & Mon, all Sun & Bank Holidays. Amex, MasterCard,* ***VISA***

SW15 Gavin's

Tel 0181-785 9151 **Fax 0181-788 1703** Map 17 B5 **JaB**
5 Lacy Road Putney SW15 1NH

This restaurant has maintained its winning formula of good-value brasserie-style food, bustling surroundings and strong management. Starters range in style from salami with Italian pickles and ciabatta bread (£3.20) to crab cakes with peanut and sweet coconut salsa (£3.30). The house speciality is fresh pasta, perhaps with pancetta, wilted rocket, red onion, cream and parmesan (£6.20), smoked salmon, prawns and dill (£6.40) or more simply with a chili-flavoured tomato sauce (£5.50). Interesting main-course salads are joined by roasted cod with a horseradish crust with mash (£7.50), poached chicken with baby leeks with a pimento sauce (£7.50) or for real carnivores chargrilled rump steak with chunky chips (£9.80). Lighter dishes such as omelettes are on offer at lunchtime with a three-course lunch on Sunday (£8.75). Candle-lit in the evening. One room for non-smokers. ***Seats** 70. **Open** 12-3.30 & 6-11 (Sun till 10.30). **Closed** some Bank Holidays. Amex, Diners, MasterCard,* ***VISA***

W8 Geales £35

Tel 0171-727 7969 **Fax 0171-727 7969** Map 18 A3 **R**
2 Farmer Street Notting Hill Gate W8 7SN

Fresh fish delivered daily is the hallmark of this ever-popular fish and chip restaurant. The fish is listed on a blackboard and regulars include halibut, salmon, skate, plaice, haddock, cod, lemon sole and salmon fishcakes. Prices start at £4.75 and depend largely on the catch and the size of the portions. From time to time, more exotic ideas join the fray: try Thai king prawn rolls, deep-fried clams or even shark! Good batter coats the fish, which is then fried in beef dripping. Chips are the business. No bookings (except for parties), so the occasional wait may be necessary. ***Seats** 100 (+10 outside). **Open** 12-3 & 6-11. **Closed** Sun, Mon, Bank Holidays (and Tuesday after), last 2 weeks Aug & 2 weeks Christmas. Amex, MasterCard,* ***VISA***

SW1 The Goring 81% £195

Tel 0171-396 9000 **Fax 0171-834 4393** Map 19 D4 **HR**
17 Beeston Place Grosvenor Gardens Victoria SW1W 0JW

Continuing a tradition begun in 1910, this civilised, stylish, family-owned hotel maintains very high standards which are exemplified by meticulous attention to detail (repaid by the loyalty of its clientele) and an ongoing programme of refurbishment and improvements. At the helm are George Goring himself and Director William Cowpe, one or both of whom personally greet guests at lunchtime, setting an example that is followed by all the staff. Elegance and immaculate house-keeping ensure that any visitor here feels special, no matter how long or short the sojourn. Polished marble floors and chandeliers in the entrance set the style, which is maintained throughout, especially in the handsome air-conditioned bedrooms, some with balconies overlooking the garden, that have modernised bathrooms offering splendid fittings, fine toiletries and good towels. The bedrooms, properly serviced in the evenings, are watched over by the hotel's trademark wooden ducks, and though they have a habit of disappearing, a proliferation of sheep from Devon seems to have taken up residence! 24hr room service. Children up to 14 stay free in parents' room. Morning coffee and afternoon teas (3.30-5) are served in the Garden Lounge, with its big chesterfields and armchairs set around low tables. Tea is still an occasion here – finger sandwiches and delicate pastries are brought on silver trays for you to choose from and excellent home-made scones are served with strawberry or raspberry jam. Rich chocolate gateau or Goring fruit cake finishes the feast. A selection of teas, tisanes, hot chocolate and soft drinks complements the set tea (£9.50). A good selection of salads (Caesar £6.50), carpaccio of beef with sweet peppers and mushrooms (£8) and carefully-made desserts are available all day. Covered parking for seven cars (£15 per day). ***Rooms** 78. Valeting. Amex, Diners, MasterCard,* **VISA**

Restaurant £95

An elegant and formal dining-room is the setting for John Elliott's classically-based fixed-price menus. Traditional English fare features prominently, as in a daily lunchtime special of roast leg of English lamb followed by steamed chocolate sponge pudding with a white chocolate sauce. The extensive dinner menu offers dishes such as steak and kidney pie, braised oxtail wrapped in Savoy cabbage and salmon fishcakes with a sorrel sauce. More modern items could be a fillet of sea bream with crispy Parma ham and a piquant tomato sauce or a vegetarian option of tagliatelle with shiitake mushrooms, sun-dried tomatoes and pesto. ***Seats** 65. Parties 10. Private Room 12. L 12.30-2.30 D 6-10. Set L £20/£24 Set D £30.*

SE1 The Gourmet Pizza Company

Tel 0171-928 3188 **Fax 0171-401 8583** Map 20 B3 
Gabriels Wharf 56 Upper Ground Southwark SE1 9PP

This busy pizzeria on the banks of the Thames enjoys a lively atmosphere enhanced by the open-plan kitchen which enables diners to watch their food being prepared. Some of the best pizzas in town (from £4.70) are to be had, with such imaginative toppings as wild mushrooms, Californian vegetable and camembert as well as the more traditional standards. A small selection of starters and salads might include antipasto – sun-dried tomatoes, grilled artichokes, salami and olives (£4.30), spinach, bacon and garlic salad (£2.95) and avocado, pine kernels with mixed leaves (£3.35). Those who prefer pasta can choose from four or five dishes (from £5.95). Puddings are good too, choose from ice creams, chocolate fudge cake and raspberry and almond tart (all £3.05). A post-prandial wander around the art and crafts shops in the complex aids digestion. Ten high-chairs provided along with separate baby-changing facilities and disabled toilet. Children's entertainers feature on Sundays from 12.30-2.30pm. Children's-size pizzas and pasta dishes on the menu. ***Seats** 82. **Open** 12-10.45 (Sun till 10.30). **Closed** 24-26 Dec.*

Also at:

18-20 McKenzie Walk Canary Wharf E14 Tel 0171-712 9192 Map 17 D4

The 1929 Building Merton Abbey Mills Watermills Way SW19 Tel 0181-545 0310 Map 17 C6

7-9 Swallow Street W1 Tel 0171-734 5182 Map 18 D3

The latest branch has now opened just off Regent Street.

Branches also in South Holmwood (nr Dorking, Surrey) & Oxford.

W1 Govindas

Tel 0171-437 4928 **Fax 0171-437 5875** Map 21 A1 JaB
9/10 Soho Street Soho W1V 5DA

Off Soho Square, just south of Oxford Street, this vegetarian restaurant is owned by the International Krishna Organisation. Some dishes are vegan and the kitchen uses no onions, garlic or mushrooms. Despite these apparent limitations the food is full of flavour. Choose from a selection of salads (£2/£3.75), pakoras – cauliflower deep-fried in batter (£1.25/£1.95) or lasagne (£3.50, £4.50 with a salad). Desserts (£1.75) range from apple crumble and crème caramel to a slice of vegan fruit cake. An all you can eat buffet is available Monday-Friday between 12 and 8 (£4.99). Natural juices and about 20 different herbal teas are available. No smoking. Unlicensed. ***Seats*** *75.* ***Open*** *12-8.* ***Closed*** *Sun, 25 Dec, 1 Jan & some other Bank Holidays. No credit cards.*

W1 The Granary

Tel 0171-493 2978 Map 18 D3 JaB
39 Albermarle Street off Piccadilly W1X 3FD

Deservedly as popular as ever, this excellent and unpretentious self-service restaurant has its dishes advertised on a blackboard. Although meat-eaters are not forgotten – with dishes such as Moroccan lamb casserole (£7.90), the real strength is in their vegetarian offerings: stuffed avocado with prawns and cheese, farfalle pasta with sun-dried tomatoes or maybe mozzarella-stuffed aubergines (all priced between £7 and £8). There are also plenty of attractive salads on offer. In an expensive area, it is one of the best value-for-money addresses in the Guide. Half-portions for children. Patio for fine-weather eating. ***Seats*** *100 (+16 outside).* ***Open*** *11.30-7.30 (Sat & Sun 12-4).* ***Closed*** *24-26 Dec. No credit cards.*

N1 Great Northern Hotel 60% £89

Tel 0171-837 5454 **Fax 0171-278 5270** Map 16 C3 H
Kings Cross N1 9AN

London's first purpose-built hotel, opened in 1854, stands in the forecourt facing Kings Cross main-line station. St Pancras is across the road. Improvements are continuing to upgrade the accommodation which now offers all rooms en suite. All have satellite TV. Children under 14 share parents' room free. Function facilities for 100 in 11 meeting rooms. Private parking limited to 12 spaces. No dogs. ***Rooms*** *78. Coffee shop 7am-10pm (Sat & Sun 8am-9pm). Closed 25-27 Dec. Amex, Diners, MasterCard,* ***VISA***

Many hotels offer reduced rates for weekend or out-of-season bookings. Always ask about special deals and family rooms.

NW8 Greek Valley £40

Tel 0171-624 3217 Map 16 B3 
130 Boundary Road St John's Wood NW8 ORH

Prices are still as reasonable as ever at this excellent and popular Greek-Cypriot restaurant next to the Saatchi gallery. Start with taramasalata (£1.75), tiropittes – fried cheese pastries (£2), or home-made lamb sausages (£2); perhaps follow with lamb and chicken kebabs (£6.50), stuffed vine leaves (£5.95) or their excellent moussaka (£5.95). Particularly good value set meals (2 courses – £7.50, 3 courses £7.95). Live music every Friday from 8pm .There is a more informal café, under the same ownership (*Café 100* – see entry) just along the road. ***Seats*** *62.* ***Open*** *D only 6-12.* ***Closed*** *Sun (except parties by arrangement). MasterCard,* ***VISA***

SW1 Green's Restaurant & Oyster Bar

Tel 0171-930 4566 **Fax 0171-930 2958** Map 18 D3 JaB
36 Duke Street St James's SW1Y 6DF

Tradition reigns supreme in this clubland address with separate bar and restaurant menus. From the bar come splendid sandwiches such as smoked salmon or fresh Dorset crab (from £5) along with Galway Bay rock oysters, (£7.50), native oysters in season (£9.75) and potted shrimps (£7). Other options might include salmon fishcakes with tomato sauce (£9.75) or calf's liver with bacon, mash and onion gravy (£13). Carefully cooked fish and chips (£9.50) and a selection of cheeses from Paxton & Whitfield (£6) are also offered. Aberdeen Angus is the only beef used and Sunday lunch includes it with all the trimmings. ***Seats*** *90.* ***Open*** *11.30-3 & 5.30-11.* ***Closed*** *Sun (except during the native oyster season), 25 & 26 Dec, 1 Jan. Amex, Diners, MasterCard,* ***VISA***

SW3 Grill St Quentin £65

Tel 0171-581 8377 **Fax 0171-584 6064** Map 19 B4 
3 Yeoman's Row Knightsbridge SW3 2AL

Entering here is like being transported to a stylish Parisian brasserie. Occupying a smart, spacious basement with very charming staff to provide exemplary service, this is one of Knightsbridge's hidden gems. The menu runs through the classic repertoire including goose rillettes, roasted goat's cheese salad and duck foie gras terrine among the starters. A prominent feature is the splendid selection of shellfish. Main courses include grilled halibut with spinach, veal cutlet with rosemary, and rib of beef with bone marrow. Round things off perfectly with the likes of lemon tart, prune and armagnac cheesecake or tarte tatin. ***Seats*** *140. Parties 25. L 12-3 (Sun till 3.30) D 6.30-11.30 (Sun till 11). Set menu £10. Amex, Diners, MasterCard,* ***VISA***

WC2 Häagen-Dazs on the Square

Tel 0171-287 9577 Map 21 A2 JaB
14 Leicester Square WC2H 7NG

A total revamp has transformed this convenient family pit-stop for a visit to the Leicester Square cinemas; nevertheless, it's still much of the same! Don't be discouraged by the long queue in front of the shop at weekends; it is probably for the take-away counter. For those wanting to eat from the à la carte menu, tables are available in the attractive, bright and lofty-ceilinged restaurant which has a Continental ambience. The ice creams are, of course, the main attraction, in 1, 2 or 3-scoop portions (£1.30/£2.20/£2.93) with all sorts of toppings, or in splits and sundaes (£3.95). The patisserie items are not in the same class as the ice creams. Three high-chairs are provided. Small portions are available for little ones. No smoking. ***Seats*** *80. Open 10am-midnight (Fri & Sat to 1am). Closed 25 Dec. Amex, MasterCard,* ***VISA***

W1 Harbour City £40

Tel 0171-439 7859 **Fax 0171-734 7705** Map 21 A2 
46 Gerrard Street Soho W1E 7LP

Set on three floors, the restaurant is extremely busy, and well patronised by the local Chinese community. The friendly staff take good care of their customers and offer advice on the long menu. Dim sum (priced from £1.50) are among the best in London, some dishes being comparatively rare: duck's tongues in black bean sauce, pickled chicken feet or perhaps tripe in a chili sauce – all at bargain prices. Various set meals (for 2 people or more) are priced from £10.50, and include an interesting one for vegetarians. Tempting dishes from the carte include Cantonese hot pots (£7-£8) and sizzling hot platters. Ingredients are fresh and of excellent quality. ***Seats*** *160.* ***Open*** *12-11.15.* ***Closed*** *25 Dec. Amex, Diners, MasterCard,* ***VISA***

W1 Hard Rock Café

Tel 0171-629 0382 **Fax 0171-629 8702** Map 19 C4 JaB
150 Old Park Lane Piccadilly W1

Still London's trendiest and best-known burger joint and almost a compulsory stop on the tourist circuit for both the young and the nostalgic. The walls are decorated with the instruments and signed photographs of rock and pop legend. The queues are often long, the music loud, the T- shirts (sold from their own shop) sell like hot cakes and the burgers likewise. The burgers all cost around £7 with fries and salad, and have been joined this year by extra temptations such as grilled marinated chicken breast with garlic mash (£7.95) and grilled Mexican fajitas (from £10.50). Upstairs is no-smoking. ***Seats*** *260.* ***Open*** *11.30am-midnight (Fri & Sat till 1am).* ***Closed*** *25 & 26 Dec. Amex, MasterCard,* ***VISA***

SW1 Harrods

Tel 0171-730 1234 **Fax 0171-225 5903** Map 19 C4 JaB
Knightsbridge SW1X 7XL

Numerous outlets provide a wealth of choice for in-store eating. Here they are in ascending order:
⋆ **Health Juice Bar** – lower ground floor. **Green Man Pub** – lower ground floor via man's shop. Pies, ploughman's and sandwiches. ⋆ **Bar Fromage** – next to cheese counter. Cheese on platters or toasted sandwiches. ⋆ **Sushi Bar** – in the Food Hall. ⋆ **Café Espresso** – by the fruit and vegetable department. Pastries, sandwiches and salads. ⋆ **Salt Beef Bar** – in the Fish and Meat Hall. Salt beef, pastrami, tongue, sausages. ⋆ **Rotisserie** – spit roast meat and poultry at on end of the Meat Hall. ⋆ **Champagne & Oyster Bar** – by the fish counter. Oysters, seafood, caviar, champagne. ⋆ **Pizzeria** – alongside the bakery. Pizza, pasta, salads. **Dress Circle** – 1st floor ladies fashion. Light meals, pastries (self-service). ⋆ **Café Harrods** – 2nd floor by luggage department. Espresso, cappuccino, pastries, sandwiches. ⋆ **Harrods Café** – 3rd floor by lighting department. Espresso, cappuccino, pastries, sandwiches and set teas. **Georgian Restaurant** – 4th floor. Buffet lunch with carved meats 12-3. Traditional afternoon tea , with waiter service 3.45-5.15. ⋆ **Ice Cream Parlour & Creperie** – 4th floor. Ice cream sundaes, crepes, light lunches. Waiter service. **Terrace Restaurant** (less formal than the Georgian) – 4th floor. Breakfast till 11. Lunch 11-3. Tea 3-5.15. Waiter service. ⋆ **Way In** – 4th floor. Hot and cold light meals, desserts and pastries. Waiter service. Baby-changing facilities can be found in the Dress Circle toilets, and in the Baby Shop and Junior Collections on the fourth floor. Harrods also has ramps for push-chairs on all floors where stairs are the only means of access. All the restaurants offer suitable items for children although they are not listed separately. The latest addition is ⋆ **Planet Harrods**, an essential refuelling stop for junior space travellers, with vivid chrome, purple and orange decor; 'mini crew meals' (£4.95 with solar fries or salad and a soft drink) are served for under-12s: astro burgers, chicken meteors, galactic pizzas, flying fish fingers, satellite lasagne and captain hot dogs. A video wall shows cartoons and educational material on space is provided on the place mats; high-chairs provided for even the smallest of astronauts. ⋆ No smoking. ***Store open*** *10-6 (Mon/Tue/Sat), 10-7 (Wed/Thu/Fri). Amex, Diners, MasterCard,* ***VISA***

W13 Haweli

Tel 0181-567 6211 Map 17 A4 JaB
127-129 Uxbridge Road West Ealing W13 9AU

Just past the fire station between Ealing Broadway and West Ealing, this bright Indian restaurant offers a varied menu ranging from palak pakora – fresh spinach leaves coated in spicy flour and deep-fried (£2.75) and paneer korma – diced cheese with fresh tomatoes and mild spices (£3.95) to murg chili masala – chicken cooked with fresh ginger, garlic and green peppers (£4.35) or sag gosht – lamb cooked with spinach and herbs (£4.95). Good breads and an excellent choice for vegetarians, all at kind prices; especially the all-day Sunday buffet (£6.50, children under 8 half that price). ***Seats*** *70.* ***Open*** *12-3 & 6-12 (Sun 12-12). Amex, Diners, MasterCard,* ***VISA***

W1 Heals, The Café at Heals

Tel 0171-636 1666/ext 250 **Fax 0171-636 7095** Map 18 D2 JaB
The Heals Building 196 Tottenham Court Road W1P 9LD

At the back of the second floor of Heals department store, this café is a quiet, relaxing spot for croissants and baguettes in the morning and tea with cakes in the afternoon (£5.60). Lunchtime brings dishes such as home-made vegetable soup (£3.30), stir-fried sesame beef salad (£3.85/£7.75) or pasta of the day (£7.30). Various items such as fresh fruit tart (£3.10), coffee and walnut cake (£2.95) and sandwiches are available throughout the day. On Saturdays a light lunch menu is served all day. ***Seats*** *60.* ***Open*** *10-5.30 (Thu till 7.30)* ***Closed*** *Sun, 25 Dec. Amex, MasterCard,* ***VISA***

SW3 Henry J Bean's Bar & Grill

Tel 0171-352 9255 **Fax 0171-351 4734** Map 19 C5 
195 Kings Road Chelsea SW3

Converted pub themed as a large American bar with an American/Mexican menu. 'Loaded potato skins' (£3.50), nachos deluxe (£4.25), voodoo wings (£3.75) and vegetarian (or beef) chili (£4.25) are starter choices, followed by 'gourmet' burgers (from £5.25), hot dogs (£3.95), salads and deli sandwiches (from £5.25). Finally, try their pecan pie (£2.95), ice cream (£2.50) or Californian cheesecake (£2.95). 'Luncheonette specials' (12-3 Mon-Fri only) offer a main course, salad and fries for £4.95 (or chili and fries for £2.95). The atmosphere is young and buzzy. To the rear is a large open-air area - one of London's most surprising settings for alfresco eating. ***Seats*** *136. Open 11.45-11 (Sun 12-10.30). Closed 25 & 26 Dec. Amex, MasterCard,* ***VISA***

JaB is short for 'Just a Bite'. The majority of these establishments are also recommended in our *Bistros, Bars & Cafés* Guide which features establishments where one may eat well for less than £15 per head.

SW5 Hogarth Hotel 62% £95

Tel 0171-370 6831 **Fax 0171-373 6179** Map 19 A5 
Hogarth Road Earls Court SW5 0QQ

A modern hotel located in a quiet stretch of Hogarth Road with modestly furnished bedrooms all of which have the usual selection of amenities. A proportion of the bathrooms have been refurbished, with the rest to follow by the end of 1996. Children under 12 stay free in their parents' room. Secure, charged, underground parking. ***Rooms*** *86. Amex, Diners, MasterCard,* ***VISA***

WC1 Holiday Inn Kings Cross/Bloomsbury 68%

Tel 0171-833 3900 **Fax 0171-917 6163** Map 16 C3 
1 Kings Cross Road WC1X 9HX

Located to the south of Kings Cross station his striking modern hotel features spacious public rooms including Charings cocktail bar and a comfortably furnished lounge. Bedrooms include the Holiday Inn hallmarks such as queen-size beds (even in single rooms), TV with in-house movies, direct-dial phone, hairdryer, trouser press, good work space and en suite bathroom. Mini-bars are stocked only on request. Executive rooms are similar, but with upgraded furnishings, complimentary soft drinks/mineral water and a basket of fresh fruit. There are ramps for disabled guests, wide lifts and four purpose-built bedrooms. All rooms are air-conditioned and half are designated non-smoking. 24hr room and lounge service. Children under 19 stay free in parents' room. No dogs. ***Rooms*** *405. Indoor swimming pool, gym, squash, sauna, spa bath, steam room, solarium, beauty & hair salon, news kiosk. Amex, Diners, MasterCard,* ***VISA***

SE16 Holiday Inn London Nelson Dock 69% £136

Tel 0171-231 1001 **Fax 0171-231 0599** Map 17 D4 H
265 Rotherhithe Street SE16 1EJ

Impressive modern hotel (formerly the Scandic Crown) in the revitalised Nelson Docks. The stylish building offers three restaurants, a bar, a small leisure centre and comprehensive function/conference facilities (the two major rooms each have a capacity of 350). Rooms are spacious and well equipped, with desk, seating area, mini-bar, trouser press, tea and coffee facilities, satellite TV and in-house movies. Children up to 16 stay free in parents' room. Executive bedrooms are larger, with a view of the Thames. A 60-seat hotel river bus offers a 15-minute trip to Embankment throughout the day. No dogs. ***Rooms** 390. River terrace, indoor swimming pool, gym, sauna, spa bath, solarium, tennis, games room, snooker. Closed 4 days Christmas. Amex, Diners, MasterCard,* ***VISA***

WC2 Hong Kong £50

Tel 0171-287 0324 **Fax 0171-287 9028** Map 21 A2 
6 Lisle Street Leicester Square WC2

A cavernous setting for a daytime selection of dim sum popular with snackers and a Cantonese and Pekingese menu of proverbial favourites like sculptured squid and prawn balls, fried noodles with roast pork, sizzling platters and hot pots (including exceptional braised lamb with dried bean curd). The more adventurous might choose crispy pig's intestines, fried fillet of eel, fried oyster with scrambled egg or even stir-fried carp with superior soup. Finish with a fruit fritter or tapioca cream. ***Seats** 200. Parties 15. Private Room 60. Meals 12-11.30. Closed 25 & 26 Dec. Set D from £8.50 (min 2). Amex, MasterCard,* ***VISA***

SE1 Horniman at Hay's

Tel 0171-407 3611 Fax 0171-357 6449 Map 20 D3 
Hay's Galleria Tooley Street London Bridge SE1 2HD

Right at the entrance of Hay's Galleria on the south bank overlooking the Thames by London Bridge, Horniman's is a modern interpretation of Victorian style in the premises of the family's tea-packing company. The tribute to Frederick John Horniman's travels is discreetly paid through a painted mural on top of the bar. It's part pub, part café and the tables on the gallerias have views of the river and the City in the background. The Pantry restaurant offers hot and cold English pub fare (steak and kidney pie, turkey and ricotta pasta, curries) at lunchtime. Families are welcome in a special area in the Pantry restaurant and children are offered special portions at special prices. *HMS Belfast* is moored nearby - perfect for ship-mad kids! *Open 10-11 (Sat 10-4, Sun 10-3).* ***Bar Food** 12-3 only.* ***Beer** Burton, Timothy Taylor's Landlord, Eldridge Pope Traditional, Tetley Bitter, Adnams Broadside, guest beers. Pub closed weekend evenings. Amex, MasterCard,* ***VISA***

SW1 Hyatt Carlton Tower 87% £366

Tel 0171-235 1234 **Fax 0171-245 6570** Map 19 C4 
2 Cadogan Place Knightsbridge SW1X 9PY

Towards the Knightsbridge end of Sloane Street and overlooking Cadogan Gardens, this ranks as one of London's smartest hotels and features the fashionable Chinoiserie (all-day snacks and afternoon tea served 3-5.30pm) on the ground floor, where enormous flower arrangements burst out of colourful Chinese glazed pots, creating an air of elegance which is continued throughout the hotel. The most sought-after bedrooms are those with balconies overlooking the verdant splendour of the square below. The 16 bedroom floors include 62 enormous suites and an 18th-floor (the top) Presidential suite which enjoys both splendid views and high levels of security. Standard rooms are spacious and well appointed, and king-size beds are a feature of the majority. Decor throughout is a timeless pale cream and beige with elegant furniture to match. The style is typified by the brass carriage clock placed on every desk, and the comfortable armchairs. All rooms have full air-conditioning and there are wall safes for valuables and umbrellas in the wardrobes for rainy days. Bathrooms in marble have fine toiletries as well as thick towels, bathrobes and scales. Excellent standards of housekeeping include a twice-daily maid service with evening turn-down. The Peak Health Club is a bright, spacious and airy, state-of-the-art 9th-floor rendezvous for fitness fanatics; there's a Club Room for post-exertion wind-down and a separate work-out studio with sprung floor. The Health Club is now served by a new external panoramic lift which also stops off for the new 20m indoor swimming pool on the first floor. Guests have use of the tennis courts in Cadogan Square. Banqueting/conference facilities for 400/250. One child up to 18 may stay free in his/her parents' room. Covered parking (£20 overnight). No dogs. ***Rooms*** *224. Indoor swimming pool, gym, work-out studio, sauna, steam room, solarium, beauty & hair salon, valeting, Chinoiserie (7am-11pm), news kiosk. Amex, Diners, MasterCard,* ***VISA***

Rib Room £110

An elegantly appointed, split-level room with rich mahogany panelling and a discreet, clubby ambience. A very traditional and classic carte offers simple, well-prepared dishes, the speciality being roast ribs of Aberdeen Angus beef served with crisp Yorkshire puddings and jacket potato with sour cream. Lunchtime daily specials include steak and kidney pie on Tuesday and cod dugléré on Friday. Service is very, very civilised but can still get you in and out in an hour if you're in a hurry. ***Seats*** *84. Parties 10. Private Room 16. L 12.30-2.45 D 6.30-11.15 (Sun 7-10.15). Closed D 25 Dec, all 1-3 Jan. Set L £24.50 Set D £30.50.*

Pubs – note that food is only recommended in those pubs with ***Bar Food*** times in the statistics at the end of an entry. Restaurant food in pubs is *never* recommended unless specifically mentioned. Some pubs are recommended for B&B or Atmosphere only – each entry's statistics indicate our recommendation.

W8 Il Portico £55

Tel 0171-602 6262 Map 19 A4 
277 Kensington High Street W8 6NA

A friendly neighbourhood restaurant *par excellence*, with a large and loyal following built up over 30 years. The menu is straightforward, traditional Italian, with plenty of choice at each stage. Note the antipasto trolley, the home-made pasta and the daily specials (ask about these). Summer eating on a semi-sheltered pavement terrace. Il Portico is a few yards west of the Odeon High St Ken. ***Seats*** *55 (+ 12 outside). Parties 24. L 12-3 D 6-11.30. Closed Sun & Bank Holidays. Amex, Diners, MasterCard,* ***VISA***

W1 Inter-Continental Hotel, Coffee House

Tel 0171-409 3131 **Fax 0171-409 7460** Map 19 C4 
1 Hamilton Place Park Lane W1V 0DQ

The Coffee House menu at this luxurious Park Lane hotel offers, along with more expensive dishes, light meals such as tomato soup with croutons (£3.50), various omelettes (all £8.50) and a main-course Caesar salad (£7.20) plus a range of sandwiches (from £8.50). A few dishes are marked as being suitable for vegetarians and healthy eaters: avocado and tomato salad (£7.50) and Japanese soba noodles with crisp vegetables (£7.80) are two such. Between 12 and 3 a few light Japanese-style dishes are added to the all-day menu. Afternoon tea, served between 3 and 6, is either à la carte or fixed-price £9.95. Live music Sunday lunchtime and Friday evening. Ask for children's portions; five high-chairs, balloons, colouring menu and crayons are all provided on request - just ask. A large shelf is available for baby-changing in the disabled toilet. ***Seats*** *125.* ***Open*** *7am-11.30pm. Amex, Diners, MasterCard,* ***VISA***

NW3 Jack Straw's Castle

Tel 0171-435 8885 **Fax 0171-794 4805** Map 16 B2 
North End Way Hampstead NW3 7ES

The Inn was built in 1721 on the site of what used to be the hay wagon from which Jack Straw addressed the peasants during the 1381 revolt. Damaged during the Second World War, it was rebuilt in the early sixties. It has a clean country pub look with a cream and white weatherboard frontage, and an agreeable paved-and-cobbled courtyard where barbecues and an arts and craft fair takes place at weekends. Being one of the highest points in London, the second-floor restaurant has beautiful panoramic views over Hampstead Heath. *Open 11-11 (Sun 12-10.30). **Beer** Bass, Fuller's London Pride, guest beer. Courtyard, outdoor eating area. Amex, Diners, MasterCard,* ***VISA***

Any person using our name to obtain free hospitality is a fraud.
Proprietors, please inform the police and us.

SW6 Joe's Brasserie

Tel 0171-731 7835 Map 17 B5 JaB
130 Wandsworth Bridge Road SW6 2UL

Friendly brasserie/wine bar, particularly popular during the evening. The interior is quite rustic and includes a conservatory area that is somewhat quieter than the main dining-area. The monthly-changing menu is modern British in style, and includes something for everyone. Soup of the day is a regular (£3), so too the popular Thai fishcakes with various accompaniments (£5.25/£7.50). Other choices might include pressed chicken, shallot and pancetta terrine (£4.50) or smoked tomato and pesto tart (£4.50) as starters; perhaps fresh grilled tuna niçoise (£11.50), root vegetable tart tatin (£7.50) or Cumberland sausages and mash (£7.50) as main courses. Desserts offer the likes of sticky toffee pudding and crème brulée (£4). A brunch menu is offered at weekends and a set-price menu Mon-Fri (£7.50 for 2 courses) offers choices from the carte. A reduced menu is available from the bar between 3 and 7. Children's menu. ***Seats** 65 (+20 outside). **Open** 12-11 (main menu 12-3 & 7-11). **Closed** 4 days Christmas. Amex, Diners, MasterCard,* ***VISA***

W1 John Lewis, The Place to Eat

Tel 0171-629 7711 **Fax 0171-629 0849** Map 18 C2 JaB
Oxford Street W1 IEX

Seven separate food counters offer a splendid choice in this third-floor restaurant, where everything is home-made except the pastries (whose pedigree, Nadels, is also excellent). Breakfast is served all day (full £6.25, healthy option £5.45, steak breakfast £8.25, savoury croissants with mushroom and cheese £3.25, vegetarian £5.50). From the cold counter try their excellent salads: maybe roast turkey (£5.95) or dressed crab (£7.25). The crockpot offers some good hot dishes – meat from £6.25, a daily vegetarian special £5.50. The fresh fish from the seafood counter is as popular as ever, offering, typically, griddled plaice (£8.45) and halibut (£8.75), both served with vegetables. For those in a rush, a 'meal of soup' is always available (£3.35). Children's themed menu. Full baby-changing facilities (for mums and dads) are provided on the fourth floor. No smoking. Wine and lagers served from 11am with meals. Eight high-chairs are provided; set children's menus include the 'crockpot' (£2.85) and a child's breakfast (£3.85). Full baby-changing facilities (for both mums and dads) are provided on the 4th floor where there is also a Coffee Shop. ***Seats** 299. **Open** 9.30-5.30 (Thu till 7.30). **Closed** Sun & Bank Holidays. No credit cards.*

Any person using our name to obtain free hospitality is a fraud.
Proprietors, please inform the police and us.

WC2 Joy King Lau £50

Tel 0171-437 1132 **Fax 0171-437 2629** Map 21 A2 R
3 Leicester Street Soho WC2H 7BL

Scallop dumplings, beef with ginger and spring onions and duck's tongues in black bean sauce are typical offerings among the good-value dim sum selection, available during the day at this Soho restaurant spread over four floors. Snackers should find plenty to please – the deep-fried selection includes the ever-popular sesame prawn toasts and sweet-and-sour wontons. Almond cold bean curd and egg custard tart are among the desserts. The long menu including all the usual favourites cooked to a high standard. ***Seats*** *200.* ***Open*** *12-11.30 (Sun 11-10.30) Dim sum till 5pm daily.* ***Closed*** *24 & 25 Dec. Amex, Diners, MasterCard,* **VISA**

SW17 Kastoori

Tel 0181-767 7027 Map 17 C6 JaB
188 Upper Tooting Road Tooting SW17 7EJ

The Thanki family's vegetarian restaurant offers Indian and Indo-African specialities whose colourful combinations might include *pani puri* (potatoes, chick peas and moong beans £1.90) and *dahi vada* (spiced black lentil balls in yoghurt sauce £1.95) alongside the regular curries (from £2.75) and specials like green pepper curry (£3.75), *kasodi* (a Swahili dish of sweetcorn in coconut with a peanut sauce £3.50) and chili banana (£3.75). Thalis start from £6.25 for a Sunday special and go up to £11.50 for the Kastoori special and desserts include *gulab jambu* (milkballs in sugar syrup with nutmeg and cardamom £1.75). Dishes are freshly prepared, so you might wait a few minutes for the excellent food. £4 minimum charge. ***Seats*** *82.* ***Open*** *12.30-2.30 & 6-10.30.* ***Closed*** *L Mon (except Bank Holidays) & Tue. Access,* **VISA**

SW10 Ken Lo's Memories of China

Tel 0171-352 4953 **Fax 0171-351 2096** Map 19 B6 JaB
Harbour Yard Chelsea Harbour SW10 0QJ

The lunchtime bar snack menu provides ample choice and best value for light eaters at this restaurant overlooking the marina. A plate of sesame prawn toast and crispy won tons (£3.85) heads the menu, followed by a short selection of dishes such as crabmeat soup (£3), stir-fried beef in satay sauce (£3.85), Sichuan sautéed courgettes (£3.85) or Singapore noodles (£4.10). A quarter of crispy duck with pancake, plum sauce, spring onion and cucumber still provides good value at £5.50. More expensive menus available lunchtime and evening. Disabled toilet. Children welcome, and it's particularly popular on Sundays when there's a buffet (children under 5 free of charge), and kids have space to play in the atrium. No high-chairs, but parents are welcome to bring their own booster seats, or there's an armchair and a couple of cushions that the little ones can use. ***Seats*** *175 (40 in bar).* ***Open*** *12-2.30 (Sun till 3) & 7-10.45 (Sun till 10).* ***Closed*** *25 & 26 Dec, 1 Jan. Access, Amex, Diners,* **VISA**

W8 Kensington Close Hotel 59% £151

Tel 0171-937 8170 **Fax 0171-937 8289** Map 19 A4 H
Wrights Lane Kensington W8 5SP

A minute's walk from the shops of High Street Kensington, the hotel boasts fine leisure/keep-fit facilities and its own underground car park (£18 for 24 hours). Top of the bedroom range are the Executives, which all have sitting areas. There are 11 function and meeting rooms, and a staffed business centre. Children up to 16 share parents' room free. ***Rooms*** *531. Garden, indoor swimming pool, gym, squash, sauna, solarium, beauty salon, news kiosk. Amex, Diners, MasterCard,* **VISA**

A jug of fresh water!

SW5 Kensington Court Hotel £87

Tel 0171-370 5151 **Fax 0171-370 3499** Map 19 A5 **B**
33 Nevern Place Earls Court SW5 9NP

Convenient for Earls Court exhibitions, this modern hotel is in a relatively quiet location. All bedrooms are double or triple bedded and have simple en suite facilities. No dogs. ***Rooms*** *35. Amex, MasterCard,* ***VISA***

W1 Kettners

Tel 0171-734 6112 **Fax 0171-434 1214** Map 18 D3 **JaB**
29 Romilly Street Soho W1

Founded by Auguste Kettner, chef to Napoleon the Third, this is now (along with *Pizza on the Park*) the flagship of the Pizza Express empire. The pizza oven provides the bulk of the menu (napoletana £6.35, potato-based King Edward £5.95, quattro formaggi £6.35) but there are also charcoal grills (burgers from £5.10, Salisbury steak £5.40, grilled or poached halibut £12.95), BLTs (or CLTs for the vegetarian!), salads, chili, ham and eggs (£5.50) and desserts (from £2.05) of sherry trifle, home-made apple pie, chocolate fudge cake and ice creams. Morning coffee and afternoon tea. Live music nightly and lunchtime Thur-Sun. ***Seats*** *300.* ***Open*** *11.30am-midnight. Amex, Diners, MasterCard,* ***VISA***

W11 Ladbroke Arms

Tel & Fax 0171-727 6648 Map 18 A3 **P**
54 Ladbroke Road Notting Hill Gate W11 3NW

Opposite Notting Hill police station, on the corner of Ladbroke Road and the charming Willby Mews. The front terrace is resplendent with flowers in summer and welcomes you with open arms; built a few steps above street level, it is well stocked with tables, benches and parasols (and thus very popular in good weather). Inside is a traditional mixture of mahogany panelling, yellow velvet-covered banquettes, large etched mirrors, a semi-circular bar with pillars and a split-level area at the back. There's a very civilised atmosphere with smiling faces and classical music softly playing in the background. Scottish Courage. *Open 11-3, 5.30-11 (Sat 11-11, Sun 12-3, 7-10.30).* ***Beer*** *Courage Best & Directors, John Smith's, Wadworth 6X, guest beer. Closed 25 Dec eve. MasterCard,* ***VISA***

NW1 The Landmark London 88% £273

Tel 0171-631 8000 **Fax 0171-631 8080** Map 18 C2 
222 Marylebone Road NW1 6JQ

Built at the front of Marylebone Station in 1899, this was originally the Great Central Hotel. It then became British Rail Headquarters before reverting to a hotel in 1993. The transformation was dramatic, involving the complete reconstruction of the interior, and the result is a hotel which now ranks among London's best. A glass-canopied entrance leads into a spacious lobby with a polished cream stone floor with steps up to the Winter Garden, where all-day snacks are available. This is the heart of the hotel and has a very impressive eight-floor-high glass-roofed atrium. A mezzanine gallery features a shopping arcade as well as a quiet lounge area. Two other notable features are the lofty palms and the amazing cathedral-like acoustics. There are six floors of spacious, well-designed bedrooms of which half look on to the atrium and are blissfully peaceful. Each room has very attractive maple veneer furniture including a cupboard which houses a satellite TV and a well-stocked mini bar. There are also three phone lines and a fax/modem line as well a good-sized desk. Bathrooms are as splendid as the bedrooms; lined with white marble, most have a separate shower cubicle, but only the suites have a bidet. Thick towelling bathrobes, a pair of scales, a wall safe and an umbrella are among a host of thoughtful touches provided to pamper guests. A 15-metre swimming pool is a feature of the Health Club located at the rear of the basement, the front portion being occupied by the magnificent oak-panelled Cellar Bar, which is more clubby than pubby. A business centre is available for guests' use and children up to 14 stay free in their parents' room. Almost every family accoutrement can be provided: from electric socket guards to playpens and thermometers. No dogs. ***Rooms*** *305. Indoor swimming pool, gym, sauna, steam room, spa bath, beauty & hair salon, news kiosk, shopping arcade. Amex, Diners, MasterCard,* ***VISA***

The Dining Room £105

A grand, lofty dining-room dominated by three huge silver and crystal chandeliers is the opulent setting for some accomplished and enjoyably imaginative cooking. Even the breads to begin are very moreish, especially the pizza-like, thin, crisp herb bread. TV chef and writer Ken Hom has collaborated with head chef George Heise to produce an exciting menu including Oriental and Mediterranean influences. There is also a short carte of dishes created by Ken Hom, the latter including fresh crab and lemon grass quiche with parmesan, crispy chicken and sun-dried tomato spring rolls and parchment paper fish with ginger and Parma ham among the starters. Main dishes could be steamed salmon in Chinese leaves with lemon sauce, orange duck Peking-style or peppered beef with basil. The main menu follows a very similar theme, including fillet of beef coated with Vietnamese curry paste and iced tomato, and steamed poussin with wild garlic and *gailan* in a Chinese basket. There's an excellent choice of well-prepared desserts: Oriental rice pudding with mango sorbet, millefeuille of peanut and banana cream with anise sauce and deep-fried lychees with chocolate sauce. Well-balanced wine list. ***Seats** 80. Parties 10. L 12-2.30 D 7-11. Closed D Sun. Set L £21.50 Set D from £38.*

> We endeavour to be as up-to-date as possible, but inevitably some changes to data and key personnel may occur at restaurants and hotels after the Guide goes to press. Prices should also be taken as indications rather than firm quotes.

NW1 Lemonia £40

Tel 0171-586 7454 **Fax 0171-483 2630** Map 16 C3 R
89 Regent's Park Road NW1 8UY

Roomy though this lively Greek restaurant certainly is, it's still full to bursting at peak evening times. Outside and in there's a Mediterranean air, with lots of light and masses of hanging flower baskets. The meze selection at £11.25 is great value offering a selection of hot and cold starters and Greek salad which are brought in a seemingly unending procession. Look, too, for the special three-course lunch (Mon-Fri) and daily specials that supplement the regular menu. *Limani*, opposite at 154, is in the same ownership. ***Seats** 140. Parties 14. Private Room 40. L 12-3 D 6-11.30. Set L (not Sun) £7.95. Closed L Sat, D Sun, 25 & 26 Dec. MasterCard,* **VISA**

> We welcome bona fide complaints and recommendations on the tear-out pages at the back of the Guide for Readers' Comments. They are followed up by our professional team.

NW11 Local Friends

Tel 0181-455 9258 **Fax 0181-458 0732** Map 16 B1 
28 North End Road Golders Green NW11 7PT

Conveniently situated opposite Golders Green tube station, this friendly restaurant offers dim sum and Cantonese cooking normally only found in Soho. Dim sum are available between noon and 4.30, and include delicacies such as cold spiced chicken feet, fried yam cake and char siu pork buns (each £1.70). For the sweet-toothed, egg custard tart, fried water chestnut cake and lotus seed buns (£1.70) are particularly delicious. The Cantonese dishes provide all the familiar choices at equally reasonable prices, for example chicken and sweetcorn soup (£1.70), chicken with black pepper, chili and black bean sauce (£5.50) and spare ribs (£4). Set meals are available for two people or more (from £9.50 per person). Drink tea at 50p a pot. ***Seats** 100. **Open** 12-11. **Closed** 25 & 26 Dec. Amex, MasterCard,* **VISA**

W1 Lok Ho Fook £35

Tel 0171-437 2001 Map 21 A2 
4-5 Gerrard Street Soho W1V 7LP

A near twelve-hour daily trade in Cantonese cooking takes place at this popular restaurant at the east end of Chinatown's main street. After the starters and soups (chicken with cashew nuts, crabmeat and sweetcorn soup) comes a vast selection of 'Popular Chinese Dishes' including some unusual ones like chicken blood with ginger and spring onion (£4.50), plus a long vegetarian list and 'Popular Provincial Dishes' (Szechuan pork £4.30, fried squid cake £4.50, crispy aromatic duck (quarter £5) and a hot pot of belly pork and yam £5.10). Chef's specials include beef with wood fungus in a hot pot (£6.50) and deep-fried stuffed duck with minced cuttlefish (£6.90). Bargain-hunters in groups should watch for the range of set menus (from £6.60) – most for a minimum of 5 people. A 10% service charge is added to all bills. ***Seats*** *100.* ***Open*** *12-11.30.* ***Closed*** *25 & 26 Dec. Amex, Diners, MasterCard,* **VISA**

W4 Mackintosh's

Tel 0181-994 2628 Map 17 A4 JaB
142 Chiswick High Road W4 1PU

The eclectic brasserie-style menu at this busy Chiswick eaterie offers plenty of choice for all tastes, from pastries at breakfast (from £1) and a full English breakfast (£4.95) to all-day grills – marinated mixed meat brochette (£8.95). Pasta dishes (from £4.50) include a delicious vegetarian lasagne, with sun-dried tomatoes, goat's cheese and roasted vegetables (£4.95); pizza (from £3.75) and interesting main-course salads (from £4.95) spread their nets wide and there are substantial sandwiches (£3.25-£3.95, until 5pm only). House specialities include grilled Cajun chicken, with tomato and chili pepper sauce (£9.50) and pork stuffed with apricots with a red wine sauce (£9.25). A long list of desserts include Belgian chocolate mousse and Key lime pie (both £2.95). Space is at a premium, but the place is enhanced by bright, theatrical murals. Afternoon tea (with scones and home-made desserts) is served from 4 to 5.30 and brunch from 12 to 3 Saturday and Sunday. A children's menu is advertised in the window and crayons are provided for doodling on the paper tablecloths; Sunday night (5.30-9) is family pasta night with an all-in family spaghetti meal for four (£20). ***Seats*** *54.* ***Open*** *8am-midnight.* ***Closed*** *25 & 26 Dec. Amex, MasterCard,* **VISA**

W2 Maison Péchon Patisserie Française

Tel 0171-229 0746 Map 18 A3 
127 Queensway W2 4BQ

This one of the four is the only branch to offer a full menu in addition to the marvellous array of cakes and bread. Full English (£4.85) and Continental breakfasts are served until 3pm, while lunchtime snacking runs from croissants and vol-au-vents through savoury pancakes, quiches and pizzas, jacket potatoes, pastas and salads, to a full roast dinner, as well as specials such as chicken chasseur (£3.90 with salad) or lasagne (£3). Those with a sweet tooth will enjoy their cinnamon slices, fruit tartlets or French-style apple flan (£1.20 per slice with cream). A few wines are served by the glass. ***Seats*** *30 (+6 outside).* ***Open*** *8-8 (Mon-Wed to 7, Sun 7.30-7).* ***Closed*** *25 Dec. No credit cards.*

W8 Malabar £40

Tel 0171-727 8800 Map 18 A3 
27 Uxbridge Street Notting Hill Gate W8 7TQ

Unusually, for an Indian restaurant, this one has a smart, cool, Mediterranean decor; it's located in the narrow street that runs behind the two cinemas at Notting Hill. Its unchanging menu offers a largely familiar selection though with one or two more unusual offerings. These include *hiran* (venison slices marinated in tamarind), devilled *haleja* (charcoal-grilled chicken livers, marinated in yoghurt and spices) and *jeera* chicken (chicken pieces cooked with roasted cumin). Sunday buffet lunch £6.95. Menu prices all include service. ***Seats** 56. Parties 16. Private Room 20. L 12-2.45 D 6-11.15. Closed last week Aug & 4 days Christmas. MasterCard,* ***VISA***

W11 Manzara

Tel 0171-727 3062 Map 18 A3 JaB
24 Pembridge Road Notting Hill W11 3HL

A visual feast greets the visitor, comprising a vast array of cakes and pastries, all baked freshly on the premises. Many are French, but there is also a good selection of the sweeter Turkish variety. To the rear is a small and neat modern restaurant where regional Turkish specialities appear on a six-week rota. As well as the familiar houmus (£1.95), taramasalata (£2.35) and imam bayildi (£2.35) there are more unusual hot starters such as a selection of good, crisp fried filo pastry triangles with fillings of feta cheese and egg (£1.95) or seasonal lamb or chicken (£1.95). Kebabs (from £4.15) are deliciously tender and well cooked, served with a good salad and basmati rice (or pommes noisettes if preferred). Real imported Turkish Delight is on offer with a cup of fine Turkish coffee (95p). ***Seats** 43. **Open** 8am-11.30pm. Amex, Diners, MasterCard,* ***VISA***

W1 Marché Mövenpick

Tel 0171-494 0498 Fax 0171-494 2180 Map 21 A3 JaB
Swiss Centre Leicester Square W1V 7FJ

Watching the cook prepare your dish is an entertaining spectacle here in the basement of the Swiss Centre, where the dining spaces are divided into areas of French, German and Italian influence. Each counter has its own speciality: salads, salami and Swiss cheeses sliced to order; bloomer, cheese, walnut and onion breads kneaded and baked on the spot. Rösti is prepared to order (with broccoli and a cheese sauce £4.20, with pork or with smoked salmon and sour cream £5.90), and pasta, freshly out of the pasta machine, is cooked on demand and tossed in frying pans with fresh ingredients of the day (pasta dishes £4.20-£5.50). there are also various grills and roasts: lamb steak with gratin dauphinois and green beans (£9.50) and roast turkey, pork or lamb with vegetables (all £6.20). There is, of course, Mövenpick ice cream by the scoop and a special pastries counter with freshly baked strudel (£2.10), fruit squares or chocolate marbled cake (£2.40). There's beer, wine, cocktails and Mövenpick's own brand of coffee served as espresso, cappuccino or the Swiss way with whipped cream and chocolate flakes. In the bistro upstairs a good selection of Swiss specialities, sandwiches (from £2.50), a daily soup (£1.70) served with bread, salads, light snacks and ice creams are on offer. The bar offers a good range of cocktails and has a short snack menu. Children are welcome and high-chairs, balloons, crayons and paper plus bibs are provided. Large no-smoking area. Happy hour Mon-Fri 5-7pm. ***Seats** 400. **Open** 8am-midnight (Sun from 9), bistro from 11.30am. **Closed** 25 Dec. Amex, MasterCard,* ***VISA***

NW3 Marine Ices

Tel 0171-485 3132 Fax 0171-485 3982 Map 16 C2 JaB
8 Haverstock Hill Chalk Farm NW3 2BL

The name gives no clue that part of this operation comprises a conventional Italian restaurant serving pizzas (from £4.85), pasta, veal, chicken and house specialities including penne with salmon in a cream, white wine and smoked salmon sauce (£6.40), linguine with veal meatballs in a tomato sauce (£6.25) and pasta with clams, prawns, squid and mussels in a garlic and tomato sauce (£6.50).There is a £6 minimum charge in the restaurant (excluding drinks and ice cream). The ices are superb; try 3 scoops of ice cream topped with cassis, zabaglione or their excellent espresso coffee. Children's helpings and plenty of choice for vegetarians. Marine Ices is located more or less opposite the Roundhouse. ***Seats** 142. **Open** 12-3 & 5.30-11 (Sat 12-11, Sun 12-10). **Closed** 3 days Christmas. MasterCard,* ***VISA***

SW11 Mariners

Tel 0171-223 2354 Map 17 B5 JaB
30 Northcote Road Battersea SW11 1NZ

Fresh fish from Aberdeen is served in this traditional restaurant, from filleted cod (£3.75) to plaice, haddock (£4.20) and scampi (£4). The chips are authentic and really hot and all the fish comes with lemon wedges and a salad garnish, bread, butter, tartare sauce and either gherkins or pickled onions. You might choose home-made apple pie or lemon cheesecake for pudding (£1.60- £1-70). ***Seats*** *36.* ***Open*** *12-2.30 & 5-10 (Fri & Sat 12-10).* ***Closed*** *Sun, Mon, 24 Dec-2 Jan. No credit cards.*

W1 Merryfield House £62

Tel 0171-935 8326 Map 18 C2 B
42 York Street W1H 1FN

A friendly, family-run bed-and-breakfast hotel with compact, simply furnished bedrooms, with comfortable hide-away beds, remote-control TV and hairdryers. There's a telephone, and tea/coffee-making facilities on each landing. Bathrooms, which are all en suite, now have shower attachments. Full English breakfast is served in bedrooms only. Unlicensed. No dogs. ***Rooms*** *8. Closed Feb. No credit cards.*

W6 Mr Wong Wonderful House £50

Tel 0181-748 6887 Map 17 A4 R
313-317 King Street Hammersmith W6 9NH

A splendid pair of white Chinese lions greets diners entering this large restaurant on Hammersmith's 'restaurant row'. There is a selection of over 30 items on the dim sum list, cooked to order at lunchtime during the week (all day at the weekend): perhaps taro croquettes, mooli radish mousse, char siu roast pork or chicken buns, nine types of dumpling and even chicken feet in black bean sauce should you feel so inclined (prices start at £1.80). Dishes are served in steamer baskets, a pre-set selection can be chosen on weekday evenings (£5.50). A long à la carte menu offers a standard range, but among these baked lobster with chili and steamed Dover sole take Mr Wong away from the main stream with regard to both dishes and prices. But stick to the dim sum or choose carefully from the menu and you will remain satisfied in both purse and stomach! A 10% service charge is added to bills ***Seats*** *200.* ***Open*** *12-3 & 6-11.45 (Sat/Sun noon-midnight).* ***Closed*** *25 & 26 Dec. Amex, Diners, MasterCard,* ***VISA***

Our inspectors *never* book in the name of Egon Ronay's Guides. They disclose their identity only if they are considering an establishment for inclusion in the next edition of the Guide.

WC2 Le Mistral

Tel 0171-379 8751 Map 21 B2 JaB
Thomas Neal Centre 16a Shorts Gardens Covent Garden WC2

A short all-day snack menu is available at this basement wine bar, which opens on to an atrium shedding daylight on to the ochre walls and white marble tables. A selection of open sandwiches might include brie and avocado (£3.25), prosciutto and emmental (£4.50) and roast chicken with mango chutney (£4.50) all served on ciabatta bread. Salads are also offered: frisée with bacon and croutons (£4.95), Caesar (£5.50) or chicken (£6.95) and a mixed summer salad. Croissants (£1.25) and a Continental breakfast (£3.25) are on offer in the mornings. Over 10 different types of coffee include double cappuccino, mocha, macchiato and espresso romano (with a twist of lemon). The bar opens on to an atrium with additional seating and though roofed it has a charming alfresco Continental café ambience. Children are welcome, with crayons and colouring books provided! ***Seats*** *90.* ***Open*** *9.30am-9pm (Thur, Fri, Sat till 11, Sun 10- 7).* ***Closed*** *25, 26 Dec & 1 Jan. Amex, Diners, MasterCard,* ***VISA***

W5 Momo

Tel 0181-997 0206 **Fax 0181-997 0206** Map 17 A4 JaB
14 Queens Parade North Ealing W5 3HU

Good-value one-dish lunches are served at this cosy Japanese restaurant just off the Hanger Lane (by North Ealing tube). *Korokke* is deep-fried minced beef and potato with breadcrumbs (£7.50); *buta shogayaki* is sliced pork grilled with a ginger sauce (£8.30).There is, too, a choice of ten set lunches based around either sashimi, tonkatsu, tempura or other main dishes with the addition of boiled rice, miso soup, pickles and a piece of fresh fruit for dessert. Lunch prices range from £7.20 to £16 for sushi (with a special children's offering for £6.50); evenings are more expensive. Attentive service and hot hand-towels are indicative of a well-run venture in an unexpected setting. ***Seats*** *30.* ***Open*** *12-2.30 & 6-10.* ***Closed*** *Sun, Bank Holidays, 1 week Aug & 10 days Christmas. Amex, Diners, MasterCard,* **VISA**

W8 Muffin Man

Tel 0171-937 6652 Map 19 A4 JaB
12 Wrights Lane off Kensington High Street W8 6TA

A traditional teashop, where the waitresses' dresses match the flowery tablecloths, is a treat indeed in bustling London, where traditions are oft forgot! A choice of set teas includes Devon cream tea (£3.80) and Muffin Man tea (£3.70/£4.70). Sandwiches prepared to order (from £1.90) and light lunches are also available: home-made soups (£2), muffin rarebit (£2.80) and salads (from £3.95). Other good home-made dishes include moussaka (£4.95 with a small bowl of salad) and spaghetti bolognese (£4.50). Breakfast, like everything else, is served all day (£5.50 full English). No cheques under £10. ***Seats*** *72.* ***Open*** *8-5.45.* ***Closed*** *Sun & a few days Christmas. No credit cards.*

NW6 Nautilus

Tel 0171-435 2532 Map 16 B2 JaB
27-29 Fortune Green Road West Hampstead NW6 1DT

Matzo meal is used to make the batter which surrounds the fish, fried in groundnut oil – served with excellent chips. 15 to 18 different types of fish are usually offered, including a selection of boned, grilled fish. Fresh rainbow trout (£7), haddock (£8), Cornish rock salmon (£7), grilled cod/plaice (£9) and Dover sole (£10) are just a few. Simple starters include prawn cocktail (£3), melon (£2) and cod's roe (£1). Portions are enormous and the chips generously sized. Gherkins, peas, pickled onions and roll and butter are charged extra (70p). Goujons make good meals for children (1 portion will cater for 3-4 youngsters). Busy fish'n'chip take-away next door. ***Seats*** *48.* ***Open*** *11.30-2.30 & 5-10.30.* ***Closed*** *Sun, 3 days Christmas & New Year Bank Holidays. No credit cards.*

WC2 Neal's Yard Bakery

Tel 0171-836 5199 Map 21 B2 JaB
6 Neal's Yard Covent Garden WC2 H9DP

This well-known bakery offers good vegetarian snacks as well in the upstairs tea room. Filled croissants (£1.90), filled pitta bread, beanburgers (£1.90) and small salad bowls are joined by daily specials such as mushroom stroganoff, cashew nut biryani and aubergine and mango korma (all priced between £2.70/£3.20). All cakes are 80p – banana and hazelnut, carrot and coconut, vegan fruit and nut and many more. Unlicensed, but you can bring your own wine, with no corkage charged. No smoking. ***Seats*** *20.* ***Open*** *10.30-4.30 (Sat till 4).* ***Closed*** *Sun, Bank Holidays & Christmas. No credit cards.*

W1 New World £35

Tel 0171-434 2508 **Fax 0171-287 3994** Map 21 A2 R
1 Gerrard Place Soho W1V 7LL

A 20-page à la carte menu can be a little confusing at this traditional Chinese restaurant, where a lunchtime dim sum and snack menu is good value at between £1 and £6 per dish (available between 11 and 6). Aromatic duck with pancakes (£6) and lobster with chili and black bean or ginger and spring onion is an almost permanent special at £10.50. Scallops and crabs are other seafood specialities. Desserts offer the likes of egg custard tart or sesame roll with lotus-seed paste (£1.50). Good set menus start at £11 (for a minimum of two people). ***Seats*** *700.* ***Open*** *11am-11.45pm (Fri till 12, Sun till 11).* ***Closed*** *25 & 26 Dec. Amex, Diners, MasterCard,* ***VISA***

SW4 Newtons £65

Tel 0181-673 0977 **Fax 0181-673 0977** Map 17 C6 
33 Abbeville Road South Side Clapham Common SW4 9LA

This brasserie-style Clapham restaurant offers good value for snackers with its set meals: a two-course weekday lunch (£6.95) may propose French onion soup or goat's cheese, roasted aubergine and thyme crostini as starters, followed by blackened cod fillet with tomato and ginger dressing and coriander mash, Thai vegetable curry with jasmine rice and baked loin of pork wrapped in bacon and cabbage. On Sunday the choice is wider and might include field mushrooms with garlic butter and grilled polenta (£3.95), eggs Benedict (£3.95/£5.95), tempura cod and chips (£6.95), grilled sardines (£3.95/£6.95) and spaghetti with feta cheese, roasted garlic, green beans and mint (£6.95). A three-course Sunday lunch, including a roast, is also available (£9.95). A terrace outside is great for sunny days. Children are especially encouraged on Saturdays (12.30-5.30) with a special menu to colour, a clown and a Club menu for mums and dads. A 12% service charge is added to bills. ***Seats*** *85 (+25 on the covered terrace).* ***Open*** *12.30-2.30 & 7-11.30 (Sat & Sun 12.30-11.30).* ***Closed*** *3 days Easter & 3 days Christmas. Amex, MasterCard,* ***VISA***

A jug of fresh water!

SE1 Novotel (Waterloo) 65% £140

Tel 0171-793 1010 **Fax 0171-793 0202** Map 17 C4 
113 Lambeth Road SE1 7LS

Be not deceived by the Euro-inspired name as Novotel's latest addition stands on the site of the 15th-century Norfolk House at the south end of Lambeth Bridge, but with no river views beyond the turrets of Lambeth Palace opposite. Beyond a marble-floored foyer open plan public areas include an in-house pub, The Flag & Whistle, and a bright all-day brasserie. Bedrooms are modestly furnished to a nonetheless comfortable standard, have modern ensuite bathrooms with tub and shower and separate WCs; extras include satellite TVs and mini-bars. Bedrooms on two floors are reserved for non-smokers. Children up to 16 stay free in their parents' room. Conferences for up to 40. ***Rooms*** *187. Keep-fit equipment, sauna, steam room, kiosk. Amex, Diners, MasterCard,* ***VISA***

W6 Novotel 64% £127

Tel 0181-741 1555 **Fax 0181-741 2120** Map 17 B4 
1 Shortlands Hammersmith W6 8DR

Large modern hotel, alongside (though not accessible from) Hammersmith flyover. The open-plan public areas include an in-house pub – The Frog & Bulldog – and an all-day restaurant. Comfortable bedrooms have air-conditioning and the usual range of amenities. Extensive conference facilities for up to 900. Two non-smoking floors. Children up to 16 stay free in parents' room. ***Rooms*** *635. Amex, Diners, MasterCard,* ***VISA***

SW5 Hotel 167 £82

Tel 0171-373 0672 **Fax 0171-373 3360** Map 19 B5 
167 Old Brompton Road SW5 0AN

A Victorian private house with characterful double-glazed and centrally-heated bedrooms. Original modern pictures abound, but some period features also survive, including the black-and-white mosaic in the hall. Continental breakfast only. Unlicensed. No dogs. The hotel is located on the corner of Cresswell Gardens. ***Rooms*** *19. Amex, Diners, MasterCard,* ***VISA***

SW11 Osteria Antica Bologna £60

Tel 0171-978 4771 Map 17 C6 R
23 Northcote Road SW11 1NG

With its darkwood strip decor and plain wooden tables and chairs the place has the ambience of a rustic Italian hostelry. The menu too reflects the sort of cooking found in rural Italy and some dishes are taken from ancient recipes. The end result is simple food that captures the character of this cuisine. The choice is long and enticing, offering a range from all parts of Italy; *assaggi dell'osteria* (Bolognese tasting portions – the Italian version of tapas) are a fun way to start a meal, or can be combined into an excellent light meal. These include a chick pea, artichoke, spinach and egg *torta* with rocket pesto, and fried balls of polenta, spinach and parmesan with a fish sauce of *baccala*, milk and garlic. Other sections are devoted to salads, pasta, middle dishes (*capretto alle mandorle* is a speciality – goat cooked with rich tomato and almond pesto) and desserts. Good-value Italian wines – hardly a bottle over £20. Special Easter menus. Free parking in side streets. ***Seats*** *75. Parties 30. L 12-3 (Sat & Sun from 10) D 6-11 (Fri & Sat till 11.30, Sun till 10.30). Set L (not Sun) £7.50. Closed 10 days Christmas/New Year. Amex, MasterCard,* ***VISA***

W11 Osteria Basilico

Tel 0171-727 9372 **Fax 0171-229 7980** Map 16 B3 
29 Kensington Park Road W11 2EQ

The traditional rubs shoulders with the modern on the menu at this Italian restaurant. A table groans with dishes bearing the hors d'oeuvre selection (£4.50) while the carte might offer deep-fried squid and prawns (£4.70), pasta quills with mixed vegetables and a tomato sauce (£5.50) and fresh minestrone (£3.50) to start. Main courses include good meat dishes (chargrilled entrecote with spinach, radicchio and sweet pepper (£8.50) and traditional pizzas. Amicable service and good coffee to finish. ***Seats*** *70.* ***Open*** *12.30-3 (Sat till 4.30, Sun till 3.15) & 6.30-11 (Sun till 10.30).* ***Closed*** *25, 26 Dec, 1 Jan & last Sun in Aug. MasterCard,* ***VISA***

WC2 PJ's Grill

Tel 0171-240 7529 Map 20 A2 
30 Wellington Street Covent Garden WC2

Uncle PJ's Fun Club comes into action on Sundays (from 11-4), when there's a children's party atmosphere at this American-style brasserie. The dining-room is long and narrow and stretches from its entrance on Wellington Street through to Catherine Street, opposite the Theatre Royal. On Sundays a clown sets up shop with balloon bending, face painting (£1.50), indoor play equipment (bike, slide), a box of Duplo and padded baby playrings. Food is hardly the main attraction, with a pretty standard menu of grills and popular dishes, plus a Sunday Brunch menu offering eggs Benedict (£5.25), pancakes with maple syrup (£4.75), Cumberland sausages and mash (£5.75), rib-eye steak and eggs (£6.45) and the like. Staff try hard to go about their business (given the distractions), catering for both the needs of the little ones and parents alike. Uncle PJ's Children's Menu (£4.25) offers a Kiddies Combo with peanut butter sandwichman, carrot and cucumber sticks, Sun Maid raisins, chicken finger, fries and a muesli bar, all served on a plastic plate; hamburger, pasta, home-made fish fingers or Southern-fried chicken for the older children. Drinks come in a Mickey Mouse cup with a bendy straw - guaranteed to please! Funny face ice cream cones, milk shakes and chocolate brownies (£1.95) complete the picture. High-chairs, crayons, colouring menu and balloons are all provided. Our Henry the Duck award is awarded for Sundays only, although children's helpings are offered at other times whenever possible. ***Seats** 120. Open Noon-midnight (to 1am Thu-Sat, to 5pm Sun). Closed 3 days Christmas. Amex, Diners, MasterCard,* ***VISA***

SW10 Parsons

Tel 0171-352 0651 Map 19 B5 JaB
311 Fulham Road SW10 9QH

Fond memories of this Fulham landmark can still be captured some 25 years on, as little has changed. Good-quality beef from Lower Hurst Farm in the Peak District is used to make the excellent burgers which form part of the carte; these come in 4, 8 and 12oz sizes and prices range from £5.20 for a small regular to £8.75 for a giant cheese and bacon burger. Other options are steak, mushroom and Guinness pie (£7.20), vegetarian chili with garlic bread (£5.20), Cumberland sausages with mash, onion gravy and peas (£6.25), fish and grills, and pasta dishes (from £4.15). There is a children's menu for £3.95 and free second helpings of the pasta dishes. A specially designed roof at the back opens in warm weather. Discounts for students and cinema-goers. ***Seats** 76. **Open** noon-12.30am (Sun till midnight). **Closed** 25 & 26 Dec. Amex, Diners, MasterCard,* ***VISA***

W1 Pasta Fino

Tel 0171-439 8900 Map 21 A2 JaB
27 Frith Street Soho W1V 5TR

Fresh home-made pasta is the draw here, and it is offered in a number of different guises: spaghetti marinara (£4.30), ravioli filled with spinach and ricotta in a tomato sauce (£5.50) and fettuccine carbonara – to name a few. Starters include salads, salami and stuffed mushrooms. There is also a range of pizzas (10 choices including margherita £3.75, fiorentina and americana £5.25). Also daily meat and fish specials. Chocolate pasta (£3), drenched in chocolate fudge sauce, is a novel dish on the dessert menu; or try *bongo bongo* (£3.15), which is Italian profiteroles. ***Seats** 55. **Open** 12-3.30 & 5.30-11 (Thu & Fri till 12, Sat 12-12). **Closed** Sun & Bank Holidays. Amex, Diners, MasterCard,* ***VISA***

SE1 People's Palace £70

Tel 0171-928 9999 **Fax 0171-928 2355** Map 20 A3 
Royal Festival Hall South Bank SE1 8XX

Gary Rhodes has moved on and the kitchen at this much-publicised restaurant is now in the hands of Stephen Carter. Great river views accompany the food and customers are free to choose just one course if they wish. Try mixed leaf salad with sweet potato chips, alfalfa shoots and a herb dressing (£4.50), ceviche of tuna with coriander chutney (£6.50) or a terrine of sardines, roast pepper and cream cheese with a tapénade mousse (£5) as a starter or light meal; perhaps grilled fillets of mackerel with cumin, lemon and garlic (£10.50) or roast cod with clam and chive butter (£13.50) for a more filling option. Vegetarians are not forgotten with dishes like beetroot tarte tatin with crème fraiche and chives (£8) on offer. Desserts all cost £4 and might include peach melba, lemon brulée and rhubarb and custard. An interesting venue for Sunday lunch, although a traditional roast is not served. High-chairs are provided and there are baby-changing facilities within the Festival Hall complex. ***Seats** 220. **Open** 12-3 & 5.30-11. **Closed** Bank Holidays. Amex, Diners, MasterCard,* ***VISA***

SW1 Peter Jones

Tel 0171-730 3434 **Fax 0171-730 9645** Map 19 C5 JaB
Sloane Square SW1W 8EL

The fourth-floor dining-room is a popular venue for shoppers and for meeting friends, so expect lunchtime queues. Simply decorated, it is a light, airy, open-plan space with pretty floral tablecloths. The selection of dishes available from 9.30 till 11.30 and from 3 till 5.30 is illustrated by two poached or scrambled eggs on toast (£3.25), full English breakfast (£5.95), Greek yoghurt with honey and nuts (£2.25) or just a warm croissant with butter and preserves (£1.65). Alongside this is the all-day menu with fashionable Mediterranean-style offerings such as Provençal vegetarian tart with a yellow pepper coulis and mixed leaf salad (£7.95), spinach and ricotta gnocchi with a tomato and basil dressing (£7.50) or an Italian platter including bresaola, salami and Parma ham with roasted peppers (£7.95). Lunchtime blackboard specials might combine with the charcoal grill to produce potato pancakes with chargrilled fillet steak and a sun-dried tomato and rocket salad (£10.95). Desserts include sticky toffee pudding and summer pudding (both £3.50) and Rocombe farm organic ice cream (£2.50). Afternoon tea (£5.95). Children's menu. A children's menu (for the under-11s) offers small portions of dishes of the all-day and lunchtime specials plus fun food for the little ones, including banana or peanut butter sandwiches with crisps (£2.45) and the Junior's Grill (£3.55) with individual pizza, fish fingers or chicken pieces served with baked beans and fries. Six high-chairs are provided and there's a Mother & Baby Room on the third floor; plenty of room in the restaurant for buggies. ***Seats*** *150.* ***Open*** *9.30-5.30 (Wed till 5).* ***Closed*** *Sun & Bank Holidays. No credit cards.*

Coffee Shop

Great views are part of the attraction at the fifth-floor coffee shop. A self-service counter offers sandwiches, open sandwiches (from £3.75), salads, stuffed baked potatoes (from £3.25) and hot dishes such as spinach and ricotta cannelloni (£4.75). Wide range of pastries, tea breads and cream cakes from £1.75. Good coffee. ***Open*** *9.45-6 (Wed till 7).*

SW7 Pizza Chelsea

Tel 0171-584 4788 **Fax 0171-584 4796** Map 19 B5 JaB
93 Pelham Street South Kensington SW7 2NJ

In an area of town in which restaurants abound, this pizzeria is popular with locals. The pizza dough is made freshly each day and the bases are crisp and thin, with a variety of interesting toppings such as grilled aubergine and peppers with sun-dried tomatoes and rosemary (£5.95), Thai duck with oyster mushrooms (£6.95), and country calzone with spinach, gorgonzola, aubergines and garlic (£5.75). A few other dishes are available such as marinated peppers stuffed with tomatoes, black olives and fresh basil (£3.05), spinach, mushroom and bacon salad (£3.50/£6.50) and fettuccine with smoked chicken, tiger prawns, roasted peppers and Jamaican seasoning (£7.25). A small selection of good desserts might include bitter chocolate cake with cream or ice cream (£3.50). Children's dishes and a magician on Sundays make this a popular venue for families. The front area is designated non-smoking. ***Seats*** *110.* ***Open*** *12-11.30.* ***Closed*** *25, 26 Dec & 1 Jan. Amex, Diners, MasterCard,* ***VISA***

SW1 Pizza on the Park

Tel 0171-235 5273 **Fax 0171-235 6858** Map 19 C4 JaB
11 Knightsbridge Hyde Park Corner SW1

This former Lyons Tea Shop now serves breakfast (English £4.95, Continental £4) all day, as well as an excellent range of sandwiches (£2), salads (from £5.50) and of course a range of Pizza Express pizzas. Try perhaps a smoked salmon or patum peperium (Gentleman's Relish) sandwich, a tuna fish or fresh crab (£8.40) salad or a marinara (£5.80), Four Seasons (£6.25) or American hot (£6.15) pizza – extra toppings are offered for 95p per item. Afternoon tea is served from 3.15 in the west wing, with its view of Knightsbridge and Hyde Park – choose à la carte or set at £6.75. Sunday brunch has live music. Seating in the forecourt. Ten high-chairs are provided along with a table for baby-changing in the disabled toilet. It's a cavernous place and children are unlikely to feel constrained either gastronomically or vocally! Within easy walking distance of the Knightsbridge shops and, of course, Hyde Park. ***Seats*** *240 (+ outside).* ***Open*** *8am-midnight (Sat & Sun from 9.30).* ***Closed*** *25 Dec. Amex, Diners, MasterCard,* ***VISA***

SE1 Pizzeria Castello

Tel 0171-703 2556 Fax 0171-703 0421 Map 17 D4 JaB
20 Walworth Road Elephant & Castle SE1 6SP

The queues are long here at peak times for both take-aways and tables, so for thge latter booking is advisable. A huge stainless-steel pizza oven dominates the front of the restaurant and good doughy-based pizzas are the main attraction. Toppings might include napoletana (£4.60), fiorentina (£4.90) and Sicilian – hot and spicy (£5.40). Alternatively, a standard range of starters such as minestrone (£2.10), avocado vinaigrette (£1.80) and antipasto misto (£3.30) could also be followed by a pasta dish: lasagne (£4.40), spaghetti bolognese (£4.20) and cannelloni (£3.95). Good, strong espresso follows puddings such as tiramisu. ***Seats*** *150.* ***Open*** *12-11 (Sat from 5).* ***Closed*** *L Sat, all Sun & Bank Holidays. Amex, MasterCard,* ***VISA***

W1 Pizzeria Condotti

Tel & Fax 0171-499 1308 Map 18 D3 
4 Mill Street W1R 9TE

Pizzas are the main attraction at this Mayfair trattoria, whose tiled floor and starched white napery are matched by smart and smiley staff. Try a basic margherita (£4.95), a veneziana -with capers, olives, pine kernels and sultanas (£5.40) or the unusual King Edward pizza, made with a potato base and four cheeses (£5.40); an interesting selection of main-course salads (from £5.70) is also offered. You can watch the food being prepared in the open-plan kitchen. Good ice creams and coffee. ***Seats*** *100.* ***Open*** *11.30am-midnight (Sun 12-11).* ***Closed*** *Bank Holidays. Amex, MasterCard,* ***VISA***

W1 Planet Hollywood

Tel 0171-287 1000 Fax 0171-734 0835 Map 21 A3 
Unit 75 Trocadero Centre Coventry Street W1V 7FE

Probably the most flamboyant eaterie among those that surround Leicester Square. Planet Hollywood's owners Arnold Schwarzenegger, Sylvester Stallone and Bruce Willis have enough box office cred to ensure the success of this venture. A no-bookings policy may mean that you will sometimes queue, with a further wait in the bar. The main dining-room is dramatically decorated with palm trees, a 'Hollywood Hills' set and a midnight-blue ceiling with star-like spotlights. The long menu runs the fast food gamut from burgers to pizzas, salads to sandwiches. Perhaps soup of the day (£2.95), nachos (£4.95) or buffalo wings – hickory smoked deep-fried chicken wings (£4.95) to start; 6oz hamburger with chips (£8.45), Mexican shrimp salad (£9.95) or vegetarian pasta (£8.95) to follow. A selection of wicked desserts offers such temptations as caramel crunch pie (£4.95) and butter pecan rum cake (£4.95). No reservations. A children's daily special offers a choice of about three dishes, which usually includes a vegetarian option as well as burgers or fish with fries. No children's portions, but one of the appetizer baskets can make a good child-size meal. Baby food and bottles can be heated on request. A grand total of 20 high-chairs, and baby-changing facilities in the disabled toilet. ***Seats*** *500.* ***Open*** *11am-1am.* ***Closed*** *25 Dec. Amex, Diners, MasterCard,* ***VISA***

WC2 Poons

Tel 0171-437 1528 Fax 0181-458 0968 Map 21 A2 JaB
4 Leicester Street Soho WC2H 7BL

This cheerful and busy restaurant is owned by a member of the same family who own the homely Lisle Street one and yet another in charge at the elegant Whiteley's establishment. The food differs as well, Leicester and Lisle Street offering the most diverse selection for snackers. Although Whiteleys offers a good selection of dim sum between 12-4pm (from£2), overall the variety and value is to be had at the other establishments, which offer one-plate noodle and pot-rice specials. A familiar mix of Cantonese dishes is supplemented by their trade-mark wind-dried foods and barbecued meats. ***Seats*** *80.* ***Open*** *12-11.30.* ***Closed*** *4 days Christmas. Amex, MasterCard,* ***VISA***

Also at:

50 Woburn Place Russell Square WC1 Tel 0171-580 1188 Map 18 D1

2nd Floor Whiteleys Queensway Bayswater W2 Tel 0171-792 2884 Map 18 A3

Open 12-11.

27 Lisle Street WC2 Tel 0171-437 4549 Map 21 A2

No credit cards.

WC2 Porters

Tel 0171-836 6466 Fax 0171-379 4296 Map 21 B2 JaB
17 Henrietta Street Covent Garden WC2E 8QH

"Purveyors of excellent English food for more than 16 years" claims the menu. Soup and bread (£2.95) is the only starter – a choice of six could include split pea and ham or cider and white onion. Porters' pies (£7.95) come with either salad, chips, vegetables, or mashed, boiled or baked potatoes; try lamb and apricot, chicken and broccoli or the favourite steak and mushroom. Other choices could include, fish and chips or beef with herb dumplings (both £7.95). Nursery puddings like Spotted Dick or steamed syrup sponge are £2.95. Porters is family-friendly even to the extent that there are baby-changing facilities in the ladies' loo. Minimum charge £6 per person. ***Seats*** *200.* ***Open*** *12-11.30 (Sun till 10.30).* ***Closed*** *25 Dec. Amex, Diners, MasterCard,* ***VISA***

WC1 President Hotel £72

Tel 0171-837 8844 Fax 0171-837 4653 Map 18 D2 B
Russell Square Bloomsbury WC1N 1DB

Close to the British Museum, this is a large hotel on the corner of Guilford Street and Russell Square, catering mainly for tour parties and delegates, whose conferences take place at neighbouring sister hotels. Bedrooms have all the simple artefacts including en suite facilities with both bathtubs and showers. Underground (charged) car park. ***Rooms*** *447. Coffee shop (10am-2am). Amex, Diners, MasterCard,* ***VISA***

W1 Ragam £35

Tel 0171-636 9098 Map 18 D2 
57 Cleveland Street Fitzrovia W1P 5PQ

Mainly vegetarian, this small South Indian restaurant is not far from the Telecom Tower and Great Portland Street. Popular dishes include fish curry (£6.50), egg bhuna (£3.30) and vegetable kurma (£2.50); other interesting options include masala dosai (£3.30 – rice and lentil flour pancake with a potato and onion filling, and excellent chutney), adai (£3.70 – spicy pancake made of mixed lentils) and chili chicken, meat fry or king prawn fry – all £6.90. There is a £6.50 minimum charge, and a 10% service charge is added to bills. ***Seats*** *36.* ***Open*** *12-3 & 6-11.30 (Fri till 12, Sun till 11).* ***Closed*** *25 & 26 Dec. Amex, Diners, MasterCard,* ***VISA***

N3 Rani £40

Tel 0181-349 4386 **Fax 0181-349 4386** Map 16 B1
7 Long Lane Finchley N3 2PR

One of London's top Gujerati restaurants, Rani is a five-minute walk from Finchley Central tube station. A long, entirely vegetarian menu includes Gujerati dal (£2.20), vegetable bhajias (£2.80) and bean papri chat (£3.80 – spicy beans on crispy pooris with a tamarind sauce) to start; and slow-cooked Gujerati curries such as cauliflower and pea (£4.40), spinach and aubergine (£4.50) or black eye beans (£4.20) as main courses. It is possible to devise your own set menu at £12.90 to include a starter, curry, bread and rice. There is a children's menu at £4.90 for the under-12s and a traditional one-course Rani masala dosa (£8.40) which involves a folded rice and black lentil pancake with potatoes and accompanying vegetables and chutneys. These chutneys are terrific (coriander, date, coconut, green chili, mango, pineapple) but everything here should be sampled and the variety is amazing for a vegetarian place. Young, professional staff. Desserts are home-made and might include kulfi (£2.50) – Indian ice cream or carrot halva (£2.60) served hot sprinkled with nuts. No smoking on Saturdays. Two high-chairs are provided; buffet menus are half-price for the under-10s, and there's a special children's set menu at £5.50. "Children under six years old allowed strictly under management discretion." Nevertheless, it's ideal for vegetarian children who enjoy Indian food. A 10% service charge is added to bills. See also under Richmond, Surrey. ***Seats*** *90.* ***Open*** *6pm-10.30pm & L Sun 12.15-2.30.* ***Closed*** *25 Dec. Amex, MasterCard,* ***VISA***

SW11 Ransome's Dock £70

Tel 0171-223 1611 **Fax 0171-924 2614** Map 19 B6
35 Parkgate Road Battersea SW11 4NP

Attractive modern premises that are part of a development alongside a small dock close to Battersea Bridge. The menu is short but the dishes are varied and very well put together. The style is modern, with Mediterranean and Oriental influences sitting happily side by side. Seared scallops with orecchiette pasta and saffron cream and terrine of duck with pistachios and pickled kumquats are typical starters from the monthly-changing carte. For a main course there's Elizabeth David's lamb and aubergine stew with pilaf rice, and calf's liver, smoked Cumbrian bacon, celeriac-potato gratin and spinach. Lovely desserts, too, like prune and armagnac soufflé with armagnac custard. Except for fizz and the house selection, wines are presented by style and more or less in price order, offering quite a lot under £20. Smaller portions are always available for children, as are crayons and colouring paper; there are five high-chairs. Close to Battersea Park zoo, tennis courts, ponds and herb gardens. Friendly and informed service. ***Seats*** *65. Parties 20. Meals 12-11 (Sat till 12, Sun till 3.30). Closed D Sun, 1 week Christmas. Set L £11.50 (not Sat or Sun). Amex, Diners, MasterCard,* ***VISA***

N16 Rasa £40

Tel 0171-249 0344 **Fax 0181-802 6695** Map 16 D2
55 Stoke Newington Church Street N16 OAR

South Indian vegetarian food, from the states of Kerala, Tamil Nadu and Southern Andra Pradesh is what's on offer here in prettily decorated premises which feature gleaming brass chandeliers and a cinnamon and cream decor. The spicing is subtle, with dishes being generally mildly spiced. Friendly service. No smoking. ***Seats*** *42. Parties 20. L 12-2.30 D 6-12. Closed L Mon, all 25 & 26 Dec. Amex, Diners, MasterCard,* ***VISA***

W1 Rasa Sayang £40

Tel 0171-734 8720 **Fax 0171-734 0933** Map 21 A2 R
10 Frith Street Soho W1V 5TZ

Take care not to over-order at this popular Malaysian/Singaporean restaurant – this way you'll stay within a budget and able to finish your meal – as portions are generous! *Char kway teow* (broad rice noodles, fried Singapore-style, with mixed vegetables £4.60), squid with a coconut sauce (£4.90), *gado gado* (popular cooked vegetable salad, garnished with spicy peanut sauce £4.20) and the house special of chicken pieces cooked in an orange sauce (£5.90) typify the style. A buffet lunch at the weekend is good value at £6.50 (children half-price). ***Seats** 150. **Open** 12-2.45 & 6-11.30 (Thu-Sat till 12.30am, Sun 1-10). Amex, Diners, MasterCard,* ***VISA***

Also at:
38 Queensway Bayswater W2 Tel 0171-229 8417 Map 18 A3
Open 12-11.15.

W1 Royal Academy of Arts, Milburns Restaurant

Tel 0171-494 5608 Map 18 D3 JaB
Burlington House Piccadilly W1V ODS

Fabulous murals adorn the walls of this ground-floor café, where the food matches the splendour of the surroundings. Displayed on a series of islands, both hot and cold dishes are available. Among the cold you might encounter escalope of salmon with lime and ginger glaze; chicken, fennel and tarragon cream raised pie or honey-roast chicken salad with beans, pasta and an almond pesto dressing. Hot offerings might include roast leg of lamb with flageolets; pork casserole with black olives and sun-dried tomatoes or a good paella. Vegetarians are not forgotten with plenty of choice: perhaps pasta with roast aubergine with a spring onion and herb dressing or Thai summer vegetable curry with coconut rice (all main courses are priced at around £5.90). Desserts are of an equally high standard, and home-made cakes, flapjacks and scones appear as the afternoon progresses. Sunday lunch offers a roast (£6.30) with plenty of vegetables. In summer there's an ice-cream bar in the forecourt, which also sells a choice of cold individual quiches (£2). Daily newspapers No smoking. ***Seats** 140 (+45 ice cream bar). **Open** 10-5.30. **Closed** 24-26 Dec & Good Friday. Amex, Diners, MasterCard,* ***VISA***

> **JaB** is short for 'Just a Bite'. The majority of these establishments are also recommended in our *Bistros, Bars & Cafés* Guide which features establishments where one may eat well for less than £15 per head.

SW1 Royal Horseguards Thistle 71% £146

Tel 0171-839 3400 **Fax 0171-925 2263** Map 18 D3 
2 Whitehall Court SW1A 2EJ

An imposing Portland stone pile, backing on to gardens alongside the Thames Embankment. The foyer, with its marble floor and elegant crystal chandeliers, is dominated by a Wedgwood-style, plaster-moulded ceiling; this and the comfortable lounge, with its country house feel, set the tone for the rest of the hotel. Bedrooms range from a single above Whitehall Court to spacious air-conditioned Executive rooms with private balconies overlooking the Thames. All have en suite bathrooms and the expected modern amenities. 24hr room service. Breakfast is buffet-style only. Impressive conference rooms cater for up to 300 delegates. Children up to 12 stay free in parents' room. No dogs. ***Rooms** 377. Coffee shop (11am-10.45pm). Amex, Diners, MasterCard,* ***VISA***

SW1 Seafresh

Tel 0171-828 0747 Map 19 D5 JaB
80-81 Wilton Road Victoria SW1

Endearingly traditional, with decorative fishing nets, fake beams and saloon chairs – this is a restaurant for those who take their fish seriously. Flown in from Scotland on ice (not frozen), the fish is served fried in groundnut oil, or grilled on request. You might begin with fish soup (£2.95), which is the house speciality. Then choose, cod (£6.75), haddock (£6.85) or even Scottish salmon (£7.85) all served with proper chips and pickles. Carnivores are not forgotten, with Southern fried chicken (£4.95) and pork sausages or saveloys (£3.55) on offer. Children's meals are served from 5pm. Friendly service and a take-away counter. ***Seats** 120. **Open** 12-10.30. **Closed** Sun, 25 Dec-6 Jan. Amex, Diners, MasterCard,* ***VISA***

NW1 Seashell

Tel 0171-724 1063 **Fax 0171-724 9071** Map 18 B2 JaB
49 Lisson Grove Marylebone NW1 6UH

Darkwood booths, polished tables and tapestry-weave upholstery provide the setting for this rather up-market fish and chip joint. A good selection of fish is available, mainly fried – although some options are available grilled or poached. The City branch, just off Cheapside, is located in a basement – cheerfully lit though – and offers a wider selection including chicken and a vegetarian dish. Nice old-fashioned puddings such as Spotted Dick and syrup pudding come with cream, ice cream or, of course, custard. Prices range from £13.95 for halibut to £8.95 for a fillet of cod, the fish coming with a choice of chips, new or mashed potatoes. There's a simple selection of wines and spirits. ***Seats** 150. **Open** 12-2 (Sun till 2.30) & 5.15-10.30 (Sat 12-10.30). **Closed** D Sun, all 25, 26 Dec & 1 Jan. Amex, Diners, MasterCard,* ***VISA***

We do not accept free meals or hospitality – our inspectors pay their own bills.

W1 Selfridges

Tel 0171-629 1234 **Fax 0171-409 3168** Map 18 C2 JaB
400 Oxford Street W1N 1AB

With a choice of ten different eating places within the store – it's a wonder Selfridges find room for the more customary wares of the department store! Sir Terence Conran has left his mark on the newly-opened third-floor Premier restaurant, which offers a modish menu. The set lunch is £17 for two courses and £19 for three, but the afternoon menu (available between 3.30 and 6) offers interesting dishes which might include curried chicken won tons (£8), saffron tagliatelle and calamari (£7) and Caesar salad with fresh white crab meat (£8). Set tea is £5.25. Other restaurants include the Food Garden Café on the 4th floor – pasta and international cuisine; in the basement Arena offers salads, sandwiches and children's dishes. Cafés are represented by the Brass Rail (ground floor), best described as an American salt beef diner; and the Gallery Coffee Shop – on a mezzanine over the ground floor – a coffee shop, serving light snacks, throughout the day, for non-smokers. A Dome café/bar is now open on the ground floor, part of the London chain; it is open until 11pm (separate entrance in Duke Street) and reflects the menu of its sister outlets. Gordon's Café Bar (1st floor) offers a selection of wines and beers plus bagels and cakes and tea-time sandwiches. The Balcony Wine Bar (ground floor) serves light lunches; Coffee on Two (second floor) is a convenient stopping point for the weary shopper. Just in case . . . there's a Mister Donut in the basement and an Oyster Bar in the food hall. Foreign currency accepted throughout the store. The Mother & Baby room is on the third floor. ***Store hours** Mon-Sat 9.30-7 (Thu till 8); also open Sundays leading to Christmas. Amex, Diners, MasterCard,* ***VISA***

WC2 Sheila's Bar Barbie

Tel 0171-240 8282 **Fax 0171-240 8882** Map 21 B2 
41 King Street Covent Garden WC2E 8JS

Good fun to be had by all at this Australian themed-to-the-hilt bar/restaurant run by the successful Pelican Group (who also run *Café Rouge* and *Dôme*) - now part of Whitbread. As the Aussie name suggests, tucker relies heavily on the char-grill: chook wings (£3.95), steaks (from £9.75) or delicious ribs (£5.25 half, £7.25 full rack). There are also bonza pork chops (£8.95), 'beef and reef' (£10.25), an 'Aussie orgy' barbie for six or more (£9.95 per person), salads, snake and pygmy pie (£5.95), cobberburgers, catch of the day (blackened or barbied), Ayers Rock tucker nucker pie (chocolate pastry topped with peanut caramel, peanut toffee mousse and drizzled with chocolate and roasted peanuts – £3.95) and boomerang baked chocolate bread pudding (£3.50). Service is friendly in true Antipodean style and the helpings are generous. The short 'ankle-biter's menu' for Joeys offers fish fingers, sausages or a burger in pitta bread plus Aussie fries, juice and ice cream for £2.50. On Saturdays and Sundays (until 5pm) the same menu is offered free when a child eats with an adult diner (one ankle biter/one oldie). Four high-chairs are provided, but no changing facilities. ***Seats*** *90. Open 11.30-11. Closed 25 & 26 Dec. Amex, Diners, MasterCard,* ***VISA***

SW1 Sheraton Park Tower 79% £314

Tel 0171-235 8050 **Fax 0171-235 9099** Map 19 C4 H
101 Knightsbridge SW1X 7RN

One of the most distinctive of London's hotels, a circular high-rise tower convenient for Knightsbridge shopping and Hyde Park. Bedrooms, apart from the 31 luxury suites, are identical in size and feature rather pleasing burr walnut-veneered furniture. Thick quilted bedcovers, turned down at night, match the curtains; TVs and mini-bars are discreetly hidden away. There are telephones by the bed, on the desk and in the bathrooms, which have marble-tiled walls, good shelf space, towels and toiletries. Children up to 14 stay free in parents' room. Extra services on Executive floors include valet unpacking, two-hour laundering, a special check-out service and fax machines. Libraries of books, videos and games (even Super Nintendo machines – very popular with airline crews as well as kids!) are kept to amuse youngsters. If you forget baby's nappies, powder, lotion or soap then housekeeping will happily sell you supplies. A baby bath and high-chair can also be provided. A children's menu of favourites is served in the room via 24hr room service. Secure parking for 100 cars – £9 for 24 hours. The busy *Restaurant 101* has a smart conservatory feel and is recommended for adults once the children are in the Land of Nod; it's also a stylish haven for the weary Knightsbridge shopper at lunchtime (£12.50 for two courses including coffee, plus 12½% service). Secure parking for 70 cars. ***Rooms*** *295. Beauty & hair salon, coffee shop (7am-7pm). Amex, Diners, MasterCard,* ***VISA***

SW18 The Ship

Tel 0181-870 9667 Map 17 B5 
41 Jews Row Wandsworth SW18 1TB

Tucked away by the river behind Wandsworth bus garage, the McDonald's drive-thru and by a ready-mix concrete plant, The Ship's setting doesn't sound in the least bit inviting. Nevertheless, once you've made your way round the one-way maze (the slip-road turning off the Wandsworth Bridge is from the south side heading north), thing do begin to look up! A delightful terrace, complete with rose-covered rustic trellis, stretches on several levels all the way to the riverside; an outside bar helps cater for the drinkers who horde here on fine days. The conservatory bar makes a pleasant, airy, most un-London-like venue, with its motley collection of old wooden tables, benches, chairs and pews; there's also a public bar, very much a locals' haunt. A recent extension (45 seats, bookings taken, waiter service) to one side is where you'll find an open kitchen and the food servery, with one menu served throughout. Last year a new chef took over – along with a new management team – and the menu now offers the likes of New Zealand green-lipped mussels in a rich cheese and brandy sauce, smoked haddock and Red Leicester fishcakes with a tangy orange and fennel coulis, and chargrilled burgers alongside steaks (sirloin, lamb, tuna) and perhaps sautéed chicken breast with a blue cheese sauce, glazed walnuts and mace-spiced apple potato. However, they're not too grand to serve just a bowl of chips or cheese-topped garlic bread. When weather permits, a spit-roast or barbecue on the terrace is very, very popular (chicken and fig kebabs, chargrilled lamb steak). The Ship is a Young's pub, under a joint tenancy with the nearby *The Alma, The Coopers Arms* in Chelsea and *The Castle* in Battersea (see entry). The beer is always good – it's about as close to the brewery as you'll get – and there are lots of wines sold by the glass. Bonfire Night (November 5th) and the Last Night of The Proms (early September) are celebrated in style. London pubs are generally unsuitable for children but The Ship is a rare exception, particularly in summer – just outside the pub's gate is an enormous old ship's anchor on a safe riverside walkway. *Open 11-11 (Sun 12-10.30).* ***Bar Food*** *12.30-3 (Sat & Sun till 4), 7-10.30 (Sun till 10).* ***Beer*** *Young's. Riverside terrace, outdoor eating, summer barbecue. Amex, MasterCard,* ***VISA***

W1 Smollensky's Balloon Bar & Restaurant

Tel 0171-491 1199 **Fax 0171-409 2214** Map 18 D3 JaB
1 Dover Street Mayfair W1X 3PJ

The split-level basement bar and dining-room, where there is live piano music every night, offers an American-style menu where steak and fries (£11.25) remain a popular choice. A more eclectic image is being built, with new dishes such as filo chicken parcels with Chinese hoi sin sauce (£4.10) and smoked salmon tartare, caper and chive crème fraiche with bagel toast (£4.95) among the starters; then maybe Thai chicken and prawn salad with chili, soy and ginger dressing (£8.95) or blackened Cajun chicken sandwich with salad with fries (£7.75). Happy hour is between 5.30 and 7 Monday to Friday for some of the best cocktails in London. Lighter lunch options (Mon-Fri to 3.30pm) might offer Chinese five-spice pork with creamed spinach (£5.85), Cajun chicken sandwich (£5.40), a pasta dish (£5.50) and a steak sandwich with fries (£5.95). Weekend lunchtimes and Bank Holidays are dedicated to children, with their own menu and entertainment (face painter, magician, cartoon videos and a clown on Sundays). Lunchtimes at weekends and Bank Holidays are dedicated to children who are offered their own menu and entertainment (face-painter, magician, cartoon videos and a clown on Sundays). Limitless number of high-chairs and booster seats available, and a changing table in the Ladies is provided. Previous joint-winner (with *Smollensky's Balloon)* of our 1993 Family Restaurant of the Year award; the Balloon is perhaps better for the over-7s, while the Strand has more to amuse and distract tinier tots. Nursing mothers are offered the privacy of the Manager's office. ***Seats*** *220.* ***Open*** *12-12 (Sun till 10.30).* ***Closed*** *25 Dec. Amex, Diners, MasterCard,* ***VISA***

WC2 Smollensky's On The Strand

Tel 0171-497 2101 **Fax 0171-836 3270** Map 17 C4 JaB
105 The Strand WC2R 0AA

This basement restaurant and bar throbs to the sound of live music every night, and on Thursdays, Fridays and Saturdays you can dance off your supper! Sunday is jazz night in conjunction with Jazz FM (£3.50 door charge). The layout is open-plan with split-level partitions. Executive chef Lawrence Keogh has overseen a successful broadening of the menu selection at both this and its sister restaurant in Dover Street. Apart from steak and fries, which remains a popular choice, you could begin with sweetcorn Washington soup with polenta croutons (£2.95), deep-fried camembert with gooseberry compote (£3.95) or a box of crudités – serves with any two dips from the choice of taramasalata, houmus, aïoli and tapénade (£3.95); and follow with spinach and goat's cheese tart with rocket and shaved parmesan (£6.95), blackened Cajun chicken sandwich with salad and fries or one of their excellent steaks (£11.25) which come with fries and a choice of sauces. All their meat is encouragingly additive-free. A good-value two-course set deal is available for £10.95. Desserts (all £3.85) might include tiramisu, lemon tart with raspberry coulis and despite the cutesy name Grandma Smollensky's peanut butter cheesecake is well worth saving room for!

Happy hour between 5.30 and 7 Monday to Friday. Children's entertainment at lunchtimes on weekends with magician, clown, kids' videos, raffles and magic show at 2.30pm. A play area with mini-slide, seesaw and bikes helps the under-7s throughout the cooking times of their parents' main courses; colouring sheets and pens and cartoon videos help, too. There are heaps of high-chairs and booster seats available; a changing mat is provided in the toilet and a manager's office for feeding in privacy. Previous joint-winner of our 1993 Family Restaurant of the Year award. Note that both Smollensky's restaurants mix business and pleasure during the week, so don't expect bells and whistles for the children other than at weekends. However, the positive attitude of the staff towards children and the child-friendly food is what makes Smollensky's stand out from the crowd in this part of town. ***Seats*** *250.* ***Open*** *noon-midnight (Thu, Fri, Sat till 12.30am, Sun till 10.30).* ***Closed*** *25 & 26 Dec. Amex, Diners, MasterCard,* ***VISA***

W1 Soho Pizzeria

Tel 0171-434 2480 Map 18 D3 JaB
16-18 Beak Street Soho W1R 3HA

Live music (Tue-Sat evenings) adds to the clamour at this busy Soho pizzeria, with movie star posters, black furniture, and fresh flowers on each table. Garlic mushrooms (£2.45) or onion rings with tomato and horseradish dip (£2) are typical starters. A range of generously-topped pizzas (£4.05-£5.75) is available with or so vegetarian options. A few pasta dishes, salads and chili con carne (£6.95) complete the carte. Desserts comprise chocolate fudge cake, apple strudel (both £2.50) and tiramisu (£2.65). ***Seats*** *105.* ***Open*** *12-12 (Sun 2-10).* ***Closed*** *25, 26 Dec & 1 Jan. Amex, Diners, MasterCard,* ***VISA***

SW13 Sonny's £65

Tel 0181-748 0393 Fax 0181-748 2698 Map 17 A5 
94 Church Road Barnes SW13 ODQ

The café menu at this ever-popular restaurant offers very good value as well as lots of choice and is available between noon and 6pm. Lighter dishes might include fish soup with cod and mussels (£3.95), a plate of crostini (£4.50) and Caesar salad (£4.50); or perhaps lamb and bean stew (£6), Italian sausage with lentils and salsa verde (£6) or a steak sandwich with béarnaise sauce and frites (£5.50) for something more substantial. Muffins (95p), croissants with butter and jam (£1.95) and smoked salmon blinis with sour cream (£5), plus tea and coffee are available before 12 and after 4. There is an excellent lunch menu for £10 and a more expensive à la carte menu in the restaurant – into which the café is absorbed in the evenings. ***Seats*** *100.* ***Open*** *12.30-2.30 (Sun till 3) & 7.30-11.30.* ***Closed*** *D Sun, Bank Holidays. Amex, MasterCard,* ***VISA***

SW17 Sree Krishna £25

Tel 0181-672 4250 Map 17 C6 
192-194 Tooting High Street Tooting Broadway SW17 OSF

Unique and exotic combinations of freshly-ground spices and herbs are the hallmark of this good-value Indian restaurant and the vegetarian cooking of Kerala in South India is its speciality. There is a list of these specialities on the menu including various items stuffed inside traditional dosai pancakes made from rice and lentil flour – rava dosai (vegetables, served with sambhar and coconut chutney £4), masala dosai (potatoes and fried onions £2) and meat masala dosai (their own creation, with minced meat added to the above £3) plus delicious avial (a Kerala dish of vegetables cooked with coconut, curry leaves and spices £2). The remainder of the menu offers standards such as lamb Madras, chicken dansak (both £3.30) and vegetable biryani (£3.50). For dessert there is home-made kulfi (almond or mango), or if you have a really sweet tooth, you can have gulab jamun for just £1.50. One no-smoking room. ***Seats*** *120.* ***Open*** *12-3 & 6-11 (Fri & Sat till 12)* ***Closed*** *25 & 26 Dec. Amex, Diners, MasterCard,* ***VISA***

W8 Sticky Fingers

Tel 0171-938 5338 **Fax 0171-937 7238** Map 19 A4 JaB
1 Phillimore Gardens off Kensington High Street W8 7QG

The popularity of this diner, with Rolling Stones memorabilia-clad walls, has not diminished and this is in no small way due to the friendly, clued-up and very hard-working staff. Breaded mushrooms with aïoli (£3.50), beef chili with corn chips (£3.55) or guacamole (£3.95) are among the ten or so starters; and you could follow with one of the excellent burgers – with a choice of beef or lamb – (from £6.45), chargrilled hot dogs, served with heaps of onions (£5.25) or grilled fish of the day (£8.95). Puddings include frozen yoghurt with honey and almonds, brown sugar apple pie and sticky cake (all £3.15). Half-price drinks in the bar during happy hour 5.30-6.30 (Mon-Fri). No bookings in the evening. Children are made very welcome here; a special menu offers the likes of kiddies' burgers, or ribs and fries. No half portions, but extra plates can be provided if a little one can only manage a bit of mum or dad's meal. Children's parties catered for. Balloons, colouring books and stickers are all provided, and on Sundays there's a magician. ***Seats*** *150.* ***Open*** *12-11.30 (Sun till 11).* ***Closed*** *25 & 26 Dec. Amex, Diners, MasterCard,* ***VISA***

W6 Sumos

Tel 0181-741 7916 Map 17 A4 JaB
169 King Street Hammersmith W6

This small but neat *yzakaya* (snack) restaurant is a perfect introduction to Japanese food. Five budget set menus (3-course set lunch £6.90-£10.90 and 3-course dinner from £10 to £12). Also miso soup £1, griddle-fried dumplings £3, beef with ginger £2.50, chicken yakitori £2. ***Seats*** *40.* ***Open*** *12-3 & 6.30-10.45.* ***Closed*** *L Sat, all Sun, Bank Holidays & 1 week Christmas. No credit cards.*

> If we recommend meals in a hotel a *separate* entry is usually made for its restaurant. Pub and inn entries include bar food details where recommended.

SW4 Tea Time

Tel 0171-622 4944 Map 17 C5 JaB
21 The Pavement Clapham Common SW4 OHY

Frantically busy, especially at the weekend, this endearingly bizarre tea room is a firm Clapham favourite furnished as it is in a homely, higgedly-piggledy style. Choose from a selection of freshly-made sandwiches from a choice of breads (smoked salmon and cream cheese £3.35, BLT £2.35), salads, and good-looking cakes and pastries (from £1.40) in the window display. The all-day breakfasts offer the full works, including freshly squeezed orange juice, and is good value at £5.40, as is the 'Tea-time Special' (sandwiches, two scones, drink) at £6.95. Several loose-leaf teas, fruit teas, infusions and assorted ground coffees (no cafetières at weekend). Warming soups and jacket potatoes make an entry in winter. No smoking in the basement. Unlicensed. ***Seats*** *60.****Open*** *10-6 (Sat & Sun till 6).* ***Closed*** *25, 26 Dec, 1 & 2 Jan. No credit cards.*

SW5 Terstan Hotel £54

Tel 0171-835 1900 **Fax 0171-373 9268** Map 19 A5 B
29 Nevern Square Earls Court SW5 9PE

Standing in a quiet residential square just up from Earls Court Exhibition Centre, this modest bed-and-breakfast hotel is celebrating its ruby anniversary. The Polish Tabaka family has been here since 1957 and run the place with care. The majority of bedrooms have private bathrooms. All have TV and phone. Licensed bar and games room with a pool table. No dogs. ***Rooms*** *48. Closed 24-26 Dec. Amex, MasterCard,* ***VISA***

SW7 Texas Lone Star Saloon

Tel 0171-370 5625 Map 19 B5 JaB
154 Gloucester Road SW7

A wooden Red Indian indicates the entrance to this busy restaurant whose theme is inspired by a Western saloon, complete with Country and Western music and videos. A confusing layout on the Tex-Mex menu requires concentration. Caesar salad (£3.25), peel-outs with chili and guacamole (£3.95) and Coyote Pete's spicy onion rings (£2.30) are typical starters. Ribs, enchiladas, burritos and burgers (prices between £4.85 and £9), chilis and steaks make up the main-course menu. Pecan pie (£2.65) or apple pie with Häagen-Dazs ice cream (£3.65) to finish. Great fun (but noisy) and the cocktail list is worth investigating! Children's menu available. A 12½% service charge is added to bills. ***Seats*** *160.* ***Open*** *noon-midnight (Mon-Wed till 11.30pm). Amex, Diners, MasterCard,* ***VISA***

Also at:

117 Queensway W2 Tel 0171-727 2980 Map 18 A3
Open 12-3 & 6.30-1am (Sat & Sun open all day).

50 Turnham Green Terrace Chiswick W4 Tel 0181-747 0001 Map 17 A5
Open 12-3 & 6-12.30am (Sat & Sun noon-midnight).

SW4 Tiger Lil's

Tel 0171-720 5433 **Fax 0171-622 5995** Map 17 C6 JaB
16a Clapham Common Southside SW4 7AB

This uncommonly busy restaurant draws a lively crowd. Tables and chairs are made of wood, and there are also wooden partitions in the window and carved wooden lanterns hanging from the ceiling. The concept behind the food is that you can either have it fried by one of the wok chefs while you watch or cook it yourself in a steaming firepot at your table. There is a huge display of food on offer from which to choose: pork, squid, chicken, spare ribs, beef, turkey, mussels, wind-dried sausage, tofu, fish cakes, fried bean curd, and mung beans with chick peas which you pile on to your plate alongside some of the 16 vegetable dishes: shaved carrot with Japanese seaweed, watercress with water chestnuts, bok choy with mangetout, three colours of peppers with sesame seeds, cloud ear fungus with mushrooms and bamboo shoots with wild flowers. The wok chefs offer six sauces: teriyaki, curried coconut, satay, black bean, sweet and sour or Lil's Special (a spicy tom yam sauce of chili, lemon grass and ginger) and you can have extra garlic, chili, spring onions, coriander and ginger. For a set price of £10 (including rice or noodles) you can return and create as many combinations as you like – older children will love it (younger ones might, too, especially as it's half-price for under-10s). The dessert menu (£3.50) includes tropical fruits and a pot of hot melted chocolate to dip them into as well as tropical ice creams and sorbets served in a lotus flower basket. To drink there are Lil's juices (lychee cocktail, mango and apple, carrot, celery and apple £1.80) alongside wines and Tiger, Giraf and Elephant beers! The service is friendly and informative, particularly if it's your first visit. Booking advisable. Two high-chairs are provided (but no changing facilities). ***Seats*** *90. Open 6-11.30 (Fri till 12, Sat 12-12, Sun 12-11). Closed 25 & 26 Dec, 1 Jan. Set menu £10. Diners, MasterCard,* ***VISA***

Also at:

500 Kings Road Chelsea SW3 Tel 0171-376 5003 Map 19 B6
At World's End, on the corner of Slaidburn Street.

270 Upper Street Islington N1 Tel 0171-226 1118 Map 16 C3

N10 Toff's

Tel 0181-883 8656 Map 16 C1 JaB
38 Muswell Hill Broadway N10 3RT

Old prints of Billingsgate market adorn the walls of this popular fish and chip restaurant, which the Toffalli family continues to run with great success. The fish is coated in batter or matzo meal (60p extra), then fried in groundnut oil. Prices start at £7.95 (cod and chips), with plaice fillet at £8.50 (£9.50 on the bone), Dover sole (£16.50) and halibut (£13) top the range. Nearly everything is also available grilled – which takes a little time and costs £1 more. Add fish soup, fisherman's pie, daily specials, traditional puds and a children's menu and in Toff's you have the ideal family fish restaurant. ***Seats*** *32.* ***Open*** *11.30-10.* ***Closed*** *Sun, Mon, 2 weeks Aug-Sept. Amex, MasterCard,* ***VISA***

W4 Tootsies

Tel 0181-747 1869 Map 17 A4 JaB
148 Chiswick High Road W4

A popular burger chain sharing the same decor of cane bistro chairs and walls covered with enamel signs and colourful mirrors. Beefburgers (from £4.95) are offered with a choice of different toppings. Salads (£3.95-£6.50) are made freshly from good ingredients: chargrilled chicken served with different toppings (£7.50) or in a sandwich (£5.50) and English breakfast (with freshly-squeezed orange juice and unlimited tea or coffee – £5.95) is available all day. 'Tootsies tots' under 10 are given balloons, special plates and a menu of mini hamburger with cheese, egg or beans and fries; small chicken sandwich or sausage, fries and baked beans; finish with TT's ice cream. Grown-ups can set into lattice apple pie, hot chocolate fudge cake or a banana split (all £3.50). High-chairs and booster seats are provided. Tables on the pavement in good weather. ***Seats*** *72. Open 12-11.30 Mon-Thu, 12-12 Fri & Sat, 11-11 Sun. Closed 5 days Christmas. MasterCard,* ***VISA***
Also at:
196 Haverstock Hill NW3 Tel 0171-431 3812 Map 16 B2
177 New Kings Road Parsons Green SW6 Tel 0171-736 4023 Map 17 B5
107 Old Brompton Road South Kensington SW7 Tel 0171-581 8942 Map 19 B5
147 Church Road Barnes SW13 Tel 0181-748 3630 Map 17 A5
48 High Street Wimbledon Village SW19 Tel 0181-946 4135 Map 17 B6
120 Holland Park Avenue W11 Tel 0171-229 8567 Map 17 B4

N1 Tuk Tuk £30

Tel 0171-226 0837 Map 16 D3 R
330 Upper Street Islington N1 2XQ

Find Tuk Tuk at the Islington Green end of Upper Street. The chic Thai restaurant, named after the little canopied cycle-taxis in South East Asia, models itself on the small family shops which sell one-pot dishes to the taxi drivers. Order a number of dishes – maybe *tom yum kung* (spicy prawn soup £5.95), chicken satay (£3.50) to start. Follow with a red curry with rice (*kang ped* £5.50) or Thai rice noodles (£4.95) and some vegetable dishes. Specialities include rice and chicken cooked in a clay pot (£5.25) and Thai fishcakes (£3.50). ***Seats*** *60.* ***Open*** *12-3 & 6-11 (Sun till 10).* ***Closed*** *L Sat & Sun, some Bank Holidays. Amex, MasterCard,* ***VISA***

SW17 Tumbleweeds

Tel 0181-767 9395 Map 17 C6 JaB
32 Tooting Bec Road SW17

Straightforward vegetarian and vegan restaurant with a daily-changing menu. Perhaps carrot and coriander or Armenian soup (£1.90), broccoli filo parcels with cashew and ginger sauce (£6.90), leek and mushroom curry in a coconut and lime sauce (£5.90) and tomato bake (polenta, cheese, peppers and olives £5.95) might be the day's offerings, each with an accompanying salad. There are a few puddings such as spiced banana cake to finish. Organic wines and beer are served. ***Seats*** *46.* ***Open*** *6.30-10.30 (Sat & Sun 12-10.30).* ***Closed*** *Mon, Easter, 25 & 26 Dec, 1 Jan. No credit cards.*

SW5 Tusc

Tel 0171-373 9082 **Fax 0171-244 6401** Map 19 A5 JaB
256 Brompton Road SW5 9HP

Tusc is the revamped *Pontevecchio*, a long-established Italian restaurant in the ownership of Walter Mariti, restaurateur and racehorse owner. It's now owned by his son, Riccardo Mariti, who also has *Riccardo's* in Fulham Road. This is a roomy, comfortable place, and 30 of its seats are on an enclosed terrace protected from the street by hedges and greenery. The menu concept, as at *Riccardo's*, is that all portions are starter size, with the suggestion that two or three dishes should be ordered.

A recent meal of cannelloni bean and cabbage soup (£3.25), filled polenta with prosciutto and asparagus (£4.25) and grilled spring chicken with chilis and lemon (£4.95) proved enjoyable and more than adequate with some bread (95p) to dip in the olive oil, a little bottle of which is on each table. The most expensive item on the menu is chargrilled sea bass at £8.50. A 12½% service charge is added to bills. ***Seats*** *100 (+30 outside).* ***Open*** *12.30-3 & 6.30-12. Amex, Diners, MasterCard,* ***VISA***

WC2 Tuttons Brasserie

Tel 0171-836 4141 **Fax 0171-379 9979** Map 20 A2 **JaB**
11-12 Russell Street Covent Garden WC2B 5H2

A reliable brasserie amidst the profusion of Covent Garden eateries – Tuttons starts the day early with breakfast, English (£5.50) or Continental (£3.90), and then offers an all-day menu until 11.30pm with such tempting ideas as spinach and goat's cheese tart (£3.80) or spicy fishcakes with tomatoes and fresh coriander (£4.30). Main courses such as baked cod, pesto mash and fresh tomato and basil sauce (£8.90) and tagliatelle with smoked salmon and red pepper sauce (£7.90), run alongside burgers, steaks and a standard range of puddings, crème brulée or home-baked cheesecake (from £3.50). There is a list of daily specials from which you can choose a prix-fixe menu – two courses for £10.90, 3 for £14.50. Tea is served from 3pm and is £3.90 for sandwiches, scone and tea. A large terrace extends over the Covent Garden pavement in fine weather. ***Seats*** *100 (+70 outside).* ***Open*** *9.30am-11.30pm (Fri/Sat till 12, Sun till 10.30).* ***Closed*** *24 & 25 Dec. Amex, Diners, MasterCard,* ***VISA***

SW1 22 Jermyn Street £247

Tel 0171-734 2353 **Fax 0171-734 0750** Map 18 D3 **PH**
22 Jermyn Street SW1Y 6HL

In one of London's most select shopping streets, only yards from the hubbub of Piccadilly Circus, this delightfully genteel town house offers peace and seclusion in spacious, elegantly furnished suites and studios. Every thought has gone into the creation of high-calibre accommodation with fine furniture, beautiful fabrics and fresh flowers creating a very pleasant home from home. Each room has two direct-dial phone lines and a fax/modem line with a Windows-compatible CD-ROM reference library. 24hr room service, from enthusiastic staff, provides everything from breakfast and dinner (there is no restaurant) to personal shopping. Laundry/dry-cleaning service. Business and secretarial service. Car parking can be arranged nearby. "We really do welcome children at 22 Jermyn Street", says Henry Togna, providing them with a newsletter that gives recommendations for shopping (the Disney Store and Tower Records are only a short walk away), eating out (Planet Hollywood - ask about their Platinum Card to beat the queues) and entertainment (Rock Circus, SegaWorld, West End shows). Computer whizz-kids can even cruise the Internet or browse through a collection of CD-ROMs in the hotel's business office; Gameboys are available and a Sega Mega drive can be connected to your room TV; more traditional entertainment like Monopoly, Scrabble and jigsaws are also provided. Children should insist on taking away (at a small charge) one of their collectable teddy bear bathrobes! 24hr room service; 24hr medical and dental support is advertised. ***Rooms*** *18. Amex, Diners, MasterCard,* ***VISA***

SW16 Uno Plus

Tel 0181-764 3007 Map 17 C6 **JaB**
1538 London Road Norbury SW16 4EU

This cheerful wine bar, owned by the Caterino family, is next door to the their main restaurant. A wide selection of tapas (from £1.30) is available alongside pasta dishes – helpfully offered in two sizes (£2.90-£5.90); pizzas (from £4.45) as well as soups, salads, baked potatoes and even hamburgers. A lunchtime buffet only on Sunday. Parking to the rear of the premises. ***Seats*** *50.* ***Open*** *(meals) 12-3 & 6-11.30 (Sun 1-4pm).* ***Closed*** *L Mon, Sat & Bank Holidays. Amex, Diners, MasterCard,* ***VISA***

N1 The Upper Street Fish Shop

Tel & Fax 0171-359 1401 Map 16 D3 JaB
324 Upper Street Islington N1 2XQ

Crowded with both eaters-in and takers-away, the Conways' splendid fish and chip restaurant has been going strong for some 15 years now. Excellent fish and chips are the main attraction; plaice (£7.50), cod and haddock (£7). But daily specials might include whole lemon sole with chips (£8.50), fried squid with chips (£6.50) or whole crab with salad and brown bread (£9). Tempting starters might include Irish rock oysters (£5.50 for half a dozen), fish soup and smoked salmon paté (both £2.50). Home-made puddings are served with cream or custard. Unlicensed, so bring your own wine – no corkage charge. Minimum food charge £7.50. ***Seats** 50. **Open** 12-2.15 (Sat to 3) & 6-10.15 (Fri & Sat 5.30-10.15). **Closed** L Mon, all Sun, Bank Holiday weeks & 3 weeks Christmas. No credit cards.*

WC1 Wagamama £25

Tel 0171-323 9223 **Fax 0171-323 9224** Map 21 B1
4 Streatham Street off Bloomsbury Street WC1 1JB

'Not so much a noodle bar – more a way of life!' might well be the motto here, where there is a page-long dissertation on positive eating and positive living, preceding the menu. Nothing, however, detracts from the popularity of this Japanese-style restaurant which is now open all day and has spawned a second branch in Lexington Street. *Ramen* (Chinese), *soba* and *udon* (Japanese) noodles all feature on the menu (from £4.50): chicken ramen in a clear broth with slices of chicken, seasonal greens, memma and spring onions. *Yaki udon* are pan-fried thick white noodles with shiitake mushrooms, eggs, leeks, prawns, chicken, red pepper and Japanese fishcake in curry oil (£4.50). Side dishes include *gyoza* – dumplings (from £3). Three set meals make choosing easy for the beginner, and the most expensive 'Absolute Wagamama' (£7.50) includes a beer or raw juice. Jasmine green tea is served free of charge. No smoking. No bookings are taken, expect queues at peak times. ***Seats** 104. **Open** 12-11 (Sat from 12.30, Sun 12.30-10). **Closed** 1 week Christmas. Diners, MasterCard, **VISA***
Also at:
10a Lexington Street W1R 3HS Tel 0171-292 0990 Map 18 D3
This branch has a more extensive menu with yakitori and tempura dishes. Prices are a little higher.

WC2 Waldorf Meridien 83% £247

Tel 0171-836 2400 **Fax 0171-379 3463** Map 20 A2 HR
Aldwych WC2B 4DD

Opened in 1908, the Waldorf is a hotel of world renown, though it isn't linked to New York's Waldorf Astoria. Public areas include the Club Bar with its polished wood panelling, leather chesterfields and marble fireplaces, the pubby Footlights Bar and traditional Aldwych Brasserie. The hotel is equally well known for the magnificent Palm Court Lounge which retains its splendid original Edwardian character and is a very special place for afternoon tea (£6.50-£25). Saturday and Sunday tea dances (from £22) are a veritable institution, with their origins in the Waldorf's famous Tango Teas of the 1920s and 30s. Music from a five-piece band is one of its added attractions. Bedrooms all have air-conditioning, secondary sockets for fax or modems and even 110-volt outlets for the convenience of transatlantic guests. Every bedroom has its own entrance lobby, handsome darkwood furniture and one of nine bold decorative schemes. Elaborately draped curtains and chandeliers hark back to the opulence of the hotel's Edwardian origins, as do the period-style washstands in marble-trimmed bathrooms that all have both fixed and hand-held showers over the tubs; bathrobes, speaker extensions and good toiletries are also provided. Well-turned-out staff provide a proper turn-down service in the evenings and valet parking, but overnight room service is limited to sandwiches and snacks. ***Rooms** 292. Brasserie (11-11). Beauty & hair salon, gift shop. Amex, Diners, MasterCard, **VISA***

Restaurant **£90**

A grand, high-ceilinged room with Corinthian columns and French doors opening on to the Palm Court. The menu mixes traditional and modern: pan-fried Dover sole with asparagus, olives and mixed green salad, roast rabbit with spinach and mushrooms, roast turbot with artichokes and roast rack of lamb. The wine list is very modest for a hotel of this class. ***Seats*** *60. Parties 10. L 12.30-2.30 D 6-11 (Sun 7-10). Set L £20 Set D £26/£32. Closed L Sat & Sun.*

SW1 Wilbraham Hotel 55% £94

Tel 0171-730 8296 **Fax 0171-730 6815** Map 19 C5 H
Wilbraham Place Sloane Street SW1X 9AE

Occupying three Victorian houses, this charmingly old-fashioned hotel enjoys a peaceful location close to Sloane Square. Most of the simply furnished bedrooms have TVs and en suite bathrooms. No dogs. ***Rooms*** *52. No credit cards.*

SW1 Willett Hotel £94

Tel 0171-824 8415 **Fax 0171-730 4830** Map 19 C5 B
32 Sloane Gardens SW1W 8DJ

Just south of Sloane Square, the Willett offers modest bed and breakfast accommodation. Bedrooms, all with satellite TVs, direct-dial phones, hairdryers and trouser presses are undergoing gradual refurbishment with six rooms completed to a comfortable standard. ***Rooms*** *19. Amex, Diners, MasterCard,* ***VISA***

W8 Windsor Castle

Tel 0171-727 8491 Map 19 A4

114 Campden Hill Road Kensington W8 7AR

A charming Georgian pub built in 1828 when (the entrance on Campden Hill Road being at the same height as the top of St Paul's Cathedral) one could see Windsor Castle 20 miles away. The original panelling and built-in benches still remain and the three small bars have separate entrances. Traditional English cooking throughout the day; Sunday lunch roast rib of beef with Yorkshire pudding. A shaded and paved beer garden (one of London's busiest) at the rear is the main attraction in summer (and gets really packed), while a cosy country inn atmosphere prevails inside in winter. Both oysters (£5 for half a dozen) and champagne (£20 for Lanson Black Label) are sold at sensible prices. Not suitable for children inside. Bass. *Open 12-11 (Sun 12-10.30).* ***Beer*** *Bass, Adnams Extra, Hancock's HB, guest beer. Garden. Amex, MasterCard,* ***VISA***

> Always ring ahead and inform establishments of your exact requirements when travelling with children. Unannounced can, sadly, still mean unwelcome.

W5 Wine & Mousaka £40

Tel 0181-998 4373 Map 17 A4

33 Haven Green Ealing W5 2NX

Traditional Greek favourites are to be found on the menu at this taverna, with views of the charcoal grill and rotisserie. Try such classics as kleftiko (£6.60), shish kebabs (£6.60) and indeed moussaka (£5.75), or opt for a set menu (available lunchtime and Mon-Thu evenings for £8.95) offering tsatsiki with hot pitta, taramasalata or dolmades to begin; smaller helpings of the above dishes as main courses; and Greek pastries or ice cream to finish. Half-portions available for children. Good air-conditioning. A 12½% service charge is added to bills. Sister restaurant in Kew (see entry). ***Seats*** *92* ***Open*** *12-2.30 & 6-11.30.* ***Closed*** *Sun & Bank Holidays. Amex, Diners, MasterCard,* ***VISA***

W2 Winton's Soda Fountain

Tel 0171-229 8489 Map 18 A3 JaB
2nd Floor Whiteleys Queensway Bayswater W2 4SB

The multi-unit shopping complex that occupies the magnificent Whiteley's building has many fast-food outlets. This one is an ice cream soda fountain with parquet floors, marble-topped tables and a Wurlitzer juke-box. A 'Whiteley's Dream' consists of three scoops of ice cream of your choice with fruit salad, nuts and whipped cream (£4.20). A wide range of flavours is available – fresh malted banana, Dime bar crunch, chocolate chip or lemon mousse among them and these form the base for sundaes such as Monkey Madness (£4.50), Jolly Giant (£7) and Children's Delight (£2.50). Milkshakes (£2.80), cakes (£1-£1.95) and biscuits are also available. High-chairs available, and a Mother & Baby room is one floor up in the shopping centre. Children's portions on request. A multi-screen cinema on the same floor will keep older children happy for an afternoon. ***Seats*** *100.* ***Open*** *11-10.30 (Fri & Sat till 11).* ***Closed*** *25 Dec. No credit cards.*
Also at:
58 Queensway W2 Tel 0171-243 2975 Map 18 A3
Open 10am-12.30am 7 days a week.

WC2 Wolfe's Bar and Grill

Tel 0171-831 4442 Map 21 B2 JaB
30 Great Queen Street Holborn WC2B 5BB

Wolfburgers (perhaps Little Red Riding Hood might have ended differently?) feature on an extensive menu here at this converted club/cocktail bar. Try old American favourites from £7.85 with Roquefort cheese or barbecue sauce; Continental wolfburgers include such exotic varieties as provençale with herbs, onions, tomatoes and garlic (£7.85) or pepperburger with green peppercorn sauce. Alternatives to burgers include pasta, salads, omelettes and grills or perhaps Continental veal sausages with sauerkraut (£9.25) or goujons of sole with tartare sauce (£11.50). Minimum charge £9, £10 on Saturday. Good selection of wines by the glass. 30% off at the bar as there's an all-day happy hour. ***Seats*** *100 (+ terrace seating).* ***Open*** *11.30am-midnight.* ***Closed*** *Sun, 25 Dec. Amex, Diners, MasterCard,* ***VISA***
Also at:
25 Basil Street SW3 Tel 0171-589 8444 Map 19 C4
Open 7 days (hours as above). Same menu. Behind Harrods.

W1 Woodlands

Tel 0171-486 3862 Fax 0181-908 5182 Map 18 C2 JaB
77 Marylebone Lane W1M 4GA

South Indian vegetarian food displaying skilful use of herbs and spices, is the stock-in-trade of this smart, comfortable but unpretentious restaurant. Thalis provide the best value and are a complete meal in themselves, beginning perhaps with a soup and following with a curry, rice, chapati and dessert – prices for these start at £8.95. Dishes to be enjoyed from the carte include *rasa vada* (lentil cakes in a spicy sauce £2.50) and *idli* (steamed rice cakes with *sambal* and coconut chutney £2.75). The light, crisp *dosa* pancakes have fillings of spiced potato, onion or cottage cheese (from £3.25). The pizza-like *uthappams* – made of lentils not flour – are enjoyable too (from £3.75). An excellent set lunch (£4.95) mght offer a choice of *masala dosa* or a curry, with pickles and dal. There is a minimum charge of £5 in the evening. A 12½% service charge is added to bills. ***Seats*** *70.* ***Open*** *12-3 & 6-11.* ***Closed*** *25 & 26 Dec. Amex, Diners, MasterCard,* ***VISA***
Also at:
37 Panton Street SW1 Tel 0171-839 7258 Map 21 A3
Open 12-3 & 5.30-11.
402a High Road Wembley Tel 0181-902 9869 Map 15 E2

WC2 World Food Café

Tel 0171-379 0298 Map 21 B2 JaB
First Floor 14 Neal's Yard Covent Garden WC2H 9DP

A small selection of vegetarian dishes from across the globe is served here in the relaxed café above the herbal shop. Large wooden tables are shared or you can sit at the bar. 'Meals' are £5.95; for example *Indian* is a thali of coconut chutney, cucumber raita, carrot and lime salad, steamed brown rice and vegetables cooked with fresh ground spices. There are *West African, Mexican* and *Turkish* meals too. Half a dozen starters (or light meals) might include Egyptian falafel in pitta bread with tabbouleh, salads and houmus (£4.25) or a soup of the day with pitta bread (£3.50). Puddings are likewise eclectic at £2.95; maybe tiramisu or mango kulfi ice cream. No smoking. Bring your own wine, no corkage. Afternoon teas. Take-aways available.***Seats*** *42.* ***Open*** *12-5 (Tue-Fri till 7.30 & on some summer evenings, phone for details).* ***Closed*** *Sun & Bank Holidays. No credit cards.*

> **JaB** is short for 'Just a Bite'. The majority of these establishments are also recommended in our *Bistros, Bars & Cafés* Guide which features establishments where one may eat well for less than £15 per head.

N16 Yum Yum £65

Tel 0171-254 6751 **Fax 0171-241 3857** Map 16 D2 
26 Stoke Newington Church Street N16 0LU

Regular trips to Thailand by Atique Choudhury and his Thai wife have resulted in a delightful local restaurant whose walls are crammed with beautiful carvings and artwork from that part of the world. Complementing the intricacy of the ornamentation, the food is also beautifully presented, with carved vegetable flourishes offered with the starters and all served on pretty china. The menu encompasses a wide range of well-prepared, enjoyable Thai dishes, some hot and very fiery, others soothingly milder and gentler. Other choices could be sweet and sour prawns with vegetables, duck with crab meat and a cashew nut sauce, roasted baby chicken in a red wine sauce and sliced pork with fresh basil leaves and onion. The portions are quite generous. Vegetarians have an extensive choice, too. Staff are willing and pleasant. Booking is advisable, particularly at weekends. ***Seats*** *120. Parties 22. Private Room 30. L 12-2.30 D 6-10.45 (Fri & Sat till 11.15). Closed 2 weeks Christmas. Set L £13 (min 2) Set D £29. Amex, Diners, MasterCard,* ***VISA***

W1 Zoe (Café)

Tel 0171-224 1122 **Fax 0171-935 5444** Map 18 C2 
St Christopher's Place off Wigmore Street W1M 5HH

Tables spill on to the pavement, in fine weather, at this Mediterranean-inspired café with a brasserie downstairs. The menu offers a modish choice: maybe Tuscan bread soup (£3.95), sun-dried tomato and mozzarella tart (£4.25) or oysters with Worcestershire sauce, crème fraiche and chives (£7.95/£12) for something light; penne pasta with pesto and parmesan shavings (£6.25), rosemary chicken with olive oil potato skins and chive sour cream (£9.95) or chargrilled squid with bok choy and bean sprouts (£7.95) for something weightier. Salads and side orders are interesting and tempting, but push up prices – herb leaf salad £3.95. Good puds. ***Seats*** *75.* ***Open*** *11.30-11.30.* ***Closed*** *Sun & Bank Holidays. Amex, Diners, MasterCard,* ***VISA***

> A jug of fresh water!

ACCEPTED IN
HOTELS AND R
THAN MOST PE
EVER HAVE HO

VISA IS ACCEPTED FOR MORE TRANSACTIONS

England

The addresses of establishments in the following former **Counties** now include their new Unitary Authorities:

Avon
North Somerset, Bath & North East Somerset

Cleveland
Redcar & Cleveland, Middlesbrough, Stockton-on-Tees, Hartlepool

Greater Manchester
Wigan, Bolton, Bury, Rochdale, Salford, Manchester, Trafford, Tameside, Oldham

Humberside
East Riding of Yorkshire, Kingston-upon-Hull, North Lincolnshire, North East Lincolnshire

Middlesex
Harrow, Hounslow, Hillingdon (also certain London Unitary Authorities like Brent and Ealing)

Tyne & Wear
Newcastle-upon-Tyne, North Tyneside, Gateshead, South Tyneside, Sunderland

West Midlands
Wolverhampton, Walsall, Dudley, Sandwell, Birmingham

South Yorkshire
Barnsley, Sheffield, Rotherham, Doncaster

West Yorkshire
Bradford, Leeds, Calderdale, Kirklees, Wakefield

All other counties remain the same

ABBOTS BROMLEY Marsh Farm Tea Rooms

Tel 01283 840323 Map 6 C3 JaB
Uttoxeter Road Abbots Bromley Staffordshire WS15 3EJ

Featured in the first edition of the *Just a Bite Guide* in 1965, Mrs Hollins's tea rooms are situated in the main house of her former working farm. Stop in on weekends and Bank Holidays in summer to sample her scones, fruit or plain, with clotted cream and home-made jam, or her fine home baking and celebrated fruit loaf (50p). There are sandwiches (from £1) and salads (from £2.50) for heartier teas, and trifle or apple pie to follow. Cooking to order is limited to poached eggs, beans or cheese on toast (£1); and to tempt the littlest ones boiled eggs and soldiers on request. ***Seats** 42. **Open** 3-6 weekends and summer Bank Holidays. **Closed** Mon-Fri & end Oct-Easter Sun. No credit cards.*

ALFRISTON Toucans Restaurant at Drusillas Zoo

Tel 01323 870656 **Fax 01323 870846** Map 11 B6 JaB
Drusillas Park Alfriston East Sussex BN26 5QS

One mile north of the Brighton-Eastbourne road, Drusillas Zoo continues to attract hordes of families and it is rewarding to see them so well catered for when the little ones get hungry. Our 1991 Family Restaurant of the Year has a play corner, designed to combat the long stretches of boredom that visit children at mealtimes, and is always well used. There are paper tablecloths, ample room for prams and push-chairs, excellent nursing and changing areas, high-chairs galore; every facility is provided. The staff are young, friendly and attentive and deliver maximum portions of food, usually with a minimum wait. Baby meals can be ordered, bottles heated and jars warmed. The regular menu offers the usual array of children's favourites, from jacket potatoes to fish fingers, scampi (£5.65) and chips, burgers (£4.25) and vegetarian pasta (£4.65); 'Little Monkeys' under 10 pay £2.35 for main courses and around £1.40 for kids' cocktails (fancy a muddy puddle?); ask for children's portions of puddings like soft fudge brownies (£2.45). A roast (£5.95, children under 10 £3.25) is offered on Sunday in winter (barbecues in summer), often with children's entertainment. A good local brew, Harveys from Lewes, is served for dads who find the zoo thirsty work. Talking mechanical animals help teach the little monkeys their manners. No smoking; no dogs. The open-plan *Inn at the Zoo* in the same thatched building caters well for adults (from 10-5), offering a short menu of typical snacky pub food and teas. Themed children's parties. No reservations after 12.30; "it does get very busy and it's unfair on other diners waiting if a table reservation fails to turn up". Free car parking. ***Open** all year weekdays (no waitress service or indoor restaurant entertainment), weekends and school holidays 10-6 (Oct-Mar 11-5). Zoo open every day (10am-4pm, last entry 5pm in summer) except 24-26 Dec; under-3s free, 3-12s £4.50 inc train and playland (adults £5.50, OAP £3.50). Closed Dec 24-26. MasterCard,* ***VISA***

ALNMOUTH Village Gift and Coffee Shop

Tel 01665 830310 Map 5 D2 JaB
West Tower 58 Northumberland Street Alnmouth Northumberland NE66 2RS

Formerly a Customs Post Office, this 18th-century oak-beamed building now houses a traditional coffee shop also selling much of its home-made produce (fudge, preserves, biscuits) as gifts from the shop. In addition to good home baking, some local seafood specialities are featured along with a selection of hot and cold dishes – popular items include fisherman's lunch (prawns, crab meat, smoked mackerel and salad £4.50), and coast and country lunch (cheese, ham, prawns and crab £4.50). Popular too is the special warmer of Northumbrian broth (£1.50), toasted sandwiches (with a filling of your choice) and filled baked potatoes (£2.50 – £3.95). There are plenty of home-made goodies for the sweet-toothed (scones 80p, ginger cake 95p) and tempting fresh fruit meringues (£1.85). Cream teas are substantial and good value, with sandwiches, scones, cake and a pot of tea for £3.50. The hot chocolate warmer (warmed chocolate fudge cake with custard or ice cream accompanied by a drink of hot chocolate with whipped cream and marshmallows £2.65) might well have earned Alnmouth its reputation as a place 'famous for all kinds of wickedness'

(J.Wesley)! Attached to the coffee shop is an art gallery housing paintings and works by local artists and craftsmen. Unlicensed. No smoking. ***Seats*** *35.* ***Open*** *8-6.30 (extended during high season).* ***Closed*** *25 Dec (and in very bad weather). MasterCard,* ***VISA***

ALPHINGTON Double Locks

Tel 01392 56947 Map 13 D2 
Alphington Exeter Devon EX2 6CT

The Double Locks isn't easy to find but it's well worth the effort. First find the Marsh Barton Trading Estate and drive through it to the council incinerator – don't worry, the pub is some way yet – until you reach the plank canal bridge, which is made for vehicles, although it may not appear to be. Once across, turn right, and a single-track road will bring you to the red-brick Georgian Double Locks in a splendid canalside location within sight of the Cathedral. Equally popular with business people and students, this is a fine summer pub: there are swans on the canal next to the lock, a large garden shaded by huge pine trees, and a barbecue both lunchtime and evening in summer, weather permitting. Inside is very informal. Several rooms have black- and white-tiled floors, draw-leaf domestic dining-room tables and lots of posters advertising local events – not far removed from a student bar at University. Nine real ales are drawn straight from the cask and chess, draughts, Monopoly, Scrabble and bar billiards are all keenly played. A huge blackboard displays the day's offerings, featuring almost as many options for vegetarians as for carnivores. Start, perhaps, with mushroom and coriander soup, garlic mushrooms and Stilton on toast or a selection of garlic breads with Cheddar, Stilton or goat's cheese topping, followed perhaps by turkey and mushroom pie, lasagne, baked potatoes, lamb kebabs and late breakfasts. Families welcome. *Open 11-11 (Sun 12-10.30).* ***Bar Food*** *11-10.30 (Sun 12-10).* ***Beer*** *Smiles Brewery Bitter, Best & Exhibition, Adnams Broadside, Greene King Abbot Ale, Wadworth 6X, Everards Old Original, two guest ales. Riverside garden, outdoor play area, outdoor eating, summer barbecue. Family room. MasterCard,* ***VISA***

ALTON Alton Towers Hotel 67% £100

Tel 01538 704600 **Fax 01538 704657** Map 6 C3 
Alton Staffordshire ST10 4DB

This extraordinary new resort hotel has 175 non-smoking family bedrooms and suites (sleeping up to 6) and specialises in packaged mini-breaks that include daily admission (both 1- and 2-day passes; 1996 daily entry was around £59 for a family of four) to Alton Towers Theme Park, of which it's an integral part. Magical touches in the rooms include a giant teddy bear, duck-shaped hairdryer, watering-can lamps with floppy-hat shades and an antique, freestanding pedestal telephone (ours was positively dusty!). Six bedrooms are equipped for disabled guests. The constant presence of clowns, costumed eccentrics and woman-sized teddy bears ensures a subtle degree of adult supervision around the hotel and the constant tide of entertainments, magical, musical and otherwise recreational, are reflected in the overall room tariff. Mother and baby comfort stations, the availability of baby food and snacks all day, high tea from 5pm and universally-available baby-listening all contribute towards lessening the load. However, parents who are unused to being totally outnumbered by others' offspring may find this all a trifle overpowering; foreign visitors, meanwhile, can observe a thoroughly British propensity for queuing, which will stand them in good stead upon entering the Theme Park proper. The real bonus for youngsters topping 1.4 metres (and some brave parents) is preferential early-morning admission to the park's current *dernier cri* in white-knuckle rides, Nemesis; one inspector still can't believe he really rode it and lived (his daughter, of course, was thrilled). Although the marketing, sales and reservations is slick, the operation can be let down by poor housekeeping, under-trained staff and check-out queues. Breakfast may be a bit of scrum (despite the queues) and our experience of room service was not worth bothering with – so much for 'family breakfast in bed'! The food is certainly not a major attraction! No dogs. Central reservations 0990 001100. ***Rooms*** *175. Garden, indoor swimming pool, sauna, spa bath, children's play rooms, games room, kiosk. Amex, Diners, MasterCard,* ***VISA***

ALTRINCHAM — Bowdon Hotel — 61% — £99

Tel 0161-928 7121 **Fax 0161-927 7560** Map 6 B2 H
Langham Road Bowdon Altrincham Trafford WA14 2HT

Created out of two Victorian houses with the gap between filled by a modern extension in identical style, the Bowdon offers practical, if not always very spacious, accommodation reached via a maze of corridors. The reception/lounge area and restaurant with its integral cocktail bar have recently been refurbished in a rich Victorian style. If flying from Manchester Airport ask about the special package which includes parking while you are away and transport to the terminal. Children up to 12 stay free in parents' room. Lyric Hotels. ***Rooms*** *82. Amex, Diners, MasterCard,* ***VISA***

ALTRINCHAM — Francs — £50

Tel 0161-941 3954 **Fax 0161-929 0658** Map 6 B2 R
2 Goose Green Altrincham Trafford WA14 1DW

Friendly French bistro with a wide à la carte choice of dishes both classic and more innovative: onion soup, bourride, roasted pepper filled with turkey confit, sole florentine, magret de canard, gigot d'agneau, pasta cooked with oyster mushrooms, tomatoes, courgettes, basil, pine nuts and crème fraiche. Sunday lunches with a fixed-price menu and a short à la carte are very popular, with 1 child under 12 eating free per adult. ***Seats*** *90 (+12 outside). Parties 25. Private Room 12. L 12-3 D 6-10.30 (Fri & Sat till 11). Closed D Sun. Set Sun L £8.95 Set L & D (Mon-Fri) £9.95 Set D (6-7.30) £6.95. Amex, Diners, MasterCard,* ***VISA***

ALTRINCHAM — The French Brasserie

Tel 0161-928 0808 **Fax 0161-941 6154** Map 6 B2 JaB
24 The Downs Altrincham Trafford WA14 2QD

This large, friendly, and very French brasserie offers a wide choice of eating possibilities. At lunchtime (Mon-Sat) £4.95 will buy you two courses of typically rustic fare: *champignons à l'ail* (mushrooms in garlic butter) or smoked salmon terrine to start, then maybe a classic coq au vin or boudin lyonnaise (game sausage braised in onion gravy and served with potatoes). Three courses at dinner time (Sun-Fri) are on offer at £10.95 and could include chicken liver paté, folowed by *l'agneau d'Artagnan* (lamb shoulder braised in garlic, rosemary and red wine jus), with tarte aux pommes to finish. On Sundays, the brasserie is ideal for families and the three-course lunch (£7.95) is similar to the other menus but children eat free when accompanied by an adult. Live jazz Thu-Sat evenings. ***Seats*** *140.* ***Open*** *12-12 (Thu-Sat till 2.30am). Amex, MasterCard,* ***VISA***

ALVELEY — Mill Hotel — 72% — £65

Tel 01746 780437 **Fax 01746 780850** Map 6 B4 H
Birdsgreen Alveley nr Bridgnorth Shropshire WV15 6HL

The D'Aniello family has created, from a 16th-century mill, a fine hotel set in beautifully landscaped grounds with unusually spacious public areas that include a comfortably furnished lounge and cocktail bar. The mill workings can still be seen in the public bar. Upstairs, dado-panelled corridors are broad, and well-appointed bedrooms generally large, with phones at both desk and bedside. Superior rooms (rates ascend to £95) are particularly large and have either four-posters or elaborate bedhead drapes plus sofa and armchairs. Good bathrooms, with either corner or alcoved tubs, boast large bath sheets, and often have twin basins; five have separate shower cubicles. A well-run hotel with notably friendly staff, 24hr room service and turn-down service in the evenings. Conference/banqueting facilities for up to 230; ample parking. No dogs. ***Rooms*** *21. Garden, games room. Amex, Diners, MasterCard,* ***VISA***

Amberley Black Horse

Tel 01453 872556 Map 14 B2 **P**
Amberley Gloucestershire GL5 5AD

Teetering on the very edge of the escarpment just below Minchinhampton Common, the pub's westerly aspect comes into its own on glorious summer evenings. Behind the bar itself is a picture window, and beyond it a prominent conservatory from which to soak in the panoramic views. Below are a tiered patio and garden, though parents should be mindful of a steep drop from the bottom wall to the meadow below. The upper garden has swings and picnic tables, and there's a separate games room with pool table and darts. A wide and regularly-changing range of real ales draws aficionados from far and wide. *Open 12-3, 6-11 (Sat 12-11, Sun 12-10.30). Free House.* ***Beer*** *Smiles, Hook Norton Best, Fuller's London Pride, Tetley, Archers Best, three guest beers. Garden. MasterCard,* ***VISA***

Ambleside Rothay Manor 71% £118

Tel 015394 33605 **Fax 015394 33607** Map 4 C3 **HR**
Rothay Bridge Ambleside Cumbria LA22 0EH

An attractive Regency-style building on the Coniston road, handy for Ambleside yet well protected from its bustle in beautiful, secluded grounds. The Nixons have been here since it opened 30 years ago and personal touches are evident throughout; service is very friendly and attentive. Guests have free use of a nearby leisure club (swimming pool, sauna, steam room, spa bath) and permits may be obtained for trout fishing. Traditional afternoon tea is served every day between 3.30 and 5.30. Phone about the special themed holidays and weekends. A suite and a ground-floor room are equipped for the use of disabled guests. No dogs. ***Rooms*** *18. Garden, croquet. Closed 3 Jan-7 Feb. Amex, Diners, MasterCard,* ***VISA***

Restaurant £70

The setting of polished mahogany tables and soft candle-light is thoroughly traditional, and both cooking and service are in keeping. Lunchtime sees a cold buffet and a few hot dishes of the day, with roasts on Sunday (book), while dinner is a fixed-price meal. Typical dishes on the evening list include vol-au-vent filled with ham, asparagus and sweetcorn in a cream sauce, poached salmon with a mushroom and chive sauce, Basque chicken and, for dessert, a chocolate, rum and raisin tart. A vegetarian menu is available. There are some almost giveaway prices on the wine list. The list is splendid – diverse, good growers, and those prices! No smoking. ***Seats*** *70. Parties 14. Private Room 32. L 12.30-2 (Sun 12.45-1.30) D 7.45-9. Set L £14 (Sun £16) Set D £24/£27/£30.*

Ambleside Sheila's Cottage Country Restaurant

Tel 015394 33079 **Fax 015394 34488** Map 4 C3 **JaB**
The Slack Ambleside Cumbria LA22 9DQ

Since the early 60s Stewart and Janice Greaves have been running this restaurant in a 250-year-old cottage and converted barn which were formerly part of the coaching stables and used to accommodate the drivers. Everything is home-baked, including delicious tea breads like Borrowdale or bara brith (a Welsh spiced bread with fruit and peel) and cakes. The à la carte menu allows you to eat as little or as much as you like, dishes such as potted trout with wholemeal rolls (£4.75), roasted vegetable and goat's cheese salad (£5.50), Welsh rarebit with home-made fruit chutney and an open Niçoise-style sandwich. There's also a soup of the day like cream of carrot and orange or chilled cucumber and mint as well as chicken liver paté with brioche. The Barn restaurant menu offers fuller meals with some seven principal dishes such as seafood platter (£7.95), vegetarian wild mushroom or Emmental and smoky bacon rösti (£7.75), salmon and local shrimp fishcake, oak-smoked chicken salad (£7.50) and Provençal tart with roasted vegetables and green salad. Puddings might include lemon ice cream (£2.50 – a speciality) and summer pudding (£3.75) and there's a selection of farmhouse cheeses (£3.25). Three-course dinner menu £22 including coffee. Freshly-made lemonade. Loose-leaf tea. Small portions and a limited children's menu (available lunchtime only). Youngsters dining in the evening are charged for what they eat. Three high-chairs, and a box of toys provided. Large Ladies toilet has a bench for baby-changing and an armchair suitable for nursing. No smoking. ***Seats*** *68.* ***Open*** *12-5 & 7-10 Mon-Sat.* ***Closed*** *Sun (in summer), 25, 26 Dec & all Jan. Amex, MasterCard,* ***VISA***

AMBLESIDE Zeffirellis

Tel 015394 33845 **Fax 015394 31771** Map 4 C3 JaB
Compston Road Ambleside Cumbria OA22 9DP

Zeffirellis is an unusual complex comprising a shopping arcade, a cinema, a pizzeria done out in Japanese Art Deco style and a leafy café (both the Pizzeria and café are totally vegetarian). The pizza bases are kneaded wheatmeal rolled in sesame seeds and the basic toppings (from £4.75) can be supplemented by various other ingredients (40p each, £1 for 3). The pizzas come in two sizes plus a small one for children. There are also pasta dishes (all £5.95), main-course salads and, for dessert, fruit salad, frozen yoghurt (£2.45) and tiramisu. There's a special deal combining a three-course candle-lit dinner and a reserved cinema seat. No smoking. ***Seats*** *80.* ***Open*** *5-9.30, also Sat & Sun 12-2.* ***Closed*** *Mon & Tue in winter. MasterCard,* ***VISA***

AMPNEY CRUCIS Crown of Crucis £74

Tel 01285 851806 **Fax 01285 851735** Map 14 C2 I
Ampney Crucis Cirencester Gloucestershire GL7 5RS

One of four Gloucestershire Ampneys, Crucis stands by the A417, 3 miles east of Cirencester. Established over 400 years, the refined, upmarket Crown has seen rapid growth in the last handful of years with the building of 25 hotel-style bedrooms, refurbishment of the oak-beamed bar and two-tiered restaurant and now a conservatory extension. Furnishings and decor in the bedrooms are uniform, as are up-to-date amenities and neat, fully-tiled bathrooms with over-bath showers. Fourteen ground-floor rooms are especially handy for those needing easy access; one room is specifically equipped for disabled guests; the clever courtyard lay-out affords most rooms a view over Ampney Brook, connected to the cricket ground opposite by a wooden footbridge. All-day room service shows that this is more inn than pub. Good selection of real ales and wines by the glass in the bar. *Open 11.30-10.45 (Sun 12-10.30).* ***Beer*** *Boddingtons, Ruddles County, Archers Village. Patio, stream-side garden.* ***Accommodation*** *25 bedrooms, all en suite, £74 (from £52 single). Children welcome overnight (£17.50 if sharing parents' room), additional bed & cot available. Accommodation closed 24-30 Dec. Amex, Diners, MasterCard,* ***VISA***

APPLEBY-IN-WESTMORLAND Appleby Manor 66% £98

Tel 01768 351571 **Fax 01768 352888** Map 5 D3 HR
Roman Road Appleby-in-Westmorland Cumbria CA16 6JB

A friendly, family-owned hotel overlooking Appleby Castle and the Eden valley. Most of the original (1870s) architectural features remain, including the main fireplace and old hooks that used to carry rods to hang tapestries and pictures. Bright and cheerful bedrooms, whether those in the main house and modern wing or the seven in the coach house annexe, provide everything you need, from powerful hairdryers to in-house video films; four-poster beds attract a small supplement. Sink into one of the comfortable armchairs in the three lounges, warm yourself in front of a real log fire and sample one of the 71 single-malt whiskies on offer. Dogs in annexe rooms only. ***Rooms*** *30. Garden, croquet, indoor swimming pool, keep-fit equipment, sauna, steam room, spa bath, solarium, snooker. Closed 3 days Christmas. Amex, Diners, MasterCard,* ***VISA***

Oak Room Restaurant £55

A panelled room (with a hand-painted tiled fireplace), where interesting food from Britain and further afield is served in decent portions on the now all à la carte menus. Oven-baked mushroom caps, sweet black pudding skillet or calamari and smoked haddock tartlet might precede chargrilled skate with fried cabbage, baked lamb fillet in oatmeal or a Mediterranean aubergine roulade. Sweets from the trolley or a choice of six local Cumbrian cheeses that come with a selection of home-baked breads. There's a fixed mark-up on wines (excluding champagnes and three French classics), so nothing exceeds £16 on the list. Youngsters' menu served in the restaurant from 5 to 7.30. ***Seats** 70. Parties 30. L 12-1.45 D 7-9.*

ARNOLD — Burnt Stump

Tel 0115 963 1508 Map 7 D3 

Burnt Stump Hill Arnold Nottingham Nottinghamshire NG5 8PA

It is the location, in 30 acres of country park on the fringe of Sherwood Forest, which makes the evocatively-named Burnt Stump such a popular spot. Four miles out of Nottingham, turn off the A60 Mansfield road a mile or so north of its junction with the A614. There's a wealth of open space for one or more of the family to exercise the dog, a cricket pitch below the terrace for others to watch Ravenshead cricket club at play, while children can act out their latest Robin Hood adventures in an extensive playground under the trees. In summertime there are bouncy castles and barbecues and a covered pop and crisps counter. Indoors, hungrier little outlaws have their own menu and non-alcoholic cocktail list, while at lunchtime the peckish in-laws are promised a 'Hot Hoagie' in less than nine minutes. *Open 11-11 (Sun 12-10.30). **Beer** Mansfield Riding Mild, Bitter & Old Baily. Garden, children's play area. Family room. Amex, MasterCard,* ***VISA***

ASCOT — Berystede Hotel — 67% — £145

Tel 01344 23311 **Fax 01344 872301** Map 15 E2 H

Bagshot Road Sunninghill Ascot Berkshire SL5 9JH

Just south of Ascot, this hotel is based on a large Victorian house standing in its own 6 acres of wooded grounds. As popular with racegoers as business people, the public rooms and the best of the bedrooms are in the original house and share its period feel. The majority of the bedrooms, however, are in a modern extension. The hotel has its own conference centre, including a business centre and can cater for up to 120 delegates. ***Rooms** 91. Garden, croquet, outdoor swimming pool, putting. Amex, Diners, MasterCard,* ***VISA***

ASHBOURNE — Ashbourne Gingerbread Shop

Tel 01335 343227 Map 6 C3 JaB

St John Street Ashbourne Derbyshire DE6 1AY

Gingerbread men (65p) and chocolate men (75p) head the parade of home baking at a characterful old coffee shop in the town centre which has been in the same family ownership since Victoria was on the throne. Staunch support is provided by scones and teacakes, biscuits, fresh cream cakes and puddings; Cream Tea £2.95. ***Seats** 45. **Open** 8.30-5 (Sat till 5.30, Jan & Feb till 4.30). **Closed** 25 Dec. No credit cards.*
Also at:

Matlock Street Bakewell Tel 01629 814692 Map 6 C2

Open 9.30-5.

ASHBOURNE — Ashbourne Lodge Hotel — 66% — £82

Tel 01335 346666 **Fax 01335 346549** Map 6 C3 H

Derby Road Ashbourne Derbyshire DE6 1XH

On the A52 from Derby to Leek, this modern redbrick hotel is lent some old-world style by rustic-designed public areas. There are three bars, including one in pub style. Bedrooms are neat and light but not over-large, although family rooms for two adults and two children are available. Two rooms have spa baths. Banqueting/conference facilities for 200/220. Children up to 12 stay free in parents' room. No dogs. ***Rooms** 50. Garden, indoor swimming pool, gym, sauna, steam room. Amex, Diners, MasterCard,* ***VISA***

We do not accept free meals or hospitality
– our inspectors pay their own bills.

ASHBY ST LEDGERS Olde Coach House Inn

Tel 01788 890349 **Fax 01788 891922** Map 15 D1 **P**
Ashby St Ledgers Rugby Warwickshire CV23 8UN

Despite its Warwickshire address, Ashby St Ledgers is just across the county border in Northants, 3 miles from the M1, J18; alternatively, take the single track road signed off the A361, 4 miles north of Daventry. At the centre of this once-feudal village (population now 70) is Brian and Philippa McCabes' admirable pub where, from outside, you'd least expect to find one. Behind its ivy-covered facade is the cavernous, hollowed-out interior of a row of former cottages. Stone chimney breasts and cast-iron ranges still point to a certain antiquity. The jokey printed menu encompasses chargrills, pasta dishes (seafood tagliatelle, lasagne) vegetarian options, chicken and fish dishes. Separate children's menu (puzzles, crayons, high-chairs, booster seats and baby-changing facilities are all provided). The warm welcome to families extends to special children's activities on summer Sundays. The Coachman's Fayre menu lists a short selection of more adventurous meals: spiced lamb kebab with onion and mint salad, strips of pork with a creamy leek and cider sauce and trout baked with olive oil, basil and tomato. There are half a dozen bedrooms, all en suite, with TVs and tea trays, pine bedsteads and floral drapes plus abundant peace and quiet. A multi-purpose children's adventure climbing frame is a popular attraction in the protected, walled garden, allowing parents to get a break; once tired out, the children will hopefully sleep soundly in the main family bedroom, which offers a double and two single beds plus en suite bathroom; two further rooms feature both double and sofa beds. With a happy mix of mid-week corporate customers, weekend function overnighters and those seeking out good pub food and exceptional real ales, the Olde Coach House Inn is a busy place. Winner of our Family Pub of the Year award in 1996. *Open 12-2.30, 6-11 (Sat 12-11, Sun 12-4, 7-10.30).* ***Bar Food*** *12-2, 6-9.30 (Sun 12-3, 7-9). Free House.* ***Beer*** *St Ledger Ale (Chiltern Brewery), Flowers Original, Boddingtons, Everards Old Original, guest beers. Garden, outdoor eating.* ***Accommodation*** *6 bedrooms, all en suite, £56 (four-poster £61, single £46). Children welcome overnight (under-5s stay free in parents' room), additional bed (£5) & cot supplied. Disabled WC. Amex, MasterCard,* ***VISA***

ASHFORD-IN-THE-WATER Ashford Hotel

Tel 01629 812725 **Fax 01629 814749** Map 6 C2 **P**
1 Church Street Ashford-in-the-Water Bakewell Derbyshire DE45 1QB

The former Devonshire Arms stands at the head of this picturesque Derbyshire village, just off the A6 and a mere stone's throw from the historic stone Sheepwash Bridge. Much original oak is retained in the beamed bar where log fires burn in winter; residents have use of their own cosy lounge, which opens on to a rear courtyard and enclosed garden. Each of the seven bedrooms (two with four posters) have been carefully remodelled in appropriately country style with floral-patterned wallpapers and bed linen; all are well equipped with direct-dial phones, TVs, clock radios and trouser presses. *Open 11-11 (Sun 12-10.30). Free House.* ***Beer*** *Mansfield Cask Bitter & Riding Bitter, guest beers. Garden. Family room.* ***Accommodation*** *7 bedrooms, all en suite (three with bath), £75 (four-poster & family room £85, single £50). Children welcome overnight, additional bed & cot (£10) supplied. Amex, Diners, MasterCard,* ***VISA***

ASHFORD-IN-THE-WATER The Cottage Tea Room

Tel 01629 812488 Map 6 C2 **JaB**
3 Fennel Street Ashford-in-the-Water Derbyshire DE45 1QF

Betty and Bill Watkins' tea shop is a very popular place to relax and refresh. Everything is home-made – brown bread, currant bread, sultana and cheesy herb scones, preserves and cakes – and everything is vegetarian. Special cakes and preserves are available for customers with diabetic or cardiac problems. There are six set teas, ranging from a pot of tea with a portion of cake (£2.50) to savoury scone tea (£3.25) and Derbyshire cream tea with scones and cake (£3.75). The weekend morning menu covers speciality coffees and teas, scones both sweet and savoury, and traditional

English cakes. Children and babies welcome: the owners' private parlour is made available to nursing mothers. Children's play area at the top of Fennel Street by the car park. Feeding the ducks on the river is also popular with youngsters. No smoking. ***Seats*** *20.* ***Open*** *Mon, Wed, Thu 2.30-5, also Sat & Sun 10.30-12.* ***Closed*** *Tue, Fri, 25 Dec, 1 Jan & 1 week Sep. No credit cards.*

ASHPRINGTON Waterman's Arms

Tel & Fax 01803 732214 Map 13 D3 **P**

Bow Bridge Ashprington Totnes Devon TQ9 7EG

Delightfully situated on the banks of the River Harbourne, at the top of Bow Creek, the Waterman's is a favourite summer venue for alfresco riverside imbibing with resident ducks and – if you are lucky – kingfishers to keep you company. Bow Bridge is recorded in the Domesday Book and the inn until recently was a smithy and prior to that a brewery and a prison during the Napoleonic Wars. Recently purchased by Discovery Inns, who intend to maintain the successful formula – home-cooked food and quality overnight accommodation – that makes this friendly inn so popular. 'Tardis'-like inside, a series of neatly-furnished rooms radiates away from the central servery, all filled with a mix of rustic furniture, old photographs, brass artefacts and other memorabilia. Home-cooked bar food caters for all tastes, from hearty snacks such as sandwiches, salads and platters to regular menu favourites – served in both the bar and candlelit restaurant – including fresh pasta dishes, steak and kidney pie, rack of Devon lamb and steaks. A daily-changing blackboard enhances the choice by offering the likes of huntsman's pie, whole gurnard with crab and ginger sauce and the very popular mixed seafood salad platter (crab, prawns and fresh salmon). Good-value table d'hote menu at £15. A separate pudding board may highlight home-made banoffi pie and crème brulée. Ten beautifully fitted-out bedrooms have floral, cottagey fabrics and co-ordinating friezes around the walls, attractive dark-stained modern furniture and spotlessly-kept bathrooms with shower cubicles and efficient, thermostatically-controlled showers. Added comforts include telephone, cabinet-housed TV and tea-making facilities. Front rooms overlook the river and surrounding valley sides while the five newest rooms, complete with en suite bathrooms, overlook the gardens; two family rooms have a double and a single bed plus room for a cot or further bed. *Open 11-3, 6-11 (Sun 12-3, 7-10.30).* ***Bar Food*** *12-2.30, 6.30-9.30 (Sun 7-9.30). Free House.* ***Beer*** *Dartmoor Best, Palmers IPA, Tetley Bitter, Bass. Riverside terrace, garden, outdoor eating. Family room.* ***Accommodation*** *15 bedrooms, all en suite, £54-£70 (family room £58-£88, single £32-£39 according to season). Children welcome overnight (under-3s free, 3-5s £5, 6-10s £10, 11-14s £15), additional bed & cot supplied. MasterCard,* ***VISA***

ASHSTEAD Superfish

Tel 01372 273784 Map 15 E3 **JaB**

2-4 Woodfield Lane Ashstead Surrey KT21 2UP

Part of an excellent Surrey-based chain serving fish and chips fried in beef dripping, the traditional Yorkshire way. See Morden entry for more details. Licensed. ***Seats*** *56.* ***Open*** *11.30-2 (Sat till 2.30), & 5.30-10.30 (Fri & Sat from 5).* ***Closed*** *Sun, 25, 26 Dec & 1 Jan. Amex, MasterCard,* ***VISA***

ASHURST Manor Court Farm

Tel 01892 740210 Map 11 A6 **JaB**

Ashurst nr Tunbridge Wells Kent TN3 9TB

The garden of this attractive Georgian farmhouse is particularly perfect for tea on a sunny summer's day. Chickens strut freely through the rustic tables and chairs, and the resident golden retriever remains oblivious! Many footpaths cross this 350-acre working farm, which includes woodland and extends to the River Medway; a stroll along these is the perfect way to summon an appetite for an excellent cream tea (£3.25) including home-made jam from a neighbouring farm, freshly baked scones and home-made cake. There are toasted tea-cakes, cheese and chive or lemon and raisin scones (both 95p). Dogs and children are most welcome. ***Seats*** *20 (+ 35 outside).* ***Open*** *Sat, Sun & Bank Holidays only 2-5.45.* ***Closed*** *end Sep-Easter. No credit cards.*

Avebury — Stones

Tel 01672 539514 Map 14 C2 JaB
Avebury nr Marlborough Wiltshire

Local produce (some of it from their own one-acre garden) is at the heart of the cooking in this outstanding vegetarian restaurant by the historic stone circle. Dishes are difficult to itemise, as they are proud of the fact that they change daily – so scarcely a complete meal has been repeated in twelve years. But the style is set by various cold savouries (around £2.30) and superb baking (ginger people 45p, date slice 95p, carob fudge cake with Guernsey cream £1.85) all available throughout opening hours; these are joined at lunchtime by terrific soups (maybe broccoli and Stilton, Canadian split pea with red wine £2.50) and a couple of main courses (£5.25) such as sorrel and lovage frittata with courgette and roast aubergine tian with Pernod, mixed leaves and olive-garlic bread, or Oriental spring rolls with lime-ginger sauce, pineapple-cashew rice, sesame broccoli and stir-fried strips of carrot and red pepper. Afternoon tea (£3.25) is served from 2.30. They are particularly proud of their cheeses, most from local suppliers and made with vegetarian rennet. ***Seats*** *80 (+80 outside).* ***Open*** *10-6 (Sat & Sun only Nov- end of March, 10-5).* ***Closed*** *Christmas & all Jan. No credit cards.*

Axbridge — Almshouse Bistro

Tel 01934 732493 Map 13 F1 JaB
The Square Axbridge Somerset BS26 2AR

Tim Collins' cosy bistro is housed within a 15th-century almshouse and overlooks the charming village square. The old beams, rough stone walls and flagged floors are softened by pretty matching fabrics. There is a home-made pasta dish each day with a dressed leaf salad (£4.95), a three-course Italian supper (£10.95), or a two-course table d'hote (£9.95), featuring asparagus and balsamico, followed perhaps by chicken with *vin santo* and wild mushrooms. The à la carte menu changes daily and might offer Tuscan minestrone with pesto (£2.45) or Sicilian sardines (£4.95) followed by Venetian salmon fillet (£8.95) or magret duck with strawberry vinegar sauce (£12.95). Puddings such as strawberry and brandy crème brulée or dark chocolate cheesecake are a tempting finale. Half-helpings for children. No smoking in the dining area. ***Seats*** *32. Open 12-2 & 6.45-10. MasterCard,* ***VISA***

Ayot St Lawrence — Brocket Arms

Tel 01438 820250 **Fax 01438 820068** Map 15 E1 
Ayot St Lawrence Hertfordshire AL6 9BT

Splendid medieval pub – an unspoilt 14th-century gem – set within an equally splendid village close to Shaw's Corner, where George Bernard Shaw lived for forty years (now National Trust-owned). Classic unadulterated three-roomed interior with a wealth of oak beams, an inglenook fireplace, a rustic mix of furniture and tasteful piped classical music. Those wishing to experience the historic charm further can stay upstairs in one of the four characterful bedrooms built into the timbered eaves. Furnished in traditional style – one with a four-poster bed – the rooms are simple and homely, and reputedly haunted by a monk from the local abbey. All share two adequate bathrooms. Those guests craving more modern creature comforts can book one of the three newer bedrooms housed in a converted old stable block across the courtyard. These are neatly carpeted and comfortably furnished in modern pine (one also boasts a four-poster bed), and (unlike main building rooms) they have central heating. Two have rather compact shower rooms, the third a clean en suite bathroom, and all are equipped with tea-makers and clock radios. Pleasant walled garden for peaceful alfresco drinking and for enjoying a summer cream tea (3-6pm May-Oct). Families welcome. *Open 11-11 (Sun 12-10.30). Free House.* ***Beer*** *Greene King Abbot & IPA, Wadworth 6X, Theakston Best, Adnams Broadside, Ruddles Best, guest beer. Garden.* ***Accommodation*** *7 bedrooms, 3 en suite, £55-£70 (single £40). Children welcome overnight, additional bed (£10) & cot supplied. Amex, MasterCard,* ***VISA***

BAKEWELL Chatsworth House, Carriage House

Tel 01246 582204 Fax 01246 583464 Map 6 C2 JaB
nr Bakewell Derbyshire DE45 1PP

In beautiful grounds, behind the main house stands the old carriage house, surrounded by the stable blocks and their courtyard and fountain. The high-ceilinged room has impressive hanging lights and is decorated with large pictures of the estate; the original arches have been filled in with plate glass. The long pine self-service counter displays the food on refrigerated shelves and uniformed staff are friendly and efficient. Among the typical choice are soup of the day (£1.35), garlic bread (75p), assorted salads – maybe salmon (£4.70) or ham (£5.15), cottage pie (£4.35), fried cod and roast chicken; vegetarians are not forgotten with a vegetarian pasta bake (£4.45) on offer on a summer visit; strawberries and cream (£1.65), various gateaux and treacle tart, might be other temptations. Good cream teas are also available. There's a roast every Sunday and children's portions are available. £1 car parking. ***Seats*** *250.* ***Open*** *10.15-5.30.* ***Closed*** *end of Nov-mid Mar. Amex, MasterCard,* ***VISA***

BALDWIN'S GATE Slater's

Tel 01782 680052 Fax 01782 680136 Map 6 B3 P
Marfield Gate Farm Baldwin's Gate Newcastle under Lyme Staffordshire ST5 5ED

Five miles from Junction 16 on the M6, this skilful conversion of former outbuildings on a working farm (they still have a 100-head milking herd) has created a stylish accommodation pub with super facilities for youngsters. In addition to the family/function room there's a safe, enclosed rear garden full of play equipment and a pair of ducks and geese to talk to. Set around a cobbled courtyard behind the pub proper, three self-contained cottagey suites contain just about everything for overnight or longer stays: en suite bathrooms with over-bath showers, fitted kitchenettes and breakfast area, plus extra beds and cots at no extra charge. Two further en suite bedrooms for overnight guests complete the picture. Breakfast in the dining-room if self-catering residents prefer. Music on Tuesday and Sunday evenings. *Open 11-3, 5.30-11 (Sun 12-10.30 summer). Free House.* ***Beer*** *Marston's Bitter & Pedigree, Boddingtons. Garden, children's play area. Family room.* ***Accommodation*** *5 bedrooms, all en suite, £47, (four-poster & family room £50). Children welcome overnight (stay free if sharing parents' room), additional bed & cot available. Amex, Diners, MasterCard,* ***VISA***

BAMFORD Yorkshire Bridge Inn

Tel 01433 651361 Fax 01433 651812 Map 6 C2 
Ashopton Road Bamford Derbyshire S30 2AB

In the heart of the Derbyshire Peak District, this inn dates from 1826 and is named after an old packhorse bridge on the River Derwent. Views from the central bar take in the peak of Win Hill – a beautiful setting in which to enjoy some good, reliable cooking. Bar food is split between a lunchtime and an evening menu. Lunchers may choose from hot or cold sandwiches, ploughman's lunches, traditional hot dishes of the home-made steak and kidney pie variety, or from four vegetarian dishes (broccoli and cream cheese bake); fresh fish is listed on a blackboard on market days. In the evening similar fare is supplemented by chargrilled steaks and salmon and additional specials like roast lamb with mint gravy, chicken and mushroom pie and barbecue pork chops. Accommodation takes the form of an adjoining hotel converted from barns, now housing ten en suite bedrooms, all with satellite TVs, radios, telephones, and beverage-making facilities; for those wishing to escape the hurly-burly there is a peaceful lounge and a residents-only dining-room. Non-smokers have the pleasure of the conservatory and children are well catered for both on the menu (fish fingers, sausages or burgers) and outside where there is a slide and climbing frame.
Open 11-11 (Sun 12-10.30). ***Bar Food*** *12-2, 6-9 (till 9.30 Sat), Sun 12-9. Free House.* ***Beer*** *Stones, John Smith's Magnet, Bass, Boddingtons. Garden, outdoor eating, children's play area. Family room.* ***Accommodation*** *10 bedrooms, all en suite, £49.50 (single £38). Children welcome overnight (under-4s stay free in parents' room, 5-12s £5), additional bed & cot available. No dogs. MasterCard,* ***VISA***

BANBURY Banbury House Hotel 62% £99

Tel 01295 259361 **Fax 01295 270954** Map 15 D1 **H**
27-29 Oxford Road Banbury Oxfordshire OX16 9AH

A Georgian house on the main road into town from Oxford; the main entrance and parking are to the rear of the building in Lucky Lane. The reception/lounge area, which has been given a period feel with plaster mouldings on the ceiling and glass chandeliers, has several groups of good-quality sofas. Gulliver's Bar offers a less formal setting. Refurbishment continues in decent, practical bedrooms (with good work space) that come with all the usual modern comforts including satellite TV. Two 'junior suites' come with spa baths and one boasts a four-poster bed. Children up to 16 share parents' room free. Parking for 35 cars. ***Rooms** 49. Amex, Diners, MasterCard,* ***VISA***

> **JaB** is short for 'Just a Bite'. These majority of these establishments are also recommended in our *Bistros, Bars & Cafés* Guide which features establishments where one may eat well for less than £15 per head.

BARDWELL Six Bells Country Inn

Tel 01359 250820 Map 10 C2 **P**
The Green Bardwell Bury St Edmunds Suffolk IP31 1AW

Approached via a track (once the original coaching highway) off the village green, this rather plain, cream-painted 16th-century inn (Grade II listed) is surrounded by open countryside, views of which can be appreciated from both the warm and comfortable beamed bars and the converted stable-block bedrooms. Reliable home-cooked food listed on different lunch and dinner blackboard menus – served in both bar and restaurant – encompasses potted shrimps and warm tandoori chicken salad for starters, with main-course options like prawn and pesto pasta, seafood pithiviers and breast of Barbary duck with cranberry and port sauce. Fresh fish and shellfish feature strongly on Fridays – try their deep-fried cod with hand-cut chips at lunch or lobster in the evening. The interesting, 30-bin list of wines from Adnams includes eleven half bottles. Peaceful and homely overnight accommodation is in converted barn and stable buildings; the eight en suite bedrooms are furnished with modern pine and co-ordinating bedcovers and fabrics. All have clean, compact shower rooms, TVs, telephones and tea-makers and all are on the ground floor. In the past year a new conservatory extension to the restaurant has been built and serves as the venue for live classical music evenings. Children are well catered for, with a Wendy House in the much improved garden, high-chairs inside and a vanity unit for baby-changing in the Ladies. *Open 12-2.30, 7-11 (till 10.30 Sun & winter).* ***Bar Food** 12-1.45, 7-9.15. Free House.* ***Beer** John Smith's Bitter, Adnams Southwold, guest beer. Garden, outdoor eating, children's play area.* ***Accommodation** 8 bedrooms, all en suite shower, £55 (four-poster £60, single £40). Children welcome overnight, additional bed (£5) available. Closed all 25 & 26 Dec. MasterCard,* ***VISA***

BARKING Colonel Jasper's

Tel 0181-507 8481 Map 11 B4 **JaB**
156 Longbridge Road Barking & Dagenham

Candle-light, mahogany furniture and a sawdust – covered floor gives a rustic feel to a Davy's old ale, port and wine house near Barking Station and below the Spotted Dog. Favourites from a simple menu include cod, chips and mushy peas (£5.30), beefsteak, kidney and mushroom pie (£6.95) and rack of lamb with barbecued sauce (£7.95). Weekly-changing blackboard specials might include chicken satay with peanut sauce (£4.20) or home-made sherry trifle (£1.60), washed down perhaps with a tankard of Old Jollop or Davy's 1870. Live jazz on Friday and Saturday evenings from 8.30 till 11. ***Seats** 140 (+ 20 outside).* ***Open** 12-4 (Sat till 3, Sun 12.30-5) & 5.30-10.30 (Sat from 7).* ***Closed** D Sun-Wed, Bank Holiday Mons, 25 & 26 Dec. Amex, Diners, MasterCard,* ***VISA***

Barley — Fox & Hounds

Tel 01763 848459 Map 15 F1 P

High Street Barley Royston Hertfordshire SG8 8HU

Pleasingly traditional white-painted 15th-century village local, with rambling, low-ceilinged rooms, splendid open fires and a separate dining area and conservatory. A beer drinker's favourite – the Fox & Hounds has 10 handpumps in constant use. Diners have the choice of a short lunchtime only bar menu offering the usual popular snack meals and a longer main menu which operates throughout the pub at lunchtime and in the evenings (bar and restaurant): steak, Flame Thrower and Stilton pie, 16oz stuffed plaice, paella and a daily fish special – swordfish braised in tomatoes. Vegetarians are well catered for with their own extensive menu which may well feature cashew nut paella and vegetable korma. Ice creams and sundaes are a speciality (9 varieties are on offer), as well as puddings such as strawberry flan and paw-paw cheesecake. Traditional pub games are very popular with indoor and outdoor skittles, bar billiards, shove-ha'penny, darts and dominoes; there's also a boules pitch. The children's play area has a multi-purpose climbing frame with slide and swing; inside the pub there are baby-changing facilities and a children's menu is offered. *Open 12-2.30, 6-11 (Sun 12-3, 7-10.30).* ***Bar Food*** *12-2, 6.30-10 (Sun 7.15-9.30). Free House.* ***Beer*** *home-brewed Nathaniel's Special (3.3%) & Flame Thrower (4.4%), Boddingtons, Adnams Southwold, six guest beers. Garden, outdoor eating, children's play area. Family room. Disabled WC. MasterCard,* ***VISA***

Barnard Castle — Priors Restaurant

Tel 01833 638141 Map 5 D3 

7 The Bank Barnard Castle Durham DL12 8PH

Hidden by an arts and crafts shop, and offering dishes to tempt even the most hardened carnivore, Mark Prior's counter-service restaurant and take-away offers international vegetarian cuisine that continues to draw the faithful and convert newcomers. The menu might include two or three soups, perhaps carrot and lentil or tomato and cauliflower (both £1.25), aubergine stuffed with rice, mushrooms, onions and walnuts or butter bean and vegetable cobbler (both £2.95); meals priced at £2.95 or over come with potatoes or rice and salad. Desserts might include banana and walnut roulade (£1.75) and there's some excellent patisserie, including flapjacks, carrot cake and chocolate oat crunchies (85p). Good organic wines and beers. Young families very welcome, children's menu available, with dishes like 'awfully abominable bronto burger' (75p). Vegan, gluten-free and other special dietary requirements are also catered for. Two high-chairs, cushions, potty and changing mat are all provided. No smoking throughout. ***Seats*** *50.* ***Open*** *10-5 (Sat to 5.30, Sun 12-5 Christmas to Easter, 12-5.30 Easter to Christmas).* ***Closed*** *25 & 26 Dec, 1 Jan. Amex, Diners, MasterCard,* ***VISA***

> We endeavour to be as up-to-date as possible, but inevitably some changes to data and key personnel may occur at restaurants and hotels after the Guide goes to press. Prices should also be taken as indications rather than firm quotes.

Baslow — Cavendish Hotel 71% £117

Tel 01246 582311 **Fax 01246 582312** Map 6 C2 HR

Baslow Derbyshire DE45 1SP

A solid, local stone-built former inn backing on to the A619. The front, in contrast, commands superb views over acres of green pasture that form part of the Chatsworth Estate. Eric Marsh took over the leasehold in 1975 and has created a splendid hotel radiating comfort and hospitality. Public rooms include a bright, sunny conservatory, flower-filled chintzy lounge and dark, intimate bar where log fires burn in the winter. A major feature is Eric's eclectic collection of over 300 paintings. Bedrooms are very attractive, each with a view of the estate and a full complement of homely comforts including good beds, armchairs and writing desks. Two have four-posters and several feature antiques from Chatsworth. No dogs. ***Rooms*** *23. Garden, putting, fishing. Amex, Diners, MasterCard,* ***VISA***

See over

Restaurant £75

During the day, a bright, sunny dining-room with super views over part of the Chatsworth estate. At night, the soft pastel colours of the decor come into their own with subtle light creating an elegant setting for imaginative and carefully constructed dishes, prepared by Nick Buckingham, also here since 1975. Pan-fried duck livers in sesame seeds with an orange salad and grenadine dressing; marinated salmon and vegetable terrine with cheese paté; and venison steak with a port and five-spice sauce show his very individual style. Old favourites are available on a supplementary menu at an additional charge: caviar with warm pancakes, scampi in tempura batter with three dipping sauces, saddle of rabbit with a mustard and white wine sauce, hot passion fruit soufflé. British cheeses are a fine alternative to dessert. The wine list is presented immaculately but differently – by price and colour. There are some superb bottles to choose from, and you can even buy fine clarets and ports by the case. No smoking. ***Seats*** *50. Private Room 16. L 12.30-2 D 7-10. Set menu £24.75/£28.75/£33.*

Garden Room £75

The panoramic view from this conservatory provides a charming backdrop, while crisp linen, fresh flowers and bistro chairs complete the scene for this relaxed and informal dining-room. The Garden Room offers all-day informal eating, from a plate of smoked salmon (£8.75) to designer sandwiches: triple decker (£6) – vegetables, nuts and fruit with a cream cheese dressing. Breakfasts include the City breakfast (£4.95) or Country breakfast (£9.20) and, from mid-morning, Late Breakfasts (from £6.50). Lunchtime might see the likes of vichyssoise (£3.25), seafood lasagne (£9.50) or venison sausages wrapped in puff pastry with a cranberry and thyme sauce (£6.75). Hot and cold desserts of the day (£4.20) could be bread-and-butter pudding with cinnamon and apples, fresh strawberry meringue (£3.75) or lemon rice pudding, and there's a selection of farmhouse cheeses. Teas (3-6pm) are generous, with Welsh rarebit on onion bread (£4.25), scrambled or poached eggs (£3.50), scones or toasted teacakes (£2.85) and a choice of cakes plus a good selection of coffees and teas. In summer guests can eat on the lawn, where children are kept busy with mini-golf and swings. ***Seats*** *32 (+ 18 outside).* ***Open*** *11-11.*

Baslow — Derbyshire Craft Centre, Eating House

Tel 01433 631583 Map 6 C2 **JaB**
Calver Bridge Baslow Derbyshire S30 1XA

Adjoining a now extensive craft centre, this is an ideal spot for snacking, set alongside the A623 north-west of Baslow. Paintings of the Dales and Derbyshire's stately homes hang on the walls. Carefully prepared food includes home-made soup (£1.75) served with bread, home-baked ham with potato and salad and a daily pasta bake served with salad (both £4.50). Jacket potatoes are offered with a choice of fillings, plus a quiche of the day. Lighter dishes include cakes (from 95p) and sandwiches (from £1.65). Extra dishes are listed on a blackboard. A real effort is made to stock local cheeses. No smoking. Cream teas (£1.95) are served all day, not just at tea time. Unlicensed. Two high-chairs; ask for children's portions. There's a playroom with a small easy chair (ideal for baby-feeding), Wendy house, blackboard, toys and things-on-wheels. Calver village has riverside walks, a garden centre and park. ***Seats*** *36.* ***Open*** *10-5.* ***Closed*** *25 Dec, 1 Jan & middle 2 weeks Jan. No credit cards.*

Bassenthwaite — Armathwaite Hall 65% £110

Tel 01768 776551 **Fax 01768 776220** Map 4 C3 **H**
Bassenthwaite Lake nr Keswick Cumbria CA12 4RE

After 20 years as resident owners, the Graves family remain the most welcoming of hosts at their historic stately house set in splendid grounds leading down to the lake. Best bedrooms have fine views as well as plenty of space, the latter attribute shared by rooms in the coach house/stable block. There are extensive leisure facilities, and the equestrian centre offers hacking and lessons. Families are well catered for, with accommodation free for under-12s when sharing parents' room and various other attractive options. An animal park with a variety of farm animals and rare breeds is open between April and October. Three self-catering units are within the grounds. ***Rooms** 43. Garden, croquet, tennis, riding, mountain bikes, 9-hole pitch & putt, coarse & game fishing, indoor swimming pool, gym, sauna, steam room, solarium, spa bath, beauty & hair salons, snooker. Amex, Diners, MasterCard,* **VISA**

BATCOMBE — Batcombe Inn

Tel 01749 850359 **Fax 01749 850615** Map 13 F1
Batcombe Shepton Mallet Somerset BA4 6HE

Tucked away down a web of country lanes in the very rural Batcombe Vale, Derek and Claire Blezard's old honey-coloured stone coaching inn enjoys a peaceful position away from the main village, next to the church. The long and low-ceilinged main bar has exposed stripped beams and is warmly and tastefully decorated; terracotta sponged walls with ivy leaf stencilling are hung with several old paintings, creating a relaxed and homely atmosphere. A mix of individual chairs, deep window seats and darkwood furniture fronts a huge stone inglenook with log fire. Adjoining the bar is a high-ceilinged, no-smoking dining area in what used to be the old barn and toll-house. Bar food is reliably good with blackboards listing daily-changing specials such as bream with tomato and fresh basil, skate wing with capers and lemon butter, home-made spring and crab rolls with chili sauce and good vegetarian dishes – basil roulade. The printed menu is better than most, offering a range of hearty snacks, starters and main dishes, from duck and sun-dried tomato salad and home-made salmon and watercress fishcakes to lamb topped with mint stuffing and asparagus and baked in filo pastry. Accompanying salads are enormous and imaginative and main-dish vegetables are served separately and generously. Traditional Sunday lunch is always popular, as are non-alcoholic drinks such as elderflower pressé and a tasty ginger brew. Bookings are taken anywhere in the pub. A big welcome is made to families: children not only have their own 'Kiddies Corner' menu with a choice of nine items but they also have their own fully-equipped room complete with mini-trampoline, doll's house, drawing board, books, toys (including a Nintendo games console) and a video recorder with a good choice of films – enough to placate any child while relaxed parents enjoy their meal. Children's facilities extend to the rear garden play area for fine-weather activity; there is also a changing and feeding area in an ante-room to the Ladies. *Open 12-2.30, 7-11 (Sun 12-2.30, 7-10.30).* ***Bar Food** 12-2, 7-10 (till 9.30 Sun). Free House. **Beer** Butcombe Bitter, Wadworth 6X. Garden, patio, children's play area. Family room. MasterCard,* **VISA**

BATH — Bath Spa Hotel — 87% — £206

Tel 01225 444424 **Fax 01225 444006** Map 13 F1 **HR**
Sydney Road Bath Bath & North East Somerset BA2 6JF

General Manager Robin Sheppard and his superb staff generate a relaxed and friendly atmosphere in elegant country house surroundings in a building of handsome proportions. The original house dates back to the 1830s with a Grecian facade, a Georgian portico, and a classical entrance hall, resplendent with Oriental carpets, flower displays, antiques, a fine plasterwork ceiling and mice....! The mice, it must be said, are of the pastry and chocolate variety and something of a hotel trademark. The gracious drawing-room affords panoramic views of the landscaped grounds and gardens – seven acres in all – while past the distinctive murals and greenery of the Colonnade, you'll find the clubby bar. Walk a little further and chance upon the water collection, a display of mineral and spring waters from around the world, including the hotel's own brands of Bath Spa and canned Alfresco. Individually decorated bedrooms, including nine suites, are models of good taste, providing a host of extras, with particularly luxurious bathrooms in mahogany and marble. Two bedrooms have been adapted to the needs of disabled guests. There's a splendid health and leisure spa, a purpose-built staffed nursery for children between the ages of 2 and 9 (ask for rates – open 8am-6pm weekdays, 10am-3pm weekends, advise you requirements to the hotel in advance) and several functions rooms. 24hr room service. ***Rooms** 98. Garden, croquet, tennis, indoor swimming pool, gym, sauna, spa bath, sun beds, beauty & hair salons. Amex, Diners, MasterCard,* **VISA**

See over

Vellore Restaurant £90

The formal, non-smoking restaurant of the hotel, with a pianist playing at weekends, often with accompaniment. With a varying clientele, it's always difficult to design and balance menus to suit everyone, though chef Jonathan Fraser succeeds by not only changing them monthly, but also by combining traditional British cuisine with exotic elements. Thus you might find Oriental crispy duck salad with vermicelli noodles, daikon and pickled ginger alongside asparagus and chervil soup; or a classic crown of beef with a Stilton and walnut farce, smoked bacon and port jus side by side with peppered monkfish tail with Singapore black noodles. There are daily-changing fixed-price menus, a separate vegetarian menu and themed menus for two persons. End with choice British farmhouse cheeses or perhaps a Granny Smith soufflé laced with calvados or a Fatboys chocolate pudding. There's a very fine wine list, with quite fair prices and authoritative tasting notes. Gentlemen are respectfully requested (though it's not insisted upon) to wear a jacket and tie. ***Seats** 120. Parties 12. L (Sun only) 12.30-2 D 7-10. Set Sun L £16.50 Set D £35.*

Alfresco Restaurant £65

In the Colonnade, overlooking the patio rose garden (outdoor seating 30), eating is more informal with seasonal and eclectic dishes on a menu that mixes English, Mediterranean and Oriental influences. Typical choices run from creamy black mushroom and herb broth with rosemary sippets (croutons) to ribbon noodles carbonara, rich man's cod and chips (with mushy peas) and crispy duck teriyaki with yellow rice and stir-fry vegetables. For a dessert try the sticky toffee pudding and vanilla ice cream, baked caramel custard or even the Spa Pudding Club - tastings of everything! Splendid home-made bread, good coffees, and an easy-to-use wine list with most available by the glass. Children's menus are available here (the Vellore restaurant is more formal and not so suitable for youngsters), and on the 24-hour room service menu. High-chairs provided. ***Seats** 80. L 12-2 D 6-10. Closed Sun.*

Our inspectors *never* book in the name of Egon Ronay's Guides. They disclose their identity only if they are considering an establishment for inclusion in the next edition of the Guide.

BATH Café René

Tel 01225 447147 Fax 01225 448565 Map 13 F1 JaB

Unit 2 Shires Yard Milsom Street Bath Bath & North East Somerset BA1 1BZ

Situated in the trendy Shires Yard (former livery stables) alongside small designer shops, Café René is run by an Englishman but everything else about it aspires to be French. The café has its own bakery and patisserie which supplies croissants, brioches, *pains au chocolat* and traditional French cakes – religieuse, millefeuille and tartelettes (from £1.75). Continental breakfast (£3.95) is available from 8am and the self-service lunch offers light meals (filled potatoes from £3.35 including salad) as well as four hot and cold specials daily: maybe ratatouille filled crepes (£4.75), chicken with peppers in a fresh tomato sauce (£4.75) or tagliatelle carbonara (£3.95) all served with mixed salad. There's a counter service of a selection of baguettes (from £2-£3.95) with fillings such as chicken or tuna mayonnaise, cream cheese or prawn and crab and toppings of avocado, crispy bacon or a Mediterranean option with green beans, red and green peppers, sweetcorn and black olives. There's a very large courtyard which is popular for alfresco eating in summer *and* winter. Nearest parking is at Broad Street car park. ***Seats** 60 (+ 120 outside). **Open** 8-5 (Sun 10-5). **Closed** 25 & 26 Dec. No credit cards.*

We welcome bona fide complaints and recommendations on the tear-out pages at the back of the Guide for Readers' Comments. They are followed up by our professional team.

BATH The Canary

Tel 01225 424846 Map 13 F1 JaB
3 Queen Street Bath Bath & North East Somerset

Well worth a stop-off for a quick bite, this café/tea room is set in one of Bath's earliest cobbled streets. Breakfast is full English £6.50, Continental £3.95 or individual dishes such as eggs Benedict (£3.25) or afternoon tea offers Clotted Ceam Tea £3.60 or the Anniversary Tea £6.75 – minimum two persons and booked in advance. The display of cakes and pastries is matched by a truly remarkable range (50) of Ceylon, Indian, China, fruit and herbal loose-leaf teas. They also serve filled bagels, sandwiches (from £2.45) and various dishes throughout the day such as lime chicken (£6.65) steak and kidney pudding (£6) and Russian lamb pie with apricots, honey and fenugreek (£6), all with vegetables. Children's portions. Traditional Sunday lunch September-May £7.95. No-smoking room. Parking available at Charlotte Street car park. ***Seats** 70. **Open** 9-7 (summer till 9, Sun 10.30-6). **Closed** 25, 26 Dec & 1 Jan. Amex, MasterCard,* ***VISA***

BATH Fountain House £120

Tel 01225 338622 **Fax 01225 445855** Map 13 F1 
9/11 Fountain Buildings Lansdown Road Bath BA1 5DV

An 'all-suite hotel', Fountain House comprises one-, two- and three-bedroom suites with sitting room, good-quality furnishings and a smart, fully-equipped kitchen, within a Palladian mansion on the northern edge of the city centre. The idea is that you get plenty of privacy and space but there are no public rooms and no restaurant. Continental breakfast and a daily newspaper are left outside the door at 7am and a maid provides fresh linen and kitchen servicing daily. A same-day valet service and laundry facilities are also available. Reception staff can organise most things from car hire and theatre tickets to a personal in-room fax or shooting on the owners' own 750-acre estate. Unlike in a serviced apartment there is no minimum stay and indeed many guests stay for just one night. A lock-up garage is available at £11.75 per night. ***Suites** 14. Amex, Diners, MasterCard,* ***VISA***

BATH Green Park Brasserie

Tel 01225 338565 **Fax 01225 460675** Map 13 F1 
Green Park Road Bath Bath & North East Somerset BA1 2JB

With free parking at the adjacent Sainsburys the glass-arched former Green Park station contains a colonnade of craft shops and Andrew Peters' family-friendly brasserie under a single roof. Menus are all-encompassing, from cappuccino to a three-course lunch (£9.95), with sandwiches, salads, snacks and fresh pasta available all day. Snacks in the bar could be a vegetarian club sandwich (£4.95), mixed grill (£7.95) salad niçoise (£3.95). English and Continental breakfast (with newspapers) and traditional roast lunch fill Sunday to the accompaniment of live jazz in a careful Victorian recreation of the old ticket office. ***Seats** 65 (+ 32 outside).*
Open** 10am-10.30pm Tue-Sat (Sun 10-3pm). **Closed** Mon 25 Dec & 1-3 Jan. Amex, Diners, MasterCard,* ***VISA

BATH The New Moon £50

Tel 01225 444407 **Fax 01225 318613** Map 13 F1 R
Seven Dials Sawclose Bath Bath & North East Somerset BA1 1EN

The set lunch at the New Moon is great value – enjoy it in the bright modern atmosphere of this sister restaurant to the Broad Street original. You might begin with crab meat, bound in coriander mayonnaise with marinated tomatoes, followed maybe by lamb's liver with a Madeira and shallot sauce. Perhaps banana and Kahlua bread-and-butter pudding to round off (£7.50 for two courses, £9.50 for three). A pre-theatre menu is served on weekdays between 5.30 and 7 (£9.50 for two courses). There is a wider choice on the à la carte evening menu, including maybe Chermoula marinated tiger prawns with spicy egg plant and tabbouleh (£8.50) or salad niçoise (£6.45). Mainly no smoking. ***Seats** 70 (+ 12 in courtyard). **Open** 12-11 (Sun till 10.30). **Closed** 25, 26 Dec & 1 Jan. Amex, MasterCard,* ***VISA***

BATH — Pump Room, Milburns

Tel 01225 444488 **Fax 01225 447979** Map 13 F1 **JaB**
Stall Street Bath Bath & North East Somerset BA1 ILZ

The famous Pump Room was built in the late 18th century and was the haunt of fashionable folk who came to take the waters. Now the tourists are attracted in the same way since the tables overlook the Roman baths; giant Corinthian columns stand guard all around and a great chandelier hangs overhead. A trio plays morning and afternoon, bracketing a lunchtime classical pianist. The food ranges from Continental breakfast (£4.60) to brunch (£6.50), Georgian Elevenses (hot chocolate, Bath bun, cinnamon biscuits and spa water), lunch, snacks and five variations on the afternoon tea theme (clotted cream tea £5.20, high tea £6.95). The lunchtime menu includes soups (£3.00), salads (salmon and chive tart with mixed leaf salad £8.50), baguettes (tuna, red pepper and celery, salami and gherkins, or rare roast beef tomato and watercress – from £2.95) or filo pastry nest filled with chicken and oyster mushroom in a tarragon cream sauce (£8.50). At midday a good deal is to be had from the soup and baguette lunch (£7.50) featuring the soup of the day (spinach and nutmeg for example) plus a choice of one of the filled baguettes. Children's portions are available; there are four high-chairs, and mothers will find a pull-down baby-changing shelf in the Ladies. Close to the Roman Baths and Museum of Costume. ***Seats*** *96.* ***Open*** *9.30-4.30 (summer to 5).* ***Closed*** *25 & 26 Dec. Amex, Diners, MasterCard,* ***VISA***

BATH — Sally Lunn's House

Tel 01225 461634 **Fax 01225 447090** Map 13 F1 **JaB**
4 North Parade Passage Bath Bath & North East Somerset BA1 1NX

Sally Lunn, a Huguenot refugee from France, created the brioche-type Bath bun which has become a Bath tradition; famous since the 1680s, it's served today in what was her own refreshment house built in 1482, and the oldest house in Bath. Over 20 are offered in various preparations including savoury toasts with Welsh rarebit (£4.20) or with baked beans (£3.88), cold with salads or chicken curry (£6.55) or smoked salmon paté (£5.68) and sweet ones with brandy or cinnamon butter (£2.68) and lemon or orange curd (£2.78). Alongside are soup (£2.98 – when the cook thinks the weather's cold), apple pie, carrot or banana cake (£2.25), multifarious beverages and speciality teas. In the afternoons they offer a traditional Georgian cream tea (£4.28) – a toasted bun served with preserves, clotted cream and softened butter. Alone worth the trip is the basement kitchen museum, open every day. English candle-light dinners from 6pm Tuesday to Sunday also feature light bites such as toasted goat's cheese with salads (£4.20) and BLT Sally Lunn (£5.25) as well as some substantial items like smoked haddock bacon in a rich mornay sauce (£6.98), Cumberland lamb in a rosemary and vegetable sauce and venison in port with celery and mushrooms. No smoking. ***Seats*** *63.* ***Open*** *10am-11pm.* ***Closed*** *25 & 26 Dec. MasterCard,* ***VISA*** *(only in the evenings).*

BEAULIEU — Montagu Arms — 67% — £99

Tel 01590 612324 **Fax 01590 612188** Map 14 C4 **H**
Beaulieu New Forest Hampshire SO42 7ZL

A welcoming old creeper-clad inn, cosy in winter with real fires and cool in good weather with a small conservatory overlooking a paved terraced area; the latter is a fine spot for afternoon tea in summer, overlooking a circular lawn and immaculately kept, compact terraced gardens. Public rooms include an intimate, bookcase-lined bar, comfortable sitting room and a rather dark dining-room, only the front part of which benefits from the lovely garden views at breakfast. Bedrooms range from four singles overlooking the gardens to three antique-furnished suites, one with two bathrooms, another with a corner aspect and a four-poster bed heavily draped with floral fabric. Guests have the use of the health and beauty centre and indoor swimming pool at sister hotel *Careys Manor*, 6 miles away in Brockenhurst. After a visit to the National Motor Museum or the Palace, take tea in the pretty, well-kept garden or the conservatory overlooking it. A pot of tea or good cafetière coffee with home-made biscuits comes at £1.95 or there are a couple of set tea options (with home-made cakes such as chocolate dip fancies, and cake and Viennese whirls or scones £3.95, with both £5.95). Although teas are meant to start around 3.30pm it can sometimes be later if they have had a busy lunch. ***Rooms*** *24. Garden.* *Open (for teas) 3.30-5.45. Amex, Diners, MasterCard,* ***VISA***

BEAUWORTH Milbury's

Tel 01962 771248 **Fax 01962 771910** Map 15 D3 **P**

Beauworth nr Alresford Hampshire SO24 0PB

Set on a hill just to the south of the village, the site of some bronze age burial mounds or barrows, the pub's name is actually a corruption of Mill-Barrow, the name of the last remaining mound just 150 yards away. The South Downs Way passes by the front door of this old tile-hung pub. The main bar boasts old brickwork, a flagstone floor and rough-hewn three-legged tables, but the most fascinating feature is an enormous treadmill, within which a poor donkey once walked to raise water from a 300-foot well. For the price of a donation to the Guide Dogs for the Blind, you are invited to drop an ice-cube down the well and count the nearly eight seconds it takes to splash in the water far below. Children are made positively welcome, with their own small section on the menu and a large safe garden to play in. There is also a skittle alley, which must be booked. *Open 11-3, 6-11 (Sat 11-11 summer), Sun 12-3, 7-10.30 (12-10.30 summer). Free House.* ***Beer*** *Milbury's (4.3%), Hampshire Brewery King Alfred & Pendragon, guest beers. Garden, outdoor eating, children's play area. Family room. Amex, MasterCard,* **VISA**

BECKINGHAM Black Swan £60

Tel 01636 626474 Map 7 E3 **R**

Hillside Beckingham Lincolnshire LN5 0RF

A converted village pub with a country atmosphere and a charming riverside garden where light summer lunches are served. The à la carte menu provides an interesting selection of dishes, classically based but often with original touches: twice-baked cheese soufflé with mushroom sauce, pheasant terrine served on an apple and cinnamon compote, escalopes of sea bream on red cabbage, fillet of beef marinated in lavender and honey, topped with a Stilton mousse served on a bed of spinach with a port sauce. Good puds, with soufflés like hot orange, Grand Marnier and chocolate something of a speciality. Children under 11 eat Sunday lunch free (one child per adult). Parking for 10 cars. No smoking. 5% charge for credit cards. ***Seats*** *35. Private Room 28. L 12-2 D 7-9.30. Closed D Sun, all Mon, 1 week Jan & 2 weeks Aug. Set L £10.50/£13.50. MasterCard,* **VISA**

BELFORD Blue Bell Hotel 63% £84

Tel 01668 213543 **Fax 01668 213787** Map 5 D1 **H**

Market Square Belford Northumberland NE70 7NE

Creeper-clad, the Bell stands at the head of the village on a cobbled forecourt. In front are the old Market Place and stone cross (restored by English Heritage), and the Norman parish church stands on a hill behind. The pubbiest part is the Belford Tavern, licensed in old stables in the courtyard, where there's a games room, a children's menu and just one regularly-changing real ale on offer. The hotel's stone-flagged foyer leads to a stylish cocktail bar boasting a collection of miniature hand bells, and a restful residents' lounge. Bedrooms are a mix, from those in the annexe (with shower/WCs only) to superior and de luxe rooms with full bathrooms and lovely views of the Blue Bell's 2-acre "garden of 10,000 blooms". One ground-floor room is equipped for disabled guests. *Open 11-3, 6.30-11 (Sun 12-3, 7-10.30).* ***Accommodation*** *17 bedrooms, all en suite, £74-£92 (single £35-£42). Children welcome overnight (under-12s stay free in parents' room, 12-16s £4) additional bed & cot available. Amex, MasterCard,* **VISA**

Pubs – note that food is only recommended in those pubs with ***Bar Food*** times in the statistics at the end of an entry. Restaurant food in pubs is *never* recommended unless specifically mentioned. Some pubs are recommended for B&B or Atmosphere only – each entry's statistics indicate our recommendation.

BELTON — Belton Woods Hotel — 72% — £125

Tel 01476 593200 **Fax 01476 74547** Map 7 E3 H

Belton nr Grantham Lincolnshire NG32 2LN

Just off the A607, north of Grantham, a modern De Vere-owned complex standing in 475 acres of grounds, with outstanding sports facilities that are matched by equally impressive accommodation. Ambassador rooms are particularly spacious, and some of them, like the suites, have patios or balconies affording views over the golf course (one of three). Three bedrooms are adapted for disabled guests. A spacious, high-ceilinged lounge leading off the main foyer is filled with parlour plants and hanging baskets, and also overlooks one of the golf courses. The cocktail bar on the first floor is more club-like, with easy chairs and rich decor; there's a conservatory and a 'spike bar' for golfers. Excellent facilities for children. 24hr room service. Parking for 500 cars. No dogs. ***Rooms*** *136. Garden, croquet, tennis, golf (2 18-hole, 1 9-hole), golf driving range, putting green, indoor swimming pool, splash pool, gym, squash, sauna, steam room, spa bath, solarium, beauty & hair salon, playroom, playground, snooker. Amex, Diners, MasterCard,* ***VISA***

BIBURY — The Swan — 78% — £140

Tel 01285 740695 **Fax 01285 740473** Map 14 C2 

Bibury Gloucestershire GL7 5NW

A splendid hotel on the banks of the River Coln. The setting, in neatly kept gardens, is a real delight, and the first impressions continue throughout, from the foyer through to the comfortably furnished parlour (for non-smokers) and the charming writing room, which was once the village post office. Explore further through and you find a splendid long bar with pale oak panelling, leather tub chairs on flagstone floor, log fire and one wall covered with a mural depicting various folk involved in the hotel's transformation. Press on and the mood changes yet again in a stylish all-day brasserie complete with Italian wrought-iron furniture. There are all sorts of fine decorative fabrics throughout the hotel including a collection of Charles Rennie Mackintosh chairs. Upstairs even the standard bedrooms have great appeal with antique furniture and individual decor; the best might have a four-poster bed, crystal chandelier, spa bath or luxuriously large, old-fashioned freestanding tub. Fine toiletries and bathrobes are standard. No dogs. For sale as we went to press. ***Rooms*** *18. Garden, croquet, fishing, brasserie (10am-10pm). Closed 5 days Christmas. Amex, MasterCard,* ***VISA***

BICKLEY MOSS — Cholmondeley Arms

Tel 01829 720300 **Fax 01829 720123** Map 6 B3 

Bickley Moss Malpas Cheshire SY14 8BT

Virtually opposite Cholmondeley Castle and gardens on the A49 and still part of the Viscount's estate is this redbrick former schoolhouse replete with family heirlooms, educational memorabilia, bell tower without and blackboards within. These last provide interesting reading, the daily-changing list possibly featuring goat's cheese soufflé with devilled tomato sauce, Mediterranean fish soup, and terrine of sweetbreads with bacon and garlic among the starters, followed by chicken breast in a mushroom, Dijon mustard and cream sauce, rabbit braised in red wine, monkfish provençale or Kashmiri lamb curry. Finish, perhaps, with rhubarb and ginger crumble or bread-and-butter pudding. Overnight accommodation is across the car park in what must have been the head teacher's house. Four recently refurbished and two new self-contained bedrooms (five doubles and a family room) are bright and cottagey with en suite WC and shower rooms (one with bath); one of the two new bedrooms having French doors leading out into the garden. All have telephones, television and clock radios, tea trays and hairdryers. It's back to school in the morning to report in for a slap-up breakfast. *Open 11-3, 7-11 (from 6.30 Sat), Sun 12-3, 7-10.30.* ***Bar Food*** *12-2.15, 7-10 (from 6.30 Sat, till 9.30 Sun). Free House.* ***Beer*** *Boddingtons, Flowers IPA & Original, guest beer. Garden, outdoor eating. children's play area. Family room.* ***Accommodation*** *6 bedrooms, all en suite, £53.50 (family room £80, single £38.50). Children welcome overnight (£7.50 if sharing parents' room), additional bed & cot available. Check-in by arrangement. Closed 25 Dec. MasterCard,* ***VISA***

Biddenden — Claris's

Tel 01580 291025 Map 11 C5 JaB
High Street Biddenden Kent TN27 8AL

Originally a row of 15th-century weaver's cottages, this cosy tea room and gift shop has been in the capable hands of the Winghams for more than 12 years now. Claris's is open from 10.30am, so although tea is the main attraction, there is also a range of snacks. Unlicensed. No smoking. ***Seats*** *24 (+ 16 outside).* ***Open*** *10.30-5.20.* ***Closed*** *Mon (except Bank Holidays) & 1st 2 weeks Jan. No credit cards.*

Bingley — Bankfield Hotel — 61% — £96

Tel 01274 567123 **Fax 01274 551331** Map 6 C1 H
Bradford Road Bingley Bradford BD16 1TU

Behind an eye-catching castellated Gothic frontage are handsome Victorian day rooms, an up-to-the-minute bar and mainly modern, decent-sized bedrooms. Conference facilities for up to 300. The hotel stands on the A650 Bradford-Skipton road. Jarvis Hotels. ***Rooms*** *103. Garden, croquet. Amex, Diners, MasterCard,* ***VISA***

Birch Vale — Sycamore Inn

Tel 01663 742715 **Fax 01663 747382** Map 6 C2 P
Sycamore Road Birch Vale Hayfield Derbyshire DE55 6FG

Surrounded by woods of sycamore and silver birch, this quietly located pub at the fringe of the village (turn off the A6015 at Station Road) is built precariously into the side of a steep hill. In ten acres of grounds, the paddock slopes steeply down to the River Sett (although you can't see it), while beyond the lower car park there are a barbecue terrace, dovecotes, mini-aviary and a children's Tarzan trail playground. There are bars at two levels, the lower with regular entertainment and a clubby atmosphere while that above is given over largely to eating in neatly partitioned dining areas which include non-smoking and family rooms. With one exception, bedrooms look out across the valley; they're neatly appointed with whitewood furniture and patchwork quilts; all have en suite facilities (four with baths), satellite TVs, radios, beverage trays and trouser presses. For those with other pressing business, the only telephone provided is on the upper landing. New chalet-style family B&B accommodation is being built in the grounds; two will come on line at the end of 1996. Children welcome indoors. *Open 11-11 (Sun 12-10.30).* ***Beer*** *John Smith's, Marston's Pedigree, Sycamore Bitter, guest beer. Garden.* ***Accommodation*** *6 bedrooms, ll en suite, £45 (family room sleeping four, £55, single £29.50, weekend reductions). Children welcome overnight, additional bed (£10) & cot supplied. MasterCard,* ***VISA***

> If we recommend meals in a hotel a *separate* entry is usually made for its restaurant. Pub and inn entries include bar food details where recommended.

Birdlip — Air Balloon

Tel & Fax 01452 862541 Map 14 B2 
Crickley Hill Birdlip Gloucester Gloucestershire GL4 6JY

A prominent 17th-century inn adjacent to the A417/A436 junction, equidistant from Gloucester and Cheltenham, amusingly named to commemorate the exploits of a local balloonist. He took off from the top of nearby Crickley Hill on a maiden flight in 1802 and promptly vanished into thin air (or so the story goes). Today's tale is of a busy Whitbread Wayside Inn which packs in the families year-round. In winter there are large log fires; on summer days hill-top gardens set out with play equipment and a bouncy castle. There are also picnic tables on the sheltered rear patio under a permanent awning. *Open 11-11 (Sun 12-10.30).* ***Beer*** *Wadworth 6X, Flowers Original, Boddingtons, Whitbread Castle Eden Ale. MasterCard,* ***VISA***

BIRDLIP Kingshead House £70

Tel 01452 862299 Map 14 B2 **RR**
Birdlip nr Cheltenham Gloucestershire GL4 8JH

On the Cotswold Way and about eight miles from both Cheltenham and Gloucester, this informal and very welcoming country restaurant began life in the 17th century as a coaching inn. Since 1986 it has been run in fine style by Judy and Warren Knock. Judy offers fixed-price-only dinner menus in a style that's modern British with some French influences. Watercress soup or a trio of smoked poultry with celeriac rémoulade could be your starting option, then perhaps (if you're taking four courses) a risotto of field and button mushrooms. The centrepiece dish (five choices including one vegetarian) might be fillet of lemon sole with a herb crust and a hot parsley sauce or pork fillet with Stilton, walnuts and red cabbage. Desserts are no less appealing, and there's an alternative of British and French cheeses. Lunch Monday to Friday is a simpler à la carte affair served in the restaurant or bar (you can take one dish or a full meal) while Sunday lunch always includes traditional roasts. Prices are fair on a short but enterprising hand-written wine list with sensible tasting notes and plenty of halves. Smoking is discouraged by table cards. ***Seats*** *32. L 12.30-1.45 D 7.30-9.45. Closed L Sat, D Sun, all Mon. Check Christmas closures. Set Sun L £17.50 Set D £24/£26. Amex, Diners, MasterCard,* ***VISA***

Room £60

The one and only en suite double bedroom is a delightful place to stop over for a night.

> Always ring ahead and inform establishments of your exact requirements when travelling with children. Unannounced can, sadly, still mean unwelcome.

BIRMINGHAM Adil £30

Tel 0121-4490335 Map 6 C4 
148 Stoney Lane Sparkbrook Birmingham B12 8AQ

It's been open for more than 20 years so some credence must be given to the claim that this is Birmingham's first balti house. The menus are displayed beneath the glass table tops. Balti refers to the hemispherical dishes in which the food is both cooked and served. Try the ever-popular chicken tikka masala (£4.50) here served in a balti dish, balti meat with dal (£4.30) or balti prawn rogan josh (£4.40) among almost 100 variations including a sizeable vegetarian section. Use the excellent naan breads to eat with: the small size is probably enough for one, medium does two people and the large size (it really is huge) is enough for a table of four. No smoking in the upstairs room. Car parking opposite. ***Seats*** *100.* ***Open*** *12-11.45.* ***Closed*** *25 Dec. Amex, Diners, MasterCard,* ***VISA***

Also at:

Waterfront Balti House 127 Dudley Road Brierley Hill Map 6 C4
Tel 01384 76929
Open 5pm-1am.

BIRMINGHAM California Pizza Factory

Tel 0121-428 2636 Map 6 C4 **JaB**
42 High Street Harborne Birmingham B17 9NE

Large, colourful, bustling pizza house with a wood-block floor, exposed ducting high overhead cultivate the factory theme. First-rate pizzas, with a slightly charcoal flavour, emerge from a special wood-fired kiln, imported from Italy, with a range of inventive toppings such as Peking duck (£6.50), Cajun chicken (£7.50), and breakfast (with Gloucester sausage, black pudding and a fried egg among other things £6.25). Other options include pasta (they make their own), with dishes like spaghetti Thai chicken

(£8.25), angel-hair with chicken and black beans (£7.95) and spaghetti vegetable provençale (£3.25/£5.95) priced as either starter or main dish. Some salads are similarly priced, among them: Caesar (£2.35/£4.65), bacon and spinach (£3.25/£6.50) and Greek (£2.95/£5.75). For afters try their range of Baskin Robbins ice creams (from £2.35), tiramisu or Californian carrot cake (both £3.25). Children are made very welcome with toy box, crayons and colouring sheets and their own menu – baked bean and cheese pizza (£1.75). Friendly, smiling service provides the finishing touch. The lower level is reserved for non-smokers. Own car park. ***Seats*** *110.* ***Open*** *12-10.45.* ***Closed*** *25 & 26 Dec. Amex, MasterCard,* ***VISA***
Also at:
10 Poplar Road Solihull West Midlands B91 3AB Tel 0121-693 6339
20 Victoria Street Nottingham NG1 2AS Tel 0115 985 9955

BIRMINGHAM Chung Ying £40

Tel 0121-622 5669 **Fax 0121-666 7051** Map 6 C4 R
16 Wrottesley Street Birmingham B5 4RT

The Chinese flock to this well-established, traditionally appointed restaurant for its long Cantonese menu. The choice extends to well over 300 dishes, including more than 40 dim sum items and a 'special dishes' section with steamed pork pie with fresh or dried squid, fishcakes with mangetout and fried frogs' legs with bitter melon. Also of note are the casseroles and the Sunday lunchtime hot pots from which you help yourself. ***Seats*** *220. Parties 18. Meals 12-11.30 (Sun till 11). Closed 25 Dec. Set menus from £12.50 (min 2). Amex, Diners, MasterCard,* ***VISA***

BIRMINGHAM Chung Ying Garden £40

Tel 0121-666 6622 Map 6 C4 R
17 Thorpe Street Birmingham B5 4AT

The main menu at this first-floor restaurant has a choice of over 300 items, though the lighter eater would do well to choose from the 50 or so dishes offered on the good-value dim sum menu (fewer after 5pm). All the favourites are here – paper-wrapped prawns, deep-fried won ton, beef with ginger and spring onion, crispy spring rolls, char siu buns – plus the likes of assorted braised ox tripe and steamed duck webs in black bean sauce. Most come in at £1.80 with the most expensive being £2.20. Sister restaurant to the nearby *Chung Ying (qv)*. Parking is at the Euro car park. ***Seats*** *300.* ***Open*** *12-12 (Sun till 11).* ***Closed*** *25 Dec. Amex, Diners, MasterCard,* ***VISA***

BIRMINGHAM Gaylord

Tel 0121-236 0445 Map 6 C4 JaB
51 Dale End Birmingham B4 7LS

The name of this North Indian restaurant has changed (it was formerly Rama) but it's still in the same ownership. It's situated between Dale End and Albert Street car parks, so where to leave the car should present no problems. A hot buffet lunch is available during the week, offering two starters, three different curries, naan bread and rice for £7.50. From the carte, fish tikka or chicken chat are among the starters. Main courses such as chicken jalfrezi or roghan josh are good value at £5.95. There is a good vegetarian selection, too. ***Seats*** *100.* ***Open*** *12-2.30 & 6-11.30.* ***Closed*** *L Sat, all Sun. Amex, Diners, MasterCard,* ***VISA***

JaB is short for 'Just a Bite'. The majority of these establishments are also recommended in our *Bistros, Bars & Cafés* Guide which features establishments where one may eat well for less than £15 per head.

Birmingham — Hudson's Coffee House

Tel 0121-643 1001 Map 6 C4 **JaB**
City Plaza Centre (1st floor) Cannon Street Birmingham B2 5EF

On the first floor of a circular atrium shopping centre, Hudson's (the name comes from an 18th-century coffee house in Covent Garden) aims to provide an oasis of 1930s elegance and calm amid the bustle of the city. Waiters are smart in tail-coats, there are newspapers and magazines (Dandy and Beano for kids of whatever age) and even a few armchairs amongst the bentwood chairs that surround the glass-topped tables. The menu ranges from New York-style filled bagels (from £2.65) and sandwiches made with a choice of breads (from £2.95) to various platters (seafood £7.50, rare beef £4.95) and desserts like lemon and sultana cheesecake £2.45 and apple strudel plus Dundee cake (made in Sutton Coldfield) served with clotted cream, and Häagen-Dazs ice creams. The selection of loose-leaf teas and coffees is particularly notable. The centre's baby-changing room is 50 yards away. Unlicensed. No smoking, air-conditioned. ***Seats*** *75.* ***Open*** *9-6.* ***Closed*** *Sun, most Bank Holidays & 25 Dec. Amex, MasterCard,* ***VISA***

Birmingham — Hyatt Regency — 75% — £146

Tel 0121-643 1234 **Fax 0121-616 2323** Map 6 C4 **HR**
2 Bridge Street Birmingham B1 2JZ

A canalside setting in the heart of Birmingham for the impressive, mirrored, 25-storey Hyatt Regency, which has a direct link to the International Convention Centre next door. Inside, the huge glazed atrium is the epitome of style and elegance, bedecked with plants, and awash with marble. The luxuriously appointed bedrooms include 12 suites; all have quality modern furniture and fashionably uncluttered decor, plus equally splendid, marble-floored bathrooms. Three rooms are adpated for the disabled and three floors make up the Regency Club of superior rooms; the latter has its own Club Lounge on the 22nd floor. Floor-to-ceiling windows afford fine views over the City. Excellent leisure facilities. Conference and banqueting facilities for up to 240, plus a business centre. Children up to 16 stay free in parents' room. Parking £8 for 24 hours (£10 valet). ***Rooms*** *319. Indoor swimming pool, gym, sauna, solarium, steam room, spa bath, café (6.30am-11.30pm). Amex, Diners, MasterCard,* ***VISA***

Number 282 — £80

Tagged as the Brasserie on Broad Street, with a menu that incorporates the day's news headlines, weather, entertainment and even a personalised message on the paper place mat. The menu itself (on the same sheet) ranges from French onion soup, Caesar salad and curried artichoke hearts to fish & chips (deep-fried monkfish with sweet potato chips), pan-fried duck breast with poached dried fruits and a honey-flavoured Madeira sauce, and sirloin steak with a peppercorn sauce. To finish, perhaps poached pear or Tahitian crème brulée. Plenty of New World as well as European wines. Other eating venues include the all-day Court Café. ***Seats*** *75. Parties 16. L 12.30-2.30 D 6-10.30. Set L £14.75 (3-course) Set D from £16 (2-course). Closed L Sat, all Sun.*

Birmingham — New Happy Gathering — £35

Tel 0121-643 5247 **Fax 0121-643 4731** Map 6 C4 **R**
43 Station Street Birmingham B5 4DY

The Chan family claims that theirs was the first (1970) Cantonese restaurant in Birmingham, and it can be found a short walk from Chinatown, above street level at the back of New Street Station. A tented fabric ceiling above the staircase and carved wood panels within the restaurant lend an opulent air, while traditional Chinese cuisine holds few surprises on a neatly laid-out menu that runs to nearly 200 items; many of these are included in the various set menus for two or more diners. Dim sum head the main menu with a choice of more than two dozen, available unusually in the evening as well as lunchtime. Other sections of the menu cover soups, sizzling dishes, beef, pork, duck, chicken, king prawns, seafood, curries and Cantonese casseroles. ***Seats*** *90. Private Room 100. L 12-1.45 D 5-11.15 (Fri to 11.45, Sun to 11) Sat all day 12-11.45. Set meals (min 2) from £10. Amex, Diners, MasterCard,* ***VISA***

Birmingham — Wild Oats

Tel 0121-471 2459 Map 6 C4 JaB
5 Raddlebarn Road Selly Oak Birmingham B29 6HJ

Modest vegetarian café run in cheerfully unpretentious style by Mo Marshall. Cashew nut paté, various dips with crudités or tortilla chips, marinated mushrooms (£1.40) or soup of the day (such as cream of broccoli or carrot and orange £1.10) is followed by the day's main dishes – chick pea casserole, Italian beans and pasta (both £3.80), savoury mushroom tart (£3.50) perhaps – before puds like banana and apple crunch, fruit crumble, and blackcurrant or chocolate cheesecake (all £1.40). Everything is freshly made and served in generous portions. Unlicensed. No smoking. ***Seats*** *25.* ***Open*** *12-2 & 6-9.* ***Closed*** *Sun, Mon, Bank Holidays (except Good Friday) & 2 weeks Christmas. No credit cards.*

Blackburn — Tiggis

Tel 01254 667777 Map 6 B1 JaB
71 King William Street Blackburn Lancashire BB1 7DT

Good use has been made of the vaulted semi-basement of the old Corn Exchange. Granite table tops, art nouveau cloths and lots of gleaming brass complete the scene and provide a setting for traditional Italian fare. The menu has something for everyone with pizzas (from £4.20 for a margherita), pasta dishes including penne alla carbonara (£5.90), antipasti like *fegatini di pollo* (chicken liver with onions, pepper, chili and wine, £3.95) and deep-fried mushrooms with garlic mayonnaise (£2.95), plus old favourites such as grilled trout and chicken kiev (£9.95). Children can have half portions whenever possible, and they have their own Italian-style menu with pizzas, pasta and beefburgers, a helium-filled balloon and free birthday cake for birthday boys and girls. Four clip-on high-chairs are available for really tiny tots. Vegetarian main courses include *pappardelle alla Tiggis* – pasta ribbons with wild mushrooms with avocado in a tomato sauce (£5.70). ***Seats*** *150.* ***Open*** *12-2 & 6-11.* ***Closed*** *Mon (but open Bank Holiday evenings), 25, 26 Dec & 1 Jan. MasterCard,* ***VISA***
Also at:
63 Bradshawgate Bolton Tel 01204 363636
See entry

Blackpool — Pembroke Hotel — 67% — £139

Tel 01253 23434 **Fax 01253 27864** Map 6 A1 H
North Promenade Blackpool Lancashire FY1 2JQ

A modern conference hotel with facilities for up to 900 delegates (theatre-style) and up to 650 for banqueting. In the main holiday season families are well catered for, with extra beds and cots, a playroom and a separate children's menu. A large swimming pool and Springs night club are among the leisure amenities. Parking for over 300 cars. Metropole Hotels. ***Rooms*** *274. Indoor swimming pool, games room, news kiosk. Amex, Diners, MasterCard,* ***VISA***

Blakeney — Blakeney Hotel — 64% — £132

Tel 01263 740797 **Fax 01263 740795** Map 10 C1 
The Quay Blakeney nr Holt Norfolk NR25 7NE

On the Heritage Coastline, in an area of outstanding natural beauty, this family-owned-and-run hotel is favoured by conservationists, holidaymakers and business travellers alike. Most rooms are in the main building but a few are in an annexe. All the bedrooms are comfortably furnished and top-of-the range rooms usually have a feature such as four-poster bed, jacuzzi, antique furniture or a balcony. Rooms with an estuary view are priced £6 higher per person. Children under 16 sharing adults' rooms are charged £6 a night (free during summer holidays). Car parking for 70. ***Rooms*** *60. Garden, indoor swimming pool, keep-fit equipment, sauna, spa bath, hair salon, snooker. Amex, Diners, MasterCard,* ***VISA***

BLANCHLAND Lord Crewe Arms £105

Tel 01434 675251 **Fax 01434 675337** Map 5 D2
Blanchland Consett Durham DH8 9SP

Wild and remote, Blanchland lies some 3 miles below Derwent Water in a deep valley. Blanchland Abbey can trace its origins back to 1165 – despite dissolution in 1576 the layout of its surrounding village remains unchanged to this day. At its heart is one of England's finest inns, containing relics of the abbey lodge and kitchens and set in a cloister garden which is now an ancient monument. Lord Crewe purchased the entire estate in 1704 from one Tom Foster, a Jacobite adventurer; the ghost of his sister Dorothy is claimed still to be in residence. A sense of history pervades the building's remarkably modernised yet largely unchanged interior, no more so than in the Crypt bar. The meals served here are substantial: German pork sausage with sauerkraut and warm potato salad and wild boar and pheasant pie with salad do not constitute the average pub lunch. Evening options of baked salmon, minute steak or cheese-filled pasta are rather more traditional. Ploughman's and filled brown rolls are lunchtime alternatives, while Sunday lunch features a hot and cold buffet. A three-course Sunday lunch is also served in the stylish first-floor restaurant overlooking the garden. Bedrooms, needless to say, are splendidly individual; suitably traditional in the old house with stone mullion windows and restored fireplaces and mantels, yet up-to-date with accessories from colour TVs to bespoke toiletries and thoughtful extras from mending kits to complimentary sherry. Altogether more contemporary are the style and furnishings of rooms in the adjacent Angel Inn – once a Wesleyan Temperance House – a mere newcomer dating from the 1750s. *Open 11-3, 6-11 (Sun 12-3, 7-10.30).* ***Bar Food*** *12-2, 7-9. Free House.* ***Beer*** *Vaux Samson. Garden.* ***Accommodation*** *20 bedrooms all en suite from £105 (single from £75). Children welcome overnight (under-14s stay free if sharing parents' room). Amex, Diners, MasterCard,* ***VISA***

BLEDINGTON Kings Head Inn

Tel 01608 658365 **Fax 01608 658902** Map 14 C1 P
The Green Bledington Kingham Oxfordshire OX7 6HD

A more delightful spot would surely be hard to find: facing the village green with its brook and border-patrolling ducks, this is surely the quintessential Cotswold pub. Dating back to the 15th century, it stands on the Gloucester border with its easterly wall resident in Oxfordshire. Inside, the low-ceilinged bar is full of ancient settles and simple wooden furniture and there's a separate lounge and dining-room – all equally agreeable settings in which to enjoy the Royces' imaginative pub food. Lunchtime 'bar fayre' offers a wide range, from unusual sandwiches (vodka-soused red mullet with mayonnaise, cucumber and tarragon) to basil and mozzarella pancake, steak, mushroom and wine pie, a wide range of salads in summer (perhaps feta and olives or black pudding and walnuts), bowls of pasta with shredded beef and horseradish, and interesting weekly-changing specials like artichoke, asparagus and feta pithiviers on tomato coulis and salmon, scallop and prawn pie. These might be supplemented in winter by the likes of jugged hare, local rabbit and venison. An à la carte evening menu sees plenty of variety without undue elaboration among the deftly-sauced main courses; the ever-popular half honey-roasted duck may come with a green pepercorn sauce and apple purée. Sweets like toffee and walnut flan and rum flavoured bread pudding are genuinely home-made. A set-price 'Snippets menu' is a monthly-changing, three-course table d'hote with alternative choices at each stage – particularly good value for residents at £9.95. Excellent overnight accommodation in twelve superbly furnished en suite bedrooms. Meticulous attention has been paid to their detail; the three ground-floor rooms in the rear extension are an added bonus for less mobile guests. The older, cottagey bedrooms (no-smoking) over the pub should not suffer by comparison (though they may be less suitable for an early night) although the floorboards may be a little creaky. Their appointments nonetheless are top class, with direct-dial phones, TVs, clock radios and an array of extras. Residents here enjoy the use of a quiet smokers' lounge and a private patio. A changing mat and facilities are available on request in the Ladies. *Open 11-2.30, 6-11 (from 5.30 Sat), Sun 12-2.30, 7-10.30.* ***Bar Meals*** *12-2, 7-10 (from 6.30 Fri & Sat, till 9.30 Sun).* ***Beer*** *Hook Norton Best, Wadworth 6X, four guest beers. Garden, outdoor eating. Family room.* ***Accommodation*** *12 bedrooms, all en suite, £60-£75, (single £40). Children welcome overnight, (under-5s stay free if sharing parents' room, 5-15s £10), additional bed & cot supplied (both £5). No dogs. Closed 25 Dec. MasterCard,* ***VISA***

BLICKLING Blickling Hall Restaurant

Tel 01263 733474 Map 10 C1 JaB

Blickling nr Aylsham Norfolk NR11 6NF

Housed in one of the brick stable blocks flanking the magnificent 17th-century red-brick house and overlooking the expanse of front lawn, this charming tea room and restaurant (free access) is a popular refreshment stop with the usual high standard of decor, service and cooking that one expects from the National Trust. Two attractive beamed rooms with leafy patterned oilcloth-covered tables are the setting in which to enjoy a light lunch comprising home-made soup – vegetable (£2), a wholesome vegetarian dish such as vegetable gratin (£4.50), or a warming farmhouse beef casserole (£4.95). Home-made desserts (£2) might include hot sticky apple and suet puddings. Traditional Sunday roast lunch (£5.75). Afternoon tea visitors can choose from a mouthwatering range of scones, biscuits and freshly-made cakes (from 75p). Children's menu and crockery, high-chairs, baby food, scribbling sheets and changing area. No smoking. ***Seats*** *90 (+25 outside).* ***Open*** *10.30-5.* ***Closed*** *Mon-Wed Nov-Mar, Mon & Thu Mar-end Jun & Sept/Oct. MasterCard,* ***VISA***

BLICKLING Buckinghamshire Arms Hotel

Tel 01263 732133 Map 10 C1 

Blickling Aylsham Norfolk NR11 6NF

Splendid Grade I listed 17th-century inn which stands deferentially at the gates of the even more magnificent Blickling Hall. Once the estate builders' house and later the servants' quarters to the fine National Trust property. The three charming and well-furnished bars have open fires and are typically National Trust in style of decor and taste. No children overnight. Recently acquired by Humble Inns who intend revamping the accommodation and improving the food – watch this space!
Open 11-3, 6-11 (11-11 school holidays), Sun 12-3, 7-10.30. Free House.
Beer *Adnams Bitter & Broadside, two guest beers. Garden. MasterCard,* ***VISA***

BODIAM Knollys

Tel 01580 830323 Map 11 C6 

Main Street Bodiam East Sussex

Just next to the splendid castle at Bodiam, Gloria Barratt bakes and cooks splendid teas and lunch-type dishes, all available throughout the day. Freshly prepared sandwiches plain or toasted (from £1.85) and cakes (fudge cake 95p, chocolate cake with double cream £1.45) accompany morning coffee and afternoon tea, while favourites on the full menu include smoked salmon paté (£3.45), cod in crisp batter (£4.50), jacket potatoes (from £2.65), main-course salads and chicken and leek pie with potatoes (£5.25). Fruit pies and ice creams are the most popular desserts, plus strawberries and cream in season (£2.05). Fast and friendly service. Children's portions available. ***Seats*** *53 (+50 outside).* ***Open*** *10.30-5.* ***Closed*** *Mon (except Bank Holidays), Oct-Mar. No credit cards.*

BOLTON Beaumont Hotel 58% £75

Tel 01204 651511 **Fax 01204 61064** Map 6 B2 

Beaumont Road Bolton BL3 4TA

Looking very much like an older-style Posthouse, which is what it actually once was, this modern hotel stands on the outskirts of Bolton near J5 of the M61. There's a two-level bedroom block and conference/banqueting facilities for 120/90. ***Rooms*** *96. Garden, play area. Amex, Diners, MasterCard,* ***VISA***

We endeavour to be as up-to-date as possible, but inevitably some changes to data and key personnel may occur at restaurants and hotels after the Guide goes to press. Prices should also be taken as indications rather than firm quotes.

BOLTON — Last Drop Village Hotel — 68% — £107

H

Tel 01204 591131 **Fax 01204 304122** Map 6 B2
Hospital Road Bromley Cross Bolton BL7 9PZ

About 30 years ago, a collection of 18th-century moorland farm buildings was skilfully turned into a village with cottages, gardens, craft shops, a pub, a tea shop and bakery and, at its heart, a comfortable and well-equipped hotel. Day rooms retain some original features, while bedrooms (three more since last year) are bright and modern with all the expected amenities. Children stay free in parents' room, paying for meals as taken. The hotel is well signposted from the A666. ***Rooms** 86. Garden, indoor swimming pool, gym, sauna, steam room, spa bath, sun beds, squash, beauty and hair salons, snooker, tea shop (10am-5pm). Amex, Diners, MasterCard,* **VISA**

BOLTON — Tiggis

JaB

Tel 01204 363636 Map 6 B2
63 Bradshawgate Bolton

See entry under Blackburn. The children's menu includes buttered corn on the cob, a choice of three pizzas, beefburger and chips or a pasta dish and ice cream. If it's a birthday (adults included!) a complimentary birthday cake is presented in a gold box while lights are dimmed. Three high-chairs, a booster seat, small plates and straws are all provided, and children leave Tiggis clutching a balloon, probably 'well happy'. Chair in Ladies for baby-changing. ***Seats** 110. **Open** 12-2 & 6-11. Closed L Bank Holidays, all 25, 26 Dec & 1 Jan. MasterCard,* **VISA**

Our inspectors *never* book in the name of Egon Ronay's Guides. They disclose their identity only if they are considering an establishment for inclusion in the next edition of the Guide.

BONCHURCH — Winterbourne Hotel — 64% — £106*

H

Tel 01983 852535 **Fax 01983 853056** Map 15 D4
Bonchurch Isle of Wight PO38 1RQ

Charles Dickens wrote most of *David Copperfield* here, and the bedrooms are named after characters in the novel. The setting is one of great charm, with waterfalls in the wooded, terraced garden and lovely sea views. Inside is no less appealing, and the main day room has French windows opening on to the terrace and garden. Bedrooms, most with sea views, vary considerably in size and appointments, the best perhaps being five in the converted coach house. A family-friendly place, with extra beds and cots available, and a children's menu. The village of Bonchurch is near Ventnor, on the southern tip of the island. *Half-board terms only. ***Rooms** 14. Garden, outdoor swimming pool. Closed Nov-Mar. Amex, Diners, MasterCard,* **VISA**

BOREHAM STREET — White Friars Hotel — 57% — £75

H

Tel 01323 832355 **Fax 01323 833882** Map 11 B6
Boreham Street nr Herstmonceux East Sussex BN27 4SE

The oldest part dates back to the 15th century, but most of this tile-hung, redbrick hotel was built in the 1700s. Inside there is a cottagey, homely feel to the main lounge and bar area with its old black beams, floral soft furnishings, pot plants and a real fire in winter. Bedrooms, which vary in size and shape, are modestly furnished with dark-stained built-in units plus a scattering of traditional (old rather than antique) pieces. All are light and bright, however, and come with all the usual modern comforts. Of the functional bathrooms, two have showers only and several of the others have tubs without showers. Eight rooms, in identical style, are in a separate building. Family-run and children are welcome (under-16s sharing parents' room free – meals charged as taken) except over Christmas and the New Year. ***Rooms** 20. Garden. Amex, Diners, MasterCard,* **VISA**

BORROWDALE Stakis Keswick Lodore Hotel 71% £112

Tel 01768 777285 **Fax 01768 777343** Map 4 C3 H
Borrowdale Keswick Cumbria CA12 5UX

Overlooking Derwentwater and set in 40 acres of wooded grounds, the hotel is an ideal lakeland retreat for families, with an extensive range of leisure facilities and a nursery for under-6s. The best bedrooms take full advantage of the splendid lake views. There are numerous price packages available from overnight bed and breakfast to stays of five nights or more (these are on half-board terms). Children are charged according to age. Conference/banqueting facilities for 80. Free golf midweek at Keswick golf club. Lock-up garage £4 a night. ***Rooms** 70. Garden, croquet, tennis, indoor & outdoor swimming pool, gym, squash, sauna, sun beds, games room, nursery. Amex, Diners, MasterCard,* **VISA**

BOTTLESFORD Seven Stars

Tel 01672 851325 **Fax 01672 851583** Map 14 C3 
Bottlesford Woodborough Pewsey Wiltshire SH9 6LU

Set in a charming rural location, almost lost down narrow lanes deep in the Vale of Pewsey with views across country to the White Horse, is the splendid thatched and creeper-clad Seven Stars. Make for Woodborough from the A345 at Pewsey (past the hospital), or from the mini-roundabout at North Newnton. Delightful rambling interior of beams and black oak panelling and a central brick bar with quarry tile flooring. There's plenty of room to enjoy some masterfully produced bar food from the ever-enthusiastic, sometimes inspired Philippe Cheminade. Moules marinière, confit of duck and pork fillet normande attest equally to his Gallic origins as to a broad range of skills, which also extend to fine presentation of the more traditional venison and mushroom pie, jugged hare and lamb moussaka. Daily fish deliveries in summer from Cornwall satisfy the popular seafood platters (encompassing both lobster and winkles) and unusual dishes like Merlin steak with garlic and tomato sauce and pan-fried blue shark; both sandwiches and ploughman's lunches are also available. Two self-contained rooms at either end of the building double up for evening dining à la carte. The pub also boasts splendid gardens and grounds; a nine-acre tranche of land borders a shallow stream which winds down to the River Kennet; there are picnic tables here and hampers can be organised by arrangement. *Open 11.30-3, 6-11 (Sun 12-3, 7-10.30). Closed Sun eve Oct-Easter.* ***Bar Food** 12-2, 7-9.30 (no food ßSun eve & all Mon Oct-Easter). Free House.* ***Beer** Bunces Pigswill, Wadworth 6X, two guest beers. Garden, outdoor eating. children's play area, Family room. MasterCard,* **VISA**

We welcome bona fide complaints and recommendations on the tear-out pages at the back of the Guide for Readers' Comments. They are followed up by our professional team.

BOURNEMOUTH Beales Coffee Shop

Tel 01202 552022 **Fax 01202 295306** Map 14 C4 
36 Old Christchurch Road Bournemouth Dorset BH1 1LJ

The coffee shop in Beales department store is on the lower ground floor. The choice is extensive and everything is made on the premises. Choose from cottage pie, cauliflower cheese, quiche and baked potato filled with cheese and ham or curry (all around £3). Lunchtime choices (11.30-2) could include fresh salmon, baked ham, filled jacket potatoes (from £2.45) steak and kidney pie and a roast of the day (£6.75). In summer there are salads – cold meat (£5.90), salmon (£6.99). Set breakfast is served between 9 & 10.30 (£3.75), but a similar meal can be had all day under the title 'breakfast grill'. Sweet choices might be caramel cream, apple pie and fruit salad. Two high-chairs and two booster seats are available; no children's portions. Space in Ladies for baby-changing, but full facilities on the fourth floor. ***Seats** 125.* ***Open** 9-4.45.* ***Closed** Sun & some Bank Holidays. Amex, Diners, MasterCard,* **VISA**

BOURNEMOUTH Chez Fred

Tel 01202 761023 Map 14 C4 JaB
10 Seamoor Road Westbourne Bournemouth Dorset BH4 9AN

Terrific fish and chips make Fred's a cut above the rest and a lunchtime special of cod, chips, bread and butter and a drink (£3.95) provides excellent value. A 'small fry' menu for children under 10 at £2.99 offers a choice of cod, fishcake or sausages with chips and mushy peas, followed by ice cream and a soft drink. Treacle sponge and custard and variously sauced New Forest ice creams turn simple fish and chips into a family meal. Bright lights, lively music and friendly staff mark Fred's out from the crowd: look for Westbourne off the Wessex Way (A35) west of town towards Poole. No smoking. No bookings. ***Seats** 46. **Open** 11.30-1.45 & 5-10 (Sun from 5.30). **Closed** L Sun, 25-27 Dec. MasterCard, **VISA***

BOURNEMOUTH Chine Hotel 65% £96

Tel 01202 396234 **Fax 01202 391737** Map 14 C4 
Boscombe Spa Road Bournemouth Dorset BH5 1AX

In the same ownership since 1945, the Chine, built in 1874, occupies a fine position overlooking Poole Bay to the south. Large bedrooms, nearly half with private balcony or patio, have light-oak units and a pleasing pale-green colour scheme. Spacious public areas include a cosy residents' lounge overlooking the pine-fringed outdoor swimming pool. Business people are attracted by a number of well-equipped conference rooms (in an adjacent building) and families appreciate the playroom, games room, coin-operated laundry room and, during school holidays, a children's activities organiser. Some of the family rooms have kitchenettes. Children up to 14 stay free in parents' room. No dogs. Sister hotels are the *Haven* (Chine guests may use its leisure facilities) and *Sandbanks* at nearby Poole. ***Rooms** 86. Garden, putting, outdoor & indoor swimming pools, sauna, solarium, playroom and playground, games room. Amex, Diners, MasterCard, **VISA***

BOURNEMOUTH De Vere Royal Bath Hotel 73% £140

Tel 01202 555555 **Fax 01202 554158** Map 14 C4 
Bath Road Bournemouth Dorset BH1 2EW

A splendid Victorian hotel combining traditional values (courteous and helpful staff for example) and modern amenities for both business and leisure. The hotel stands in an immaculately kept three-acre garden with clifftop views out to sea, enjoyed by many of the bedrooms (some with terraces) which vary in style and size but are all smartly furnished with good bathrooms. Excellent housekeeping, including a turn-down service at night, is evident throughout. The vast public areas (bars and lounges) are comfortable and well appointed, and breakfast in the Garden Restaurant will not disappoint. Children up to the age of 14 stay free in parents' room. Covered parking for 70 cars. No dogs. ***Rooms** 131. Garden, croquet, indoor swimming pool, mini-gym, sauna, steam room, spa bath, solarium, beauty & hair salon. Amex, Diners, MasterCard, **VISA***

Restaurant £60

The Garden Restaurant is only open in the evenings and for Sunday lunch, offering a cuisine of English, French and International inspiration. Oscar's, a more intimate setting with Oscar Wilde memorabilia all around, offers a French-orientated carte and set menus, which at lunchtime include a roast carved from the trolley. ***Seats** 300. L (Sun only) 12.30-2.15 D 7-9.15. Set L £16.50 Set D £23. Oscar's (closed Sunday): Seats 40. L 12.30-2.15 D 7.30-10.15. Set L £15.50 Set D £28.50.*

A jug of fresh water!

BOURNEMOUTH Norfolk Royale 70% £140

Tel 01202 551521 **Fax 01202 299729** Map 14 C4 H
Richmond Hill Bournemouth Dorset BH2 6EN

Bournemouth's Edwardian heyday is recalled most notably at the Norfolk Royale in the splendid two-tier cast-iron verandah that looks proudly over the town. Twin conservatories – one housing the pool and the other part of the all-day Orangery restaurant – extend into the pretty garden to the rear and several interconnecting rooms provide plenty of lounge/bar space. Pretty, well-maintained bedrooms have good bathrooms. Fourteen rooms are reserved for non-smokers, others are equipped for lady travellers, yet more are adapted for disabled guests. Children up to age 12 can be accommodated free in parents' room. Valet parking for 85 cars in a secure underground park is a big plus given the hotel's central location. Well-motivated staff. No dogs. Banqueting/conferences for up to 100. ***Rooms*** *95. Garden, indoor swimming pool, sauna, spa bath, steam room. Amex, Diners, MasterCard,* ***VISA***

Any person using our name to obtain free hospitality is a fraud.
Proprietors, please inform the police and us.

BOURNEMOUTH Swallow Highcliff Hotel 69% £125

Tel 01202 557702 **Fax 01202 292734** Map 14 C4 H
St Michael's Road West Cliff Bournemouth Dorset BH2 5DU

Aptly named hotel set high on the West Cliff, above the Bournemouth International Centre, giving some rooms fine marine views. In summer a funicular lift opposite the hotel gives direct access to the promenade. Brass chandeliers feature in public rooms, which include a large lounge with lots of sofas and be-cushioned rattan chairs, an equally comfortable lounge bar and, in a separate part of the building, the less formal Plantation Inn. Generally good-sized bedrooms are furnished with fairly standard polished-wood hotel furniture with matching bed-covers and curtains, and all come with mini-fridges (containing complimentary fresh milk and mineral water - stocked as a mini-bar on request), satellite TV and iron and ironing board among other amenities. Bathrooms, of which 13 have shower and WC only, all boast towelling robes. A row of converted coastguard cottages contains 16 slightly less spacious but equally well-appointed bedrooms. Children under 15 stay free in parents' room. ***Rooms*** *157. Garden, croquet, tennis, golf practice net, putting green, indoor & outdoor swimming pools, children's splash pool, gym, volley ball, spa bath, sun beds, sauna, playground, playroom (school summer holidays only), games room, snooker, gift shop. Amex, Diners, MasterCard,* ***VISA***

Any person using our name to obtain free hospitality is a fraud.
Proprietors, please inform the police and us.

BOURTON-ON-THE-WATER Bo-Peep's Tea Rooms

Tel 01451 822005 Map 14 C1 
Riverside Bourton-on-the-Water Gloucestershire GL54 2DP

This ever-popular tea room continues to pack in the crowds, both local and visitors. It occupies a corner site across one of the footbridges over the Windrush (opposite the High Street at the Post Office end). A range of snacks such as scones (90p), pastries (95p) and sandwiches (from £1.70 – with healthy options clearly marked) is available all day. Lunch dishes range from garlic chicken goujons (£5.25) to seafood platter (£4.95) and vegetarian options like mushroom stroganoff (£5.25). The Cornish clotted cream tea (£2.95) is available all day with a huge choice of leaf teas.Children's items. ***Seats*** *80 (+12 outside).* ***Open*** *10.30-5 (till 8 in summer).* ***Closed*** *25 Dec. Amex, Diners, MasterCard,* ***VISA***

Bovey Tracey Devon Guild of Craftsmen, Granary Café

Tel 01626 832223 **Fax 01626 834220** Map 13 D3 **JaB**
Riverside Mill Bovey Tracey Newton Abbot Devon TQ13 9AF

Evidence of the Devon Guild of Craftsmen's output abounds throughout the Granary, housed in a restored mill perched on the River Bovey. Watercolours for sale alongside hand-thrown pottery and colourful cookbooks add tone to the bright, airy service counter and dining area. A team of five enthusiasts produces an imaginative and well-prepared selection of dishes including soup – perhaps courgette and bean (£2.25) salads with houmus and a wide range of hot dishes such as ham, mushroom and broccoli or creamy crab and mushroom bakes (both £3.95) and broccoli, walnut and apple crumble. Excellent cakes and desserts range from chocolate marshmallow slice and pineapple fruit cake to Dartmoor rocky road (£1.25); speciality teas and coffee are sold by the mugful; cider and apple juice are organic (as are all the meat and vegetables used), and wines include Bovey Tracey's own Whitstone (£1.55 glass). Large summer courtyard. Children welcome, with a high-chair available and baby-changing facilities in the Ladies. Children's toys are also provided. Children's portions. No smoking. ***Seats*** *40 (+ 50 outside).* ***Open*** *10-5 (lunch 12-2.30).* ***Closed*** *25 & 26 Dec, 1 Jan. MasterCard,* ***VISA***

Bowland Bridge Hare & Hounds

Tel 01539 568333 Map 4 C4 **P**
Bowland Bridge Grange-over-Sands Cumbria LA11 6NN

Truly rural, good-looking old inn owned by ex-international soccer player Peter Thompson and his wife Debbie. The bar successfully blends ancient and modern, with its rough stone walls, discreet farming bric-a-brac and simple wooden furniture; open fires spread warmth in winter weather. The dramatically high-ceilinged dining-room is for residents only; the residents' lounge is rather more chintzy. Bedrooms are immaculately kept, beamy, floral, and on the small side. Delightful garden. *Open 11-11 (till 10.30 Sun). Free House.* ***Beer*** *Tetley. Garden, children's play area.* ***Accommodation*** *16 bedrooms, 13 en suite (showers), £48 (single £34). Children welcome overnight (under-2s stay free in parents' room, 3-5s £5, over-5s £10), additional bed & cot available. MasterCard,* ***VISA***

Bowness-on-Windermere Belsfield Hotel 62% £107

Tel 015394 442448 **Fax 015394 46397** Map 4 C3 **H**
Kendal Road Bowness-on-Windermere Cumbria LA23 3EL

Six acres of neat gardens provide an attractive setting for the white-painted Belsfield, and its elevated position offers splendid views over Lake Windermere (the best bedrooms, with Lake views, are priced at £105). Family rooms have either bunk beds or an adjoining child's room. Leisure facilities include a heated indoor swimming pool with sliding roof. ***Rooms*** *64. Garden, pitch & putt, tennis, indoor swimming pool, sauna, sun beds, snooker. Amex, Diners, MasterCard,* ***VISA***

Bracknell Coppid Beech Hotel 72% £140

Tel 01344 303333 **Fax 01344 301200** Map 15 E2 **HR**
John Nike Way Bracknell Berkshire RG12 8TF

Of striking Swiss chalet design, the Coppid Beech is in the same private ownership as the adjacent John Nike Leisuresport complex with its dry ski slope, toboggan run and Olympic-sized ice rink. Within the hotel further leisure opportunities include Waves health and fitness centre and the Après disco night club (over-25s only). The main open-plan public area is spacious enough to incorporate a comfortable bar/lounge and the reception desk with plenty of room to spare. When you approach the lifts look up to find a triangular shaft, extending the entire height of the building, lined with aquaria (the largest in Europe apparently) and mirrors creating a mesmerising, watery kaleidoscope. Bedrooms are roomy and well planned, all with a special triple-mirrored make-up table, proper armchairs, good-sized beds and an advanced TV system that includes an account review and check-out facility in addition to various satellite channels and in-house movies. Accommodation includes 16 suites and 6 family rooms with two additional single beds in an alcove. Children under 12 stay free in parents' room and get to join the Bobby Beech Nut club which involves filling in their own fun form (listing their favourite foods and drinks) while mum and dad are checking in, and getting a rucksack of goodies. Extensive 24hr room service. ***Rooms*** *205. Dry ski slope, toboggan run, ice rink, indoor swimming pool, splash pool, gym, sauna, steam room, sun beds, night club (disco). Amex, Diners, MasterCard,* ***VISA***

Rowans Restaurant £75

Large, comfortably-appointed hotel restaurant where food is taken seriously, the smoked salmon being sliced at the table for example, and served at a pace more appropriate to a leisurely dinner than a quick lunch. Chef Alan Blenkinsop's style is refined and inventive with great care taken over the presentation of dishes such as a tian of crab that came topped with caviar and grapefruit segment and surrounded with artistically placed saffron rouille and olive oil dressing. A purist at a nearby table decried the addition of brandied apricots to a lobster bisque and a cauliflower soup flavoured with vanilla was not a great success but watercress mousse-stuffed breast of chicken with tarragon sauce worked well as did a delightful little complimentary starter of langoustine in an intensely flavoured sauce with spinach noodles. In addition to desserts like millefeuille of figs with honey cream, pastilla of chocolate with crème brulée ice cream and a consommé of melons with almond milk ice cream there are more familiar offerings (displayed on the buffet at night) like lemon tart, chocolate gateau and a traditional sherry trifle. The well-balanced wine list is clearly laid out with useful tasting notes and offerings from the New World as well as the Old. ***Seats*** *125. L 12-2.30 (Sun till 3) D 6-10 (Sun 7-10). Set menus £25 & £39.50 (Sun buffet L £15.95).*

BRACKNELL Hilton National 69% £137

Tel 01344 424801 **Fax 01344 487454** Map 15 E2 
Bagshot Road Bracknell Berkshire RG12 0QJ

A modern hotel handy for the M3 (J3) and M4 (J10). 90 bedrooms are reserved for non-smokers. Children up to 14 can stay free in their parents' room. 24hr room service. Large conference and banqueting facilities for up to 400. ***Rooms*** *167. Keep-fit equipment, sauna, coffee shop (8am-11pm). Amex, Diners, MasterCard,* ***VISA***

BRADFORD Cocina

Tel 01274 727625 Map 6 C1 
64 Manningham Lane Bradford BD1 3EP

This fun, buzzy Mexican cantina offers good value for money – any two tacos for £5.95 or burritos (£4.95-£5.75), enchiladas (any two for £6.25) and fajitas (strips of chicken or rump steak marinated, fried and served with salsa and roll your own pancakes – £9.95). Unusually there are some half dozen vegetarian house specials too. Puddings somewhat lose the Mexican accent: toffee pudding (£2.95), chocolate cake (£2.65) or capirotada – almonds, raisins and apples baked in a cinnamon sugar. Service is friendly. Children's menu available. Very welcoming to the tots-and-toddlers brigade. Three high-chairs are provided, and a bucket of toy animals is a popular extra. A £7.95 set dinner – starter, main course and either ½ bottle of wine or a ½ pitcher of beer – is on offer Mon-Fri 5.30-7pm. ***Seats*** *85.* ***Open*** *12-2 & 6-10.30 (Fri/Sat to 11, Sun 5.30-9.30).* ***Closed*** *L Sat-Mon, all 25 & 26 Dec, 1 Jan. MasterCard,* ***VISA***

Pubs – note that food is only recommended in those pubs with ***Bar Food*** times in the statistics at the end of an entry. Restaurant food in pubs is *never* recommended unless specifically mentioned. Some pubs are recommended for B&B or Atmosphere only – each entry's statistics indicate our recommendation.

Bradford-on-Avon The Bridge Tea Rooms

Tel 01225 865537 Map 14 B3 **JaB**
24a Bridge Street Bradford-on-Avon Wiltshire BA15 1BY

These tea rooms built in the 17th century stick firmly to tradition – even to the waitresses in mob caps and frilly aprons. An old sideboard is home to a splendid display of Kevin Nye's baking: delicious cakes such as walnut, fresh lemon, chocolate and peppermint or soft meringue roulade with raspberries and cream (all at £2.75). Set teas are £4.25 for scones and clotted cream, £9.95 for the Bridge full afternoon tea with sandwiches, crumpets, scones, cake and tea of your choice. There are salads (£5.25), toasted sandwiches (from £3.25), pancakes (£5.25) and a daily hot special. No smoking. Well-behaved children welcome! ***Seats*** *52.* ***Open*** *9.30-5.30 (Sun from 10.30).* ***Closed*** *25 & 26 Dec. No credit cards.*

Bradford-on-Avon Scribbling Horse

Tel 01225 862495 Map 14 B3 **JaB**
34 Silver Street Bradford-on-Avon Wiltshire BA15 1JX

This cheerfully decorated coffee shop, named after an old device for processing wool, stands next to the tourist information centre in the town centre.The day starts with breakfast, served until 11.30: English breakfast here is the full works including fresh orange juice (£4.90); a vegetarian option (£4.70) replaces the bacon and sausage with two veggie sausages. At lunchtime salad bowls (from £3.55), filled jacket potatoes (from £2.25), and sandwiches (from £1.80) are joined by blackboard specials such as broccoli and Stilton quiche with new potatoes or cod bake and salad (all priced at about £3.25). A few cakes and gateaux (£1.45) are baked on the premises, the rest bought in from a good local baker (95p-£1.35). Cream teas are £3.25. They also sell locally produced free-range eggs, Belgian chocolates and excellent Sidoli ice cream. Tables on the patio in summer. A flexible approach to children, rather than any special facilities; small drinks and small portions are readily available on request and there are delights such as Winnie The Pooh sandwiches (with Wiltshire honey) to keep sweet-toothed tiddlers happy. No smoking inside. ***Seats*** *44 (+ 12 outside).* ***Open*** *9.30-5 (Sat from 9.15, Sun from 10.30).* ***Closed*** *25 Dec. No credit cards.*

Bradford-on-Avon Woolley Grange 75% £145

Tel 01225 864705 **Fax 01225 864059** Map 14 B3 **HR**
Woolley Green Bradford-on-Avon Wiltshire BA15 1TX

The Grange is a handsome 17th-century country mansion whose comfortably lived-in day rooms are full of character, with antiques, paintings and real fires. There's a Victorian Gothic conservatory, an oak-panelled drawing-room and various other rooms for whiling away a few quiet moments, and friendly young staff imbue the whole place with a friendly, relaxing feel that's a major part of the attraction. Bedrooms vary considerably in size but all have great character with a beamed bathroom here (mostly with Victorian-style fittings), a rugged stone fire breast there (about half have working gas coal fires), brass bedsteads, patchwork bedcovers, antiques and fresh flowers all helping to create an appealing 'country' feel. Two extra bedrooms have recently been created in one of the outbuildings. Don't miss the collection of interesting bicycles and be sure to say hello to Susie and Rosie, the Vietnamese pot-bellied pigs. The smallest doubles are priced considerably below the rate quoted above. An ideal family location; the aim at Woolley Grange is to provide an environment in which 'parents and children can enjoy each other – and not get on top of each other'. Children sharing with their parents are accommodated free of charge (there is a nominal charge for children's breakfast), with many rooms, including interconnecting rooms and suites, being suitable for families – extra beds and cots provided. The old Coach House is now 'Woolley Bear's Den' with full-time nanny (10am-6pm, 7 days) and large indoor games room; both early children's lunch (at noon) and high tea (at 5pm) are served in the nursery (with a varied selection that might include everything from a simple boiled egg with soldiers, hot dog or fish fingers, to a fresh daily dish such as lamb kebabs or grilled fish, and even their own roast of the day, with sweet puddings and cakes to follow; orders at least one hour ahead). Ten high-chairs, children's cutlery, baby baths, baby-listening and sitting (by arrangement) are all available on request. 14 acres of gardens and paddocks extends beyond the stable yard where there is a play area with a large sandpit and long grass in which the young ones can romp; 2 gardens (one with resident pigs) include a children's garden, complete with swing, slide, climbing frame and an array of Little Tikes toys, and now also a children's flower and vegetable garden. They also offer high-season Saturday entertainment, perhaps a magic show, for the young ones. Woolley Grange won our Family Hotel of The Year award in 1992 and is very suitable for parents who want to stay in a civilised, adult hotel where the owners understand that children really *can* come too. Mother's changing area provided. ***Rooms*** *22. Garden, croquet, tennis, badminton, bicycles, outdoor swimming pool, games room. Amex, Diners, MasterCard,* ***VISA***

Restaurant £75

An elegantly-appointed dining-room with antique chairs and colourful paintings. The three-course (+ coffee) fixed-price dinner menu (five choices at each stage) offers an appealing selection of dishes, often with a contemporary ring: salad of seared tuna with avocado, crème fraiche and chili salsa, stir-fried calf's liver with Thai spices and pickled garlic, escalope of salmon with sorrel butter sauce, pot-roast chump of lamb with celeriac mash and tapénade jus, breast of chicken with creamed leeks and bacon. Good desserts (hot plum tart and vanilla ice cream). The Terrace menu (served lunch and evening in the Conservatory) and lunch menu are rather less formal, involving the likes of salmon fishcakes, Club sandwich, goat's cheese crostini and hamburger with barbecue relish. No smoking in main restaurant. ***Seats*** *54. Parties 8. Private Room 22. L 12-2 D 7-10. Set L (Sun) £18 Set D £29.*

Bradley Green — Malt Shovel Inn

Tel 01278 653432 Map 13 E1 

Blackmoor Lane Bradley Green Cannington Somerset TA5 2NE

Located beside a tiny lane just outside Cannington, this rambling 300-year-old pub enjoys a peaceful rural position surrounded by open farmland. Traditional homely interior with settles and sturdy elm tables and chairs in the main bar and a cosy snug bar with quarry-tiled floor. Two upstairs bedrooms (one en suite) are clean and comfortable – one being a spacious family room – with modern furnishings, TVs, tea-makers and views across fields to the Quantock Hills, their proximity making this a useful base from which to explore. *Open 11.30-2.30 (till 3 Fri & Sat), 6.30-11 (from 7 winter), Sun 12-3, 7-10.30. Free House.* ***Beer*** *Butcombe Bitter, John Smith's Bitter, Morland Old Speckled Hen, guest beer. Garden. Family room.* ***Accommodation*** *2 bedrooms, 1 en suite (bath), £38 (family room sleeping four £46, sleeping three £39.50, single £21.50). Children welcome overnight (under-3s stay free in parents' room,). Closed 25 Dec. No credit cards.*

Branscombe — Masons Arms 64% £54

Tel 01297 680300 **Fax 01297 680500** Map 13 E2 

Branscombe Seaton Devon EX12 3DJ

Picturesque Branscombe lies in a steep valley, deep in National Trust land and only a ten-minute walk from the sea. Occupying most of the village centre is this delightful 14th-century, creeper-clad inn and its neighbouring terraces of cottages, which house most of the comfortable bedrooms. Beyond the pretty front terrace is a most charming bar with stone walls and floors, an assortment of old settles and a huge inglenook with open fire, which not only warms the bar but also cooks the beef or lamb spit-roasts that appear on the evening menu. Reliable bar food from the extensive regular menu includes various sandwiches and ploughman's lunches (lunchtime only), New Orleans stewed pork, salmon parcels, jambalaya and baked marinated rack of lamb. Daily dishes are listed on a blackboard and features good fish (grilled lemon sole and plaice), beautifully fresh crab caught off Branscombe beach that morning, as well as turkey and ham pie, beef bourguignon and home-made chili. On Sundays there's also a roast for lunch. Attractive and tastefully-decorated restaurant (dinner only) with an old-world ambience. Exposed beams and the odd piece of antique furniture add to the charm of attractive bedrooms in the inn and old cottages opposite the pub; TVs, phones and clock/radios are standard throughout.

Conference/function room. Two miles off A3052, between Sidmouth and Colyford. *Open 11-3, 6-11 (Sat 11-11 winter, Mon-Sat 11-11 summer, Sun 12-10.30).* ***Bar Food*** *12-2, 7-9.30. Free House.* ***Beer*** *Bass, Otter Bitter, three guest beers. Terrace, outdoor eating.* ***Accommodation*** *21 bedrooms, 19 en suite, £74 (hotel), £54-£64 (cottages), £80 (The Linny), single from £22. Children welcome overnight (2-10s £10), additional bed & cot available. Dogs welcome (£3 + food per night). MasterCard,* ***VISA***

BRAUNSTON Old Plough

Tel 01572 722714 **Fax 01572 770382** Map 7 E4 **P**
Church Street Braunston Leicestershire LE15 8QY

Well-regarded local innkeepers Amanda and Andrew Reid have brought a wealth of experience also to their tastefully modernised inn on the fringe of the village. Healthy eating options and vegetarian alternatives (cauliflower and chickpea curry) are well interspersed throughout an extensive menu encompassing 'famous Plough crusties' (large home-baked granary filled rolls) through pasta meals (seafood tagliatelle) and steaks to chef Nick Quinn's specials. Pork ribs with barbecue sauce, liver and bacon, sage chicken, and beef and mushroom pie might arrive with chef's potatoes of the day and crisp, fresh vegetables. There is a separate ice cream menu but better options might be lemon and cream cheese roulade and sticky toffee pudding. With light lunches on the terrace and candle-lit dining in the picturesque conservatory a sense of occasion is easily engendered. Children are allowed in the bar to eat at lunchtime only. *Open 11-3.30, 6-11 (Sun 12-3.30, 7-10.30).* ***Bar Food*** *12-2, 7-10 (till 9.30 Sun). Free House.* ***Beer*** *Theakston XB, Oakham JHB, Ten Fifty & Triple B, Ruddles Best, guest beer. Garden, outdoor eating. Family room. Amex, Diners, MasterCard,* ***VISA***

BRENT KNOLL The Goat House Café

Tel 01278 760995 Map 13 E1 **JaB**
Bristol Road Brent Knoll Somerset TA9 4HJ

A couple of minutes' drive from Junction 22 of the M5 (stay on the A3 – don't turn off at the signpost to Brent Knoll). Don't be put off by the transport caff exterior – inside is bright and airy with pine fittings, friendly service and a warm welcome for families. Your kids will be fascinated by their kids – around a dozen goats and their offspring inhabit stables across the open-air courtyard where there are a shop and pub-style tables for good weather. Goat's milk products (including ice cream) are offered alongside sandwiches, jacket potatoes, home-made pastries and pizzas; more substantial homely fare is also on the menu with specials like spinach and ricotta cannelloni or sausage casserole (£3.95). Get there before 11.30 and there are good solid breakfasts to be had (bacon, egg, sausage, tomato, beans and fried bread £2.85). Set Sunday lunch is £5.50 for two courses or £4.50 for one. A bistro menu with speciality pizzas is served Thu, Fri & Sat evenings. Two no-smoking areas. ***Seats*** *50 (+ outside).* ***Open*** *8-5 (Bistro menu 7-10 Thu-Sat). MasterCard,* ***VISA***

BRETFORTON Fleece Inn

Tel 01386 831173 Map 14 C1 **P**
The Cross Bretforton Evesham Hereford & Worcester WR11 5JE

The stone, thatch and half-timbered Fleece has been owned by the National Trust since 1977, bequeathed by retiring landlady Lola Taplin on strict condition that the pub remained unaltered, and potato crisps weren't sold. It stands out today as a living, yet very lived-in, museum whose three interior rooms, the Brewhouse, the Dugout and the smoking-free Pewter Room (with unique pewter collection on an oak dresser), are now preserved for posterity. There's an array of antiquities and all the interior is original – grandfather clock, settles, rocking chair, inglenook fireplaces, beams, timbers, flagstone floors, cheese moulds et al. Children get a look in, except in the tiny bar, and are catered for superbly outside: there's a thatched heraldic barn, barbecue, extensive orchard garden and adventure playground. The wealth of hanging baskets and flower-filled stone tubs which adorn the central flagged and pebbled yard are an absolute picture in summer. It's always busy, so get there early at lunchtime to ensure a table. *Open 11-2.30, 6-11 (Sun 12-2.30, 7-10.30). Free House.* ***Beer*** *M&B Brew XI, Everards Beacon, Uley Old Spot & Pig's Ear, guest beers. Garden. No credit cards.*

BRIDGEMERE Bridgemere Garden World Coffee Shop

Tel 01270 520381 **Fax 01270 520215** Map 6 B3 JaB
Bridgemere nr Nantwich Cheshire CW5 7QB

The conservatory coffee shop is a popular haunt at this large garden centre. There is a good selection of snacks and hot meals, starting with breakfast at £2.95; then cheese and bacon puffs (£1.29), hot cheese and onion scones (99p), salads (from £3.75) or a main dish such as lamb hot pot, turkey and cranberry pie or cod mornay (from £3.75). For puds or afternoon tea there is a range of cakes and ice creams (from 99p). Children's meals are offered. A Garden Café is now open for light snacks. For those of a horticultural bent – an all-inclusive day with talks, a tour of the garden centre, flower arranging class and lunch costs from £5.99. Six high-chairs; separate Mother & Baby room. No smoking. ***Seats*** *300.* ***Open*** *9-7.30 (till 5 in winter).* ***Closed*** *25 & 26 Dec. Amex, MasterCard,* ***VISA***

BRIDGWATER Nutmeg House

Tel 01278 457823 **Fax 01278 428802** Map 13 E1 JaB
8-10 Clare Street Bridgwater Somerset TA6 3EN

Just off the main street in a quiet corner of town, Michael Gibson's café and bistro offers a good selection of carefully-prepared dishes which change on a daily basis. Typical choices include carrot and orange soup (£1.75), home-made lasagne (£5), grilled liver with bacon (£4.40) and gammon steak with fried egg (£5.20), all served with petits pois and fries/new potatoes. Filled baked potatoes (from £2.30) are popular, and seafood tagliatelle (£4.50) can appear in the winter along with venison with mushrooms and cream or rump steak with Stilton and port (£4.95-£7 in the evening). Coffee, cakes, home-made pastries and desserts are served throughout the day, and slightly more expensive bistro meals Friday and Saturday evenings. Parking in Sedgmoor Splash swimming pool car park. ***Seats*** *45 (+30 outside).* ***Open*** *9-5.30 & 7-12 (Thu-Sat).* ***Closed*** *D Mon-Wed & Bank Holidays, all Sun. MasterCard,* ***VISA***

BRIDPORT Riverside Restaurant & Café

Tel 01308 422011 Map 13 F2 JaB
West Bay Bridport Dorset DT6 4EZ

A friendly restaurant/café that is dedicated to excellent locally caught fish and shellfish with an additional snack menu for those who don't care for seafood. The menu extends all the way from humble fish and chips (from £6) to delicious lobster dishes. Grilled local black bream with lime and chili butter (£10.95) is typical of the more elaborate dishes with snacks ranging from Caesar salad (£3.75) and extending to omelettes (from £4), burgers, sandwiches (£2-£2.80) and a Dorset cream tea (£2.95). Opening times can vary with the seasons, so check when booking. As we went to press a new oyster and seafood bar, with seating on stools, was about to open next door. ***Seats*** *70 (+ 20 outside).* ***Open*** *11-2.30 & 6.30-9.* ***Closed*** *D Sun, all Mon (except Bank Holidays), late Dec-early Mar. MasterCard,* ***VISA***

BRIGHTLING Jack Fuller's £35

Tel 01424 838212 **Fax 01424 838666** Map 11 B6 R
Brightling nr Robertsbridge East Sussex TN32 5HD

From Robertsbridge, take the Brightling road and drive about 3½ miles to the crossroads to find Jack Fuller's – if you reach Brightling church you've gone a mile too far. It's about five miles north-east of Battle. John Fuller, also known as Mad Jack of Brightling, was a Georgian builder of follies, and these are scattered around the local area, drawing visitors and locals alike to Roger and Shirl Berman's former pub. The fun atmosphere of follies extends to the interior (or the terrace for fair-weather eating) and the Bermans have a warm welcome for both adults and children ("we cook anything for children at their parents' request"). The menu majors on main courses and puddings, and the style is generous traditional English, with the likes of gammon and onion pudding, steak and kidney pudding or pie, prawn pancakes, chicken pie and always a vegetarian selection such as cauliflower crumble and cashew, spinach and aubergine bake. Side dishes are particularly enticing – honeyed carrots, bubble and squeak, cheesy leek and potato bake – and it's equally hard to resist rounding things off with a sticky treacle tart or a chocolate mousse. There's an excellent choice of wines by the glass. No children's menu as such, but they will provide children's meals or smaller portions on request; five high-chairs, booster seats and children's cutlery available, plus a separate bathroom for nappy-changing. ***Seats** 70 (+ 40 outside). Private Room 30. L 12-2 D 7-11. Closed D Sun, all Mon & Tue, Bank Holidays & 2 weeks Jan. Set Sun L £7.95. Amex, Diners, MasterCard,* ***VISA***

Brighton — Al Duomo & Al Forno

Tel 01273 326741 **Fax 01273 749792** Map 11 B6 JaB
7 Pavilion Buildings Brighton East Sussex BN11EE

These two restaurants, 100 yards apart, separated by busy North Street, have similar menus and have been attracting pizza aficionados since 1979. A fairly standard range of starters is available – Parma ham with melon or avocado (£4.40), chicken livers with crispy bacon and wilted salad (£3.80) or a delicious hot mixture of ham with mushrooms, tomato and garlic (£3.75) – and as well as excellent pizzas (both restaurants have brick wood-burning ovens – so you can enjoy the smell even if you choose something else) you might try spaghetti carbonara (£4.85), potato gnocchi with a fresh tomato sauce (£4.60) or excellent penne in a meat sauce with mushrooms, ham and cheese (£4.90) from their range of pasta dishes. Fish- and meat-eaters are not forgotten, with standard trattoria offerings: fritto misto (£7.20), saltimbocca (£7.75) and bistecca pizzaiola (£8.95). There is a three-course set menu for £7.50, and a two-course student menu for £5 (called menu C); but these may not be produced unless you ask! Always bustling and fun. It is advisable to book in the evening, as there can be long queues. No booking at weekends except for large parties. The 65-seat *Al Forno* is at 36 East Street, and has a few open-air seats: Tel 01273 324905. ***Seats** 120. **Open** Al Duomo 12-2.30 & 6-11.30 (Sat/Sun 12-11.30). Al Forno 12-3 & 6-11 (Fri/Sat/Sun 12-11). **Closed** 25 Dec. Amex, Diners, MasterCard,* ***VISA***

Brighton — Browns

Tel 01273 323501 **Fax 01273 327427** Map 11 B6 JaB
3-4 Duke Street Brighton East Sussex BN1 1AH

Open all day, this bustling, family-friendly brasserie has found a winning formula, now replicated across southern England. Start with breakfast (£5.65) and continue to munch your way through the day! Starters such as moules marinière (£3.95), chicken liver paté with melba toast (£3.25) or roast red peppers with fresh basil, garlic and olive oil (£3.75) might be followed by country chicken pie (£7.55), roast pork ribs with barbecue sauce (£8.45) or chargrilled lamb steak with Oxford sauce (£10.45). There is a choice of hot sandwiches (from £5.45), salads and pasta dishes (from £6.85). A blackboard offers daily specials, and a wide range of generous puddings provide for just about every taste. Vegetarian options could include mushroom stroganoff £6.95). Teatime (3-5.30) brings scones, sandwiches and toasted snacks. There's a good selection of wine and some 15 cocktails to choose from. An earlier breakfast (from 8 to 10) is served in the nearby Browns Bar in Ship Street.
Pay & Display park in Ship Street. Other *Browns* are in London, Bristol, Cambridge and Oxford (see entries). ***Seats** 120. **Open** 11am-11.30pm (Sun from noon). **Closed** 25 & 26 Dec. Amex, MasterCard,* ***VISA***

Brighton — China Garden

Tel 01273 325124 Map 11 B6 JaB
88-91 Preston Street Brighton East Sussex BN12HG

Peking specialities with an emphasis on fish are the attraction at this spacious restaurant. A range of dim sum dishes is available (from £1.50) until 4pm. From the carte mixed hot hors d'oeuvre (£9.95 for two) or paper-wrapped prawns (£5.50) might precede a sizzling dish such as lamb with stir-fried ginger and spring onions (£7.95) or a mixture of oysters, scallops, prawns, squid and sole (£8.50). A karaoke room and a pianist in the evening make for a boisterous night out. Children welcome (but no under-9s after 8pm). Parking in Regency Square. ***Seats*** *130.* ***Open*** *12-11.* ***Closed*** *25 & 26 Dec. Amex, Diners, MasterCard,* ***VISA***

BRIGHTON Cripes

Tel 01273 327878 Map 11 B6 JaB
7 Victoria Road Brighton East Sussex BN1 3FS

Savoury buckwheat galettes with a variety of fillings are the popular staple at Joy Leader's welcoming restaurant. Try chicken and ratatouille (£5.70), cheese and asparagus (£5.10) or prawn and beansprouts with a chili and ginger sauce (£6), all served with mixed salad. If the set combinations don't take your fancy, you can create your own from a list of ingredients. House specialities include spicy minced beef creole with Cheddar, onion, chili and sour cream (£7.15) or chicken livers cooked in red wine, basil, garlic, spinach and sour cream (£6.60). Sweet crepes for pudding have delicious fillings like lemon and honey (£2.50) or bananas in rum with whipped cream (£3.70). A number of Breton and Normandy ciders are on offer, also the excellent bière de Garde (£4.87 for 75cl). One no-smoking room. Street parking. ***Seats*** *50.* ***Open*** *10.30-2.30 & 6-11.30 (Sun till 11).* ***Closed*** *25 & 26 Dec. Amex, MasterCard,* ***VISA***

BRIGHTON Dig In The Ribs

Tel 01273 325275 Map 11 B6 JaB
47 Preston Street Brighton East Sussex

This Tex-Mex restaurant offers a wide selection of dishes, perhaps guacamole (£3.25) poppers – mild jalapenos filled with black beans and cheese, with an orange and ginger dip (£4.55) to start. Then there are tacos and nachos (£2.95), hickory smoked ribs (from £6.45) or burritos (£7.85) and enchiladas (£7.85). Texan T-bone steaks (£12.95) and some salads are available for plainer eating. There is also a list of light bites, available from lunch until 6pm, such as stuffed baked potatoes (£4.10) or steakwich – a 6oz rump steak, salad, ranch dressing and a sesame bun (£6.75). Puddings include banchanga – a banana fritter including toffee and ice cream (£2.55) or bunuelos – cinnamon tortillas with honey and ice cream (£2.25). Everything for the younger client has been thought of, from high-chairs to colouring books. The kid's menu is £2.85 for a sombrero – mini Mexican pizza or goldfish toes (prawns and fries) and includes a soft drink and fruit or ice cream. The menu also includes pages of pictures to colour in, 'join the dots', 'spot the difference' and other amusements. For the very young there are plenty of high-chairs, a supply of emergency nappies and changing facilities in the Ladies loo. If you would like them to 'warm up, sterilise, customise, liquidise or carry out some other childish wish' – just ask. Sundays are particularly busy. ***Seats*** *110.* ***Open*** *12-11.30 (Sun till 10.30).* ***Closed*** *25 & 26 Dec. Amex, MasterCard,* ***VISA***

BRIGHTON Donatello

Tel 01273 775477 **Fax 01273 775477** Map 11 B6 JaB
3 Brighton Place The Lanes Brighton East Sussex BN1 1HJ

Fun for all the family at this busy Italian restaurant, which specialises in pizza and pasta. There are two good-value set menus (£5.95 or £8.95 for three courses), perhaps prawn cocktail or minestrone followed by the pizza of your choice and a pudding from the main carte – the nore expensive has a wider choice at each stage. The à la carte menu offers Parma ham with melon and avocado (£3.85), prawn cocktail (£2.95) or deep-fried squid (£3.30) among the starters; spaghetti bolognese (£4.15), breast of chicken in a garlic, mushroom and white wine sauce (£8.45) and fritto misto (£9.80) among the main courses. Or you can make your own salad from the display for £2.35 (main course £3.95). Otherwise an impressive range of pasta and pizza completes the picture. A 10% service charge is added to bills. ***Seats*** *140 (+ 60 outside).* ***Open*** *11.30-11.30.* ***Closed*** *25 Dec. Amex, Diners, MasterCard,* ***VISA***

BRIGHTON The Dove Hotel

Tel 01273 779222 **Fax 01273 746912** Map 11 B6 

18 Regency Square Brighton East Sussex BN1 2FG

On arriving you can expect to be greeted like long lost friends and presented with a welcome drink. Owner Mr Peter Kalinke is happy to do almost anything to keep his junior house guests happy – from the provision of a toy box to a guided tour of the hotel. The hospitality for families is almost second to none: even at breakfast a new selection of toys can be provided for early risers who have already reached the boredom threshold. The atmosphere is informal and low key and in such a small place you feel as if you are in a private home (fire doors notwithstanding). Bedrooms are comfortable and bright with a well-chosen mix of antique furniture and modern fabrics; travel cots and small beds are provided. Room three is the largest (£78) with two double beds and room for a further single; rooms one, five and seven are also family rooms (£65) and front-facing; slightly cheaper, less spacious rooms are also available; under-2s free, 2-12 £8, 13-17 £15 (reductions for longer stays). Baby-listening and baby-sitting are on offer, the latter only by prior arrangement. Early high teas (either in the dining room or in your room), nappies, potties and baby bottles all provided. Three-course dinner is £13.50, but lighter meals are always available. Mr Kalinke is only too happy to oblige. Sea World, on the sea front by Palace Pier, is a short walk away. ***Rooms** 10. Closed 1 week Christmas. Amex, Diners, MasterCard,* ***VISA***

> We do not accept free meals or hospitality
> – our inspectors pay their own bills.

BRIGHTON Food for Friends

Tel 01273 202310 **Fax 01273 202001** Map 11 B6 JaB

17-18 Prince Albert Street Brighton East Sussex BN1 1HF

This vegetarian and vegan restaurant, simply decorated with pine furniture and potted plants, is welcoming and hospitable and an established part of the Brighton culinary scene. Among interesting hot dishes on offer might be Chinese stir-fry with noodles (£3.45), lentil burger, with garlic mayonnaise and tomato/sweetcorn salsa (£3.35) or lasagne and salad (£3.95). There is a good selection of quiches/salads such as red onion quiche (£2.15, £3.95 with salad) or Florentine quiche (£1.95/£3.65). Excellent organic bread selection including croissants and *pain au chocolat*, lots of dips and salads, and plenty of cakes and puddings (from £1.20). Children particularly welcome. Large no smoking area. ***Seats** 50 (+ 16 outside).* ***Open** 8am-10pm.* ***Closed** 25 & 26 Dec. Amex, MasterCard,* ***VISA***

BRIGHTON Old Ship Hotel 65% £125

Tel 01273 329001 **Fax 01273 820718** Map 11 B6 H

King's Road Brighton East Sussex BN1 1NR

Centrally located on the seafront, with covered parking for 70 cars, the Old Ship has a long and interesting history. Public areas include a surprisingly spacious oak-panelled lobby dotted with antiques, a pair of quiet lounges with Adam-style ceilings and the panelled Tettersell's Bar. The Paganini Ballroom (from whoe balcony the maestro played his violin in 1831) is the largest of 16 rooms available for conferences or banquets (max 300/200). About two-thirds of the bedrooms (mostly those in the east wing) are smartly furnished and have up-to-date bathrooms. The remainder vary somewhat in age and style. Friendly staff. 24hr room service. Children under 12 stay free in parents' room. A children's playroom operates at weekends. ***Rooms** 152. Amex, Diners, MasterCard,* ***VISA***

> Many hotels offer reduced rates for weekend or out-of-season
> bookings. Always ask about special deals and family rooms.

BRIGHTON Pinocchio

Tel 01273 677676 **Fax 01273 734001** Map 11 B6 **JaB**
22 New Road Brighton BN1 1UF

Framed Brighton Festival posters, Pinocchio masks, a framed display of dried pasta shapes, and red plastic check tablecloths set the tone for this large, informal Italian trattoria. There are two floors, the upper of which is delightfully bright and airy under a conservatory roof; one half of the long upstairs room is for non-smokers. Cheap menus and cheerful service are the main attractions. The vast menu offers pasta and pizza (£3.40-£5.70) every which way – plus make-your-own salad, veal escalope, chicken, monkfish and Dover sole dishes. Best bet are the fixed-price 2/3 course menus (£4.95/£5.95) with a choice of the more straightforward dishes; an £8.95 3-course menu includes meat and fish dishes at unbeatable prices. Families are well catered for, with high-chairs provided; youngsters will love the profiteroles with chocolate sauce (£2.05). On the same side of the street as the Theatre Royal, opposite the Dome and Pavilion Theatres. Sister restaurant to *Donatello* – see entry. ***Seats*** *200. Open 11.30-11.30. Closed 25 Dec. Amex, Diners, MasterCard,* ***VISA***

BRIMFIELD The Roebuck

Tel 01584 711230 **Fax 01584 711654** Map 14 A1
Poppies Restaurant Brimfield Ludlow Shropshire SY8 4NE

Carole Evans's pub and restaurant has been a leading light since 1983. It's a very individual pub and worthy of an exceptional detour just to savour the superb hospitality on offer. It takes so much effort to run a quality establishment at this level that Carole's energy simply has to be admired. There is certainly no finer pub restaurant (recommended in our *1997 Hotels & Restaurants Guide*) round these parts than Poppies at the Roebuck. The public bar retains a pubby atmosphere, whereas the lounge bar – a characterful room with a 15th-century beamed ceiling and dark oak panels – could be the restaurant. It isn't – there's a separate dining-room which is a bright and cheery room with parquet floor and cane-back chairs in chintzy style, in keeping with the rest of the building. You can, however, book tables in the lounge bar, where Carole's food can be enjoyed at less than the restaurant prices. Her command of composition and subtle blends of colour and flavour are frankly bewildering. The long, exciting bar menu might encompass mushroom and herb risotto, coarse duck liver paté with melba toast, confit of duck on a bed of red cabbage with an orange sauce, monkfish with mustard dressing, whole lemon sole with limes and capers, and cider chicken pie. There's a comprehensive list of hot and cold desserts to follow: chocolate soufflé with a bitter chocolate sorbet, bread-and-butter pudding with apricot sauce, and steamed marmalade pudding with whisky-flavoured custard – leave room! Some twelve cheeses are listed on a tip-top cheese menu, from Longridge Fell (oak-smoked Lancashire cheese) to Shropshire Blue. Ploughman's lunches are served with home-made pickles; a selection of cheeses is served with home-made oat cakes and walnut and sultana bread. The excellent wine list has a large selection of half bottles. There are three lovely cottage bedrooms (two doubles with showers and a twin with full bathroom) in which to stay overnight. Here, you'll find home-made biscuits, cake, cafetière coffee and quality teas – an example of the care you're likely to receive. A wonderful country breakfast, including Herefordshire apple juice, honey from the garden and Carole's home-made sausages, will set you up for the day and set the seal on a memorable stay. *Open 12-3, 7-11 (Sun 12-3, 7-10.30). Closed all Sun & Mon.* ***Bar Food*** *12-2, 7-10 (no food Sun & Mon) Free House.* ***Beer*** *Morland Old Speckled Hen, guest beer. Patio/terrace, outdoor eating.* ***Accommodation*** *3 bedrooms, all en suite, £60 (single £45). Children welcome overnight. Check-in by arrangement. Pub & accommodation closed 25 & 26 Dec. MasterCard,* ***VISA***

JaB is short for 'Just a Bite'. The majority of these establishments are also recommended in our *Bistros, Bars & Cafés* Guide which features establishments where one may eat well for less than £15 per head.

BRISTOL Arnolfini Café Bar

Tel 0117 927 9330 Map 13 F1 JaB
Narrow Quay Prince Street Bristol BS1 4QA

Adjacent to the Arnolfini Gallery in a thriving complex created out of dockside warehouses, this roomy, airy café bar is an ideal stop-off for a light lunch or afternoon tea. The blackboard menu changes daily to offer 8-12 dishes such as chilled cucumber and celery soup, or leek and potato soup £2.90 with garlic bread); mains (all with salad) might include roast grilled marinated goat's cheese salad, prawns in garlic butter, cauliflower gratin, chicken with a creamy pesto sauce on a bed of pasta, or Cumberland sausages with mash (£4.95-£5.95); jacket potatoes (£2.95) are popular, and always available; fillings might include tuna mayonnaise or blue cheese. Home-made puddings (all £2.20) include lemon tart and summer pudding. There's a wide choice of teas and if it's sunny the benches out on the docksde provide a very pleasant place to sit and sip. ***Seats*** *50 (+ 30 outside).* ***Open*** *12-3 & 5-9 (Sun till 8).* ***Closed*** *10 days Christmas. No credit cards.*

BRISTOL Aztec Hotel 74% £124

Tel 01454 201090 **Fax 01454 201593** Map 13 F1 H
Aztec West Business Park Almondsbury Bristol BS12 4TS

On the outskirts of Bristol, this is a smart, well-run, modern hotel, in the Shire Inns group.It offers a good balance of facilities between mid-week conferences – a business centre provides secretarial services – and weekend family breaks. All bedrooms are of Executive standard with a sitting area, writing desk and fax point; a good proportion are reserved for non-smokers. Syndicate rooms convert to family use at weekends with wall-mounted let-down beds; children under 16 are accommodated free in their parents' room. Day rooms are spacious, with lounges on two levels in the central 'lodge' and a smart snooker room. The hotel also has a fine leisure club and its own Black Sheep pub. The location is a modern business park near J16 of the M5 (south of the M4/M5 interchange). ***Rooms*** *109. Garden, indoor swimming pool, splash pool, gym, squash, sauna, solarium, steam room, spa bath, snooker. Amex, Diners, MasterCard,* ***VISA***

BRISTOL Browns

Tel 0117 930 4777 Map 13 F1 JaB
38 Queen's Road Clifton Bristol Avon

London, Brighton, Cambridge and Oxford all now also boast a branch of the ever-popular Browns. A winning brasserie-style formula is relaxed and popular with both students and business people. The bar is busy too, where a piano takes centre stage and is played during the evenings. There is a long list of starters including grilled sardines with tomato salsa (£3.55), roast red peppers with fresh basil, garlic and olive oil (£3.75) and Caesar salad (£3.15); follow with pasta (from £6.75), salads (vegetarian £7.25, hot chicken liver and bacon £7.85), hot sandwiches, generously served fisherman's pie (£7.65) or roast poussin with bacon, lemon and tarragon (£8.45). Plenty of puddings, too, including sherry trifle (£2.95) and bread-and-butter (£2.75). Breakfast is served till noon; afternoon tea 3-5.30. Twelve high-chairs and a large mother's changing area (shelf and wipes provided). ***Seats*** *240 (+summer terrace 40).* ***Open*** *11am-11.30pm (Sat from 10am, Sun from 12).* ***Closed*** *25 & 26 Dec. Amex, MasterCard,* ***VISA***

BRISTOL Café Première

Tel 0117 973 4892 **Fax 0117 908 1127** Map 13 F1 JaB
59 Apsley Road Clifton Bristol BS8 2SW

The Nirmani family's all-day café projects a cosmopolitan air, with its striped awnings and pavement tables clearly visible off Whiteladies Road, just above Clifton Down. Within, the potted plants, ceiling fans and light classical music create a pleasant atmosphere and bustling and generally slick table service keeps things moving. Breakfasts come in 11 different types, with names like Irish fries (£5.95), Blackstone egg – lightly poached eggs over English toasted muffin, with tomatoes, bacon and cheese sauce (£4.95) – and veggie brekki (£5.95); these are available all day. There are also avocado and feta salad (£3.95),Thai chicken (£4.95), chargrilled sardines (£5.95) and goat's cheese salad (£3.95) and the popular Cajun spiced chicken sandwich with salad and fries (£5.95). Other offerings include smoked salmon on bagel (£5.75), Roquefort and asparagus tart (£5.95), bread-and-butter pudding (£2.45) and sticky toffee pudding. Good care is taken of families a half-floor below, with high-chairs and a booster seat provided. The children's menu departs from the run-of-the-mill with the likes of pasta 'wiggly woos', and children's portions can be ordered from the breakfast menu. Changing mat and emergency nappies provided in the Ladies. Bottles and baby-food can be heated on request. No-smoking area. Street parking. ***Seats*** *42 (+30 outside).* ***Open*** *8-8.30 (Sat/Sun from 9, Sun till 6).* ***Closed*** *25, 26 Dec & 1 Jan. MasterCard,* ***VISA***

BRISTOL — Jameson's Restaurant — £50

Tel 0117 927 6565 Map 13 F1 
30 Upper Maudlin Street Bristol BS2 8DJ

Carole Jameson's popular bistro has a 30-seat conservatory in addition to the two-level set-up and is adorned with plenty of greenery throughout. Fresh fish is the main feature in summer and cooking is of a good standard. Red snapper with capers, parsley and brown butter, salmon escalopes with an avocado salsa, duckling with an orange and port sauce and beef Wellingtion show the style. There are usually a couple of vegetarian alternatives, and Sunday lunch always includes traditional roasts. ***Seats*** *70. Parties 24. L 12-2 (Sun till 4) D 6.30-11.30. Closed L Sat, D Sun, 26 Dec. Set D £14.95/£18.90. Amex, Diners, MasterCard,* ***VISA***

BRISTOL — Rainbow Café

Tel 0117 973 8937 Map 13 F1 
10 Waterloo Street Clifton Bristol BS8 4BT

This arts-orientated café remains a popular lunchtime favourite with both meat-eaters and vegetarians since the middle of the day brings the greatest choice: tomato and basil soup (£1.45), chicken, grape and tarragon salad (£4.50) cheese and asparagus quiche (£1.90) or carrot and cashewnut paté with toast and side salad (£3.90). Good fresh salads accompany main courses, such as chicken with lime and fresh coriander (£5.60). Finish with Breton pudding or raspberry and redcurrant tart with cream (both £2.10). Outside lunch hours, the baking extends to bagels with smoked salmon and cream cheese (£1.75), fruit, cheese or cheese and leek scones (65p), cakes and slices (from 65p). Interesting home-made ice cream like lemon with mint is always available along with such goodies as walnut brownies and banana and walnut tea bread. One room is no-smoking. ***Seats*** *38 (+ 10 outside).* ***Open*** *10-5.30 (full meals 12-2.30).* ***Closed*** *Sun, Bank Holidays & 1 week Christmas. No credit cards.*

BRISTOL — Redwood Lodge — 64% — £98

Tel 01275 393901 **Fax 01275 392104** Map 13 F1 H
Beggar Bush Lane Failand Bristol BS8 3TG

Approximately ten minutes from the city centre (via Clifton Bridge) and quite close to exit 19 of the M5, Redwood Lodge offers conference facilities (for up to 250 delegates) and an impressive choice of leisure activities, notably five floodlit tennis courts and nine squash courts. Bedrooms, most of which are designated non-smoking, include 28 Executive rooms. Children up to 12 stay free in parents' room. Whitbread Country Club Resorts. ***Rooms*** *108. Garden, croquet, indoor, outdoor & children's swimming pools, gym, sauna, steam room, solarium, tennis, squash, badminton, snooker, playroom & playground, sports shop, 175-seat cinema, coffee shop (10.30am-10.30pm). Amex, Diners, MasterCard,* ***VISA***

BRISTOL Rocinantes

Tel 0117 973 4482 Map 13 F1 **JaB**
85 Whiteladies Road Bristol BS8 2NT

Rocinantes is fun, noisy, frantic and almost always busy, with loud Spanish music and murals whose pictorial decibels rate fairly high too! The café area offers a list of tapas which are great as snacks or choose two or three together for a main meal: *patatas bravas* – crispy fried potatoes in a spicy red wine and tomato sauce (£2) – marinated fresh anchovies (£4.75) or *pan Catalan* – home-made bread grilled with olive oil, tomatoes and garlic (£2.50) – and, for meat-eaters, chicken wings baked with chili, honey and almonds (£4.25) or *pincho moruno* – grilled skewered lamb marinated in olive oil, saffron, cumin and lemon juice (£4.95). Moving away from the Spanish influence, bacon and eggs with toast and butter (£4) and other breakfast dishes are served between 9.30 and 10.30am Mon-Sat or brunch on Sundays until 3pm. The à la carte menu is a more international affair, with starters from mushroom and tarragon soup (£2.95) to a selection of charcuterie (£5.95). Snackers can choose just a main course (£7.95-£13.50). Outdoor eating on a terrace. ***Seats*** *60 (+ 32 outside).* ***Open*** *9am-11pm (Sun 9.30am-10.30pm).* ***Closed*** *25, 26 Dec & 1 Jan. Amex, MasterCard,* ***VISA***

BRISTOL Swallow Royal Hotel 76% £125

Tel 0117 925 5100 **Fax 0117 925 1515** Map 13 F1 **HR**
College Green Bristol BS1 5TA

A Victorian building in one of the most favourable locations in Bristol next to the Cathedral and overlooking the neat lawns of College Green. The original Victorian grandeur has been enhanced by a decor with firmly traditional leanings but which also has an elegantly fashionable touch. The polished red marble-floored foyer has beautiful lounges on each side furnished in a comfortable country house style with deep-cushioned settees arranged in well-spaced groups. The cocktail bar features huge Oriental murals at either end and a bar with gleaming glass and silverware. There's also the recently opened Queen Vic pub. All the bedrooms, apart from a few smaller, inward-facing rooms, are spacious, with two armchairs and a writing desk. Every room has a whole host of extras from mini-bars with complimentary mineral water and fresh milk to irons and ironing boards. Coloured marble bathrooms have super-strong showers and most have bidets though a few, where space is more limited, have large corner baths instead. There are several suites with cosy sitting-rooms and spa baths in their bathrooms. ***Rooms*** *242. Indoor swimming pool, sauna, steam room, spa bath, sun beds, beauty & hair salons, keep-fit equipment, news kiosk. Amex, Diners, MasterCard,* ***VISA***

Palm Court Restaurant £90

The grand Palm Court extends up through three floors lined in Bath stone with curved balustrades and topped by stained-glass skylights. The à la carte is modern in style, taking inspiration from numerous sources: basil and crab conchigliette, butternut squash soup with a pumpkin tartlet, Brecon Court venison, sautéed duck breast with artichoke and truffle potatoes and glazed baby beets. Service is formal yet unfussy. ***Seats*** *60. Parties 8. D only 7.30-10.30. Closed Sun & Bank Holidays. Set D from £22.50.*

BRISTOL Watershed Café-Bar

Tel 0117 921 4135 **Fax 0117 921 3958** Map 13 F1 **JaB**
1 Cannons Road Cannons Marsh Bristol BS1 5TX

Looking down on the old dock basin, theis excellent first-floor café is in the Watershe arts and cinema complex. Food orders are made and paid for at a busy counter and pretty promptly delivered. Although meat eaters are catered for, the emphasis is on vegetarian food: maybe home-made split-pea and tarragon soup (£2), potato wedges with sour cream and salsa (£2.10) or hot nachos with melted cheese (£2.40) to begin; breast of chicken in a smoked garlic, paprika and lemon sauce

(£4.55), fresh mackerel fillet with a Provençal glaze (£4.35) or wild mushroom risotto with shaved parmesan (£4.35) to follow. Notably grease-free chips are a popular choice of the littlest ones and can come with a child's portion of almost anything. While the rafters echo a bit to the sound of jazzy, though scarely intrusive tapes, there are plenty of exhibits to browse over in the adjacent galleries. There's use of a side-entrance lift, on request, for wheelchairs and buggies (the café's up two flights of stairs); baby-changing facilities in the disabled toilet. Two high-chairs. On the ground the Watershed sandwich bar dispenses made-to-order sandwiches (from £1.50), filled baguettes, jacket potatoes and salads. ***Seats*** *100 (sandwich bar 20 + 20 outside).* ***Open*** *10.30-9 (Sun 12-6) (Sandwich bar 9-5 everyday).* ***Closed*** *25, 26 & 27 Dec. Amex, Diners, MasterCard,* ***VISA***

BROADWAY Dormy House 69% £120

Tel 01386 852711 **Fax 01386 858636** Map 14 C1 **HR**
Willersey Hill Broadway Hereford & Worcester WR12 7LF

Privately owned converted 17th-century farmhouse just off the A214, with views over the Vale of Evesham. Beams, exposed stonework and tiled floors set the tone in the main house, whose two homely lounges have fine bay windows. Converted outbuildings house cottagey, comfortable bedrooms, many also with timbered ceilings; two rooms have four-posters. There's a purpose-built conference centre. ***Rooms*** *49. Garden, croquet, putting, mountain bikes, mini-gym, sauna, steam room, games room. Closed 25 & 26 Dec. Amex, Diners, MasterCard,* ***VISA***

Restaurant £90

A conservatory overlooks the garden and surrounding countryside, giving a brighter alternative to the more formal, dimly-lit dining-room. Alan Cutler is in charge of the kitchens, producing a wide range of English/French-inspired dishes on à la carte, table d'hote, gourmet and vegetarian menus. Biggest choice comes à la carte, with such dishes as woodland mushrooms, baby spinach and Jerusalem artichoke tart on a coriander cream sauce, steamed mousseline of scallops and crayfish with a cucumber and lime sauce, supreme of Barbary duckling with a fig and ginger confit and loin of venison accompanied by a gin and juniper berry sauce and sautéed spätzle. British farmhouse cheeses are served with warm sultana and walnut bread, and desserts include speciality crepes Suzette and a hot soufflé. A decent wine list includes 20+ champagnes. Less formal lunch and dinner menus are served in the Barn Owl bar. ***Seats*** *85. Parties 18. L 12.30-2 D 7-9.30 (Sun till 9). Closed L Sat, all 25 & 26 Dec. Set Sun L £17 Set D £26.50/£34.*

BROADWAY Lygon Arms 80% £173

Tel 01386 852255 **Fax 01386 858611** Map 14 C1 **HR**
High Street Broadway Hereford & Worcester WR12 7DU

Part of the Savoy Group, the hotel is quintessentially English in all the best possible ways. For the most part, the interior enjoys real old-world charm with polished stone floors, low-beamed ceilings, wood panelling and imposing open fireplaces (even lit in summer) while the splendidly maintained bedrooms are furnished with antiques and country-style fabrics, yet provide modern amenities such as state-of-the-art satellite TV and wall safe. The bathrooms are modern too, with good toiletries, bathrobes (mini-robes for children and their own toilet bag) and vases of flowers. In fact, there are flowers everywhere – wonderful arrangements made up daily in the flower room. This is a good place to bring children (alebit at a price), who are warmly welcomed on arrival with their own play kits; there's a decent children's room service (or they can eat informally in the cosy and atmospheric hotel-owned Goblets wine bar next door - families are most welcome in the Tankard Room; high-chairs provided, and half portions are served on request), table tennis in the leisure complex, baby-sitting is available, and the family suites sharing a bathroom are ideal. Staff, under the dedicated and watchful eye of Managing Director Kirk Ritchie, succeed in being helpful and caring, and discreet and courteous, exemplified by the nightly-turn down service, the offer of a glass of sherry on arrival, and cleaning of car windscreens. Standards of housekeeping are superb throughout, and breakfast in the restaurant is a cut above the usual. Elegant conference rooms for up to 80, and a magnificent leisure complex.

Ample parking, including some lock-up garages (£10 a day – book in advance). ***Rooms*** *63. Garden, croquet, tennis, indoor swimming pool, gym, spa bath, sauna, steam room, solarium, beauty salon, snooker, valeting. Amex, Diners, MasterCard,* ***VISA***

The Great Hall Restaurant £85

A grand room with barrel-vaulted ceiling and a 17th-century minstrel's gallery. In the kitchen first-rate ingredients are used to good effect in dishes that are full of interest and quite often elaborate without resort to gimmickry: fish soup with garlic croutons, pithiviers of smoked Cotswold game with peas and roasted tomato, spiced sea bass with scampi brochettes and salsa, honey-roasted duckling with port and beetroot gravy and braised faggot. Plain dishes from the chargrill are always available. A separate vegetarian menu (£28.50) offers three courses and no choice. There's a variety of British and Irish farmhouse cheeses, and desserts might include apple cake with clotted cream and a hot soufflé. There's a good wine list here, with excellent house selections. No young children at night. No smoking. ***Seats*** *120. Parties 20. Private Room 80. L 12.30-2 D 7.30-9.15. Set L £20.50 Set D £32.*

BROCKENHURST Le Blaireau Café/Bar

Tel 01590 623032 Fax 01590 622799 Map 14 C4 **JaB**
Brockenhurst Hampshire SO42 7QH

This very French brasserie is situated next to the entrance to Carey's Manor Hotel (and under the same ownership), set back just off the Brockenhurst – Lyndhurst road. The prix-fixe menus at £9.95 or £12.95 offer the likes of watercress soup, beef bourguignon and crème caramel. The curved bar has a *pression* beer tap and is decorated with posters and the rear end of a Citroen 2CV on one wall – no doubting the Gallic influence here! The snack menu offers croissants, sandwiches, salads and other tempting snacks. Prices are modest: £2.35 for a croque monsieur or £4.95 for tagliatelle with ham, cream and mushrooms. There is a more elaborate à la carte menu with dishes such as soupe de poissons (£4.95), salmon hollandaise (£8.75) and rib-eye steak with red wine sauce and chips (£11.75) and maybe tarte aux pommes (£3.25) to finish. Plenty of dishes available for the under-7s. There is a pétanque pitch for those with the energy! ***Seats*** *120 (+ 50 outside).* ***Open*** *10-2.15 & 6-8. Amex, Diners, MasterCard,* ***VISA***

BROCKHAMPTON Craven Arms

Tel 01242 820410 Map 14 C1 
Brockhampton Gloucestershire GL54 5XQ

A deservedly popular pub hidden down winding lanes deep in the rolling Gloucestershire countryside: Brockhampton is 2 miles north of the A436 Cheltenham to Gloucester road. Approached under a stone lych gate, the garden extends to an enclosed paddock with a children's play area which includes a small summer house containing games for soggier days. Revealed within the Craven Arms are stone-flagged floors and a warren of rooms given over primarily to eating. Real ales are well represented in the bar, where the less adventurous may order gammon, egg and chips or steak pie. Look to the the daily blackboard menu for good quality dishes like poached salmon with lemon and thyme, beef bourguignon and aubergine and mushroom bake with Stilton sauce. Round off a value-for-money meal with traditional home-made treacle tart or banana and peach crumble. Dining tables are predominantly pine, their evening adornment of fresh carnations and candles quite in keeping with the pub's relaxed environment. *Open 11-2.30, 6-11 (Sun 12-3.30, 7-10.30.* ***Bar Food*** *12-2 (from 12.30 Sun), 7-9.30. Free House.* ***Beer*** *Butcombe Bitter, Hook Norton, Best Wadworth 6X, Worthington Best, occasional guest beer. Garden, outdoor eating, children's play area. MasterCard,* ***VISA***

If we recommend meals in a hotel a *separate* entry is usually made for its restaurant. Pub and inn entries include bar food details where recommended.

BROMLEY — Bromley Court — 66% — £91

Tel 0181-464 5011 **Fax 0181-460 0899** Map 11 B5 H

Bromley Hill Bromley Kent BR1 4JD

With fine gardens to the rear, this substantial hotel, comprising a period building and large 1970s extension, has recently benefited from a complete and high-quality refurbishment of public areas which include a spacious foyer lounge with split-level bar, armchair-furnished cocktail bar and brand new health and fitness suite neatly fitted into a vaulted basement. A rolling programme of bedroom refurbishment, which is due to start at the beginning of 1997, will bring bedrooms up to the standard of the day rooms. All the bathrooms have already been re-tiled. Families are well catered for with cots, extra beds and high-chairs available, and a magician at the family Sunday lunch; children up to the age of 8 stay free in parents' room; family rooms available. The hotel is located one street back from the A21 (look out for the hotel sign) on the London side of town. Ample parking. ***Rooms** 116. Garden, croquet, putting, gym, steam room, spa bath, ironing room. Amex, Diners, MasterCard,* **VISA**

BROMSGROVE — Pine Lodge Hotel — 64% — £97

Tel 01527 576600 **Fax 01527 878981** Map 14 B1 H

Kidderminster Road Bromsgrove Hereford & Worcester B61 9AB

Spot the bright Mediterranean look just out of town on the A448 towards Kidderminster. The theme is continued in the foyer, which has a terracotta-tiled floor and timbered ceiling. There's a more English feel in the cane-furnished Terrace Lounge, where snacks are available throughout the day. Bedrooms (of which the majority are very spacious Club rooms) feature darkwood furniture and boldly patterned fabrics. 24hr room service. Children are very welcome, and under-16s stay free in parents' room. Conference facilities for up to 200. ***Rooms** 114. Patio, playground, indoor swimming pool, gym, sauna, steam room, spa bath, sun bed, snooker, playroom (weekends). Amex, Diners, MasterCard,* **VISA**

BROOM — Broom Tavern

Tel 01789 773656 **Fax 01789 772983** Map 14 C1 

High Street Broom Warwickshire B50 5HL

Pretty, timbered village pub dating back to the 16th century with virginia creeper clinging to the outside and lots of black beams and brass within. The bar menu (mostly home-made although some puds and soups are not) offers plenty of choice, from ploughman's lunches, sandwiches and starters like smoked salmon mousse and black pudding with hot mustard sauce to main-course dishes such as whole grilled plaice, chicken, gammon and mushroom pie, rack of lamb with rosemary, and various pasta dishes. Children are catered for with a special menu, high-chairs and, on summer weekends and during school holidays, a 'bouncy castle' out in the garden. *Open 11-3, 6-11 (Sun 12-3, 7-10.30).* ***Bar Food** 12-2, 6.45-9.30 (Sat 6.30-10, Sun 7-9).* ***Beer** Hook Norton Best Bitter, two guest beers. Garden, outdoor eating. Family room. Amex, MasterCard,* **VISA**

BROXTED — Whitehall — 69% — £110

Tel 01279 850603 **Fax 01279 850385** Map 10 B3 

Church End Broxted Essex CM6 2BZ

Ask directions from J8 of the M11 when booking at Whitehall, which stands on the outskirts of a village overlooking rolling Essex countryside. The original Elizabethan manor house has been much extended, in keeping with the original style, and creates a comfortable country hotel. The interior is characterised by ancient oak beams and rough plaster walls which have been skilfully combined with modern amenities. There's a quite simply appointed bar which leads into a small sitting-room dominated by the lounge behind it. Bedrooms are of good size and are furnished in a uniform scheme of cream fabrics and blond woods, each possessing thoughtful extras like bathrobes and quality toiletries in the spacious bathrooms, some of which have separate shower cublicles. Free parking for 60 cars. No dogs. ***Rooms** 25. Garden, outdoor swimming pool, tennis. Closed 26-31 Dec. Amex, Diners, MasterCard,* **VISA**

See over

Restaurant £80

The ancient timbered dining-room features a huge redbrick inglenook fireplace and a pretty, summery decor with just a few tables having views over a neat walled garden. The modern menus vary considerably in choice and content: typical items on the carte could include a rustic lamb shank and celery soup, smoked chicken and pasta terrine with a basil dressing, baked salmon with a crust of walnuts and grapes on a champagne sauce and fillet of lamb encased in puff pastry with a Madeira jus. An extensive selection of vegetables accompanies. To finish, there's a hot soufflé of the day along with perhaps four more choices, and a cheese platter. Very fine wine list. ***Seats*** *40. Private Room 18. L 12.30-2 D 7.30-9.30. Closed L Sat. Set menus from £13.50 to £37.50 (menu surprise).*

Buckland Newton — Gaggle of Geese

Tel 01300 345249 Map 13 F2 P
Buckland Newton Dorset DT2 7BS

Formerly the Royal Oak, The Gaggle of Geese is so named since a previous landlord bred geese as a hobby; the building dates back to 1834 when it started life as the village shop. Twice-yearly goose charity auctions still take place here. Located on the B3143, about halfway between Dorchester and Sherborne, this tranquil village pub has a civilised and attractive main bar and pretty garden complete with pond. Children are allowed in the skittle alley and dining-room. *Open 12-2.30, 6.30-11 (Sun 12-3, 7-10.30). Free House.* ***Beer*** *Hall & Woodhouse Badger Best, Bass, Wadworth 6X, Butcombe Bitter, two guest beers. Garden, children's play area. Family room. No credit cards.*

Burcot — Chequers

Tel 01865 407771 Map 15 D2 
Abingdon Road Burcot Oxfordshire OX14 3DP

Originally a staging post for River Thames barges and their crews, until what is now the A415 was built outside. Charming, part 16th-century beamed and thatched building with unspoilt quarry-tiled bars, open fires and a choice of books for customers to read. A daily-changing blackboard menu is the same for the bar and dining-room. Cook Mary Weeks offers simple home-made fare (including bread) – chicken, sage and mushroom or seafood pies, tomato and aubergine crumble, lamb and courgette lasagne and (genuine old-fashioned suet) steak and kidney pudding – followed by melting meringues filled with peaches and cream and Mary's disaster cake! Sunday lunch is served on the first Sunday of every month. Piano music on Friday and Saturday nights. *Open 11-2.30, 6-11 (Sun 12-3, 7-10.30).* ***Bar Food*** *12-2, 6.30-9 (no food Sun eve). Free House.* ***Beer*** *Ruddles County, Ushers Best, Archer's Village Bitter. Garden, outdoor eating. MasterCard,* ***VISA***

Burley — Burley Manor 61% £85

Tel 01425 403522 **Fax 01425 403227** Map 14 C4 H
Burley nr Ringwood Hampshire BH24 4BS

A Victorian manor house surrounded by 54 acres of parkland in the heart of the New Forest. Families and dogs are encouraged. Period decor includes stone fireplaces, a creaky staircase with carved balustrade and unusual commode side-tables. Bedrooms are simply decorated and have smart bathrooms; converted stable-block rooms are the largest and have the best views over open fields, plus a couple of steps leading directly down to the lawns. Riding stables in the grounds offer rides in the New Forest for both novices and experts. Children up to 15 stay free in parents' room. ***Rooms*** *30. Garden, croquet, riding stables, outdoor swimming pool, hairdressing, putting. Amex, Diners, MasterCard,* ***VISA***

BURLEY Manor Farm Tea Rooms

Tel & Fax 01425 402218 Map 14 C4 JaB
Ringwood Road Burley New Forest Hampshire BH24 4AB

A picture-postcard come alive is how this tea shop might be described; the roof is thatched, and the log fire roars in winter. Teas and coffees with scones, pastries and cakes (from 95p) are available in the morning. At lunchtime, sandwiches (from £1.95), baked potatoes and maybe haddock and chips (£5.50) or sausages and chips (£3.95) are supplemented by daily blackboard specials such as cold poached salmon with salad and Jersey royals (£6.25) or shepherd's pie (£3.95). Set teas in the afternoon cover most tastes and appetites (£3.50-£5.75). Children's lunches offer fish fingers, sausages or chicken nuggets with chips and beans or peas, and a children's tea menu ('the little one's treat') includes a fizzy drink or orange squash, ice cream and home-made cake. Three high-chairs; baby food and bottles can all be provided, and a Mother & Baby room has changing mats, nappy bins and wipes plus an armchair for feeding. ***Seats** 84 (+ 12 outside). **Open** 10-5 (Sun from 10.30, Mon from 2.30). **Closed** Mon Nov-Jun. No credit cards.*

A jug of fresh water!

BURNHAM MARKET Hoste Arms

Tel 01328 738257 **Fax 01328 730103** Map 10 C1 IR
The Green Burnham Market Norfolk PE31 8HD

A handsome, pale yellow-painted 17th-century inn (now much extended to the rear) occupying a prime position overlooking the green and parish church of a most picturesque village. Paul Whittome's relentless enthusiasm for the property (and the business) over the past six years has transformed the Hoste into one of the most popular inns along the Norfolk coast. It goes from strength to strength, with a new block of six elegant, extremely comfortable bedrooms only recently added. Two carefully-renovated front bars feature dark wood panelling, open brick fireplaces with winter log fires, rustic wooden floors and cushioned bow window seats with village views. Of note are the original paintings by wildlife artist Bruce Pearson illustrating a series of rural walks from the inn, Lord Decies' shell collection displayed in cabinets, and a permanent exhibition of Stephen Heffer's Norfolk coastal photographs. Live traditional jazz and R&B are popular Friday and Monday night events in the comfortably furnished piano bar. Tip-top bar food draws on supplies of fresh local and seasonal produce from within a twenty mile radius and everything is prepared on the premises. Varied menu choices range from open sandwiches, local Burnham Norton oysters, smoked chicken salad with mango dressing and pan-fried black pudding on a salad of beetroot with hazelnut oil to risotto of smoked haddock with saffron and chives, millefeuille of monkfish and mangetout with langoustine butter sauce, grilled lamb's liver and bacon, and penne pasta with chargrilled vegetables. To finish, try the apple crumble, chocolate and hazelnut torte, a selection of three English cheeses or Prospero ice creams, made locally in Holt. Vegetarians might enjoy braised cos lettuce with vegetarian oyster sauce and toasted sesame seeds. Sunday roasts. Look out also for beef from Wroxham Broads, mussels from Brancaster Staithe or sea bass and sea trout from Scolt Head Island. The global list of well-priced wines has sensible prices, useful notes and a selection of half bottles; well-kept ales are drawn straight from the cask. Upstairs, beyond the small gallery/lounge, are the majority of the charming bedrooms, four of which now boast four-posters. The rooms are all individually decorated, some with freestanding pine, others with antique pieces, designer fabrics and fittings. Spotless en suite facilities and TV, radio, tea-maker, telephone and hairdryer are all provided. The six newest rooms offer superb comfort and one can really look forward to a good night's sleep after exploring the Norfolk's north-coast salt marshes and sand dunes. Top of the range of bedrooms is a huge room with custom-built four-poster and luxurious bathroom – a bargain in low season! First-rate breakfasts are served in the conservatory, which is also the venue for

…s (free to residents). Year-round tariff reductions are offered for stays …ts and over; the best deal is half price (Sun-Thu) from November to …f March. Quite delightful garden with rustic benches and dry hop-filled …atory. Winner of our 1996 Pub of the Year Award. *Open 11-11 (Sun 12-3, …0).* ***Bar Food*** *12-2, 7-9. Free House.* ***Beer*** *Morland Old Speckled Hen, Greene …g IPA & Abbot Ale, Woodforde's Wherry Bitter, guest beers. Garden, outside …ating.* ***Accommodation*** *21 bedrooms, all en suite, £84-£108 (single £60). 2+ night rates: £60-£76 (weekends £66-84), £42-£54 Nov-Mar (exc. Christmas and New year). Children welcome overnight (under-2s free if sharing parents' room), additional bed & cot provided (£15). Amex, MasterCard,* ***VISA***

BURNHAM THORPE Lord Nelson

Tel 01328 738241 Map 10 C1 **P**

Walsingham Road Burnham Thorpe Norfolk P31 8HN

Unspoilt rural cottage located in a sleepy village close to Burnham Market and named after England's most famous seafarer, who was born in the nearby rectory. A narrow, worn brick-floored corridor leads to two rooms; a timeless, old-fashioned bar on the left boasting some magnificent high-backed settles and a few sturdy tables and plain chairs on a re-tiled floor. Nelson memorabilia in the form of prints and paintings adorn the walls. There is no bar; excellent Greene King ales are drawn straight from the cask in the adjacent cellar room and brought to the table. Also available is a popular rum concoction called "Nelson's Blood", which is made to a secret recipe by the previous long-serving landlord who still resides near the pub. A further warmly decorated and simply furnished room is ideal for families. The adjacent barn has recently been renovated to provide more seating and the new toilets, including disabled facilities. Good-sized garden with bowling green, bat & ball, football net, basketball net, swing and slide for active youngsters to let off steam. *Open 11-3, 6-11 (Sun 12-3, 7-10.30), longer hours in summer.* ***Beer*** *Greene King. Garden. Family room, children's play area. No credit cards.*

BURY Est Est Est

Tel & Fax 0161-766 4869 Map 6 B2 **JaB**

703 Manchester Road Bury BL9 0ED

A large member of the north-west chain of Italian trattorias, this one can cater for up to 200. The menu is the same as at Knutsford. Pizza pasta pronto (£7.95) is a special deal for 2 before 7.30pm (not Saturday) offering one pizza and one pasta dish plus a mixed salad. Live music Wednesday and Thursdays. Children's menu up to 7.30pm daily. ***Seats*** *200.* ***Open*** *12-2.30 & 6-11 (Sat 6-11.30, Sun 12-10.30).* ***Closed*** *25, 26 Dec & 1 Jan. Amex, MasterCard,* ***VISA***

BURY ST EDMUNDS Angel Hotel 66% £89

Tel 01284 753926 **Fax 01284 750092** Map 10 C2 **H**

Angel Hill Bury St Edmunds Suffolk IP33 1LT

Right across a sloping square from the Abbey Gardens, the Angel is an integral part of the town, and has been in continuous use as a hotel since 1452. It comprises several adjacent buildings (the oldest part dating back to the 12th century) that gained a unifying facade in Georgian times, and is now completely covered in Virginia creeper. Bedrooms come in all shapes and sizes from large rooms with four-poster beds and antique furniture to small singles with simple white-painted fitted units; all are in good order and individually decorated – often quite stylishly. Bathrooms are decorated to match each room. Room 15, where Charles Dickens stayed, is preserved as it was in his day. 24hr room service. Ample parking. ***Rooms*** *42. Amex, Diners, MasterCard,* ***VISA***

BURY ST EDMUNDS Butterfly Hotel 62% £66

Tel 01284 760884 **Fax 01284 755476** Map 10 C2 **H**

Symonds Road Bury St Edmunds Suffolk IP32 7BW

Take the Bury East exit from the A14 to the Butterfly, a modern low-riser with other outlets in Colchester, King's Lynn and Peterborough. Practical accommodation, function facilities for up to 50, ample free parking. ***Rooms*** *66. Amex, Diners, MasterCard,* ***VISA***

Cadeby — Cadeby Inn

Tel 01709 864009 Map 7 D2 P

Main Street Cadeby Doncaster DN5 7SW

This atmospheric old inn was clearly once an elegant country farmhouse and stands today in a mature orchard garden full of flowering shrubs. There's plenty of space here for little ones to play safely, and the picnic tables are especially popular when there's a barbecue on. Original flagstones and fireplaces survive in the two bars whose counters are built in brick, while the walls are hung with horse collars, brasses and webbing. *Open 11.30-3, 5-11 (Sat 11-11, Sun 12-3, 7-10.30). Free House.* ***Beer*** *Tetley Best, Courage Directors, John Smith's Best & Magnet, Samuel Smith's Old Brewery, guest beer. Garden, children's play area. Family room. MasterCard,* ***VISA***

Cadnam — White Hart

Tel 01703 812277 **Fax 01703 814632** Map 14 C4 P

Cadnam Lyndhurst Hampshire SO40 2NP

The Emberley family run this attractive and smartly-refurbished old coaching inn, located on the edge of the New Forest beside the A31 and convenient for Junction 1 of the M27. A big welcome awaits familes either in the extensive sheltered garden, complete with a paddock of animals, or in the spacious interior which boasts plenty of exposed brick, open fires and a comfortable mix of old and new furniture. Well worth stopping for is the reliable selection of bar food on offer here. As well as tried and tested dishes (freshly battered cod and chips, mixed grill, prawn open sandwich, noisettes of lamb with fresh herb jus) listed on the varied printed menu, blackboard specials improve the choice further with game in season (venison with spring onion, bacon and oyster mushrooms) and fresh fish dishes such as sea bass with home-made lobster sausages, brill with pistou salad, and tournedos of hake with pesto dressing. For pudding try the chocolate and banana strudel or the brioche butter pudding. Set three-course Sunday roast lunch, good selection of real ales and at least nine wines available by the glass. *Open 11-2.30, 6-11 (Sun 11-3, 7-10.30).* ***Bar Food*** *11.30-2, 6-9.30 (Sun 12-2, 7-9).* ***Beer*** *Morland Old Speckled Hen, Wadworth 6X, Courage Best, Flowers Original. Garden, outdoor eating. MasterCard,* ***VISA***

Camberley — Frimley Hall — 68% — £136

Tel 01276 28321 **Fax 01276 691253** Map 15 E3 

Portsmouth Road Camberley Surrey GU15 2BG

Signposted off the A325 and set in six acres of mature grounds, this hotel is based on a mansion built by the Wright family (of coal tar soap fame) at the turn of the century. Reception is located in the galleried main hall with its coffered ceiling and splendid carved oak staircase leading up past large stained-glass windows. Other public areas, all in the original building as are the various function rooms, include a pleasing lounge with red and green upholstered armchairs and a recently refurbished mock rustic bar. Ten manor bedrooms in the main house are spacious, excellent bathrooms especially so, and appealing with individual decor and antique furniture; one boasts particularly fine fitted furniture original to the house. Remaining rooms, in a 1960s extension to the rear, are more standardised with good, solid wood furniture and bedcovers and curtains in matching floral fabrics; bedroom corridors, with rather tired hessian-like wall coverings, let the side down a bit. Children up to 16 stay free in parents' room. 24hr room service. ***Rooms*** *66. Garden. Amex, Diners, MasterCard,* ***VISA***

Cambridge — Arundel House — 62% — £63

Tel 01223 367701 **Fax 01223 367721** Map 15 F1 H

53 Chesterton Road Cambridge Cambridgeshire CB4 3AN

On the city-centre ring road overlooking the River Cam, Arundel House is popular with business people as well as tourists. Privately owned, the hotel is well maintained throughout, with pleasing traditional standards of accommodation, and managing director Robert Norfolk oversees a constant programme of refurbishment and improvement. Top floor bedrooms enjoy splendid views, some others are in the converted coach house behind the main building. A Victorian-style Conservatory housing an all-day restaurant opens on to an enclosed garden. No dogs. ***Rooms*** *105. Garden, laundrette & ironing room. Closed 25 & 26 Dec. Amex, Diners, MasterCard,* ***VISA***

CAMBRIDGE Browns

Tel 01223 461655 Map 15 F1 JaB
23 Trumpington Street Cambridge Cambridgeshire

This branch of the successful and popular Browns chain, with other outlets in London, Brighton, Bristol and Oxford, is situated opposite the Fitzwilliam Museum, and shares much of the menu with its siblings. It offers breakfast until mid-day, when the main menu comes into play. This proposes a long list of starters including grilled sardines with tomato salsa (£3.55), roast red peppers with fresh basil, garlic and olive oil (£3.75) and Caesar salad (£3.15); follow with pasta (from £6.75), salads (vegetarian £7.25, grilled goat's cheese £7.15), hot sandwiches (BLT £5.45) roast poussin with bacon, lemon and tarragon (£8.45) or a generously filled fisherman's pie (£7.65). Something then for everyone, and all dished up with a smile. There is tea in the afternoon from 3 to 5.30, a children's menu and tables on the pavement in fine weather. Ten high-chairs, and a changing room with table, mat and baby wipes are all provided; bottles and baby food can be heated on request. Joint winner of our Family Restaurants of the Year award in 1994. Park at the Pay & Display in Trumpington Street. ***Seats*** *230 (+ 30 outside).* ***Open*** *11am-11.30pm (Sun and Bank Holidays from 12). Access, Amex,* ***VISA***

CAMBRIDGE Cambridgeshire Moat House 63% £98

Tel 01954 249988 **Fax 01954 780010** Map 15 F1 H
Bar Hill Cambridge Cambridgeshire CB3 8EU

Well-designed modern hotel on the A604 with plenty of free parking, extensive leisure facilities, function suites, a business centre and a variety of bars and restaurants. Bedrooms are well equipped, with all the usual gadgets. Children up to 15 can stay free in parents' room. ***Rooms*** *99. Garden, croquet, tennis, golf (18), putting, indoor swimming pool, children's splash pool, gym, squash, sauna, spa bath, steam room, solarium, pool table. Amex, Diners, MasterCard,* ***VISA***

CAMBRIDGE Hobbs Pavilion

Tel 01223 367480 Map 15 F1 JaB
Hobbs Pavilion Park Terrace Cambridge Cambridgeshire CB1 1JH

Tucked behind the University Arms and bordering the cricket squares of Parker's Piece, Hobbs Pavilion is a real winner. Stephen and Susan Hill have been cooking their savoury pancakes on circular cast-iron plaques since 1978. Interesting toppings include leeks, cashews, ginger and cheese (£4.95), hot chili lamb (£5.80) and the bumper vegetarian – cheese, spinach, tomatoes and mild horseradish (£4.95). Sweeter versions, deftly turned into crispy fans, containing stem ginger and cream (£3.75) or the 'perils of praline' topped with hazelnut crème (£4.50) are served alongside the famous home-made ice creams, honey and lavender or ginger (£3.50 for 2 scoops). There are also various set menus – £5 & £6.75 at lunchtime, £8.75 & (wine incl) £12.75 at any time. New this year – chargrilled Mars Bar Parcel (wrapped in batter, thrown on the chargrill, served with whipped cream and dark chocolate sauce £3.95). Multifarious wines by the glass, fruit juices, speciality teas and coffees. The terms under which parents may bring their children into the restaurant is printed on the menu remains the same, with the intention of encouraging rather than discouraging: "as you can see from the provision of high-chairs, we are pleased to have children among our guests. Out of concern for the welfare of everyone, however, we must insist that the child in your care is reasonably quiet. (This does not mean silent). All children have 'bad days', but it is unreasonable to expect other customers to have to share the consequences of them. It is also unreasonable to wait for us to tell you when the child in your care is dominating the restaurant's atmosphere and then take offence at that request". Weather permitting, fidgety toddlers can play outside on the grass while parents wait for their meal on the pavilion steps. No special changing facilities but a room can usually be made available to nursing mothers on request. Baby food and bottles can be heated on request, and children's crockery is available (but not of the unbreakable type). No smoking. Outdoor eating in good weather. ***Seats*** *60.* ***Open*** *12-2.15 & 7-9.45.* ***Closed*** *Sun, Mon, Bank Holidays & mid Aug-mid Sep. No credit cards.*

CAMELFORD Lanteglos Country House Hotel

Tel 01840 213551 **Fax 01840 212372** M

Camelford Cornwall PL32 9RF

Lanteglos is set in 15 acres of gardens and woodland and on entering are immediately made aware of the presence of children, by road signs warn children at play. There are ten rooms in the 19th-century main hotel building, four chalet suites (three bedrooms), three cottage suites (two/three bedrooms), 21 self-catering lodges and 45 self-catering villas (sleeping five and also marketed by Hoseasons) plus one house sleeping up to nine. Along with 100 cots and high-chairs, baby baths, potties, safety gates and nappy buckets and baby-listening devices are all provided. Family rooms have a double bed, single bed and cot plus en-suite facilities. It is an absolute paradise for children, with secret play areas in the woods, four playgrounds, an adventure playground and a games room. The outside pool is well heated (May to mid-Sept) and the shallow children's pool has a central island with a fountain. Bedrooms are tastefully furnished, spacious and comfortable. Children's teatime is a carefree affair when children can choose dishes like roast chicken and gravy or Cornish pastie, as well as the usual beefburger and spaghetti bolognese. Don't be late finishing supper (5.30-6.30pm) or you'll miss the seasonal children's entertainment (5 nights weekly in Jun-Aug). The minimum stay is two nights and with so much to do this is probably just as well. No dogs or pets. *Half-board terms: low-season rates start from £38 per room per night on the standard tariff, £43 on the premier tariff; high-season rates range from £55-£60; B&B rates less £10; 10% discount for 7 day+ bookings. Youngest child under 5 stays free; additional children: under-5s £20 per day, 5-14s £20 per day. Special golfing packages available throughout the year; Bowood Park golf course (concessionary rates for hotel guests) surrounds the hotel and nine other courses are within easy driving distance. ***Rooms** 17 + 66 villas. Closed Dec-Feb. MasterCard,* **VISA**

CANTERBURY Ebury Hotel 59% £60

Tel 01227 768433 **Fax 01227 459187** Map 11 C5 H

65 New Dover Road Canterbury Kent CT1 3DX

Set back from the New Dover Road (A2) a mile south-east of the city centre, the Ebury is made up of two adjoining Victorian houses. There are two acres of garden, an antique-furnished lounge and a small, indoor swimming pool. Light, airy bedrooms are simply but neatly appointed. Four self-catering flats and bungalows in the grounds are also available. Owned and run by the Mason family since 1979. ***Rooms** 15. Garden, indoor swimming pool, spa bath, keep-fit equipment. Closed mid Dec-mid Jan. Amex, MasterCard,* **VISA**

CANTERBURY Falstaff Inn £90

Tel 01227 462138 **Fax 01227 463525** Map 11 C5 I

8 St Dunstan's Street Canterbury Kent CT2 8AF

A centuries-old coaching inn by the outer walls of the city. Day rooms, including the good pubby bar, get character from original beams, leaded windows and polished oak tables. Bedrooms are neat and pretty and the majority use solid modern furniture that suits the feel of the place perfectly; two rooms feature a four-poster bed (small supplement to the regular tariff). Within easy walking distance of the town centre and historic cathedral, near the Westgate Tower. Good pubby bar. Country Club (Whitbread) Hotels. *Open 11-11 (Sun 12-10.30). **Beer** Flowers Original, Wadworth 6X, guest beer. **Accommodation** 24 bedrooms, all en suite, £75 (single £68, room only – breakfast £7.50-£8.95). Children welcome overnight (under-16s stay free in parents' room), additional bed & cot available. Amex, Diners, MasterCard,* **VISA**

We endeavour to be as up-to-date as possible, but inevitably some changes to data and key personnel may occur at restaurants and hotels after the Guide goes to press. Prices should also be taken as indications rather than firm quotes.

TERBURY — Il Vaticano Pasta Parlour

l 01227 765333 Map 11 C5 **JaB**
5 St Margarets Street Canterbury Kent CT1 2TG

A dining-room with poster-adorned walls, or a charming walled garden (weather permitting) is the setting for a simple mix-and-match selection of pasta dishes – choose from four varieties of pasta and a range of a dozen sauces: *casareccia* (diced chicken breast and vegetables in a tomato and red wine sauce – £6.95), *campagnola* (black olives and mushrooms in a tomato sauce – £5.95) or perhaps *vongole* (baby clams in a tomato, garlic and herb sauce – £6.50). A list of starters includes *agliata* (raw vegetables with garlic dip – £2.85) and minestrone (£2.35). Gateaux or ice creams to finish. A blackboard displays daily specials. Two high-chairs; children's portions, and changing facilities in Ladies. Walled garden. Parking at Watling Street car park. ***Seats*** *50 (+ 26 outside).* ***Open*** *11.30-10.30 (Sun 12-10).* ***Closed*** *25 & 26 Dec. Amex, Diners, Mastercard,* ***VISA***

CARLISLE — The Grapevine

Tel 01228 46617 Map 4 C2 **JaB**
22 Fisher Street Carlisle Cumbria CA3 91Q

The YMCA building plays host to this friendly counter-service restaurant. Brightly decorated with pictures (mostly by local artists) and hanging baskets, it is a popular spot for visitors and locals alike. An all-day menu offers good-value main dishes (all £3.25) such as lamb lasagne, Middle Eastern vegetable bake, chili and baked potatoes or Malayasian chicken curry. There is also a colourful array of salads – Bombay potato, spinach, carrot and ginger or perhaps sweet and sour beansprouts. On two evenings a month there is a hot and cold buffet where you can eat as much as you like for £9.70 including corkage (it's unlicensed, so bring your own wine). Upstairs, the owners offer a crèche/nursery for the little ones while the grown-ups eat in peace. There is a garden terrace for alfresco eating in fine weather. City centre car parks are the nearest. ***Seats*** *70 (+ 12 outside).* ***Open*** *9-4 (Fri/Sat till 4.30, Mon 10-2).* ***Closed*** *Sun & Bank Holidays. No credit cards.*

CARLISLE — Zapotec

Tel 01228 512209 **Fax 01228 593100** Map 4 C2 **JaB**
18 Fisher Street Carlisle Cumbria CA3 8RH

Menus at this basement restaurant divide the cuisine distinctly into Spanish and Mexican. On the Mexican side come salsa, guacamole and chargrilled spring onions (all £2.50) before several styles of *nachos* (from £3.90), *burritos pescados* (£8.30) and *pollo asado con rajas* (barbecued chicken with onion, chili and coriander £8.50). Desserts come in the form of ice creams or fresh mango in a cinnamon ginger syrup and can be washed down with various tequila-based cocktails. The Spanish menu bases itself mainly on tapas (25 different dishes, priced between £1.90 and £4.20) although there are always also main courses, typically paella and fillet of Aberdeen Angus beef with blue cheese sauce (£11.90). Courtyard for summer eating. Two no-smoking rooms. ***Seats*** *44 (+ 18 outside).* ***Open*** *12-2 & 7-10.30 (Sat 6.30-10.30), also open some Sun eves – please enquire.* ***Closed*** *L Sun, 14 days from Christmas eve. MasterCard,* ***VISA***

CARLYON BAY — Carlyon Bay Hotel — 68% — £136

Tel 01726 812304 **Fax 01726 814938** Map 12 B3

Sea Road Carlyon nr St Austell Cornwall PL25 3RD

Families are particularly well catered for at this handsome 1930s' creeper-clad hotel, which stands in 250 acres of sub-tropical gardens and grounds. It also offers extensive conference and function rooms (up to 250/220) and boasts fine leisure facilities including its own championship golf course. Large-windowed lounges, furnished in traditional style, make the most of the splendid setting, as do most of the light, attractive bedrooms (a supplement is charged for sea-facing rooms). ***Rooms*** *73.*

Garden, croquet, 18-hole golf course, 9-hole approach golf course, tennis, indoor & outdoor swimming pools, spa bath, sauna, solarium, snooker, playground & playroom. Amex, Diners, MasterCard, ***VISA***

CASTLE ACRE — Willow Cottage Tea Room

Tel 01760 755551 Map 10 C1 JaB
Stocks Green Castle Acre Norfolk PE32 2AE

Charmingly situated in an 18th-century brick-and-flint building next to the parish church, this tea room offers good home-made light snacks as well as cakes and cream tea (£1.80). Filled baked potatoes (from £1.90), freshly made sandwiches (from £1.35), salads (from £2.80) and Welsh rarebit (£1.90) set the style. Their home-made waffles (£2) are popular, and come with maple syrup plus cream or ice cream. The village is popular with walkers and tourists, as it boasts a Norman castle and a ruined 11th-century priory. No smoking. ***Seats*** *28 (+ 16 outside).* ***Open*** *10.30-5.30.* ***Closed*** *Mon except Bank Holidays, all Nov-mid Mar. No credit cards.*

CASTLETON — Rose Cottage Café

Tel 01433 620472 Map 6 C2 JaB
Cross Street Castleton nr Sheffield Derbyshire S30 2WH

Rose Cottage Café is a charming white-painted building comprising three village cottages, bedecked with baskets of flowers and offering a warm welcome to all-comers. Mrs Woodget and her daughter offer home-made dishes from a self-service counter. Soup (£1.85), chicken and mushroom pie (£4.95) and a range of sandwiches (£2.45 for home-cooked ham) are some of the lunchtime offerings, a list of which is on the blackboard behind the counter. Home-made fruit crumbles and puddings are £2.25, and cream teas in the afternoon £2.80. Helpful, friendly staff. ***Seats*** *50 (+ 30 outside).* ***Open*** *10-5.* ***Closed*** *Fri, Jan, Feb & 24-26 Dec. No credit cards.*

CHADDESLEY CORBETT — Brockencote Hall 75% £110

Tel 01562 777876 **Fax 01562 777872** Map 6 B4 HR
Chaddesley Corbett nr Kidderminster Hereford & Worcester DY10 4PY

Surrounded by 70 acres of pastureland, the Georgian-looking original has spawned an almost identical building next door where most of the spacious bedrooms are to be found. Stylish individual decor, fine cherrywood furniture and extras like sherry, fruit and mineral water make for very comfortable accommodation; one room has been specially adapted for disabled guests. Large bathrooms with alcoved tubs (three with spa baths and six with separate walk-in showers) are equally luxurious. A conservatory lounge links the two buildings. No dogs. ***Rooms*** *17. Garden, croquet. Amex, Diners, MasterCard,* ***VISA***

Restaurant £80

The park and the lake provide classic English views from the elegant chandeliered restaurant, but the kitchen is in French hands. Sound skills are applied to local and regional produce to create interesting dishes that combine classical and modern elements: pan-fried duck foie gras with caramelised oranges, asparagus mousse served with warm Loch Fyne oysters and roasted asparagus tips, tartlet of braised monkfish tails with tapénade served with a sweet pepper coulis, roast best end of lamb topped with a tomato and courgette rosace served with pan-fried sweetbreads, bitter chocolate tart served with a toffee and fudge clotted ice cream. There's a fine cheeseboard, and a separate menu of lighter and vegetarian dishes. No smoking. ***Seats*** *50. Parties 12. Private Room 28. L 12-1.30 D 7-9.30 (Sun from 7.30). Closed L Sat. Set L £17.50 & £37.50 Set D £22.50 & £37.50.*

> Always ring ahead and inform establishments of your exact requirements when travelling with children. Unannounced can, sadly, still mean unwelcome.

CHADLINGTON Tite Inn

Tel 01608 676475 Map 14 C1 **P**
Mill End Chadlington Oxfordshire OX7 3NY

This warm 16th-century Cotswold-stone pub is as pretty as a picture, complete with cottage roses clambering up the walls. Inside, the original rough stone walls remain, but otherwise it is almost too neat and tidy, with its modern carpeted floor and wheelback chairs. A table displaying newspapers and magazines is a nice touch, though, and there is also a garden room which features bunches of grapes hanging from a vine covering the roof. Michael Willis behind the bar looks after the real ales, while Susan looks after the kitchen. Hearty home-made soups, haddock smokey with salad, lambs kidneys braised in port, bobotie (spicy South African dish) and spinach and ricotta lasagne are amongst the offerings listed on the regularly-changing blackboard menu, and there are always several vegetarian dishes available.
A traditional roast is served on Sundays. Popular puddings include fruit crumble, hot sticky toffee pudding and chocolate and rum mousse. Children are made genuinely welcome and small portions are no problem. *Open 12-3, 6.30-11 (Sun 12-3, 7-10.30). Closed Mon (except Bank Holidays).* ***Bar Food*** *12-2, 7-9 (no food Mon). Free House.* ***Beer*** *Archers Village, Wychwood The Dog's Bollocks, two guest beers. Garden, outdoor eating. No credit cards.*

CHAGFORD Mill End 63% £79

Tel 01647 432282 **Fax 01647 433106** Map 13 D2 **H**
Sandy Park Chagford Devon TQ13 8JN

An old white mill (the wheel still turns in the courtyard) with 600 yards of fishing on the River Teign. The setting, on the edge of Dartmoor, is particularly beautiful and peaceful. Bedrooms are furnished with a mixture of traditional, antique and modern pieces and rooms on the ground floor have patios leading to the gardens. Children up to 16 sharing their parents' room are accommodated free; good facilities for young families include a long children's supper menu. ***Rooms*** *16. Garden, game fishing. Closed 10 days mid-Dec, 10 days mid-Jan. Amex, Diners, MasterCard,* ***VISA***

CHALE Clarendon Hotel & Wight Mouse Inn £70

Tel & Fax 01983 730431 Map 15 D4 **I**
Chale Isle of Wight PO38 2HA

John and Jean Bradshaw's frenetic family hotel and pub is set well back from the A3055 overlooking Chale Bay and the Needles; an object lesson in good innkeeping it continues year-round to pull in the crowds from near and far, even providing for those from afar private transport, the Mousemobile, by arrangement. The pub's interior, full of ships' beams, antique artefacts and musical instruments includes a cluster of family rooms and play areas matched only by outdoor facilities which include adventure playground and barbecue terrace where there are Punch and Judy shows in summer and pony rides to be had on Syd the Welsh cob and Arthur the Shetland pony. For a kitchen producing hundreds of meals all day, every day, output is remarkably consistent; anything goes, from a child's egg and chips through local crab for grandma to Wiener Schnitzel with potato salad and fried egg and the giant Clarendon mixed grill for trenchermen. There's a free lucky bag given with every child's meal ordered, while to keep the grown-ups happy there are as many wines as there are weeks in a year, a different real ale for every day of the week and 365 different whiskies on sale, including "Famous Mouse", and 366 again next Leap Year – 2000 AD! Fully half the en suite bedrooms have three or more beds, and there are two self-contained family suites with sitting areas and two full-size bedrooms, one of them (for parents only!) containing a water-bed. Everything from early teas to mid-evening entertainment is designed to be as flexible as possible, as reflected by charges for children, inclusive of all meals, on a graduating scale from £14 weekly for 2-year-olds to £25 per day at age thirteen. *Open 11-midnight (Sun 12-10.30).* ***Bar Food*** *11.30-10 (Sun 12-9.30). Free House.* ***Beer*** *Marston's Pedigree,*

Wadworth 6X, Boddingtons, Whitbread Fuggles Imperial, Strong Country Bitter, Morland Old Speckled Hen, guest beer. Garden, outdoor eating, children's play area. 3 Family rooms. ***Accommodation*** *13 bedrooms, 10 en suite (3 with bath), £66 (suite £89, single from £35, higher in season). Children welcome overnight (0-2 £3.50, 3-7 £8, 8-13 £25, 14-16 £33), additional bed & cot available. Dogs £3.50. MasterCard,* ***VISA***

CHARLBURY Bell Hotel £75

Tel 01608 810278 **Fax 01608 811447** Map 14 C1 I
Church Street Charlbury Oxfordshire OX7 3PP

Historic Charlbury with its 7th-century St Mary's Church was royally chartered to hold cattle markets in 1256: the last one was held behind the Bell some 700 years later. With its own datestone of 1700, the mellow stone inn is full of character. The small flagstoned bar and sun-lounge makes guests feel much at home and in fair weather the patio looking down a long, sloping garden is a picturesque spot. Access to bedrooms is by steep staircases and narrow passageways yet the rooms themselves are spacious and neatly appointed with matching fabrics and up-to-date accessories which include hairdryers, trouser presses and welcome clock-radios. The three smaller doubles have en suite WC/showers only and one single is not en suite, though its adjacent bathroom is private. Conference facilities in the converted stable block accommodate up to 55. *Open 10.30-11 (Sun 12-10.30). Free House.* ***Beer*** *Hook Norton Best, Wadworth 6X. Family room.* ***Accommodation*** *14 bedrooms, all en suite, £75 (single £50). Children welcome overnight (under-16s stay free in parents' room), additional bed & cot available. Amex, Diners, MasterCard,* ***VISA***

CHARMOUTH Fernhill Hotel £45

Tel & Fax 01297 560492 Map 13 E2 
Charmouth nr Lyme Regis Dorset DT6 6BX

Whether you stay in the hotel itself, or one of the self-catering bungalows (not really bungalows but blocks of rooms), Fernhill is suitable for budget B&B family holidays. Although the accommodation is extremely modest, the hotel's fourteen acres have excellent facilities for children – its own heated swimming pool, paddling pool, games room, crazy golf, fishing pond and an outdoor play area. There is even a launderette for when you are forced to remember what you came to get away from. The bungalows (bring your own towels) have at least a double bedroom and a separate twin-bunk room along with a galley kitchen, bathroom, child-listening and TV; these attract a tariff from £87.50-£250 according to size (from 2 to 6 persons) and time of year (minimum three days' stay). There's also a lively bar. ***Rooms*** *50 (35 bungalows, 15 hotel). Closed end October-March. MasterCard,* ***VISA***

CHATTON Percy Arms

Tel 01668 215244 Map 5 D1 
Chatton Alnwick Northumberland WE66 5PS

"A romantic retreat, situated in a favourite neighbourhood, several miles of free fishing water in the Till. Half an hour's walk from Chillingham Castle, Park and wild cattle. Well-aired beds. Good stabling". Posted prominently at the bar, the words of John Fitzgerald, proprietor at the turn of the century, ring equally true today. Stabling – for residents – is as good as ever with beds as well-aired: one wonders what the former landlord would have made of en suite WCs and showers, colour TVs and beverage trays, let alone the guests' private sauna and solarium. The sole village pub since 1874, today's black oak bar is many times bigger than that of yesteryear, with a children's games room to the rear and a tiny garden in front. *Open 11-3, 6-11 (Sun 12-3, 7-10.30). Free House.* ***Beer*** *Theakston XB, guest beer. Garden. Family room.* ***Accommodation*** *7 bedrooms, 5 en suite (showers), £40 (family room £50, single £20). Children welcome overnight (under-3s free and 4-12s £10 if sharing parents' room), additional bed & cot available. Accommodation closed 25 Dec. MasterCard,* ***VISA***

CHAWTON Cassandra's Cup

Tel 01420 83144 Map 15 D3 JaB
The Hollies Winchester Road Chawton nr Alton Hampshire GU34 1SB

This popular tea shop is directly opposite Jane Austen's house in a pretty village. Ena Goodman is well known for her home baking, with scones (60p) and gateaux (£1.85) to the fore. There are also hot savoury snacks: baked potatoes (from £2.50), some with elaborate fillings such as chicken with tarragon (£3.20); vegetarians have their own section of the menu, which includes spinach and mushroom lasagne with salad and macaroni cheese with salad (both £4.95). Breakfast (£3.60) is served till noon, cream tea (£2.75) all day. No smoking. One high-chair. Next to a park with swings. ***Seats*** *38 (+ 16 outside).* ***Open*** *10.30-4.30 (restricted opening in winter – phone to check). No credit cards.*

CHEAM Superfish

Tel 0181-643 6906 Map 15 E3 JaB
64 The Broadway Cheam Surrey SM3 8BD

Part of the excellent Surrey-based chain of traditional British fish and chip restaurants, the frying done the Yorkshire way, in beef dripping . See Morden entry for more details. This, the Cheam branch, is unlicensed. ***Seats*** *22.* ***Open*** *11.30-2 (Sat till 2.30) & 5-10.30 (Thu-Sat till 11).* ***Closed*** *Sun, 25, 26 Dec & 1 Jan. Amex, MasterCard,* ***VISA***

CHEDDAR Wishing Well Tea Rooms

Tel 01934 742142 Map 13 F1 JaB
The Cliffs Cheddar Somerset BS27 3QA

Operating for nearly 30 years, a mother-and-daughter team produce consistently good afternoon teas: plain tea (£2, children under 8 £1.25) with bread and butter, cake and tea; cream tea (£2.65, child £1.55). There is also a fruit tea, offering fresh fruit salad or peaches with clotted cream, bread, butter and jam (£2.80). The lunchtime menu (12-2) offers filled jacket potatoes (£3.30), salads – including home-cooked gammon (£4) – and omelettes (from £2.80) along with toasted snacks and freshly prepared sandwiches (from £1.10). Book for the Sunday roast lunch, three courses for £5.70, child £3.95). Unlicensed. Four high-chairs and booster seats provided; changing mat and shelf in Ladies. Children's portions. Close to the Cheddar Gorge caves. Fenced garden. ***Seats*** *66 (+ 10 outside).* ***Open*** *10-6.* ***Closed*** *Mon-Fri mid-Oct to mid-Mar, all Dec & Jan. MasterCard,* ***VISA***

CHESTER Chester Grosvenor 84% £205

Tel 01244 324024 **Fax 01244 313246** Map 6 A2 HR
Eastgate Chester Cheshire CH1 1LT

A really superb hotel, which in its present form has graced the city's main street since 1866. The interior decor is as graceful and elegant as you could wish, with sweeping staircases, the magnificent Grosvenor chandelier, panelled library and draped drawing room all providing an air of timelessness. Suites and bedrooms are equally luxurious, with attention to every possible detail. Hand-made furniture from Italy and silks and other fabrics from France and the USA combine with quality British craftsmanship to create a reassuring feeling of solidity. Children up to 14 share their parents' room free; stylish banqueting and conference facilities cater for up to 250 delegates; and there is direct access to the hotel from Newgate Street car park. 24hr room service. ***Rooms*** *86. Closed 25 & 26 Dec. Sauna, sun beds, gym, valeting. Amex, Diners, MasterCard,* ***VISA***

Arkle Restaurant £110

Named in honour of the triple Gold Cup-winning steeplechaser, this elegant, thoroughbred restaurant is deep in the heart of the hotel beyond the library lounge, where pre-prandial drinks are served, but with a skylight providing natural illumination. Paul Reed heads the kitchen brigade, producing high-quality dishes such as globe artichoke with a whipped mousseline of crab, roasted Scottish lobster and gazpacho, pot-roasted Bresse pigeon with savoy cabbage and thyme-scented juices, and loin of lamb with kidney, grilled seasonal vegetables and tarragon. Super desserts and a fine French/English cheeseboard. Perhaps the best bread trolley in the country generally carries about 14 different breads – all from the hotel's own bakery. The wine list is splendid indeed, but mostly at prices to make you weep! The Sommelier's Selection suggests that a 1990 Opus One from California's Napa Valley is value for money at £100 - we beg to differ and, incidentally, the 1991 vintage is £25 cheaper. Moreover, a Krug Rosé NV champagne priced last year at an elevated £175 is now a stratospheric £200. Is there really any justification for those price hikes? Polished, assured service. ***Seats*** *45. Parties 16. L 12-2.30 D 7-9.30. Closed D Sun, L Mon, Bank Holidays & 2 weeks from 25 Dec (except 31 Dec). Set L £22.50 Set D £35/£42.*

La Brasserie £50

French-styled with a polished wood floor, painted glass dome ceiling, leather banquette seating and black bentwood chairs, this is the informal arm of the hotel. It's open for breakfast, lunch and dinner or just a drink, and the main menu runs from the day's soup, crab and ginger risotto and penne with ham, leeks and parmesan to sea scallops and monkfish with saffron, chargrilled liver and bacon, and pork cutlet with braised red cabbage and sage. As may be expected, prices are much friendlier on the wine list than in the Arkle. Separate children's menu with the likes of soup, prawn cocktail, French bread pizza, sausage and mash, spaghetti bolognese, fish and chips, banana split and ice creams. Children are welcome at all times; changing can easily be managed in one of the hotel's cloakrooms and heating bottles and baby foods is all part of the service. A good supply of high-chairs. ***Seats*** *100. Meals 7am-10.30pm (Sun till 10). Closed 25 & 26 Dec.*

Chester Francs

Tel 01244 317952 Fax 01244 661422 Map 6 A2 JaB
14 Cuppin Street Chester Cheshire

Set on two floors of a converted warehouse, this cheerful, bustling brasserie has old timber beams, ceiling fans and French rock music. The menu, on a French provincial theme, changes monthly, featuring seasonal products – asparagus in May, wild mushrooms in autumn. Eating choice is wide and those wanting just one course or a more serious meal are equally welcome. Start perhaps with boudin blanc (£3.80), moules marinière (£3.85) or house paté, with pork dijonnaise (£6.95), steak and chips (£8.95) or a beef casserole (£8.70) to follow. Desserts include tarte tatin (£2.75), crème caramel (£1.95) and fresh fruit salad (£2.75). A two-course bargain set menu (£7.50) is offered between 6 and 7, and again after 10. Sundays are family days, when part of the first floor is given over to a play area for children; a three-course set menu (£8.45) is offered, with one child under 10 eating free for each accompanying adult. They also offer during the week a special children's menu at £2.50 which includes a soft drink, starter, main course and a dessert. Six high-chairs and changing facilities for nursing mums, with wipes and nappies provided. The restaurant now extends over three floors and there are small creche facilities on each floor. Booking almost essential. ***Seats*** *110.* ***Open*** *11-11.* ***Closed*** *D 25 Dec. Amex, MasterCard,* ***VISA***

Chester Mollington Banastre 67% £111

Tel 01244 851471 Fax 01244 851165 Map 6 A2 
Parkgate Road Chester Cheshire CH1 6NN

A mile and a half from the M56 (J16) stands an extended Victorian mansion surrounded by gardens. Comfortable overnight accommodation is allied to good leisure and conference facilities (up to 300 delegates) and ample free parking. One room is adapted for disabled guests. Children up to 16 can stay free in their parents' room. ***Rooms*** *64. Garden, croquet, indoor swimming pool, gym, squash, sauna, solarium, whirlpool bath, beauty salon, hairdressing, coffee shop (11am-11pm). Amex, Diners, MasterCard,* ***VISA***

CHESTER Rowton Hall 64% £88

Tel 01244 335262 **Fax 01244 335464** Map 6 A2 **H**

Whitchurch Road Rowton Chester Cheshire CH3 6AD

Built as a private residence in 1779, and since considerably extended, the hall stands three miles out of Chester on the A41 on the site of a Civil War battle. There's a spacious reception area and a lounge bar looking out on to the smart indoor pool. Rooms in the old house are stylish and individual, those in the adjoining wing more functional. Good amenities (Hamiltons Leisure Club) and conference facilities for up to 200 – also parking for 200 cars. ***Rooms*** *42. Garden, croquet, tennis, indoor swimming pool, mini-gym, sauna, steam room, spa bath, sun beds, squash, coffee shop (10am-10pm). Closed 25-27 Dec. Amex, Diners, MasterCard,* ***VISA***

CHESTER Ye Olde King's Head

Tel 01244 324855 **Fax 01244 315693** Map 6 A2 **P**

48/50 Lower Bridge Street Chester Cheshire CH1 1RS

A striking black and white timber-framed building just a stone's throw from the Roman walls and river, yet handy for high street shopping. Residents find evening refuge from popular all-day bars in a first-floor lounge bar and Hudson's restaurant. Second-floor bedrooms have recently been refurbished and house some remarkable features, the superb 16th-century roof trusses fortunately reinforced with forged steel pins. Dark hardwood fittings and co-ordinated fabrics stay in keeping, while comforts are plentiful with dial-out phones, TVs, tea trays and trouser presses: en suite bathrooms are necessarily small, but are neatly appointed. Premier Inn (Greenalls). *Open 12-11 (from 11 Sat, till 10.30 Sun).* ***Beer*** *Greenalls, guest beer. Family room.* ***Accommodation*** *8 bedrooms, all en suite, £51.40 (four-poster £59.90, single £41.50). Children welcome overnight (£5, under-5s free), additional bed & cot available. No dogs. Amex, Diners, MasterCard,* ***VISA***

CHICHESTER Comme Ca

Tel 01243 788724 **Fax 01243 530052** Map 11 A6 

67 Broyle Road Chichester West Sussex PO19 4BD

It's the bar – small, with green plush seating, swathes of dried flowers and log fire – of this popular French restaurant that is of particular interest for light meals. Although the menu is set out in courses there's no minimum charge or obligation to have more than a single dish. The starters are perfect as snacks with offerings such as fish soup (£4.25), pan-fried prawns and mussels with a saffron dressing (£5.25), goat's cheese in filo pastry with honey and almonds, with a tomato and mushroom sauce (£4.25) or pan-fried scallops with bacon, prawns and mushrooms on a bed of salad (£4.85). More substantial are the main-course dishes, which might include skate with capers in a meunière sauce (£8.75), grilled parrot fish with a tarragon sauce (£9.25) and grilled noisettes of lamb with garlic confit (£9.45). There's an excellent selection of salads too, accompanied by new potatoes (from £4.95 as a starter to £8.95 as a main). Open from 11 for coffee and biscuits. All dishes served are half-price for children under ten. Safe, enclosed garden. One high-chair. The restaurant stands north of town on the A286, convenient for the Festival Theatre. Smoking in the bar only. ***Seats*** *Restaurant 74 (+ 30 outside), Bar 20.* ***Open*** *12-2 & 6-11.* ***Closed*** *D Sun, all Mon & Bank Holidays. Amex, MasterCard,* ***VISA***

> **JaB** is short for 'Just a Bite'. The majority of these establishments are also recommended in our *Bistros, Bars & Cafés* Guide which features establishments where one may eat well for less than £15 per head.

CHICHESTER East Side Café

Tel 01243 783223 Map 11 A6 JaB
Eastgate Square Chichester West Sussex PO19 1ED

In a tiny arcade on the edge of the town's shopping area, this modest brasserie-style café offers a wide variety of eating throughout the day. Sandwiches (from £3.50 – with a good salad garnish) range from turkey, brie and cranberry to fresh Selsey crab with lemon mayonnaise and frankfurter, chili and cheese. There's always a vegetarian and a meat soup, for example carrot and coriander or chicken and leek (both £2.75 with fresh or garlic bread). For larger appetites there are hot dishes (all around £5) like penne with mascarpone, tomato and bacon, seafood crepes or fresh vegetable and ricotta strudel on a tomato coulis. Salads include Greek and bacon, brie, avocado and strawberry (both £4.95). Hot snacks include focaccia with anchovy tapénade, mozzarella and artichoke hearts (£4.95) and for the sweet-toothed there's pecan and butterscotch cheesecake and chocolate truffle torte (both £2.20). Breakfasts, both cooked (£3.75) and Continental (£2.75), are officially only available till 12.30 but, unless the place is very busy, will often be served later. One high-chair; children's portions, and children's meals on request. Space in the Ladies for baby-changing, and bottles or baby food can be heated. A few children's books can also be provided. All outdoor tables are under cover. ***Seats** 56 (+ 16 outside). **Open** 7.30-5. **Closed** Sun & Bank Holidays. No credit cards.*

CHICHESTER St Martin's Tea Room

Tel 01243 786715 Map 11 A6 JaB
3 St Martin's Street Chichester West Sussex

Keith Nelson and his chefs take great care to produce health-orientated foods at this charming, old-fashioned tea room with two pretty gardens for outdoor summer eating. With the exception of a few fish dishes, the food here is vegetarian and all the vegetables are organic; the blackboard announces the soup special, dish of the day, and the regular dishes; a typical menu could include leek, carrot and potato soup (£2.80), smoked wild salmon (£4.90), spinach and mushroom lasagne (£3.90), open egg and salmon sandwich (£3.30), mackerel and coley pie with salad (£3.95) and Welsh rarebit and salads (£4.20). Sultana scones (£1.20), bread and cakes (from £1.50) are all home-baked, as are flapjacks, apricot slice, banana and lemon or carrot cake. Fresh orange juice. Loose-leaf teas. No smoking except in garden. Classical pianist some Saturday afternoons. Park in St Martin's car park opposite. ***Seats** 100. **Open** 9-6. **Closed** Sun. No credit cards.*

CHICHESTER Salad House

Tel 01243 788822 Map 11 A6 JaB
14 Southgate Chichester West Sussex PO19 1ES

Fresh flowers are always liberally used in the decor of this otherwise plain and unfussy self-service vegetarian restaurant where the emphasis is very firmly on the freshness of the food on offer. Alison Ellis, the owner, insists that nothing is bought in and that everything is home-made in the true sense of the word. The day could begin with the Old English Breakfast (£2.95) and end with a cream tea (£3.30) but the choice at lunchtime is varied, offering the likes of cheese paté on toast or avocado and prawn platter as light snacks, as well as more substantial dishes like mushroom, spinach and pasta bake, eggs provençale, chestnut casserole on brown rice or macaroni cheese (all £2.95) and a choice of seven different salads (£1.90-£2.50) worthy of the distinction in the establishment's name. On Fridays there's a fish dish such as fish melody – a mix of fresh and smoked fish with prawns on a bed of rice – or poached salmon with new potatoes and salad (both £5.75). Fresh baking will bring bread, scones, lemon meringue pie or treacle tart, blackcurrant cheesecake and pavlova (45p-£1.10). Children's portions. No smoking downstairs. Orchard Tea Rooms at 47 North Street is in the same ownership. ***Seats** 48. **Open** 8-5.30. **Closed** Sun, Bank Holidays. No credit cards.*

CHICHESTER Shepherds Tea Rooms

Tel 01243 774761 Map 11 A6 JaB
35 Little London Chichester West Sussex PO19 1PL

Richard and Yvonne Spence opened their lace-clothed tea room, just off the main shopping street, to provide "a haven of peace and tranquillity". Today you may have to queue at busy times to enjoy their excellent sandwiches – chicken salad with mayonnaise (£3.75), or open sandwiches served with a salad (£5.25) and savoury snacks like filled jacket potatoes (from £4.25) and various rarebits (a speciality of the house, and priced between £4.75 and £5.25) including Hawaiian (with pineapple), Stilton and tomato, buck (with poached egg) and shepherd's (with brie and tomato) as well as the traditional Welsh rarebit, all with salad and chutney. An all-day breakfast is popular (£4.75). There are also excellent tea cakes, croissants, muffins and crumpets to accompany the fine selection of loose-leaf teas that include gunpowder, Lapsang Souchong, fruit teas and their own English Breakfast Tea blend – a mixture of Assam, Ceylon and African. No smoking. ***Seats** 55. **Open** 9.15-5 (Sat from 8). **Closed** Sun & Bank Holidays. No credit cards.*

CHICKSGROVE Compasses Inn

Tel & Fax 01722 714318 Map 14 C3 JaB
Chicksgrove Tisbury Salisbury Wiltshire SP3 6NB

A timeless air pervades this attractive, 16th-century thatched inn, set on a peaceful lane, deep in rolling Wiltshire countryside. An old cobbled path leads to the entrance of the charmingly unspoilt bar, which has a low-beamed ceiling, partly flagstoned floor and an assortment of traditional furniture arranged in many secluded alcoves. Various farming tools and tackle from bygone days adorn the bare walls and a 100-year-old set of table skittles maintain the old-world atmosphere. Sarah Lethbridge produces a short, regularly-changing blackboard list of home-cooked dishes which may highlight cream of carrot and leek soup and avocado and crispy bacon salad for a starter or snack. More substantial offerings may include steak and Guinness pie, breast of chicken with stem ginger, medallions of pork with paprika and cream and chargrilled steak with garlic butter, all served with crisp vegetables. A separate board lists the lunchtime sandwiches and ploughman's platters. A small adjoining dining/children's room leads out to a sheltered rear garden with rural views – ideal (as is the front brolly- and bench-filled lawn) for a peaceful summer alfresco pint. Reached via a covered outside staircase are three homely, simply furnished bedrooms, one tucked beneath the heavy thatch. Two have en suite shower rooms, the third having its own private facilities across the communal lounge, which has easy chairs, tea-making equipment, TV and bookcases. A peaceful, rural base from which to explore this beautiful area. *Open 11-3, 6.30-11 (Sun 12-3, 7-10.30). Closed Mon (except Bank Holidays, then closed following Tue). **Bar Food** 12-2, 7-9 (till 9.30 Fri & Sat). Free House. **Beer** Tisbury Old Wardour, Bass, Wadworth 6X, Adnams Southwold. Garden, children's play area. Family room. **Accommodation** 3 bedrooms, 2 en suite, £45 (single £25). Children welcome overnight (under-2s stay free in parents' room), additional bed (£10) available. Check-in by arrangement. No dogs. MasterCard, **VISA***

CHILHAM Woolpack

Tel 01227 730208 **Fax 01227 731053** Map 11 C5 P
The Street Chilham Kent CT4 8DL

Dating from 1420, this pretty salmon pink-painted inn lies within 100 yards of Chilham's charming square and castle. A historic place with a refurbished olde-worlde bar, an attractive dining-room and thirteen en suite bedrooms. A new landlord since last years guide has redecorated and upgraded most of bedrooms which vary in size and location, the sole main building bedroom and one of the three wool store rooms boasting fine four-poster beds. Good overnight accommodation for families, one of the decent-sized family rooms having access to a sheltered garden with seating. All have clean bath or shower rooms and TVs, tea-makers, telephones and clock-radios for added comfort. The suite has three separate rooms: a double, single and twin plus a bathroom; priced up to £110 for 6 adults. *Open 11-11 (Sun 12-3, 5-10.30). **Beer** Shepherd Neame. Garden, courtyard. **Accommodation** 13 bedrooms, all en suite, £49.50 (family room with garden £65-£85, four-poster £65, suite from £85, single £38.50). Children welcome overnight, additional cot available. Amex, MasterCard, **VISA***

CHILLINGTON Chillington Inn

Tel 01548 580244 Map 13 D3
Chillington Kingsbridge Devon TQ7 2JS

The front door of this white-painted 16th-century inn opens directly on to the main road through the village, with no pavement in between, so take care when leaving after a convivial evening. Inside, the unpretentiously snug bar has some unusual carved oak wall benches and tables, a warming open fire and two blackboards listing the monthly-changing selection of bar food. The highlight of the menu is the splendid range of up to nine home-made soups (mushroom and hazelnut, broccoli and Stilton), which are a lunchtime favourite. Other good-value and hearty home-prepared snacks include French bread sandwiches, ploughman's lunches, curries, grilled sardines, spicy crab parcels and local scallops. For more substantial meals the small attractive restaurant, boasting a fine stone fireplace, provides a short hand-written menu listing interesting dishes like roast duck with cranberry and orange sauce, herb-crusted rack of lamb with damson sauce, good steaks from a local butcher and popular fresh fish (brill with tarragon and prawns, monkfish kebabs). Home-made puddings – bread-and-butter pudding and and sticky toffee pudding – come with thick clotted cream. Two charming bedrooms have matching wallpaper and fabrics and a clean, good-sized bathroom across the corridor. A stable-block conversion houses a family suite which is available (by prior arrangement) for daily B&B or weekly lets. No immediate off-street parking for residents, but you can park right outside on the road or 50 yards away. *Open 12-2 (till 3 Sat), 6-11 (Sun 12-3, 7-10.30).* ***Bar Food*** *12-2 (till 2.30 Sat) & 7-10. Free House.* ***Beer*** *Bass, Palmers IPA, occasional guest beer. Small garden, outdoor eating.* ***Accommodation*** *2 bedrooms, £39 (single £23.50). Children welcome overnight, additional bed (£10) and cot (£5) available, family suite by arrangement. Check-in by arrangement. Diners, MasterCard,* ***VISA***

CHOBHAM Blubeckers

See entries under Odiham and Shepperton

CHORLEYWOOD Sportsman Hotel

Tel 01923 285155 **Fax 01923 285159** Map 15 E2
Station Approach Chorleywood Hertfordshire WD3 5NB

The Sportsman was built on a hillside across the road from the underground station and dates from the late 19th century. Popular with visiting businessmen during the week, the 18 bedrooms are a bit of a mix, but all are generally comfortable with modern darkwood furniture (some have modern pine) and brass light fittings; all are well equipped with TV, direct-dial telephones, radio-alarms, tea-making kits and trouser presses. En suite bath/shower rooms are fully tiled. Light attractive decor extends to the public areas and the Garden Bar with its airy, plant-filled conservatory overlooking the spacious garden, terrace and children's play area. The hotel has a children's certificate. *Open 11-11 (Sun 12-10.30).* ***Beer*** *no real ale. Garden, children's play area. Family room.* ***Accommodation*** *18 bedrooms, all en suite, £67.50 (single £57.50). Children welcome overnight, additional bed & cot (both £15) available. Amex, Diners, MasterCard,* ***VISA***

CHURCH STRETTON Acorn Restaurant

Tel & Fax 01694 722495 Map 6 A4

26 Sandford Avenue Church Stretton Shropshire SY6 6BW

The front door to this first-floor wholefood restaurant is down a tree- and plant-lined passage just off the town's main square. Soup and garlic bread (£2), quiches (onion £1.55), pitta sandwiches (£1.60) and scone-based pizzas (cheese, tomato and herb £1.90) are regulars on the menu, and there's always a vegetarian dish (vegetables in a peanut butter sauce £4) and fish/meat dish of the day (Normandy beef £4.25). A selection of 30 teas is available and several home-made puddings (ice creams, crumbles, rice pudding) and cakes (cider and nut, carrot and cinnamon, tea bread, bread pudding, apple strudel). On fine days, the garden is open. Unlicensed (BYO, corkage 99p). No smoking. ***Seats*** *44 (+ 24 outside).* ***Open*** *10-6 (winter 9.30-5.30).* ***Closed*** *Tue & Wed (except during school summer holidays), 2 weeks Feb & 2 weeks Nov. No credit cards.*

CIRENCESTER Brewery Arts Coffee House

Tel 01285 654791 **Fax 01285 644060** Map 14 C2 JaB
Brewery Court Cirencester Gloucestershire GL7 1JH

Pictures adorn the exposed Cotswold-stone walls of an attractive coffee shop specialising in home baking, and wholefood and vegetarian food. Staff serve at the counter, where cold dishes prevail in summer and hot meals are available in winter. Start with soup – maybe carrot and leek, parsnip and apple or tomato, orange and ginger (£2.05 including bread). Home-baked ham is a firm favourite (£3.65 with a mixed salad) and other lunchtime savouries might include rice and mushrooms in a Stilton sauce or Somerset chicken, patés, quiches and filled jacket potatoes. The cake menu is particularly enticing: spiced apple and yoghurt cake; marmalade and ginger cake; sticky fig and almond slice; rosewater, currant and coconut cake (80p). Good choice of teas. One high-chair; children's portions and toys are set aside in the craft shop for children to play with. Museum, leisure centre and waterparks nearby. No smoking. ***Seats** 49. **Open** 10-5. **Closed** Sun, 24, 25 & 26 Dec, 1 Jan. No credit cards.*

CIRENCESTER Stratton House 64% £85

Tel 01285 651761 **Fax 01285 640024** Map 14 C2 H
Gloucester Road Cirencester Gloucestershire GL7 2LE

On the A417 to the north of town this former wool merchant's house dates back to the 17th century. The period feel has been retained in public areas like the flagstoned entrance hall, the beamed bar with real log fire and leather chairs and the comfortable lounge overlooking a walled garden. Pretty bedrooms are individually decorated, those in the original building often retaining original fireplaces. Good bathrooms. Limited room service. Children under 14 are accommodated free of charge when sharing with two adults. ***Rooms** 41. Garden, croquet. Amex, Diners, MasterCard, **VISA***

CLARE Peppermill Restaurant

Tel 01787 278148 Map 10 C3 JaB
Market Square Clare Suffolk CO10 8NH

This unpretentious little restaurant is housed in a charming 15th-century cottage, and offers lots of choice, from omelettes (from £2.75) to stroganoff (£9.95) or one of the daily specials such as liver and bacon parcels with onion, cranberry and wine gravy (£6.95) for lunch. Afternoon tea is popular and includes scones, cakes and sandwiches. Children's portions available. One high-chair is provided but it's a small place and little folk are welcome only if on their very best behaviour. Country park, riverside walks and play area close-by. No smoking. ***Seats** 20. **Open** 11.30-2.30 (Sat 11-4, Sun 12-5). **Closed** Wed, also 2 or 3 days after Bank Holidays. No credit cards.*

CLAVERING Cricketers

Tel 01799 550442 **Fax 01799 550882** Map 10 B3 P
Clavering Saffron Walden Essex CB11 4QT

Comfortable 16th-century dining pub located 200 yards from the cricket green with a good local reputation for well-prepared home-made food. The main restaurant menu (also available in the bar) is changed every two months and is supplemented by chalk-board specials and regular theme nights – Tuesday highlights fish and Wednesday is 'Pudding Night' – steak and kidney, Yorkshire and sweet steamed puds – all, of course, home-made. Good starters/snacks to choose from may include home-cured gravad lax with dill and yoghurt, prawn and courgette provençale, coarse pork and chicken liver paté with Cumberland sauce, and filo parcels of duck with sweet and sour sauce, followed by rack of lamb with Madeira and rosemary sauce, chargrilled sirloin of beef with brandy and peppercorn sauce or fresh tuna steak with basil beurre blanc. Up to a dozen desserts are offered daily – try the treacle tart or lemon meringue pie. The restaurant offers a 3-course Sunday lunch with choice of 10 starters and main courses for £16.50. Well-appointed overnight accommodation is offered in the house next door, where six individually decorated en suite bedrooms are equipped to a high standard with added comforts like TVs, direct-dial phones, tea-makers, radio-alarms and a thoughtful extras like a decanter of sherry and a tray of petit fours on arrival. Ten minutes from Stansted Airport. *Open 12-2, 7-11 (Sun 12-3, 7-10.30).* ***Bar Food*** *12-2 (till 2.30 Sun), 7-10 (till 9.30 Sun). Free House.* ***Beer*** *Flowers IPA & Original, Wethered Bitter, Boddingtons. Terrace, outdoor eating. Family room.* ***Accommodation*** *6 bedrooms, all en suite £60 (single £50). Children welcome overnight, additional bed (£10) & cot available. No dogs. Amex, MasterCard,* ***VISA***

CLAWTON Court Barn 64% £66

Tel 01409 271219 **Fax 01409 271309** Map 12 C2 **H**
Clawton Holsworthy Devon EX22 6PS

This small country house has 17th-century origins but was significantly rebuilt in Victorian times. Today it is a homely hotel run in friendly fashion by Robert and Susan Wood. The two domestic-scale lounges are comfortable and homely with fresh flowers, magazines and all sorts of knick-knacks. One is the TV lounge and it and the small bar are the only places in the hotel (accommodation included) where smoking is allowed. The bedrooms, which are all non smoking, have a variety of furniture from antiques (particularly in the larger rooms) to hotel-style units. All have pleasant decorative schemes and nice touches like fresh flowers along with the usual amenities like beverage tray (although there is light room service throughout the day and evening), TV and telephone. Bathrooms (two with shower and WC only) are all in good order and beds are turned down in the evening. Two rooms are suitable for family use, and children up to 14 stay free in parents' room; cots and high-chairs are available. The house is set in five acres of gardens beyond which can be seen the village church. It's also just the place for a traditional afternoon tea (£2-£5). Sit in the comfortable lounge, or out on the patio when it's fine, and enjoy Susan's scones, featherlight meringues and delicious cakes (marsala and almond, honey, cherry and almond, date and walnut, coffee, chocolate). A tea specially blended to suit the local water is one of the many listed. Morning coffee is served from 10am, bar snacks throughout the day in the old dining-room and bar lunches from 12 to 2 – home-made soups, maybe orange and leek or spicy parsnip (£2) and patés (£2.75), salads, curried nut roast (£4.95), chicken and Stilton roulade (£7.95), fresh local trout (£7), and home-made desserts (£3). There's a three-course lunch (£11.95 Mon-Sat) and traditional four-course Sunday lunch. More elaborate evening meals. No smoking. ***Rooms*** *8. Garden, croquet, badminton, tennis (lawn), pitch & putt, putting. Closed 1 week early Jan. Amex, Diners, MasterCard,* ***VISA***

CLEARWELL Wyndham Arms £65

Tel 01594 833666 **Fax 01594 836450** Map 14 B2
Clearwell Coleford Gloucestershire GL16 8JT

The Stanford family, here since 1973, are the imperturable hosts of the tranquil 600 year-old Wyndham Arms. Traditional hand-pulled real ales, 17 wines served by the glass and a notable malt whisky collection are indicators of the public bar's civilised style, to which the menu is entirely apposite. A lunch still favoured by many is the 18-dish hors d'oeuvre trolley, the daily special might be hot seafood platter or guinea fowl Montmorency, while main bar menu choices include Stilton stuffed pears with orange sauce and home-made soup (cream of asparagus). Accommodation is divided between original bedrooms in the evocative main building and a stone extension where room sizes, decor and comforts are altogether more modern. There's plenty of space for young children (cots, high-chairs and baby-listening are all readily available), and the less mobile appreciate use of 6 ground-floor bedrooms with easy ramps into the pub. Early evening turn-down and dawn shoe-cleaning patrol aren't found in every pub: along with a hearty breakfast, it's all part, here, of the Wyndham service. Secure car-parking. *Open 11-11 (Sun 12-10.30).* ***Bar Food*** *12-2, 7-9.30. Free House.* ***Beer*** *Flowers Best, Boddingtons, Bass. Garden, patio, outdoor eating.* ***Accommodation*** *17 bedrooms, all en suite, £65 (single £49.50). Children welcome overnight (stay free if sharing parents' room), additional bed & cot available. Amex, Diners, MasterCard,* ***VISA***

CLEY-NEXT-THE-SEA George & Dragon

Tel 01263 740652 **Fax 01263 741275** Map 10 C1 **P**
High Street Cley-next-the-Sea Holt Norfolk NR25 7RN

Standing head and shoulders above its neighbouring whitewashed cottage, this striking brick inn was rebuilt in 1897 in Edwardian style and enjoys an enviable position close to Cley's fine windmill overlooking an expanse of unspoilt salt marsh. For decades the inn has been a popular base for visiting naturalists, walkers and holidaymakers, and the good pubby bars have witnessed the forming of the Norfolk Naturalists Trust in 1926 and today daily bird observations are recorded in the "bird bible" – a large volume placed on a lectern in the main bar. Upstairs, most of the homely, simply furnished bedrooms, including the four-poster room, have far-reaching salt marsh views and six have clean, adequate en suite facilities. TVs and tea-makers are standard. The residents lounge is the internal hide, complete with scrape-facing window and a pair of binoculars. Good-sized garden across the lane with pétanque pitch. Being a well-visited coastal village, families are very welcome and well catered for if staying overnight. Good-sized family rooms, extra beds and cots, early evening meals from 6pm, and young diners have their own menu and use of a high-chair. However, children must be carefully supervised in the garden. Summer afternoon cream teas. *Open 11-2.30, 6.30-11 (from 6 Sat, 11-11 in high summer), Sun 12-3, 7-10.30. Free House.* ***Beer*** *Greene King IPA, Abbot Ale & Rayments Bitter. Garden.* ***Accommodation*** *8 bedrooms, 6 en suite, £40-£50 (four-poster £65, family room sleeping four £55-£75, single £30). Children welcome overnight (babies free), additional bed & cot available. Check-in by arrangement. Accommodation closed 25, 26 & 31 Dec. No credit cards.*

> Any person using our name to obtain free hospitality is a fraud.
> Proprietors, please inform the police and us.

COATHAM MUNDEVILLE Hall Garth 66% £91

Tel 01325 300400 **Fax 01325 310083** Map 5 E3 **HR**
Coatham Mundeville nr Darlington Co Durham DL1 3LU

A 16th-century house with 18th- and 19th-century wings, situated just off the A167 within two minutes of the A1(M). Day rooms include three most civilised country house-style lounges warmed by real fires in winter while for a change of mood there's the separate Stables Bar with a more lively, pubby atmosphere. Best of the bedrooms are perhaps those furnished with antiques in the original building; the majority have darkwood freestanding pieces and co-ordinating fabrics while those in the annexe above the bar feature solid lightwood furniture. ***Rooms*** *41. Garden, tennis, golf (9), putting green, indoor swimming pool, sauna, steam room, spa bath, solarium, children's outdoor playground. Closed night of 25 Dec. Amex, Diners, MasterCard,* ***VISA***

Hugo's £60

Choose between the dark-red dining-room or conservatory extension to enjoy generally soundly cooked dishes from fixed-price and à la carte menus that offer a good choice. Mussel, onion and cider stew, salad of pigeon with blackcurrant vinaigrette, turbot with wild mushrooms and a red wine butter sauce, and roast lamb rump on a gratin of grilled vegetables illustrate the range. Shorter lunch menu, and informal lunches and suppers in the Stables Bar. ***Seats*** *80. Parties 12. Private Room 20. L 12-2 D 7-9.30. Closed L Sat, D Sun & D 25 Dec. Set L £11.95 Set D £15.95/£19.95 (Fri £10.95).*

> Pubs – note that food is only recommended in those pubs with ***Bar Food*** times in the statistics at the end of an entry. Restaurant food in pubs is *never* recommended unless specifically mentioned. Some pubs are recommended for B&B or Atmosphere only – each entry's statistics indicate our recommendation.

Coggeshall White Hart 69% £97

Tel 01376 561654 **Fax 01376 561789** Map 10 C3

Market End Coggeshall Essex CO6 1NH

A centuries-old inn that still retains all its character with flagstone floors, low beams, inglenook fireplace and not one but two resident ghosts. One bay of the original (1420) Guildhall is now the residents' lounge, whose decor adds style and comfort to the atmospheric surroundings. Individually decorated bedrooms, 12 in an extension, offer little extras like fresh fruit and mineral water. ***Rooms*** *18. Garden. Amex, MasterCard,* ***VISA***

Restaurant £60

A long, low and narrow dining-room with sturdy beams and cheerful staff. The main menu is Italian, running from antipasti and home-made pasta to risotti, *fritto misto di mare*, *pollo marengo*, *piccata di vitello al limone* and T-bone steaks. Traditional Sunday lunch and a good selection of desserts. ***Seats*** *70. Private Room 20. L 12-2 D 7-10. Closed D Sun, all 25 & 26 Dec. Set Sun L & Set D £14.95.*

Colchester Butterfly Hotel 61% £67

Tel 01206 230900 **Fax 01206 231095** Map 10 C3

Old Ipswich Road Ardleigh Colchester Essex CO7 7QY

Part of a small chain offering practical accommodation (there is separate work space in all the bedrooms) that includes four rooms specially equipped for ladies (door-chains, spy-holes) and 14 reserved for non-smokers. Located on the A12/A120 near the Business Parks. Others in the group are in Bury St Edmunds, King's Lynn and Peterborough. ***Rooms*** *50. Amex, Diners, MasterCard,* ***VISA***

Colchester Poppy's Tea Room

Tel 01206 765805 Map 10 C3 JaB

17 Trinity Street Colchester Essex CO1 1JN

Tucked away in the narrow old streets close to the shopping precinct is Mrs Sexton's tea shop/café. The bright little rooms make a charming setting for relaxing with a drink and a snack – maybe a coffee and walnut cake – from the enticing display. Sandwiches (from £1.90), jacket potatoes (plain £1.45, cream cheese and chives (£1.90) and liver, onion and bacon (£2.55) are among savoury favourites, along with paté (£2.15), quiche (£2.10) and salads. Daily specials might be spaghetti bolognese (£3.25) or cauliflower cheese in winter months; avocado salad in warmer weather. Teas, scones and home-made cakes are served all day and meringues (a house speciality) come in five different flavours. No smoking. ***Seats*** *33.* ***Open*** *9.30-5 (Fri & Sat till 5.30).* ***Closed*** *Sun, 25, 26 Dec & some other Bank Holidays.* ***VISA***

Colchester Rose & Crown Hotel

Tel 01206 866677 **Fax 01206 866616** Map 10 C3 I

East Street Colchester Essex CO1 2TZ

Magnificent ancient black-and-white timbered inn that has stood on the corner of the old Ipswich and Harwich roads since the 15th century. Once an old posting house, it is now a well-appointed inn having been carefully extended and refurbished over the past few years. A pubby bar attracts a busy local trade and is full of character with open fires, heavy beams and antique, cushioned pews and settles. Old-world charm extends upstairs into the main-building bedrooms – three of which boast sturdy four-poster beds – with leaded windows, wall timbers and uneven floors. Newer extension bedrooms are uniform in size, decor and furnishings, all being very comfortable and well equipped with older-style darkwood furniture and quality co-ordinating fabrics. Fully-tiled bathrooms have overhead showers. Full complement of added comforts from remote-controlled TVs (with satellite channels) to trouser presses. *Open 12-2.30, 6-11 (Sun 12-3, 7-10.30). Free House.* ***Beer*** *Tetley Bitter.* ***Accommodation*** *30 bedrooms, all en suite, £58-£119 (single £58). Children welcome overnight (under-12s stay free in parents' room), additional bed & cot available. No dogs. Closed 27-29 Dec. Amex, Diners, MasterCard,* ***VISA***

CONGRESBURY White Hart

Tel 01934 833303 Map 13 F1 

Wrington Road Congresbury North Somerset BS19 5AR

Combined quaint village pub and dining venue hidden down a long lane off the A370 (follow the Wrington Road). A conventional line in snacks and salads is supplemented by some more promising home-cooked fare: crab parcels, chicken korma, lasagne, chicken and mushroom pie and tuna pasta bake served with a choice of potatoes and vegetables or salad. An increasing attraction is Sunday lunch, especially with families, who have use of a neat conservatory looking across the large pub garden and away towards the Mendips; no children are allowed in the bars. With plastic bottles of pop from the bar youngsters can amuse themselves in full view on the play equipment. There's also an aviary by the terrace. *Open 11-2.30, 6-11 (Sun 12-3, 7-10.30).* ***Bar Food*** *12-2, 6-9.30 (from 7 Sun).* ***Beer*** *Hall & Woodhouse. Garden, patio, children's play area. Family room. MasterCard,* ***VISA***

CONISTON Bridge House Café

Tel 01539 441278 Map 4 C3 JaB

Coniston Cumbria LA21 8HJ

Cheerful cottagey café on two floors, with flowered tablecloths, pictures for sale and old beams. Home-made baking includes toffee shortbread, fruit cakes, crumbles, scones, slices (almond or coconut), flapjacks and gingerbread (from 65p). A small selection of savoury snacks offers jacket potatoes (from £2), soup (£1.60 – maybe pea and ham, curried parsnip, carrot and orange), salads (£3.50), sandwiches (£1.60) and pizzas (from £3) with a choice of toppings including garlic sausage, peperoni and vegetarian. Full cooked breakfast is also served (£3.50). On summer evenings a supper menu is offered, with maybe prawn cocktail (£2.25), egg mayonnaise (£1.75) or breaded mushrooms with a cucumber and garlic dip (£2) to begin; whole breaded plaice (£4.75), chicken Kiev (£4.95) or quiche to follow – all served with vegetables or salad. Children have their own three-course meal for £2.50. Alfresco eating on the pavement or in the courtyard overlooking the village. Bed and breakfast accommodation is available. ***Seats*** *50 (+ 20 outside).* ***Open*** *10-5 (Jul & Aug also 6-10pm).* ***Closed*** *25, 26 Dec & 1 Jan. No credit cards.*

CONISTON COLD Coniston Hall Tea Room

Tel 01756 748136 **Fax 01756 749551** Map 6 B1 

Coniston Cold nr Skipton North Yorkshire BD23 4ED

Set in the beautiful Dales National Park, this family-friendly café/restaurant is on a privately-owned 1200-acre estate (by the A65) which includes a 24-acre lake and a large stretch of the River Aire. From its own trout farm and smokehouse comes much of the produce sold in the estate farm shop, while prodigious volumes of goodies whet appetites in the Tea Room. An all-day menu offers tea and coffee, scone and butter (85p), scrambled egg on toast (£2.95) and a wide variety of sandwiches (from £2.95). More substantial dishes are introduced and noon, and available for the rest of the day: jacket potatoes with various fillings (from £3.50), ploughman's lunch (£4.95), and blackboard specials such as smoked trout paté (£3.50), steak and kidney pie (£5.95) and a splendid venison, port and cranberry pie (£6.65). Fruit crumbles, pies, ice creams and tarts (all £2.25). Cream tea £2.75. Booking advised at weekends. Traditional roast on Sundays (£6.95 for one course). An outdoor play area has swings, slide and climbing frame. ***Seats*** *96 (+ 20 outside).* ***Open*** *10-6. MasterCard,* ***VISA***

We endeavour to be as up-to-date as possible, but inevitably some changes to data and key personnel may occur at restaurants and hotels after the Guide goes to press. Prices should also be taken as indications rather than firm quotes.

Constantine Trengilly Wartha Inn

Tel & Fax 01326 340332 Map 12 B4 P
Nancenoy Constantine Helston Cornwall TR11 5RP

One mile due south of Constantine down country lanes, the Inn sits in a beautiful wooded valley looking down towards Polpenwith Creek on the Helford River. The unpretentious main bar is happily unmodernised with games machines and pool table relegated to a separate room and another tapestry upholstered 'lounge' area where families are welcome; there's a small children's section on the menu too. For summer there are tables on the vine-covered patio and in the garden beyond. A further alfresco area is around a lake in the valley bottom. There is a long list of 'Trengilly Classics' (smoked chicken strudel, and cassoulet) on the bar food menu but the most interesting options appear on the blackboard. This features fresh fish from Newlyn like baked cod with chive cream sauce, monkfish in a piquant tomato sauce and Thai fish soup; in addition there might be rabbit pie, tagliatelle with avocado and smoked trout and homely puddings. Lighter bites include crab open sandwiches and ploughman's lunches. The separate restaurant offers a two- or three-course dinner. Good range of wines by the glass selected from a list of 160, regularly-changing real ales and three strong scrumpy ciders. Six cosy bedrooms are light and pretty with good, modern carpeted bathrooms and up-to-date conveniences such as remote-control TV and direct-dial telephones. Well maintained and comfortable accommodation. *Open 11-3 (till 2.30 winter), 6-11 (Sun 12-3, 7-10.30).* ***Bar Food** 12-2.15 (till 2 Sun), 6.30-9.30 (from 7.15 Sun). Free House. **Beer** Sharp's Cornish Coaster, Furgusons Dartmoor Best, St Austell HSD, two guest beers. Garden, outdoor eating. Family room. **Accommodation** 6 bedrooms, 5 en suite, £60 (single £40). Children welcome overnight, additional bed (£8) & cot (£2) provided in one larger room. Amex, Diners, MasterCard,* ***VISA***

Constantine Bay Treglos Hotel 65% £103

Tel 01841 520727 **Fax 01841 521163** Map 12 B3 H
Constantine Bay St Merryn Padstow Cornwall PL28 8JH

In the same ownership since 1965, this is a friendly, well-run hotel just five minutes from the sea, overlooking Constantine Bay and Trevose Golf Course, where concessionary rates are available to residents. It's a popular place with many regular guests, so balcony rooms are booked well in advance. All the public rooms except the bar have sea views; the three comfortable and traditional lounges are bright and airy. Bedrooms have simple white laminate units, large windows and compact bathrooms. In the hotel jackets and ties are requested after 7pm. ***Rooms** 44. Garden, croquet, indoor swimming pool, spa bath, games room, playroom, snooker, lock-up garages (£1.50 a day). Closed early Nov-early Mar. MasterCard,* ***VISA***

Cooden Jarvis Cooden Beach Hotel 60% £102

Tel 01424 842281 **Fax 01424 846142** Map 11 B6 H
Cooden Beach Bexhill-on-Sea East Sussex TN39 4TT

Leisure and business visitors are equally welcome at this half-timbered 30s' hotel, which looks across Pevensey Bay from its setting right on the beach. There are facilities for up to 160 conference delegates, a health and leisure club, a modern lounge, a cocktail bar and the Sovereign Tavern serving real ale. One of the bedrooms has been adapted for disabled guests; 12 are suitable for family use. Under-16s share parents' room free. ***Rooms** 41. Garden, croquet, indoor & outdoor swimming pools, keep-fit equipment, sauna, spa bath, sun beds, beauty salon. Amex, Diners, MasterCard,* ***VISA***

JaB is short for 'Just a Bite'. The majority of these establishments are also recommended in our *Bistros, Bars & Cafés* Guide which features establishments where one may eat well for less than £15 per head.

Cookham Dean Inn on the Green

Tel 01628 482638 **Fax 01628 487474** Map 15 E2 P
The Green Cookham Dean Marlow Berkshire SL6 9NZ

Tucked away in one corner of the large village green, this interesting pub has four dining areas but only a small bar. Two small drinking rooms (with just seven tables) lead through to a Swiss chalet-style dining-room, off which the high-ceilinged Lamp Room restaurant and a small conservatory lead. The bar menu (and daily blackboard specials) might offer reliable snacks like home-made soup (white onion, vegetable), various open sandwiches, home-cured bresaola with balsamic vinegar and olives, grilled sardines and home-made burgers. From a more adventurous dining-room menu (also available in the bar) start with seafood sausage or Caesar salad and move on to venison with juniper, sea bass pan-fried in fennel and Pernod or corn-fed chicken with aubergine and pesto noodles. Finish off with strawberry and mascarpone tart or summer pudding. Outside, there's a large walled courtyard barbecue area (lit by wall lights and heated by tall gas burners, Apr-Oct) and an acre of paddock behind the car park. It's a wonderful summer pub for families with youngsters: the rear grassed area features picnic tables, a tree house, a chalet-style 'Nut House', double slide, climbing frame and rubber tyre swings. Overnight accommodation now comprises six cottagey pine-furnished bedrooms (£60 double, £40 single) – not yet inspected. *Open 12-3, 6-11 (Sun 12-3, 7-10.30).* ***Bar Food*** *12-2, (till 2.30 Sun), 7-10. Free House.* ***Beer*** *Brakspear Bitter, Boddingtons, Fuller's London Pride, guest beer. Garden, terrace, outdoor eating, children's play area. Amex, MasterCard,* **VISA**

Cookham Dean Jolly Farmer

Tel 01628 482905 Map 15 E2 P
Cookham Dean Marlow Berkshire SL6 9PD

Homely and traditional village pub located opposite the parish church and close to the vast village green. Two simply furnished interconnecting bars with open fires, and a separate small and cosy dining-room in which to enjoy wholesome, home-cooked pub food. Blackboard choices may range from Stilton and cider soup and warm goat's cheese on beef tomato salad to ham, egg and chips, chicken and mushroom stroganoff, poached salmon in white wine and dill sauce, and calf's liver, bacon and onions. Sandwiches and ploughman's at lunchtime only. Apple pie and crème brulée are typical pudding options. Good summer garden with children's play area. Well-behaved children only inside. *Open 11.30-3, 5.30-11 (from 6 Sat), Sun 12-3, 7-10.30.* ***Bar Food*** *12-2.30, 7.30-9.30, (no food Mon eve). Free House.* ***Beer*** *Courage Best, two guest beers. Garden, outdoor eating, children's play area. Closed 25 & 26 Dec eve. MasterCard,* **VISA**

Corfe Castle Corfe Castle Restaurant & Tea Rooms

Tel 01929 481332 Map 14 C4 JaB
National Trust Tea Rooms The Square Corfe Castle Dorset BH20 5EZ

The tea room is suitably old and beamed, with lattice windows and floral drapes. At the back is a garden with views up to the brooding ruins of the castle. Coffee and various cakes are served from 10.30, then at lunchtime come home-made soup (always vegetarian £2.05), sandwiches (£2.25) and filled jacket potatoes (from £2.50 to £3.50). Traditional ploughman's with half a pint of Scrumpy Jack is £5.20, and a few hot specials come at £4.95: leek and ham crumble with cheese sauce, cottage pie. Choices for afternoon tea include the Dorset cream tea with local home-made jam and Cornish clotted cream (£3.25) or the Purbeck tea comprising two slices of locally baked bread, jam and a choice of cakes. Home-made cakes are also on offer (coffee walnut sponge or rich sticky fruit cake). There's a roast on Sundays (£4.95) and the staff are happy to cater for children (two high-chairs, children's cups, bottles, small portions and a short children's menu are all provided). Large bench with wipe-over surface in Ladies, suitable for baby-changing. No smoking inside. ***Seats*** *70 (+ 70 outside).* ***Open*** *10-5.30 (10-4 Nov-23 Dec).* ***Closed*** *24 Dec-2 Jan. Amex, Diners, MasterCard,* **VISA**

Crathorne — Crathorne Hall — 72% — £140

Tel 01642 700398 **Fax 01642 700814** Map 5 E3 H
Crathorne nr Yarm Cleveland TS15 0AR

The last of the great stately homes built in the Edwardian era, Crathorne Hall enjoys a beautiful, serene setting in 15 acres of grounds just a short drive from the A19. Most of the original features have been lovingly preserved or restored, inluding magnificent panelling. The drawing room is of classical proportions with a fine carved overmantel, large portraits in oil and brass chandeliers. Knoll sofas and buttoned leather Queen Anne-style armchairs form part of a comfortable and very traditional decor. The cocktail bar has the air of a gentleman's club with its bottle-green walls, mahogany panelling and pillars and plush red velour chairs. Bedrooms are splendid though top-floor and back rooms are smaller. Furniture is period style in keeping with the character of the building and all rooms are well equipped, superior rooms in particular. Bathrooms, some with bidets, have quality toiletries and bathrobes. Children under 12 share parents' room free. Conference/banqueting facilities for 140/120. A Virgin hotel. ***Rooms** 37. Garden, croquet, riding, fishing, clay-pigeon shooting. Amex, Diners, MasterCard,* **VISA**

Cray — White Lion Inn

Tel 01756 760262 Map 5 D4 
Cray Buckden Skipton North Yorkshire BD23 5JB

Titular headquarters of the Wharfdale Head Gun Club, the Lion nestles in a deep valley on the road (B6160) between Wharfdale and Bishopsdale at the foot of Buckden Pike. For droves of fell walkers and families it's a sure shot in all weathers. Flagstoned within by a huge open range, the bar is a chummy place to dry off over a welcome pint of Moorhouse's (leaving muddy boots outside, please!). A sun-soaked front patio comes into its own in summer; parents can relax while across the road children in their dozens splash in and around the Beck, seemingly oblivious of the true purpose of its aged stepping stones. Children and well-behaved dogs are welcome indoors. *Open winter 11-3, 6-11 (Sat 11-11), Sun 12-3, 7-10.30, summer 11-11 (Sun 12-10.30). Free House.* ***Beer** Tetley Best, Moorhouse's Premier & Pendle Witches Brew, guest beer. Family room. Amex, Diners, MasterCard,* **VISA**

Crowborough — White Hart

Tel 01892 652367 **Fax 01892 662656** Map 11 B6 
1 Chapel Green Crowborough East Sussex TN6 2LB

In July 1994 after several failed leases, including the Beefeater chain, the future of the run-down White Hart – a large mock-Tudor and suburban-looking pub located on top of Crowborough Hill – seemed very uncertain. Against all the odds in come Carl and Judith Martin, a confident and enterprising couple who, having done their homework, knew the exact potential of the property as a family-orientated pub. Within weeks this big 'white elephant' of a pub was transformed through the hard work and dedication of the Martin family and now, come rain or shine, the White Hart is foremost in local parents' minds when considering a family meal out. Whether parents arrive with babes-in-arms or hyperactive youngsters every conceivable facility has been thought of and provided to satisfy their needs or keep them amused. Inside, a series of well-refurbished inter-connecting rooms feature some exposed brick, pine furnishings, plenty of plants and bygones and, ideally placed between the bar and restaurant, a splendid indoor play area for inclement days. While mum and dad tuck into reliable and generously-served bar food, from filled jacket potatoes and ploughman's to home-made steak and ale pudding, lamb and mint pie, sausage casserole with mushrooms and red wine and large battered cod, accompanied by a pint of one of the eight real ales on handpump or a glass of good English wine, children can amuse themselves in the kitchen playhouse, watch a video on TV, play with multiplication tables and chalkboards or read one of many books available. For peckish children their are jars of baby food and an imaginative kids menu offering fishcakes, pizza, Speldhurst sausages and mash and a nourishing lunch box with sandwiches, crisps, apple and kit-kat. In addition, sugar-free drinks are listed on a board, several high-chairs/booster seats are readily available and a spotless and well-equipped baby-changing area is located in the disabled toilet. Sunny summer days attract hordes of children and the safe rear garden is paradise for all ages. Those with the energy can explore the well-equipped play area (due to be upgraded further in 1997), which features a bouncy castle, a wooden fort, a climbing rope ladder, a Wendy house full of toys, a sandpit with bucket and spade and, for the tots, a baby-swing suspended from a holly tree. However, the most popular feature by far is the Wibbly Wobbly Farmyard or mini-zoo that houses an ever-growing collection of animals, from Shallwe the pot-bellied pig and Cash 'n' Carry the pygmy goats to numerous rabbits, ducks, chickens and guinea-pigs. Children can access the pens and pet the animals at certain times and notices explain the animals and warn of the dangers of too much intrusion. And, if this is not enough family entertainment, Carl and Judith stage various fun events to mark Easter and Hallowe'en, as well as summer family barbecues and a special party with games and fireworks to celebrate each anniversary at the pub. Winner of our Family Pub of the Year 1997. *Open 11-11 (Sun 12-10.30).* ***Bar Food*** *11-10 (from 12 Sun). Free House.* ***Beer*** *Morland Old Speckled Hen, Young's Special, Pot-bellied Bitter (brewed for pub), Flowers Original, Wadworth 6X, Fuller's London Pride, Greene King Abbot Ale, guest beers. Garden, outdoor eating, children's play area, mini-zoo. Disabled facilities. Amex, Diners, MasterCard,* ***VISA***

Croydon — Hilton National — 69% — £116

Tel 0181-680 3000 **Fax 0181-681 6171** Map 11 B5 **H**

Waddon Way Purley Way Croydon Surrey CR9 4HH

Space, style and comfort combine at a commendably high level in this polished-granite hotel at the Croydon end of Purley Way. Good bedrooms offer large beds and ample work space plus wing armchairs and proper breakfast table. White marble features in equally good bathrooms. Suites (actually just large rooms) have sophisticated wide-screen TVs that incorporate CD players and a video games feature, spa baths and separate shower cubicles in addition to the tub. Some rooms are adapted for disabled guests. Children up to 12 can stay free in parents' room. Room service is available round the clock, and there's a same-day laundry and dry cleaning service. Conferences for up to 400 and a business services centre. ***Rooms*** *168. Indoor swimming pool, gym, sauna, spa bath, steam room, sun beds, beauty salon, coffee shop (7am-11pm). Amex, Diners, MasterCard,* ***VISA***

Croydon — Hockney's

Tel 0181-688 2899 Map 11 B5 **JaB**

98 High Street Croydon Surrey CRO 1ND

The little empire that is Hockney's includes a gift shop and wholefood store as well as a vegetarian café and restaurant. From 10 to 6 the coffee shop offers a selection of drinks, cakes (chocolate £1.40, banana and cashew £1.10, coffee and walnut £1.25) and parfaits (rum and raisin or crème de menthe £1.50). In the main restaurant, there is counter service at lunchtime offering lasagne, curries and maybe patatas bravas – potatoes fried with olive oil and paprika, served with chick peas and chutney (all at £4.95) among other appealing salads and hot dishes. At dinner, there is table service and a wider menu selection. Starters include soup or houmus (£1.95/£2.50) and the weekly changing main courses are interesting and good value, maybe spanokopitta – spinach, feta and pine nuts in filo pastry with a garlic béchamel (£6.95) or cavatappi veneziana – pasta with olives, capers and a tomato and basil sauce (£5.95). Finish with sherry trifle (£2.95) or fruit salad (£3.50). Unlicensed. Small garden.
Seats *70 (+ 20 outside).* ***Open*** *10am-10pm.* ***Closed*** *Sun, Mon & Bank Holidays. Amex, MasterCard,* ***VISA***

Our inspectors *never* book in the name of Egon Ronay's Guides. They disclose their identity only if they are considering an establishment for inclusion in the next edition of the Guide.

CROYDON Selsdon Park 68% £144

Tel 0181-657 8811 **Fax 0181-651 6171** Map 11 B5 H
Addington Road Sanderstead Croydon Surrey CR2 8YA

200 acres of parkland 13 miles south of Central London are the setting for ivy-clad Selsdon Park, whose amenities combine those of hotel, golf course, leisure club, conference venue and business centre. It's also a good place for weekending families, who enjoy special rates. The baronial-style entrance hall has stone walls, an elaborate plaster ceiling and leather armchairs that are also to be found in the oak-panelled bar-lounge with its heavily carved antique furniture and brass ornaments. Bedrooms come in a variety of sizes and appointments from freestanding lightwood furniture to fitted units, and soft floral to bright fabrics. All have mini-bars and room safes. The very best rooms enjoy views across the Surrey Hills. Dinner dances Friday and Saturday. Unusual 40m circuit indoor swimming pool. Reservable lock-up garages (£5 a night) and courtesy car service to East Croydon station. ***Rooms** 170. Garden, croquet, boules, golf (18-hole), putting green, driving range, golf shop, tennis (grass and all-weather), indoor & outdoor swimming pools, gym, squash, sauna, spa bath, sun beds, beauty salon, snooker, playground, news kiosk. Amex, Diners, MasterCard,* ***VISA***

CUCKFIELD Murray's £60

Tel 01444 455826 Map 11 B6 
Broad Street Cuckfield West Sussex RH17 5LJ

Several cottagey rooms, one reserved for non-smokers, provide a cosy setting in which to enjoy Sue Murray's excellent cooking. Influences are varied, but almost every dish is just that little bit different: Stilton cream with candied pear, warm pigeon salad, cod and minestrone sauce, pepper-crusted lamb, sweetbreads in pasta. Park in the village car park opposite. Short wine list with nearly everything under £20. ***Seats** 32. Parties 12. L 12-1.30 D 7.15-9.30. Closed L Sat, all Sun & Bank Holidays. Amex, MasterCard,* ***VISA***

CULLOMPTON Manor House Hotel

Tel 01884 32281 **Fax 01884 38344** Map 13 E2 
2/4 Fore Street Cullompton Devon EX15 1JL

Built as the town house for a rich wool merchant, this hotel-cum-inn dates in part to 1603, and fine old casement windows jut out from the freshly-painted black and white facade. Inside has an attractive mix of styles, the knotty pine bar Victorian in feel but with a distinct, pubby atmopshere. The appealing bedrooms are all individually decorated, with stylishly co-ordinated fabrics, nicely framed botanical prints, plenty of pieces of china and plates on the walls and good freestanding furniture in mahogany or an orangey pine finish. All the usual modern comforts: TV (with satellite), radio, telephone, tea/coffee-making facilities and a trouser press. Carpeted bathrooms have good thermostatically-controlled showers over the baths, and nice touches like cotton wool, pot-pourri and decent toiletries. Most rooms are at the front of the building facing the main road (double-glazing helps to reduce the traffic noise) and one of the two quieter rooms to the rear has a pair of bunk beds for families. Excellent-value overnight accommodation. *Open 11-11 (Sun 12-10.30). Free House.* ***Beer** Boddingtons, Flowers IPA, Morland Old Speckled Hen. Patio/terrace. Family room.* ***Accommodation** 10 bedrooms, all en suite, £53.50 (family room sleeping 4 £68.50, single £41.50). Children welcome overnight, additional bed (£7.50) & cot available. Amex, MasterCard,* ***VISA***

We welcome bona fide complaints and recommendations on the tear-out pages at the back of the Guide for Readers' Comments. They are followed up by our professional team.

CUMNOR Vine Inn

Tel 01865 862567 **Fax 01865 200303** Map 15 D2 **P**
11 Abingdon Road Cumnor nr Oxford Oxfordshire OX2 9QN

Situated just off the A420 south-west of Oxford, this homely 18th-century village pub is leased by the proprietors of Whites Restaurant in Oxford, so it is understandable that the emphasis here is on producing above-average pub food. Beyond the vine-covered stone facade the original low-ceilinged and plainly furnished core has been extended to incorporate a more modern dining-room, but what it lacks in atmosphere it makes up through the choice and quality of the food on offer. An extensive and interesting blackboard menu should not disappoint, with starters available in small or large portions (priced accordingly) so as to satisfy hearty appetites. Choose from fresh crab soup, marinated duck salad and hoi sin sauce, mussels in white wine and garlic, or pigeon breast salad with onion marmalade for starters, followed by stir-fried spicy lamb, Thai beef curry, fillet of pork with sherry and green peppercorn sauce, good fresh fish (monkfish, halibut, turbot) with maybe basil and tomato or tarragon sauce and various grills like tandoori lamb kebab and spare ribs. A short list of puddings may highlight sticky toffee pudding and baked vanilla cheesecake. Good summer garden in which to enjoy a well-kept pint and a game of Aunt Sally, while children expend some energy on the play equipment. *Open 11-2.30, 6-11 (Sun 12-3, 7-10).* ***Bar Food*** *12.30-2.15, 6.30-9.15 (from 7 Sun).* ***Beer*** *Greene King Abbot Ale, Adnams Bitter, Tetley, Wadworth 6X, guest beer. Garden, outdoor eating, children's play area. Family room. MasterCard,* ***VISA***

DAMERHAM Compasses Inn

Tel 01725 518231 **Fax 01725 518880** Map 14 C3 **P**
Damerham Fordingbridge Hampshire SP6 3HQ

Attractive 16th-century coaching inn located in the heart of the village with a splendid flower-filled garden next to the cricket green – ideal for watching an innings or two with a pint on sunny summer Sunday evenings. Spartan public bar with traditional games and a carpeted open-plan lounge bar with pine furniture, central woodburner, pretty wallpaper and a short blackboard menu listing reliable home-cooked specials. Choose from a daily soup (chicken and herb), sardines with Cajun spices, pork chops with garlic, coriander and lemon, or maybe red mullet with an orange and herb crust. Impressive ploughman's lunch list with a choice of over seven cheeses, served with home-made pickle, and good standard pub dishes (sandwiches, various curries, steak and mushroom pie, lasagne, steaks) featured on a printed menu. Overnight accommodation in six cottagey bedrooms (one family room); these are light and airy with small print wallpapers, co-ordinating fabrics, comfortable furnishings and tiled en suite facilities plus TVs and tea-makers. A warm welcome extends to children with the provision of a play area, menu and baby-changing facilities. *Open 11-2.30, 6-11 (Sat 11-11, Sun 12-3, 7-10.30).* ***Bar Food*** *12-2, 7-9.30 (Sun 12-2.30, 7-9). Free House.* ***Beer*** *Wadworth 6X, Flowers Original, Ringwood Best, Hampshire Brewery Compasses Ale, guest beer. Garden, Family room, children's play area.* ***Accommodation*** *6 bedrooms, all en suite (two with bath), £50 (four-poster £60, single £29.50). Children welcome overnight (under-2s free, 2-12s half-price if sharing parents' room). MasterCard,* ***VISA***

DARTINGTON Cranks Health Food Restaurant

Tel 01803 862388 Map 13 D3 **JaB**
Shinners Bridge Dartington nr Totnes Devon

Cranks continues to cater in fine style for visitors to the ever-popular Cider Press Centre. Service is courteous and efficient at the self-help counter, and seating ample if closely spaced at varnished pine tables. There are four different salads (£1.30) each day as well as dishes like leek and smoked cheese jalousie, Mediterranean roasted vegetables with a choice of two salads (£4.25) and stuffed peppers (£1.90, £3.40 with salads). Baking weighs in with pizza slices and homity pie (£1.90) and a wealth of such sweets as banoffi or lemon and raisin pie, fruit pavlovas and coffee and walnut gateau. For children they do a mini-pastry or pizza with baked beans and fruit juice. Especially handy parking and disabled access. Take-away service also. Four high-chairs and two clip-on seats; baby food and bottles will be heated. A pull-down table in the Ladies' lobby is provided for baby-changing, and a garden at the back (away from the road) has access for push-chairs and wheelchairs. No smoking. ***Seats*** *80 (+ 30 outside).* ***Open*** *9.30-5 (Sun from 10.30).* ***Closed*** *Sun Jan-Easter, 25, 26 Dec & 1 Jan. MasterCard,* ***VISA***

DARTMOUTH Stoke Lodge 60% £77

Tel 01803 770523 **Fax 01803 770851** Map 13 D3 **H**
Stoke Fleming Dartmouth Devon TQ6 0RA

A popular family-run holiday hotel at the top of a village two miles south of Dartmouth.Leisure facilities are good (a mixture of indoor and outdoor, including giant chess), while public areas and bedrooms are comfortable and well maintained. Parking for 50 cars. Reduced green fees at Dartmouth Golf Club. ***Rooms*** *24. Garden, indoor & outdoor swimming pools, putting, keep-fit equipment, sauna, spa bath, snooker. MasterCard,* ***VISA***

DEDHAM Dedham Centre Vegetarian Restaurant

Tel 01206 322677 Map 10 C3 **JaB**
Arts & Crafts Centre High Street Dedham Essex CO7 6AD

The former United Reform church in the delightful village of Dedham has been remodelled (but has retained the organ) to house the Arts & Crafts Centre – various open-plan shops selling clothes, jewellery, paintings, pottery plus a toy museum on the first floor – and a vegetarian self-service restaurant. Made-to-order sandwiches (from £2), jacket potatoes (£1.95-£3.40) and snacks on toast are supplemented by main dishes such as quiche (with salad or baked potato £4.55), cashew nut risotto (£5.35), aubergine pasta bake and leek croustade (£5.35 with a mixed salad bowl). Home-made German apple tart (£2.50) is a favourite sweet. Children, babies and nursing mothers are very welcome throughout the restaurant, and there's a children's section on the menu - small portions are also available; beakers and two high-chairs provided. Unlicensed. No smoking. ***Seats*** *58.* ***Open*** *10-5 (Sat & Sun to 5.30).* ***Closed*** *Mon Jan-Mar, middle 2 weeks Oct. No credit cards.*

DENT Dent Crafts Centre

Tel 01539 625400 Map 5 D4 **JaB**
Dent Crafts Centre Helmside Dent Cumbria LA10 5SY

This former barn built of Lakeland stone is part of a smallholding which stands at the heart of Dent Dale in spectacular walking country just about 6 miles from Sedburgh. As well as housing a gallery, the centre sells a wide array of arts and crafts from the locality, including pottery and Lakeland stone ornaments. Tables are widely spaced by large picture windows affording lovely views of the Dale. The menu is based on home baking and until 12 offers a selections of cakes such as carrot, sachertorte, banoffi fudge pie or brownies. From midday the choice extends to include soup and a roll (fresh tomato with diced courgettes £1.80), sandwiches (from £1.70), salmon salad (£5.50), stir-fried spicy chicken on frisée salad (£5.50) and oven-roast peppers, aubergines and tomatoes with a mixed salad (£5.50). For dessert try the creamy marbled orange and blueberry mousse (£1.50) or apple crumble and cream. Scones, fresh from the oven, are available in the afternoon and are served with jam and cream (£1). No smoking. ***Seats*** *30 (+ 20 outside).* ***Open*** *9.30-5.30 (Sun 10.30-5).* ***Closed*** *weekdays Jan/Feb. MasterCard,* ***VISA***

DERBY International Hotel 62% £58

Tel 01332 369321 **Fax 01332 294430** Map 6 C3 **H**
Burton Road Derby Derbyshire DE23 6AD

Once a Victorian school, now a privately-owned hotel with an important conference and exhibition business. Bedrooms are well equipped and the suites have spa baths. 24hr room service. Children up to 12 can stay free in their parents' room. The hotel stands on the A5250 south-west of the city centre. ***Rooms*** *60. Amex, Diners, MasterCard,* ***VISA***

DEVIZES Wiltshire Kitchen

Tel 01380 724840 Map 14 C3 JaB
11 St John's Street Devizes Wiltshire SN10 1BD

Behind a corner shop just off the market square lies a very special eating place, run since 1985 by Ann Blunden, who also specialises in outside catering. Customers help themselves and can sit downstairs, on ground level or outside at tables on the pavement. The day begins with breakfast (full £3.95), which continues through till 11.30am. The set lunch menu (£4.95) offers the roast of the day plus a pudding, and stands alongside choices such as carrot, tomato and basil soup or cream of mushroom (both £1.60), Thai chicken (£4.85), tipsy duck with plum and wine sauce £5.50, bean cakes with onion and ginger marmalade (£4.50), salads such as smoked chicken with a mango and melon sauce or turkey with tuna and anchovy mayonnaise (both £4.60) and their speciality sweet and savoury roulades – maybe salmon (£4.50). Fruit meringue is a fine dessert (£2.25). At teatime, choose one of the many options (£2.50 with scones, cream, jam and cake). No smoking. ***Seats** 50 (+ 12 outside).* ***Open** 8.30-5.* ***Closed** Sun, 25 Dec-2 Jan & Bank Holidays. No credit cards.*

DIDSBURY Est Est Est

Tel 0161-445 8209 Map 6 B2 JaB
756 Wilmslow Road Manchester M20 2DW

A large and friendly Italian restaurant decorated in light, white trattoria style and divided across a centre curve giving a raised stage effect to the rear seating section. Tables with parasols on the pavement in summer. More details under Knutsford. Branches also in Bury, Hale and Liverpool. Very much a child-friendly group of restaurants. Five high-chairs and the children will love the 'make your own pizza menu' where they get to 'push the dough', and put on a topping of their own choice, and then carry it back to the kitchen ready to be cooked, sporting their own special chef's hat - the biz! Access for push-chairs and wheelchairs and plenty of space for buggies. Half portions are available and balloons are all part of the service. ***Seats** 200 (+ 16 outside).* ***Open** 12-2.30 & 6-11 (Fri, Sat till 11.30, Sun 12-10.30).* ***Closed** 25, 26 Dec & 1 Jan. Amex, MasterCard,* ***VISA***

DISS Weavers Wine Bar and Eating House

Tel 01379 642411 Map 10 C2 JaB
Market Hill Diss Norfolk IP22 3JZ

This pretty restaurant is housed in a former chapel, retaining some original beams and cosy alcoves for intimate dining. A good-value set lunch (2/3 courses £7.95/£10.75) is offered, starting with perhaps a sauté of chicken livers with Madeira and cream on toast or filo pouches of crabmeat with sweet and sour sauce and Oriental salsa. To follow, you might choose venison faggots in port with caramelised onions or steamed fillet of cod with asparagus and beurre blanc. Desserts include banana and toffee flan or steamed marmalade sponge and custard. Dinner is £12 for three courses (not available on Saturday evenings) or à la carte if you prefer. There's a separate vegetarian menu. No smoking before 2pm or in the evening before 9.30pm. Ask for children's meals. Two high-chairs and baby-changing facilities, with mat, disposable nappies and wipes provided. ***Seats** 80.* ***Open** 12-1.30 & 7-9.* ***Closed** L Sat, all Sun & Mon, Bank Holidays, 1 week Christmas & 10 days Aug. Diners, MasterCard,* ***VISA***

DORCHESTER Kings Arms

Tel 01305 265353 **Fax 01305 260269** Map 13 F2 
30 High East Street Dorchester Dorset DT1 1HF

A substantial Georgian inn dominating the busy main street of this attractive county town, famous for its associations with the author Thomas Hardy, who resided in the nearby village of Lower Bockhampton. Locals fill the comfortable, low-ceilinged bar, while good-value overnight accommodation is proving popular among businessmen, families on the move (each room sleeps two adults and two children under 16) and tourists following the Hardy trail. Bedrooms are uniformly decorated in restful pastel colours and floral fabrics, with easy chairs and well-equipped bathrooms (all with bath/shower) enhancing a relaxing stay, although bow-fronted rooms overlooking the High Street could suffer from traffic noise. Tea-makers, satellite TV, trouser press, hairdryer and telephone are standard extras. Housed in an adjacent building are two unusual 'theme' rooms; the Tutankamun room and the Lawrence of Arabia room (£99 a night including champagne and breakfast). Residents' lounge. Premier Lodge (Greenalls). *Open 11-3, 6-11, (Fri & Sat 11-11), Sun 12-3, 7-10.30.* ***Beer*** *Wadworth 6X, Boddingtons, Flowers Original, Bass, Courage Directors, weekly guest beer.* ***Accommodation*** *33 rooms, all en suite, £41.50 excluding breakfast (Fri-Sun £34.50) Children welcome overnight (under-12s stay free in share parents' room), additional cot available. No dogs. Amex, Diners, MasterCard,* ***VISA***

DORCHESTER Potter In

Tel 01305 260312 Map 13 F2 JaB

19 Durngate Street Dorchester Dorset DT1 1JP

Sue Collier's welcoming establishment offers plenty of choice, and everything on the menu is available all day in a charming dining-room, cosily filled with fresh flowers and warmed by a real fire in chilly weather. Full English breakfast (£3.70) is on offer alongside filled rolls with white or wholemeal bread (£1.70-£2.60). Order from the counter and choose from an excellent salad bar to accompany omelettes, jacket potatoes or maybe home-made chicken pie (£2.70), curry and rice (£3.50), macaroni cheese (£2.15) or perhaps a hot bacon roll (£1.50). Hot Dorset apple cake and cream (£2) tops a short dessert menu, though the main attraction is the home-made ice cream selection – at least 20 flavours (from 80p), and Mrs Collier is now making yoghurt ice cream too. High-chairs and children's drinking mugs are available for the younger customers plus smaller helpings. The patio garden is open in fine weather. Close to the Dinosaur museum. ***Seats*** *64 (+ 40 outside).* ***Open*** *9.30-5 (Sun 10-4 in the summer only).* ***Closed*** *Sun Sep-Jun, 7 days July/Aug & 4-5 days Christmas. No credit cards.*

DORKING The Atrium

Tel 01306 876616 **Fax 01306 888930** Map 15 E3 JaB

Denbies Wine Estate London Road Dorking Surrey RH5 6AA

Housed within an imposing, chateau-style complex at the heart of a vast 600-acre estate featuring a 250-acre vineyard (reached via a long driveway off the A24 north of Dorking), this up-market eating house makes a fitting refreshment stop after a fascinating tour of the winery, or just a relaxing destination for lunch. Seating for 200 fills a really splendid glass-covered atrium with tables and chairs and a wealth of tropical plants. The self-service operation includes urns of good home-made soups (wild mushroom £2.25), cold cabinets displaying smoked salmon and avocado or marinated herrings with red onions and sour cream (£5.65-£6.50), and a range of freshly-filled baps. Interesting hot dishes like oak-smoked venison with parmesan and tomato salsa, tagliatelle of baby vegetables, chargrilled tuna steak with fresh lime and coriander and roast leg of lamb with honey thyme sauce (£5.95) are ready plated under the hot lights. Any venison or lamb on offer comes from the estate. Puddings (£2.95) change daily and may include marshmallow with fruits of the forest or tiramisu with pistachio *anglaise*. The full complement of Denbies wines can be sampled by the glass. Families are most welcome with little 'tuck boxes' for children, baby-changing facilities, high-chairs and kiddie-sized seats. No smoking. ***Seats*** *200 (+ 30 outside).* ***Open*** *10-5 (Sun from 12).* ***Closed*** *25 & 26 Dec. Amex, MasterCard,* ***VISA***

If we recommend meals in a hotel a *separate* entry is usually made for its restaurant. Pub and inn entries include bar food details where recommended.

DOVEDALE Izaak Walton Hotel 59% £98

Tel 01335 350555 **Fax 01335 350539** Map 6 C3 **H**
Dovedale nr Ashbourne Derbyshire DE6 2AY

Owned by the Duke of Rutland, the 17th-century farmhouse building, where Izaak Walton once stayed, affords rolling views of Thorpe Cloud and Dovedale in the Peak District Park. The River Dove flows through the estate, and fly fishing is available on a 2-mile stretch. Leather chesterfield sofas and open fires add comfort and warmth to the public rooms; bedrooms are more noteworthy for the vistas without than the space within. Conference facilities for up to 60. Under-16s stay free in parents' room. ***Rooms*** *32. Garden, fishing. Amex, Diners, MasterCard,* ***VISA***

DULVERTON Carnarvon Arms 60% £80

Tel 01398 323302 **Fax 01398 324022** Map 13 D2 **H**
Dulverton Somerset TA22 9AE

Five miles of salmon and trout fishing on the Rivers Exe and Barle bring anglers to the Carnarvon Arms, which was built in 1874 by the 4th Earl to accommodate travellers arriving by train. The railway disappeared long ago, but the station buildings survive as a feature. Walking and riding are other favourite outdoor activities, while relaxing in the old-fashioned lounges is a popular indoor pastime. Bedrooms are modest but comfortable enough and children under 12 are accommodated free during low season when sharing their parents' room. Owner Mrs Toni Jones has run the hotel since 1958. ***Rooms*** *25. Garden, croquet, outdoor swimming pool, children's splash pool, tennis, fishing, snooker, hair salon. Amex, MasterCard,* ***VISA***

DURHAM Station House Hotel

Tel 0191-384 6906 **Fax 0191-386 6007** Map 5 E3 **JaB**
High Shincliffe Durham

At Joan McGuiggan's sympathetically restored old station building you can enjoy good-value eating in either the bar or the restaurant. A modestly priced à la carte menu offers tempting suggestions such as cream of Stilton soup (£2.25) or prawns in Pernod (£2.95) to start. Main courses could include honey-baked ham with Dijon sauce (£7.99) or rack of lamb with apricot and ginger (£8.45) most of the steak dishes are on the expensive side. Desserts comprise gateaux and ice creams or perhaps a fruit crumble. Sundays bring a three-course lunch menu (£6.50), always including a roast, and Sunday dinner's three-course menu is £10.50. Garden tables in the summer. One room is designated no-smoking. ***Seats*** *50 (+30 outside).* ***Open*** *12-3 (Sat & Sun only, but Mon-Fri by arrangement), 5-11.30 (Sun from 7).* ***Closed*** *26 Dec. MasterCard,* ***VISA***

EASINGWOLD Truffles

Tel 01347 822342 Map 5 E4 **JaB**
Snowdon House Spring Street Easingwold North Yorkshire YO6 3BN

A pretty little cottage tearoom near the market square. Business is moving more towards the restaurant side of things and away from the tea shop trade, but cakes and snacks are still available. Breakfast is served all day Mon-Sat (£3.60), while lunchtime dishes run from soup and garlic mushrooms to crunchy vegetable pancake (£5.25), omelettes, salmon salad, roast chicken and lasagne. From the full à la carte come deep-fried brie with cranberry sauce (£3.20), salmon and broccoli bake and pan-fried pork fillet strips in a brandy, mushroom and cream sauce (£7.85). There's always a roast on the Sunday lunch menu (£5.50). Free parking in the market square. No smoking. Children get their own special menu; one high-chair, one booster seat and nursing mothers seeking privacy will be offered the use of a private lounge. Close to Flamingo Land and Lightwater Valley. ***Seats*** *32.* ***Open*** *10-2.30 (Sun from 12-2) also open for supper Fri/Sat in winter, Tue-Sun in summer.* ***Closed*** *some Bank Holidays. No credit cards.*

East Horsley — Jarvis Thatchers Hotel — 63% — £108

Tel 01483 284291 **Fax 01483 284222** Map 15 E3

Epsom Road East Horsley Surrey KT24 6TB

The hotel is based on a charming, original Tudor building with first-floor verandah, which, together with pretty gardens, makes a popular wedding venue. Fairly standard bedrooms are either in a Tudor-style extension to the main building, arranged around an open-air pool (Terrace rooms) with patio doors opening onto the pool or (just a few) in a separate cottage. The main public area, recently refurbished, serves as both bar and lounge, with plenty of comfortable armchairs as well as chairs around eating/drinking-height tables. Breakfast is served in the characterful restaurant located in the oldest part of the building. 24hr room service. Children up to 16 are free in parents' room. ***Rooms*** *54. Garden, outdoor swimming pool (May-Sep), 24hr lounge service. Amex, Diners, MasterCard,* ***VISA***

East Ilsley — The Swan

Tel 01635 281238 **Fax 01635 281791** Map 15 D2

East Ilsley Newbury Berkshire RG16 0LF

A well-run, friendly family pub at the heart of an attractive Berkshire village: turn off the A34 just 3 miles north of the M4, Junction 13. The Swan is operated by Morlands, the brewers from nearby West Ilsley, and by the bar is posted a record of their landlords, unbroken since 1865. The pub, however, was a coaching inn in the early 1700s and despite today's open-plan interior many original features remain within its many rooms and alcoves, alongside collections of brewery artefacts, cartoons, local photographs and miniature bottles which have been accumulated over the years. Residents overnight enjoy the best of the old building's charm in carefully modernised en suite bedrooms, all neatly equipped with beverage trays, colour TVs and direct-dial phones – two are non-smoking. In summer, the trellised rear patio is a picturesque spot where parents can sit while the children let off steam in the adjacent garden. *Open 11-2.30, 6-11 (Sun 12-3, 7-10.30).* ***Beer*** *Morland, guest beer. Patio, garden, children's play area. Family room.* ***Accommodation*** *10 rooms, all en suite (three with bath), £47 (family room £60, single £34). Children welcome overnight. Check-in by arrangement. Amex, MasterCard,* ***VISA***

East Molesey — Superfish

Tel 0181-979 2432 Map 15 E2

90 Walton Road East Molesey Surrey KT8 ODL

Part of the excellent Surrey-based chain serving traditional British fish and chips, cooked the Yorkshire way, fried in beef dripping. See Morden entry for more details. Licensed. ***Seats*** *30.* ***Open*** *11.30-2 (Sat till 2.30) & 5-10.30 (Thu-Sat till 11).* ***Closed*** *Sun, 25 & 26 Dec, 1 Jan. Amex, MasterCard,* ***VISA***

Eastbourne — De Vere Grand Hotel — 75% — £150

Tel 01323 412345 **Fax 01323 412233** Map 11 B6

King Edward's Parade Eastbourne East Sussex BN21 4EQ

At the west end of the seafront, the hotel maintains much of the style and grace of its Victorian origins with marble pillars, crystal chandeliers, vast corridors and high-domed day rooms evoking a more leisurely, bygone age, with everything kept in good order. Some of the more expensive sea-facing bedrooms have balconies and are huge, with bright furniture and up-to-date fabrics, though other rooms are smaller, so it's best to check when booking. 24hr room service, comprehensive leisure and exercise facilities, themed weekend breaks and family facilities. ***Rooms*** *164. Garden, putting green, indoor & outdoor swimming pools, spa bath, sauna, steam room, solarium, beauty & hairdressing salons, keep-fit equipment, snooker. Amex, Diners, MasterCard,* ***VISA***

See over

Mirabelle Restaurant £70

In elegant, formal surroundings professional staff serve fixed-price lunch (2- or 3-course) and dinner (4-course, priced by choice of main course) menus offering a small but varied choice, and in addition there's an à la carte option. Showing the interesting, eclectic style are lentil soup with Moroccan spices; terrine of smoked chicken with wild mushrooms and pickled vegetables; brill fillet and mousseline cooked in Parma ham glazed with a lemon and chive cream sauce; and a trio of pasta dishes - spinach tortellini, mushroom tagliatelle and Thai vegetable lasagne. British and French cheeses are served with home-made walnut and raisin bread, and desserts could include hot mango tatin served with a water-melon and lime sorbet or a plate of Belgian chocolate creations. ***Seats** 50. Parties 12. Private Room 40. L 12.30-2.30 D 7-10. Closed Sun, Mon, Bank Holidays, 2 weeks Aug & 1st 2 weeks Jan. Set L £15.50/£18.50 Set D from £24.*

EASTBOURNE Wish Tower Hotel 66% £96

Tel 01323 722676 **Fax 01323 721474** Map 11 B6 **H**
King Edward's Parade Eastbourne East Sussex BN21 4EB

The hotel stands on the seafront opposite the Wish Tower, a martello tower that is now a Napoleonic and World War II museum. Bedrooms are in attractively up-to-date style, with modern comforts like double-glazing, and many enjoy sea views. Children up to 14 stay free in parents' room. Residents have free use of the David Lloyd Tennis and Sports Leisure Centre (10 minutes drive). Park on the street or in the NCP, or book one of the hotel's three lock-up garages (£3 per day). Principal Hotels. ***Rooms** 65. Amex, Diners, MasterCard, **VISA***

EASTGATE Ratcatchers Inn

Tel 01603 871430 Map 10 C1 **P**
Eastgate Cawston Norfolk NR10 4HA

A pleasantly old-fashioned free house, dating from 1861, standing in a rural spot just off the B1149 one mile south of Cawston. A warm and friendly atmosphere pervades the neatly furnished bar and restaurant areas which are both laid up for diners, for food is very much the thing here. The appeal is the extensive range of home-cooked meals listed in a veritable tome of a menu, a 14-page epic of jokily-named dishes. Nevertheless, additional imaginative daily specials and a packed pub – it is advisable to book – instills confidence in the enthusiastic kitchen. Use of fresh local produce is clearly evident – fish from Lowestoft, shellfish direct from the North Norfolk coast, produce from local smokehouses and naturally-aged cuts of meat from a nearby butcher. The 'home-made' policy extends to freshly-baked bread, herb oils, chutneys, stocks and pickled samphire plus the use of fresh herbs from the garden. Fish comes in a variety of forms (duo of salmon and cod wrapped in bacon on baby spinach, brill with sun-dried tomato and saffron sauce, tempura of scallops with a beurre blanc sauce) and dipping into the menu might reveal fowl and funghi pie served with either a short-crust or puff-pastry top, Jaffri's madras curry, Shylock's tagliatelle carbonara, salads, doorstep sandwiches, at least 15 vegetarian, vegan or diabetic options, plus grills named after film stars. Having digested the main menu selection, look to the specials board for even more tantalising dishes such as fresh oysters, melon and squid cocktail and venison with a wild mushroom and port wine sauce. Home-made puddings have Dickensian titles like Mr Micawber's cake (Belgian chocolate cheesecake). Separate cheese menu listing twelve varieties, six of them British. An interesting list of wines has at least a dozen available by the glass. Plans are to build some bedrooms. East of England Regional Winner of our 1997 Seafood Pub of the Year award. *Open 11.45-2.30, 5.45-11 (Sun 12-3, 7-10.30). **Bar Food** 11.45-2, 6-10 (Sun 12-2, 7-10). Free House. **Beer** Hancock's Best Bitter, Bass, Adnams Extra. Garden, outdoor eating. Closed all 26 Dec. No credit cards.*

Many hotels offer reduced rates for weekend or out-of-season bookings. Always ask about special deals and family rooms.

EASTLEIGH Forte Posthouse Southampton 66% £87

Tel 01703 619700 **Fax 01703 643945** Map 15 D3 
Leigh Road Eastleigh Hampshire SO50 9PG

Modern low-rise hotel just off junction 13 of the M3. Features include a leisure club, nine conference rooms, family facilities (chidren free in parents' room, family rooms, playrooms, playground) and four bedrooms with access for disabled guests. The majority of the bedrooms (74) are designated non-smoking. ***Rooms** 116. Indoor swimming pool, keep-fit equipment, sauna, steam room, solarium, beauty salon, playroom. Amex, Diners, MasterCard,* **VISA**

EBBESBOURNE WAKE Horseshoes Inn

Tel 01722 780474 Map 14 B3 P
Ebbesbourne Wake Salisbury Wiltshire SP5 5JF

The Ebble valley and more especially the village of Ebbesbourne Wake seem to have escaped the hustle and bustle of modern day life, as it nestles among the folds in the Downs, close to the infant River Ebble. This peaceful unspoilt rural charm is reflected in the village inn that has been run "as a proper country pub" by the Bath family for over 20 years. Its 17th-century brick facade is adorned with climbing roses and honeysuckle, while inside the traditional layout of two bars around a central servery still survives. The main bar is festooned with an array of old farming implements and country bygones and a mix of simple furniture fronts the open log fire. Well-kept real ales are served straight from the cask and both local farm cider and free-range eggs are also sold across the bar. Bar food is good value and homely, the best choice being the freshly-prepared dishes that are chalked up on the blackboard menu, featuring liver and bacon casserole, beef in ale, duck with gooseberry sauce, and home-made game pie. Fresh fish to order. The standard printed menu highlights the range of sandwiches, ploughman's lunches and other hot dishes. The set 3-course Sunday lunch at £9.25 is superb value for money, extremely popular and served throughout (booking necessary). The flower- and shrub-filled garden is perfect for summer alfresco eating and safe for children, who also have access to view the four goats in the pets area. Those wanting to explore this tranquil area further can stay overnight in one of the two modest bedrooms at either end of the inn; both are decorated in a cottagey style with pretty fabrics and wallpaper and have TVs, tea-making kits and their own private facilities. A peaceful night's sleep is guaranteed. *Open 12-3, 6.30-11, (Sun 12-3, 7-10.30). **Bar Food** 12-2, 7-9 (till 9.30 Sat). No food Sun & Mon eve. Free House. **Beer** Adnams Broadside, Wadworth 6X, Ringwood Best, guest beer. Garden, outdoor eating, pet area. **Accommodation** 2 bedrooms, both en suite (one with bath), £40 (single £25). Children welcome overnight, (under-2s stay free in parents' room, 3-12s by arrangement), additional bed & cot available. No credit cards.*

EGHAM Runnymede Hotel 74% £170

Tel 01784 436171 **Fax 01784 436340** Map 15 E2 
Windsor Road Egham Surrey TW20 0AG

Leave the M25 at J13 and take the A308 Egham/Windsor road to find this modern redbrick building set in 12 acres of gardens running down to the Thames at Bell Weir Lock. Public areas are light and airy and accommodation is comfortable, stylish and well maintained. The best (Executive) bedrooms are most appealing with yellow and blue colour scheme, good armchairs and fine marble bathrooms; some have jacuzzis (£5 supplement). Standard rooms (the rate quoted above) are more variable in size (a few are on the small side) and decor, but all have the same amenities – air-conditioning, mini-bars, bathrobes – and benefit from the same high standards of housekeeping. Numerous, well-equipped conference rooms can cope with up to 400 delegates theatre-style. Children (up to the age of 12 £10 when sharing parents' room) are made welcome with their own menu in the hotel's informal restaurant, Charlie Bells, and a large children's pool in the Spa. ***Rooms** 171. Garden, croquet, indoor swimming pool, splash pool, gym, dance studio, sauna, steam room, spa bath, solarium, beauty salon, hair salon, snooker. Amex, Diners, MasterCard,* **VISA**

ELLERBY — Ellerby Hotel

Tel 01947 840342 **Fax 01947 841221** Map 5 E3 P
Ellerby nr Saltburn-by-Sea Redcar & Cleveland TS13 5LP

David & Janet Alderson have transformed a run-down village pub into a country inn. The much-extended main bar and attendant dining-room provide plenty of space in which to enjoy a wide range of substantial fare, of which a large proportion is changed daily and posted on prominent blackboards. From starters encompassing home-made soup and lamb samosa with curry dip, progress to steak pie, chargrills and interesting specials like medallions of beef, fillet of pork wrapped in smoked gammon with a sweet pepper sauce, and rabbit, hare and grouse pie. Freshly-cut sandwiches and ploughman's lunches are also available. Monthly Chinese banquets have proved highly popular. Nine bedrooms are furnished to a commendably high standard with varnished pine furniture and bright floral drapes; all have TVs, dial-out phones, trouser presses and hairdryers. Bathrooms are fully tiled and carpeted, with large baths and separate shower stalls (two have shower only). Refurbishment to all bedrooms was underway as we went to press. *Open 12-3, 6.30-11 (till 10.30 Sun).* ***Bar Food*** *12-2, 6.30-10 (till 9.30 Sun). Free House.* ***Beer*** *John Smith's Bitter & Magnet, Courage Directors. Garden, outdoor eating.* ***Accommodation*** *9 bedrooms, all en suite, £54 (single £32). Children welcome overnight (under-5s stay free in parent's room, 6-13s £11, over-14s £16), additional bed & cot available. Accommodation and pub closed all 25 Dec. MasterCard,* ***VISA***

ELSENHAM — The Crown

Tel 01279 812827 Map 10 B3 P
High Street Elsenham Bishop's Stortford Hertfordshire CM22 6DG

Once a row of three 300-year-old character cottages, this attractive, flower-decked and well-cared-for village inn has a traditional carpeted and low-ceilinged interior complete with brasses, beams, open fires and a relaxing atmosphere. Separate lively public bar offering a variety of games. Bar food relies primarily on an extensive and varied printed menu featuring good pub favourites – lasagne, stuffed pancakes and fisherman's pie – as well as interesting home-cooked dishes like hot smoked haddock pots, turkey and mushroom pie, chicken in red wine and mushroom sauce, pork fillet with apples and calvados, and fresh fish dishes like monkfish with watercress and cream, and seafood mixed grill. To accompany them, there are well-cooked vegetables or choose a selection of fresh salads from the self-service salad bar. Large granary baps, freshly-made Crownburgers served with home-made whisky relish, and ploughman's platters are served at lunchtime only. Home-made puddings include the tireless landlady Barbara Good's unusual ice creams such as stem ginger, marmalade and gin and toffee fudge – up to 14 at any one time; rhubarb crumble with proper custard, summer pudding, fresh fruit trifle. Barbara also hand-makes the pub's chips and crisps every day! South-facing front patio with benches and a beer garden to the rear (with children's play area). Children welcome in the pub to eat. *Open 11-2.30, 6-11, (Sun 12-2.30, 7-10.30).* ***Bar Food*** *12-2, 7.30-9.30 (no food Sun).* ***Beer*** *Crouch Vale Bitter, Marston's Pedigree, Benskins Bitter, Nethergate Bitter, guest beer. Garden, children's play area. Amex, Diners, MasterCard,* ***VISA***

ELSLACK — Tempest Arms

Tel 01282 842450 **Fax 01282 843331** Map 6 B1 P
Elslack Skipton North Yorkshire BD23 3AY

Just off the A56 near its junction with the A59 and only three miles from Skipton, the pub nestles in a verdant hollow with its own stream winding picturesquely round the garden. To the rear of the pub proper, and with its own secure entrance, a purpose-built block houses well-appointed bedrooms that are fully equipped for the '90s with TVs, telephones and plenty of well-lit workspace for the business guest. En suite bathrooms are a little small, but being fully tiled with strong over-bath showers they are more than adequate. Two rooms have three beds. Double-glazed and well back from the road, accommodation here promises less Tempest than Midsummer Night's Dream. *Open 11-11 (Sun 12-10.30).* ***Beer*** *Jennings Bitter, Cumberland Ale, Mild & Cocker Hoop, two guest beers. Garden.* ***Accommodation*** *10 bedrooms, all en suite, £54 (family room sleeping three/four £66, single £47). Children welcome overnight (under-5s stay free in parents' room), additional bed (£12) & cot available. No dogs. Amex, Diners, MasterCard,* ***VISA***

ELSTEAD Woolpack

Tel 01252 703106 Map 15 E3 

The Green Elstead Surrey GU8 6HD

Originally built as a wool-bale store in the 18th century, the attractive tile-hung Woolpack is now comfortably countrified and adorned with various artefacts relating to its previous use: bobbins and spindles of yarn, a lamb's fleece and a partly woven rug. Today folk flock here to enjoy the famously-generous portions of home-cooked dishes chosen from a long blackboard menu which might encompass duck casseroled in sherry, gammon with honey, mustard and caper cream sauce, pork steak with apples and cider, and good fresh seafood like dressed crab salad, mussels, and swordfish in apricot wine and mint sauce. No sandwiches, but ploughman's platters are popular. Genuinely home-made puddings might include fruit pavlovas, raspberry and hazelnut roulade and crème brulée. Arrive early on Sundays, especially if intending to tuck into a decent roast, as it gets very busy. Children can have smaller portions at smaller prices, or opt for baked beans and tinned spaghetti on toast. A family room has nursery rhyme murals and bunches of flowers hung up to dry from the ceiling; there's also a slide, swing and climbing frame in the pretty garden. *Open 11-2.30, 6-11 (Sun 12-3, 7-10.30).* ***Bar Food** 12-2, 7-9.45 (Sun 7.30-9).* ***Beer** Green King IPA, Young's Bitter, Ansells Bitter, guest beers. Garden, outdoor eating, children's play area. Family room. Diners, MasterCard,* ***VISA***

ELSTED MARSH Elsted Inn

Tel 01730 813662 Map 15 D3 

Elsted Marsh Midhurst West Sussex GU29 0JT

Unprepossessing Victorian roadside pub built to serve the railway in the steam age (when there was a station here), but later left stranded by Dr Beeching's 'axe' in the 1960s. This explains the old railway photographs that adorn the thankfully unmodernised and unpretentious bars, in what is very much a local community pub, free of background music and electronic games but with plenty of traditional pub pastimes like shove ha'penny, darts, cards, dominoes and even conversation. There are two small bars with lots of original wood in evidence, original shutters and open fires. A small dining-room, candle-lit in the evening, boasts an old pine dresser and colourful cloths on a few dining tables surrounded by a motley collection of old chairs. Tweazle Jones and her partner Barry Horton produce varied menus with dishes that are always home-made and based on good local produce – hand-made bread from the National Trust bakery at Slindon and free-range eggs, ducks and chicken from a nearby farm, to name but a few suppliers. Local specialities listed on the daily-changing blackboards may include Ron Puttock's hand-made sausages, Sussex bacon pudding, downland rabbit in mustard, Sussex cassoulet, and boiled mutton in caper sauce. Choices extend to home-made soups (creamy onion), mussels baked with garlic and cheese, salmon fishcakes, and vegetarian bean korma, alongside good snacks like hand-cut sandwiches, ploughman's lunches and filled baked potatoes. The sweet-toothed can indulge in a gooey treacle tart, dark chocolate mousse or home-made banana and chocolate ice cream. Winter Wednesday nights are popular curry nights. Booking essential at weekends. Children can have half portions at half price, and there's a wooden playhouse in the shady garden to keep them amused, plus pétanque for the adults. The rear coach house is due to be converted into four en suite letting rooms. *Open 11-3, 5.30-11(from 6 Sat), Sun 12-3, 6-10.30.* ***Bar Food** 12-2.30, 7-9.30 (till 10 Fri & Sat, till 9 Sun). Free House.* ***Beer** Ballard's Best, Trotton, Nyewood, Gold & Wassail, Fuller's London Pride, guest beers. Garden, outdoor eating, boules. Family room. MasterCard,* ***VISA***

Pubs – note that food is only recommended in those pubs with ***Bar Food*** times in the statistics at the end of an entry. Restaurant food in pubs is *never* recommended unless specifically mentioned. Some pubs are recommended for B&B or Atmosphere only – each entry's statistics indicate our recommendation.

ELTON Loch Fyne Oyster Bar

Tel 01832 280298 **Fax 01832 280170** Map 7 E4 **JaB**
The Old Dairy Elton Peterborough Cambridgeshire PE8 6SH

An old dairy with a courtyard is the picturesque setting for this splendid restaurant. The day begins with a snack menu which includes an all-day kipper breakfast (£5.95), scrambled eggs and smoked salmon (£4.20), and open sandwiches of cheese or smoked salmon paté. Soups such as tomato or mushroom (£2.95) could precede dishes which can be ordered as starters or light dishes, including Loch Fyne oysters (£2.60 for 3, £8.90 for 12) and herring fillets in four marinades (£4.95). Shellfish of the day (from £7.20) could be langoustines, scallops or whole lobster and the speciality Bradhan Rost smoked salmon comes either hot with a whisky sauce or cold with horseradish (£8.50) – Bradhan Orach is a more strongly flavoured version. A specials board offers white fish, which varies according to the day's catch and could be whole lemon sole (from £6), and the vegetarian dish of the day. Other options include sirloin steak (£9.95) and occasionally venison. Mull Cheddar, Dunsyre Blue and Inverlochy goat's cheese (£3.50) are a good alternative to a pudding, unless of course you cannot resist sticky toffee pudding, fruit crumble or banoffi pie (all £3.50). There is level access for prams and wheelchairs. Landscaped courtyard for outdoor eating. One room no-smoking. Booking recommended. ***Seats** 80 (+40 outside). **Open** 9-9 (Sun till 4). **Closed** D Sun, 25, 26 Dec & 1 Jan. MasterCard, **VISA***

ELY Old Fire Engine House £50

Tel 01353 662582 Map 10 B2 **R**
25 St Mary's Street Ely Cambridgeshire CB7 4ER

An 18th-century town house, near the Cathedral, that gained its present name at the turn of the century when Ely's horse-drawn fire engine was kept here. It's a place of enormous charm and friendliness; you pass through the kitchen to reach the main eating-room with its uneven tiled floor, kitchen tables and pew seating. All rooms (one non-smoking) boast a changing collection of pictures by various artists, many local, as the whole house is as much an art gallery as a restaurant. Cooking tends towards the homely rather than the sophisticated but does not lack interest with dishes, often from local recipes, such as herrings pickled in dill with yoghurt and cucumber, mitoon of pork, beef and mushroom casserole with Guinness and port, and lemon sole with prawn sauce plus a vegetarian dish like baked avocado stuffed with brazil nuts with a black-eyed bean stew. Good fresh ingredients are drawn as much as possible from the surrounding Fens and the bread is home-made. Tempting puds might include meringues with cream, sherry trifle, apple pie (made with delicious, sugary, melt-in-the-mouth short pastry), and apricot and brandy ice cream. Very long notes accompany each wine on a fairish list. No special children's menu, but half-portions are always available. A private room can be made available for nursing mothers, and a safe garden has a swing and lots of space for the young ones. Indoors, there's a sitting-room with books and toys. In summer some tables are set out in a pretty walled garden. ***Seats** 36. Private Room 22. L 12.30-2 D 7.30-9. Closed D Sun, all Bank Holidays & 2 weeks Christmas. MasterCard, **VISA***

EMERY DOWN New Forest Inn

Tel & Fax 01703 282329 Map 14 C4 **P**
Emery Down Lyndhurst Hampshire SO43 7DY

Prettily set in woodland, the building of the inn was the result of the first successful establishment of squatters' rights on Crown land in the early 18th-century. The original caravan that used to sell ale forms part of the front lounge porchway. Much extended since, it has a big, modern open-plan bar with effective country touches and real fires. The reliable bar food available here aims to please all tastes, and the regular printed menu features old favourites and chips, as well as some interesting home-cooked dishes. A daily-changing specials board enhances the choice further with possibly rabbit in peaches and cream, rack of lamb with Cumberland sauce and sautéed pork in green peppercorn and cream sauce. Home-made puddings like sticky toffee pudding and cheesecake round off the meal. Recently redecorated bedrooms are clean, comfortable and homely, three having en suite facilities (two with bath), the fourth having its own private, but not en suite, bathroom. The three-level rear garden is a super summer spot for alfresco imbibing. Whitbread Wayside Inn. *Open 11-11 (Sun 12-10.30).* ***Bar Food*** *12-9.30 (till 9 Sun).* ***Beer*** *Flowers Original, Strong Country Bitter, Greene King Abbot Ale, Boddingtons, Garden, outdoor eating, summer barbecue.* ***Accommodation*** *4 bedrooms, 3 en suite, £50 (single £25). Children welcome overnight (under-5s stay free in parents' room), additional bed (£10) available. MasterCard,* ***VISA***

EMPINGHAM — White Horse

Tel 01780 460221 **Fax 01780 460521** Map 7 E3 P
2 Main Street Empingham Oakham Leicestershire LE15 8PR

A stone's throw from serene Rutland Water, Roger Bourne's civilised pub (including a newly-refurbished bar area) is the centre of village life, a meeting-place for walkers and birdwatchers and convenient for access from the A1 at Stamford and the market town of Oakham. In attempting to be all things to most callers its day stretches from morning coffee and croissants through lunches and cream teas to late evening suppers. Central to the three eating areas, which include a family room, is the food counter displaying cold meats and home-made sweets backed by a blackboard of daily dishes offering the likes of beef chasseur, Rutland chicken, sweet and sour prawns, and cod mornay, plus baked ham, self-served salads, junior pizzas and filled baguettes (lunch only). The best bedrooms are in the stables, kitted out in varnished pine and each with its own well-appointed bathroom. In the main building, rooms are bright and neat though more modest, with shared bathing facilities. One room has a four-poster. *Open 11-11 (till 10.30 Sun).* ***Bar Food*** *12-2.15, 6.30-9.45 (till 10 Sat, till 9.30 Sun).* ***Beer*** *John Smith's, Courage Directors, Ruddles Best, guest beer. Garden, outdoor eating. Family room.* ***Accommodation*** *14 rooms, 9 en suite, £55 (four-poster £60, family room sleeping three £55-£65, single £32). Children welcome overnight (under-2s stay free in parents' room), extra bed & cot available. Disabled WC. Amex, Diners, MasterCard,* ***VISA***

ESKDALE GREEN — Bower House Inn

Tel 01946 723244 **Fax 01946 723308** Map 4 C3 
Eskdale Green Holmbrook Cumbria CA19 1TD

The Connors' informal, friendly inn is a delightful place to stay for peace and quiet in the beautiful Eskdale valley, as the growing numbers of returning guests will vouch for. Comfortable bedrooms are divided between the main house, where they are abundant in character, the converted stables and garden cottages, subtly extended and thoughtfully equipped to meet modern-day demands. In the clubby bar, incidently the Headquarters of the Eskdale cricket team who play in the adjacent field, there is a warming winter fire and country furnishings, and opens on to an enchanting, enclosed garden of pine and shrub, with a tiny wooden bridge traversing the village stream. For the best choice of home-cooked food look to the specials board for such dishes as wild boar cooked in cider, guinea fowl with cranberry sauce, nut roast with tomato sauce and puddings like lemon mousse and sticky toffee pudding. A fixed-price dinner menu is the preferred choice of residents. A warm welcome extends to families; there are three large rooms suitable for family occupation and children can play safely in the garden. After a restful night, it's traditional to tuck into a hearty Lakeland breakfast. *Open 11-11 (Sun 12-3, 6.30-10.30).* ***Bar Food*** *12-2, 6.30-9.30. Free House.* ***Beer*** *Theakston Best, Hartleys XB, Courage Directors, Younger Scotch Bitter, guest beer. Riverside garden, outdoor eating, children's play area.* ***Accommodation*** *24 rooms, all en suite, £60 (family room £72, single £47). Children welcome overnight (under-5s £6, 5-12s £10 in parents' room), additional bed & cot available. No dogs. Amex, MasterCard,* ***VISA***

We endeavour to be as up-to-date as possible, but inevitably some changes to data and key personnel may occur at restaurants and hotels after the Guide goes to press. Prices should also be taken as indications rather than firm quotes.

ETTINGTON Houndshill

Tel 01789 740267 Map 14 C1 **P**

Banbury Road Ettington Stratford-on-Avon Warwickshire CV37 7NS

A friendly, family-operated roadhouse which includes children's play areas and a licensed campsite in its extensive grounds. The clean, tidy decor of the lounge bar and adjoining dining-room is repeated in the pine-clad bedrooms and compact bathrooms with over-bath showers. Up-to-date direct-dial phones and remote-control TVs ensure a degree of comfort commensurate with the price range. Very useful to know, as it's beside the A422 Banbury road, four miles south of Stratford. *Open 12-3, 6-11 (from 7 Sat), Sun 12-3, 7-10.30. Free House.* ***Beer*** *Theakston Best, & XB. Garden, children's play area. Family room.* ***Accommodation*** *8 bedrooms, all en suite, £45 (family rooms sleeping up to four £60, single £28). Children welcome overnight, additional bed (from £10) & cot (£5) available. Pub and accommodation closed all 25 & 26 Dec. MasterCard,* ***VISA***

EVESHAM Evesham Hotel 65% £86

Tel 01386 765566 **Fax 01386 765443** Map 14 C1 **HR**

Cooper's Lane off Waterside Evesham Hereford & Worcester WR11 6DA

A largely Georgian hotel, with Tudor origins, set in several acres of secluded grounds on the edge of town and run in their own jolly style by the Jenkinson family for over 20 years. The 'Jenkinson' humour breaks out all over the place, from a what-the-butler-saw' machine by the pool (Evesham-by-the-Sea) to the padlocked perfume in the (award-winning) public loos, which also have magazines and a portable radio in each cubicle. Bedrooms (keys are attached to a teddy bear) have a traditional feel with candlewick bedspreads and all sorts of extras from playing cards to rubber ducks and clothes-washing liquid in the bathroom. Some rooms have characterful beams and others a period feel with painted Georgian panelling. Public rooms centre around a comfortable, chintzy bar. Freephone reservation number: 0800 716969. ***Rooms*** *40. Garden, croquet, indoor swimming pool, playground. Closed 25 & 26 Dec. Amex, Diners, MasterCard,* ***VISA***

Cedar Restaurant £60

The weekly-changing menu is jokey, but the setting is elegant (Regency style) and the results on the plate quite satisfactory with dishes like roulade of salmon in filo pastry, the popular dhal soup, braised lamb's hearts on a paté croute or gammon with wild mushrooms. Separate menus provide for vegetarians, children and those looking for simpler dishes – smoked salmon, grills, cold meats and salads. Good selection of British cheeses. At lunchtime there is a buffet option (£6.85) in addition to the regular menu. The French and Germans probably won't appreciate the wine list here since neither of their countries is represented! On the other hand, everyone else will, since the choice is huge and the prices are low. If you didn't know, even Sweden and Luxembourg are wine-producing countries. ***Seats*** *55. Parties 8. Private Room 15. L 12.30-2 D 7-9.30.*

EWELL Superfish

Tel 0181-393 3674 Map 15 E3 **JaB**

9 Castle Parade Bypass Road Ewell Surrey KT17 2PR

Part of the excellent Surrey-based chain serving traditional British fish and chips fried in beef dripping. See Morden entry for more details. Licensed. ***Seats*** *36.* ***Open*** *11.30-2 (Sat till 2.30) & 5-10.30 (Thu-Sat till 11).* ***Closed*** *Sun 25, 26 Dec & 1 Jan. Amex, MasterCard,* ***VISA***

Always ring ahead and inform establishments of your exact requirements when travelling with children. Unannounced can, sadly, still mean unwelcome.

…TH St Michael's Hotel 63% £76

…1326 312707 **Fax 01326 211772** Map 12 B4 H
…acey Road Falmouth Cornwall TR11 4NB

…ocated directly opposite Gyllyngvase beach (reached through the garden), this hotel provides basic yet comfortable accommodation for the tourist or business visitor. Banquets/conferences for 200/250. There's a spacious bar/lounge with a sun terrace which overlooks award-winning gardens. Children's entertainment in high season. No dogs. ***Rooms** 65. Garden, indoor swimming pool, keep-fit equipment, sauna, spa bath, sun beds, outdoor play area. Amex, MasterCard,* ***VISA***

FAREHAM Solent Hotel 75% £120

Tel 01489 880000 **Fax 01489 880007** Map 15 D4 H
Solent Business Park Whiteley Fareham Hampshire PO15 7AJ

By J9 of the M27 (10 miles from both Portsmouth and Southampton) this gabled hotel dating from 1990 almost has the feel of a New England inn, successfully balancing wood and brick in its design and happily satisfying the contrasting needs of business and leisure guests, with conference facilities for up to 250, a business centre and a stylish leisure club. All the bedrooms are of Executive standard, in traditional style, with both working and relaxing space plus comprehensive comforts – from bathrobes to mini-bars. Children up to 16 are accommodated free in their parents' room. Committed young staff and expert management show good direction throughout. Plenty of easy parking. Shire Inns. ***Rooms** 88. Garden, tennis, indoor swimming pool, keep-fit equipment, squash, sauna, steam room, solarium, snooker. Amex, Diners, MasterCard,* ***VISA***

FAWKHAM Brandshatch Place 64% £111

Tel 01474 872239 **Fax 01474 879652** Map 11 B5 H
Fawkham Valley Road Fawkham Kent DA3 8NQ

A Georgian country house in red brick, standing in 12 acres of gardens and parkland not far from the entrance to Brands Hatch racing circuit. Conferences (up to 150 delegates) are big business, and there's a health and leisure club. There are two lounges (one with a bar counter) and a bar, roof terrace and informal restaurant in the club. Bedrooms are generally of a good size with armchairs and all the usual amenities. One room in the Mews is adapted for disabled guests. No dogs. ***Rooms** 41. Garden, indoor swimming pool, gym, squash, sauna, steam room, spa bath, solarium, snooker. Closed 25 Dec. Amex, Diners, MasterCard,* ***VISA***

FELBRIGG Felbrigg Park Restaurant & Tea Room

Tel 01263 838237 Map 10 C1 JaB
Felbrigg Hall Felbrigg Roughton Norfolk NR11 8PR

Located within the converted courtyard stabling area adjacent to the magnificent 17th-century hall, these National Trust refreshment rooms (no access charge) make ideal destinations after a long parkland stroll or at the end of a tour of the hall (admission fee unless members). Lunchtime visitors can enjoy a good home-made light lunch – soup (usually beef or chicken and vegetable) and roll (£2.10), steak pie, pork casserole (£6.15), salads (from £4.95), blackcurrant crumble, ginger sponge pudding with lemon sauce and custard, lemon and coconut sponge (all £2.50) – in the neat and tastefully decorated Park Restaurant, where waitresses attend to every need. In the adjacent, light and airy, self-service Turret Tea Room are snacks such as broccoli and cream cheese quiche or sausage and apple plait with side salad (£2.95). There are delicious home-made cakes like chocolate, coffee, various tea breads, scones and a spicy cherry cake to celebrate the Trust's 100th Anniversary – National Trust Centenary cake (80p). Warm summer days see the courtyard tables and chairs with parkland views filled to capacity. Very much a children-friendly place, offering a colouring menu, on which are also listed special children's events and activities provided during the summer months. The usual favourites are supplemented by half portions of many of the other dishes from the main menu; bottle warming, a high-chair, a limited selection of baby food, feeder cup, children's crockery, scribbling sheets and crayons are all part of the service, and 'if there is anything else we can do to make your children's visit more enjoyable, please ask for assistance'. A family room for inclement days, and a mother's changing area also available. Sunday roast (£6.25). No smoking throughout. ***Seats*** *54 Restaurant, 56 Tea Room, 28 Family Room (+ 44 outside).* ***Open*** *Tea Room 11-5.15 (Mar-Nov till 4). Restaurant L 12-2.* ***Closed*** *Tue & Fri, also Mon, Wed, Thu Nov-end Mar. Amex, MasterCard,* ***VISA***

FELIXSTOWE Hamiltons Tea Rooms

Tel 01394 282956 Map 10 D3 JaB
134 Hamilton Road Felixstowe Suffolk IP11 7AB

There's a traditional look to these tea rooms above a row of shops, aided by dried flowers, a Victorian fireplace and waitresses in black and white uniforms. Scones (62p) and cakes (chocolate or coffee sponge, flapjacks, shortbread – 68p) make an alluring display on the sideboard, and more substantial savoury dishes could include pork and apple hotpot, beef cobbler and home-made quiche with salad and baked potato (all £3.95). Follow with steamed pudding, apple pie or lemon crunch (from £1.25). A two-course special lunch is offered on Wednesdays only for £3.95. Children's portions are available and there are two high-chairs provided. A private room can be made available for nursing mums. Children's toys are provided indoors. Unlicensed. No smoking. ***Seats*** *50.* ***Open*** *9.30-4.30 (Wed till 1.45).* ***Closed*** *Sun, Mon, Bank Holidays. No credit cards.*

FEOCK Trelissick Garden Restaurant

Tel 01872 863486 Map 12 B3 JaB
Feock nr Truro Cornwall TR3 6QL

An idyllic setting overlooking the River Fal on a wonderful National Trust estate makes the Trelissick Garden restaurant perfect for a light snack, lunch or tea. A good selection of salads with ham or a meat pie (£5.95), a hot dish of the day (£5.30) and maybe smoked mackerel with horseradish sauce (£3.05) are typical lunchtime fare. In the morning you can have coffee and biscuits and afternoon tea is served from 2.15 – traditional Cornish Cream Tea (£3.20) or Trelissick Garden Tea (£4.50) with sandwiches and a slice of cake. There is a converted farm building known as the courtyard room with a counter-service snack bar. Children will enjoy the Woodcutter's Lunch of jacket wedges, sausages and baked beans (£2.60). High-chairs, booster seats, children's crockery, cutlery and place mats all provided. Changing facilities in the disabled toilets. Don't miss the garden and wonderful surrounding parkland. No smoking. ***Seats*** *65.* ***Open*** *10.30-5.15 (Mar & Oct to 4.45, Nov & Dec to 3.45) L 12-2.15.* ***Closed*** *23 Dec-1 Mar. Amex, MasterCard,* ***VISA***

FINCHINGFIELD Jemima's Tea Rooms

Tel 01371 810605 Map 10 B3 JaB
The Green Finchingfield Essex CM7 4JX

Jemima's is a 900-year-old beamed cottage in the picturesque village of Finchingfield and could not have been cast better than as a tea room. Simple, wholesome fare is on offer, from a variety salads (ham, cheese, paté or quiche) and sandwiches (£1.60) to blackboard specials of good-value snacks like toasted bacon or sausage sandwich with salad and tea or coffee (all for £2.50). Winter Warmer Specials (October-March) offer soup, followed by maybe an omelette or a stuffed baked potato, with tea or coffee (£4.95-£5.50). Cream tea is £3.25 and all the scones and cakes (coffee and walnut, chocolate and cherry etc) are home-made. There is a courtyard for alfresco summer eating. Unlicensed. No smoking. ***Seats*** *76 (+ 16 outside).* ***Open*** *10-5.30 (Sat & Sun till 6) (Nov-Feb till 4.30).* ***Closed*** *Mon & Fri Nov-Feb, 25 & 26 Dec. No credit cards.*

FITTLEWORTH The Swan

Tel 01798 865429 **Fax 01798 865546** Map 11 A6 P
Lower Street Fittleworth Pulborough West Sussex RH20 1EN

One can luxuriate in the peaceful beauty of the lovely award-winning garden of flowers and herbs of this 14th-century tile-hung inn, and see where the River Arun meets the Rother by taking a peaceful river walk. Inside, fresh flowers adorn the hallway and reception and the dark panelled picture lounge boasts a fine collection of early 19th-century paintings embedded in the upper panels. Spotless Laura Ashley-style bedrooms are comfortable and well appointed – TVs, tea-makers, trouser presses, telephones, hairdryers – and feature modern pine furniture, although two rooms have fine mahogany four-poster beds. Good en suite facilities, with three of the bedrooms sharing two smart bathrooms. A warm welcome awaits families; children can eat with parents anywhere in the bar, choose from their own menu or request smaller portions of adult dishes and eat at any time of the day. A wooden climbing frame in the safe garden will keep the more active offspring amused on fine days. Whitbread Wayside Inn. *Open 11-11 (Sun 12-10.30).* ***Beer*** *King & Barnes Sussex, Boddingtons, Wadworth 6X, Flowers Original, Gales HSB. Garden, children's play area.* ***Accommodation*** *10 bedrooms, 7 en suite, £40-£50 (single £25.50). Children welcome overnight (stay free in parents' room), additional bed & cot available. No dogs. Amex, Diners, MasterCard,* ***VISA***

FLETCHING Griffin Inn

Tel 01825 722890 **Fax 01825 722810** Map 11 B6 P
Fletching East Sussex TN22 3NS

Simon de Montfort's army camped outside Fletching church prior to the Battle of Lewes in 1256. These days visitors with a more peaceful intent are made more than welcome at the 16th-century Griffin Inn, which is at the heart of Saxon Fletching's picturesque main street, and is everything a village local should be. The main bar has old beams and wainscot walls, a copper-hooded brick fireplace and a motley collection of old pews and wheelback chairs; the public bar provides a pool table and fruit machine for the amusement of the local youth and there's a pretty restaurant. Good home-made food is a major attraction, with a varied blackboard menu available in the bar and a short, more imaginative daily-changing à la carte menu on offer in the restaurant (more extensive Fri and Sat evenings) – all draw on local, mostly organic, suppliers. An eclectic choice in the bar might range from celery, leek and Stilton soup, potted shrimps with hot ciabatta and local asparagus to Thai-spiced salmon fishcakes for starters, followed by main-course options like fish pie, lamb shank braised in Moroccan spices on couscous, steak and ale pie, roast Mediterranean vegetable flan or fresh cod and home-made chips. There are also chargrills, homely puddings (tarte tatin, summer pudding, white chocolate and Baileys mousse) and generous ploughman's platters. Excellent wine list with at least eight available by the glass. There are four charming, bedrooms, three with four-poster beds purpose-built to counteract the sloping floors and to ensure a level night's rest. All have en suite power showers (one with bath and shower), tea- and coffee-making kits and TVs. The substantial breakfast is worth getting up for. In summer, the rear garden offers outstanding views across rolling Sussex countryside and delicious weekend barbecues. *Open 12-3, 6-11 (till 10.30 Sun, maybe 12-11 Sat in summer – if fine).* ***Bar Food*** *12-2.30, 7-9.30. Free House.* ***Beer*** *Harveys Sussex Bitter, Hall & Woodhouse Tanglefoot, Fuller's London Pride, Hog's Back Traditional English Ale. Garden, patio, outdoor eating, summer weekend barbecue.* ***Accommodation*** *4 bedrooms, all en suite, £55-£65 (weekends £75, single £40). Children welcome overnight (stay free on sofa bed in parents' room). Check-in by arrangement. Pub & accommodation closed all 25 Dec. No dogs. Amex, MasterCard,* ***VISA***

FORD Plough Inn

Tel 01386 584215 Map 14 C1 
Temple Gutting Ford Gloucestershire GL54 5RU

A gregarious pub in something of an agrarian setting on a bend in the B4077. There's an old well in the walled garden and a mixture of abandoned filling station and farmyard behind. The simply furnished bars recall the pub's past days as a farmhouse with flagstone floors, pine tables and high-backed settles, and diners move easily

FROME — The Olde Bath Arms

Tel 01373 465045 Map 13 F1 

1 Palmer Street Frome Somerset BA11 1DS

A friendly family-owned restaurant in what was a 17th-century coaching inn, running a range of excellent home-made cakes and pastries. At lunchtime a blackboard menu might offer chicken supreme with cream sauce, vegetables or salad, roast beef with Yorkshire pudding or a salmon and prawn flan (all £3.95) and there are filled jacket potatoes with salad (£2.95). Lots of tempting puddings, maybe steamed syrup sponge or rhubarb crumble (£1.60). Sunday lunch is a bargain £6.95 for three courses. Two high-chairs, and half-portions (under-5s charged only for what they eat); a bedroom is available to change or feed baby. Close to Longleat wildlife park, zoo, and caves. ***Seats** 72. **Open** 10-3 (also Fri & Sat for dinner). **Closed** D Sun, all Mon & Bank Holidays. Diners, Mastercard, **VISA***

FYFIELD — White Hart

Tel 01865 390585 **Fax 01865 390671** Map 15 D2 

Main Road Fyfield Abingdon Oxfordshire OX13 5LN

John and Sherry Howard's 500-year-old former chantry house (abolished in 1548) has been a pub since 1580 when St John's College in Oxford, large local landowners, leased it to tenants but reserved the right to 'occupy it if driven from Oxford in pestilence' – so far this has not been invoked! At some time in its history the large hall was divided into two floors, but in 1963 this was removed, thereby restoring the main hall's original proportions and exposing the 15th-century arch-braced roof to view. There's still a splendid 30-foot-high minstrel's gallery overlooking the main bar and the interior features original oak beams and flagstone floors. The very large, rambling lawned garden includes a children's play area. Just off the A420, seven miles from Abingdon and eight miles from Oxford. *Open 11-3, 6-11 (Sun 12-3, 7-10.30). Free House. **Beer** Boddingtons, Hook Norton Best, Wadworth 6X, Theakston Old Peculier, two guest beers. Garden, children's play area. Family rooms. Closed all 25 & 26 Dec. Amex, MasterCard, **VISA***

GATESHEAD — Marks & Spencer Restaurant & Coffee Shop

Tel 0191-493 2222 **Fax 0191-493 2130** Map 5 E2 

Unit 46 Metro Centre Gateshead NE11 9YE

Fresh, imaginatively designed, and spotlessly clean, Marks & Spencer has created a delightful setting for its in-store restaurant. The food is simple, covering a wide selection of sandwiches (£1.75-£2.25), pies and salads. Hot food includes both meat and vegetarian dishes: steak and kidney pie (£2.99), chicken in basil sauce (£3.99) and leek and mushroom pastie (£3.39) all served with chips; plus some ethnic dishes such as sweet and sour chicken with egg rice (£4.99) or vegetable tikka and rice (£3.99). There are some delicious desserts: maybe double chocolate cheesecake, carrot cake (both £1.39) and peach and apricot torte (£1.09). A full English breakfast (£2.50) is served from 10 to 11.30. Ten high-chairs; a children's menu offers the usual favourites plus daily fresh dishes, available from breakfast onwards. There's also a parent and baby room with changing facilities and a nursing area. No smoking. ***Seats** 260. **Open** 10-6 (Thu till 7, Sat 9-5, Sun 11-4). **Closed** 25 Dec & 1 Jan. No credit cards.*

GATESHEAD — Newcastle Marriott — 70% — £125

Tel 0191-493 2233 **Fax 0191-493 2030** Map 5 E2 

MetroCentre Gateshead NE11 9XF

A tall, modern hotel faced in dark glass, just off the A1 and opposite the impressive MetroCentre. The spacious and modern white marble-floored foyer is stylishly appointed with wide brown leather settees and armchairs. Bedrooms (half designated non-smoking) have smart lightwood furniture and soft pastel colour schemes; all are well equipped – even to the extent of having video recorders with a selection of video cassettes for hire. Bathrooms have power showers and good towels. Ten highly distinctive, themed rooms are very original, well thought out and popular. Children can stay free in their parents' room. 24hr room service. Conference facilities for up to 450. ***Rooms** 148. Indoor swimming pool, spa bath, gym, sauna, steam room, solarium, beauty salon. Amex, Diners, MasterCard, **VISA***

Gatwick Airport — Forte Posthouse Gatwick — 63% — £77

Tel 01293 771621 **Fax 01293 771054** Map 15 E3 H
Povey Cross Road Horley Surrey RH6 0BA

On the A23 a mile north of the airport. Good modern bedrooms (where refurbishment is under way) include family rooms where two children can share with two adults free. Choice of conference and meeting rooms (up to 150 delegates), large long-term car park. Courtesy airport coach every 30 minutes (6.15am-11.45pm). ***Rooms*** *210. Coffee shop (7am-10.30pm). Amex, Diners, MasterCard,* **VISA**

Gerrards Cross — Santucci

Tel 01753 889197 Map 15 E2 JaB
24 Packhorse Road Gerrards Cross Buckinghamshire SL9 7DA

A spacious restaurant specialising in home-made pasta dishes. Flexible combinations of pasta and sauces are served to suit customers requirements. Particularly recommended are *trenette al pesto* – noodles in a cream and basil sauce, *fusilli al fumo* – pasta twists with smoked bacon, vodka, tomato and cream and *tagliolini verdi gratinati* – green noodles with ham and cheese (all £5). A daily list of specials might include the likes of fresh artichoke (£2.95), lamb's kidneys in garlic sauce (£9.50) and calf's liver with an onion and white wine sauce (£9.50). Excellent coffee. ***Seats*** *50.* ***Open*** *12-2.30 & 6.30-10.30.* ***Closed*** *D Sun, 25 & 26 Dec. MasterCard,* **VISA**

Gittisham — Combe House — 73% — £100

Tel 01404 42756 **Fax 01404 46004** Map 13 E2 H
Gittisham nr Honiton Devon EX14 0AD

Signposted off the A30, Thérèse and John Boswell's fine Elizabethan mansion enjoys a glorious setting in 3000 acres of Devon countryside. Guests have peace and relaxation a-plenty, and everywhere are interesting architectural features, antiques and personal touches by painter and sculptress Thérèse and her mother. There's some handsome panelling in the entrance hall and pictures of the family's horse-racing activities in the cosy bar. Bedrooms vary in size and price, larger rooms tending to have better views and more interesting furniture and pictures. One suite and two rooms have four-poster beds. The hotel owns fishing rights on the River Otter, with a season running from April to the end of September. ***Rooms*** *15. Garden, croquet, fishing. Closed 1st 2 weeks Feb. Amex, Diners, MasterCard,* **VISA**

> Any person using our name to obtain free hospitality is a fraud.
> Proprietors, please inform the police and us.

Glastonbury — Rainbow's End Café

Tel 01458 833896 Map 13 F1 
17a High Street Glastonbury Somerset BA6 9DP

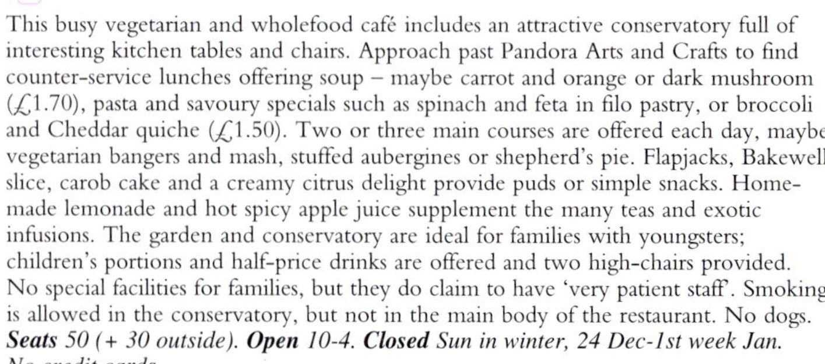

This busy vegetarian and wholefood café includes an attractive conservatory full of interesting kitchen tables and chairs. Approach past Pandora Arts and Crafts to find counter-service lunches offering soup – maybe carrot and orange or dark mushroom (£1.70), pasta and savoury specials such as spinach and feta in filo pastry, or broccoli and Cheddar quiche (£1.50). Two or three main courses are offered each day, maybe vegetarian bangers and mash, stuffed aubergines or shepherd's pie. Flapjacks, Bakewell slice, carob cake and a creamy citrus delight provide puds or simple snacks. Home-made lemonade and hot spicy apple juice supplement the many teas and exotic infusions. The garden and conservatory are ideal for families with youngsters; children's portions and half-price drinks are offered and two high-chairs provided. No special facilities for families, but they do claim to have 'very patient staff'. Smoking is allowed in the conservatory, but not in the main body of the restaurant. No dogs. ***Seats*** *50 (+ 30 outside).* ***Open*** *10-4.* ***Closed*** *Sun in winter, 24 Dec-1st week Jan. No credit cards.*

GLEMSFORD Black Lion

Tel 01787 280684 **Fax 01787 280817** Map 10 C3 P
Lion Road Glemsford Suffolk CO10 7RF

On entering the Lion, it turns out to have a treasure of a Tudor interior complete with half-timbered walls and rehabilitated timbers, quarry-tiled floors, country prints, leather armchairs and bay-window seats, all of which is at once both uncluttered and charming. Licensee Anne Curran concentrates on producing good home cooking: Suffolk hotpot, chili, speciality pizzas, traditional Indian curries, fisherman's pie and pork steaks in cider and apple sauce are good examples on the straightforward menu and specials board that serve both bar and dining-room. Their fruit pies and toffee apple tart are also home-made. A three-course traditional Sunday lunch is also offered. *Open 11-3, 6-11 (Sun 12-3, 7-10.30).* ***Bar Food*** *12-2.30, 6-9.30 (from 7 Sun).* ***Beer*** *Greene King. Garden, outdoor eating, summer barbecues, children's play area. Family room. No credit cards.*

GOATHLAND Mallyan Spout Hotel 61% £75

Tel 01947 896486 **Fax 01947 896327** Map 5 F3 H
Goathland Whitby North Yorkshire YO22 5AN

Goathland village is tucked into a fold in the moors two miles off the A159 and some 9 miles from Whitby. The unusual name of Peter and Judith Heslop's inn derives from the waterfall which cascades down the wooded valley just yards from the pub garden; hugging the valley's contours runs the North Yorkshire Moors Railway. Lunchtime in the Spout Bar can be a busy occasion with customers regularly overflowing into the Hunt Bar and hotel lounge next door. Hearty and ever-popular dishes are the lamb and barley broth, casserole of oxtail and butterbeans in red wine, Whitby codling and chips, and pot-roast knuckle of lamb with flageolet beans. Sandwiches and ploughman's lunches are also available. Puddings to follow may include rhubarb crumble and baked banana with caramel sauce. Evenings see the hotel restaurant move up a gear, with bar food restricted to the Spout public bar only. Bedrooms, indubitably upmarket in a purely pubby context, are housed to the rear and the side of the Jacobean-style, ivy-covered hotel; of the four small and cottagey rooms in the coach house, two are on the ground floor for those with mobility problems. Four large bedrooms (no dogs or children in these) have splendid views of the valley – two rooms have balconies; some rooms have half-tester or Laura Ashley coronet-draped beds. En suite bathrooms are generally on the small side, except in the four newest rooms. Negotiate, if you can, a larger room if arriving with a family; no reduction for children's meals in the restaurant at dinner (when children under 10 are not welcome); high-tea served from 6-7pm. *Open 11-11 (Sun 12-10.30).* ***Bar Food*** *12-2, 6.30-9 (from 7 Sun). Free House.* ***Beer*** *Malton Best Bitter. Garden, patio, outdoor eating.* ***Accommodation*** *24 bedrooms, all en suite, £75/£80 (family room £90 single). Children welcome overnight, additional bed (£10) & cot (£5) available. Closed all 25 Dec. Amex, MasterCard,* **VISA**

GOODWOOD Marriott Goodwood Park Hotel 69% £145

Tel 01243 775537 **Fax 01243 533802** Map 11 A6 H
Goodwood nr Chichester West Sussex PO18 0QB

A much modernised and extended old mansion, recorded in 1780 as Waterbeach House, stands at the heart of the newly refurbished Marriott Country Club complex within the 12,000 acre grounds of Goodwood Estate. A wealth of leisure facilities is included in complimentary Club membership afforded to all residents, and golf is available on the 18-hole course set against the backdrop of Goodwood House. While residential conferences are the mainstay of mid-week business, weekend breaks include tickets to the nearby Chichester Festival and events such as Goodwood races and the June Festival of Speed. A new business centre, staffed throughout normal office hours, is an added facility for conferences, whose capacity has increased to 150. Parking for 300 cars. 24hr room service. Children under 16 stay free in parents' room. ***Rooms*** *95. Garden, tennis, indoor swimming pool, sauna, solarium, spa bath, squash, gym, beauty salon, children's playground, golf course (18), drivng range, golf shop, coffee shop (9.30am-10pm). Amex, Diners, MasterCard,* **VISA**

GOUDHURST Star & Eagle £48

Tel 01580 211512 **Fax 01580 211416** Map 11 B5 I

High Street Goudhurst Kent TN17 1AL

Behind the splendid timbered and gabled facade vintage charm and modern comfort blend harmoniously in a fine 14th-century hostelry owned by Whitbread. Period appeal survives in exposed beams, vaulted stonework and old brick fireplaces in the public rooms, while creaking floors and odd angles are the order of the day in the bedrooms. These vary in size and shape and the majority are furnished in pine, though the four-poster room has some antiques. The inn is less than two miles from the A21. *Open 11-11 (Sun 12-10.30).* ***Beer*** *Flowers Original, Fremlins. Garden. Family room, children's playroom.* ***Accommodation*** *11 bedrooms, 9 en suite, £48 Sun-Thur, £53 Fri & Sat (four-poster £60-£70 Fri & Sat, single £35-£40). Children welcome overnight (under-5s stay free in parents' room, 3-16s £15), additional bed & cot available. Amex, MasterCard,* **VISA**

GRASMERE Wordsworth Hotel 72% £128

Tel 015394 35592 **Fax 015394 35765** Map 4 C3 HR

Grasmere nr Ambleside Cumbria LA22 9SW

Situated in the centre of the village in its own peaceful grounds, next to the churchyard where Wordsworth is buried, this hotel offers a pleasant haven from the constant tourist rush around the Lakes. Comfortable lounges, with deep armchairs and sofas, include one for non-smokers. Individually decorated bedrooms all have tubs and showers, and are of a good size, except for a few singles on the top floor, which are smaller and have showers only. Many rooms are suitable for family use and there's a children's menu plus high tea served between 5.30 and 6.30, in either the bedrooms or the Conservatory. Free golf at Keswick during the week. No dogs. ***Rooms*** *37. Garden, indoor swimming pool, keep-fit equipment, spa bath, solarium, games room. Amex, Diners, MasterCard,* **VISA**

Prelude Restaurant £75

At lunchtime Bernard Warne's menu is a tempting three-course affair, starting perhaps with a monkfish and prawn sausage with sauté potatoes and spring onion fondue, followed by medallions of beef fillet flamed in brandy, finished with cream and mushrooms. What better way to finish than a warm peach soufflé with a passion fruit sauce. At dinner a few more dishes are on the menu, and the four-course option is ideal after a day's lakeside walk - give in and be tempted by smoked trout and mango tart with horseradish sauce, followed by maybe prawn and scallop chowder and then perhaps Lunesdale duck breast stuffed with prunes on a Dubonnet and green peppercorn sauce. Save space for summer pudding with Lakeland cream or a plate of chocolate desserts with cherry compote. The mainly British cheeses are always in peak condition and worthy of consideration by those with a little red wine to finish. An easy-to-use wine list has good house recommendations. The latter include tasting notes, while the rest of the list does not, so you might have to seek advice. ***Seats*** *65. Parties 12. L 12.30-2 D 7-9 (Fri & Sat till 9.30). Set L £9.50/£12.50 Set D £29/£31.*

GRASSINGTON Dales Kitchen Tearooms & Brasserie

Tel 01756 753208 Map 6 C1 JaB

51 Main Street Grassington North Yorkshire BD23 5AA

The blueberry and marzipan pie (£2.80) is still a firm favourite here, along with deliciously soft scones and their famous Yorkshire rarebit (made with Black Sheep ale, Cheddar and mustard £3.95). In fact there is little on the menu at this 200-year-old former apothecary's house in the main street that will not please. The choices range from soup of the day (cucumber and mint or carrot and coriander £2.40), sandwich platters (from £3.05), salads and hot dishes such as Mediterranean vegetables with marinated feta on couscous (£5.45), spinach and feta cheese in filo pastry with salad and new potatoes (£4.95) to toasted teacakes (£1) and scrumptious home-made cakes like coffee and walnut, carrot or rich chocolate (all £1.75). Puds include a zesty lemon mousse pie and hot baked banana with brandy and cinnamon cream (both £2.80). This is not a place to bring kids who are hungry for burgers, chicken nuggets or fish fingers and chips, but they display a caring attitude towards families and are sensitive to children's needs. A range of simple sandwiches for little ones (from £1.30), children's cups, beakers, straws, bibs and wipes can all be provided; baby food and bottles will be heated, and there is a small lobby area that can be used for baby-changing. ***Seats*** *38 (+ 8 outside).* ***Open*** *10-5 (Sun to 5.30, 10.30-4pm weekdays in winter) & 7-9 (Fri-Sat only).* ***Closed*** *D Sun-Thu (advisable to phone and check during Dec-Feb, as times can vary), 24-27 Dec. MasterCard,* ***VISA***

GRAYS R Mumford & Son

Tel 01375 374153 Map 11 B5 JaB

6-8 Cromwell Road Grays Essex RM16

Fish is bought on a daily basis from Billingsgate market at this excellent fish and chip shop, which has been run by the same family for over 70 years. Traditional offerings such as cod and chips, plaice (both £7.75), sole (£10.50) and skate (£11) are backed up by starters such as prawn or crab cocktail. Chicken and steaks for meat-eaters. More elaborate menu in the evening. Children's menu. ***Seats*** *68.* ***Open*** *11.30-2 (Sat till 2.45) & 5.30-10 (Mon 5.30-9pm) (Sat till 10.30).* ***Closed*** *Sun, Bank Holidays & 25 Dec-6 Jan. No credit cards.*

GRAYSWOOD Wheatsheaf Inn

Tel 01428 644440 Map 11 A6 P

Grayswood Haslemere Surrey GU27 2DE

Victorian village inn, located beside the busy A286 near the parish church, cricket pitch and green (where there's a children's playground), run by Rex and Janet Colman. There's a neat and comfortable bar area with older-style furniture, quality prints and fabrics, with the adjacent spacious L-shaped restaurant sporting artistic plants, marble-topped tables, a terracotta-tiled floor and cushioned rattan chairs, creating a relaxing 'Italian-style' ambience. Quality of cooking and food presentation matches the stylish surroundings, with both the regularly-changing lunch and dinner menus listing imaginative pub fare; one menu is served throughout. Typical dishes might include Parma ham and melon, cod in home-made beer batter, warm salad of mushrooms, garlic and chicken, and freshly-prepared soups – parsnip and ginger – as well as lighter snacks like sandwiches, a mixed-cheese ploughman's and ham, egg and bubble and squeak. Specials might encompass rack of lamb with chargrilled vegetables and rosemary jus, fishcakes with lemon butter, fillet of cod with herb crust and fresh tomato sauce and rib-eye steak. Round off the meal with a home-made pudding: perhaps lemon cheesecake with strawberry coulis or summer pudding. Short, global list of keenly-priced wines. Seven comfortable, en suite bedrooms are housed in a rear brick extension. Uniformly modern in decor and furnishings, they have clean, marble-floored bathrooms, as well as TVs, telephones and tea-makers for added comfort. Children welcome. *Open 11-3, 6-11 (Sun 12-3, 7-10.30).* ***Bar Food*** *12-2, 6.30-10. Free House.* ***Beer*** *Ballard's Best & Wassail, Wadworth 6X, Wheatsheaf Bitter, Hall & Woodhouse Badger Best, occasional guest beer. Garden, outdoor eating.* ***Accommodation*** *7 bedrooms, all en suite, £60 (single £45). Children welcome overnight (under-5s stay free in parents' room), additional bed (£5) & cot available. Check-in by arrangement. No dogs. Amex, MasterCard,* ***VISA***

GREAT BIRCHAM Windmill Tea Room

Tel 01485 578393 Map 10 B1 JaB

Great Bircham nr King's Lynn Norfolk PE31 6SJ

This carefully restored windmill is a delight to visit and the 200-year-old coal-fired bakery oven is still producing bread rolls daily. There is a mill and bakery museum to wander around, after which one of Gina's teas is just the ticket. £2.50 buys you scones jam and cream, and there's a range of teacakes and other home-made cakes (65-80p). A few savoury snacks are available at lunchtime, such as rolls and sandwiches (from 90p) filled with cheese, ham or salmon and cucumber. Vegetable pasties (65p), sausage rolls (45p). Children's portions; changing facilities in the Ladies with table, mat, wipes and chair. Pony rides and a children's play area in the garden (for under-7s) with a small swing can be enjoyed by young families. A patio and small garden are open on fine days. The mill is situated on the B1155 Bircham-Snettisham road. Unlicensed. No smoking. ***Seats*** *78 (+30 garden/terrace).* ***Open*** *10-5.30.* ***Closed*** *1 Oct-Easter. No credit cards.*

Great Chesterford Plough

Tel 01799 530283 Map 10 B3 **P**
High Street Great Chesterford Essex CB10 1PL

Delightful 18th-century village pub with a traditional, unspoilt and well-cared-for interior, despite the addition of a more modern rear extension which houses the bar. Original cottagey bars feature exposed standing timbers and ceiling beams, two warming winter fires in inglenooks and neatly arranged tables. The airy extension leads out on to an attractive patio and lawn for summer alfresco drinking. Children can enjoy the large adventure playground with its aerial runway, wooden climbing frames and swings. *Open 11-3, 6-11 (Sun 12-4, 7-10.30). **Beer** Greene King. Garden, children's play area. Family room. MasterCard,* ***VISA***

Great Rissington The Lamb

Tel 01451 820388 **Fax 01451 820724** Map 14 C1 **P**
Great Rissington Cheltenham Gloucestershire GL54 2LP

Enjoying views over the village and rolling Cotswold countryside, this mellow stone-built pub dates back some 300 years to when it was a farmhouse. Well extended over the years by the Cleverly family, the interior comprises two civilised and comfortable bars, both decorated with plates, pictures and collections of old cigarette tins; above one of the fireplaces is a propeller from a wartime bomber which crashed in the garden. Home-cooked bar food is listed on a blackboard and ranges from French onion soup and chicken liver paté for a snack or starter to steak pie, liver and bacon, lamb curry and whole lemon sole. A separate menu operates in the neat rear restaurant. Tranquil overnight accommodation is offered in fourteen charming bedrooms. All are individually decorated with pretty fabrics and wall coverings, antique furnishings and two sport carved four-poster beds. Maintained to a good standard with good en suite facilities (five with showers rather than baths), they make a virtue out of not having television or radios in most of the rooms, but addicts will find a television (and log fire) in the cosy residents' lounge as well as in the six top-of-the-range suites. Two new spacious suites 'Millie's House' and 'Jemmima's House' are located at the bottom of the garden on the site of the indoor swimming pool. The peaceful summer hillside garden makes the most of the views, as do some of the bedrooms. *Open 11.30-2.30, 6.30-11 (Sun 12-2.30, 7-10.30). **Bar Food** 12-1.45, 7-9 (till 9.30 Fri & Sat). Free House. **Beer** Morland Old Speckled Hen, guest beer. Garden, outdoor eating. **Accommodation** 14 bedrooms, all en suite, £52 (four-poster £60, suite £65-£75, single from £30). Children welcome overnight (under-2s free if sharing parents' room), additional bed (£10) & cot available (£3.50). Dogs £1.50. Pub and accommodation closed 25 & 26 Dec. Amex, MasterCard,* ***VISA***

Great Yarmouth Carlton Hotel 67% £79

Tel 01493 855234 **Fax 01493 852220** Map 10 D1 **H**
Marine Parade Great Yarmouth Norfolk NR30 3JE

The Carlton has a fine seafront location directly opposite Wellington Pier. The hotel's impressive interior houses conference facilities for up to 180. Bedrooms (refurbished during 1995) have bright colour schemes and smart tiled bathrooms. Children up to 12 free in parents' room. Covered parking for 22 cars. Free admission to a nearby leisure centre. ***Rooms** 95. Games room, hair salon. Amex, Diners, MasterCard,* ***VISA***

Gretton Royal Oak

Tel 01242 602477 **Fax 01242 602387** Map 14 C1 **P**
Gretton Winchcombe Gloucestershire GL54 5EP

Extensive gardens and playing areas (including a tennis court for rent) and regular summer visits by the steam train from Winchcombe all contribute to the irresistible summer attractions of the Royal Oak. Low hop-hung beams adorned with pewter mugs and chamber pots and open log fires, whose glow is reflected in polished flagstones, make it equally appealing in winter. Add to this a good range of real ales and a vast blackboard menu and you have unravelled the secrets of this Cotswold pub's popular success. Mussels grilled with Stilton, chicken liver paté and garlic mushrooms can be either snacks or starters. Main courses run from Gloucester sausages with Cumberland sauce and ham, cheese and mushroom pasta bake to lamb cutlets with mint sauce. Twice-weekly fish deliveries may yield halibut with yoghurt and Cajun spices, alongside the usual trout and mackerel dishes. No sandwiches, but ploughman's platters are served all day. Finish off, perhaps, with chocolate fudge cake or caramelised Granny's apple. Children welcome. *Open 11-3, 6-11 (Sun 12-3, 7-10.30).* ***Bar Food*** *12-2, 7-9.30. Free House.* ***Beer*** *Smiles Best, John Smith's, Wadworth 6X, Ruddles County, Morland Old Speckled Hen, Marston's Pedigree. Garden, outdoor eating. Closed all 25 & 26 Dec. Amex, MasterCard,* ***VISA***

GRIMSBY — Leon's

Tel 01472 356282 Map 7 F1 JaB

Riverside 1 Alexandra Road Grimsby North East Lincolnshire DN31 1RD

Full use of the local fishing boats provides the excellent raw materials for the menu at this family-run fish restaurant. Plaice on the bone (£5.50), home-made fishcakes (£3.35), skate (£5.50) and haddock (£4.75) are all popular choices, each served with chips and bread and butter. Family-friendly, with a children's menu for the under-12s; children's early evening meals are served from 5pm daily (except Mondays). Three high-chairs and three booster seats. ***Seats*** *80.* ***Open*** *12-2 (Fri from 11.30) & 5-9.30 (Sat 11.30-9.30, Sun 12-6.30).* ***Closed*** *Mon, Bank Holidays (exc Good Friday) & 2 weeks Christmas. No credit cards.*

GRINDLEFORD — Maynard Arms Hotel — £65

Tel 01433 630321 **Fax 01433 630445** Map 6 C2 I

Main Road Grindleford Derbyshire S30 1HP

A solid-stone roadside inn located in the Peak National Park, on a hillside outside the village. There's a spacious and attractive public bar, and the Longshaw cocktail bar exudes a stylish and comfortable ambience for the enjoyment of some simply conceived and reliably produced bar food. Regular dishes include almond chicken, seafood linguine and original Yorkshire puddings filled with beef stew or Cumberland sausage. More adventurous choices may include swordfish steak with lemon butter, braised steak with a rich red wine sauce and half rack of ribs with barbecue sauce. All comers are invited also to leave room for the traditional Bakewell pudding served hot with cream. As befits an old coaching inn, the grand style, large, airy bedrooms overlook the Derwent Valley through elegant stone mullion windows. Suitably up-to-date accessories include direct-dial phones, remote-control TVs and trouser presses. Residents' lounge and conference/function facilities. *Open 11-3, 6-11, (Sun 12-10.30).* ***Bar Food*** *12-2, 6-9.30 (Sun 12-9.30). Free House.* ***Beer*** *Flowers Original, Morland Old Speckled Hen, Boddingtons. Garden, outdoor eating. Family room.* ***Accommodation*** *11 bedrooms, all en suite, £65-£75 (weekend £85-£95, single £49-£55, weekend £60). Children welcome overnight, additional bed (£15) & cot available. Amex, MasterCard,* ***VISA***

HAILEY — Bird in Hand

Tel 01993 868321 **Fax 01993 868702** Map 14 C2

Whiteoak Green Hailey Witney Oxfordshire OX8 5XP

A delightful 'residential country inn' in a rural setting, one mile north of Hailey on B4022. The neat, low-walled roadside garden gives an indication of the standards aimed for inside and the large car park shows its popularity as a dining pub. Inside, four stone-walled bar rooms include one with a long bar, sofa, pews and old tables, plus another with an inglenook where a wood fire burns during winter; the rooms are candle-lit at night. Ivan Reid's menu offers a long list of dishes that might include smoked goose breast with pickled red cabbage and pear, smoked salmon fishcake with home-made pesto, three or so pasta dishes (linguine with queen scallops, salmon and prawns in a wine and dill sauce), rack of lamb with aubergines and tomato in a redcurrant sauce, and confit of duck with potato rösti and pulses. These are supplemented by a blackboard of daily fresh fish (roast shark steak with pimentos and sweet chili sauce, grilled octopus and fennel with tomato salsa, turban of salmon and sole with scallops and chives) and other specials like globe artichoke with smoked salmon and scrambled egg, and roast lamb hock with garlic, rosemary and honey. The snack card offers the likes of ploughman's lunches, sandwiches, scampi, home-cooked cold ham and children's favourites. Sixteen spacious and comfortable, cottagey rooms are in a U-shaped, two-storey building with wooden balconies overlooking a central grassed courtyard. Two ground-floor twin rooms for the disabled; two large, family rooms have a double and a single bed plus a sofa bed and room for a cot. Pine furnishings, thoughtful touches and good housekeeping bring all rooms up to an above-average pub standard. Room-only prices are quoted, but the prices we quote here include cooked breakfasts (as for all the entries in this Guide). *Open 11-11 (Sun 12-3, 7-10.30).* ***Bar Food*** *12-1.45, 7-9.30 (till 9.15 Sun). Free House.* ***Beer*** *Boddingtons, Marston's Pedigree, Wadworth 6X. Patio, outdoor eating.* ***Accommodation*** *16 bedrooms, all en suite, £53.95 Sun-Thu, £65 Fri & Sat (single £46.95, £53 Fri & Sat). Children welcome overnight (under-3s stay free in parents' room, over-3s £15), additional bed & cot available. Check-in by arrangement on Sun afternoon. Closed all 25 & 26 Dec. MasterCard,* ***VISA***

HALE — Est Est Est

Tel 0161-928 1811 Map 6 B2 **JaB**
183 Ashley Road Hale Trafford WA15 9FB

The menu is the same throughout the chain (see under Knutsford) although charcoal grills also available here. Two high-chairs and 'make your own pizza menu' offered; plenty of floor space for push chairs - and air space for balloons! ***Seats*** *90.* ***Open*** *12-2.30 & 6-11 (Sat 12-11.30, Sun 12-10.30).* ***Closed*** *25 & 26 Dec. Amex, MasterCard,* ***VISA***

HALIFAX — Holdsworth House 69% £103

Tel 01422 240024 **Fax 01422 245174** Map 6 C1 **H**
Holdsworth nr Halifax Calderdale HX2 9TG

A 17th-century manor house three miles north of Halifax has for some time been a charming hotel in the hands of the Pearson family. Period appeal remains in the day rooms, notably the three handsome oak-panelled rooms that make up the restaurant. The entrance hall also features polished panelling, and the lounge opens on to an attractive courtyard. The best bedrooms are four split-level suites and the rest are both neat and comfortable, with colourful fabrics and mainly period furniture. Two rooms are specially adapted for disabled guests. Characterful meeting rooms, the largest of which can hold 150. ***Rooms*** *40. Garden. Closed 1 week Christmas. Amex, Diners, MasterCard,* ***VISA***

HALLATON — Bewicke Arms

Tel 01858 555217 Map 7 D4 **P**
1 Eastgate Hallaton Leicestershire LE16 8UB

400-year-old thatched country inn standing above the Welland Valley in the heart of fine Leicestershire countryside. Hallaton itself is locally renowned for the parish church's Norman tower, the conical butter cross on the village green – right across the road from the pub – and the tiny village museum which offers a unique insight into its rural past. The pub is a cracking good local and a predictable printed menu lists the usual steaks and grills, ploughman's lunches and sandwiches – look to the specials board for more adventurous options. Starters typically include a 'help yourself' crock of home-made soup (carrot and tomato) and deep-fried Brie, while top-sellers among the main courses include beef goulash, orange chicken, and salmon with lemon and dill butter. Vegetarians get a good look in, too, with aubergine and chick pea moussaka, and there's a fair choice of home-made puddings of the banoffi pie and treacle sponge and custard genre. The pub is consistently busy and the Bottom Room, stone clad with a bow window, Austrian blinds and an effective library theme, opens when demand dictates. At weekends it's almost certain to be full, so better book. Children welcome. *Open 12-2.30 (till 3 Sun), 7-11.* ***Bar Food*** *12-2, 7-9.45. Free House.* ***Beer*** *Marston's Pedigree, Ruddles Best & County, Bass. Garden, patio, outdoor eating. MasterCard,* ***VISA***

HAMPTON COURT Blubeckers

See entries under Odiham and Shepperton

HAREWOOD Harewood Arms

Tel 0113 288 6566 **Fax 0113 288 6064** Map 6 C1 
Harrogate Road Harewood Leeds LS17 9LH

A fashionable address opposite the gates of Harewood House and convenient location on the A61 halfway between Leeds and Harrogate ensure particular mention for this elegant inn. Formerly a coaching house, with a history dating back to 1815, it has been meticulously restored by Sam Smith, the brewers of Tadcaster. Though fully carpeted and rather studiously appointed, the three lounge bars retain an essentially pubby feel and are much frequented by a business, golfing and race-going fraternity. Traditional oak bed frames and freestanding furniture have been used as a unifying theme in individually designed bedrooms, the majority of which are in the former coachhouse wing overlooking the terrace, formal rose garden and rolling Yorkshire countryside. Four are conveniently located on the ground floor. A full range of room accessories – from remote-control TVs and trouser presses to bidets and over-bath showers – is impressive, a factor reflected in their rather higher-than-average room prices. *Open 11-11 (Sun 12-10.30).* ***Beer*** *Sam Smith's Old Brewery Bitter. Garden, terrace. Family room.* ***Accommodation*** *24 rooms, all en suite, £78 (reduced weekend tariff, single £50). Children welcome overnight, additional bed (£12) & cot (£8) available. Amex, Diners, MasterCard,* ***VISA***

HARROGATE Bettys

Tel 01423 502746 **Fax 01423 565191** Map 6 C1 
1 Parliament Street Harrogate North Yorkshire HG1 2QU

Originally a family business founded in 1919 by a Swiss confectioner, this traditionally decorated café has expanded to include establishments in Ilkley, Northallerton and York (see those towns for addresses and phone numbers; see also entry under York for *Taylors Tea Rooms* in the same group). Bettys prides itself on the baking of over 400 specialities both sweet and savoury. At lunchtime, there is a wide range of sandwiches plain or toasted from egg mayonnaise and cress (£2.85) to club (£5.85). There are also hot dishes such as Swiss alpine macaroni with melted raclette (£5.95) or Taylor's rarebit (£5.98) made with Theakston's Yorkshire ale. Traditional Yorkshire afternoon tea is an elaborate affair with ham or chicken sandwich, sultana scone with cream and jam and Yorkshire curd tart (£8.30). There is plenty of choice in the pastry/cake department, including Normandy pear torte (£2.15), chocolate cream puff (£1.85), perhaps a fresh fruit tart (£2.80), as well as cinnamon muffins (£1.35), toasted currant teacakes (£1.38) and wholemeal date scones (£1.15). A pianist plays in the evenings, here and in York. Children's menu offering a good variety of sandwiches, savoury snacks and hot dishes, with a choice of cakes, ice creams and drinks. The Ladies toilet offers changing facilities and a play pen, and they can supply beakers, bibs, and nappies on request. They also provide a range of preservative- and additive-free foods for small babies and are happy to heat up customers own milk. High-chairs are available, but they 'cannot be held responsible for any accidents which might occur during their use'. ***Seats*** *156.* ***Open*** *9-9.* ***Closed*** *25, 26 Dec & 1 Jan. MasterCard,* ***VISA***

Also at:

32 The Grove Ilkley West Yorkshire Tel 01943 608029 Map 6 C1
Seat 110. Open 9-6

188 High Street Northallerton North Yorkshire Tel 01609 775154 Map 5 E3
Seat 58. Open 9-5.30 (Sun from 10)

6 St Helen's Square York Tel 01904 659142 Map 7 D1
Seats 174. Open 9-9.

Taylors Tea Rooms 46 Stonegate York Tel 01904 622865 Map 7 D1

A jug of fresh water!

HARROGATE Imperial Hotel 65% £95

Tel 01423 565071 **Fax 01423 500082** Map 6 C1 **H**
Prospect Place Harrogate North Yorkshire HG1 1LA

Overlooking the Stray in the centre of town, the hotel looks out over flower-filled borders with balconied first-floor bedrooms at the front making the most of the view. Public areas are smart with white marble-tiled floors, the bar and lounge having buttoned, dark red-upholstered settees and armchairs. Bedrooms, which span four floors, have traditional style darkwood furniture are neat and come with a range of useful amenities. Half have recently been refurbished. Bathrooms are simple, with vinyl floors. ***Rooms** 85. Amex, Diners, MasterCard,* ***VISA***

HARWICH Pier at Harwich £70

Tel 01255 241212 **Fax 01255 551922** Map 10 C3 **RR**
The Quay Harwich Essex CO12 3HH

Overlooking the harbour (and within a mile of the ferry port), the first-floor restaurant is just the place to enjoy good, fresh seafood which comes both plain (dressed crab, oysters, Dover sole with nut brown butter and lemon, fish and chips, grilled sea bass) and sauced (crab ravioli in a vermouth and saffron sauce, poached paupiettes of Dover sole stuffed with a mousseline of salmon on leaf spinach served on a lobster and brandy sauce). Steaks and a chicken dish also on the menu. Several inexpensive bottles figure on an excellent wine list that is longer on quality than quantity - cleverly comprehensive. The Ha'penny Pier on the ground floor is a second, family-orientated restaurant also with a mainly fish menu. Begin with pier haddie – smoked haddock in a parmesan sauce with mushrooms (£3.50), local dressed crab with lemon mayonnaise (£3.95) or American-style ribs with barbecue sauce (£3.50); maybe Ha'Penny fish and chips (£5.50), fish pie, served with a side salad (£5.95) or chargrilled chicken teriyaki, with chips and salad (£6.95) to follow. Children's menu, also a few meat and vegetarian options. ***Seats** 70. Parties 30. Private Room 50. L 12-2 D 6-9.30. Set L £9.50/£12.50 (Sun £14.95) Set D £13.25/£16.50. Closed D 25 & 26 Dec. Amex, Diners, MasterCard,* ***VISA***

Rooms £71

The third-floor accommodation comprises six bedrooms of varying standards, all with a nautical theme, some with views down the estuary. All have en suite bathrooms and televisions.

HATHERLEIGH George Hotel £70

Tel 01837 810454 **Fax 01837 810901** Map 13 D2 **I**
Market Street Hatherleigh Okehampton Devon EX20 3JN

Dating from 1450, this ancient cob-and-thatch town-centre inn was once a rest house and sanctuary for the monks of Tavistock. In later years it became a brewery, tavern, a law court and a coaching inn before developing into what is now a most comfortable and historic small hotel. Off the central cobbled courtyard in the converted brewhouse and coachman's loft is the main bar and family area extension, while the original inn's bar oozes charm and antiquity with old beams, an oak-panelled wall, an enormous fireplace and an assortment of cushioned seats and sofas. It is now largely confined to residents or waiting diners, as the attractive restaurant is next door. The Farmers Bar across the courtyard is like a small bistro and locals' bar and opens on Thu-Sat nights only. Sloping floors and low 'head-cracking' doorways lead to eleven individually furnished bedrooms with pretty chintz fabrics, pieces of old or antique furniture and generally good clean en-suite facilities. Three rooms have elegant four-poster beds. TVs, telephones and tea-making facilities are the added comforts and residents also have the use of a charming lounge and the outdoor swimming pool. Eight/ten wines available by the glass. New owners took over just as we went to press. *Open 11-3.30, 6-11 (Sun 12-3, 7-10.30). Free House.* ***Beer** Bass, Boddingtons, two guest beers.* ***Accommodation** 11 bedrooms, 9 en suite, £69.50, four-poster £82, single £48-£55. Children welcome overnight, additional bed (£6) & cot supplied. Amex, MasterCard,* ***VISA***

HAWKSHEAD Queen's Head Hotel

Tel 01539 436271 **Fax 01539 436722** Map 4 C3 
Hawkshead Cumbria LA22 0NS

The Queen's Head here is that of Elizabeth I; at the heart of this traffic-free village the black and white painted 16th-century frontage hides a cavernous pub within, full of period character and camaraderie. Food from the wide-ranging menu can be enjoyed anywhere in the panelled bar areas and adjacent dining-room, although at busy times it's certainly advble to find a free table first! Begin with seafood risotto or Queen's club salad (black pudding and shredded duck), then, for main course, try the Westmorland pie, braised rabbit with apple and gooseberry sauce, smoked chicken and tarragon with pasta, or choose from the weekly-changing fish board (fresh fish and chips, poached halibut with vermouth, lobster and prawn salad). Lunchtime only snack menu offering sandwiches, ploughman's and filled jacket potatoes. Residents and others wishing to eat in the dining-room at night or for Sunday lunch (served all day) are advised to book in advance. Ten bedrooms within the pub have low beams, modest furnishings and compact en suite bathrooms; two have old-fashioned four-posters and there are a couple of family rooms sleeping three. The balance of the accommodation is in two adjacent cottages which are only yards away. *Open 11-11 (Sun 12-10.30).* ***Bar Food*** *12-2.30, 6.15-9.30 (Sun 12-9.30).* ***Beer*** *Hartleys XB, Robinson's Bitter & Frederic's Bitter. Family room.* ***Accommodation*** *13 bedrooms, 11 en suite, £59.50 (four-poster £70, single £35). Children welcome overnight (under-10s £12.50, 10-16s £17.50), additional bed & cot available. Diners, MasterCard,* ***VISA***

> If we recommend meals in a hotel a *separate* entry is usually made for its restaurant. Pub and inn entries include bar food details where recommended.

HAY-ON-WYE Old Black Lion

Tel 01497 820841 Map 9 D5 
26 Lion Street Hay-on-Wye Hereford & Worcester HR3 5AD

Owners John and Joan Collins run this ever-popular 17th-century coaching inn situated close to what was once the Lion Gate, one of the entrances to the old walled town. On the extensive main bar menu dishes range from ploughman's lunches (try the Continental with salami, soft cheese and garlic sausage) to home-made venison burger, chicken and ham pie and vegetarian options (nut roast with leek, watercress and mustard sauce). The daily specials board might extend the range further to include prawn and bacon chowder, beef Wellington, loin of pork with caramelised apples and oranges, or ragout of wild boar with cranberries and marsala, finishing with chilled lemon tart with iced lime parfait, or apple and calvados pie. A separate bar menu is devoted solely to steaks, sauced or plain. In the evening the equally imaginative Cromwell restaurant menu is available throughout the dining areas. Bedrooms within the main building, of 17th-century origins, render the Black Lion justifiably famous. Refurbishment has generally enhanced the building's character and comforts of high degree that include direct-dial phones, TVs, radios, beverage trays and bright duvets (traditional bedding provided on request). Rooms in the annexe are more modern, though no less comfortable; all rooms (with the exception of one single with a private bathroom) have entirely acceptable en suite facilities. Families particularly enjoy the Cromwell Room with its gallery and two additional beds. Speciality breakfasts include a salmon fisherman's version with smoked eel and aquavit plus one for romantics: scrambled egg with caviar and a quarter bottle of champagne (for two). The whole pub is candle-lit at night and there's no smoking in the restaurant. Not suitable for children under 5 (over-8s in the restaurant only). *Open 11.30-11 (Sun 11.30-10.30).* ***Bar Food*** *11.30-2.30, 7-9.30 (Sun 12-2.45, 7-9). Free House.* ***Beer*** *Flowers Original, Fuller's London Pride, Wye Valley Hereford Bitter. Small patio, outdoor eating.* ***Accommodation*** *10 bedrooms, 9 en suite, £45.90 (family room sleeping 4 £67.90, single from £19.95). Children over 5 welcome overnight (5-12s £10, over-12s £14 if sharing parents' room). Amex, MasterCard,* ***VISA***

HEATHROW AIRPORT Forte Posthouse (Ariel) 65% £97

Tel 0181-759 2552 **Fax 0181-564 9265** Map 15 E2 **H**
Bath Road Hayes Hounslow UB3 5AJ

A long-established airport hotel with practical accommodation and a variety of meeting and conference rooms. ***Rooms** 180. Amex, Diners, MasterCard,* ***VISA***

HEATHROW AIRPORT Holiday Inn Crowne Plaza 74% £153

Tel 01895 445555 **Fax 01895 445122** Map 15 E2 **H**
Stockley Road West Drayton Hounslow UB7 9NA

Holiday Inns' top-of-the-range Crowne Plaza brand offers higher levels of service – 24hr table service in the lounge/bar, extensive room service with a good range of hot meals available throughout the night, a turn-down service in the evenings, valet parking – and generally more comfort than one might expect in a more standard Holiday Inn. Spacious bedrooms have proper armchairs and breakfast table plus plenty of work space – even more in the Business Study rooms (£175 B&B); half the rooms are non-smoking. Three rooms are specially designed for disabled guests. Most luxurious of the bedrooms are the Directors and Presidential suites. Under-19s are accommodated free in family rooms. There's a large swimming pool in the leisure centre, where there are also facilities for disabled guests and mothers with babies. The hotel stands just north of J4 of the M4. Frequent courtesy coach service to Heathrow Terminals 1, 2 and 3. ***Rooms** 374. Golf (9), indoor swimming pool, splash pool, gym, sauna, steam room, spa bath, solarium, beauty & hair salon, coffee shop (6.30am-midnight), gift shop. Amex, Diners, MasterCard,* ***VISA***

HEATHTON Old Gate

Tel 01746 710431 Map 6 B4 **P**
Heathton Claverley Shropshire WV5 7EB

A much-extended 17th-century inn down country lanes some five miles from Bridgnorth on the Staffordshire border. There's plenty to amuse antiquarians in the parlour: hanging from the beams are decorative Toby and water jugs, from the walls and lintels framed watercolours, old prints and brass flat irons. The Old Stable snug contains more suitable seating for families when the weather precludes use of the garden's picnic tables and play area. Eight miles from Junction 2 of the M5 and near Halfpenny Green Airport. *Open 12-2.30, 6.30-11 (Sun 12-3, 6.30-10.30).* ***Beer** Tetley Bitter, Holts (HP&D) Entire & Enville Ale, guest beer. Garden, children's play area. Family room. Amex, Diners, MasterCard,* ***VISA***

HELMSLEY Feathers

Tel 01439 770275 **Fax 01439 771101** Map 5 E4 **P**
Market Place Helmsley North Yorkshire YO6 5BH

'Elmslac', a Saxon village on the river Rye settled in 600 AD was listed in Domesday, and as Helmsley, renowned for its Norman castle, had a well-documented history throughout the Middle Ages. Feathers was once a merchant's house with the highest rent in town, later it was split into two cottages and is now re-unified by the friendly Feather family. There are, of course, two entrances, two bars – with a unifying theme of the local 'Mouse Man' furniture – two dining-rooms and two stair-wells. Two floors of bedrooms provide accommodation that is more practical than luxurious; TVs and tea trays are provided, alarm clocks and hairdryers available on request. Family rooms (sleeping up to 4) with en suite bathrooms offer good value, with under-12s accommodated free (meals charged as taken). Several smaller rooms have en suite WC/shower rooms only, and the three remaining unconverted singles share adequate facilities. *Open 11-11 (Sun 12-10.30). Free House.* ***Beer** John Smith's, Theakston Best & Old Peculier, guest beer. Garden. Family room.* ***Accommodation** 17 bedrooms, 13 en suite, £60 (single £35). Children welcome overnight (under-12s stay free in parents' room), additional bed & cot available. Accommodation closed 24 Dec-2 Jan. Amex, Diners, MasterCard,* ***VISA***

Any person using our name to obtain free hospitality is a fraud.
Proprietors, please inform the police and us.

HELMSLEY Monets

Tel 01439 770618 Map 5 E4 **JaB**
19 Bridge Street Helmsley North Yorkshire YO6 5BG

The Dysons' little restaurant with rooms is a charming setting in which to enjoy some splendid home-made fare. Morning and afternoon teas offer fruit scones (99p), delicious cinnamon toast and chocolate éclair among the choices. At lunchtime the menu includes sandwiches: egg and cress (£2.25), crab and cucumber (£4.20) or smoked chicken and coleslaw (£3.50); filled croissants (£5.50) and more substantial dishes such as chicken, ham and mushroom pie with sweet pickle and salad (£5.99), fillet of smoked mackerel with summer leaves and horseradish (£5.50) or home-baked cheese and broccoli quiche with salad (£4.99). Good puddings include lemon tart with vanilla *anglaise* (£2.75) and Dutch apple flan (£1.95). More elaborate evening meals. No smoking in the dining-room. ***Seats*** *20.* ***Open*** *10-5 (Oct to Mar from 11)* ***Closed*** *Mon & 25-27 Dec. Mastercard,* ***VISA***

HEMEL HEMPSTEAD The Gallery Restaurant

Tel 01442 232416 **Fax 01442 234072** Map 15 E2 **JaB**
The Old Town Hall High Street Hemel Hempstead Hertfordshire HP1 3AE

Located in the heart of the old town on the first floor of the former town hall, now a theatre and arts complex, the Gallery is a cheerful, welcoming, informal restaurant offering a selection of some rather well-prepared foods. Dishes change daily and are chosen from a blackboard. Typical are deep-fried brie with plum sauce, crostini with mozzarella, anchovy and roasted Mediterranean vegetables £3.95, smoked salmon paté (£2.95) or avocado, artichoke and grilled red peppers (£4.50). Main dishes could include grilled fresh tuna niçoise, chicken schnitzel with lemon and chive sauce, new potatoes and French beans (both £8.50), a vegetarian dish of Mediterranean vegetables with spaghetti (£6.95) or pasta with fresh asparagus, tomatoes and cream (£6.95). Sweets, all £2.75, might offer fromage frais cheesecake with gooseberry sauce, pavlova roulade, hazelnut meringue and hot puddings such as rhubarb crumble or a totally irresistible chocolate truffle torte decorated with crushed amaretti biscuits. From 2pm to 5pm sandwiches, scones, teacakes and cakes (chocolate with almond, passion) are served and in the evening there are set meals (two courses for £10). Next door to the children's theatre, it's a festive place to be if there's a special kid's tea-party on (Saturday afternoons tend to be busiest). Four high-chairs are available, and there's space in the staff facilities for baby-changing, if required. ***Seats*** *60.* ***Open*** *10.30am-11pm (Mon till 4.30pm)* ***Closed*** *Sun & Bank Holidays. MasterCard,* ***VISA***

HENLEY-ON-THAMES Red Lion 67% £117

Tel 01491 572161 **Fax 01491 410039** Map 15 D2 **HR**
Hart Street Henley-on-Thames Oxfordshire RG9 2AR

A former coaching inn, dating back in part to the 15th century, this wisteria-clad hotel has benefited from considerable refurbishment in recent years. A flagstoned entrance hall leads into a reception area boasting waxed-pine panelling and fresh flower displays. There's no longer a lounge as such (it's become an informal brasserie) but an appealing bar with more flagstones, old timbers and black leather-upholstered seating makes a good spot for socialising. Antique-furnished bedrooms, which are decorated in warm dark blue and burgundy colours, are generally of a good size and all come with proper armchairs. Good bathrooms, many with marble tiling, have chunky suites that suit the period of the building, almost all have bidets and are supplied with Roger & Gallet toiletries. There are three Economy single rooms (about half the standard room rate) that share a bathroom across the corridor. Families are made welcome with three rooms having an extra 'pull-down' bed hidden in the wardrobe and a children's menu in addition to the usual cots and high-chairs being available. On winter evenings beds are turned down, curtains drawn and bedside lights lit. Room service offers meals at mealtimes and, although not advertised, drinks and sandwiches throughout the 24 hours. In the same ownership as *Durrants Hotel* in London. The Red Lion is located by the bridge near the finishing post for the Henley Royal Regatta. No dogs. Parking for 26 cars. ***Rooms*** *26. Terrace. Amex, MasterCard,* ***VISA***

See over

Regatta Brasserie £60

The hotel's only restaurant, which successfully combines both formal and informal eating with a menu that includes fairly sophisticated dishes like ravioli of two salmons with basil and coriander sauce, prawns thermidor, hare fillet with raspberry vinegar and bitter chocolate sauce, and fresh-water trout in puff pastry with a cider, thyme and apple sauce along with a selection of sandwiches including tuna and caper mayonnaise, baked ham with grain mustard and smoked salmon. Desserts range from millefeuille of nougatine and chocolate mousse to apple turban with pineapple sauce and cheese with home-made walnut bread. Interesting range of coffees (try a *caramel latte macchiato* – espresso poured over caramel, filled with foamed milk and topped with cream). Decor features old beams, yellow rag-rolled walls, coir matting, and wicker-seated chairs along with crisp white napery and silver cutlery. Friendly staff. ***Seats** 34. Parties 10. Private Room 18. L 12-2.30 D 6-10.*

Hethersett Park Farm Country Hotel 64% £90

Tel 01603 810264 **Fax 01603 812104** Map 10 C2 H
Hethersett nr Norwich Norfolk NR9 3DL

Five miles south of Norwich, the Gowing family's hotel has expanded considerably over the years from the original Georgian farmhouse. Bedrooms in various styles (Executives have four-posters and whirlpool baths) are arranged around the landscaped gardens, some in the old buildings, others in a renovated Norfolk barn. Also in outbuildings is a stylish, well-equipped leisure complex. No dogs. ***Rooms** 38. Garden, croquet, tennis, putting, indoor swimming pool, gym, sauna, spa bath, steam room, solarium, beauty & hair salon, games room, snooker. Amex, Diners, MasterCard,* ***VISA***

Hexham The Rowan Tree

Tel 01434 601234 Map 5 D2 JaB
19 Market Place Hexham Northumberland

Mrs Nairn supervises a hard-working kitchen in her bright first-floor café overlooking Hexham's market square. Sound home baking is in evidence throughout the day with an imaginative variety of nicely presented lunchtime specials – a casserole of venison (£5.25), lamb chops with cranberry sauce (£4.25) and crepes filled with mushrooms, herbs and cream (£3.75) set the lunchtime style. Small portions of virtually anything are available for children and high chairs are provided, but it's a bit of a climb (up two flights) for toilet facilities. Licensed with main meals. Plans are afoot to open during the evening – please enquire. No smoking. ***Seats** 33. **Open** 10-5. **Closed** 25 & 26 Dec. MasterCard,* ***VISA***

Higham The Knowle £70

Tel 01474 822262 Map 11 B5 R
School Lane Higham nr Rochester Kent ME3 7HP

Set in three acres of secluded gardens, Lyn and Michael Baragwanath's large Victorian rectory is both an easygoing restaurant and a family home. It's also licensed to hold marriage ceremonies and is a popular place for receptions and parties. Sit in the eclectically furnished bar to choose from an equally varied menu of dishes served simply in generous proportions: cheese soufflé royale, salmon and cucumber mousse, king prawns thermidor, pot-roast pheasant, lamb fillet on a crisp potato cake, and various ways with steak. Lunchtimes (except Sunday) and Tuesday to Thursday evenings there is an additional 'Bistro' menu that is considerably less expensive than the standard carte. No formal arrangements are made for children's meals but this is the kind of place where you only have to ask (in advance, preferably) and they will make sure that the children will be happy; the adaptable kitchen is likely to serve up fish goujons rather than fish fingers and chicken bites rather than chicken nuggets, and you can always get chips and fresh vegetables. Popular for traditional Sunday lunches. Children are welcome to play in the garden, although there are no special facilities. Access and facilities for the disabled. ***Seats** 70. Private Room 40. L 12-1.30 D 6.30-10. Closed D Sun, all Mon & Bank Holidays. Set L £14.95. MasterCard,* ***VISA***

Highclere — Yew Tree

Tel 01635 253360 **Fax 01635 255035** Map 15 D3
Andover Road Hollington Cross Highclere Berkshire RG15 9SE

Former 16th-century coaching inn situated just south of the village on the A343 and self-styled by owner Jenny Wratten as a 'restaurant with rooms'. Full of charm and character with huge logs smouldering in the inglenook fireplace while old scrubbed pine tables and the odd sofa sit beneath ancient beams. Several interconnecting rooms comprise the main dining area but the same menu is served throughout. Seasonally-changing choices (plus dishes of the day) might include hot chicken Caesar salad, duck liver paté with a delicious spicy onion marmalade, Stilton and celery soup, salmon fishcakes with parsley sauce, beef and stout cobbler, smoked salmon and watercress pasta and daily fish dishes. Finish, perhaps, with steamed ginger pudding and custard, Emma's chocolate cheesecake or farmhouse cheeses served with apple, celery, water biscuits and their own walnut bread. Ten wines are offered by the glass, including a champagne. Six cottagey bedrooms offer overnight accommodation with direct-dial telephones, remote-control TVs, beverage trays and little extras like books and magazines; all have en suite bathrooms, half with shower and WC only. No under-14s in bar area. *Open 11-3, 5.30-11 (Sun 12-3, 7-10.30).* ***Bar Food*** *12-2.30, 6.30-10 (Sun 12.30-3, 7-9.30). Free House.* ***Beer*** *Fuller's London Pride, Wadworth 6X, Hampshire King Alfred Bitter. Garden, patio, outdoor eating.* ***Accommodation*** *6 bedrooms, all en suite, £60 (single £45). Children welcome overnight (under-5s stay free in parents' room). Amex, MasterCard,* ***VISA***

Higher Burwardsley — Pheasant Inn

Tel 01829 770434 **Fax 01829 771097** Map 6 A3
Higher Burwardsley Tattenhall Cheshire CH3 9PF

The Pheasant is best located by following signs to the candle factory from the A534. It is tucked into the hillside amongst the Peckforton hills, and on arrival, it's plain to see that the place was once a farm, and the more surprising, therefore, to find that there has been a pub here since the 17th century. The oldest part, a half-timbered sandstone farmhouse, is the venue for the bar, which claims to house the largest log fire in Cheshire. Adjacent is the Highland Room which in turn leads to an imposing conservatory that looks over a tiered patio and, beyond this, right across the Cheshire plain towards North Wales. Bar snacks encompass a broad range from hot avocado with seafood and lasagne to fresh fish (a speciality) and cold platters (ploughman's, salads). A selection of ten sandwiches is listed and children are offered the usual list of favourites. Daily specials extend the kitchen's repertoire to the likes of baked monkfish wrapped in bacon with a cream sauce and noisettes of lamb with Provençal onions. Sunday lunch is always popular as it's such good value and as space is limited it is advble to book at all times. The old barn has been skilfully converted into eight very comfortable bedrooms, including two suites, equipped with televisions, clock-radios, hairdryers, mini-bars and roomy bathrooms. Stonework interiors are eye-catching, and nights tranquil. Two further bedrooms, housed in the pub proper, boast original beams and brighter bathrooms, as well as memorable views. It is an ideal spot for keen walkers, as the inn stands midway along the Sandstone Trail. Credit cards taken for amounts of £20 and over only. *Open 12-3, 7-11 (Sun 12-3, 7-10.30).* ***Bar Food*** *12-2.30, 7-9.30. Free House.* ***Beer*** *Bass, guest beer. Garden, outdoor eating, children's play area. Family room.* ***Accommodation*** *10 bedrooms, all en suite, £70 & £80 (single £40-£45). Children welcome overnight (under-10s stay free in parents' room, over-10s £10), additional bed & cot available. Amex, Diners, MasterCard,* ***VISA***

JaB is short for 'Just a Bite'. The majority of these establishments are also recommended in our *Bistros, Bars & Cafés* Guide which features establishments where one may eat well for less than £15 per head.

HIMLEY Crooked House

Tel 01384 238583 Map 6 B4 P

Coppice Mill Himley Dudley DY3 4DA

This is not a particularly attractive setting; turning off B4176 between Womborne and Dudley, the long lane runs down through woods past urban forest, landfill and quarry. Yet the sight at the lane's end is simply extraordinary. Once the Glynne Arms, the 250-year-old building was a victim of subsidence in Victorian times and teeters alarmingly from right to left. One bar door opens out at an oblique angle and instills an uneasy feeling of collapsing through it – and this is on the way in! Meanwhile, in the upper bar, (for a charitable donation) customers can watch a ball-bearing apparently roll upwards along the dado. Despite some recent levelling of the floor, many's the customer who appears all at sea with his legs. A more recent extension houses a family-friendly conservatory overlooking a small adventure playground. Saturday barbecues. No children under 14 in the bars. *Open 11-11 (Sun 12-10.30) Apr-end Aug, 11.30-2.30, 6.30-11 (Sun 12-3, 7-10.30) Sep-Mar,* ***Beer*** *Banks's Mild & Bitter, Marston's Pedigree, guest beer. Patio, children's play area. No credit cards.*

HINDON Lamb at Hindon

Tel 01747 820573 **Fax 01747 820605** Map 14 B3 P

Hindon Salisbury Wiltshire SP3 6DP

Wisteria clings to one corner of this mellow 17th-century coaching inn. At its height, 300 post horses were kept here to supply the great number of coaches going to and from London and the West Country. Prime Minister William Pitt was apparently most put out to find no fresh horses available when he stopped off in 1786. Inside, the long bar is divided into several areas and is furnished with some sturdy period tables, chairs and settles, and a splendid old stone fireplace with log fire creates a warm, homely atmosphere, especially on cold winter nights. The blackboard bar menu is sensibly not over-long, but still manages to offer a reasonable choice – fresh mussels, grilled hake with capers and garlic, game casserole, lamb and mint casserole and, for pudding, lemon tart with raspberry coulis and orange and nectarine brulée. Granary sandwiches, ploughman's platters and salads are always available. The emphasis is fishy on Wednesday and Fridays, and in winter there's also plenty of game from the estate of the local landowner who bought the inn a few years ago. No-smoking restaurant. Upstairs, there are thirteen en suite bedrooms, which are furnished and decorated to varying styles and standards. *Open 11-11, (Sun 12-10.30).* ***Bar Food*** *12-2, 7-10. Free House.* ***Beer*** *Wadworth 6X, Hook Norton Best, Ashvine Bitter, Ringwood. Best, guest beer. Garden, outdoor eating.* ***Accommodation*** *13 bedrooms, all en suite, £55 (four-poster £65, single £38). Children welcome overnight (under-3s stay free in parents' room), additional bed & cot (both £10) available. Amex, MasterCard,* ***VISA***

HOLT Byfords – Le Café

Tel 01263 713520 Map 10 C1 

1-5 Shirehall Plain Holt Norfolk NR25 6BG

Occupying a prime position in the centre of a charming market town and set within a superbly restored Elizabethan manor, Le Café appeals to all tastes and moods. A table laden with home-made cakes and other goodies entices folk into the oldest room, which boasts beams, exposed brick, bare boards, an open fire and a rustic mix of pine furniture. Light classical music enhances the relaxing atmosphere in which to savour a choice of cakes – apple, carrot, coffee, chocolate, lemon or plain Victoria sponge as well as chocolate fudge brownies (from 85p). Soup of the day could be mixed bean or fennel and potato (£2.95), and there are daily hot dishes such as grilled fillet of salmon with olive oil and balsamic vinegar dressing with a side salad (£6), risotto with sun-dried tomatoes (£4.75) or feta cheese kebab with sambal salad and crème fraiche (£4.95). Children's portions and one high-chair; shopping parents who are desperate for a sit-down and sustenance will find the café an ideal haven for a snack. A high-chair is available for very young diners who can chose a smaller portion of gooey cake, pasty or baguette. ***Seats*** *80 (+ 30 outside).* ***Open*** *9-5.30.* ***Closed*** *Sun, 25, 26 Dec & 1 Jan. No credit cards.*

HOLT The Owl Tea Room

Tel 01263 713232 Map 10 C1 JaB
Church Street Holt Norfolk NR25 6BB

A splendid tea room behind the Owl Bake Shop in the centre of town. A band of local ladies prepare fresh scones, pies and quiches which are served on plates made by the owners in their own pottery. Coffee is served between 9 and 11.45, while lunch begins at noon; regular menu items include country pie (£4.50), steak and kidney pie (£4.85) and home-baked ham (£4.90), all served with locally grown vegetables, organic whenever possible. There are excellent salads, including cheese (£3.95), smoked mackerel (£4.45) and fresh crab (£4.95). Specials are listed on a blackboard. Vegetarians should not be disappointed, with vegetarian country pie (£4.50) and nut roast with herbs (£4.05) among the offerings. A traditional selection of desserts: ginger sponge pudding, treacle tart (both £2.45) or banana split (£2.80) is backed up by speciality sundaes such as 'brown owl' – chocolate ice cream, sauce, nuts, chocolate slice, wafer and cream (£2.65). Set teas are good value (from £2.05), and the range of mouthwatering cakes (from 70p) is hard to resist. All the jams, marmalades and chutneys are made here, jars of which can be purchased in the Bake Shop. Small, cottagey walled garden for fine days. No smoking. ***Seats*** *36 (+ 16 outside).* ***Open*** *9-5.* ***Closed*** *Sun & Bank Holidays. No credit cards.*

HOPE The Hopechest

Tel 01433 620072 Map 6 C2 JaB
8 Castleton Road Hope nr Sheffield Derbyshire S30 2RD

A cosy tea room converted from a stable in the heart of the Hope Valley provides a splendid setting for enjoying some delicious home-made snacks. Tea comes with scones, cream and jam (£1.75) or a selection of cakes: brandy cake, fruit cake, Bakewell or cheesecake (all £1). Savouries (all served with salad) could offer quiche (£3.30), cheese omelette (£3.25), filled rolls (£1.50) or home-baked ham (£3.30). Children's portions on request. Small patio in walled garden for outdoor eating. No smoking. ***Seats*** *15 (+14 outside).* ***Open*** *9-4.30.* ***Closed*** *Sun, Mon & Christmas. MasterCard,* ***VISA***

HOPE COVE Cottage Hotel 56% £102*

Tel 01548 561555 **Fax 01548 561455** Map 13 D3 H
Hope Cove nr Kingsbridge Devon TQ7 3HJ

The village of Hope Cove rests in the curve of Bigbury Bay and this popular family hotel makes the most of the views. The sun terrace is the place to be in summer, while inside there are three lounges and a cocktail bar which was built from timbers salvaged from a wrecked windjammer, the *Herzogin Cecilie*. The rate quoted above is for a double/twin with sea view. Rooms with balconies are priced slightly higher and there are some budget rooms without sea views and with shared bathroom facilities. *Half-board terms only. ***Rooms*** *35. Garden, games room. Closed Jan. No credit cards.*

HORAM Gun Inn

Tel 01825 872361 Map 11 B6 
Gun Hill Horam Heathfield East Sussex TN21 0JU

Extended 16th-century tiled and timbered pub, resplendent in summer with colourful hanging baskets, enjoying a peaceful rural location just off the A22 north-west of Hailsham. Neat open-plan interior with a series of comfortably furnished alcove seating areas, several open fires and an old kitchen Aga. Head for the blackboard menu for the daily-changing selection of home-cooked dishes, which supplements a standard printed menu of pub favourites. Good reliable choices may include decent pies – Sussex fidget, rabbit and lamb, apricot and rosemary – shank of pork, salmon parcels, and Sussex smokie in white wine and mustard sauce. Fresh fish – whole plaice and lemon sole – comes from Newhaven. Keen to cater for all tastes there is the choice of fresh vegetables, chips, jacket potatoes or a selection of fresh, imaginative salads from the regularly replenished salad bar. For a home-made pudding try the treacle tart or apple crumble. Cream teas are available each afternoon between April and October. Overnight accommodation comprises three homely, simply furnished bedrooms with TVs, tea-makers and rural views. One has en suite facilities, the others share a clean bathroom and two toilets. Continental breakfasts are served in the room. *Open summer 11-11, (Mon-Fri 11-3, 6-11 in winter), Sun 12-10.30.* ***Bar Food*** *Apr-Oct 12-10, (12-2, 6-10 in winter), Free House.* ***Beer*** *Larkins Chiddingstone, Harveys Sussex Bitter, Flowers original, guest beer. Garden, outside eating, children's play area. Family room. Closed all 25 & 26 Dec. MasterCard,* ***VISA***

HORNDON Elephant's Nest

Tel 01822 810273 Map 12 C3 **P**
Horndon Mary Tavy Tavistock Horndon Devon PL19 9NQ

Isolated 16th-century inn located on the flanks of Dartmoor and reached via narrow, high-hedged lanes from the A386 Tavistock to Okehampton road at Mary Tavy (signposted). Named after a portly landlord with a bushy beard it is a character pub for wild winter weather with its window seats, rustic furnishings, old rugs, flagstones, heavy beams and open fires. The large garden has open views across the moor and picnic tables for summer days; rabbits, ducks, goats, geese and chickens in pens should keep the children interested. It is a busy dining pub with an extensive blackboard menu listing popular pub favourites as well as a range of home-cooked daily dishes – perhaps local game pie, lamb and lentil hotpot, seafood ragout and steak and kidney pie. 'Pete's Puds' include chocolate and brandy crunch cake and treacle and walnut tart. *Open 11.30-2.30, 6.30-11 (Sun 12-2.30, 7-10.30).* ***Bar Food*** *11.30-2 (from 12 Sun), 6.30-10 (till 9.30 Sun). Free House.* ***Beer*** *St Austell's HSD, Palmers IPA, Boddingtons, guest beers. Garden, outdoor eating. Family room. No credit cards.*

HORTON-IN-RIBBLESDALE Crown Hotel

Tel 01729 860209 **Fax 01729 860444** Map 5 D4 **P**
Horton-in-Ribblesdale Settle North Yorkshire BD24 0HF

Sandwiched between two road bridges on the B6479 where Bransgyll runs into the Ribble, the Crown is centrally located amid the Three Peaks at the heart of the Ribble Valley. At the pub, three generations now come into play. Landlady Norma Hargreaves moved here over 30 years ago with her parents; now, daughter Helen is in charge of the kitchen. She makes home-made pies and puddings, plus an extended range that might include pheasant and port pie, lamb and apricot pie, seafood pancake and Stilton and spinach quiche. Freshly-baked 'crusties' (small baguettes, lunchtime only) and ploughman's lunches are also offered. In terms of accommodation, to term the bedrooms modest is not to decry them, as an absence of TVs and phones remains intentional. Internal dimensions of this unaltered 17th-century inn dictate, though, against much modernisation and there are but two rooms with en suite bathrooms and a further five with added shower stalls. However, plans are afoot to add more en suite facilities. Two adjacent cottages offer self-contained private accommodation for larger parties. Being an altogether family-run affair there's also a special promise that "parents with children are welcome here to do exactly what other normal people like to do". *Open 11-11 (possibly closed earlier mid-week eves in winter), Sun 12-10.30.* ***Bar Food*** *12-2, 6-9.30.* ***Beer*** *Theakston XB & Old Peculier. Garden, outdoor play area.* ***Accommodation*** *9 bedrooms, 2 en suite, £34-£42 midweek, £39-£48 Fri, Sat & Bank Holidays (single from £17). Children welcome overnight (0-12s 75% adult tariff), addtional bed & cot available. No credit cards.*

HUNGERFORD The Tutti Pole

Tel 01488 682515 Map 14 C2 **JaB**
3 High Street Hungerford Berkshire RG17 0DN

Located a few yards from the Kennet and Avon canal, The Tutti Pole tea room is housed in a cottage dating back to 1634. A full English breakfast (£4.50) is served all day alongside a light snack menu offering a large assortment of sandwiches (from £1.30), cheese on toast with two poached eggs (£3.70), sardines on toast (£2.90), ham, mushroom and sweetcorn quiche (£4.70) and Cheddar or Stilton ploughman's (£2.90/£3). Canal-walkers stop by in the afternoon for the Tutti Pole Cream Tea

(£3.50) – two home-made scones and jam ("with stones" – a wonderful mixture of raspberries, strawberries, loganberries, gooseberries, blackcurrants, redcurrants, apples, rhubarb, damsons and plums all grown on the premises), Guernsey cream and pot of tea – two crumpets with butter (95p) or perhaps a fresh cream gateau (£1.85) – Black Forest or strawberry. Home-made cakes (lemon, banana or chocolate almond) and meringues are also on sale at the counter. Three-course traditional roast Sunday lunch £9.75 or £5.95 for just the roast. Children and babies are frequent visitors to the Tutti Pole and though they do not have their own menu, the owners will do their best to satisfy children's requests wherever possible and are happy to provide a smaller portion of something if asked. There's space for push-chairs and prams, and three high-chairs are available. Baby food can be blended, bottles heated and there's space in the Ladies/disabled toilets for baby-changing. Patio for outdoor eating in fine weather. ***Seats*** *80 (+ 48 outside).* ***Open*** *9-5.30 (Sat/Sun till 6).* ***Closed*** *25, 26 Dec & 1 Jan. No credit cards.*

HUNTINGDON — Old Bridge Hotel — 68% — £90

Tel 01480 452681 **Fax 01480 411017** Map 7 E4 **HR**
1 High Street Huntingdon Cambridgeshire PE18 6TQ

A town-centre hotel overlooking the River Ouse, the creeper-clad Old Bridge Hotel caters to business and leisure customers equally well. The lounges and public rooms have an air of comfort and elegance – a highlight is the continuous mural in the Terrace, a single work of art (extending over all walls) which took Julia Rushbury over four months to complete. Bedrooms are furnished with regard to the overall atmosphere of the place, but are also well equipped with modern amenities. Free parking for 80 cars. ***Rooms*** *26. Garden. Amex, Diners, MasterCard,* ***VISA***

Restaurant — £80

One menu is available throughout the hotel, in either the more relaxed setting of the Terrace or the more formal, bookable, no-smoking Restaurant. However you can eat as much or as little as you wish from the menu, regardless of location. The cooking is modern and multi-cultural, with such dishes as warm potato latkes with crab and crème fraiche, carpaccio, chicken satay, duck confit salad, salted cod fishcakes and braised lamb shank wrapped in cabbage with mashed potato, capers, tomatoes, beans, rosemary and thyme. There are always two roasts on Sundays, and from Monday to Friday a lunchtime buffet of cold roast meats, poached salmon and fresh salads. Cheeses are from Neal's Yard and the dessert side of the menu (the day's soufflé is well worth the wait) lists suggested sweet wine by the glass, plus digestifs. John Hoskins is too modest, suggesting he's 'lucky' to win our accolades for his wine lists. Luck doesn't come into it: he knows his onions, buys shrewdly, and adds the lowest mark-ups in the country, so you're drinking the best at the fairest prices of all: a glass of *marque* champagne at under £4, a bottle well under £25. One bottle here is not enough, drink several. ***Seats*** *44. Private Room 28. L 12-2.30 D 6.30-10.30. Closed D 25 Dec.*

HUNTSHAM — Huntsham Court — 68% — £115

Tel 01398 361365 **Fax 01398 361456** Map 13 D2 **HR**
Huntsham nr Bampton Tiverton Devon EX16 7NA

The ultimate antidote to chain hotels, a rather gaunt Victorian Gothic pile run in friendly, very casual style by owners Mogens and Andrea Bolwig (motto 'dulce nihil facere'). Eating is communal, there's an honour system in the bar, and you just wander into the kitchen if you need anything. There's great atmosphere in the day rooms (log fires, a panelled great hall, splendid pieces of furniture) and in the roomy bedrooms, with Victorian beds and baths. The rooms are named after composers – the rate quoted above is for Haydn, Handel, Bellini and Donizetti. The hotel is dedicated to music, with the classical variety played forte in the evening. The day starts with an excellent breakfast. No dogs. Private house parties and group functions are a speciality and their mood is likely to determine the atmosphere. ***Rooms*** *14. Garden, croquet, tennis, sauna, snooker. Closed 2 weeks in winter. MasterCard,* ***VISA***

See over

Restaurant £75

Five-course dinners (no choice, but variations possible in advance) are served by candle-light in leisurely fashion at an often convivial, communal table. Non-residents must book in advance as if the house is full there are no spare seats around the table. There's no wine list as such – guests choose during a trip to the cellar before dinner. ***Seats** 30. D only 8-10. Set D £30.*

HYTHE Hythe Imperial 71% £115

Tel 01303 267441 **Fax 01303 264610** Map 11 C5 **H**

Princes Parade Hythe Kent CT21 6AE

Built right on the seafront at Hythe in 1880, the Imperial is set in 50 acres of grounds and its wide frontage means that all bedrooms face the gardens or sea. Bedrooms range from singles to doubles, Executive doubles and suites, some with jacuzzis, some with four-posters or half-testers; interconnecting rooms are particularly suitable for families and both cots and extra beds are provided. The polished mahogany panelled reception area is adorned with brown leather chesterfields and leads through to comfortable bars and lounges. Pleasant staff and excellent leisure facilities that include a permanent children's play room and outdoor play area. Families are particularly well catered for with baby-listening and baby-sitting (the latter available by prior arrangement) along with creche facilities available on Saturday mornings (10am-1pm); they can eat informally in the leisure centre bistro. Parents can relax in the 15m swimming pool and enjoy the health and beauty facilities of the Inner Sanctuary; no green fee charges are made on weekdays for golf (handicap required). The Marston Minor Diner menu offers everything from finger fun food and commercial baby foods to 'reduced salt and sugar' beans on toast, cottage pie, macaroni cheese, pizza and vegetarian yeast paté sandwiches; puzzles and quizzes at meal times help keep the peace while parents finish their own meal. 'Sunday Plus' is an excellent idea – extend a weekend stay (keeping the use of your room) until 5pm on Sunday for £10 per adult including Sunday lunch (half portions and half price for children). The hotel thoroughly deserved our 1996 Family Hotel of the Year award, but it is particularly recommended for holiday periods when special promotions enhance the family-friendly atmosphere even further. Dancing to a band every Saturday night. Local attractions include the Romney, Hythe and Dymchurch miniature railway, Port Lympne Zoo, picturesque Rye and rowing boat hire on the Royal Military Canal – ask for a Marston Mini Guide. *Le Shuttle* (to Calais) Cheriton drive-in road/rail terminal is 10 minutes away; the *Eurostar* passenger rail terminal in Ashford has easy parking and is ideal for a short hop over to France. 600 metres along the seafront is the sister hotel, Stade Court, with whom the Imperial shares its facilities; families with dogs are welcome here. Ask about short-stay and Bank Holiday special tariffs. No dogs. Marston Hotels. ***Rooms** 100. Garden, croquet, indoor swimming pool, gym, spa bath, sauna, sun beds, steam room, beauty & hair salons, squash, all-weather floodlit tennis, games room, snooker, 9-hole golf course, putting, bowls, children's climbing frame, helipad, coffee shop (10am-10.30pm). Amex, Diners, MasterCard,* ***VISA***

IBSTONE The Fox

Tel 01491 638289 **Fax 01491 638873** Map 15 D2 **P**

Ibstone High Wycombe Buckinghamshire HP14 3GG

Much modernised and extended 300-year-old inn located on the Chiltern ridgeway opposite Ibstone Common, and close to acres of beechwood rambles. With the M40 (Junction 5) only a mile away, this rural inn is a handy overnight stop for travellers, for the nine en suite rooms are comfortable and well equipped. All rooms feature co-ordinating fabrics, modern pine furniture, clean fully tiled shower rooms and a full complement of added comforts – tea-makers, TVs, direct-dial telephones, clock-radios, trouser presses and hairdryers. Rear rooms have soothing views across fields and woodland. The oldest part of the building houses the relaxing, comfortably modernised lounge bar with wood-burner, and the simply furnished Country Bar with adjacent games/family room. Delightful sunny front terrace and well-tended garden. *Open 11-3, 6-11 (Sun 12-3, 7-10.30). **Beer** Brakspear Bitter, Fuller's London Pride, Marlow Rebellion IPA, Flowers Original, guest beer. Garden. Family room. **Accommodation** 9 bedrooms, all en suite (shower), £58-£76 (single from £44). Children welcome overnight, additional bed (£10) available. Amex, Diners, MasterCard,* ***VISA***

ILKLEY Bettys

Tel 01943 608029 Map 6 C1 JaB
32 The Grove Ilkley West Yorkshire LS29 9EE

Part of a very succesful and well-run chain of café tea rooms established in 1919; see entry under Harrogate for full menu details. The bright, sunny Ilkley outlet has windows inset with stained glass through which one can see the moors in t he distance; the interior boasts a collection of antique and contemporary teapots displayed around the walls. A huge marquetry picture, *La Chasse*, depicts a medieval hunting scene and was made in Alsace using unstained natural wood veneers. Rarebits and savoury dishes with a Swiss accent are specialities and uniformed waitresses will guide you through the delights of their speciality teas, coffees and tempting cake trolley. Eight high-chairs are provided, along with beakers and bibs. Children's are offered smaller portions or their own separate menu (Masham sausages, banana and honey or peanut butter sandwiches, ginger biscuits, ice cream clown and more). In the Ladies there's a changing shelf with a mat, chair and play pen; nappies are available for emergencies. Most of the café is no-smoking. A pianist plays on Fri, Sat & Sun afternoons from 4.30-6pm and from 10.30am-12.30pm on Thursdays. Pay and display parking to the rear of the café. Other outlets in Northallerton and York (see entries). ***Seats** 110. Open 9-6. Closed 25 & 26 Dec. MasterCard,* ***VISA***

ILKLEY Rombalds Hotel £95

Tel 01943 603201 **Fax 01943 816586** Map 6 C1 HR
West View Wells Road Ilkley Bradford LS29 9JG

Just yards from the edge of Ilkley Moor, this hotel occupies part of a Georgian terrace; if arriving by car head for their car park to the rear. Under the new ownership of Colin and Jo Clarkson, the main day room, a combined bar/lounge, has been refurbished with good new sofas and easy chairs and attractive sunny decor. Bedrooms vary somewhat in size (from two full and two smaller suites to a small single) and furnishings but all come with the usual amenities plus bathrobes in bathrooms of which nine have shower and WC only. Good cooked breakfasts and friendly staff. The coach-house meeting room combines character with high-tech facilities. 24hr room service. For children up to 16 staying in their parents' room there is a charge of £10 which includes breakfast. Limited service (ie B&B only) 27-30 Dec. ***Rooms** 15. Garden. Amex, Diners, MasterCard,* ***VISA***

Restaurant £60

A comfortable dining-room with blue decor and brass chandeliers where Jason Shaw provides some interesting and well-conceived dishes. The main à la carte (starters and desserts all £4 and mains £10) is always available and ranges from a good tarte tatin of home-dried tomatoes topped with Brillat-Savarin cheese and surrounded by a basil dressing to French onion soup; fillet of cod with a brioche crust, tomato fondue and cep mushroom linguine; braised pork shank with pommes dauphinoise, apple fritter and sage jus, and poussin cooked en cocotte with creamed potatoes and watercress sauce. An equally tempting list of desserts runs from a hazelnut and Baileys Cream vacherin with poached berries to an individual apple, ginger and sultana pie with vanilla and white chocolate sauce. Good cheeses too. Only the bread disappointed. Despite the change of owner and chef the Edwardian Brunch is still the main event on Sunday. There's also still a buffet lunch from Monday to Saturday. No smoking. Limited service 27-30 Dec. ***Seats** 35. Private Room 14. L 12-2 (Sun 9am-2) D 7.30-9.30. Set L £6.95 (Tues only, traditional roast) £7.75 (Mon-Sat, buffet) £10.95 (Sun only, traditional roast) £10.95 & £13.95 (Sun only, brunch).*

IPSWICH — Marlborough Hotel — 65% — £78

Tel 01473 257677 **Fax 01473 226927** Map 10 C3 **H**
73 Henley Road Ipswich Suffolk IP1 3SP

North of the town centre opposite Christchurch Park, the Marlborough is a friendly, comfortable little hotel in private hands (the *Angel Hotel* in Bury St Edmunds is in the same ownership). The tasteful public areas and the comfortable bedrooms (the best have antique furniture) are both well kept. 24hr room service. Ample own parking. ***Rooms*** *22. Garden. Amex, Diners, MasterCard,* ***VISA***

KENDAL — The Moon — £35

Tel 01539 729254 Map 4 C3 **R**
129 Highgate Kendal Cumbria LA9 4EN

Eye-catching bistro opposite the Brewery Arts Centre (park here) where attention to quality and loyalty to local produce are paramount. The monthly-changing blackboard menu offers dishes with a wide-ranging inspiration, from parsnip, carrot, lentil and fennel soup and creamy spiced curried mushrooms to wild boar with garlic and juniper in a home-made brioche; prawn, monkfish and whisky thermidor; and chicken supreme stuffed with rice, lime and ginger with Thai creamed coconut and coriander sauce. Vegetarian main courses (about three) and some fairly wicked puds such as rich fruit steamed suet pudding and home-made damson ice cream. The monthly pudding club and starters club menus remain a popular feature. No smoking. ***Seats*** *38. Parties 22. Private Room 40. D only 6.30-10 (Sat from 6). Closed 24, 25 & 31 Dec, 1 Jan & 2 weeks Jan/Feb. MasterCard,* ***VISA***

KENDAL — Waterside Wholefoods

Tel 01539 729743 Map 4 C3 **JaB**
Kent View Kendal Cumbria LA9 4HE

This wholefood and vegetarian restaurant with adjoining shop is housed in a converted mill with low ceilings and plaster walls. Snackers can look forward to scones – cheese, date and mixed fruit; delicious cakes, maybe banana and raisin, fig and ginger or lemon; and tarts, rum and raisin and various varieties of Bakewell, as well as home-baked breads. Lunch brings soups: carrot and orange, fennel and tomato or split pea and mint – all served with a cheese roll; Turkish pilaf; leek and mushroom croustade or moussaka. An excellent range of salads is available, plus stuffed jacket potatoes and quiches. Among the puddings you might find plum and apple nutty crumble served with cream, custard or yoghurt (£1.85). Tables with parasols are set up outside in summer on the banks of the River Kent, in a traffic-free walkway. Unlicensed but a comprehensive range of teas is refreshing in the summer; or BYO wine (£1 corkage). No smoking. ***Seats*** *34 (+ 12 outside).* ***Open*** *9-4.* ***Closed*** *Sun. No credit cards.*

KESWICK — Bryson's Tea Room

Tel 01768 772257 **Fax 01768 775456** Map 4 C3 **JaB**
38-42 Main Street Keswick Cumbria CA12 5JD

Above Bryson's bakery shop, with its tempting display, is their busy tea room, where the day starts with a bacon or Cumberland sausage roll, Continental breakfast or the full English version (£5.25). The output of the bakery features prominently throughout the day, and at teatime the Lakeland Cream Tea (£4.80) and the Cumberland Farmhouse Tea (£4.05) are very popular. Filled rolls (from £2.85), baked potatoes, omelettes (from £4.55) and salads are other options, along with ham and eggs (£6.10), fried haddock and cold home-roasted meats. Children's portions. No smoking. Municipal car park at rear. ***Seats*** *84.* ***Open*** *8.30-5.30 (Sun 11-5 Apr-Dec).* ***Closed*** *Sun Jan-Mar, 25, 26 Dec & 1 Jan. No credit cards.*

Many hotels offer reduced rates for weekend or out-of-season bookings. Always ask about special deals and family rooms.

KEW — Original Maids of Honour

Tel 0181-940 2752 Map 15 E2 JaB
288 Kew Road Kew Richmond-upon-Thames TW9 3DU

This lovely old tea shop has been in the Newens family since 1887, and can be found opposite the Cumberland Gate entrance to Kew Gardens. Round wooden tables, wrought-iron light fittings and bold rose-print curtains make a very atmospheric setting in which to indulge in the results of the hard work in the bakery to the rear. Most famous of the baking are the Maids of Honour (£1), Henry VIII's favourite sweetmeat. Cream cakes, baps, almond slices, éclairs and millefeuilles are other sweet temptations. A full cream tea including a Maid of Honour costs £4.20. Lunch (served between 12.30 and 2.15) offers a roast of the day, poached salmon and spinach quiche and vegetarian pasty among main-course choices (£6.95 including a dessert). All the meats are organically produced. Children's portions. No smoking. ***Seats*** *50 (+ 12 outside).* ***Open*** *9.30-5.30 (lunch Tue-Sat 12.30-2.15).* ***Closed*** *Mon pm, all Sun & Bank Holidays. MasterCard,* ***VISA***

KEW — Wine & Mousaka

Tel 0181-940 5696 Map 15 E2 JaB
12 Kew Green Kew Richmond-upon-Thames TW9 3BH

Overlooking Kew Green and opposite Kew Gardens, this bustling Greek restaurant has closely-packed tables and an informal atmosphere enhanced by candle-light in the evenings. Oregano-scented meats and fish fresh from the charcoal grill are a popular choice – try souvla (lamb marinated in red wine, and grilled £6.60), or chargrilled squid with dill mayonnaise (£6.95). Moussaka comes in both meat and vegetarian versions (£5.75/£5.45). Starters include taramasalata, tsatsiki and houmus (all £1.95) alongside stuffed courgettes or peppers (£2.65), squid cooked in wine (£3.50) and mushrooms à la grecque (£2.60). For a minimum of two, the Grand Meze (£11.45 per person) provides 4 hors d'oeuvre, 8 taster dishes, sweet and coffee. There is a garden for outdoor eating. Half portions for children. The painter Pissarro lived next door. ***Seats*** *48 (+ 20 outside).* ***Open*** *12-2.30 & 6-11.* ***Closed*** *Sun & Bank Holidays. Amex, Diners, MasterCard,* ***VISA***

KEYSOE — Chequers Inn

Tel 01234 708678 Map 15 E1 P
Pertenhall Road Keysoe Bedfordshire MK44 2HR

Dating back to 1520, the Chequers' one bar is divided into two by an unusual pillared fireplace; log fires in cold weather. The separate lounge opens on to a large, lawned garden complete with a Wendy House, playtree and swing. *Open 11.30-2.30, 6.30-11 (Sun 12-3, 7-10.30). Closed all Tue. Free House.* ***Beer*** *Hook Norton Best Bitter, guest beer. Garden, children's play area. MasterCard,* ***VISA***

KILNSEY — Kilnsey Park, Garden Room

Tel 01756 752150 **Fax 01756 752224** Map 6 C1 JaB
Kilnsey nr Skipton North Yorkshire BD23 5PS

At the heart of Kilnsey Leisure Park and Trout Farm, the Garden Room has been a hit since its opening in 1993. Home baking is the speciality, ranging from lunchtime pies to luscious Victoria sponges and the commendable speciality, Dales Treacle Tart (95p). The farm weighs in with its fine products: paté, fishcakes, oak-smoked and plain grilled trout (the last served with lemon and herb butter £4.75). Local suppliers add Wensleydale cheeses and Yorkshire ham for the high teas served daily from 4.30 to 7.30 in school holidays. It's a place that takes young families very much into account; a children's menu and small helpings are provided, as are three high-chairs and a shelf in the Ladies for baby-changing. An outdoor play area with swing, slide and climbing frame for toddlers to let off steam. Much of the surrounding activity is designed with children in mind: even if they're not hungry themselves, they need little enough encouragement to feed the fish! Facilities for disabled visitors are also excellent. Book on Sundays. ***Seats*** *50.* ***Open*** *9-4.30.* ***Closed*** *25 Dec. MasterCard,* ***VISA***

KILVE Meadow House 70% £75

Tel 01278 741546 **Fax 01278 741663** Map 13 E1 **H**
Sea Lane Kilve nr Bridgwater Somerset TA5 1EG

Howard and Judith Wyer-Roberts operate a civilised home-from-home at their former rectory set in eight acres of gardens and grounds that include a water garden and duck pond. It's just five minutes from a quiet, fossil-strewn beach (the inspiration for Wordsworth's *On Kilve's Beach*). It's a peaceful setting and the main-house bedrooms are spacious, attractive and well appointed. Stable rooms across the car park have sitting-rooms and a pleasant, cottagey look.Antiques, original paintings and log fires are features in the drawing-room, lounge and study. No dogs in the main house. Turn right off the A39 at the Hood Arms when coming from Bridgwater. ***Rooms*** *10. Garden, croquet. Amex, MasterCard,* ***VISA***

A jug of fresh water!

KIMBOLTON The Tea Room

Tel 01480 860415 Map 15 E1 **JaB**
9 East Street Kimbolton Cambridgeshire PE18 0HJ

Right next to Kimbolton Castle, where Catherine of Aragon spent her last months in captivity (it's now a school), is this cosy tea room with a menu that's strong on sandwiches, from tuna mayonnaise with chopped walnuts on iceberg lettuce (£1.85) to turkey Waldorf with a side salad (£3.25) and home-cooked ham (£1.95). Salads are also available: chicken, ham or game pie (£6.95 including tea/coffee or a cold drink, bread and butter and a slice of cake); plus an assortment of vegetarian quiches and pizzas. There's a good selection of home-made cakes such as chocolate fudge, Dundee, coffee, ginger with vanilla icing, lemon and passion (from £1.60) plus, in summer, meringues with strawberries and cream. Two set teas: Gateaux (£3.20) and Strawberry Cream Tea (£4.50). A lovely courtyard in York stone with redbrick wall and flower baskets comes into its own in summer. Good, conscientious service in a calm, relaxing atmosphere. No smoking. ***Seats*** *24 (+ 20 outside).* ***Open*** *10.30-5.* ***Closed*** *Mon & mid Nov-mid Jan. No credit cards.*

KING'S LYNN Butterfly Hotel 62% £69

Tel 01553 771707 **Fax 01553 768027** Map 10 B1 **H**
Beveridge Way Hardwick Narrows King's Lynn Norfolk PE30 4NB

A modern, town-fringe hotel at the A10/A47 roundabout; part of a small East Anglian group (other outlets in Bury St Edmunds, Colchester and Peterborough) aiming at the middle market. ***Rooms*** *50. Garden. Amex, Diners, MasterCard,* ***VISA***

KINGSCOTE Hunters Hall

Tel 01453 860393 **Fax 01453 860707** Map 14 B2 **P**
Kingscote Tetbury Gloucestershire GL8 8XZ

Five miles from Tetbury on the A4135 Hunters Hall is an ideal spot for a family day out. It sports a lovely tree-lined garden with extensive play areas and assault course, while on wet days parents and little ones use the gallery room, almost hidden above the pub's interlinked beamed and flagstoned bars. Standing separately, a Cotswold stone block of recent construction houses the bedrooms, residents' lounge and a conference facility. With roomy en suite bathrooms, remote-control TV and dial-out phone, neither space nor comfort is stinted: two ground-floor rooms incorporate facilities for the disabled, and a large suite has two double bedrooms. Good selection of wines by the glass. New management (Old English Pub Company), head chef and menus since last year's guide. *Open 11-11 (Sun 12-10.30). Free House.* ***Beer*** *Bass, Hook Norton Best, Marston's Pedigree, Uley Old Spot. Garden, barbecue, children's play area. Family room.* ***Accommodation*** *12 bedrooms, all en suite, £60 (four-poster £70, family room for three £70, for four £85, single £45). Children welcome overnight (under 4s stay free in parents' room, 5-14s £10), additional bed & cot available. Amex, Diners, MasterCard,* ***VISA***

KINGSTEIGNTON Old Rydon Inn

Tel 01626 54626 **Fax 01626 56980** Map 13 D3
Old Rydon Road Kingsteignton Newton Abbot Devon TQ12 3QG

Hermann Hruby (pronounced Ruby) continues to maintain his high standards in producing some of the best pub food in the South West, and in that respect little has changed since the Hrubys bought the Old Rydon in 1978 except for the building of a splendid, and large, heated conservatory, leafy with vines, jasmine, bougainvillaea and other plants. It's a Grade II listed former farmhouse, converted in the 1960s with an original old cider loft forming an attractive part of the bar, previously the farm stables. Underneath the plank and beam ceiling adorned with pewter mugs is a raised log fire; the whitewashed stone walls are hung with antlers and horns. Tables here are drinking style, too small and cramped for relaxed dining, and many of the seats are converted barrels. The place to dine is in the comfortable conservatory, or on warm sunny days at a table on the patio or in the sheltered walled garden – an ideal summer venue for lunch. Separate from the bar, a relaxing diners' lounge leads through to the charming little restaurant, in the oldest part of the building. Most visitors come for the delicious and interesting food (including sandwiches and ploughman's platters) which, in the bar, is listed on twice daily-changing blackboards and might include seafood pancake in shellfish sauce, goujons of Brixham fish with a spicy coating and lime mayonnaise, strips of pollock with lemon, honey and ginger with stir-fried vegetables, grilled lamb neck fillet with rosemary scented rice and red pepper sauce, venison or hare pie, various pasta specials (chargrilled vegetables with tapénade), and vegetarian options like large local flat mushrooms with tomato, red pepper and basil sauce. Excellent puddings range from spiced banana cake to home-made lemon layer pudding. Service is polite and very efficient. No children under 8 in the pub after 8pm. The pub is awkward to locate as it now hides within a modern housing estate, but it is best approached along Longford Lane off the A381, then take Rydon Road which lies on your left. *Open 11-2.30, 6-11 (Sun 12-3, 7-10.30).* ***Bar Food*** *12-2, 7-9.30. Free House.* ***Beer*** *Wadworth 6X, Bass, guest beer. Garden, outdoor eating. Family room. Amex, Diners, MasterCard,* ***VISA***

We welcome bona fide complaints and recommendations on the tear-out pages at the back of the Guide for Readers' Comments. They are followed up by our professional team.

KINGSTON The Juggs

Tel 01273 472523 **Fax 01273 476150** Map 11 B6
The Street Kingston Lewes East Sussex BN7 3NT

Just off the A27, a short distance from Brighton, you will find this picturesque little 15th-century inn made from two tiny cottages. The name 'Juggs' originates from the leather jugs the women used to carry on their heads to collect fish from the market. The main bar is particularly characterful with its low ceilings, rough black timbers, rustic benches and yellowing walls; there's also a small no-smoking dining area (same menu in both, bookings taken) and a rear no-smiking family room. Daily specials like mushroom, spinach and garlic lasagne or tuna, sweetcorn and spring onion quiche are prominently displayed. The home-made steak and kidney puddings have a reputation for being enormous and good value, the Sussex bangers are made by a local butcher and served with proper chips, and puddings, all home-made, are considered a speciality: perhaps apple strudel lemon cheesecake or redberry crème brulé. Open sandwiches, ploughman's platters, home-made soups and salads are also offered, as well as a Sunday lunch buffet (limited hot food). Large outdoor seating area on a bricked terrace and underneath a pergola. In addition to the pub's wooden climbing frame there's a new playground on the other side of the car park. Head up the lane past the church and you'll find yourself right at the bottom of the Downs. *Open 11-2.30, 6-10.45 (till 11 Fri & Sat, 11-11 July & Aug), Sun 12-3, 7-10.30,* ***Bar Food*** *12-2, 6-9.30 (from 7 Sun). Free House.* ***Beer*** *Harveys Best, King & Barnes Festive, guest beer. Garden, outdoor eating, children's play area. Family room. Closed all 26 Dec. MasterCard,* ***VISA***

KINGSTON La La Pizza

Tel 0181-546 4888 Map 15 E2 **JaB**
138 London Road Kingston-upon-Thames KT2 6QJ

The owners of this cheerful Italian pizzeria offer an imaginative range of 32 pizzas, ranging from £3.30 to £9.50 (for their special King pizza). Many of them are named after famous people, mainly classical singers and composers: Ascari (after the great racing driver) has asparagus, pastrami, Italian salami, smoked bacon and mortadella sausage with tomato and herbs; and amongst the others, Vivaldi – (four seasons, what else!). If you can manage a starter as well you could choose from baked dough sticks, borlotti bean and tuna fish salad or Mediterranean seafood salad. For dessert try Mama's mousse (£2.25), made with chocolate, eggs and brandy, topped with whipped cream. Children are welcome 'anytime, anywhere' in typical Italian style, and the kitchen will do their best to please their younger customers; ten high-chairs are provided. There is no minimum charge. Fenced-in garden. ***Seats*** *50 (+30 garden).* ***Open*** *D only 5.30-11.30.* ***Closed*** *1 Jan, Easter Sunday & 4 days Christmas. Amex, MasterCard,* **VISA**

KINGTON Penrhos Court £75

Tel 01544 230720 **Fax 01544 230754** Map 9 D4 **RR**
Penrhos Kington Hereford & Worcester HR5 3LH

Set back from the A44, an ancient farm with parts dating back to 1280 is the setting for a marvellous restaurant with rooms. Owners Martin Griffiths and Daphne Lambert have spent many years rebuilding and refurbishing the site. The dining-room is the restored 13th-century Cruck Hall, complete with heavy beams and flagstone floors. Menus change daily and consist of a short selection of well-prepared dishes using locally produced ingredients, organic and additive-free where possible, and there's an excellent vegetarian choice. Good desserts;Welsh cheeses. Bread baked fresh daily on the premises. No smoking. ***Seats*** *70. Private Room 20. D only 7.30-10. Closed Sun & 2 weeks Jan. Set D £25. Amex, Diners, MasterCard,* **VISA**

Rooms

Fifteen bedrooms are individual in style and specifications. Eight rooms are in skilfully converted Elizabethan barns; of a fair size, they use lightwood and mahogany furniture, and co-ordinated contemporary fabrics contribute to a bright, clean decor. The Swallow Room features a four-poster bed and private balcony; Kingfisher is a family room with two double beds and bathroom with shower. No smoking. No dogs. Garden.

KIRKBY LONSDALE Snooty Fox Tavern

Tel 01524 271308 **Fax 01524 272642** Map 4 C4 **P**
Main Street Kirkby Lonsdale Cumbria LA6 2AH

Completely refurbished former Jacobean coaching inn near the town square. Inside, the various bars and eating areas sport all sorts of interesting bits and pieces from a collection of period clothing to numerous stuffed animals and birds in glass cases. Chef-manager Gordon Cartwright, who runs things with wife Joanna, operates a long menu with a wide range of around 40 dishes, from smoked salmon and dill mousse, home-made soup (with apricot and walnut bread) and Cumberland sausage with an onion and mignonette sauce and mashed potato to leek and Brie tart with tomato sauce, honey roast lamb with Madeira and caramelised onions, sweet and sour pork and chargrilled medallions of Angus fillet with chips; not forgetting jacket potatoes, salads, spotted dick and much else besides. Everything is home-made and enjoyable and bookings are suggested for Sunday lunches. There is a small walled beer garden to the rear across a cobbled courtyard. Children are made welcome with small portions and high-chairs. Well-refurbished bedrooms, of which there are now nine (and all no-smoking), boast a variety of furniture (sometimes antique) and pretty duvet covers with co-ordinating curtains. Many have characterful exposed timbers and all are en suite; just one has a bath, the others fully-tiled shower rooms. No telephones in the bedrooms. Breakfasts show that Gordon Cartwright's experience in the kitchens at Sharrow Bay in Ullswater has paid dividends: choose from pan-fried apple rings, sautéed mushrooms, hash browns and Berry black pudding to go with the more usual egg, smoked bacon, local pork sausage, roasted tomato and fried bread – all served on elegant Villeroy & Boch plates. *Open 11-11 (Sun 12-10.30). **Bar Food** 12-2.30, 6.30-10 (Sun 7-9.30). Free House. **Beer** Hartleys XB, Theakston Best, Timothy Taylor's Landlord. Garden, outdoor eating. **Accommodation** 9 rooms, all en suite (one with bath), £49.50-£52.50 (single £29). Children welcome overnight, additional beds (£10) & cot (£5) available. Accommodation closed all 25 Dec, 31 Dec & 1 Jan. Amex, Diners, MasterCard,* **VISA**

KNAPP Rising Sun

Tel 01823 490436 Map 13 E2 P

Knapp North Curry Taunton Somerset TA3 6BG

Directions here are hard to give and just as hard to follow. Meander down the lanes from the hamlet of Ham (six miles west of Junction 25 on the M5), right on the lip of the Somerset levels, and then keep a lookout for the arrows. Built as a Longhouse in 1480 and 'rediscovered' since the arrival of Tony Atkinson in 1989, the Rising Sun attracts its fill of worshippers of fine, fresh fish these days, and diners should mark out their spot especially early at weekends. Separated by a lounge bar with deep sofas in front of a cast-iron stove, two cottage dining areas are now given over to some serious eating with top billing given to fresh fish from Brixham and elsewhere – Tony self-styles the Rising Sun as a 'restaurant with a bar', although there are no table cloths and the service is not formal. Chef Wendy Repton's prodigious output from the kitchen might include chunky bouillabaisse or crab fishcakes to start, following with John Dory with sun-dried tomatoes, anchovies and capers, brill topped with salmon mousse and cucumber with a white wine sauce, and crevettes pan-fried with cajun spices; so popular are the megrims (Torbay sole), lobsters and langoustines that availability cannot be promised to later arrivals. Meat eaters may prefer a steak or chicken with mushroom and garlic sauce. More traditional, pubby lunchtime snacks (open sandwiches, ploughman's platters, ham, egg and chips) are also available; in the evening the place steps up a gear and the snackier items are not served. Half portions for children, popular Sunday lunch with roast rib of beef, Yorkshire pudding and hot fishy bits on the bar and flowery summer patios are all added draws. *Open 11.30-2.30, 6.30-11 (Sun 12-3, 7-10.30). **Bar Food** 12-2, 7-9.30. (no food Sun eve Oct-Apr). Free House. **Beer** Boddingtons, Bass, Exmoor Ale. Patio. Family Room. MasterCard,* **VISA**

KNIGHTWICK Talbot Hotel

Tel 01886 821235 **Fax 01886 821060** Map 14 B1 

Knightwick Worcester Hereford & Worcester WR6 5PH

On the banks of the River Teme, on which it has fishing rights, the Talbot stands by a disused road bridge and conveniently back from the new crossing on the busy A44. Dating in parts from the 14th Century, it retains an evocative interior of oak beams and blackened brick, the bar's finest feature being the back-to-back open fire and cast-iron, wood-burning stove which share a central chimney. There's a whizz in the kitchen, producing commendably varied home-cooking on a daily menu that services both bar and dining-room. For a snack, try the crab and mushroom tart, four cheese tagliatelle or fresh scallop beignets, while diners may satiate themselves on a three-course meal of pigeon breast salad, venison Wellington or pan-fried wild salmon with a sorrel and cream sauce with, to follow, Normandy apple flan or sticky date and toffee pudding. Fish (mackerel with confit of spring onions, ginger and garlic) is becoming increasingly popular. The bedrooms' up-to-date amenities include colour TVs, tea trays and dial-out telephones with little other obeisance to ostentation or modernity. Furnishings and decor are generally modest and comfortable in a cottagey style – best employed in the newer bedroom extension. Above the bars, three bedrooms are larger and more characterful but share their bathing and toilet facilities. *Open 11-11 (Sun 12-10.30). **Bar Food** 12-2, 6.30-9.30 (Sun 7-9). Free House. **Beer** Bass, Worthington Best, Hobson's Bitter. Patio/terrace, outdoor eating. Family room. **Accommodation** 10 bedrooms, 7 en suite, £56.50 (family room £52-£66.50, single £24-£31). Children welcome overnight (charged according to age), additional bed (£10) & cot available. MasterCard,* **VISA**

KNUTSFORD Cottons Hotel 66% £119

Tel 01565 650333 **Fax 01565 755351** Map 6 B2 **H**
Manchester Road Knutsford Cheshire WA16 0SU

Bedrooms here are not large but they boast many nice features like a really comfortable, upholstered chair at the desk (where there's a second phone) in addition to a proper armchair and fine well-lit bathrooms with chunky period-style suites and good shelf space. Recent refurbishment has introduced a fairly masculine decor with plaid fabrics and traditional polished wood furniture with the (satellite) TV neatly tucked away in a cabinet. 17 new Executive rooms are more spacious with a split-level sitting/work area and a mini-bar that includes fresh milk for the beverage tray. Smart public areas include a conservatory lounge and bar with rug-strewn wooden floor and punka overhead. Room service operates 24 hours a day. Children under seven share parents' room (and eat) free. A new, air-conditioned leisure centre includes a good-sized pool and well-equipped gym. The hotel is located five minutes from the M6 (junction 19) and just 15 from Manchester Airport. Ample parking. ***Rooms** 99. Tennis, indoor swimming pool, gym, squash, sauna, steam room, spa bath, sun beds, beauty treatment room, aerobics studio. Amex, Diners, MasterCard,* ***VISA***

KNUTSFORD Est Est Est

Tel 01565 755487 **Fax 01565651151** Map 6 B2 **JaB**
81 King Street Knutsford Cheshire

Light, bright and spacious, this is one of a small North-West chain of friendly Italian trattorias. The long menu includes all the traditional favourites from calamari fritti (£3.85) to stuffed mushrooms (£3.45) and some 18 pasta dishes including spaghetti bolognese (£4.99), farfalle al salmone (£6.25) and lasagne (£4.95). Pizzas are of interesting variety: pizza di Gourmet (£5.25 – Parma ham, dolcelatte and olives), pizza con porcini (£5.25 – wild and cultivated mushrooms) and pizza vegetariana (£4.85 – mushrooms, onion, peppers and olives). Secondi piatti are mainly variations on beef, veal and chicken, including pollo al rosmarino (£8.95 – chargrilled breast of chicken with garlic and fresh rosemary) and bistecca al pepe (£10.45 – sirloin steak with a cream, brandy and peppercorn sauce). The *menu dei bambini* brings a ball of dough and tray of toppings to the table and allows children to make their own pizzas, complete with a chef's hat! No minimum charge but you're expected to have a main-course dish at night. Six high-chairs. Baby-changing unit in the disabled toilet. ***Seats** 180. **Open** 12-2.30 & 6-11 (Sat 12-11.30, Sun 12-10.30). **Closed** 25, 26 Dec & 1 Jan. Amex, MasterCard,* ***VISA***

LACOCK George Inn

Tel 01249 730263 Map 14 B2 **P**
4 West Street Lacock Chippenham Wiltshire SN15 2LH

The virtual epitome of the traditional village pub. The George could scarcely be in a more ideal spot than the National Trust village of Lacock. Starting life in 1361 as the Black Boy with its own brewery in farm buildings to the rear, its many modernisations have preserved and re-utilised many of the original timbers. Central to the bar is a unique mounted dog-wheel built into the open fireplace and used for spit-roasting in the 16th-century (the dog was not roasted, but trained to rotate the wheel). Today's pub lives well alongside such idiosyncrasy with its close-packed tables on odd levels set beneath a wealth of old pictures at many an odd angle. From a menu of firm favourites, traditional steak and kidney pie is always popular alongside wild boar steak with sweet and sour sauce, fisherman's pie, chicken stew and dumplings and a vegetable balti curry. "You can have anything from a bowl of chips to a Dover sole", says the landlord. For pudding, try the banana and toffee crunch or the triple chocolate cheesecake. The large garden stretches out on both sides of the rear car park; beyond it is a safe play area for youngsters, close by an old stocks to restrain the most troublesome. True to its long-standing identity as a family concern, the licensees' family not only provides overnight farmhouse accommodation nearby but also lays on complimentary transport to and from the pub. Enquiries should be addressed to the pub. *Open 10-3, 5-11 (10-11 Sat summer), Sun 12-10.30.* ***Bar Food** 12-2, 6-10. **Beer** Wadworth. Garden, outdoor eating, children's play area. MasterCard,* ***VISA***

LAMARSH Red Lion

Tel 01787 227918 Map 10 C3 
Lamarsh Essex CO8 5EP

Enjoying a peaceful location overlooking the gently-rolling landscape bordering the River Stour valley, this charming little tiled Essex pub dates from the 14th century. It's a wonderful place to frequent on a sunny summer's evening when the perfectly-positioned front benches make the most of the view. Beams abound in the comfortable modernised interior with its rather ecclesiastical, carved and inscribed bar counter, restored pews, attractive walls murals of Suffolk scenes and welcoming winter log fire. The 16th-century barn holds a games room and is popular with locals. *Open 11-3, 6-11 (Sat 11-11, Sun 12-3, 7-10.30). Free House.* ***Beer*** *Greene King IPA, Fuller's London Pride, Wadworth 6X. Garden, children's play area. Family room. MasterCard,* ***VISA***

Pubs – note that food is only recommended in those pubs with ***Bar Food*** times in the statistics at the end of an entry. Restaurant food in pubs is *never* recommended unless specifically mentioned. Some pubs are recommended for B&B or Atmosphere only – each entry's statistics indicate our recommendation.

LANCASTER O'Malley's

Tel 01524 36561 Map 6 A1 JaB
Bashful Alley Lancaster Lancashire LA1 1LF

O'Malley's is a cosy café displaying tempting cakes in the window, all baked on the premises (£1.70 for a generous slice). A large menu offers crumpets, scones, cinnamon toast, teacakes and toasted sandwiches (from £2). Substantial meals include meat 'n' tatie pie with red cabbage, fisherman's pie (both £3.95), vegetable bake (£3.60) and filled jacket potatoes (from £2.45). The lunchtime specials list might bring corned beef hash with red cabbage (£2.50) or vegetable curry with rice and mango pickle (£3). There is a wide selection of teas and various coffees. Healthy-heart options include low-fat ice creams and sundaes. Children's juice cups are available on request and they are happy to heat up baby's bottle -just ask. Two high-chairs, and they now have a toilet on the premises (changing mat on request). Their new 'littl'uns' menu offers soup and a roll, followed by a choice of beans, cheese, spaghetti or scrambled eggs on toast, or a Dinky Diners' Box (sandwich, fairy cake and a soft drink in a colourful box that they can keep), with ice cream or a cake to finish. No smoking. ***Seats*** *56 (+8 outside).* ***Open*** *8.30-5.* ***Closed*** *Sun, 25, 26 Dec & 1 Jan. No credit cards.*

LANGDALE Langdale Hotel 71% £140

Tel 01539 437302 **Fax 01539 437694** Map 4 C3 H
Great Langdale nr Ambleside Cumbria LA22 9JD

Thirty-five acres of woodland make a secluded setting for a well-run hotel and country club. Bedrooms, all doubles or twins, are in several satellite blocks built of Lakeland stone, and there are some family rooms with bunk beds. Decor is either modern or Edwardian with four-posters or canopied beds (Premier rooms £170), and there are some self-catering lodges for weekly rental. 24hr room service. There's an open-plan bar-lounge, and a nearby slate-walled pub bar. Rooms overlooking Great Langdale Beck have private balconies. Guests have full use of the hotel's considerable leisure facilities. No dogs. ***Seats*** *65. Garden, croquet, tennis, squash, fishing, riding, indoor swimming pool & splash pool, gym, sauna, steam room, spa bath, solarium, beauty & hair salon, children's playground, games room, shop, coffee shop (9am-11.30pm). Amex, Diners, MasterCard,* ***VISA***

We do not accept free meals or hospitality – our inspectors pay their own bills.

LANGLEY-ON-TYNE Langley Castle 63% £89

Tel 01434 688888 **Fax 01434 684019** Map 5 D2 **H**

Langley-on-Tyne nr Haydon Bridge Northumberland NE49 0LY

A tall, square structure originally built in 1365 but gutted by fire in 1405. The castle remained a shell for 500 years until, at the turn of this century, it was rebuilt. It became a hotel 10 years ago but there still remains plenty to remind one of the castle's origins – from the four-foot-thick walls to the garde-robes, and the spiral staircases which lead to some of the bedrooms. The lounge/drawing-room occupies a large portion of the first floor. It has a tiny, cosy bar through a door in one corner. Five 'feature' bedrooms have either a four-poster or half-tester bed; additionally one has a spa bath and another a circular bath and private sauna (the tariff rises to £129). Eight Castle View bedrooms are in recently-converted outhouses with views up to the Castle; some of these bedrooms have sofa-beds – children will love the inescapable sense of history that surrounds them here. The hotel is on the A686, a mile or two south of Haydon Bridge. ***Rooms** 16. Garden. Amex, Diners, MasterCard,* ***VISA***

LANGSTONE Royal Oak

Tel 01705 483125 Map 15 D4 **P**

19 Langstone High Street Langstone Havant Hampshire PO9 1RY

Historic 16th-century pub with stunning views over Chichester Harbour. Right on the water's edge, the water reaches the front door when the tide's exceptionally high! Originally a row of cottages used in conjunction with the adjacent old mill, they later traded under a 'tidal licence' before the bridge to Hayling Island was built, allowing travellers a drink while waiting for the ebb tide. An individual rustic charm characterises the unspoilt interior. The neatly kept bars boast flagstone and polished pine floors, exposed beams, open fires and old wooden furnishings; a cosy haven on wild winter days. Warmer sunny days can be enjoyed with a drink on the front benches or in the secluded rear garden, which is a safe refuge for families and where a pet's corner runs the gamut from budgies to goats and a pot-bellied pig. No under-14s in bar areas. Whitbread Wayside Inn. *Open 11-11 (Sun 12-10.30).* ***Beer** Flowers Original, Boddingtons, Marston's Pedigree, guest beer. Garden, outdoor eating beside water's edge. MasterCard,* ***VISA***

LANHYDROCK Lanhydrock House Restaurant

Tel 01208 74331 Map 12 B3

Lanhydrock nr Bodmin Cornwall PL30 5AD

The former servants' hall of National Trust-owned Lanhydrock House (£2.50 entrance fee to gain access to the eateries) with its oak panelling and bell-boards is now the restaurant, where uniformed waitresses serve light lunches and teas. Home-made hot dishes could include West Country pork and apple casserole (£5.65) or cheese and onion pie (£5.20). Other dishes might be savoury flan (£4.85), home-cooked ham (£5.75) and mature Cheddar and Stilton salad (£4.95). Two puddings feature daily (£2.45), one hot (steamed ginger and marmalade sponge), the other cold (brown sugar meringues with cream and fruit sauce). The cream tea (£3.10) and the copious Country House Tea (£3.95) are served later in the day with a choice of home-made cakes, scones and splits (a Cornish speciality). The wine list extends to elderflower, strawberry and apple wines as well as a good selection of conventional grape wines of which about eight are available by the glass. Light lunches of jacket potatoes (from £3.10), small salads, soups and puddings are also served in the former housekeeper's and housemaids' sitting-rooms in the servants' quarters. Across the courtyard, the Stable Bar (the only outlet open on Mondays when the house is closed to visitors) serves snacks, drinks and ice cream throughout the day. Three-course traditional lunch (£10.50) on Sundays. Fire regulations do not allow push chairs into the restaurant but there are high-chairs and a special children's menu. The Stable and Harness Room is particularly suited to families and children. Five high-chairs, mealtime puzzles, children's portions and a fully equipped parent & baby room are all provided. No smoking. ***Seats** 108.* ***Open** 11-5.30 (from 10.30 Jul-Sep, till 4.30 Nov).* ***Closed** Mon-Fri (Nov) & Christmas-Good Friday. Amex, MasterCard,* ***VISA***

LAVENHAM Angel Inn

Tel 01787 247388 **Fax 01787 248344** Map 10 C3
Market Place Lavenham Suffolk CO10 9QZ

First licensed in 1420, the Angel looks on to the market place of one of the best preserved medieval towns in England. Inside, the bar has been opened up without losing any of its original charm, with half set up for eating and the other half well supplied with board games, playing cards and shelves of books. There are quiz and bridge nights and on Friday evenings Roy Whitworth (one of the partners) entertains with classical music at the piano. Leek and lentil soup, mushroom roulade, honey-roast pork fillet, rabbit braised with bacon and prunes and steak and kidney pie are typical offerings from the daily-changing evening menu; lunchtime brings similar dishes (at slightly lower prices) plus some more snacky items like ploughman's and cauliflower cheese. Good puddings include bread-and-butter pudding and lemon tart. Bedrooms are all en suite (five with shower, three with bath) and full of character with old beams, sloping floors and traditional freestanding furniture. All have TV, direct-dial phone and tea- and coffee-making kit. Children are made welcome with a couple of high-chairs, various toys, free cots and "put-u-up" beds; ask for small menu portions. For summer there are tables in a secluded garden plus benches and brollies overlooking the market place. *Open 11-11 (Sun 12-10.30).* ***Bar Food*** *12-2.15, 6.45-9.15. Free House.* ***Beer*** *Nethergate Bitter, Adnams Southwold, Mauldons White Adder, guest beer. Garden, patio, outdoor eating.* ***Accommodation*** *8 bedrooms, all en suite, £50-£60 (Sat half board only £90-£100, family room sleeping three £60-£70, single £37.50). Children welcome overnight (babies in cot free), additional bed (£10) & cot available. Closed all 25 & 26 Dec. Amex, MasterCard,* ***VISA***

Our inspectors *never* book in the name of Egon Ronay's Guides. They disclose their identity only if they are considering an establishment for inclusion in the next edition of the Guide.

LAVENHAM Great House £45

Tel 01787 247431 **Fax 01787 248007** Map 10 C3
Market Place Lavenham Suffolk CO10 9QZ

The Great House is 15th-century with a Georgian facade, and stands just opposite the historic Guildhall in this well-preserved medieval town. Frenchman Régis Crépy provides excellent food, served in cosy surroundings. A typical menu might offer carpaccio of tuna with rocket, lobster, spinach and ricotta raviolo, ever-popular mussels with a drop of cream, Dover sole fillets wrapped thinly in crispy potatoes, roasted saddle of venison with poached pear and a rich red wine sauce, creamy iced orange and Grand Marnier soufflé, and crème brulée (surely never to disappear from the menu!). Excellent French cheeseboard. Brasserie-style snack and table d'hote lunch menus (not Sun) and both fixed-price (not D Sat) and à la carte in the evening. Popular Sunday lunch, when there's a choice of around six or so dishes at each stage (not including a roast). Every wine is accompanied by tasting notes ('crunchy fruit'?); plenty under £20. Smoking is not encouraged. Children welcome until 9pm. Outdoor eating on a delightful paved patio with tables and sun umbrellas. Perhaps an unusual choice for our Family Restaurant of the Year 1997, but stay overnight and you'll see why it's an ideal destination for a family weekend away. Kentwell Hall is nearby. Long Melford will also be of interest to families with its moated manor house, 16th-century live 'time-warp' re-creations, café and rare breeds farm. See Awards pages for further details. ***Seats*** *40. Private Room 50. L 12-2.30 D 7-9.30 (Sat till 10.30). Closed D Sun, all Mon. Set L £9.95/£12.95 (Sun £16.95, children £9) Set D £16.95 (not Sat). Amex, MasterCard,* ***VISA***

Rooms £66

There are four charming, traditionally furnished bedrooms all with either a separate lounge or a sitting area; one room has two double beds. Thick beams, antique furniture and floral fabrics create the look of village England. Walled garden with swings. Breakfast may be served in the bedrooms. The tariff increases to £78 on Saturday nights and £88 on Bank Holidays; low-season single occupancy starts at £39.50. Children under 4 share free (cot supplied), 4- to 12-year-olds are charged £10.

LAVENHAM The Swan 71% £128

Tel 01787 247477 **Fax 01787 248286** Map 10 C3 **HR**
High Street Lavenham nr Sudbury Suffolk CO10 9QA

A splendid example of Elizabethan architecture in an attractive and much-visited village. Bristling with timbers, the cosy alcoves meander one into another, creating charming public areas. The lounge has long been the setting for relaxing afternoon tea, while the earthy real-ale bar has the warm feel of a much-loved local. Walkways overlooking pretty little gardens lead to the variously-sized bedrooms, designed to retain the period feel; stylish furniture and extras like fruit and chocolates set the the tone for the attention to detail in evidence throughout the hotel. If you want to get the real feel of the place, ask for a room with a four-poster bed (+£22.50) and private sitting-room; Feature rooms are larger and there also two suites. Three function suites, the largest holding 130. Ten rooms recently refurbished. No charge for children up to 16 years sharing with their parents; extra bed or cot provided. Forte Heritage. ***Rooms*** *46. Garden. Amex, Diners, MasterCard,* ***VISA***

Restaurant £75

The restaurant, though but thirty years old, is in keeping with the hotel's origins and has a lofty, open-raftered ceiling and a minstrel's gallery. Chef Andrew Barrass has a sure touch and his menus offer a good choice of carefully cooked dishes, based on traditional British methods: duck and liver parfait with brioche, fishcakes, avocado and bacon salad, fillet of salmon and herbs, breast of pheasant with wild mushrooms, peppered sirloin steak, good cheeses and the ubiquitous sticky toffee pudding. Modest wine list, fair prices. The lounge menu offers morning coffee with cakes and pastries from 10am and savoury light lunch choices from noon: freshly-made sandwiches (from £3.50), home-made soup (£2.95), steak sandwich, warm salmon and asparagus salad (both £8.95), and a daily hot dish (£8.95) – perhaps steak in local ale on a vegetarian pudding with a suet crust. Afternoon tea (from 3pm) offers a choice between Cream Tea (£4.95) and a Traditional English Tea complete with finger sandwiches (cucumber, egg and cress, ham), freshly-baked scones with jam and Cornish clotted cream, cakes and pastries (£7.95). In summer alfresco eating can be enjoyed in the sunny sheltered garden. Families and children are welcome throughout and an early evening children's meal can be provided; three high-chairs. A thoughtful, above-average children's menu offers the likes of home-made soup of the day or chilled melon, followed by six or so main courses (omelette, vegetables and fries, ham or cheese salad in addition to the usual kids' favourites) and a choice of desserts. 'For the very young', there's a selection of baby foods available, plus a boiled egg with soldiers. Some special children's drinks include the Lavenham Lullaby (pineapple, lemonade and grenadine juice). No smoking. ***Seats*** *70. Parties 20. Private Room 40. L 12.30-2 D 7-9.30. Set L £13.95/£15.95 (Sun £17.95) Set D £24.95.*

LEAMINGTON SPA Alastair's

Tel 01926 422550 Map 14 C1 **JaB**
40 Warwick Street Leamington Spa Warwickshire CV32 5JS

A cellar dining-room with bare-brick walls, stone floor and antique pine furniture where you can enjoy a decent snack or meal in a cheerful atmosphere. The menu offers bistro-type dishes such as deep-fried camembert (£3.50), taramasalata with pitta bread (£3.50) and garlic mushrooms (£3.25) to begin; lamb kleftico with a mint sauce gravy (£7.95), fillets of plaice (£7.80), or steaks – sirloin or fillet au poivre (£11.50/£12.50) – to follow. In warm weather there is a good range of salads (from £5.80). Vegetarians also have some interesting dishes, perhaps mushroom stroganoff, vegetarian tagliatelle or broccoli and Stilton quiche (all £5.50). Simple desserts. Walled garden. ***Seats*** *50 (+30 outside).* ***Open*** *12-2.30 & 7-10.* ***Closed*** *D Sun, also L Sun May-Sep, 25 & 26 Dec. Amex, MasterCard,* ***VISA***

Leamington Spa — Courtyard by Marriott — 65% — £87

Tel 01926 425522 **Fax 01926 881322** Map 14 C1 H
Olympus Avenue Europa Way Leamington Spa Warwickshire CV34 6RJ

Roomy and practical accommodation next to an industrial park, aimed mainly at the business traveller. Two suites are £102; standard rooms are £58 B&B Fri-Sun and Bank Holiday Mondays; 'twin' rooms have two double beds and there are also interconnecting rooms. ***Rooms*** *94. Keep-fit equipment. Amex, Diners, MasterCard,* ***VISA***

We endeavour to be as up-to-date as possible, but inevitably some changes to data and key personnel may occur at restaurants and hotels after the Guide goes to press. Prices should also be taken as indications rather than firm quotes.

Leamington Spa — Piccolino's Pizzeria

Tel 01926 422988 Map 14 C1 JaB
9 Spencer Street Leamington Spa Warwickshire CV31 3NE

Piccolino's is a reliable family-owned alternative to the high-street chains (there's another one in Warwick – see entry). Their specialities are pasta dishes and of course pizza; pasta (from £3.95) includes lasagne (£5.70 for meat, £5.80 for the vegetarian option); *carciofi quattro formaggi* – artichoke-stuffed pasta, with a sauce of four cheeses (£5.40), and *linguine al salmone e caviar rosso* – smoked salmon and red caviar cream sauce (£5.60). Pizzas (from £4.45) are available in great variety, the more unusual including Speedy Gonzales – mozzarella, gorgonzola and sliced tomato (£5.95) and *passione* – mozzarella, tomato, cream cheese, smoked salmon and avocado (£5.50). Chicken dishes, maybe *pollo celestine* – chicken breast, cream and Grand Marnier sauce with apples and almonds (£5.95) and steak pizzaiola – tomato and caper sauce (£8.10). Desserts include ice creams and rum baba (£2.40). Friendly service. ***Seats*** *86.* ***Open*** *12-2.30 & 5.30-11 (Sun till 10.30, Sat 12-11.30).* ***Closed*** *25, 26 Dec & Easter Sunday. MasterCard,* ***VISA***

Always ring ahead and inform establishments of your exact requirements when travelling with children. Unannounced can, sadly, still mean unwelcome.

Ledbury — Feathers Hotel

Tel 01531 635266 **Fax 01531 632001** Map 14 B1 I
High Street Ledbury Hereford & Worcester HR8 1DS

Right in the town centre, a classic timber-framed former coaching inn and corn exchange dating from 1564 with oddly-shaped, en suite, double-glazed bedrooms (including one with a lovely four-poster), original Elizabethan wall paintings, uneven, creaky floors and drunken staircases. Remote-control TV, direct-dial phones, bedside tea-tray and hairdryers are standard throughout. Lunchtime bar snacks in the hop-bedecked Fuggles bar may include spinach and ricotta tartlet and stir-fried sesame prawns with mangetout and garlic for starters, followed by chargrilled steaks, home-made hamburgers, salmon and fennel seed cakes and seafood and spinach lasagne. The simpler offerings are the best bet (more involved dishes like duck breast with five spice, garlic and sweet soy are less successful and offered at restaurant prices). For dessert you might find warm fig tartlet with almond cream and apricot and brandy syllabub. Annual real ale and cider festival on August Bank Holiday, music weekly on Wednesday and small rear patio available in good weather. Four miles from the M50 Junction 2. *Open 11-11.* ***Bar Food*** *12-2 (till 2.30 Sat), 7-9.30 (till 10 Sat & Sun).* ***Beer*** *Bass, Worthington Best, two guest beers. Patio.* ***Accommodation*** *11 bedrooms, all en suite, £65-£95 (family room £92-£100, single £49.50-£65). Children welcome overnight, additional bed & cot available. Amex, Diners, MasterCard,* ***VISA***

LEEDS Adriano Flying Pizza

Tel 0113-266 6501 **Fax 0113-266 5470** Map 6 C1 JaB
60 Street Lane Roundhay Leeds LS8 2DQ

The Flying Pizza is a bright and cheerful restaurant offering far more than pizzas, which come in fairly standard flavours (from £5.40). An enormous range of starters stretches from salads (from £3.75), to prawns in garlic butter cooked in white wine (£5.55) via starter-sized pasta dishes (£3.35). Main courses include pasta dishes: lasagne (£5.65), tagliatelle with smoked salmon and cream and vegetarian cannelloni, plus more elaborate dishes: veal with ham, white wine and fresh sage (£7.85), charcoal-grilled lamb cutlets (£7) and calf's liver with sage and butter (£9.25). Above-average puds. In good weather eat outside on the cobbled pavement under a colourful awning. ***Seats*** *140 (+56 outside).* ***Open*** *12-2.30 (Sun till 3) & 6-11.30 (Sun till 11).* ***Closed*** *25, 26 Dec & 1 Jan. Amex, MasterCard,* **VISA**

LEEDS Bibis £50

Tel 0113 243 0905 **Fax 0113 234 0844** Map 6 C1 
Minerva House 16 Greek Street Leeds LS1 5RU

Smart yet informal restaurant in Roman forum style squeezed in between city-centre office blocks. A giant menu – everything from lobster ravioli with shrimp sauce and *osso buco alla milanese* to pizzas and pasta every which way – is supplemented by daily specials. Tiramisu, lemon tart, *budino ai due ciocollati* or a trio of Italian cheeses with walnut bread to finish. Cooking is distinctly above average, as is the service, which is particularly swift at lunchtime. Children under 12 have their own 'Sunday Funday' menu; a magician or a clown entertains every Sunday lunchtime and eight high-chairs are provided. ***Seats*** *160. Parties 40. L 12-2.15 (Sun to 2.30) D 6-11.15 (Sun to10.30). Closed 25 Dec. Amex, MasterCard,* **VISA**

JaB is short for 'Just a Bite'. The majority of these establishments are also recommended in our *Bistros, Bars & Cafés* Guide which features establishments where one may eat well for less than £15 per head.

LEEDS Brasserie Forty Four £65

Tel 0113 234 3232 **Fax 0113 234 3332** Map 6 C1 
44 The Calls Leeds LS2 7EW

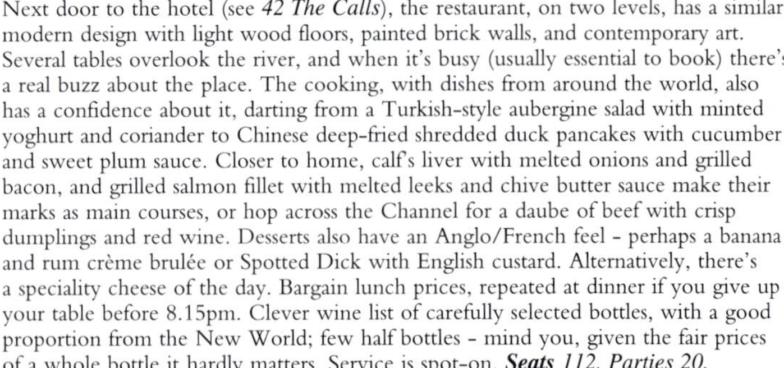

Next door to the hotel (see *42 The Calls*), the restaurant, on two levels, has a similar modern design with light wood floors, painted brick walls, and contemporary art. Several tables overlook the river, and when it's busy (usually essential to book) there's a real buzz about the place. The cooking, with dishes from around the world, also has a confidence about it, darting from a Turkish-style aubergine salad with minted yoghurt and coriander to Chinese deep-fried shredded duck pancakes with cucumber and sweet plum sauce. Closer to home, calf's liver with melted onions and grilled bacon, and grilled salmon fillet with melted leeks and chive butter sauce make their marks as main courses, or hop across the Channel for a daube of beef with crisp dumplings and red wine. Desserts also have an Anglo/French feel - perhaps a banana and rum crème brulée or Spotted Dick with English custard. Alternatively, there's a speciality cheese of the day. Bargain lunch prices, repeated at dinner if you give up your table before 8.15pm. Clever wine list of carefully selected bottles, with a good proportion from the New World; few half bottles - mind you, given the fair prices of a whole bottle it hardly matters. Service is spot-on. ***Seats*** *112. Parties 20. Private Room 50. L 12-2 D 6.30-10.30 (Fri & Sat 6.30-11). Closed L Sat, all Sun, Bank Holiday Mon & 1 week Christmas. Set L £8.75/£11.95 (also D if table vacated by 8.15pm). Amex, Diners, MasterCard,* **VISA**

LEEDS — Bryan's

Tel 0113 278 5679 **Fax 0113 224 9539** Map 6 C1 **JaB**
9 Weetwood Lane Headingley Leeds LS6 5LT

Several set deals are available at this traditional fish and chip restaurant: Senior Citizen's Special (£4.50 for two courses), a Business lunch (£8.95 for 3 courses) and Light Bites (£4.95) – perhaps a choice of salad (prawn, tuna or cheese) bread and butter and tea. Fresh fish, fried in beef dripping (as is customary in Yorkshire) is the mainstay: halibut (£6.70), plaice (£5.49) or haddock (£4.50) – any of these can be grilled to order. There is a children's menu (£3.25) and mother-and-baby facilities in the ladies loo. Breakfast (from £3.10) available Thu-Sat 9-11. Student's bargain two-course meal on Sunday (£4.50). Ten high-chairs are provided along with crayons, colouring menu, balloons, tokens to collect for T-shirts, baseball caps, badges and pencils - all part of the service. ***Seats*** *136 (+24 outside).* ***Open*** *11.30-10.30 (Thu-Sat till 11.30, Sun 12-7.30)* ***Closed*** *25 & 26 Dec. MasterCard,* ***VISA***

LEEDS — Haley's Hotel — 74% — £112

Tel 0113 278 4446 **Fax 0113 275 3342** Map 6 C1 **HR**
Shire Oak Road Headingley Leeds LS6 2DE

An unexpected find in a peaceful residential area off Headingley's main thoroughfare, the Victorian house was converted into a small hotel a few years ago. Tastefully furnished in country-house style with period pieces, it has a comfortable drawing-room and bar area, and a fine staircase leading to the individually-designed bedrooms (suites are also available at £185) with co-ordinating fabrics and polished natural wood furniture. All expected amenities are offered, from a tea tray to satellite TV, an additional desk telephone to a thoughtfully-equipped bathroom with a good shower over the bath. Each room also has its own 'Haley the Cat', a delightful life-size kitty which guests leave outside the door when they do not wish to be disturbed. Licensed for civil wedding ceremonies; banqueting facilities for 25. 24hr room service. No dogs. ***Rooms*** *22. Garden. Closed 25-30 Dec. Amex, Diners, MasterCard,* ***VISA***

Restaurant — £60

The dining-room's colour scheme is one of restful browns and creams, and the monthly-changing, modern menu (the price for the main course includes a first course) offers starters such as a terrine of mixed game and pistachio nuts, or a salad of Bayonne ham, mozzarella and sun-dried tomatoes, followed by a main course of roast widgeon with deep-fried celeriac and turnip and a sauce of Madeira and walnuts, or pastry-wrapped artichoke heart filled with a purée of mushrooms and served with a herb sauce. Finish with an iced Grand Marnier soufflé or warm bread-and-butter pudding. Mixed cheeeboard and a modest wine list that has a couple of recommendations to complement the dishes. Less choice at lunch. No smoking. ***Seats*** *45. Parties 12. Private Room 25. L 12.15-2 D 7.15-9.45. Closed (except to residents) L Mon & Sat, D Sun. Set Sun L £14.50.*

LEEDS — Salvo's

Tel 0113 275 5017 Map 6 C1 **JaB**
115 Otley Road Headingley Leeds LS6 3PX

This trattoria claims to bake the the best pizzas in the North, but their menu, based on the cooking of Southern Italy, offers much more than this! Antipasti include mushrooms in a creamy garlic sauce (£3.45), chargrilled vegetables with garlic salsa (£4.25) and popular *frittura mista* – deep-fried squid and king prawns, with spiced mayonnaise and lemon (£4.50); the menu continues with an interesting selection of pasta dishes including *penne arrabbiata con salame* – garlic, chili, salami and tomatoes (£5.35) and *tagliatelle al salmone* – smoked salmon, black pepper with a cream sauce (£5.75). *Salsicce arrostite* – roasted Italian sausages with olive oil mash and red onion gravy (£8.95) and *saltimbocca di melanzane* – chargrilled aubergine with a spicy rice and mozzarella filling, served with garlic confit, are other possibilities. Children's and braille menus. High-chairs and changing facilities provided. ***Seats*** *55.* ***Open*** *12-2 & 6-11 (Sat from 5.30).* ***Closed*** *Dec 31 & some Bank Holidays. Amex, MasterCard,* ***VISA***

Leicester — Man Ho — £45

Tel 0116 255 7700 **Fax 0116 254 5629** Map 7 D4

16 King Street Leicester Leicestershire LE1 6RJ

Comprising two houses in a low Georgian terrace behind New Walk Centre, Man Ho probably offers the best Chinese cooking in Leicester. Space, comfort and tasteful modern decor make a fine setting in which smartly-suited waitresses serve a mix of Peking, Cantonese and Szechuan cooking including sizzling dishes. Good choice à la carte or on various set menus. Sunday lunch (12-4) sees a dim sum buffet (£9 adult, £6 child under 10). Vegetarian set menu option. Private room with karaoke and disco entertainment for large parties. ***Seats*** *68. Parties 14. Private Room 90. L 12-2.30 (Sun till 3) D 6-11.30. Closed 25 & 26 Dec. Set L from £6.50 Set D from £12.50. Amex, Diners, MasterCard,* ***VISA***

A jug of fresh water!

Leicester — Welford Place — £55

Tel 0116 247 0758 **Fax 0116 247 1843** Map 7 D4

9 Welford Place Leicester Leicestershire LE1 6ZH

Follow signs for the Phoenix Arts Centre (whose car park is almost directly opposite) to find this striking Victorian building, a former Victorian gentlemen's club adjoining the Leicester magistrates' courts. Welford Place, built in 1876 and restored in 1991 still retains an aura of grandeur. Michael and Valerie Hope (who also run the *Wig & Mitre* in Lincoln) have created a spacious bar and restaurant, self-styled as a "Restaurant Pub of Rare Quality" (and they're not far off). The former is a striking semi-circular room with high windows overlooking Welford Place itself and furnished with leather armchairs and glass-topped tables, while the latter, a quietly civilised room has two great chandeliers suspended from its lofty ceiling. The menus operate throughout the day all year and any item is available at any time, but the restaurant is reserved for full meals. There is a set menu (£10.50) as well as the à la carte, both in a style of cooking that is modern while retaining traditional elements. Typical starters might include Mediterranean fish soup, creamed salt cod with grilled polenta, and baked cheese soufflé. Main dishes could be breast of duck with oranges, confit of salmon with marinated courgettes on a tomato coulis, baked guinea fowl wrapped in Parma ham and filo pastry, and fillet of sea bass with spinach and saffron butter sauce. Try the cappuccino mousse, the warm treacle tart or the interesting selection of cheeses, generally with a mix of British and French, for pudding. On-street parking during the evenings and on Sundays. *Open 11-11 (breakfast 8am-12), drinks with meals only on Sun (to 10.30).* ***Bar Food*** *all day (to 10.30 Sun), breakfast and snack menu served 8-12 & 3-6. Free House.* ***Beer*** *Ruddles Best & County. Amex, Diners, MasterCard,* ***VISA***

Lenham — Dog & Bear Hotel

Tel 01622 858219 **Fax 01622 859415** Map 11 C5

The Square Lenham Maidstone Kent ME17 2PG

This attractive coaching inn dates from 1602 and overlooks the pretty village square. Splendid oak beams combine with up-to-date decor and comfortable seating in the bar, and there is a welcoming little foyer-lounge. Centrally-heated bedrooms with darkwood furniture and bright contemporary fabrics all have direct-dial telephones, TVs, tea-making facilities and neatly-kept, en suite bathrooms. Main building rooms have more charm and character, with the rooms beyond the rear courtyard offering more space. 10 minutes from Leeds Castle. Invicta Country Inns (Shepherd Neame). *Open 11-11 (Sun 12-10.30).* ***Beer*** *Shepherd Neame. Garden, paved courtyard.* ***Accommodation*** *24 bedrooms, all en suite, £49.50 (family room sleeping four £65, four-poster £55, single £38.50). Children welcome overnight (first child free, second £15.50), additional bed & cot available. Amex, MasterCard,* ***VISA***

LEOMINSTER Royal Oak Hotel

Tel 01568 612610 **Fax 01568 612710** Map 14 A1 P
South Street Leominster Hereford & Worcester HR6 8JA

Modest accommodation in an early-18th-century coaching house on the corner of Etnam Street and South Street. Historic relics of its earlier glories are to be found in the Regency Room, complete with chandeliers and minstrel's gallery, and the brick-lined cellar bar which is a cosy spot in the evenings. The main Oak Bar boasts two enormous log fires and serves good real ales. Bedrooms come in a mixture of sizes and styles with one or two smallish singles, six spacious family rooms and a fine four-poster suite. All have carpeted bathrooms, while room comforts run through TV and intercom (for baby listening and wake-up calls) to tea and coffee makers and electric blankets. *Open 10-2.30, 6-10.30 (till 11 Fri & Sat), Sun 12-2.30, 7-10.30. Free House.* ***Beer*** *Wood's Special, Brains Bitter. Small patio. Family room.* ***Accommodation*** *18 bedrooms, all en suite, £45 (four-poster £55, single £31.50). Children welcome overnight (stay free in family rooms), additional bed & cot available. Dogs £2. Amex, Diners, MasterCard,* ***VISA***

LEWES Léonie's Restaurant

Tel 01273 487766 **Fax 01273 477714** Map 11 B6 JaB
197 High Street Lewes East Sussex

The day starts early at this smart brasserie/restaurant housed in one of Lewes's finer 17th-century High Street buildings. You can breakfast at one of the crisply-clothed tables in the pastel shades of the flower-filled dining-room: scrambled eggs with smoked salmon on toast (£5.25), croissants (95p), toast and marmalade (£1.15). At lunchtime there is a selection of sandwiches or perhaps quiche and salad (£3.75), warm garlic pitta bread with tsatsiki and houmus (£3.45) plus a few daily blackboard specials. Afternoon tea: 2 scones, jam and cream (£1.65) with a range of speciality teas. In the evening candles are lit, and a two-course (£11.95) or three-course (£14.95) set menu might offer glazed chicken livers with ginger carrots or Thai-style prawn salad to start. Main courses could include lemon and garlic chargrilled chicken or pork escalopes with spiced apples and mushroom sauce. To finish choose bittersweet chocolate tart with crème fraiche or strawberries with elderflower cordial. Piped jazz. Good-value wine list. Attentive staff make children most welcome, providing suitable cutlery and beakers and quickly retrieving the high-chair from the back of the room to make visiting toddlers comfortable. ***Seats*** *60.* ***Open*** *9-5 (Wed-Sat till 9.30).* ***Closed*** *Sun, Bank Holidays & Christmas. Amex, MasterCard,* ***VISA***

Pubs – note that food is only recommended in those pubs with ***Bar Food*** times in the statistics at the end of an entry. Restaurant food in pubs is *never* recommended unless specifically mentioned. Some pubs are recommended for B&B or Atmosphere only – each entry's statistics indicate our recommendation.

LINDAL-IN-FURNESS Chandlers Country Café

Tel 01229 468322 Map 4 C4 JaB
Lindal Business Park Lindal-in-Furness nr Ulverston Cumbria LA12 0LL

Signs off the A590 towards the candle factory will lead you to this friendly and welcoming café. At Chandlers, the menu runs the gamut from home-baked goodies (scones, teacakes 85p each), sandwiches (toasted BLT £2.85, Sloppy Joe – ham, Cheddar, lettuce and coleslaw £3.40) or baked potatoes (Blazing Saddles – with baked beans and bacon bits £2.70) to daily specials such as tarragon chicken (£4.25), spinach and feta pastry turnovers (£3.95) or smoked salmon mousse with salad and bread (£4.25). Children's menu. Two high-chairs are provided and a separate changing room. Plenty of room for buggies. Close to the wildlife park. ***Seats*** *90 (+12 outside).* ***Open*** *10-4.45 (Sun from 12).* ***Closed*** *25, 26 Dec & 1 Jan. Mastercard,* ***VISA***

LINTON Fountaine Inn

Tel 01756 752210 Map 6 C1 P
Linton Skipton North Yorkshire BD23 JHJ

An idyllic village green complete with stone bridge over a little stream is the setting for this charming mid-17th century inn. Several interconnecting rooms (one for non-smokers) feature old beams and built-in settles. A new chef has taken charge in the kitchen and is producing some interesting daily specials. Follow celery, apple and calvados soup or mousseline of salmon and oyster mushrooms with medallions of monkfish with a grain mustard sauce, Ayrshire pork with a cider and apple sauce, braised shank of lamb in red wine served with lentils and root vegetables, or wild mushroom stroganoff. A short printed menu highlights popular dishes like Whitby haddock, Cumberland grill and various open sandwich platters. For the sweet-toothed there are some good home-made puds, while for those with more savoury tastes there's the local Wensleydale cheese which comes either blue, smoked or in the traditional white style. The village green is well used in summer although the publican is not allowed to put out any tables or chairs. *Open 12-2.30, 7-10.30 (till 11 Sat). Closed Sun eve & all Mon in winter.* ***Bar Food*** *12-2, 7-9. Free House.* ***Beer*** *Black Sheep Best Bitter, Theakston Best & XB. No credit cards.*

LINWOOD High Corner Inn

Tel 01425 473973 **Fax 01425 480015** Map 14 C4 P
Linwood Ringwood Hampshire BH24 3QY

Much extended and modernised, early 18th-century inn set in seven acres of the New Forest and located along a quarter-mile gravel track off the narrow lane linking Lyndhurst and the A338 near Ringwood. A quiet hideaway in winter, mobbed in high summer, it is a popular retreat for families with numerous bar-free rooms, a Lego/Duplo room, an outdoor adventure playground and miles of Forest walks. Overnight accommodation comprises eight well-equipped bedrooms offering teletext TV, telephone, trouser press, hairdryer, tea-makers and en suite facilities. *Open 11-2.30, 7-10.30 winter, (11-3, 6-11 summer), Sat 11-4, 6-11 winter, (11-11 summer), Sun 12-4, 7-10.30 (12-10.30 summer).* ***Beer*** *Wadworth 6X, Hampshire King Alfred Bitter. Garden, outdoor play area. Family room (three rooms), indoor play room. Squash court, DIY stabling.* ***Accommodation*** *8 bedrooms, all en suite, £69 (single £47), Children welcome overnight (under-3s free), additional bed (£4) & cot available. Check-in by arrangement. Amex, Diners, MasterCard,* ***VISA***

LITTLE CANFIELD Lion & Lamb

Tel 01279 870257 Map 10 B3 P
Little Canfield Great Dunmow Essex CM6 1SR

On the A120 Colchester to Puckeridge road, three miles from Junction 8 of the M11 (3 miles west of Great Dunmow), this large family-dining pub is 200 years old in parts with more modern extensions. Open brickwork, exposed pine and artefacts inside while the fenced garden is ideal for children (bouncy castle on long weekends and an old boat has been turned into a play area). Children may eat in the restaurant and choose from their own menu. *Open 11-2.30, 6-11 (Sun 12-3, 7-10.30).* ***Beer*** *Ridleys. Garden, children's play area, disabled WC. MasterCard,* ***VISA***

LITTLE COWARNE Three Horseshoes

Tel 01885 400276 Map 14 B1 P
Little Cowarne Bromyard Hereford & Worcester HR7 4RQ

Though not immediately obvious, one can still make out the remains of a tiny two-roomed pub that once stood on this site: the newest brick is an uneven match with the old and dormers have been added to the frontage. The Shoes' interior is now a spacious dining pub, with considerable thought given equally to the needs of children and the elderly or disabled. The success of Norman and Janet Whittall in attracting both in equal measure is to be commended. Kitchen production is also prodigious from light bar snacks of red pepper and tomato soup and cider soused herrings through to a carvery Sunday lunch. Seasonally-changing main courses offer near endless variety, pheasant in Arabian spices, fresh haddock in crab sauce, fillet of pork with spiced plum sauce, and hot spicy chicken with rice. The sauté potatoes are particularly good and a local baker makes crusty bloomers and granary loaves for the sandwiches and ploughman's platters (perhaps served with home-made pickled pears, spiced damsons or apple and ginger chutney). Home-made desserts may feature damson soufflé, toffee and banana cheesecake and gooseberry crumble, and the home-made ice creams are outstanding: rhubarb and elderflower or loganberry, and one made with damsons – fresh from trees in the paddock, naturally. A pair of quiet country bedrooms (one double, one a twin) are done in an appropriate country style with a lovely rural aspect. Free from intrusive telephones, they're otherwise bang up-to-date with colour TVs, clock radios, tea-making facilities and small but effective WC/shower rooms. *Open 11-3, 6.30-11 (Sun 12-3, 7-10.30). Possibly open all day during summer.* ***Bar Food*** *12-2.30 (till 2 Sun), 6.30-10 (Sun 7-9.30).* ***Beer*** *Webster's Yorkshire, John Smith's, Ruddles County. Garden/patio, outdoor eating, barbecue.* ***Accommodation*** *2 bedrooms, both en suite, £35 (single £17.50). Children welcome overnight (under-5s stay free in parents' room, 5-11s half-price), additional bed available. Check-in by arrangement. Closed 25 Dec. MasterCard,* ***VISA***

LITTLEBURY Queen's Head

Tel 01799 522251 **Fax 01799 513522** Map 10 B3 
Littlebury Saffron Walden Essex CB11 4TD

Occupying a corner site in the village centre, this attractive yellow-painted inn dates from the early 15th-century and welcomes visitors into its carefully refurbished bar and dining-room, which preserve low beamed ceilings, some standing timbers, a rustic red-and-black tiled floor and two cosy snug areas. Reliable home-cooked food is a popular attraction here, the short daily-changing blackboard menu featuring an imaginative choice of dishes that draw on fresh herbs, vegetables and fruit grown in their extensive kitchen garden, as well as vegetables and fish hand-chosen from London markets by the landlord. A typical menu may list crab, apple and bacon broth, warm samphire with tarragon butter, and grilled sardines with fresh rosemary among the starters, followed by fresh seafood specialities – chargrilled cod fillet with warm vierge dressing, whole baked crab with ginger, pan-fried halibut with basil and cream – plus chargrilled pork with fresh apricots, gammon topped with cheese and onion and interesting vegetarian dishes like chargrilled peppers with tomato, basil and garlic coulis. Extra evening dishes generally include game options like roast pheasant brigerade. Puddings range from gooseberry pie and fresh summer fruits to chocolate ginger cake. Accommodation comprises six uniformly decorated and furnished bedrooms (including two family rooms) with clean, tiled en suite bathrooms. All – except the quiet rear room – face the main road and with no secondary glazing they could well be noisy. TVs, telephones, clock/radios and tea-makers are standard. Continental breakfasts only (the price below, along with all the B&B prices in this guide, includes cooked breakfast – £6). Sheltered walled garden with play equipment geared for younger children, also indoor games and colouring books for inclement days. *Open 12-11 (Sun 12-10.30).* ***Bar Food*** *12-2, 7-9 (no food Sun eve). Free House.* ***Beer*** *Benskins Best, Tetley, Timothy Taylor's Landlord, Bass, four guest beers. Garden, outdoor eating, children's play area.* ***Accommodation*** *6 bedrooms, all en suite, £55.95 (single £35.95). Children welcome overnight, additional bed & cot (both £5) available. No dogs. Closed 25 & 26 Dec. Diners, MasterCard,* ***VISA***

LIVERPOOL La Bouffe £50

Tel 0151-236 3375 Map 6 A2 
48a Castle Street Liverpool L2 7LQ

Informal basement restaurant, mainly self-service at lunchtime. The evening à la carte offers crispy duck and vegetable spring rolls with a mango and lime salsa, grilled fresh sardines with a Provençal sauce and a trio of Middle Eastern hors d'oeuvre among the starters. Main courses could be fillet of cod on fresh spinach with a mussel and cider sauce, noisettes of English lamb on a split-pea purée or sautéed calf's liver with smoked bacon and caramelised onions. Finish with home-made desserts or mixed cheeses. ***Seats*** *60. Parties 16. Private Room 20. L 12-3, D 6-10.30. Closed L Sat, D Mon-Wed, all Sun, Bank Holidays & 24-26 Dec. Amex, MasterCard,* ***VISA***

LIVERPOOL Casa Italia

Tel 0151-227 5774 Fax 0151 236 9985 Map 6 A2 JaB
40 Stanley Street Liverpool L1 6AL

Cheap and cheerful decor – painted brick walls and colourful check plastic cloths over rustic tables – and a noisy, bustling atmosphere at this unbookable 'pizzeria pasta' restaurant in the city centre. All the reliably cooked pizzas and pasta dishes are priced in the £4.50-£5.50 range. Afterwards, go for the good espresso coffee. Slick, speedy service. ***Seats*** *120.* ***Open*** *12-10 (Fri & Sat till 11).* ***Closed*** *Sun. Amex, Diners, MasterCard,* ***VISA***

LIVERPOOL Est Est Est

Tel 0151-708 6969 Map 6 A2 JaB
Unit 6 Edward Pavilion Albert Dock Liverpool L3 4AA

Archetypal friendly trattoria, part of a small chain with four other branches in the North-West. Plenty of high-chairs, and baby-changing facilities available. Crayons, balloons and children's portions. See Knutsford for more details. ***Seats*** *95.* ***Open*** *12-2.30 & 6-10.30 (Fri till 11, Sat 12-4 & 6-11, Sun 12-10.30).* ***Closed*** *25 & 26 Dec. Amex, MasterCard,* ***VISA***

LIVERPOOL Everyman Bistro

Tel 0151-708 9545 Map 6 A2 JaB
5-9 Hope Street Liverpool

Underneath the famous Everyman Theatre, the bistro is one of the most popular in the city. Painted brick walls are covered with old advertisements and the menu, which changes twice daily, is displayed on blackboards. Typical choices run from houmus or paté with bread (£1.75) and tomato and fennel soup (£1.15) to spicy lamb and pasta (£4.35), Italian meatballs with pasta, tomato sauce and rice (£4.20) and chicken breast in a mango and ginger sauce with yellow rice (£4.35). Good selection of vegetarian dishes, and a few simple pizzas. Finish perhaps with mango japonaise, triple chocolate cheesecake or plum soufflé (all £1.80), plus a few excellent traditional cheeses. Dishes of the day usually finish by 9pm so theatre-goers are advised to eat before the play. The café/bar is open from 10 to 2 for coffee and snacks, and home-baked cakes and sweets are always available. Popular with families; large tables, with lots of space in between, and a relaxed environment 'allow both adults and youngsters to be at ease'. Three high-chairs and baby-changing unit in Ladies. No-smoking room. ***Seats*** *200.* ***Open*** *10am-midnight.* ***Closed*** *Sun & Bank Holidays. No credit cards.*

LIVERPOOL Tate Gallery Coffee Shop

Tel 0151-709 0122 Fax 0151-709 3122 Map 6 A2 JaB
Albert Dock Liverpool L3 4BB

Look over the foyer to find this self-service coffee shop, which has a marvellous view of Albert Dock, and specialises in delicious sandwiches. Care is taken choosing breads; some bought from the *Village Bakery* (see Melmerby entry) is used for Italian tomato bread with cottage cheese, carrots, walnuts and watercress; French country bread with goat's cheese, green salad, tomato and Russian rye with pastrami, cucumber, radicchio and dill mayonnaise (all £2.25). Sandwiches (from £1.90); quiches (from £2.50) come with a green salad. Cakes, maybe espresso coffee (£1.10) or chocolate almond (£1.20), are all home-made. Häagen-Dazs ice cream. No smoking. ***Seats*** *78.* ***Open*** *10-5.30.* ***Closed*** *Mon (except Bank Holidays), 24-26 Dec, 1 Jan & Good Friday. No credit cards.*

LODE — Anglesey Abbey Restaurant

Tel 01223 811175 Map 10 B3 JaB
Anglesey Abbey Lode nr Cambridge Cambridgeshire CB5 9EJ

Access to the restaurant and National Trust shop is not restricted to those who have come to visit the famous gardens. So walkers are welcome for elevenses (cakes and scones from 75p) or light lunches such as soup and bread (£1.90), jacket potatoes with cheese, ham or tuna (£3.75) or a selection of salads (ham, smoked mackerel, quiche – all £4.95). On Sundays there is a traditional roast lunch (£5.75). Anglesey cream tea (£2.95) is served with scones and Isle of Ely honey. Children are well looked after, and as well as dishes tailored to their needs, there are high-chairs, special crockery, colouring books and pencils. Four high-chairs and changing facilities in the disabled toilet. The children's menu includes pizza faces, jacket potatoes and Marmite soldiers; small portions from the main menu are offered along with a limited selection of baby food. 'If there is anything else we can do to make your children's visit more enjoyable please ask for assistance'. There is also an enclosed garden with a play area for youngsters. No smoking. ***Seats*** *180 (+ 50 outside).* ***Open*** *11-5.30 (till 4 in winter).* ***Closed*** *Mon & Tue mid Sep-mid Jul, Wed mid Oct-Mar, Thu & Fri mid Jan-end Feb, Good Friday & 2 weeks after Christmas. Amex, MasterCard,* ***VISA***

LONG MELFORD — The Countrymen — 65% — £80

Tel 01787 312356 **Fax 01787 374557** Map 10 C3 H
The Green Long Melford Sudbury Suffolk CO10 9DN

Count the Toby jugs and admire the maps and copper collection or relax in deep sofas in the charming lounge of Stephen and Janet Errington's delightful inn. There's also a library, and games for both adults and children. Bedrooms are bright and comfortable, attractive fabrics complementing neutral walls and carpets. Each room has antique pine furniture, an easy chair or sofa and views of the village green. Several rooms (even those with four-posters) also have a sofa-bed, and one double room has an adjoining children's room with bunk beds. The top-of-the-range Green Room Suite (£95) boasts an antique mahogany half-tester bed, private sitting-room, large desk and dining-suite. Informal new wine bar/bistro (closed L Mon & D Sun). Previously known as the Black Lion. ***Rooms*** *9. Garden. Closed 23 Dec-2 Jan. Amex, MasterCard,* ***VISA***

LONGHORSLEY — Linden Hall — 75% — £125

Tel 01670 516611 **Fax 01670 788544** Map 5 D2 H
Longhorsley nr Morpeth Northumberland NE65 8XF

An imposing listed Georgian house stands at the centre of a much-extended hotel surrounded by 450 acres of mature park and woodland. For the individual guest there are choices of the imposing Inner Hall, drawing-room and two bars (one of them the Linden Pub in the grounds) in which to relax, generally uninterrupted by users of the Health Spa and Conference Centre (capacity 300). Sporting facilities are first-class, for both individuals and business groups. The Garden Rooms are set in enclosed courtyards closest to the indoor pool and afford a high degree of seclusion. State-of-the-art satellite TVs, complimentary fruit, decanted sherry and all-enveloping bathrobes are all provided (along with 24hr room service). Children up to 14 share parents' room free. A new 18-hole golf course is due to be playable by the spring of 1997. Afternoon tea is a very civilised affair here. In winter sit in front of the fire in the inner hall or drawing room; in summer the sun-soaked conservatory is the place to be or out on the patio/terrace edging the lawn with views out over Linden's mature parkland towards the Cheviots. Cream tea (£2.95) or the full works with sandwiches and cakes (£7.95). ***Rooms*** *50. Garden, tennis, croquet, pitch & putt, indoor swimming pool, mini-gym, steam room, spa bath, solarium, beauty & hair salon, snooker, mountain bikes, clay-pigeon shooting, all-weather cricket pitch. Amex, Diners, MasterCard,* ***VISA***

LORTON The Barn

Tel & Fax 01900 85404 Map 4 C3 JaB
New House Farm Lorton Cockermouth Cumbria CA13 9UU

Right by the B5289 in the Vale of Lorton (eight miles west of Keswick and six south of Cockermouth) John and Hazel Hatch's converted cattle byre is a rare find. Meticulously restored, the old cow stalls set with pine tables and benches are a unique setting for culinary rumination. Quality home baking heads the list of treats; Lakeland fruit cake (£1.45) and Loweswater gingerbread (£1.25) accompany a wide range of teas and coffees served all day; home-made quiches (£3.95) and steak and kidney pie for lunch (£5.25); set teas (Victorian with fruit cake, chocolate cake, shortbread and cucumber sandwiches; Edwardian with meringue and chocolate biscuit along with the sandwiches; Cumberland with scones, apple plate cake and Buttermere biscuits – all £5.25) and various cakes and biscuits (from 95p) to whet an afternoon appetite. Children's portions available. Two high-chairs and a mat and wipes in the Ladies for baby-changing; a bucket of toys are kept inside and outside there's a safe area in the former midden in which to romp. More elaborate evening meals (Tue-Sat, Easter-mid Sep) from 6pm by prior booking only and stylish overnight accommodation in the main farm house. No smoking. ***Seats*** *30.* ***Open*** *12-5.* ***Closed*** *Mon (except Jul & Aug) & 1st week Sep-mid Mar. No credit cards.*

LOSTWITHIEL Royal Oak

Tel 01208 872552 Map 12 C3 P
Duke Street Lostwithiel Cornwall PL22 1AH

Popular, 13th-century inn just off the main road in the original capital of Cornwall and supposedly linked to nearby Restormel Castle by a smuggling or escape tunnel. Catering for all tastes, the lively, slate flagstoned public bar (complete with juke box, modern and traditional games) attracts a good local following. In contrast, the comfortably furnished and carpeted lounge bar has tables with red and white checked cloths and is very much geared to a dining clientele. Close inspection of a fairly standard printed menu and of the additional blackboard selection of meals will reveal some good home-cooked dishes, such as fish pie, Mrs Hine's 'famous' cow pie, sautéed chicken in red wine and an authentic curry choice. Chips may arrive with the lasagne, but most main courses have the option of a full salad or a selection of four well-cooked vegetables. Plainer pub fare (no sandwiches or ploughman's platters in the evening) – Angus beef steaks, grilled trout and salads – is unlikely to disappoint in either quality or presentation. For dessert try the home-made apple pie topped with fresh clotted cream. Those wishing to explore the area will find one of the upstairs bedrooms a most comfortable base. Spacious, well-decorated and furnished with a mix of period and pine furniture, they all have TV, radio/alarms, and beverage-making facilities, with two of the rooms boasting clean, en suite bathrooms. Children welcome. *Open 11-11 (Sun 12-10.30).* ***Bar Food*** *12-2, 6.30-9.30. Free House.* ***Beer*** *St Austell Trelawney Pride, Bass, Fuller's London Pride, Marston's Pedigree, Sharp's Own, two guest beers. Terrace, outdoor eating. Family room.* ***Accommodation*** *6 bedrooms, 4 en suite, £48.74-£53.75 (single from £27.50). Children welcome overnight (under-4s free, 5-12s half-price). Closed 25 Dec. Amex, Diners, MasterCard,* ***VISA***

LOUTH Masons Arms

Tel 01507 609525 Map 7 F2 P
Cornmarket Louth Lincolnshire LN11 9PY

Useful to know in an area not highly blessed with accommodation pubs is the Masons, a former posting inn dating from the 18th century. Right in the centre of the Cornmarket, this welcoming and friendly inn is run by resident proprietors Mike and Margaret Harrison, who offer five bedrooms complete with well-equipped, en suite facilities. Five further bedrooms share two bathrooms (one a restored Victorian bathroom) and an extra WC. Bars are open all day, with fastidiously-tended real ales on handpump and six wines available by the glass. Children welcome indoors; baby-changing facilities in Ladies. *Open 11-11 (Sun and Bank Holidays 12-3, 7-10.30), Free House.* ***Beer*** *Bateman's Dark Mild, XB, XXXB & Salem Porter, Marston's Pedigree, Bass, guest beer.* ***Accommodation*** *10 bedrooms, 5 en suite (3 with bath), £49.50 (single £20). Children welcome overnight, additional bed & cot (both £5) available. No dogs. Accommodation closed 24-26 Dec; pub closed 25 Dec eve. MasterCard,* ***VISA***

LOUTH — Mr Chips

Tel 01507 603756 Map 7 F2 JaB

Ashwell Street Louth Lincolnshire ON11 9BA

A fish and chip shop has been on this site just off the Market Square since 1906 (although the building has been completely renovated), and it has been in the Hagan family ever since; look out for the Union Jacks flying the flag of British fish. The specialities of cod and haddock with crunchy chips will cost you £3.30, and are worth every penny to the dedicated fish-and-chip-lover. For vegetarians there's a meal of cauliflower, courgettes, onion rings, mushrooms and chips (£4.35). Families are especially welcomed, with a children's menu, baby-changing facilities, eight high-chairs and two booster seats all provided. The children's menu (£1.95) offers fish, sausage or fishcake and chips with peas or beans, with desserts and drinks priced individually. Children's parties catered for. Also access and facilities for disabled visitors. Kidgate car park is 2 mins walk away. ***Seats*** *300.* ***Open*** *9am-10pm (Fri & Sat till 11).* ***Closed*** *Sun, 25, 26 Dec & 1 Jan. No credit cards.*

LOW CATTON — Gold Cup Inn

Tel 01759 371354 Map 7 D1 

Low Catton East Riding of Yorkshire YO4 1EA

Five miles east of York, south of Stamford Bridge on the A166; can also be approached from east of Kexby, off A1078. Modernised but pleasant, relaxing and unpretentious pub run by Ray and Pat Hales; there are two welcoming bars, real fires and high-backed wooden pews in the rambling three-room lounge in contrast to a noisier back games room. The beer garden/paddock at the rear of the building features ponies, goats and geese to delight children and has access to the river bank. Children welcome. *Open 12-2.30, 6-11 (Sat 12-11, Sun 12-10.30). Closed Mon lunch (except Bank Holidays). Free House.* ***Beer*** *Tetley, John Smith's. Garden, children's play area. No credit cards.*

LOW NEWTON BY THE SEA — The Ship

Tel 01665 576262 Map 5 D1 

Low Newton by the Sea Alnwick Northumberland NE66 3EL

The 'village green' is just a grassy area enclosed on three sides by fishermen's cottages, one of which is the pub, and on the fourth side by the beach itself. As with so many coastal villages, public parking is restricted to an area just away from the beach, leaving you a short walk to the sand, green or pub indeed popular with holidaymakers and locals alike. The Ship is quite charming, largely as a result of the Hoppers, who run it in a very friendly fashion. Outside, there are picnic tables on the grass, while inside it has the air of somewhere from the early part of the century – creels hang over the bar to remind you of the seaside location. *Open Easter-end Oct 11-11 (Sun 12-10.30), Nov-Easter 11-3, 7-11 (Sat 11-11, Sun 12-10.30). Free House.* ***Beer*** *Ruddles Bitter, guest beer. Garden. No credit cards.*

LOWER SWELL — Old Farmhouse — £66

Tel 01451 830232 **Fax 01451 870962** Map 14 C1

Lower Swell Stow-on-the-Wold Gloucestershire GL54 1LF

Peaceful, quiet, relaxed, informal and totally unpretentious', with everything under the personal supervision of Dutch owner Erik Burger since 1989. The premises were a working farm until the 1960s, and the original 16th-century farmhouse contains the bar-lounge and restaurant. Above are neat country-style bedrooms, two of which share a bathroom. Further bedrooms are in the Old Stable House opening on to the car park; best rooms are in the Old Coach House, where there's also a quiet residents' lounge with TV, magazines and board games. Pictures and prints for sale are displayed throughout the public rooms. Mountain bikes and helmets are available for hire (with a very helpful beginner's guide and suggested routes) and air-pistol target shooting can be arranged in a corner of the garden; family games are also available for wet days. Bar snacks are available at all times except Sun L and Sat D; separate children's menu and high tea by arrangement from 6pm. Both a ground-floor family room with bunk beds and two rooms with four-poster beds attract a £10 supplement; slightly higher tariff at weekends. Cots and folding beds supplied. Lower Swell is a little Central Cotswolds village one mile west of Stow on the B4068. ***Rooms*** *14. Garden. Closed 2 weeks Jan. MasterCard,* ***VISA***

LOWSONFORD Fleur De Lys

Tel & Fax 01564 782431 Map 14 C1 **P**
Lowsonford Henley-in-Arden Warwickshire B95 5HJ

A long, low Whitbread pub dating from the 17th century, with crooked chimneys and wrinkly roof whose canalside position and outdoor tuck shop deservedly attract a family clientele. A score or more picnic tables spread out along the bank, from where parents can watch the longboats while the under-12s master the climbing frames. Galleried family dining room and atmospheric bars with low-beamed ceilings, oak furniture and stone floors. *Open 11-11 (Sun 12-10.30).* ***Beer*** *Flowers Original, Wadworth 6X, Morland Old Speckled Hen. Garden, children's play area. Family room. MasterCard,* ***VISA***

LUCCOMBE CHINE Dunnose Cottage

Tel 01983 862585 Map 15 D4 **JaB**
Luccombe Chine nr Shanklin Isle of Wight PO37 6RW

Follow the sign down a narrow lane off the Shanklin to Ventnor road to find this cottage tea room (they also do B&B) surrounded by landscaped gardens and National Trust property. Visitors can enjoy home-made snacks throughout the day: freshly made sandwiches from £1.90, scones and cakes (coffee and walnut £1.25, chocolate fudge £1.75), various ploughman's, salads and filled jacket potatoes (from £3.25). Knickerbocker Glory, chocolate nut sundae and banana split (all £2.75) are house specialities. Lunch brings chicken and mushroom pie (£4.95), lasagne, home-cooked ham, burgers (from £2.25), and a daily vegetarian special (£4.95), all with either jacket potato or chips. Children's portions of some dishes are available on request, and children eat at a reduced price for the Sunday roast. One high-chair is provided. It's a beautiful setting and parents are asked to ensure that their children respect the 3½ acres of lovely gardens with roses, herbaceous borders. ***Seats*** *45 (+ 50 outside).* ***Open*** *10.30-5.* ***Closed*** *25 & 26 Dec. No credit cards.*

LURGASHALL Noah's Ark

Tel 01428 707346 Map 11 A6 **P**
Lurgashall Petworth West Sussex GU28 9ET

450-year-old pub in a classic village green setting by the church and overlooking the cricket pitch; longer Sunday opening hours could at last assuage the afternoon thirsts of the cricketers and allow them to celebrate successes or drown their sorrows. Perhaps best in summer when the tile-hung frontage is bedecked with flowers in hanging baskets and tables are set outside on the front grassed area; cosy in winter. *Open 11.30-2.30 (till 3 summer), 6-11 (Sun 12-3, 7-10.30).* ***Beer*** *Greene King IPA, Abbot Ale & Rayments Special Bitter. Family room. Garden. MasterCard,* ***VISA***

LYDFORD Castle Inn

Tel 01822 820242 **Fax 01822 820454** Map 12 C3 **P**
Lydford Okehampton Devon EX20 4BH

Just a stone's throw from open moors, the pink-washed, wisteria-entangled Castle is certainly a pretty little pub, but it's not until you go inside that you realise how old it is. Much is 12th-century, with various later additions, and it just oozes atmosphere, with its slate floor and low sagging ceilings turned a deep amber colour by time and smoke. The place is literally crammed with bits and pieces collected by landlords over the years, including several marvellous old high-backed settles (some with little roofs), dozens of decorative plates and a fine collection of Hogarth prints (not a fruit machine or juke box in sight). Seven of only 31 remaining Lydford pennies minted by Ethelred the Unready in the 10th century are on display, the rest being held by the British Museum. The Castle's reputation for good food and a friendly welcome is safe in the hands of owners Mo and Clive Walker. Mo controls proceedings in the kitchen, producing an eclectic range of dishes listed on a daily-changing blackboard in the bar. Favourites are the Oriental-style dishes – chicken and coconut soup, Thai green curry of duck with basmati rice – and well-cooked traditional dishes like salmon and cod plait with champagne and lemon thyme sauce, Provençal chicken, steak and kidney pie and roasted red pepper roulade, all served with fresh vegetables.

At lunchtime (when there are no sandwiches, but there is a very good Devon cheese platter), this menu applies throughout the inn, but at night it's limited to the smaller bar and snug, when the main bar becomes a restaurant (bookings taken) offering a fixed-price three-course menu (with supplements). Look out for the special Asian curry nights during the winter. Bookings are also taken for dining on the covered patio outside, where five tables are a lovely spot for summer alfresco eating. Six of the modestly comfortable bedrooms are en suite while the other two share a perfectly acceptable bathroom; antique furniture features in all rooms, the Castle Room sporting a four-poster bed. By January 1997 a new extension will house two further en suite bedrooms and a residents' lounge (open Easter). Just a short walk away is the picturesque Lydford Gorge (NT) and its woodland walks. *Open 11.30-3, 6-11 (Sun 12-3, 7-10.30).* ***Bar Food*** *12-2.30, 6.30-9.30 (Sun 7-9). Free House.* ***Beer*** *Blackawton Bitter, Wadworth 6X, Fuller's London Pride, two guest beers. Garden, patio, outdoor eating. Family room.* ***Accommodation*** *8 bedrooms, 6 en suite, £44-£55 (four-poster £59, family room £71, single £28.75-£38.75). Children welcome overnight (under-5s stay free in parents' room, 6-11s £6), additional bed (from £5) & cot (£5) available. Pub & accommodation closed 25 Dec. Amex, Diners, MasterCard,* ***VISA***

LYMPSHAM Batch Country House Hotel 56% £58

Tel 01934 750371 **Fax 01934 750501** Map 13 E1 H
Lympsham nr Weston-super-Mare Somerset BS24 0EX

The setting is 50 acres of open farmland through which flows the River Axe. Traces of the former farmhouse are evident in the beams which adorn the bar and residents' lounges. The neat, practical en suite bedrooms enjoy views of either the Mendip or Quantock hills. The adjoining Somerset Suite is a popular venue for functions up to 70. Lympsham is about 3 miles from J22 of the M5. The hotel is personally run by owners Mr and Mrs Brown. Family-friendly. No dogs. Previously known as Batch Farm Country Hotel. ***Rooms*** *8. Garden, croquet, children's playground, fishing. Closed 1 week Christmas. Amex, Diners, MasterCard,* ***VISA***

We welcome bona fide complaints and recommendations on the tear-out pages at the back of the Guide for Readers' Comments. They are followed up by our professional team.

LYNDHURST Lyndhurst Park 63% £85

Tel 01703 283923 **Fax 01703 283019** Map 14 C4 H
High Street Lyndhurst Hampshire SO43 7NL

On the edge of town – where it meets the New Forest – the Georgian origins of this much-extended hotel (it boasts the largest conference/function facilities in the area – up to 500 theatre-style, although there is parking for only 85 cars) are largely lost except in the cocktail bar and chandeliered reception hall, both decorated in warm red tones. Apart from a small lounge the main public room is a characterfully rustic bar (Inn at the Park). Bedrooms are notably well kept and appealing, often with brass bedheads and always with well-lit dressing/work table. Good, fully-tiled and carpeted bathrooms. 24hr room service. Children free in parents' room to age of 14. Dinner dances on Bank Holiday weekends. Five acres of grounds include a swing for little ones; the games room has table tennis, darts and a full-size snooker table. Minimum booking of two nights at weekends. Forestdale Hotels. ***Rooms*** *59. Garden, tennis, outdoor swimming pool, sauna, games room, snooker. Amex, Diners, MasterCard,* ***VISA***

We endeavour to be as up-to-date as possible, but inevitably some changes to data and key personnel may occur at restaurants and hotels after the Guide goes to press. Prices should also be taken as indications rather than firm quotes.

LYNTON Lee Cottage

Tel 01598 752621 **Fax 01598 752619** Map 13 D1 **JaB**
Lee Abbey Lynton EX35 6JJ Devon

This enchanting cottage tea room is run by ladies from the Abbey Christian Community; to find it follow the Lee Abbey road from Lynton towards Woody Bar; although the road appears to stop at the Abbey, keep going. The setting of colourful terraced gardens, a bubbling stream and the views of the spectacular North Devon coastline are delightful, making the cottage a marvellous place to pause awhile. There is a book in which prayer requests can be left and the staff offer daily prayers before opening. Between mid-May and the end of September large numbers of visitors come to the Cottage to sit on the grass or at benches (there are only about a dozen seats indoors) and enjoy home-made rolls, filled to order with egg or tuna mayonnaise, cheese or ham (£1.50), scones and cakes (truffle log, fruit cake with almond centre, gingerbread men and ladies (60p-£1.20), cream teas (£2.60) and ploughman's (cheese, pickle and peppers from the garden £1.50). Everything except the doughnuts is home-made – even some of the herb teas are made from plants in the garden. Half portions for children (cakes included). Unlicensed. No smoking. ***Seats*** *12 (20 more on verandah + 60 outside).* ***Open*** *11-5.* ***Closed*** *Sun & mid Sep-mid May. No credit cards.*

LYTHAM ST ANNES Dalmeny Hotel 60% £85

Tel 01253 712236 **Fax 01253 724447** Map 6 A1 **HR**
19 South Promenade St Annes Lytham St Annes Lancashire FY8 1LX

A seaside hotel of wide appeal, in the ownership of the Webb family since 1945. There are several restaurants, ample roomy lounges and bars, leisure facilities, family recreational activities and accommodation that runs from singles to apartments with kitchens. Families are extremely well catered for; family rooms with kitchen facilities, cots, child-monitoring, high-chairs, high teas and entertainment at weekends and peak holiday times. There's a supervised playroom for under-5s, organised children's sports (perhaps swimming gala or volleyball), games, competitions and early evening fun shows. Ask the hotel for full details of seasonal activities and special family accommodation offers. Friendly, helpful staff add to the pleasure. ***Rooms*** *109. Garden, indoor swimming pool, gym, squash, sauna, solarium, beauty salon, playroom, games room, coffee shop (8am-10.30pm). Closed 24-26 Dec. Amex, MasterCard,* ***VISA***

C'est La Vie £60

The main restaurant is in a vaulted basement and serves an à la carte selection that ranges from fresh oysters and goujons of Dover sole to chargrilled Aberdeen Angus fillet of beef, confit of duck, a medley of seafood and traditional bread-and-butter pudding. Sunday lunch sees a traditional roast and sweets from a trolley. In addition to C'est La Vie there's a popular carvery and a snacky menu in The Patio coffee shop. ***Seats*** *40. Parties 10. L Sun only 12-6. D 6.30-10. Closed D Sun, all Mon & Tue, 3 days Christmas.*

MAIDENHEAD Holiday Inn 66% £143

Tel 01628 23444 **Fax 01628 770035** Map 15 E2 **H**
Manor Lane Maidenhead Berkshire SL6 2RA

Set in 18 acres of grounds close to J8/9 of the M4 and J4 of the M40, the hotel is usefully situated for visitors to the Thames Valley area. Top-notch, large conference and banqueting facilities (for up to 400) include the characterful, reconstructed Elizabethan Shoppenhangers Manor house in the grounds. Straightforward accommodation, but good leisure facilities, including a children's pool. Playroom provided for children at weekends (when the tariff is reduced to just £72 – exceptional value, particularly with Legoland nearby). ***Rooms*** *189. Garden, indoor swimming pool, splash pool, spa bath, sauna, sun beds, squash, gym, snooker, coffee shop (7am-11pm). Amex, Diners, MasterCard,* ***VISA***

MALDON Wheelers

Tel 01621 853647 Map 11 C4 JaB
13 High Street Maldon Essex CM9 7PB

Long established family-run fish and chip restaurant and take-away in Maldon's High Street. In tea-shop surroundings they serve plaice, cod (£3.95), haddock and rock eel, plus skate and sole when available. Some of the sweets are home-made, including apple pie. Large car park 100 yards away. ***Seats*** *52.* ***Open*** *11.30-1.45 & 6-9.30.* ***Closed*** *Sun & Mon. No credit cards.*

MALMESBURY Old Bell Hotel 69% £85

Tel 01666 822344 **Fax 01666 825145** Map 14 B2 HR
Abbey Row Malmesbury Wiltshire SN16 OAG

Beginning life in 1220 as guest house to the adjacent Abbey, this picturesque hotel with its wisteria-clad frontage has been added to over the years with a substantial proportion of the present building dating from Edwardian times. As charming within as it is pretty without, the various day rooms each have their own character – comfortable bar, Great Hall informal eaterie (rather misnamed as it is a smallish room with polished oak floor, beamed ceiling and 13th-century stone fireplace), two lounges – with the unifying theme of antique furniture (including some fine turn-of-the-century light fittings), real fires in winter and a welcoming, informal atmosphere created by friendly young staff. Bedrooms in the main house, about half the total, vary in size and shape, and include five family suites, but follow the same style with traditional furnishings. By complete contrast, smaller, more uniform rooms in a connected block to the rear have been given a decor that is strongly Japanese in inspiration. Excellent cooked breakfasts get the day off to a good start. The Old Bell is sister hotel to *Woolley Grange* at Bradford-on-Avon (see entry), so it's no surprise that children are more than welcome here with special children's meals (lunch at 12, tea at 6pm) plus, even more impressively, a fully-equipped creche, The Den, that is free to guests and operates daily from 10am (Christmas Day from 2pm) to 6pm. Parking for 30 cars. ***Rooms*** *31. Garden, playground, creche. Amex, Diners, MasterCard,* ***VISA***

Restaurant £65

A well-proportioned, Edwardian dining-room with crisp white linen, quality table settings (including candelabra at night), some fine period light fittings and good cooking from Darren Barclay, whose dishes show creativity without being gimmicky. Even one of the more esoteric dishes like langoustine ravioli on a bed of wok-roasted vegetables flavoured with tamarind, ginger and basil turned out to be most successful. Other starters could include twice-baked cheese soufflé with herbs, chicken and vegetable terrine with tomatoes and olives, and cock-a-leekie soup with scallops. Mains ranged from pot-roasted rabbit with green vegetables and a grain mustard and olive sauce to pan-fried red mullet with olive tapénade and a tian of aubergines and tomatoes. There is usually also a roast from the trolley. Among the puds look out for a hot banana soufflé with toffee sauce and caramelised rice pudding with winter fruits. The globe-trotting wine list is arranged by grape variety with useful notes on the character of each. Most bottles are comfortably below the £10 mark. ***Seats*** *60. Private Room 24. L 12.30-2 D 7.30-9.30. Set L £15 Set D £18.50 & £24.*

MANCHESTER Cocotoo

Tel 0161-237 5458 **Fax 0161-237 9188** Map 6 B2 JaB
57 Whitworth Street West Manchester M1 5WW

Cavernous Italian restaurant, built in a converted railway arch, near the Palace and Green Room Theatres. Traditional starters: perhaps salami (£4.35), avocado vinaigrette (£3.75) or oven-baked sardines (£2.25), could be followed by pizza (from £5.45), chicken with mushrooms in a red wine and tomato sauce (£7.55) or one of the many pasta dishes. At lunchtime there are also things like burgers and egg & bacon. High-chairs available; small portions can be prepared on request and there's space for baby-changing in the disabled toilet. ***Seats*** *250.* ***Open*** *12-2.30 & 5.30-11.15.* ***Closed*** *Sun & Bank Holidays. Amex, Diners, MasterCard,* ***VISA***

MANCHESTER Greenhouse

Tel 0161-224 0730 Map 6 B2 JaB
331 Great Western Street Rusholme Manchester M14 4AN

The Greenhouse has a daily-changing vegetarian menu (roughly half the items are suitable for vegans), and operates from noon till late every day of the year. The evening menu offers starters (£1.85-£2.45) such as oyster mushrooms in red wine marinade or hazelnut paté with poppyseed toast; mains courses (£4.95-£5.45) could include Greenhouse strudel with mushrooms, tarragon and white wine sauce or cashew pilau-stuffed peppers; puds (£1.85-£2.25) fresh strawberry pavlova or apple strudel. During the day the menu is more restricted with dishes such as rice-stuffed vine leaves, chili bean tacos (both £2.95) or pasta and vegetables. Country (elderflower etc) as well as grape wines (some organic) with several by the glass. No smoking. ***Seats*** *40.* ***Open*** *12-12 (Sun till 11.30). MasterCard,* ***VISA***

MANCHESTER Harry Ramsden's

Tel 0161-832 9144 Fax 0161-832 9834 Map 6 B2 JaB
Water Street Manchester M3 4JU

This renowned chippie is still packing in the crowds and a boat trip up the River Irwell is a favourite precursor to a meal here. Yorkshire pudding with onion gravy (£1.30) or soup to start; followed by fresh fried fish (£4.10-£7.95) including chips, bread and butter and tea) or for those of a strong constitution try 'Harry's Challenge' (£9.95) which offers a free pudding and a certificate for the successful consumer of the giant haddock fillet, chips, bread and butter, mushy or garden peas, beans and a choice of drink! Desserts include steamed ginger pudding (£1.55) or ice cream (£1.25). Two children's menus at £2.99 and £3.99, and even left-handed fish knives should you so desire! A few toys are provided to keep the kids amused before being seated, when the younger children receive a Postman Pat colouring mat with crayons. Plenty of room for push-chairs, lots of high-chairs and a separate baby-changing room for mums and dads, with table, mat, sink and toilet. ***Seats*** *190 (+ 25 outside).* ***Open*** *11.30-11 (Sun till 10).* ***Closed*** *25 Dec. MasterCard,* ***VISA***

If we recommend meals in a hotel a *separate* entry is usually made for its restaurant. Pub and inn entries include bar food details where recommended.

MANCHESTER Little Yang Sing

Tel 0161-237 9257 Fax 0161-237 9257 Map 6 B2 JaB
17 George Street Manchester M1 4HE

Amid the profusion of Chinese restaurants in Manchester's Chinatown, this is among the best. Of particular interest for snacking is the set daytime menu (£9.50), available between noon and 6 (Saturday until 5); this offers a four-course meal and coffee, with no choice at the starter (a dim sum platter), soup or dessert stage, but with a choice of 24 main dishes (none vegetarian). A la carte, the choice is very wide: specialities include excellent salt and pepper king prawns (£9.50), fried shredded pork with preserved vegetables (£6.95) and braised sliced duck with seasonal greens (£7.50). Children are not neglected: they have their own menu, starting with prawn crackers, followed by chicken and sweetcorn soup, a choice of main courses, and ice cream to finish. A 10% service charge is added to bills. Friendly service. ***Seats*** *90.* ***Open*** *12-11.30. Amex, MasterCard,* ***VISA***

Our inspectors *never* book in the name of Egon Ronay's Guides. They disclose their identity only if they are considering an establishment for inclusion in the next edition of the Guide.

Manchester — New Ellesmere

Tel 0161 728 2791 **Fax 0161 794 8222** Map 6 B2 P
East Lancs Road Swinton Manchester M27 3AA

Very handy (and decently-priced) accommodation – especially for families – midway between the city centre and M62 (Junction 14) on the East Lancashire Road. 'Per room' prices apply, including weekend discounts, with all the ground-floor doubles including fold-out sofa beds. While remaining furniture and fittings are a mite utilitarian, up-to-date amenities include free satellite TV and radio channels, direct-dial phones, hairdryers and trouser presses. Full en suite facilities include heated towel rails and over-bath showers. Children welcomed, with high-chairs, changing facilities, indoor play area, garden and play area all provided. Premier Lodge (Greenalls). *Open 11.30-11 (Sun 12-10.30). **Beer** Greenalls Original, Tetley, Boddingtons, guest beer. Garden. Family room. **Accommodation** 27 bedrooms, all en suite, £41.50 (per room, weekends £34.50), breakfast extra. Children welcome overnight, additional bed & cot available. No dogs. Amex, Diners, MasterCard,* **VISA**

Manchester — On the Eighth Day

Tel 0161-273 1850 **Fax 0161-273 4878** Map 6 B2 JaB
109 Oxford Road All Saints Manchester M1 7DU

Run by one of the oldest restaurant co-operatives in the country, this spacious café/shop offers an eclectic choice of vegetarian and vegan dishes prepared to a high standard. The menu is listed on a blackboard, and dishes displayed are on the self-service counter: muesli and croissant for breakfast; lunch might start with mung bean and coconut or Armenian lentil soup (£1.20), followed by woodland casserole (£2.40), Japanese kimpira stew or Mexican smoked tofu and pinto bean casserole (£2.85). Filled baked potatoes provide further choice, with delights like almond and ginger crumble to finish. Various puds – perhaps mixed fruit crumble, cakes – sometimes a very popular vegan chocolate or carrot and honey cake, are available later in the day. Gourmet nights on the last Saturday of each month; story-telling nights on the first Friday of the month. No smoking. ***Seats** 90. **Open** 10-7 (Sat till 4.30). **Closed** Sun & Bank Holidays. No credit cards.*

Manchester — Pearl City £40

Tel 0161-228 7683 Map 6 B2 
33 George Street Manchester M1 4PH

Smart first- and second-floor Chinese restaurant setting the standard for Cantonese cooking in Chinatown. The special lunch menu (£4.50) is served from noon until 2, and offers a wide choice; there is also an enormous à la carte stretching to nearly 300 dishes and including such standards as Peking hot and sour soup with prawn crackers, and chicken with green peppers, black bean sauce and delicious Chinese mushrooms. Some more unusual dishes (not listed) are often available – fried eel, or whole steamed sea bass – and worth asking about. There are about 30 dim sum, most of which are available throughout the opening hours. Booking is essential for dinner, as the queue often reaches down the stairs. Even when rushed, the service remains friendly and helpful. ***Seats** 300. Meals noon-1am (Sat till 3am, Sun till 11pm). Amex, MasterCard,* **VISA**

Manchester — Siam Orchid £60

Tel 0161-236 1388 **Fax 0161-236 8830** Map 6 B2 
54 Portland Street Manchester M1 4QU

A friendly Thai restaurant on the edge of Manchester's Chinatown, a few steps from both the *Britannia* and *Jarvis Piccadilly* hotels and with an NCP car park opposite the restaurant. A long menu of over 80 items covers the whole Thai range from soups and satay to fish cakes, spicy salads, curries from bright red to dull green, noodle platters, rice platters and many variations on pork, chicken, beef, crab, fish, prawns, lobster, squid and eggs. There's plenty of choice, too, for vegetarians (nearly 30 vegetarian dishes – if you count plain noodles as a 'dish'), plus daily-changing business lunch menus (£5, £7). ***Seats** 50. Parties 20. L 11.30-2.30 D 6.30-11.30 (Fri from 6) Meals Sat 12-11.30 Sun 12-11. Closed 25 Dec, 1 Jan. Set L from £5 Set D from £16 Set menus for two £18 & £25. Amex, MasterCard,* **VISA**

MANCHESTER Victoria & Albert Hotel 73% £154

Tel 0161-832 1188 **Fax 0161-834 2484** Map 6 B2 HR
Water Street Manchester M3 4JQ

Between their TV studios and the River Irwell, a smart hotel created from cleverly converted mid-19th-century warehousing. Original oak-timbered ceilings and cast-iron pillars feature in the galleried reception area, Watsons bar/lounge with its comfortable Victorian drawing room atmosphere and conservatory overlooking the river, and in the all-day French-style café/bistro. Bedrooms, which vary in size and shape, also boast timbered ceilings and some exposed brickwork; each is named after (and subtly themed with stills from) a different Granada TV drama or series. King- or queen-sized beds and a high level of equipment – the TV offers account review, quick check-out and breakfast-ordering facilities – make for a comfortable stay aided by keen staff offering an above-average level of service. 25 new bedrooms were completed in May 1996; these included four duplex suites (£274). Two rooms are equipped for disabled guests. Children under 12 free in parents' room. Free Granada Studios tour. 24hr room service. Breakfast served from 7am (service guaranteed within 20 minutes for 'The Rapido'). Conference and banqueting facilities now cater for up to 230/350. No dogs. Part of the Granada group. ***Rooms*** *157. Terrace, keep-fit equipment, sauna, solarium, café (7am-10.30pm), snooker, news kiosk. Amex, Diners, MasterCard,* ***VISA***

Sherlock Holmes Restaurant £75

The kitchen team under executive chef John Benson-Smith cooks with confidence and style. Menus are written in a witty mode but end up sounding rather gimmicky - does a 'terribly nice barley and any old vegetable broth' or 'Peter's goat's cheese (which sticks to your teeth)' sound enticing? Nevertheless, there's nowt wrong with a sense of humour and results on the plate are usually satisfying. Successful dishes like a simple fillet of Fleetwood halibut sat on a courgette spaghetti with a classical champagne and lobster sauce, or hay- and lavender-baked rump of English lamb sat nicely on a polite stew of ratatouille counterbalance the humour with proficiency. Good puds like 'four terribly posh lemon tastes on one plate comprising the citrus-glazed tart, the sorbet, the confit and the custard' and even 'the plebeian plain and simple caramel cream sat proudly with a little cream' or wonderful ice creams from Rocombe Farm. British farmhouse cheeses are served from a trolley and accompanied by good breads. 'Elementary' and 'Indulgence' table d'hote menus complete the picture. 'Table manners are mandatory' it says on the menu - more humour or just desperation setting in? Simple and balanced wine list. Toilet facilities for the disabled; baby-changing facilities provided. ***Seats*** *70. Parties 8. Private Room 60. L 12-2 D 7-10. Set L £14.95 & £21 D £25/£27.50 & £35.*

Café Maigret

An all-day French-style café/bistro serving an interesting variety of dishes. The main menu, which comes on stream by about 11.30, comprises a dozen or so choices, most available in small or large helpings. Dishes are amusingly described: stupidly large massive Northern chip butty with lashings of tomato ketchup (£5.25); London-style braised ducky hot pot stew with spicy, spicy sausage and white, white beans (£5.25/£8.25) and hummingly moorish cauliflower curried soup with the odd sultana and bit of naan to dip in (£4.25). A slightly more elaboarte menu operates from 5.30, with descriptions in the same style! (one dish and coffee £9.50, two £13.95). Breakfast (£10.50) is served from 8 till 10 (plus an all-day breakfast grill £5.75 small, £8.75 regular on the main menu) and a sandwich menu operates from 10 to 12 and from 2 to 5. Plenty of vegetarian options, too. ***Seats*** *80 (+ 25 outside).* ***Open*** *8am-10.30pm.*

JaB is short for 'Just a Bite'. The majority of these establishments are also recommended in our *Bistros, Bars & Cafés* Guide which features establishments where one may eat well for less than £15 per head.

MANCHESTER — Woo Sang

Tel 0161-236 3697 **Fax 0161-228 0416** Map 6 B2 JaB
19-21 George Street Manchester M1 4HE

Enormous, lively restaurant above a Chinese supermarket offering some good Cantonese dishes, over two dozen dim sum choices (cheung fun till 5.30pm only), with specials such as crispy fried asparagus or shredded beef with chili in phoenix nest (£6.95) and deep-fried chicken Cantonese-style (£6.95 half). On Saturday and Sunday lunchtimes (12-3) there is a buffet lunch (in addition to the regular menu) at £8 a head for as much as you can eat. ***Seats*** *200.* ***Open*** *12-11.30.* ***Closed*** *25 & 26 Dec. Amex, Diners, MasterCard,* ***VISA***

MANCHESTER — Yang Sing £50

Tel 0161-236 2200 **Fax 0161-236 5934** Map 6 B2 
34 Princes Street Manchester M1 4JY

Our Chinese Restaurant of the Year in 1996 added a 'Steamboat' room to its existing downstairs restaurant and upstairs banqueting rooms (for up to 220), confirming that chef-proprietor Harry Yeung stayed one step ahead of his competition in Chinatown. In this traditional way of cooking (*Da Bin Loi* – a familiar sight throughout the Far East), a divided steamer containing soy and vegetable soups is placed on the table and kept hot by a gas burner. In addition, you are brought chili oil, chili soya and oyster sauce to complement the chosen fresh ingredients - perhaps finely-sliced sirloin steak, king prawns, sliced chicken breast, won ton, fresh greens and Japanese noodles), which you cook for yourself by dipping into the liquid. Great fun and very tasty! Downstairs, of course, you can still see the tanks of live fish and shellfish (carp, eels and lobsters), further emphasising the importance of fresh, high-quality ingredients; choose from some 40 different dim sum (even more on Sundays, served 12-4.30 daily) from trolleys parked in the middle of the restaurant or order from the on-the-ball, helpful staff. The regular Cantonese menu (including two dozen or so noodles in soup dishes) is as popular as ever, making Yang Sing the most appealing restaurant in town. Booking is advisable except for Sunday lunch when you just have to join the queue (from around 11.40am) - Sunday is business day in Chinatown. Public car park to rear of restaurant. A dozen high-chairs are provided. ***Seats*** *140. Parties 20. Private Rooms 220. Meals 12-11. Closed 25 Dec. Set menus from £28 for two. Amex, MasterCard,* ***VISA***

MARLBOROUGH — Polly Tea Rooms

Tel 01672 512146 **Fax 01672 511156** Map 14 C2 JaB
26 High Street Marlborough Wiltshire SN8 1LW

The West family have been running this much-loved tea room for many years. Beams, pine dressers, pretty lace cloths and uniformed waitresses create a splendidly traditional air and there's a mouthwatering display of wonderful gateaux (tiramisu, Baileys Irish coffee cream, lemon and redcurrant cheesecake) at the entrance. Inside, croissants, brioches, Danish pastries, strudels, muesli scones, rows of biscuits and pastries are laid out – all baked on the premises. The full Polly breakfast is served from opening time till 11.30 (2 free-range eggs, bacon, Wiltshire sausages and sautéed potatoes £4.65). Individual items are also available, including excellent sausage rolls (£1.35), cheese scones and muesli. Lunch offers soup (£2.50) with home-made bread, fish mousse (£5.75 with salad), locally smoked trout (£5.75), honey-baked gammon and specials such as courgette roulade filled with carrot and cream cheese served with salad (£5.75), chicken and apricot en croute with apricot sauce and dauphinoise potatoes (£5.95). Set afternoon teas include the Polly Tea (three plain or muesli scones) and the Special Gateaux tea (both £4.10). There is also a weekend special savoury set tea (with choice of quiche, roulade or tuna croissant). Two high-chairs, and a children's menu are provided, and there's a chair and table in the Ladies for baby-changing. A large table in a separate room is particularly suited to young families. No smoking area. Minimum charge £2.50 for lunch, £4.10 for tea. ***Seats*** *100.* ***Open*** *8.30-6 (Sat 8-7, Sun 9-7).* ***Closed*** *25 & 26 Dec. Amex, Diners, MasterCard,* ***VISA***

MARSHSIDE Gate Inn

Tel 01227 860498 Map 11 C5 **P**
Boyden Gate Marshside Canterbury Kent CT3 4EB

Delightfully set beside a lane in a tiny hamlet – 2 miles from A28 Canterbury to Margate road at Upstreet – and surrounded by farmland and marshes, this unpretentious rural retreat prides itself on still being "a talkers' pub", in tandem with a thriving bar meal trade. Two welcoming and rustic interconnecting rooms have quarry-tiled floors, a central brick fireplace with winter log fire and a selection of sturdy pine tables, chairs and old pews. Fresh, local produce is used to produce homely, honest English fare (like a spicy mushroom hotpot), and perhaps a home-made cheesey salad gateburger with mild chili relish, pasta with pesto and bacon with garlic bread, black pudding ploughman's or a steak and mushroom hot torpedo. Well-kept Shepherd Neame ales are dispensed direct from the barrel and free-range eggs and local vegetables are also sold over the bar. Splendid summer garden with cottage flowers, stream and duck pond with resident ducks and geese – a constant amusement to children. Quiz night is Thursday night. ***Open** 11-2.30 (till 3 Sat), 6-11 (Sun 12-3, 6-10.30). **Bar Food** 11.45-2, 6-9.30 (Sun 12-2.30, 7-9). **Beer** Shepherd Neame. Garden, outdoor eating area, summer barbecue. Family room. No credit cards.*

MATLOCK The Strand

Tel 01629 584444 Map 6 C2 **JaB**
Dale Road Matlock Derbyshire DE4 3LT

Judith and Julian Mason run a very friendly, genuine bistro in a former Victorian draper's shop. The high-ceilinged, panelled room is lit with replica gas lamps, and attractive cast-iron pillars and balustrades lead up to more seating on the gallery. The lunchtime menu offers a variety of light, inexpensive dishes with a good selection of daily specials – celery and Stilton soup with croutons and bread (£1.75), garlic mushroom croissant (£3.75), quiche of the day with salad, chips or baked potatoes, hot New York bagel with smoked salmon and cream cheese (£3.95), goujons of lemon sole, cheese and cauliflower quiche with salad or potato (£3.95), chicken pie (£5.35) and Brooklyn tuna bake (£3.95) set the style. Smaller helpings are available for children whenever possible, plus a sandwich of chips followed by ice cream (£2.50). More comprehensive, higher-priced evening carte, but a good-value three-course menu (£11.95) is offered Mon-Wed. Live music – Thursday jazz, Friday piano and Saturday a modern jazz trio. Children's portions available on request; special lunch dish for the under-12s - perhaps a sandwich with French fries or baked beans on toast followed by ice cream. Two high-chairs; large Ladies toilet. Only well-supervised children in the evenings. Close to various family attractions including Gulliver's Kingdom and the Heights of Abraham. Smoking not encouraged. ***Seats** 65. **Open** 10-2 & 7-10. **Closed** Sun. MasterCard, **VISA***

MATLOCK Tall Trees

Tel 01629 732932 Map 6 C2 **JaB**
Oddford Lane Two Dales Matlock Derbyshire DE4 2EX

Part of a garden centre a couple miles north of Matlock on the A6. Open throughout the day for light snacks, it offers the best variety at lunchtime with dishes such as home-made soup – maybe potato and orange (£1.95), various salads and quiches, Derbyshire pie (£5.15), mushroom stroganoff (£4.80) and mackerel with apricot sauce (£4.80). The sweet-toothed will relish pineapple bombe, chocolate cheesecake and summer pudding (all £1.95) and cakes like carrot, soaked coffee, and lemon (all 95p). Sorry kids, no chips! - just good wholesome snacks and light meals, all served with fresh French bread and salad; smaller portions can be requested for the little ones. One high-chair. No smoking. ***Seats** 40 (+ 20 outside). **Open** 9-5.30 (till 5 in winter), Sun 10.30-4.30 (till 4 in winter). **Closed** 25, 26 Dec, 1 Jan & Easter Sunday. No credit cards.*

Many hotels offer reduced rates for weekend or out-of-season bookings. Always ask about special deals and family rooms.

sponge with blueberries and spice) with maple syrup ice cream and cinnamon anglaise to banana nougat glacé with crème de banane sabayon and toasted hazelnuts. Good British and French cheeses are served with celery, grapes and warm walnut bread. The excellent wine list is clearly laid out with helpful tasting notes; there's a good mix between classic France, the rest of Europe and the New World plus a new section with over two dozen wines for £15 and under; house champagne is still competitively priced and there are a dozen or so half bottles. No children in the dining-room after 8pm, however a creche facility may be offered (or a private room for families with children). Ask for details of their chauffeur service. No smoking except in pre-arranged areas. ***Seats** 65. Parties 18. Private Rooms 18. L 12.30-2.30 D 7-10.30. Closed D Sun, all Mon, 26 & 27 Dec. Set L £10/£14 (Tue-Fri) £19.95 (Sun) Set D £20/£25 (Tue-Fri). Amex, MasterCard,* ***VISA***

MELLOR Millstone Hotel £92

Tel 01254 813333 **Fax 01254 812628** Map 6 B1
Church Lane Mellor Blackburn Lancashire BB2 7JR

Daniel Thwaites, the Blackburn brewers, operate the Shire Inns chain; its original flagship, the Millstone remains true to its roots and is closest to the brewery. Pub first and foremost, it has a thriving local trade and is consistently busy for their Miller's bar food which offers the likes of fish soup, chicken liver paté and oak smoked Lune salmon as starters; main courses might extend the choice to cod in beer batter, lamb balti, steak, kidney and mushroom pie, Scottish mussels or spicy Cumberland sausage and Bury black pudding with onion gravy and apple chutney. By comparison, the à la carte restaurant and en suite bedrooms are decidedly 'hotel' and priced accordingly. At the time of going to press a new chef had just been appointed (Adrian Sedden), who intends improving the quality of the food and maintaining the style of cooking. Smart bedrooms (ten non-smoking) come in both standard and executive grades (including three suites), with satellite TV, direct-dial telephones, trouser presses and hairdryers throughout. Executive rooms receive rather more space, towelling bathrobes and top-drawer toiletries in the en suite bathrooms. Of great benefit to the less active is the wing of five ground-floor bedrooms (there is no lift) which are also appreciated by parents of very little ones. Six new bedrooms, boasting similar high standards of decor and comfort, are located in the adjacent, recently-acquired property. *Open 11-11 (Sun 12-10.30).* ***Bar Food** 12-2, 7-8.45.* ***Beer** Thwaites Mild, Bitter & seasonal beer. Patio.* ***Accommodation** 24 bedrooms, all en suite, £92-£112 (single £73-£90), weekends £58 (single £49). Children welcome overnight (under-14s free if staying in parents' room), additional bed & cot available. Amex, Diners, MasterCard,* ***VISA***

MELMERBY Shepherds Inn

Tel 01768 881217 Map 4 C3 **P**
Melmerby Penrith Cumbria CA10 1HF

Martin and Christine Baucutt have built up a fine reputation here. At the heart of their operation is Christine's cooking which draws on fresh local produce, and it's no exaggeration that regulars cross and re-cross the Pennines simply to sample the variety on offer. Ever popular dishes like chicken Leoni, Cumberland sausage hotpot, venison and Roquefort crumble and steak and kidney feature alongside new daily menus, which may offer beetroot and potato soup with home-made roll or Stilton and walnut pasta bake for starters, followed by lamb and apricot lattice pie, grilled red snapper with Cajun sauce, carrot and nut loaf or freshly battered pollock with chips and peas. Those popping in for just a quick snack may find a chicken balti pancake or an open smoked salmon sandwich on the menu. Up to a dozen sweets displayed on the counter come with lashings of 'Jersey' cream, while cheese enthusiasts can choose from some fifteen or more on offer, including interesting North Country varieties. A sensible, no-nonsense attitude towards the young enables grown-up meals as they'd like. No fish fingers here, but chips possible and scrambled egg, even, on request; high-chairs, too. A twenty-one bin wine list can be supplemented by 'tastings' from Martin's private cellar; less exotically, English country fruit wines are available by the glass and there is a selection of at least 50 malt whiskies. *Open 11-3, 6-11 (Sun 12-3, 7-10.30).* ***Bar Food** 11-2.30 (from 12 Sun), 6-9.45 (from 7 Sun). Free House.* ***Beer** Jennings Cumberland Ale & Sneck Lifter, three guest beers. Cobbled patio, outdoor eating, barbecue. Closed 25 Dec. Amex, Diners, MasterCard,* ***VISA***

MELMERBY Village Bakery £30

Tel 01768 881515 **Fax 01768 881848** Map 4 C3 **R**
Melmerby Penrith Cumbria CA10 1HE

A converted barn built of local stone with a bright, airy conservatory and pine furniture overlooks the green of a beautiful fellside village, ten miles east of Penrith on the A686 Alston road. One of the pioneers of true wholefood and organic cuisine, the bakery continues to produce superb breads and pastries which are baked on the premises in a wood-fired brick oven. Any fruit and vegetables not coming from the five-acre organic smallholding to the rear are obtained, together with the few meats on offer, from local organic and wholefood suppliers. Breakfast is served until 11am (raspberry porridge, oak-smoked Scottish kippers, free-range boiled eggs, croissants, spicy buns, full fried breakfast and a vegetarian version). Lunch (12-2) might see Swiss chard and mushroom soup, grilled Cumberland sausage with apple sauce, a Baker's lunch of North Country cheeses and their marvellous bread, plus gooseberry and elderflower fool or fruit pie. Also savoury snacks, sandwiches and super cream teas. No smoking. Family-friendly facilities include a changing area in the Ladies, a toy box, beakers and a couple of high-chairs; children can play on the village green under supervision. 'Proper children's food' includes organic beefburgers and home-made lemonade. ***Seats*** *45. Meals 8.30-5 (Sun & Bank Holidays from 9.30), till 2.30 only during Jan & Feb. Closed 25-27 Dec & 1 Jan. Amex, Diners, MasterCard,* ***VISA***

METAL BRIDGE Metal Bridge Inn

Tel & Fax 01228 74206 Map 4 C2 **P**
Floriston Metal Bridge Cumbria CA6 4HG

Pretty bed and breakfasting hostelry (formerly a fisherman's house), with old beamed bars decorated with nets and rods, enjoying a picturesque hamlet setting on the Esk estuary. The five refurbished bedrooms, four of which are en suite, are agreeably rustic with pine furniture and nice views, and all have TVs; one is a single with a separate (but private) bathroom. No smoking in the conservatory. *Open 11-3, 5.30-11 (Sun 12-3, 7-10.30).* ***Beer*** *Scottish & Newcastle Scotch, McEwan's Export, Theakston Best, Younger's Scotch. Riverside garden. Family room.* ***Accommodation*** *5 bedrooms, 4 en suite, £45 (family room £50, single £25/35 – room only rates, breakfast £5). Children welcome overnight (stay free if sharing parents' room), additional bed & cot available. Amex, Diners, MasterCard,* ***VISA***

Always ring ahead and inform establishments of your exact requirements when travelling with children. Unannounced can, sadly, still mean unwelcome.

MIDDLE WALLOP Fifehead Manor

Tel 01264 781565 **Fax 01264 781400** Map 14 C3 **JaB**
Middle Wallop nr Stockbridge Hampshire SO20 8EG

This medieval manor house, once the home of Lady Godiva, lies beside the A343 about halfway between Andover and Salisbury. Central to the house is the original dining-hall with mullioned windows where set lunch and dinner menus (£19 & £22.50) are served. The bar and lounge, however, serve excellent bar snacks for those with less serious appetites: home-made soups (£3) served with a fresh baguette; sandwiches (from £2.50); and several hot dishes – maybe stroganoff of chicken in a filo pastry basket (£7), Thai-spiced beef with vegetable stir-fry (£8) or various omelettes with interesting fillings (from £3.50 including salad). Desserts (from £3.50) might include a trio of chocolate mousses, home-made ices or stuffed apples with almonds and apricots in an apricot sauce. A platter of cheeses in top condition, is offered for £5.25. Scones, cakes (home-made caramel and chocolate shortcake £1.50), teas and coffee are served at any time (afternoon tea £3). Outdoor eating on the lawn. ***Seats*** *20 (+20 outside).* ***Open*** *12-9.30 (Sat till 7). No bar snacks Christmas and New Year. MasterCard,* ***VISA***

MILTON KEYNES Quality Friendly Hotel 61% £102

Tel 01908 561666 **Fax 01908 568303** Map 15 E1 H
Monksway Two Mile Ash nr Milton Keynes Buckinghamshire MK8 8LY

Modern, low-rise hotel at the junction of the A5 and A422. Apart from 12 Standard rooms, all come with mini-bar, teletext TVs with satellite channels and phones at the desk as well as the bedside. Twelve compact Premier Plus suites with small kitchenette and lounge also boast air-conditioning and fax machines. Children up to 14 stay free in parents' room. Hotel guests benefit from a discount on the green fees of an adjacent pay-and-play municipal golf course. ***Rooms** 88. Indoor swimming pool, gym, sauna, steam room, spa bath, sun beds. Amex, Diners, MasterCard,* ***VISA***

MINSTEAD The Honey Pot Tea Rooms

Tel & Fax 01703 813122 Map 14 C4 
Minstead nr Lyndhurst Hampshire SO43 7FX

Owned and run alongside the Honeysuckle Cottage Restaurant, in a building in the garden of the pretty black and white thatched cottage, the Honey Pot tea rooms offer a variety of delicious all-day snacks – filled rolls, baked potatoes and freshly-prepared salads are some of the savoury treats, and daily specials might offer soup of the day, Stilton ploughman's, lasagne and steak & onion pie. On the sweeter side of things are toasted teacakes, muffins, scones and cakes, and various set tea menus (from £2.95); Honey Pot Special, Queen Bee Tea and Drones Tea, and rich fruit cakes and home-made tea breads and biscuits round it all off nicely. Three high-chairs and an outdoor play area with a Wendy house and children's toys. Children's portions are available. Outdoor eating on fine days. The Honey Pot is closed during the winter but teas and light snacks are served in the restaurant from Wednesday to Sunday from 11am to dusk. ***Seats** 40 (+ 40 outside).* ***Open** (Tea Rooms) 10-5.30 (Sun till 6).* ***Closed** Mon & Tue Oct-April. MasterCard,* ***VISA***

MITHIAN Miners Arms

Tel 01872 552375 Map 12 B3 
Mithian St Agnes Cornwall TR5 0QU

Ancient inn located in a picturesque village and only a mile or so from the bustling beaches of the north coast. Built in 1577, the inn is delightfully unspoilt and typically Cornish in character for it retains its traditional layout, featuring low ceilings, wonky walls, woodblock floors and an open fire in the main bar. A cosy lounge displays a genuine Elizabethan ceiling frieze, half wood-panelled walls and shelves full of books, bottles and interesting ornaments. Also of note is the fascinating wall painting of Elizabeth I and the penance cupboard which at one time had a beautifully carved mahogany seat. The cellar bar is ideal for families and leads out into the sheltered garden. Bar food choices are limited to a short printed menu and a few daily specials, but what is on offer is good and mostly home-made. Local crab is used in preparing the crab bake which is served with walnut and dill bread, and soups (broccoli and Stilton) are freshly prepared. Main-course dishes include fish pie, Italian pasta bake, steak and kidney pie and, possibly, fresh grilled sea bass on the specials board. Attractive front cobbled terrace with picnic benches. *Open 12-3, 6-11 (Sun 12-3, 7-10.30).* ***Bar Food** 12-3, 7-9.30.* ***Beer** Marston's Pedigree, Bass. Garden, patio, outdoor eating area. Family room. No credit cards.*

MONKSILVER Notley Arms

Tel 01984 656217 Map 13 E2 
Monksilver Taunton Somerset TA4 4JB

Sarah and Alistair Cade run their white-painted roadside village pub with inimitable flair and have built up a formidably good reputation. The interior is charmingly simple: an L-shaped bar with plain wooden furniture, black and white timbered walls, candles at night, and twin wood-burning stoves; a small but bright and cheery family room leads off, and there's a stream at the bottom of the trim, cottagey garden.
The big attraction here, though, is the bar food, which roughly divides into three categories – the traditional, the Eastern or exotic, and the vegetarian – all given equal thought, using the finest fresh ingredients and cooked with sure-handed skill.
Old favourites and four or five daily hot specials are chalked up on the blackboard:

start with an excellent home-made soup, like a well-balanced, tasty tomato and fresh plum or carrot and caraway soup (served with French-flour bread). For a light but satisfying lunch, choose one of the delicious pitta bread sandwiches with garlic butter, tender meats and good crispy salad. Chinese red roast pork features well-marinated cubes of meat in a soy, five spice and hoi sin sauce, with stir-fried pimento and courgette. The fresh salmon and spinach strudel, old-fashioned lamb casserole with onion dumplings, home-made fresh pasta dishes, bacon, leek and cider suet pudding and spicy courgette kofta are equally fine, as are puddings, with light pastry and good local cream. Try the lemon and cottage cheese cheesecake, apricot bread-and-butter pudding or treacle tart, or a locally-made ice cream. A few more restaurant dishes like steaks and trout are added to the evening menu. Despite the crowds at peak times, all runs effortlessly smoothly and with good humour. *Open 11.30-2.30, 6.30-11 (Sun 12-2.30, 7-10.30). Closed 2 weeks end Jan-early Feb.* ***Bar Food*** *12-2 (till 1.45 Sun), 7-9.30 (till 9 Sun). Free House.* ***Beer*** *Exmoor Ale, Morland Old Speckled Hen, Ushers Best, Wadworth 6X. Riverside garden, outdoor eating. Family room. No credit cards.*

MONKTON COMBE — Combe Grove Manor — 71% — £110

Tel 01225 834644 **Fax 01225 834961** Map 13 F1 **H**
Brassknocker Hill Monkton Combe nr Bath Bath & North East Somerset BA2 7HS

Perched high up above Limpley Stoke valley and set within its own 68 acres of wooded grounds, the manor has extensive leisure facilities belonging to the associated country club (which even offers 7-day morning creche facilities for parents with youngsters). Elegant day rooms and the best of the bedrooms – individually decorated in some style with reproduction furniture – are in the original Georgian house beneath which, in the old cellars reached via some external steps, is an informal bar/bistro decorated in ancient Roman style. The majority of more standardised bedrooms are some 50 yards away in the Garden Lodge, designed to take full advantage of the splendid view (just four rooms are rear-facing) with most having a private patio or balcony. Beds are turned down at night. 24hr room service. Conference/banqueting facilities for 100/80 (ample parking) in the Tapestry Room of the Garden Lodge and in the Roman Room in the Manor House. Informal eating in Manor Vaults (10am-11pm). No dogs. 2 miles from Bath city centre and 18 miles from M4 J18. ***Rooms*** *40. Garden, croquet, indoor & outdoor tennis, golf (5-hole), putting, golf driving range, crazy golf, bowling green, indoor & outdoor swimming pools, squash, gym, sauna, spa baths, steam room, sun beds, beauty salon, aerobics studio, creche (9am-2pm), children's play room. Amex, Diners, MasterCard,* ***VISA***

MONTACUTE — Montacute House Restaurant

Tel 01935 826294 Map 13 F2 **JaB**
Montacute House Montacute Somerset TA15 6XP

Montacute House is a fine Elizabethan mansion owned by the National Trust and the restaurant makes use of the original bakery, dairy and laundry. Hot dishes of the day could include smoky sausage casserole, chicken cobbler, pasta bake, creamy vegetable pie and steak & kidney pie (all £5.25) and there's a ploughman's at £4.50. Cream teas are £3.25, cakes (chocolate fudge, seed, cherry, Victoria sponge) all £1.20 and slices (toffee chocolate shortbread, Bakewell, flapjack) 70p. No smoking. ***Seats*** *100.* ***Open*** *11.30-4.30 (till 5.30 Apr-end Oct).* ***Closed*** *Tue. Amex, MasterCard,* ***VISA***

MORDEN — Superfish

Tel 0181-648 6908 Map 15 E2 **JaB**
20 London Road Morden Surrey SM4 5BQ

Part of the excellent Surrey-based chain serving traditional fish and chips, cooked in beef dripping, the Yorkshire way. All dishes are served with well-cooked chips, French bread, pickles or sauces and "hopefully a smile". Fillet of cod may be small, large or a Moby Dick (£3.10, £4.10 or £5). Huss (£3.70), scampi (£5.30) and fillet of plaice (£4.35) are other regulars, while salmon, lemon sole, haddock, skate and whole plaice on the bone appear on a blackboard menu according to availablity. A children's platter of fishbites or chicken nuggets with chips costs £2.20. No reservations. Smoking discouraged. Licensed. Other outlets are in Ashtead, Cheam, East Molesey, Tolworth and West Byfleet. ***Seats*** *42.* ***Open*** *11.30-2 (Sat till 2.30) & 5-10.30 (Thu-Sat till 11).* ***Closed*** *Sun, 25 & 26 Dec, 1 Jan. Amex, MasterCard,* ***VISA***

MORETON-IN-MARSH Annie's

Tel 01608 651981 Map 14 C1

3 Oxford Street Moreton-in-Marsh Gloucestershire GL56 0LA

In a romantic, cottagey setting of candle-light and soft music, David Ellis is in the kitchen while Anne runs front of house in the most friendly fashion. David's 'French and English country cooking' is quite straightforward and without pretension. The carefully handwritten menu changes every 4 to 6 weeks and offers the likes of spiced salmon fishcakes with red pepper sauce, filo-wrapped tiger prawns pan-fried with garlic, chili and spring onions or Stilton-topped crumpet to start, followed by a home-made, puff pastry-topped pie (perhaps steak and kidney or chicken, leek, mushroom and fresh thyme), fillet of venison with brandy and peppercorn sauce, and daily fresh fish dishes. Treacle tart, toffee pudding with pecan and butterscotch sauce and clotted cream, and ratafia (whipped cream with crushed almond biscuits and whisky set in layers with biscuits and a fruit coulis) among the puddings. The Sunday lunch menu changes weekly but the format of three choices at each stage remains the same; there's always a traditional roast like loin of pork with crispy crackling and a herb stuffing as one of the main-course choices. Modest wine list with only token offerings from outside France. ***Seats** 30. Private Room 12. L (Sun only) 12-2 D 7-9.30. Set Sun L £18.50. Closed D Sun, 2 weeks Jan/Feb. Amex, Diners, MasterCard,* ***VISA***

MOTCOMBE Coppleridge Inn

Tel 01747 851980 **Fax 01747 851858** Map 14 B3 **P**

Motcombe Shaftesbury Dorset SP7 9HW

The Coppleridge Inn is a splendid example of how to convert an 18th-century farmhouse and its adjoining farm buildings into a successful all-round inn. Set in 15 acres of meadow, woodland and gardens it enjoys a lofty position with far-reaching views across the Blackmore Vale. The old farmhouse forms the nucleus of the operation, comprising a welcoming bar with stripped pine tables, attractive prints and a small gallery with seating. There's a comfortable lounge with flagstoned floor and inglenook fireplace and a delightful light and airy restaurant with open country views. Diners can choose from three menus – bar, bistro and restaurant – which are served throughout the inn. Dishes range from creamy garlic soup, smoked trout terrine, French lamb casserole and venison in wild mushroom sauce in the bar to fillet of sea bass with pernod and prawn sauce and pork fillet with tarragon and mushroom sauce on the restaurant menu. Puddings include chocolate St Emilion and ginger syllabub. Home-made pizzas are a speciality on Tuesday and Friday nights. Across the lawned courtyard are ten well-appointed, en suite bedrooms, all superbly incorporated into the single-storey old barns. Tasteful, attractive fabrics, pine furniture, mini-bar, TV, telephone, radio, sparkling clean bathrooms (one with shower only) with bidet and rural views characterise these comfortable rooms. Also part of the complex are two tennis courts, a cricket pitch, a hair salon and a magnificent barn that has been converted into a conference and function room. *Open 11-11 (Sun 12-10.30).* ***Bar Food** 12-2.30, 6-9.30 (from 7 Sun). Free House.* ***Beer** Butcombe Bitter, Hook Norton Best, guest beer. Garden, outdoor eating, children's play area. Family room.* ***Accommodation** 10 bedrooms, all en suite, £70 (single £40). Children welcome overnight (under-5s stay free in parents' room, 6-14s £10), additional bed (£10) & cot (£5) available. Amex, Diners, MasterCard,* ***VISA***

Pubs – note that food is only recommended in those pubs with ***Bar Food*** times in the statistics at the end of an entry. Restaurant food in pubs is *never* recommended unless specifically mentioned. Some pubs are recommended for B&B or Atmosphere only – each entry's statistics indicate our recommendation.

093 ...tcombe 239

Polurrian Hotel 64% £172*

...421 Fax 01326 240083 Map 12 B4 **H**

... Cornwall TR12 7EN

...ages are well catered for at this family hotel par excellence; there's a ...esident nanny for the tiny ones (£3.50 per child per hour, min 2 hours), sub... ...utdoor playground and, new in 1996, a special teenagers' room with table tennis, poo... table and multimedia PC with games. Adults can relax outside in the 12 acres of gardens or inside in one of two lounges (one for non-smokers and the larger incorporating the bar) both of which enjoy views of the sea, the secluded beach, sandy cove and National Trust coastline, 300 feet above which the hotel is situated. Bedrooms and bathrooms vary somewhat in age and appeal but there is an ongoing programme of refurbishment. At least four rooms have bunk beds (but most don't have a sea view - except the suite); many others will accommodate an extra bed and/or cot; all rooms have satellite TV. Children up to 14 share their parents' room free but with a £10 charge for breakfast and high tea (£10) for those over 6; for the younger ones it's free if parents have booked on DB&B terms. Breakfast comes with free-range eggs and honey from the breakfast chef's own bees. 24hr room service. One-night stays (B&B terms) £152. 200 yards from the hotel are cottages and bungalows let out on a weekly, self-catering basis. ***Rooms** 39. Garden, tennis, putting green, indoor & outdoor swimming pools, keep-fit equipment, squash, badminton, sauna, spa bath, sun bed, play room & playground, games room, snooker, beauty salon. Closed Jan-mid Feb. Amex, Diners, MasterCard,* ***VISA***

Mylor Bridge Pandora Inn

Tel & Fax 01326 372678 Map 12 B3 **P**

Restronguet Creek Mylor Bridge Falmouth Cornwall TR11 5ST

Yachtsmen are welcome to moor their craft at the end of the 140ft pontoon that extends out into the creek from this superbly sited and most attractive thatched 13th-century building – one of Cornwall's best-known inns. Although a boat is by far the easiest way to approach this creek-side inn, it lies at the end of a series of narrow lanes off the A39 (from which it is signposted) and it is advble to arrive early as the car park soon fills to capacity on fine days. Named after the naval ship sent to Tahiti to capture the mutineers of Captain Bligh's Bounty, the Pandora retains its unspoilt traditional layout and boasts low wooden ceilings, wall panelling, flagged floors, a good winter log fire, a black-painted kitchen range and many maritime mementoes. It is not only the pub's position, patio and pontoon that attract folk here; the range of bar food is unlikely to disappoint. Good fresh seafood and local fish is the main emphasis, with dishes like Restronguet fish pie, local crab salad and Mediterranean fish stew. Puddings include home-made treacle tart and locally-made ice creams. Very popular are the hearty sandwiches, in particular the Pandora Club and chocolate spread (with chips!) for chocoholic children! Daily specials might be chicken and apricot pie, deep-fried lemon sole, beef, mushroom and Guinness pie, or vegetable couscous. The Andrew Miller restaurant upstairs serves more imaginative dishes, especially fish, and enjoys peaceful river views. During the summer Cornish cream teas are served every afternoon in the bar or on sunny days out on the pontoon. Over a dozen wines served by the glass. *Open 11-11 (Sun 12-10.30) summer & Sat & Sun in winter, 12-3, 6.30-11 Mon-Fri in winter.* ***Bar Food** 12-2.30 (till 2 in winter), 6.30-10 (till 9.30 Sun & Mon-Thu in winter).* ***Beer** St Austell, Bass. Creekside terrace, pontoon, outdoor eating. Family room. Amex, MasterCard,* ***VISA***

Nether Langwith Goff's Restaurant £65

Tel 01623 744538 Fax 01623 747953 Map 7 D2 **RR**

Langwith Mill House Nether Langwith nr Mansfield Nottinghamshire

An old, dilapidated cotton mill forms a striking landmark alongside the A632 about a mile east of the village. Owners the Goffs converted the adjacent Mill House into a charming, homely restaurant with rooms. The front entrance is actually at the back (when approached from the road) and on the ground floor there's a simple, cosy lounge and two pretty, candle-lit dining-rooms – one spacious, the other intimate. Chef Darren Shears' fixed-price, monthly-changing menu offers five choices at each stage with starters such as grilled mackerel fillets with a rich tomato confit and dressing of anchovies and garlic or breasts of pigeon with grilled polenta and a rich orange sauce; main courses might include rack of lamb with red pesto and a rich onion sauce or fillet of salmon with basil and pepper sauce. Desserts stick to the familiar like sticky toffee pudding, tiramisu (albeit à la cheesecake), tarte tatin with crème fraiche and toffee sauce, and raspberry crème brulée. No smoking. ***Seats*** *45. Parties 12. Private Room 28. L 12-1.30 D 7-9.30. Closed L Sat, D Sun, all Mon & Tue after Bank Holidays & 26-31 Dec (but open for L 25 Dec). Set L £11.50/£14.50 (Sun £15.95, under-12s half-price) Set D £25/£29. Amex, Diners, MasterCard,* **VISA**

Rooms £50

The two bedrooms are spacious and comfortable. Storage heaters provide ample heat on chilly nights and remote-control TVs, books, magazines and fresh fruit are among the extras.

NETTLECOMBE Marquis of Lorne

Tel 01308 485236 **Fax 01308 485666** Map 13 F2 
Nettlecombe Bridport Dorset DT6 3SY

Modernised and extended 16th-century inn set in an isolated rural position at the base of Eggardon Hill and run by friendly and welcoming landlords Ian and Anne Barrett. Comfortably refurbished bar areas, named after local hills, have access to the extensive and well-maintained garden (with a much improved children's play area) and enjoy beautiful valley views across Powerstock village. Reliable, unpretentious home-cooked pub food can be found on the regularly-changing blackboard menu that serves the whole pub. Wintertime favourites include hearty casseroles – beef in port and orange, pork in mustard and ale – giant filled Yorkshire puddings (steak and kidney), while summer salads accompany fresh crab, smoked fish platter and spinach and walnut lasagne. Other notable dishes include freshly-battered cod and chips, local plaice with lime butter and grilled fresh brill. Good soups (curried parsnip), crisp vegetables and home-made puddings (sticky toffee pudding, treacle tart). Overnight accommodation in six comfortable, light and airy bedrooms, all of which have spotless shower rooms. Most have smart, modern pine furnishings, while others are kitted out, at present, with more functional furniture; all have remote-controlled TVs, telephones, hairdryers and beverage-making facilities. Most enjoy splendid views across unspoilt Dorset countryside. Best reached from the A3066 north of Bridport (5 miles), by following signs for West Milton and Powerstock along narrow country lanes. *Open 11-2.30, 6-11 (from 6.30 winter), Sun 12-3, 7-10.30.* ***Bar Food*** *12-2, 7-9.30.* ***Beer*** *Palmers. Garden, outdoor eating, children's play area. Family room.* ***Accommodation*** *6 bedrooms, all en suite, £55 (single £35). Children over 10 welcome overnight, additional bed (£10) available. No dogs. Accommodation closed 24 &25 Dec; pub closed 25 Dec eve. MasterCard,* **VISA**

NEW ALRESFORD Hunters £55

Tel 01962 732468 Map 15 D3 RR
32 Broad Street New Alresford Hampshire SO24 9AQ

Martin Birmingham's little restaurant with rooms has two distinctive bow-fronted windows and awnings, and is candle-lit within. Morning coffee is served from 11, followed an hour later by the luncheon menu. In the evenings there are both table d'hote (three choices at each stage, not available Sat evenings) and à la carte menus whose offerings include seared scallops with a gazpacho sauce and basil, boudin blanc with mashed potatoes and onions, pan-fried calf's liver with spring greens and pancetta, and Angus beef fillet with a cep and foie gras risotto. Chocolate tart with a honeycomb parfait and rhubarb tartlet with caramelised rice pudding are typical desserts. The Garden Room is a popular venue for parties, accommodating up to 75 guests; it has its own private bar and overlooks a small lawn with an ornamental fountain and patio area. New chef since last year. Children are always made welcome; two high-chairs and children's portions are available; a spare room may be found for nursing mothers. There's a safe garden for playing in, and it's convenient for the nearby Watercress Line preserved steam railway. ***Seats*** *30. Parties 12. Private Rooms 15/75. L 12-2 D 7-10. Closed D Sun, 1 week Christmas. Set menu £9.95/£12.95. Amex, Diners, MasterCard,* **VISA**

See over

Rooms £48

The three bedrooms, all with shower and WC en suite, are in an old Georgian building. TVs, radio alarms and beverage-making facilities are all provided. Children may stay free if sharing a room with their parents; an extra bed can be provided.

New York — Shiremoor House Farm

Tel 0191-257 6302 **Fax 0190-257 8602** Map 5 E2 **P**

Middle Engine Lane New York Newcastle-on-Tyne North Tyneside NE29 8D2

The Fitzgerald group discovered and restored this former set of derelict farmhouse buildings to which they felt they could attract a discerning clientele of pub-goers. Shiremoor remains unique, its circular gin-gang (a kind of horse-powered threshing machine) forming the back drop to a bar from which radiates a succession of eating areas, carefully broken up by upturned barrels, easy chairs and an assortment of Britannia and scrubbed pine tables. Outdoors are picnic tables on the patios, a wooden pill-box seat for the hardy on windy days, and plenty of safe space, albeit without play equipment, for roaming about in. *Open 11-11 (Sun 12-10.30). Free House.* ***Beer*** *Theakston Best & Old Peculier, Stones Best, Timothy Taylor's Landlord, Mordue Radgie Gadgie, various guest beers. Terrace. Family Room. Amex, MasterCard,* ***VISA***

Any person using our name to obtain free hospitality is a fraud. Proprietors, please inform the police and us.

Newark — Gannets Café

Tel 01636 702066 **Fax 01522 534660** Map 7 D3 **JaB**

35 Castle Gate Newark Nottinghamshire NG24 1AZ

Gannets Café is easy to find on the main road through Newark, almost opposite the Castle entrance. An all-day menu of carefully prepared dishes is displayed at hot and cold servery counters. Snacks such as warm muffins (from 75p), toasted plum bread (95p) and flapjacks (70p) are backed up by more serious dishes: home-made soup (£1.80), savoury quiches (£1.85) and jacket potatoes with butter and cheese (£2.80). Daily specials are chalked up on a blackboard: maybe cottage pie (£4.95), chicken and mint crumble (£5.25) or country fish pie (£5.25). Vegetarians are not forgotten, and creamy parsnip bake or vegetable curry (£3.95) is tempting even for carnivores. The afternoon brings cream tea (£2.25) and a selection of cakes. Children are welcome and small portions are available on request; two high-chairs are provided. There's plenty in the surrounding area to interest young families, including regular flea markets in the market place and free entertainments in the castle grounds (opposite Gannets) on Sunday afternoons, a couple of children's farms close by, and of course they might catch a glimpse of Robin Hood and his merry men! No smoking. ***Seats*** *60 (+ 20 outside).* ***Open*** *9.30-4 (Sat & Sun till 5).* ***Closed*** *25 & 26 Dec. No credit cards.*

Newbury — Donnington Valley Hotel 74% £118

Tel 01635 551199 **Fax 01635 551123** Map 15 D2 **H**

Old Oxford Road Donnington nr Newbury Berkshire RG14 3AG

Alongside its own golf course, this very modern, privately-owned hotel conceals a surprisingly stylish interior behind a rather less remarkable redbrick facade. Beneath a vast, steeply-pitched timber ceiling the main, split-level public areas boast a real log fire, Oriental carpets over parquet floors and numerous comfortable sofas and armchairs with intriguing antique knick-knacks dotted about. The effect created is one of Edwardian elegance (albeit air-conditioned), a theme that extends to the bedrooms, many of which have period-style inlaid furniture and hand-painted tiles in the good bathrooms. There is a turn-down service in the evenings and extensive 24hr room service. Children up to 12 stay free in parents' room. Three rooms are equipped for disabled guests. ***Rooms*** *58. Garden, golf (18), putting, tennis. Amex, Diners, MasterCard,* ***VISA***

NEWCASTLE-UPON-TYNE Fisherman's Lodge £85

Tel 0191-281 3281 **Fax 0191-281 6410** Map 5 E2 R
7 Jesmond Dene Jesmond Newcastle-upon-Tyne NE7 7BQ

In a deep wooded valley two miles from Newcastle city centre, Franco and Pamela Cetoloni's Fisherman's Lodge has been among the best north-eastern restaurants since 1979. Variety is allied to fine cooking throughout the various menus, which include one for vegetarians. A table d'hote is offered for both lunch and dinner (but not on Saturday evenings) and might start with crab risotto with fresh mussels or a smoked fish platter, following with chargrilled monkfish with garlic butter, supreme of halibut with a soy sauce, or braised and roasted lamb shank with leek pudding; crème brulée or glazed poached pear with honey ice cream to finish. A la carte might see three flavours of salmon (smoked, gravad lax and tartare), lobster dishes and 'roast turbot resting on a mussel provençale, bouillabaisse sauce', surf and turf (lobster and beef fillet), and herb-coated rack of Northumbrian lamb with a rosemary and garlic sauce. Daily specials increase the choice, and a good choice of desserts includes a wide range of home-made ice creams and sorbets. No children under 10 after 8pm. No smoking in the dining-room. Patio/garden seating for 35 in good weather. The Cradewell bypass has now been completed and there is now an easy new entrance off A1058 - follow signs for Jesmond Dene. ***Seats*** *60. Parties 14. Private Room 40. L 12-2 D 7-11. Closed L Sat, all Sun & Bank Holidays. Set L £17.80 Set D (not Sat) £26.50. Amex, Diners, MasterCard,* ***VISA***

NEWCASTLE-UPON-TYNE Mather's

Tel 0191-232 4020 Map 5 E2 JaB
4 Old Eldon Square Newcastle-upon-Tyne NE1 7JG

Rustic in character with wooden tables and chairs, wicker mats, cream crockery, a large Welsh dresser and old-fashioned till, this informal and friendly half-vegetarian bistro is located in the busy city centre. You can call in at any time to have just a coffee or perhaps a teacake or bowl of soup but more substantial offerings include robust hot-pots like a German casserole (pork with German sausage and sliced vegetables in white sauce), goulash (both £5.50), beef milanese and moussaka. Vegetarian dishes include asparagus quiche (£3.75), aubergine au gratin, cauliflower cheese, nut loaf and spicy vegburger. Patio for outdoor eating. ***Seats*** *36 (+12 outside).* ***Open*** *10-8.* ***Closed*** *Sun, Bank Holidays & 2 weeks Aug. No credit cards.*

Any person using our name to obtain free hospitality is a fraud.
Proprietors, please inform the police and us.

NEWCASTLE-UPON-TYNE Vermont Hotel 72% £146

Tel 0191-233 1010 **Fax 0191-233 1234** Map 5 E2 HR
Castle Garth Newcastle-upon-Tyne NE1 1RQ

Plumb in the city centre next to the castle and sharing the same courtyard as the Moot Hall (Law Courts), the Vermont is a highly distinctive building. Built of Portland stone in 1910 on the side of a hill, it was originally the County Hall building. It comprises 12 floors and has the unusual aspect that the main entrance, leading to reception, the spacious lounge and hotel bar and Brasserie, is on the 6th floor. A further entrance is down below on Dean Street, with Martha's bar and café on two floors. Public rooms are elegantly furnished and there are plenty of staff on hand to attend to one's needs. Bedrooms have a uniform decor of smart, contemporary mahogany furniture with ample writing space, a settee and an armchair. Of good size, they are also well equipped, featuring a mini-bar, satellite TV and fresh fruit among a range of useful amenities. 24hr room service. Bedrooms additionally offer very good views across the river, taking in the Tyne Bridge as well as the High Level Bridge – top of the range are corner-located suites (from £260) with the same wonderful views. Weekend tariff from £100. No dogs. ***Rooms*** *101. Gym, solarium, beauty salon, news kiosk. Amex, Diners, MasterCard,* ***VISA***

See over

Blue Room £85

On the third floor of the hotel, with midnight blue walls, cream upholstery and soft lighting, the main hotel restaurant is an elegant and sophisticated setting for Stephen Waites's enjoyable cooking. The imaginative, wide-ranging menu offers a particularly good choice with starters such as a salad of Gressingham duck with Oriental dressing, soy sauce and star anise, langoustine tails steamed with baby leeks, or a bisque of lobster, crab and roasted vegetables. Main-course dishes range from tournedos of beef and roast shallots layered with foie gras and truffle jus, fillets of sea bass and braised fennel coated in a tomato jus, or guinea fowl roasted in lemon thyme with a timbale of artichoke and white beans on a shiraz sauce. To finish there may be a selection of cheese with a cottage loaf and celery, a hot peach tarte tatin topped with roasted pistachio ice cream or a duo of white chocolate ice cream and sharp raspberry sorbet on a red berry coulis. Extensive wine list, particularly strong on France. ***Seats*** *90. Parties 10. D only 7-10. Closed Sat, Sun, 2 weeks Jan & 2 weeks summer. Set D £27.50.*

Brasserie £65

A smart, brightly-lit room with a varied choice of imaginative, mostly modern, Mediterranean-style dishes. Begin, perhaps, with chicken and ham terrine pressed with asparagus and tarragon or glazed smoked salmon on toasted brioche with chive salad. Main courses include king prawn and bacon brochette with cherry tomato salsa, pork loin with couscous and baby leeks, and, from the grill, good steaks or chargrilled courgettes with asparagus and tomatoes on a vermouth butter sauce. Among the desserts you might find an excellent pecan crème brulée with a whisky anglaise or warm apple and almond tart with a calvados custard. Sunday lunch is popular with families; high-chairs, beakers, small cutlery and baby-changing facilities are all provided. Disabled toilet facilities. ***Seats*** *145. Parties 20.* ***Open*** *12-3 & 6-12. Set L £13.50 (Sun £14.50) Set D £15.50.*

Newport God's Providence House

Tel 01983 522085 Map 15 D4 JaB
12 St Thomas' Square Newport Isle of Wight

Legend has it that this property, largely Georgian but with earlier elements, gained its name as a result of having several times been passed over by the plague. Now it's a haven of good-quality baking and healthy eating. In the upstairs parlour (open from 11 to 2) mainly wholefood/vegetarian dishes are served – quiche (£2.55), a hearty bean bake (£3.25), a hot vegetarian special (£3.25), filled baked potatoes (from £2.50), 'slimmers filler' (an open sandwich with all the ingredients carefully weighed not to exceed 250 calories), salads (£2.50). All these are also available on the ground floor, where there is a counter-service restaurant. At lunchtime dishes like home-made soup (95p), egg mayonnaise (£2), roast of the day (£4.90) steak pudding/pie (£4.55) and daily specials are added; main courses come complete with fresh vegetables. Savoury snacks are also available here, along with morning coffee (till 12) and afternoon tea (after 2.30). The latter includes a set cream tea (£2.65) as well as individual cakes and a 'real' lemon meringue pie. To start the day there are egg, bacon, and egg & bacon sandwiches. Smoking is allowed in just one of the several eating-rooms. ***Seats*** *100.* ***Open*** *9-5.* ***Closed*** *Sun, Bank Holidays. MasterCard,* ***VISA***

Newquay Hotel Riviera 63% £78

Tel 01637 874251 **Fax 01637 850823** Map 12 B3 H
Lusty Glaze Road Newquay Cornwall TR7 3AA

Popular for family holidays, functions and conferences (for around 120), the hotel overlooks a lovely stretch of coastline. Three bars, a lounge and a garden provide plenty of space to relax, and in summer there's evening entertainment. Most of the bedrooms enjoy sea views. ***Rooms*** *50. Garden, outdoor swimming pool & splash pool, squash, sauna, hair salon, snooker, playroom & play area, games room. Amex, Diners, MasterCard,* ***VISA***

NEWTON Red Lion

Tel 01529 497256 Map 7 E3 

Newton Sleaford Lincolnshire NG34 0EE

In a quiet hamlet tucked away off the A52, this is a civilised, neatly-kept pub with shaded rear garden and play area. Popular unchanging formula is the cold carvery/buffet of fish and carefully-cooked cold meats, from home-cooked ham and ox tongue to home-made pork pie and fresh sardines in ratatouille. Price depends on size of plate and the number of meats chosen; help yourself from a dozen or more accompanying salads. Popular hot roast carvery every Saturday evening and Sunday lunchtime, with home-cooked hot dishes, such as turkey, ham and cheese pie and chicken curry featuring on the menu during the winter months. Choose from ever-changing array of home-made desserts – Bakewell tart, treacle tart and fresh fruit pavlova. Children's prices and eating areas; informal, easy-going atmosphere. *Open 11.30-3, 6-11 (from 7 Mon), Sun 11.30-3, 7-10.30.* ***Bar Food*** *12-2, 7-10 (till 9 Sun). Free House.* ***Beer*** *Bass, Bateman's XXXB. Garden, outdoor eating, children's play area. Family room. Closed 25 Dec. No credit cards.*

NEWTON ST CYRES Crown & Sceptre

Tel 01392 851278 Map 13 D2 

Newton St Cyres Exeter Devon EX5 5DA

Alongside the A377 about two miles from Exeter, this simple roadside pub has in the past few years enjoyed a good local reputation for its food due to the presence of capable landlords Graham and Carolyn Wilson. The blackboard scripted menu lists generously-filled sandwiches like a Crown special – ham and cheese – as well as more substantial home-cooked dishes such as chicken, ham and leek pie and pork fillet with green peppercorn sauce or fresh fish from Brixham (perhaps cod in garlic butter). Puddings might include pecan and toffee cheesecake with clotted cream. Roast Sunday lunch. Recent interior improvements have included combining and refurbishing the lounge and public bars, resulting in a more spacious dining area. Children's facilities extend to a baby-changing area in the Ladies and various toys and colouring books, while in the garden (over a footbridge across a fenced-off, safe stream) there is a tree house, swings, slides and climbing frame. *Open 11.30-2.30, 6-11 (Sun 12-2.30, 7-10.30).* ***Bar Food*** *12-2, 7-9.30.* ***Beer*** *Bass, Boddingtons, guest beer. Garden, riverside patio, outdoor eating, children's play area. Family room. No credit cards.*

NORTH NEWNTON Woodbridge Inn

Tel & Fax 01980 630266 Map 14 C3 

North Newnton Pewsey Wiltshire SN9 6JZ

Akin to a 20th-century staging post, with a warm welcome to every weary traveller extended all day, every day by landlords Lou and Terri Vertessy. As well as the abundant enthusiasm that has contributed so much to the rejuvenation of this pub, their commitment and imagination has brought to these parts some truly unusual pub food. Terry's worldwide experience in the kitchen leans towards the American Deep South for her fish Creole; Mexican food has become a hot favourite, represented by sizzling beef fajitas and spicy chicken chimichangas; from the Far East comes kung po ji ding (hot and aromatic chicken stir-fry with cashew nuts). European offerings include seared salmon with fresh basil sauce, roasted marinated red peppers, and rump steak with béarnaise. Simpler bar food – sandwiches, steak and ale pie, woody vegetable pie, American-style burgers, Mexican burritos – are served all day, with the more serious restaurant fare available throughout the pub between 12-2.30 & 6-10 (from 7 Sun). Prospective weekend diners are advised to book; a self-contained back room is available for parties up to ten. The Vertessys have converted three neat and tidy bedrooms for guests' use, all with cottagey wallpapers and fabrics, freestanding darkwood or pine furniture and fresh flowers. One has en suite facilities, the others share an acceptable bathroom. Situated by the A345 bridge over the Avon, one and a half miles north of Upavon, it has a huge, colourful riverside meadow garden, part of which is fenced off to create an eating area where children can also play.

See over

Four pétanque pistes; trout fishing can be organised on the River Avon. No under-10s after 8pm and no dogs indoors. *Open 11-11 (Sun 12-10.30). **Bar Food** 11-10.30 (Sun 12-10, except 12-3, 7-10.30 Oct-Apr). **Beer** Wadworth, guest beer. Garden, outdoor eating, barbecue, children's play area. **Accommodation** 3 bedrooms, 1 en suite, £37.50 (single from £27). Children welcome overnight (under-5s stay free in parents' room), additional bed (£10) & cot available. Accommodation closed 24 & 25 Dec. No dogs. Amex, Diners, MasterCard,* ***VISA***

NORTHALLERTON Bettys

Tel 01609 775154 Map 5 E3 JaB
188 High Street Northallerton North Yorkshire DL7 8LF

In a long terrace of houses on the High Street, Bettys is the traditional tea shop that every town deserves; in fact, there are other outlets of Bettys in Ilkley, Harrogate and York (see entries). This very succesful and well-run chain of café tea rooms was established in 1919; see entry under Harrogate for full menu details. Antique teapots and pictures line the walls and the atmosphere is suitably relaxing – a perfect place to enjoy a brunch or traditional Yorkshire afternoon tea. The latter offers a roast ham or chicken sandwich, sultana scone with cream and strawberry preserve, and a Yorkshire curd tart. Rarebits and savoury dishes with a Swiss accent are specialities and uniformed waitresses will guide you through the delights of their speciality teas, coffees and tempting cake trolley. Four high-chairs are provided, along with beakers and bibs. Children's are offered smaller portions or their own separate menu (Masham sausages, banana and honey or peanut butter sandwiches, ginger biscuits, ice cream clown and more). Changing shelf with mat, chair and playpen in the Ladies; nappies are available for emergencies. Wednesdays and Saturdays see a street market bringing this delightful old town to life. ***Seats** 58. Open 9-5.30 (Sun from 10). Closed 25 & 26 Dec, 1 Jan. MasterCard,* ***VISA***

NORTHAMPTON Lawrence's Coffee House

Tel 01604 37939 Map 15 D1 JaB
St Giles Street Northampton Northamptonshire NN1 1JF

Shop and coffee house (belonging to the bakery next door) in the heart of town with a colourful window display of appetising snacks. Crusty rolls start at 93p, quiche – maybe bacon and mushroom or cheese and brocculi (£1.40), sausage rolls 72p and there are lots of bakery items from jam doughnuts to a traditional Towcester cheesecake (puff pastry tartlet with a bread-and-butter pudding-like filling. Hot snacks such as toasted sandwiches (from £1.37) and filled jacket potatoes (£2) are available most of the day. Unlicensed. No smoking. ***Seats** 40. **Open** 7.45-5. **Closed** Sun & Bank Holidays. No credit cards.*

NORTHLEACH Wheatsheaf Hotel FOOD

Tel 01451 860244 **Fax 01451 861037** Map 14 C2 P
West End Northleach Gloucestershire GL54 3E2

Quietly situated in the celebrated Wood Town (just off the A429) is the Langs' people-friendly period coaching inn. Being family-run, it's family-orientated as well, with plenty of minor diversions for the young-at-heart in the bar while meals are ordered from a daily-changing, all-embracing menu. Sandwiches, salads, cheese ploughman's lunches, a handful of vegetarian options, hot croissant with smoked chicken and cream sauce, fresh cod in a light beer batter, baked Bibury trout with parsley and butter sauce show the style. As a base for walkers and Cotswold explorers, the Wheatsheaf offers bedrooms all individually furnished to a high standard; two have king-size beds, and while four of the en suite bathrooms have WC/showers only, all the rooms have TV, beverage trays and dial-out phones. *Open 12-3, 6-11 (till 10.30 Mon-Thu), Sun 12-3, 7-10.30. **Bar Food** 12-2, 6-8.30 (till 9 Fri & Sat), Sun 12-2, 7-8.30. Free House. **Beer** Marston's Best & Pedigree. Garden, outdoor eating. **Accommodation** 10 bedrooms, all en suite, £55-£69 (single £39 midweek only). Children over 7 welcome overnight. No dogs. MasterCard,* ***VISA***

Norton — Hundred House Hotel — £79

Tel 01952 730353 **Fax 01952 730355** Map 6 B4 
Norton nr Shifnal Shropshire TF11 9EE

A creeper-covered, redbrick Georgian inn standing alongside the A442. Personally run by the Phillips family, it has great charm, with mellow brick walls, stained glass, colourful patchwork, leather upholstery and (hanging from the ceiling beams) dozens of bunches of dried flowers and herbs, all from Sylvia's splendid garden, which you are encouraged to visit. Enchanting, antique-furnished bedrooms have lots of nice touches like patchwork bedcovers (often on antique brass beds), fresh flowers, pot-pourri and even swings in some (ask about them!). All have good en suite bathrooms. Family rooms (£90) sleep two adults and two children. ***Rooms*** *10. Garden. Amex, MasterCard,* ***VISA***

Jacobean Room — £65

There's a distinctly modern touch to the dishes on a sensibly short à la carte menu prepared by joint-head chefs Stuart Phillips and Nigel Huxley. Rich fish soup with parmesan crouton, baked cod with spider crab and prawn topping and a rocket and chive salad, lamb rogan josh with home-made chutney, shin of beef braised in beer with mustard and herb dumplings, chargrilled red mullet with saffron, braised fennel and beurre blanc, and Sheila's notably good home-made puddings (tarte tatin, iced prune and armagnac terrine with hot chocolate sauce) show the style. Fish dishes appear on the list of the day's specials. A new brasserie menu has replaced the bar menu. ***Seats*** *60. Parties 15. Private Room 30. L 12-2.30 D 6.15-10 (Sun 7-9). Set Sun L £14.95.*

JaB is short for 'Just a Bite'. The majority of these establishments are also recommended in our *Bistros, Bars & Cafés* Guide which features establishments where one may eat well for less than £15 per head.

Norwich — Britons Arms Coffee House

Tel 01603 623367 Map 10 C1 
9 Elm Hill Norwich Norfolk NR3 1HN

This popular all-day restaurant/coffee shop in a building dating from 1420 is on two floors with three rooms, and a garden terrace off the first-floor room for lunchtime alfresco eating. Coffee, tea and light snacks are served until 12.15, lunch until 2.30 and afternoon tea until 5. A typical daily menu will start with soup (spiced tomato and lentil, with home-made bread (£1.60) and chicken liver and mushroom paté with toast and a salad (£3.30) and go on to the likes of Norfolk pork and apple pie (£4.10) and Cromer crab and gruyère quiche (£3.90). Home-made puddings (all £2.30) might include Spanish orange and almond cake, brown-bread-and-butter pudding or in summer, fresh raspberries with hazelnut meringue. £3 minimum charge between 12.15 and 2.30. Children's portions. Two rooms non-smoking. Monastery car park 2 mins away. ***Seats*** *60 (+ 16 outside).* ***Open*** *9.30-5.* ***Closed*** *Sun & Bank Holidays. No credit cards.*

Pubs – note that food is only recommended in those pubs with ***Bar Food*** times in the statistics at the end of an entry. Restaurant food in pubs is *never* recommended unless specifically mentioned. Some pubs are recommended for B&B or Atmosphere only – each entry's statistics indicate our recommendation.

NORWICH Norwich Sport Village Hotel 63% £74

Tel 01603 788898 **Fax 01603 406845** Map 10 C1 **H**
Drayton High Road Hellesdon Norwich Norfolk NR6 5DU

Practical, roomy bedrooms are at the centre of a very extensive sports complex situated just off the outer Norwich ring road on the A1067 to Fakenham. Sporting facilities are the most impressive feature, with over 60 sports and activities available. They include the Fitness Works gym, five squash courts, 20 badminton courts and a dozen tennis courts, seven of them indoors. Hotel guests share the all-day (7am-10pm) informal eating facilities (Desert Island Diner, Sportmans Arms and Village Market Place) with the other users of the complex. The Broadland Aquapark swimming complex includes a 6-lane 25m competition pool, a shallow, warm playpool, two 550ft flume slides and rapids and a paddling pool for toddlers. There's a soft play area for the very young. All hotel bedrooms are en suite (but some with showers only) and are large enough to take an extra bed (family rooms sleep four); up to two children under 16 may share their parents' room free. Cots, potties, nappies, high-chairs and baby food are provided on request; supervised creche for six hours a week. No dogs. Banqueting/conference facilities for up to 1500/180. Ask for their special Sporting & Leisure breaks brochure. Dinosaur Park (open mid Apr-Nov) is 9 miles away. ***Rooms*** *55. Patio, indoor swimming pool, gym, squash, sauna, steam room, sun beds, spa bath, multi-sports hall, aerobics, beauty salon, tennis, badminton, snooker. Amex, Diners, MasterCard,* ***VISA***

NORWICH AIRPORT Stakis Norwich 65% £98

Tel 01603 410544 **Fax 01603 789935** Map 10 C1 **H**
Cromer Road Norwich Airport Norwich Norfolk NR6 6JA

On the airport perimeter a few miles north of the city centre, this modern redbrick hotel offers good-sized quite comfortable bedrooms which are well equipped. There's ample writing space and deep-cushioned seating, though beds can be a bit hard. Excellent leisure facilities and in the morning there's an extensive buffet-only breakfast. Children up to 5 stay free in parents' room; purpose-built facility for conferences and banquets (up to 600/400). ***Rooms*** *108. Garden, indoor swimming pool, gym, sauna, steam room, spa bath, sun beds. Amex, Diners, MasterCard,* ***VISA***

NOTTINGHAM Higoi

Tel 0115 942 3379 **Fax 0115 970 0236** Map 7 D3 **JaB**
57 Lenton Boulevard Nottingham Nottinghamshire NG7 2FQ

Japanese chef Mr Kato, assisted by his wife, continues to educate customers in the delights of his native cuisine. Helpful and informative staff will explain all the specialities and menus, including good-value vegetarian, dombure one-pot lunches and a bento box lunch. Set lunch starts at £6.90 and set dinners run from £14.50. Families are welcome at lunchtimes, when a special children's lunch offers soup, teriyaki beef burger with rice, salad and potato croquette, and a dessert. Simple decor, lightwood tables and an assortment of Japanese artwork. ***Seats*** *35.* ***Open*** *12-2 (Sat only) & 6.30-10 (Sun till 9.30).* ***Closed*** *L Sun-Fri & Bank Hols. Amex, Diners, MasterCard,* ***VISA***

NOTTINGHAM Man Ho £40

Tel 0115 947 4729 **Fax 0115 929 0343** Map 7 D3 **R**
35 Pelham Street Nottingham Nottinghamshire NG1 2EA

A city-centre restaurant spcialising in the cooking of Canton, Peking and Szechuan; and one of the few in the City offering dim sum. Here the choice comprises some 60 items ranging from grilled pork dumplings or steamed prawns (har kau) and steamed roast pork buns (char siu bau) at £1.80 per portion to various cheung fun (here called pastries) and de-luxe siu mai (steamed chopped-meat dumplings topped with caviar and a king prawn) at £2.60 per portion. For the more adventurous there is pig's trotter in red beancurd sauce or preserved squid in satay sauce (both £2.60). A dim sum taster plate is offered for £4.50 per person (minimum of two people). Instead of the usual jasmine tea here you'll be offered a flavourful, darker brew made from a Fukien oolong leaf. ***Seats*** *150.* ***Open*** *for dim sum 12-5 (full menu available 12-12).* ***Closed*** *25 Dec & 1 Jan. Amex, Diners, MasterCard,* ***VISA***

Nottingham — Punchinello's

Tel 0115 941 1965 Map 7 D3 JaB

35 Forman Street Nottingham Nottinghamshire NG1 4AA

Good cooking, good prices, jolly staff and long opening hours in a bistro/restaurant opposite the Nottingham Theatre and Concert Hall. Breakfast starts the day (scrambled eggs on toast, muffins with bacon and melted cheese); the bistro menu comes on stream at 12 and the à la carte at 7.30. Fresh salmon with lemon and dill mayonnaise (£3.55), chili enchiladas topped with salsa and guacamole (£3.25) and various salads, smoked salmon, baked ham and quiche (all £3.85) typify a menu that is supplemented by a blackboard of daily specials like spinach ravioli (£3.25) and sausages and mash with creamy onion gravy (£3.15). Cakes and coffee are available all day. Children can benefit from the freshly prepared, wholesome food offered; children's portions available both upstairs and downstairs; one high-chair. Bottle and baby food can be warmed. A private area can be made available for nursing mothers on request. Dinner in the Balcony Restaurant is served in a slightly more formal atmosphere. ***Seats*** *90.* ***Open*** *8.30am-10.30pm.* ***Closed*** *Sun & Bank Hols. Amex, Diners, MasterCard,* ***VISA***

If we recommend meals in a hotel a *separate* entry is usually made for its restaurant. Pub and inn entries include bar food details where recommended.

Nottingham — Sonny's

Tel 0115 947 3041 **Fax 0115 950 7776** Map 7 D3 JaB

3 Carlton Street Hockley Nottingham Nottinghamshire NG1 1NL

It's the café section, just inside the entrance of this smart modern restaurant, that is of particular interest to snackers. The short menu ranges from soup (cauliflower and parmesan £3.50; fish soup with gruyère, rouille and croutons £3.75) and salads (smoked chicken with cashew nut mayonnaise £3.75, Caesar £3.50) to sandwiches and hot snacks (smoked salmon and cream cheese bagel £4.50, brandade with tapénade and bruschetta, linguine with Parma ham, mushrooms and basil cream) plus a couple of puds like crème brulée and home-made ice cream. The café is closed on Sunday but the restaurant offers a good value set Sunday lunch (£11.50 for three courses) with one of the three main-course choices generally being a roast. ***Seats*** *25 (+30 outside).* ***Open*** *11-3.* ***Closed*** *Sun, 25, 26 Dec & 1 Jan. Amex, MasterCard,* ***VISA***

Nunnington — Nunnington Hall

Tel 01439 748283 **Fax 01439 748284** Map 5 E4 JaB

Nunnington Hall Nunnington York North Yorkshire YO6 5UY

The tea room, which boasts some fine gilt-framed oils, is an integral part of this 17th-century house on the banks of the River Rye (admission £3.50 for adults). The National Trust is very much in the forefront of preserving the tradition of afternoon tea, and here proceeds from the tea rooms contribute directly to the upkeep of the Hall. Everything is baked on the premises; popular are crunchy lemon cake, caramel shortbread and Nunnington fruit loaf (all £1), and there are scones, sandwiches (from £1.75) and old-fashioned dairy ice cream. Set cream tea £2.95. A children's section of the menu includes gingerbread people, chocolate crispies and junior sandwiches. High chairs, bibs, baby food and bottle-warming and baby-changing facilities are all available and, for those at the other end of the age spectrum, special fat-handled cutlery for arthritic hands. No smoking. ***Seats*** *70.* ***Open*** *1.30-5.* ***Closed*** *Mon (except Bank Holidays) in Jun/Jul/Aug.* ***Closed*** *Mon (except Bank Holidays) & Tue Apr/May/Sep/Oct. Amex, MasterCard,* ***VISA***

Our inspectors *never* book in the name of Egon Ronay's Guides. They disclose their identity only if they are considering an establishment for inclusion in the next edition of the Guide.

Nunton — Radnor Arms

Tel 01722 329722 Map 14 C3 **P**

Nunton Salisbury Wiltshire SP5 4HS

This welcoming ivy-clad village pub dates from the 17th century and part of it once served as the village stores and post office. Locals come now for the well-kept ale and for the honest home-cooked selection of meals that are served in its low-ceilinged and simply-furnished main bar and neat, opened-out dining areas. Traditional lunchtime favourites, including ploughman's and sandwiches (also available in the evenings), can be found on the printed menu, while the changing blackboard menu advertises the lunch specials and evening choices. Look out for marinated venison steak, duck breast with orange and Amaretto, chicken breast stuffed with asparagus, and fresh fish dishes like cod and haddock grill, fresh scallops bonne femme and skate with capers and cream. For pudding try the sticky toffee pudding or the apricot and Amaretto cheesecake. The large rear garden has fine rural views, plenty of picnic benches and much to amuse energetic children. *Open 11-3, 6-11 (Sun 12-3, 7-10.30).* ***Bar Food*** *12-2, 7-9.30 (no food Sun eve).* ***Beer*** *Hall & Woodhouse Tanglefoot & Badger Best. Garden, outdoor eating, children's play area, disabled WC. Family room. No credit cards.*

Oakham — Barnsdale Lodge Hotel 69% £80

Tel 01572 724678 **Fax 01572 724961** Map 7 E3 **H**

The Avenue Rutland Water nr Oakham Leicestershire LE15 8AH

Standing above Rutland Water alongside the A606 three miles east of Oakham, this comfortable hotel was originally a 16th-century farmhouse. Recent extensions include a roomy conservatory and a wing of 12 lake-view bedrooms (£10 supplement) that have been harmoniously incorporated and cleverly retain the cottagey feel. Edwardian antiques, period prints and ornaments fill the bedrooms and public rooms; indeed, an antique centre (under the same ownership) is situated next door. Cosy bedrooms, some with four-posters, have been refurbished to a high standard with comfortable armchairs and good-quality soft furnishings. Interconnecting family rooms, four honeymoon suites and two rooms for disabled guests in the new wing. The Barn Suite has its own reception area and bar and caters for conferences and banquets. ***Rooms*** *29. Garden, playground. MasterCard,* ***VISA***

Oddington — Horse & Groom Inn

Tel 01451 830584 Map 14 C1 **P**

Upper Oddington Moreton-in-Marsh Gloucestershire GL56 OXH

A typically picturesque Cotswold inn set back from the lane in an equally appealing village close to Stow-on-the-Wold. New owners since last year's Guide have gradually set about upgrading the interior, complete with flagstones, ceiling beams, stone walls, country furnishings and log fire, as well as introducing an extensive menu that is available in both the bar and adjacent dining-room. Dominating the vast blackboard in the bar is an impressive choice of seafood dishes such as dressed Cromer crab, Scottish oysters, chargrilled tuna marinaded in soy, Cornish crab cakes with tomato coulis and garlic mayonnaise, whole lemon sole and fresh halibut poached with chive hollandaise. Carnivores are not forgotten as there is space on the menu for terrine of wild boar and juniper berries, Cajun chicken, beef Wellington, pork tenderloin with Dijon mustard sauce and various chargrilled meats. Lighter bites include sandwiches, filled baguettes and ploughman's lunches. Homely bedrooms are rather on the small side, yet are neatly kept, unencumbered by intrusive phones and due to be refurbished in the coming year. Of the four rooms in the eaves above the bar, one has a full bathroom, while the others have 'cubby-hole' shower-rooms. Two bright bedrooms, with WC/showers, are in former stables across the yard. Good sloping summer garden with ornamental pond and children's play area. *Open 11-2.30, 6-11 (Sun 12-3, 7-10.30).* ***Bar Food*** *12-2 (till 2.30 Sun), 6.30-9.30 (till 10 Fri & Sat, from 7 Sun). Free House.* ***Beer*** *Hook Norton, Wadworth 6X, Wychwood. Garden, children's play area. Family room.* ***Accommodation*** *7 bedrooms, all en suite (one with bath), £60/£70 (single £37.50). Children welcome overnight, additional bed (£10) & cot (£5) provided. Check-in by arrangement. MasterCard,* ***VISA***

ODIHAM Blubeckers Mill House

Tel 01256 702953 Map 15 D3 JaB
The Mill House North Warnborough nr Odiham Hampshire RG25 1ET

Blubeckers is in a magnificent old mill house where, in the restaurant, you can still see the huge wheel churning round. On two floors, upstairs is generally set aside for families at weekend lunchtimes when Bolly the Clown or a magician entertains; one room is always kept for adults. The children's menu (dishes around £2.75-£3.75 served with fries and baked beans unless you specify different, puds – like bananas and shark-infested custard – around £1.45) is excellent value and features cocktails (around £1.25) for youngsters. Adults are offered the likes of fish pie (£8.95), grilled lamb steak (£9.75), char-grilled steaks (from £9.95) and burgers (£7.25) plus sizzling fajitas, cream cheese, garlic and herb-stuffed chicken breast, and a mix of grilled fish (tuna, red mullet, sea bream and trout); half a dozen or so salads and other vegetarian options. The long list of puddings (all £3.35) ranges from Baileys hot chocoholic cake to kiwi, banana and toffee pavlova; ask for at least a couple of spoons! The fixed-price Sunday lunch menu always includes a choice of roasts, vegetarian dishes and those sticky puds. Monthly-changing 2/3-course blackboard menus offer particularly good value. High-chairs are set with baby cutlery and a helium balloon is tied to children's chairs, threatening to pull them up, up and away; booster seats are also provided. Children are invited to enter the menu-colouring and awful joke contest and prizes are awarded each month. At one end of the room there is a 'dungeon' play room, to which children can escape when mealtime formality becomes too much. Outside, there is boating on the pond (supervision needed), a Wendy House, climbing frame, swings and a vast, green lawn. Family changing room with bench and changing mat. This outlet of Blubeckers won our 1992 Family Restaurant of the Year award; it's half a mile from M3 J5. ***Seats*** *220. Open 12.30-2 (Sat until 2.15, Sun until 3) & 6-9.45 (Fri until 10.45, Sun from 5.30, Sat 5.30-10.15). Closed 25-27 Dec. Set menu £9.95/£12.95. Amex, Diners, MasterCard,* ***VISA***

Also at:

Chobham, Surrey Tel 01276 857580 Map 15 E3
Hampton Court Tel 0181-941 5959 Map 15 E2
Shepperton (see entry) Map 15 E2

A jug of fresh water!

OLD DALBY Crown Inn

Tel 01664 823134 Map 7 D3 P
Debdale Hill Old Dalby Melton Mowbray Leicestershire LE14 3LF

Tucked away down a lane in the village centre, this 300-year-old converted farmhouse is today the home of some enjoyable, often ambitious cooking. Cosy, antique-furnished bars are the setting for the sampling of such home-made dishes as potted chicken livers, grilled smoked salmon sausage with tagliatelle and herb cream sauce, followed by loin of lamb with basil, rosemary and red wine jus or blackened Cajun salmon on sweet potato and coconut stew, all of which may appear on the quarterly-changing menus. Puddings include baked Austrian strawberry cheesecake and treacle tart, while local Colston Bassett Stilton features amongst a good choice of cheeses. Simpler snacks like sandwiches and speciality baguettes (chicken and compote of mango) are available at both lunchtime and evening. Eat in either the restaurant or in the bar where there is a constantly-changing selection of draught bitters (up to 14) always available. A large, pleasant and secluded garden provides a haven for children and offers a terraced area for outdoor eating from which guests can watch regular games of pétanque organised by local enthusiasts. *Open 12-3, 6-11 (Sun 12-3, 7.10.30).* ***Bar Food*** *12-2, 6-10 (no food Sun eve). Free House.* ***Beer*** *up to 14 guest beers: Adnams, Marston's Pedigree, Hardys & Hansons Kimberley Bitter, Timothy Taylor Landlord, Black Sheep Bitter, Greene King Abbot Ale, Bateman's XB & XXXB. Garden, outdoor eating. Family room. No credit cards.*

Old Hunstanton — Le Strange Arms Hotel — 60% — £70

Tel 01485 534411 **Fax 01485 534724** Map 10 B1 **H**
Golf Course Road Old Hunstanton Norfolk PE36 6JJ

Clearly signposted off the A149, one mile north of the busy seaside resort of Hunstanton, an extended Victorian hotel with lawns that lead directly on to sand dunes, beach huts and a mile-long golden beach. Bedrooms vary from smart new Premier rooms in a modern wing to more traditionally-furnished rooms (one a family suite with bunk bedroom) in the original building; the best rooms have panoramic sea views and attract only a small supplement. To one side of the hotel is the Ancient Mariner pub, while across the road is an interesting craft centre. ***Rooms** 36. Garden, children's play area, snooker. Amex, Diners, MasterCard,* ***VISA***

Onecote — Jervis Arms

Tel 01538 304206 **Fax 01538 304514** Map 6 C3 **P**
Onecote Leek Staffordshire ST13 7RU

On B5053 (off A523) and positioned just at the edge of the Peak National Park, the pub stands on one bank of the Hamps river – park on the opposite bank and cross a footbridge into the garden. While the picnic tables, play area and ducks are super, parents should be mindful of the littlest ones by this fast-flowing stream. Vegetarian and children's meals both feature prominently on the printed menu (curried nut, fruit and vegetable pie; egg, chips and beans) alongside pretty standard pub grub. A little more adventure emanates from the blackboard: beef Madras, seafood tagliatelle and ocean pie. Adjacent to the pub is holiday accommodation in a converted barn. Baby-changing facilities in the Ladies. *Open 12-2.30 (till 3 Sat), 7-11 (from 6 Sat), Sun 12-10.30.* ***Bar Food** 12-2, 7-10 (from 6 Sat), Sun 12-10. Free House.* ***Beer** Theakston XB, Mild & Old Peculier, Bass, Marston's Pedigree, Ruddles County, Worthington Best. Riverside garden, children's play area. Family rooms. Closed 25 & 26 Dec. No credit cards.*

Orford — Butley Orford Oysterage

Tel 01394 450277 Map 10 D3 **JaB**
Market Square Orford Suffolk

A long-established family-run business which catches its own fish and smokes them in the family smoke-house, and also has its own oyster beds. The menu runs from oyster soup (£2.80), smoked sprats (£2.90) and mixed hors d'oeuvre to smoked fish and oysters (£6.90), pork and cockle stew (£5.50) and scalloped prawns served in a cheese sauce with potato topping (£4.90). The raison d'etre however is their excellent oysters (£4.95 for six, £9.90 a dozen). An interesting savoury includes the rarely found angels on horseback – grilled bacon with oysters, here served on toast (£3.90). Simple desserts include chocolate mousse (£2.70) and a selection of Spanish fruit ices (from £2.80). Licensed, or you can bring your own (corkage £3). One of three dining-rooms is reserved for non-smokers. ***Seats** 90.* ***Open** 12-2.15 & 7-9 (high season from 6, Nov-Apr Fri/Sat only).* ***Closed** D Sun-Thu Nov-April, 25 & 26 Dec. No credit cards.*

Oswestry — Wynnstay Hotel — 68% — £98

Tel 01691 655261 **Fax 01691 670606** Map 8 D2 **H**
Church Street Oswestry Shropshire SY11 2SZ

In the town centre opposite St Oswalds church, this is a typical Georgian building, with stylish day rooms. Besides the restaurant and lounge there are now increased conference facilities for up to 300, plus a 200-year-old crown bowling green as an unusual leisure offering. Best of the bedrooms have whirlpool baths, king-size or four-poster beds. Children up to 13 free in parents' room. The newly-built Coach House health and fitness suite offers fine sporting facilities. ***Rooms** 27. Garden, bowling, indoor swimming pool, gym, sauna, spa bath, solarium, beauty salon, coffee shop (9.30am-10pm). Amex, Diners, MasterCard,* ***VISA***

A jug of fresh water!

OTLEY — Chevin Lodge — 64% — £97

H

Tel 01943 467818 **Fax 01943 850335** Map 6 C1
York Gate Otley Leeds LS21 3NU

Set in fifty acres of woodlands and lakes and built of Finnish pine, the Lodge is the largest log construction in the country. Bedrooms are in either the main building or in most unusual log lodges scattered amongst the trees. Despite the rusticity, rooms have all the usual modern conveniences; some lodges have more than one bedroom (£16 per person extra). Executive lodges (£10 supplement) have separate lounges. 24hr room service. The well-equipped Woodlands Suite has facilities for up to 120 conference delegates. New leisure centre. ***Rooms** 52. Garden, indoor swimming pool, jogging trail, mountain bikes, sauna, solarium, spa bath, beauty salon, tennis, fishing, games room. Amex, MasterCard,* **VISA**

OVER STRATTON — Royal Oak

Tel 01460 240906 Map 13 F2
Over Stratton South Petherton Somerset TA13 5LQ

This row of three 400-year-old thatched cottages merges with its neighbours in the main street of the village and, but for the pub sign, it would be easy to miss altogether; at the South Petherton roundabout (A303) take the old Ilminster town-centre road. Cottage atmosphere is still the secret of an interior with a real sense of style. Original features like old beams, hamstone and flag floors (as well as a couple of stone pillars that look to have been there for ever but were actually salvaged from the cellars of a nearby house a few of years ago) blend successfully with dark rag-rolled walls, scrubbed wooden tables, a polished granite bar counter and extensive displays of dried flowers, hops and strings of garlic. In the safe rear garden there are swings, a junior assault course and trampolines to keep the kids amused. *Open 11-3, 6-11 (11-11 Mon-Sat in Aug), Sun 12-3, 7-10.30. **Beer** Hall & Woodhouse Tanglefoot, Badger Best & Stratton Ale (brewed for pub). Garden, children's play area. MasterCard,* **VISA**

OXFORD — Browns

Tel 01865 511995 **Fax 01865 52347** Map 15 D2
5 Woodstock Road Oxford Oxfordshire OX2 6HA

Part of the expanding Browns chain (see London, Brighton, Bristol and Cambridge), this light, airy restaurant and bar is equally popular with town and gown. Bumper hot sandwiches remain a favourite sustaining snack (BLT £5.45, vegetarian club £5.95), along with hamburgers (from £6.45), salads – hot chicken with mixed leaves £8.25 – and spaghetti (choices of four sauces, includes garlic bread and a mixed salad). Steak, mushroom and Guinness pie (£7.55), steaks and fish specials for serious main courses, lemon Bakewell tart and rich, dark chocolate cake among the tempting puddings. Traditional English breakfast (11-12 Mon-Sat), equally traditional cucumber sandwiches at tea time, roast Sunday lunch (£8.95). Fifteen high-chairs; children's menu available all day or smaller portions. Baby-changing room with shelf, changing mat, baby wipes and chair provided. Joint winner of our Family Restaurant of the Year award for 1994. Park at Pay & Display in St Giles. ***Seats** 230. **Open** 11am-11.30pm (Sun and Bank Holidays from noon). **Closed** 24 & 25 Dec. MasterCard,* **VISA**

OXFORD — Gourmet Pizza Company

JaB

Tel & Fax 01865 793146 Map 15 D2
100-101 Gloucester Green Oxford Oxfordshire OX1 2DF

An offshoot of the popular and successful pizza group based in London. See London entry for further details. Three high-chairs; children's menu comes with crayons to colour it in. Baby-changing in disabled toilet, complete with emergency supplies. ***Seats** 85 (+ 40 outside). **Open** 12-10.45. **Closed** 25, 26 Dec & 1 Jan. Amex, Mastercard,* **VISA**

OXFORD Greek Taverna

Tel 01865 511472 Map 15 D2 JaB
272 Banbury Road Summertown Oxford Oxfordshire OX2 7DY

A fairly standard menu, prepared with above-average care, is offered in this Greek-Cypriot restaurant in the Summertown shopping parade. Bean soup (£2.65), charcoal-grilled goat's milk cheese and butter beans baked in tomato and herbs (£2.95) are interesting starters, backed up by the more conventional taramasalata and houmus (both £2.95). Lamb kebabs (£7.95), moussaka (£6.95) and keftedhes – meatballs baked in tomato and herb sauce – are popular main courses. A meze sampling menu is offered from £13.95 per person (for a minimum of two). You can also choose anything from the menu, even at night, with no minimum charge. Booking is advisable at weekends. ***Seats*** *60.* ***Open*** *12-2 & 6.30-10 (Fri & Sat till 10.30).* ***Closed*** *L Mon, all Sun. Amex, Diners, MasterCard,* ***VISA***

OXFORD Le Petit Blanc £75

Tel 01865 510999 **Fax 01865 510700** Map 15 D2 R
71 Walton Street Oxford Oxfordshire OX2 6AG

Located in a quiet residential area of north-west Oxford, Raymond Blanc's second venture outside his magnificent *Le Manoir aux Quat' Saisons* at Great Milton has proved an instant success, with booking well in advance already required. The spacious, brightly-decorated two-room restaurant has a bar at the front end and an open-plan interior alongside a small Japanese-style garden at the back. Sir Terence Conran's interior design features stylishly simple decor with creams, terracotta, deep blue and old gold creating a sunny environment for a long menu of imaginative Mediterranean dishes (to which have been added a few of Oriental inspiration). It's open throughout the day, with planning permission being sought at the time of going to press to open for breakfast from 8am. The greatest choice is at main meal times, beginning with dishes like *hors d'oeuvre façon Maman Blanc* – a platter of ten extremely simple and rather basic vegetarian snippets – half an egg mayonnaise on finely-shredded carrot surrounded by cucumber and dill, sautéed button mushrooms, new potatoes, French beans, lettuce and tomato, and beetroot. A risotto millefeuille with morel jus and wafers of crusty parmesan proved more interesting - the creamy risotto layered between quite strong-tasting, crisp tuiles. Among a selection of spit-roasted meats is free-range corn-fed guinea fowl, jointed and served on a bed of lightly-roasted root vegetables with a touch of lime and a ginger sauce. Other dishes include fresh pasta, Oxford sausage with parsleyed mash and a Madeira and sweet onion sauce, confit of duck with olives, tomato and fennel, and grilled calf's liver with pecan nuts and concentrated veal jus. Desserts range from a very rich feuillantine of Valrhona chocolate with hazelnut sauce and vanilla ice cream to a beautifully-risen hot caramel soufflé. The three-course lunchtime *menu du jour* offers just alternative dishes for each course but is good value. 'Children of any age are not just accepted, they are welcome and we have created a special menu for them.' Every wine on the short list of three dozen or so bottles has helpful tasting notes. Disabled toilet. ***Seats*** *120. Parties 6. Private Room 16. L 12-3.30 D 6.30-11. Closed 25 Dec. Set L £14. Amex, Diners, MasterCard,* ***VISA***

OXFORD St Aldate's Coffee House

Tel 01865 245952 Map 15 D2 JaB
St Aldate's Oxford Oxfordshire OX1 1BP

There are seats for 72 in this self-service coffee house opposite Christ Church, plus outside seating on the patio or on the grass in front of St Aldate's Church. Home baking includes rock cakes (75p), flapjacks (85p), chocolate fudge cake (£1.15) and carrot cake (£1.40). Savoury items span sandwiches, jacket potatoes, quiches, salads and hot lunch dishes such as chicken à la king, shepherd's pie (both £4) and vegetable stir-fry (£3.50). Cream tea £2.95. No smoking. ***Seats*** *72 (+30 outside).* ***Open*** *9.30-5.* ***Closed*** *Sun. No credit cards.*

PADSTOW — Old Custom House

Tel 01841 532359 **Fax 01841 533372**
South Quay Padstow Cornwall PL28 8ED

Proudly set on the quayside with picturesque views across the b… its colourful boats and beyond over the Camel estuary, the Old … life as the Customs and Excise building in the 1800s. St Austell B… the inn, creating spacious, well-decorated and neatly furnished pu… display a good collection of prints. A light and airy conservatory (… at the front of the building has a quarry-tiled floor and cushioned … – a popular spot from which to watch harbour life. Of the 27 well-equipped, en suite bedrooms, over half enjoy harbour and estuary views and all are modern in style with fresh, co-ordinating fabrics and wallpapers. The honeymoon suite has an elegant four-poster, a double shower and a large, deep jacuzzi set in the floor. Telephone, beverage-making facility and satellite TV are standard throughout. New residents' lounge. *Open 11-11 (Sun 12-3, 7-10.30, 12-10.30 summer). Cream teas 3-5 in summer.* ***Beer*** *St Austell XXXX Mild, Tinners Ale.* ***Accommodation*** *27 bedrooms, all en suite, £90-£97 (single £67-£74). Children welcome overnight (under-3s stay free in parents room, 3-12s half-price), additional bed & cot available. Amex, Diners, MasterCard,* ***VISA***

PAIGNTON — Redcliffe Hotel — 62% — £96

Tel 01803 526397 **Fax 01803 528030** Map 13 D3 **H**
Marine Drive Paignton Devon TQ3 2NL

A round tower is the central feature of this distinctive turn-of-the-century hotel on Paignton seafront, dividing Paignton and Preston beaches, with views over Tor Bay. Day rooms enjoy the view, as do some of the bedrooms, which include seven low-ceilinged rooms of character in the tower; interconnecting/family rooms are also available. Conference/banqueting for 160/210. A private tunnel leading to the beach is of particular appeal to children (direct access in summer only). The leisure complex features a 10m pool and a jacuzzi for up to 12 people. No dogs. 24hr room service. ***Rooms*** *60. Garden, putting, indoor & outdoor swimming pools, mini-gym, sauna, steam room, spa bath, solarium, hair salon (not Mon), games room, playroom (summer only) & play area. Amex, MasterCard,* ***VISA***

PAINSWICK — St Michael's Restaurant and Guest House

Tel 01452 812998 Map 14 B2 **JaB**
Victoria Street Painswick Gloucestershire GL6 6QA

Opposite the village church, which boasts no less than 137 clipped yew trees in the churchyard, St Michael's Restaurant and Guest House (there are four well-kept bedrooms) offers good home baking – chocolate cake (£1.50), fruit cake, scones – plus snacks on toast and sandwiches, either side of a varied lunch menu. This proposes some half a dozen main dishes – lasagne al forno, beef chasseur, vegetarian crumble, tagliatelle and curry – at prices from £5.25 to £6.95. One high-chair; children are welcome and can share meals or have smaller portions. An ideal setting for high-tea. There's a pleasant walled garden for summer eating. A traditional roast is served on Sundays (£11.90 for 3 courses). ***Seats*** *36 (+ 12 outside).* ***Open*** *10-5.* ***Closed*** *Mon (except Bank Holidays) & 24-26 Dec. No credit cards.*

PELYNT — Jubilee Inn

Tel 01503 220312 **Fax 01503 220920** Map 12 C3 **P**
Pelynt Looe Cornwall Pl3 2JZ

Originally called the Axe Inn, this attractive, pink-washed, 16th-century inn patriotically changed its name in 1887 to celebrate the first fifty years of Queen Victoria's reign. Ornate crowns top the front pillars and various prints and portraits of the Queen and pieces of Victorian china decorate the characterful lounge bar. Also furnishing the smart public areas are a delightful collection of antique tables and chairs which front the fine fireplace with its gleaming copper hood. There is also a simple, flagstone-floored public bar. Ten good-sized bedrooms vary greatly in style and quality of furniture. All are individually furnished (and recently redecorated), some pleasantly

…riod-style with good antiques – one with a four-poster, another with …nd matching chest of drawers – while others are simply furnished in …style. All have en suite facilities (nine with shower-trays), and telephone, TV, …/alarm and beverage-making facilities are standard. A homely lounge is available …r residents' use. Outdoor imbibing can be appreciated on the rear patio and in the extensive garden with an adjacent terrace and barbecue area. *Open 11-3, 6-11 (Sat 11-11, Sun 12-10.30). Free House.* ***Beer*** *Bass, St Austell Trelawney's Pride. Garden, children's play area.* ***Accommodation*** *9 bedrooms, all en suite, £56-£65 (single £33). Children welcome overnight (under-3s stay free in parents' room, 4-13 half-price), additional bed & cot available. MasterCard,* ***VISA***

PENISTONE Cubley Hall

Tel 01226 766086 **Fax 01226 766361** Map 6 C2 **P**
Mortimer Road Penistone Barnsley S30 6AW

The interior of this unusual conversion from Edwardian country house to what is almost a 'stately pub' is resplendent with oak panelling, mosaic floors and ornate ceilings. It echoes a bit when empty but hums along busily when full and, with sizeable parties accommodated in the conservatory, there can be a scrum for tables to eat at. Food ranges from ploughman's platters, baguettes and hot-filled pittas (Danish smoked bacon) through to the steak and grill meals, but the daily specials enhance the choice: beef and vegetable pie, fresh jumbo cod and chips, home-made pasta with seafood, chargrilled leg of lamb steak with Provençal vegetables and a choice of fresh fish dishes are better indicators of a capable kitchen which also produces more imaginative fare for the adjacent restaurant and carvery. The well-tended gardens and grounds with play areas (even with the occasional bouncy castle) and drinking patios are a major draw for families through the summer. No smoking in the 'Green Room'. Recent refurbishment and the addition of a rear extension has created twelve en suite bedrooms, seven in the elegant main house (not inspected), and a new conservatory leading out to the extensive gardens. *Open 11-11 (Sun 12-10.30).* ***Bar Food*** *12-10 (till 9 Sun). Free House.* ***Beer*** *Tetley Bitter & Imperial, guest beers. Large garden and patio, outdoor eating, children's play area. Family room. Amex, Diners, MasterCard,* ***VISA***

PENRITH North Lakes Hotel 71% £114

Tel 01768 868111 **Fax 01768 868291** Map 4 C3 **H**
Ullswater Road Penrith Cumbria CA11 8QT

Smart modern hotel, by J40 of the M6, comfortably dividing its function between mid-week conferences and a weekend base for Lakeland visitors. Facilities for both categories are purpose-built around a central lodge of local stone with massive railway-sleeper beams, which houses bar, lounges and coffee shop. Executive-style bedrooms include a separate study and relaxation area while interconnecting syndicate rooms convert handily to family use at holiday times. Two rooms have wheelchair access. Children up to 14 free in parents' room. 24hr room service. Conference facilities for up to 300 and a staffed business centre. Plenty of activities for children at weekends and during school holidays. Shire Inns. ***Rooms*** *84. Terrace, indoor swimming pool & splash pool, gym, sauna, spa bath, sun beds, squash, gamesroom, play room. Amex, Diners, MasterCard,* ***VISA***

PENSHURST Fir Tree House Tea Rooms

Tel 01892 870382 Map 11 B5 **JaB**
Penshurst nr Tonbridge Kent TN11 8DB

Mrs Fuller-Rowell's tea room with a delightful garden is still a firm favourite with both families and those after traditional afternoon teas. Freshly made coffee and loose-leaf teas accompany scones with cream and jam, two slices from a selection of home-made cakes or the full works (scones, cream, jam, sandwiches, cake). Soup and freshly baked rolls. Families welcome throughout and the cottage garden has a swing. One high-chair; children's books to read. No smoking. ***Seats*** *45 (+ 25 outside).* ***Open*** *1.30-5.45 (Sat & Sun till 6), Jan-Mar 1.30-5.30 Sat & Sun only.* ***Closed*** *Mon, all Nov & Dec. No credit cards.*

Perranuthnoe Victoria Inn

Tel 01736 710309 Map 12 A4 P

Perranuthnoe Penzance Cornwall TR20 9NP

New enthusiastic landlords have taken over this pretty pink-washed village inn, originally built to accommodate the masons who extended the church in the 12th century, and officially described as a safe house for the clergy. With the sea and a safe beach just down the road the comfortable, typically Cornish stone-walled bar, adorned with various seafaring and fishing memorabilia, and the sheltered sun-trap rear terrace fill up early with visitors. A warm welcome is offered to families, who make use of the spacious games room. The two homely en suite bedrooms (recommended last year as a convenient stopover for walkers and for those catching the early morning ferry from Penzance to the Scilly Isles) are due to be upgraded in the coming year. *Open 11.30-3, 6.30-11 (Sun 12-3, 7-10.30).* ***Beer*** *Ushers. Garden. MasterCard,* ***VISA***

Peterborough Butterfly Hotel 63% £74

Tel 01733 64240 **Fax 01733 65538** Map 7 E4 H

Thorpe Meadows Longthorpe Parkway Peterborough Cambridgeshire

One of a small chain of modern, low-rise brick-built East Anglian hotels. Peterborough's Butterfly sits at the water's edge, overlooking Thorpe Meadows rowing lake. Neat, practical accommodation ranges from studio singles to suites with separate seating areas. Free parking for 80 cars. ***Rooms*** *70. Amex, Diners, MasterCard,* ***VISA***

Many hotels offer reduced rates for weekend or out-of-season bookings. Always ask about special deals and family rooms.

Petersfield Flora Twort Gallery & Restaurant

Tel 01730 260756 Map 15 D3 JaB

Church Path 21 The Square Petersfield Hampshire

Beneath the first-floor museum (which is devoted to the life and work of the local water colourist after whom it is named) this charming cottage tea room/restaurant offers excellent home-made fare. Throughout the day there are open sandwiches (tuna mayonnaise and tomato £3.75), salads (smoked salmon and prawn £5.80), and light snacks and lunches: home-made soup with crusty bread (£2.75), cottage rarebit (with mustard and wine £3.75) and pizza bread – French bread split and served with a pizza topping (£3.95). At teatime there are cakes (75p-£1.75), scones, teacakes and crumpets, and a cottage tea at £3.15. Lunchtime also offers a range of interesting specials, maybe breast of turkey and asparagus millefeuille, roast leg of lamb with honey glaze and a redcurrant and port sauce or perhaps home-baked gammon with sugar-glazed apricots and Madeira sauce – all priced at around £5 including fresh vegetables. There is always a vegetarian option. A more formal dinner menu on Friday and Saturday nights is very popular, offering three courses, petits fours and coffee for £18.50. No smoking. A special note on the menu offers small portions of most items on the menu for children – just ask. Two high-chairs provided. Close to the Teddy Bear Museum; a large boating lake with children's play area is a short drive away. ***Seats*** *28 (+ 8 outside).* ***Open*** *9.30-4.45, also (Fri/Sat only) 7.30-9.30.* ***Closed*** *D Tue-Thu, all Sun & Mon. Diners, MasterCard,* ***VISA***

Pubs – note that food is only recommended in those pubs with ***Bar Food*** times in the statistics at the end of an entry. Restaurant food in pubs is *never* recommended unless specifically mentioned. Some pubs are recommended for B&B or Atmosphere only – each entry's statistics indicate our recommendation.

PETWORTH — Petworth House Restaurant

Tel 01798 344080 **Fax 01798 342963** Map 11 A6 **JaB**

Petworth House Petworth West Sussex GU28 0QA

After exploring the antique shops in town or touring this magnificent 17th-century country house (paintings by Turner and Grinling Gibbons' carving are among the attractions), this delightful restaurant offers the chance of a well-deserved rest as well as some good eating. Built as a sculpture gallery in 1870, the impressive, high-ceilinged room has an uncovered wooden floor, modern pine furniture, and deep orange walls hung with enormous ancestral portraits. It is a grand setting in which to tuck into a light lunch – soup (£2.25), savoury flans (prawn and asparagus, quiche lorraine – both £1.95), sandwiches (£1.75), daily vegetarian and home-made hot dishes (courgettes provençale £3.75, Hungarian goulash £4.25), ploughman's made with local Gospel Green cheese. There is also a mouthwatering display of scones and freshly-baked cakes (the latter from 95p) and a set (clotted) cream tea (£2.80). High-chairs, baby-changing room and facilities for disabled visitors are all provided. Free parking in Petworth House's own car park. If heading for the restaurant on foot from the town access is via a roadside door near the church. No smoking. ***Seats*** *120.* ***Open*** *12-5 (from 11 Jul/Aug).* ***Closed*** *Thu, Fri, also Nov-Mar. Amex, MasterCard,* ***VISA***

Any person using our name to obtain free hospitality is a fraud.
Proprietors, please inform the police and us.

PHILLEIGH — Roseland Inn

Tel 01872 580254 **Fax 01872 580951** Map 12 B3 **P**

Philleigh Cornwall TR2 5NB

17th-century cob-built Cornish treasure peacefully positioned beside the parish church in an out-of-the-way village, two miles from the King Harry Ferry that crosses the River Fal. The front terrace is delightfully floral with colourful climbing roses, while indoors there are old-fashioned seats, lovely old settles, worn slate floors, fresh flowers, low beams and a welcoming fire. Spotlessly kept and run with enthusiastic panache by Graham and Jacqui Hill, the Roseland is a popular rural destination for reliable pub food. The menu and blackboard specials cover a range from decent sandwiches and ploughman's platters, salad niçoise and smoked fish platter to navarin of lamb, crab Newburg and bean and potato goulash. Evening extras may include Oriental monkfish and seafood 'extravaganza' (24hrs' notice); the fish is delivered daily from a local trawler. The garden is closed off from the road and has a rocking horse and slides for children. *Open 11.30-3, 6-11 (from 6.30 in winter), Sun 12-3, 7-10.30.* ***Bar Food*** *12-2.15, 7-9.* ***Beer*** *Marston's Pedigree, Greenalls Bitter, Bass. Garden. No credit cards.*

PINGEWOOD — Kirtons Hotel — 60% — £105

Tel 0118 950 0885 **Fax 0118 939 1996** Map 15 D2 **H**

Pingewood Reading Berkshire RG30 3UN

Unexceptional standardised bedrooms (those in the new wing are best), except that each has a balcony overlooking the a large water sports lake; one room is adapted for disabled guests. Residential conferences (facilities for up to 110) are the main business during the week but at weekends it's the extensive leisure facilities of the adjacent country club (also available to hotel guests) that are the big attraction. It is here that there are creche facilities in the mornings (reservations required) with a children's club on Saturdays. 24hr room service. Near J11 of the M4 but ask for detailed directions when booking. ***Rooms*** *81. Tennis, playground, water-skiing, jet-skiing, indoor swimming pool, gym, squash, spa bath, sauna, steam room, sun beds, beauty & hair salon, snooker. Closed Christmas. Amex, Diners, MasterCard,* ***VISA***

PLUSH Brace of Pheasants

Tel 01300 348357 Map 13 F2
Plush Dorchester Dorset DT2 7RQ

Originally two cottages and a forge, dating from the 16th century, this attractive collection of thatched, brick and flint buildings became an inn in the mid-1930s and must surely be one of the prettiest in Dorset. The location is idyllic, nestling in a peaceful rural hamlet, surrounded by rolling downland. A brace of glass-encased stuffed pheasants hangs above the main cottage door that leads into the charmingly unspoilt bar, complete with a huge inglenook (used for seating), a further log fire and an assortment of traditional furniture. The attraction here, other than its setting, is the bar food. Separate blackboards for both lunch and evening fare list the weekly-changing specials that supplement an extensive printed menu selection. Lunch features the usual ploughman's platters and salads, plus a range of lighter bites, including queen scallops and bacon salad, crab savoury and soft herring roes. Substantial home-cooked lunch dishes may include lamb and rosemary pie, smoked haddock mornay, lasagne, venison sausages and grilled lemon sole. Evening fare is more adventurous. Puddings, listed on a board, range from mango cheesecake to apple and plum crumble. There is a delightful garden with mature trees and shrubs. No under-14s in bar areas. *Open 12-2.30, 7-11 (Sun 12-3, 7-10.30).* ***Bar Food*** *12-1.45, 7-9.45 (till 9.30 Sun). Free House.* ***Beer*** *Smiles Best, Flowers Original, Fuller's London Pride. Garden, outdoor eating, children's play area. Family room. Closed 25 Dec eve. MasterCard,* ***VISA***

Any person using our name to obtain free hospitality is a fraud.
Proprietors, please inform the police and us.

PLYMOUTH Moat House 70% £119

Tel 01752 639988 **Fax 01752 673816** Map 12 C3 **H**
Armada Way Plymouth Devon PL1 2HJ

Day rooms at this high-rise hotel, in particular the Penthouse restaurant and bar, command spectacular views of the Hoe and Plymouth Sound. So do many of the good-sized, picture-windowed bedrooms, which have double beds (twins have two double beds), seating areas and plenty of writing space. International rooms (£126) are air-conditioned and have larger bathrooms. Conference and banqueting facilities for 300/350. Children under 16 are accommodated free if sharing their parents' room. Covered free parking below the building. ***Rooms*** *212. Indoor swimming pool, gym, sauna, steam room, solarium, games room. Amex, Diners, MasterCard,* ***VISA***

A jug of fresh water!

POLKERRIS Rashleigh Inn

Tel 01726 813991 Map 12 B3 
Polkerris Fowey Cornwall PL24 2TL

Literally on the beach in a tiny isolated cove and known locally as the 'Inn on the Beach', the Rashleigh is well worth seeking out for its magnificent setting. Once the old lifeboat station, until becoming a pub in 1924, it is a popular refreshment spot for coast path walkers and for families using the beach in the summer. Summer alfresco drinking is unrivalled in this area, for the table-filled terrace is a splendid place from which to watch the sun set across St Austell Bay. On cooler days the sea views can still be admired from the warmth of the main bar, especially from the bay-window seats. Parents enjoying a drink (possibly a well kept pint of St Austell Hicks Special tapped from wooden casks) on the terrace can keep an eagle eye on their children playing on the beach. No under-14s inside unless eating. *Open 11-3, 5.30-11 (Sun 12-3, 6-10.30). Free House.* ***Beer*** *St Austell HSD, Ind Coope Burton Ale, Bass, Bolsters Best, two guest beers. Terrace. MasterCard,* ***VISA***

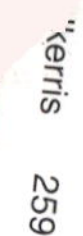

Haven Hotel 69% £165

333 **Fax 01202 708796** Map 14 C4 **HR**

lbanks Poole Dorset BH13 7QL

: Swanage ferry to find the Haven, right by the water's edge at the
rld's second largest natural harbour giving most of the bedrooms
ies) fine views either of Brownsea Island and the Purbeck Hills
it to the Isle of Wight. Comfortable rather than luxurious, with
lightwo... re and matching bedcovers and curtains, the rooms are immaculately kept, as is the whole hotel. 24hr room service. Inviting public areas include the beamed Marconi lounge (he made the first wireless telegraph broadcast from here) with leather chesterfields, and a splendid Conservatory (informal eating 10.30am-6pm) with comfortably upholstered 'garden' furniture and waterside terrace beyond. The exceptionally comprehensive Haven leisure centre includes both indoor and outdoor pools, just a few steps beyond which is the hotel's own sandy beach. There's also a fine, purpose-built business centre adjacent to the hotel catering for up to 160. Suitable for older children only: no children under 5 are allowed in the hotel (see sister *Sandbanks Hotel* below for under-5s), but 5- to 14-year-olds stay free if sharing with their parents (meals as taken). No dogs. FJB Hotels. ***Rooms** 94. Terrace, tennis, indoor & outdoor swimming pools, gym, squash, sauna, steam room, spa bath, solarium, beauty & hair salons. Amex, Diners, MasterCard,* ***VISA***

Sea View Restaurant £55

Large, 20s-style dining-room with a short but well-balanced table d'hote dinner menu supplemented by a varied grill menu. Well-thought-out dishes are reliably cooked and swiftly served – dishes like terrine of leek, salmon and sun-dried tomatoes, pan-fried calf's liver 'set upon creamed parsley potatoes, spooned over with Madeira sauce, studded with sweetbread, tomatoes and bacon' or warm pecan and bourbon steamed pudding with whisky *anglaise*. Lunch is a buffet/carvery affair, including Sunday when a traditional roast is always offered. The wine list is presented by style; for the most part, wines are not expensive; don't miss the wines of the month, fine wines, bin ends and wines by the glass at the back of the list. A dress code has evolved 'which caters for the overall benefit of all guests (and not the hotel) and if we relax the rules then we will be upsetting far more people than we will be pleasing'. No children after 7pm. Light lunches are also available in the informal conservatory and on the terrace, from where there are views of Poole Bay and Studland. ***Seats** 150. Parties 24. L 12.30-2 D 7-9.30. Set L £15 Set D £22.50.*

La Roche £80

The more intimate à la carte restaurant is where chef Karl Heinz Nagler gives full rein to his undoubted skills. The sophisticated black-edged decor is a suitable foil to equally sophisticated dishes such as a salad of tiger prawns, artichoke and smoked salmon in tarragon jelly with lobster vinaigrette, a piquant vegetable strudel with watercress and pepper sauce, poached loin of Dorset lamb topped with onion purée, set on a garlic crouton and served with a sorrel-scented lamb jus. To round off a meal there may be desserts like fluffy banana soufflé enveloped in vanilla pancakes and set with Galliano sauce or hot chocolate fondant pudding with Tia Maria-flavoured ice cream and a macedoine of fresh fruit. Same wine list as above. No children under 10. ***Seats** 26. Parties 12. D only 7.30-10. Closed Sun & 1 week Christmas.*

Poole — Sandbanks Hotel 59% £114

Tel 01202 707377 **Fax 01202 708885** Map 14 C4 **H**

15 Banks Road Sandbanks Poole Dorset BH13 7PS

Sandbanks occupies a unique position on a wonderful European Blue Flag sandy beach - ideal for a family beach holiday. The attractive patio and garden lead straight on to the beach, and holiday services include organised activities (10am-9.30pm during school holidays), a children's restaurant and a nursery. Four tiers of balconied bedrooms look either out to sea or across Poole Bay and the open-plan bar/ballroom, vast sun lounge and dining-rooms also enjoy panoramic views over the sea. There are

29 interconnecting family suites and twins/doubles with bunk beds. 24hr room service. Adult guests may use the leisure facilities at the *Haven Hotel* (see entry). Bicycle and catamaran hire adjacent to the hotel. A purpose-built wing houses five main meeting rooms holding up to 120. No dogs. FJB Hotels. ***Rooms** 105. Terrace, putting green, tennis, indoor swimming pool, gym, sauna, steam room, spa bath, solarium, creche (daily 1-2pm in summer), children's indoor play area & outdoor playground, games room, coffee shop (10am-6pm). Amex, Diners, MasterCard,* **VISA**

PORTH Trevelgue Hotel 62% £116*

Tel 01637 872864 **Fax 01637 876365** Map 12 B3 H

Porth nr Newquay Cornwall TR7 3LX

The Trevelgue commands a prime headland position (just a short walk up quite an incline from Newquay's beaches) with the rolling downs of north Cornwall behind and a 180° sea vista to the front. Its rather austere, block-like facade belies the genuine welcome and efficiently run hotel within. Self-styled as a 'parents' haven', 'children's paradise' and now 'the UK's first family health and holiday club', aiming fairly and squarely at the family market, its long-term success has been achieved by providing almost everything that families with young children really need in order to have a peaceful stay away from the comforts of home. Some hotels are described as a 'home-from-home' because they are, quite simply, homely, but there is so much more here to satisfy not only the requirements of demanding children – from babes in arms to energetic teenagers – but also parents who need a break from the incessant routine that is inherent in bringing up children. You can hire a toddler's tricycle or take the whole family on a bike ride along the Camel Trail on six miles of disused railway line; you can purchase a youngster's daily pint of milk over the counter in the tea room (and keep it fresh in your bedroom fridge) or indulge yourself at dinner with a bottle from the ungreedily priced wine list; you can even have a full top-to-toe beauty treatment while the children are looked after in carefully arranged groups. You name it, they've generally thought of it, and they bring it off with panache; particularly impressive are the arrangements for children's high tea and for parents to enjoy their modest evening meal ('homely' food is the best description; no children under 7 in the dining-room during dinner): the very young are looked after in the fully supervised Teddy Bears Club for a quiet time before bed, while older children (3-7s) can expend their final energies in an indoor playroom and 'dirty' room; constantly monitored baby-listening is provided to help release bedtime tension. The list of activities is too long to describe in detail, but there is sufficient to keep everybody happy in both good and bad weather; cots, high-chairs, bunk beds, bikes, buggies, back packs, baby walkers, baby baths, sterilisers, bottle warmers and bouncy chairs can all be booked in advance. A Hobby Club for older children offers a range of activities for kids' cookery, T-shirt printing. Surprisingly, although the Trevelgue attracts a predominance of young families, the hotel is spacious enough never to feel like a nursery and the management is clever enough to make the adult attractions as inviting as those for their junior guests. Children's teas (for the under-7s) and light lunches are served in the diner-style piazza bar. Indeed, the fitness, health and beauty treatment facilities are now a real attraction and health packages are offered in early and late season; aerobics and exercise classes are held in the gym. A very large, sandy beach is just down the hill. Lastly, and by no means least, the tariff is incredibly reasonable for all the activities provided and accommodation in the identical family suites is unusually spacious. Free child under 7 offer during certain periods; super saver weeks at beginning and end of season offer free accommodation for two youngest children. Half-board terms only – ring for special weekly rates; shorter (even better value) breaks out of season; children are charged on a sliding scale according to age – under-1s 15%, 1-2s 25%, 3-6s 50%, 7-14s 65% of adult rate. Weekly bookings commence on Thursdays, Saturdays or Sundays. No dogs or pets. Winner of our 1994 Family Hotel of the Year Award. Sister hotel to *Bedruthan Steps* in Mawgan Porth (see entry). ***Rooms** 42 family suites, 28 rooms. Garden, tennis & organised sports in high season (football, rounders, volleyball), squash, golf practice net & two practice holes, mini-golf, croquet & boules, skittles, air rifle range, adventure playgrounds, sandpit, Wendy houses, outdoor, indoor & children's splash swimming pools, health and beauty salons, gym, sauna, sun bed, sauna, mother & baby room, table football, pool table, table tennis, BMX track. Hotel open from mid Feb to end Oct (booking office open all year). MasterCard,* **VISA**

POWERSTOCK Three Horseshoes Inn

Tel 01308 485328 **Fax 01308 485577** Map 13 F2 
Powerstock Bridport Dorset DT6 3TF

'The Shoes' (as it is affectionately known locally) is a Victorian stone inn set in a sleepy village amid narrow, winding lanes and best reached from the A3066 north of Bridport. Rebuilt in 1906 after a devastating fire, but solidly old-fashioned in style with simple country furnishings in both the bustling bar and in the two pine-panelled dining-rooms. People come from miles around to this reliable old favourite for the chef/licensee Pat Ferguson's food; it's not cheap, certainly, but it is fresh and delicious, specialising in fish from local boats, Dorset lamb and seasonal game. The extensive, daily-changing blackboard list of home-cooked dishes serves both bar and restaurant. Begin, perhaps, with terrine of pork and game with chutney, cheese soufflé, mussels steamed in white wine onion and garlic, and grilled sardines with garlic butter; fish fanciers can then continue with monkfish provençale, local lobster, sea bass served on a bed of spinach with garlic sauce or fresh local crabs steamed with ginger, garlic and chili. Meat and game dishes like garlic-studded roast rack of Dorset lamb with rosemary-scented jus and marinated duck breast are all served with well-cooked vegetables. Lighter bites include interesting fresh pasta dishes, salads and freshly-baked baguettes. Traditional puddings include rhubarb crumble and fresh fruit parfait. Must book for busy Sunday lunches (£12.50). Good Palmers ales and a choice of twenty wines by the glass. Delightful terraced garden and rear patio with village and valley views for summer eating. Four simple, centrally-heated bedrooms with traditional older-style furniture, TV and tea-maker provide homely overnight accommodation. Two are spacious and comfortable with clean, en suite bathrooms, the others are rather too compact and share a bathroom. *Open 11-3, 6-11 (Sun 12-3, 7-10.30).* ***Bar Food*** *12-2, 7-10 (till 9 Sun).* ***Beer*** *Palmers BB & IPA. Garden, patio, outdoor eating, children's play area.* ***Accommodation*** *4 bedrooms, 2 en suite, £60 (single £40). Children welcome overnight, additional bed & cot available. Check-in by arrangement. Amex, MasterCard,* ***VISA***

REETH Buck Hotel

Tel 01748 884210 **Fax 01748 884802** Map 5 D3 
Reeth Richmond North Yorkshire DL11 6SW

An imposing building standing at the head of this prettiest of Dales villages; the fascinating Swaledale Folk Museum is a short walk away across the green. The Buck scores highly with families for its separate games room, safe back garden, children's menus and choices of family accommodation. All ten bedrooms have TVs, tea trays and en suite facilities (two with shower only); the best have fabulous views of the surrounding hills. Afternoon teas. *Open 11-2, 6-11 (till 1am Fri, 11am-1am Sat except 11-3, 6-11 in winter), Sun 12-2, 7-10.30.* ***Beer*** *Theakston Best & XB, John Smith's, Black Sheep Bitter. Garden. Family room.* ***Accommodation*** *10 bedrooms, all en suite £49 (family room £55-£60, single £25). Children welcome overnight (under-12s stay free in parents' room), additional bed & cot available. MasterCard,* ***VISA***

REPTON Brook Farm Tea Rooms

Tel 01283 702215 Map 6 C3 
Brook End Repton Derbyshire DE65 6FW

Brook Farm is a working dairy and arable farm and the tea rooms are housed in an old sandstone-and-brick barn beside a trout brook. There's a large, lawned and walled garden with bench seating for summer eating and the tea rooms have their own parking. A blackboard advertises the lunchtime dishes: simple starters of home-made soup (£1.50), fruit juices and melon are followed by the likes of chicken, ham and mushroom pie, courgette and mushroom lasagne or casserole of pork with orange and mushrooms; these are all priced at £4.25 to include vegetables and bread and butter. Desserts (all £1.65) might include sticky toffee pudding, bread-and-butter pudding and apple cobbler. Light refreshments are also available in abundance, from hot buttered toast, crumpets and scones to sandwiches and splendid home baking; the list (each slice 85p) might include coffee and walnut cake, nutty banana loaf, Victoria sandwich and Bakewell tart. A children's menu (£1.40) offers either baked beans or spaghetti on toast. The Brook Farm cream tea is £2.60. Large lawned, walled garden with slide, swing and swingboat. Two high-chairs provided and there's a changing mat and trainer seat in Ladies. After tea, take a stroll by the brook or explore Repton, whose history goes back to 653 A.D. No smoking inside. Unlicensed – BYO, no corkage. ***Seats** 50. **Open** 10.15-5. **Closed** Christmas-New Year. No credit cards.*

RICHMOND — The Refectory

Tel 0181-940 6264 Map 15 E2 JaB

6 Church Walk Richmond-upon-Thames TW9 1SN

Martin and Harriet Steel's pleasantly informal, cottagey restaurant and coffee shop is conveniently located just off the High Street by the church. When the sun shines the pretty little paved courtyard comes into its own, but more often than not you will opt to sit inside at the mellow pine tables. The food is served speedily, but is certainly not 'fast food': traditional British dishes like cottage, steak & kidney or fish pie (around £4.85) are accompanied by generous helpings of vegetables (£1.50, choice of four) that may be shared; a vegetarian option is always offered (leek, broccoli and courgette bake, say, or vegetable casserole £4.60). Steamed puddings (£2.85) and Loseley ice creams (£1.95) to finish, if you can find room. Normal menu (no roast) on Sundays. Booking advised. No smoking at lunchtime. Half portions, high-chairs, a booster seat and a changing area provided for children – no bells, no whistles, just a sensible place to eat en famille. ***Seats** 44. **Open** from 10am for coffee, lunch 12-2, teas 2-5 (not Sun). **Closed** Mon & Christmas. MasterCard,* **VISA**

RICHMOND — Richmond Harvest

Tel 0181-940 1138 Map 15 E2 JaB

5 The Square Richmond-upon-Thames

In the centre of town, this basement vegetarian restaurant offers a menu of international provenance, and many of the dishes are suitable for vegans. Starters, served with home-baked brown bread, could include houmus (£1.95), tamari mushrooms (£2.75) and red bean and basil paté (£1.95). Typical main courses are Greek butter bean casserole (£4.95), spicy Mexican pancakes (£5.95) and sweet and sour mixed vegetables (£4.95). Filled jacket potatoes (£3.50) and plenty of salads (from £1.50) are also available, with fresh fruit salad (£1.95) and a chocolate pudding with bananas (£2.25) to finish. A 10% service charge is added to bills after 5pm, on Sundays and Bank Holidays. ***Seats** 38. **Open** 11.30-11 (Sun 1-10). Amex, MasterCard,* **VISA**

> Always ring ahead and inform establishments of your exact requirements when travelling with children. Unannounced can, sadly, still mean unwelcome.

RICKLING GREEN — Cricketers Arms

Tel 01799 543210 **Fax 01799 543512** Map 10 B3 P

Rickling Green Saffron Walden Essex CB11 3YE

Victorian redbrick-built pub enjoying a peaceful position overlooking the village green and cricket pitch. Inside there is a homely bar and lounge, a comfortable dining-room and a small and cosy side room which has access to the delightful front terrace – a popular spot in which to relax and watch an innings or two. People needing an overnight stop close to Stansted airport (ten minutes' drive away) will find the five comfortable bedrooms, housed in a modern rear extension, most convenient and acceptable. All are uniformly equipped with reproduction darkwood furniture, decent fabrics and have clean, tiled en suite shower rooms. Added comforts include TVs, radio alarms, telephones, trouser presses, hairdryers and tea-makers. Two family rooms with additional beds. *Open 12-3, 6-11 (Sun 12-3, 7-10.30). Free House. **Beer** Flowers IPA, guest beers. Patio. Family room. **Accommodation** 7 bedrooms, all en suite, from £60 (single £50), family room £70 (sleeps 3-5). Children welcome overnight (1st child under 16 free in parents' room, each additional child £5), additional bed & cot available. Amex, Diners, MasterCard,* **VISA**

RIPLEY Boar's Head Hotel 66% £95

Tel 01423 771888 **Fax 01423 771509** Map 6 C1 **HR**
Ripley nr Harrogate North Yorkshire H93 3AY

Dating back to 1830 when the Lord of the Manor rebuilt the village next to Ripley Castle (open to the public during the summer, complimentary access to hotel guests), this former coaching inn is now a fairly up-market hotel. Oil paintings and furniture from the castle help to create the country house feel in tranquil drawing and morning rooms and the individually decorated bedrooms, which favour plain walls and stylish matching fabrics. Antique furniture features in rooms in the main building and in the larger rooms in another house across the cobbled square, while rooms in the former stable block are furnished with white-painted wicker pieces. Nice touches include porcelain ornaments and wooden toy catamarans in bathrooms that boast large soft towels and quality toiletries. 24hr room service. ***Rooms** 25. Garden, tennis, coarse fishing. Amex, Diners, MasterCard,* **VISA**

Restaurant £70

New chef Steven Chesnutt is continuing the modern English style on short, well-chosen menus. A typical set-price £30 dinner menu might offer wild mushroom ravioli and deep-fried leeks with mild mustard sauce, Stilton-glazed medallions of monkfish with black truffle vinaigrette or pressed game and redcurrant terrine with spiced figs and mixed leaves to start, followed by stuffed breast of guinea fowl on a casserole of chicken livers and bacon with honey-roasted vegetables, pan-fried loin of lamb with a Mediterranean tarte tatin and red wine sauce, or roasted tournedos of salmon with spinach, baby onions and dried tomatoes. Baked chocolate bread-and-butter pudding with cappuccino cream sauce, hot caramel soufflé with citrus sorbet or mascarpone and passion fruit syllabub with coconut shortbread may lead the tastebuds into temptation. A five-course *menu gourmand* is also offered. Informal eating and real ales in the pubby Boris Bar & Bistro. The extensive wine list is well chosen, with fair prices, a good choice of half bottles and helpful tasting notes. No children under 10 after 8pm. Disabled toilet facilities. ***Seats** 38. Parties 14. L 12-2 D 7-9.30. Set L £13.50/£17.50 (Sun £14.95) Set D £25, £30 & £35.*

ROCHESTER Bridgewood Manor Hotel 68% £110

Tel 01634 201333 **Fax 01634 201330** Map 11 B5 
Bridgewood Roundabout Maidstone Road Rochester Kent ME5 9AX

Halfway between Dover and London, virtually beside J3 of the M2, this modern brick-built hotel offers up-to-date meeting and conference facilities (for up to 200) and service that is both friendly and helpful. Public areas, including a spacious reception lounge and bar, have an ecclesiastical decorative inspiration. Bedrooms have all the expected features, remote TV, trouser presses and compact, clean, functional bathrooms. 24hr room service. Children up to 16 stay free in their parents' room; an unsupervised playroom is provided at weekends (when there are significant tariff reductions, Fri-Sun). A central courtyard area provides a sheltered alfresco area in the summer months. There's a wide range of facilities in the self-contained leisure club. Small dogs only. Marston Hotels. ***Rooms** 100. Terrace, tennis, pitch & putt, indoor swimming pool, gym, sauna, steam room, spa bath, sun beds, hair & beauty salon, children's playground, snooker. Amex, Diners, MasterCard,* **VISA**

ROMSEY Cobweb Tea Room

Tel 01794 516434 Map 14 C3 **JaB**
49 The Hundred Romsey Hampshire SO51 8GE

This homely tea room with beams and green tablecloths is where Angela Webley dispenses her delicious light lunches and afternoon teas. Temptingly-displayed baking includes old-style madeleines, rum truffles and apricot Bakewell tart, plus various sponge gateaux and other cakes and cookies. Light lunches might offer toasted sandwiches (from £1.80), sausage rolls (£1), country platters of Cheddar, Stilton or paté (£3.20) and hot specials such as chicken curry, lamb and leek casserole or turkey and ham salad. Main courses are all priced at £4, and also include daily quiches and a vegetarian option. Hot dishes are served with either vegetables or salad. Cream teas (£3), winter tea with two boiled eggs. Three high-chairs and a shelf in Ladies for baby-changing. Small toy box provided for young children, also puzzles and books. Children's portions. No smoking. ***Seats*** *34 (+ 12 outside).* ***Open*** *10-5.30.* ***Closed*** *Sun, Mon, 1 week Christmas & 2 weeks end Sep/early Oct. No credit cards.*

Rookley — Chequers Inn

Tel 01983 840314 Map 15 D4 

Niton Road Rookley Isle of Wight PO38 3NZ

Sue and Richard Holmes are the houseproud owners of this family-friendly pub just a mile off the A3020 at Rookley (take the road signed to Niton). Nestling in a shallow dell looking out over the rolling downlands, the pub makes a feature of its garden with lots of picnic tables from which parents can watch over their little ones enjoying the playhouse, toboggan run and bouncy castle; pony rides, too, in fine weather. Just outside the family room there's a ball pool and soft-shape gym, while inside are high-chairs, bibs and colouring sets in abundance, a purpose-built Lego table and, close by, a well-kept nappy-changing facility. Children's menus are a little more varied than most, with potato skins or prawn cocktail followed by 4oz steak with mushrooms and tomato for youngsters and loads of things such as bacon, onions, more mushrooms and hot chili sauce to pile on top of their burgers. There are voluminous bar snacks, grills, fish specials and à la carte main courses to keep the adults amused; beef stroganoff, casseroled game pie and salmon with puff pastry arrive with plentiful fresh vegetables. Those not travelling en famille need not despair as they have use of a youngster-free lounge bar in which to enjoy the views in relative peace, with one of five real ales to accompany their meal, or a choice from a modestly-priced wine list. ***Open*** *11-11 (Sun 12-10.30).* ***Bar Food*** *12-10 (till 9.30 Sun). Free House.* ***Beer*** *John Smith's Bitter, Courage Best & Directors, Fuller's London Pride, Morland Old Speckled Hen. Garden, outdoor eating, children's play areas. Family room. MasterCard,* ***VISA***

Ross-on-Wye — Fresh Grounds

Tel 01989 768289 Map 14 B1 JaB

Raglan House 17 Broad Street Ross-on-Wye Hereford & Worcester

A Queen Anne town house is home to Norma Snook's refined coffee shop-cum-restaurant. There's plenty for snackers throughout the day, including filled jacket potatoes (from £2.40), open sandwiches and various salads. Lunchtime brings the widest choice, with favourites like omelettes, lasagne, steak and kidney pie, Spanish chicken and the day's roast. Scrumptious home-made cakes could include coffee and walnut, banana and fudge or coffee and pecan nut pie. There are also things like freshly-baked croissants and cinnamon toast, plus a full English breakfast served until 11. One high-chair; children's portions on request. No special facilities, but a private room can be made available for nursing mothers; babies' bottles and food will be warmed on request. ***Seats*** *40.* ***Open*** *9-5.30 (Sat till 6).* ***Closed*** *Sun (but open for L before Bank Holidays). No credit cards.*

Ross-on-Wye — Meader's

Tel 01989 562803 Map 14 B1 JaB

1 Copse Cross Street Ross-on-Wye Hereford & Worcester

Meader's offers a menu of Hungarian, Continental and vegetarian dishes with counter service at lunchtime, waiter service in the evening. Lunchtime offers the better value: cream of vegetable soup (£2), home-made paté with toast (£2) and deep-fried mushrooms (£2.50) are typical starters; various goulashes (£5.50), beef stroganoff (£7.50) and mushroom and aubergine lasagne (£4) for main courses. Filled jacket potatoes (from £2.95) make ideal snacks, with the day's fillings listed on a board. Finish with apple strudel, chocolate mousse or lemon cheesecake (all £1.80). The evening menu is more ambitious: starters are all £3, vegetarian and Hungarian main courses £7.50 and flambé dishes £9.50. At both lunch and dinner there is a salad bar offering an alternative to vegetables. Children's menu £3.50. Smoking only in the coffee area at night. ***Seats*** *45.* ***Open*** *10-2.30 & 7-9.30.* ***Closed*** *Sun & Mon (except D Bank Holiday Mon and Sun before), 1 week Christmas. MasterCard,* ***VISA***

ROSS-ON-WYE Pengethley Manor 67% £100

Tel 01989 730211 **Fax 01989 730238** Map 14 B1 H

Harewood End Pengethley Park nr Ross-on-Wye Hereford & Worcester HR9 6LL

Pengethley is to be found at the end of a long drive off the A49 Ross (10 minutes to the south) to Hereford (20 minutes north) road. Fifteen acres of estate with a par-3 golf course, trout lake, vineyard and landscaped gardens enhance the tranquil country setting. Banqueting for up to 75 and conference rooms accommodating 50 are kept discreetly separate. One purpose-built bedroom for disabled guests; children up to 16 stay free in parents' room with meals charged as taken. Courtyard and Manor House (£120) bedrooms are all individually styled; 'Titled' rooms (£160) are richly classical, perhaps with a four-poster, separate lounge or spa bath. ***Rooms*** *25. Garden, croquet, golf (9), pitch & putt, outdoor swimming pool, snooker, fishing. Amex, Diners, MasterCard,* ***VISA***

A jug of fresh water!

ROTHBURY Katerina's

Tel 01669 620691 Map 5 D2 JaB

High Street Rothbury Northumberland NE65 7TQ

Super little red-and-black-decorated Italian restaurant, very popular, and suitable for families. Good-sized, crisply baked pizzas include *quattro stagione* (mushrooms, ham, peppers and sweetcorn £4.25) and funny-face (for children – mostly cheese and tomato £3.80). Also on the menu are salads, pasta, omelettes, main-course chicken and steaks, fish and vegetarian dishes and a trio headed 'calorie conscious'. No smoking. ***Seats*** *24.* ***Open*** *12-2 & 6-10.* ***Closed*** *L Wed, all Mon (except Bank Holidays) & Tue. No credit cards.*

RUDGE Full Moon

Tel 01373 830936 **Fax 01373 831366** Map 14 B3 P

Rudge Frome Somerset BA11 2QF

Conveniently located two miles from the A36 at its junction with the A361 (and equally close to the Woodland Park) is the sleepy hamlet of Rudge. It has a white-painted village inn of 16th-century origins whose interior has been meticulously restored; there's a wealth of interior stonework, old fireplaces and uneven flagstone floors in a succession of intimate nooks and alcoves; the focal point is a friendly locals' bar. All manner of local history and memorabilia provides the starting point for a tall story or two. An extension which threatens to dwarf the original has its ground floor given over to a function room. Above are the five en suite bedrooms (four with shower only), purpose-built and a little cottagey in style. All are neatly equipped with TV, direct-dial phone, radio-alarm and tea- and coffee-making facility; there's one decent-sized family room. To the pub's rear the walled garden is neatly kept and has some swings; from here, as from the bedrooms, there are lovely rural views down to Broker's Wood. *Open 12-3, 6-11 (Sun 12-10.30). Free House.* ***Beer*** *Bass, Wadworth 6X, Butcombe Bitter. Garden, children's play area. Family room.* ***Accommodation*** *5 bedrooms, all en suite, £45 (family room £60, single £35). Children welcome overnight (under-5s stay free in parents' room), additional bed (£10) & cot available. Amex, MasterCard,* ***VISA***

Pubs – note that food is only recommended in those pubs with ***Bar Food*** times in the statistics at the end of an entry. Restaurant food in pubs is *never* recommended unless specifically mentioned. Some pubs are recommended for B&B or Atmosphere only – each entry's statistics indicate our recommendation.

Rugby — Summersault

Tel 01788 543223 Map 7 D4 J…
27 High Street Rugby Warwickshire CV21 3DW

Eileen and Michael Jeffs' unusual High Street emporium with an Edwardian flavour purveys a wide assortment of goods from designer-label clothes to soaps and shampoo, confectionery, teas and coffee. There's a mellow air also in the pine-furnished café (to the rear), which is Rugby's vegetarian mecca. Breakfast is served all day (Continental £2.30), and lunchtime dishes typified by leek croustade, tomato cobbler or parsnip Dijon (all £4.45) are accompanied by any three of the colourful, tasty salads that adorn the self-service counter. Pastas and pizzas are always available. Outside main meal hours there's a creditable array of sandwiches and home baking – banoffi pie, fresh fruit pavlova, pecan toffee and apple crumble to enjoy with an assortment of beverages including speciality and herb teas. No smoking. ***Seats*** *60 (+ 12 outside).* ***Open*** *9-4.30.* ***Closed*** *Sun & Bank Holidays. Amex, Diners, MasterCard,* ***VISA***

Running Waters — Three Horseshoes Inn

Tel & Fax 01913 720286 Map 5 E3 P
Sherburn House Running Waters Durham Co Durham DH1 2SR

With fine views over open country and north-west towards Durham (4 miles), the 'Shoes' stands by the busy A181, fronted by old ploughshares and farming implements; the Running Waters of its location reflects olden times when water was carried from its underground stream by the monks of nearby Sherburn House. While none of the recently refurbished bedrooms are particularly spacious, they all have en suite facilities (two with shower-trays only), TV, tea-maker and radio-alarm, and are decorated ina bright, cottagey style. There's a small residents' lounge area and a fenced-in rear garden; front double-glazing ensures that the morning traffic will not become intrusive. *Open 11.30-2.30, 6.30-11 (Sun 12-3, 7-10.30). Free House.* ***Beer*** *Ruddles Best, Marston's Pedigree, guest beer. Garden.* ***Accommodation*** *6 bedrooms, all en suite £46 (single £35). Children welcome overnight (under-6s stay free in parents' room), additional bed & cot available. Diners, MasterCard,* ***VISA***

Ruskington — Elite Fish Bar & Restaurant

Tel 01526 832332 Map 7 E3 JaB
High Street Ruskington nr Sleaford Lincolnshire NR34 9DY

Good old-fashioned fish and chips are the stock in trade of this popular family-run establishment, a light, airy place with neatly set tables. It is a relaxing spot in which to enjoy the freshest of fish in excellent batter and good plump chips. Service is by friendly, uniformed and efficient waitresses. The choice includes generous cod, haddock and plaice with chips (£3.20-£4), plus other standard chippy favourites. Kiddie's corner menu. Large car park to the rear. ***Seats*** *60.* ***Open*** *11.30-1.30 & 4.30-7.30 (Sat 11.30-8.30).* ***Closed*** *Sun, Mon & Bank Holidays. No credit cards.*

Rye — Landgate Bistro £60

Tel 01797 222829 Map 11 C6 R
5/6 Landgate Rye East Sussex TN31 7LH

Seafood is very much a speciality on chef-patron Toni Ferguson-Lees's menu at his popular bistro. The surroundings are simple and the menu hand-written in refreshingly straightforward English: salmon and smoked haddock fishcakes with parsley sauce, scallop mousse, cod with ginger and spring onions, poached fillet of turbot with chive hollandaise. Alongside these fishy offerings might sit lamb's kidneys with a grain mustard sauce, guinea fowl, Gressingham duck and organic sirloin steak with red wine sauce. The three-course, fixed-price menu offers two or three dishes at each stage. Blood orange sorbet, honey ice cream, walnut and treacle tart, syllabub trifle among the desserts. Service is included in the menu prices. ***Seats*** *30. Parties 10. D only 7-9.30 (Sat till 10). Closed Sun, Mon, 1 week Jun, 1 week autumn & 1 week Christmas. Set D (Tue-Thu) £14.90. Amex, Diners, MasterCard,* ***VISA***

…MORE Ryton Gardens Restaurant

…7 Fax 01203 639229 Map 7 D4 JaB
…-on-Dunsmore Warwickshire CU8 3LG

…nal Centre for Organic Gardening supports this restaurant. The … devoted to coffee, tea and pastries, joined at 10 o'clock by light …ds – served until 4pm). Lunch proper is served from 12 to 2.30. Starters include a seasonal vegetable terrine (£3.50) and a daily-changing home-made vegetable soup, perhaps Oriental vegetable or leek and potato (£2). Main courses include plenty for everyone: vegetable and nut stir-fry with timbale of rice (£5.95), pork in cider and apple sauce (£6.15) and fish pie with vegetables (£6.50) are among the choices. Traditional roast beef (£7.50) and roast pork (£6.95) on Sundays. Smaller helpings for children are half price and there is a comprehensive range of organic bottled baby foods (£1 per jar). No smoking. Tables in a marquee and on a patio in fine weather. On Saturday nights only there is a full restaurant dinner. Two high-chairs; mother's changing area in disabled toilet. Children's portions or special dishes on request. Outside, there is a play area with swing, slide, climbing frame and Swiss chalet. Close to Transport Museum and Warwick Castle. Ample own parking. ***Seats*** *70 (+ 70 in marquee and outside).* ***Open*** *9-5.* ***Closed*** *25 & 26 Dec. Mastercard,* **VISA**

St Agnes Driftwood Spars Hotel

Tel & Fax 01872 552428 Map 12 B3 P
Trevaunance Cove St Agnes Cornwall TR5 0RT

Constructed in the 17th century of huge ship's timbers and spars (hence the name), with stone and slate, the hotel – once a marine chandlery and tin miners trading post – is located just 100 yards from one of Cornwall's best beaches, making it an ideal family destination for a holiday. Accommodation comprises nine neat and tidy en suite rooms – one family room with bunk beds – featuring attractive co-ordinating fabrics, and a mix of furnishings that ranges from comfortable new pine to modern-style white furniture. Rooms are well equipped with direct-dial phones, TVs, hairdryers and tea-makers and two afford peaceful sea views. Guests are treated to the sound of waves on the beach and live music on Fridays and Saturdays. ***Open*** *11-11 (Sun 12-10.30). Free House.* ***Beer*** *St Austell HSD, Sharp's Doom Bar, Tetley, Ind Coope Burton Ale, Bass, guest beer. Garden, patio. Family room.* ***Accommodation*** *9 bedrooms, all en suite, £54-£58 (single £38-£40). Children welcome overnight (under-4s stay free, 4-13s half price if sharing parents' room), cot available. Dogs (£1.50). Accommodation closed 25 Dec. Amex, Diners, MasterCard,* **VISA**

St Albans Kingsbury Mill Waffle House

Tel 01727 853502 Fax 01727 832662 Map 15 E2 JaB
St Michaels Street St Albans Hertfordshire AL3 4SJ

Adjoining Kingsbury Mill Museum, this small cottage restaurant with tightly packed tables expands in warm weather to occupy a pretty terrace by the River Ver. Delicious Belgian waffles are cooked to order (made with free-range eggs and organic flour), and offered with a variety of generous toppings. Savoury versions include ratatouille (£4), tuna mayonnaise (£4.20) and cream cheese, herbs and garlic (£4). Daily blackboard specials might include toppings such as chicken in tarragon sauce and beef in Guinness. Among the sweet choices are coconut or chopped nut (£1.95), black cherry (£2.95) and pecan nut with butterscotch sauce (£2.90). It's an ancient building, not really conducive to special facilities, but young families are very welcome throughout and there are five high-chairs. No children's portions; and no service charge - 'it's our pleasure'. No smoking. Ample parking. ***Seats*** *80 (+ 40 outside).* ***Open*** *11-6 (Sun from 12).* ***Closed*** *Mon except Bank Holidays. MasterCard,* **VISA**

St Albans Sopwell House Hotel 69%

Tel 01727 864477 **Fax 01727 844741** Map

Cottonmill Lane Sopwell St Albans Hertfordshire AL1 2HQ

Two miles south-east of the city centre, Sopwell House, once the of Earl Mountbatten, still retains a good degree of its original Geo although it is much enlarged. Eleven acres of part-wooded, part-landsc provide a peaceful rural setting. Substantial conference facilities (for up to 400; parking for 200 cars), a bedroom wing and a splendid leisure complex (with baby-changing facilities) are all fairly recent additions. Public rooms include an elegant, quite clubby bar furnished with brown leather chesterfields; this sets the tone for the drawing room and library. A new conservatory lounge/bar and patio were added last year. 22 of the bedrooms have four-posters and these, together with a number of other rooms, have a traditional ambience. The remainder are a little more modern in style. Decor in all is well co-ordinated and tasteful. Marble bathrooms are excellent, each with a power shower, scales and useful toiletries. 24hr room service. ***Rooms*** *92. Garden, croquet, indoor swimming pool & children's splash pool, gym, sauna, spa bath, steam room, sun beds, beauty & hair salon, snooker, brasserie (11.30am-10pm). Amex, Diners, MasterCard,* **VISA**

St Dominick Edgcumbe Arms at Cotehele Quay

Tel 01579 350024 Map 12 C3 JaB

The Quay Cotehele St Dominick nr Saltash Cornwall PL12 6TA

A stretch of woodland, containing a chapel built by Richard Edgcumbe during the Wars of the Roses, separates Cotehele Quay from Cotehele House (near the village of Callington). On the quayside, amid a row of 18th- and 19th-century houses, the National Trust's Edgcumbe Arms is set in a former lime-worker's cottage which later became a public house. It is now a tea room (not a pub, despite the name) where light refreshments are available all day: home-made soup (£2.50), paté, ploughman's, fisherman's lunch (£4.30 – smoked mackerel fillet), jacket potatoes (£2.95), treacle tart and clotted cream (£2.45), various cakes and biscuits, traditional Cornish Cream Tea (£3.20 with Cornish splits – soft white yeast buns – in place of scones). Cornish ice cream is sold through a window on the side. Children's portions. New this year is a small tea lawn to take advantage of sunny days. No smoking. Own parking. ***Seats*** *76 (+ 20 outside).* ***Open*** *11-5.30 (Apr-Oct), 11-4 (Sat & Sun only in Nov, Wed-Sun in Dec, Sun only Jan, Feb, Mar). Amex, MasterCard,* **VISA**

A quarter of a mile up the hill at the late-medieval Cotehele House is *The Barn* restaurant serving a similar range of snacks plus a few more substantial hot dishes. In season, visitors are required to pay an entrance fee (£2.80 grounds only) to reach the restaurant. No smoking.

St Ives Garrack Hotel 62% £102

Tel 01736 796199 **Fax 01736 798955** Map 12 A3 H

Burthallan Lane St Ives Cornwall TR26 3AA

Run by the Kilby family since 1965, the creeper-clad Garrack stands peacefully in two acres of secluded gardens overlooking Porthmeor beach, the Tate Gallery and the distant sweep of St Ives Bay (ask for directions). The main lounge is a busy family room with games and books, and there are two other more formal lounges plus a pleasant cocktail bar. Bedrooms in the main house are traditionally furnished and vary in size; those in the extension are more modern and roomy. Some rooms have four-posters, others spa baths and there are also two family rooms with bunk beds; one room is adapted for disabled guests. Guests of all ages are admirably catered for. ***Rooms*** *18. Garden, indoor swimming pool, mini-gym, sauna, solarium, spa bath, coffee shop (11am-11pm). Amex, Diners, MasterCard,* **VISA**

Tean Restaurant

The restaurant, whose walls are hung with paintings by local artists, makes good us of local fish which is landed right on the hotel's quay. Lobster is a speciality and gam and home-grown vegetables also feature on the four-course, fixed-price dinner menu. No smoking. Lighter bar lunches. ***Seats*** *50. Parties 10. L in bar only 10-5 D 7-10. Set D £29.50.*

Round Island Bar

The hotel's Round Island Bar is the scenic setting for an all-day lunch, offering anything from sandwiches including honey roast ham and pear chutney, roast sirloin and horseradish and Stilton, walnuts, celery and grapes (all £4.45 for two rounds) and crusty filled granary baguettes (called torpedoes): brie, lettuce and tomato; roast turkey and crispy bacon and mature Cheddar and pickle (all £4.95), to more elaborate dishes such as crab salad (£9.85) with crusty bread, stuffed pancakes (£5.25) and lobster salad (£12.95). A home-made soup is always available. A short list of desserts includes home-made ice creams and chocolate marmalade cake (both £2.95). ***Seats*** *30 (+ 12 tables outside).* ***Open*** *(lunch menu) 10-5.*

St Mawgan — Falcon Inn

Tel 01637 860225 Map 12 B3 

St Mawgan Newquay Cornwall TR8 4EP

In the heart of the holiday land where good unspoilt traditional pubs are an endangered breed, the Falcon survives and is a haven for the discerning pub-goer. Nestling in a most attractive village, deep in the Vale of Lanherne and a stone's throw from its tiny stream, this 16th-century wisteria-clad inn is a popular summer destination with those escaping the bucket-and-spade brigade on the beach. Inside, the main bar is neatly arranged and decorated with pine farmhouse tables and chairs, trellis wallpaper and decent prints and is thankfully music and game-free. The adjacent dining-room has a rug-strewn flagged floor, a pine dresser and French windows leading out into the bench-filled cobbled courtyard. Beyond a rose-covered arch there is a splendid terraced garden, ideal for enjoying some summer refreshment. *Open 11-3, 6-11 (Sun 12-3, 7-10.30).* ***Beer*** *St Austell. Garden, children's play area. Family room. Diners, MasterCard,* ***VISA***

St Michael's Mount — The Sail Loft Restaurant

Tel 01736 710748 Map 12 A4 

St Michael's Mount Marazion Cornwall TR17 0AT

At low tide the Mount is reached via a cobbled causeway, while at high tide you must take the ferry (weather permitting) to reach this National Trust restaurant located in a converted boat store and carpenter's shop. Hot lunches served between 12.15 and 2.30 include Hobbler's Choice (the day's fish special £6.50 – the island ferrymen are known as Hobblers), and a dish of the day (except Sunday) such as chicken and ham pie or beef in ale plus a vegetarian dish (£4.95). Cold platters include local cheese, smoked fish, seafood and ham. Home-made puddings are delicious (gooseberry and elderflower syllabub, bread-and-butter pudding with apricot sauce and clotted cream – both £2.50) and there is a good selection of home-made cakes and biscuits with the traditional Cornish Cream Tea (£3.20) featuring Cornish splits (soft white yeast buns) instead of scones. Traditional Sunday lunch (high season only, booking advisable) £6.50 for one course. Four high-chairs; separate first aid and baby-changing room. Grassed area outdoors where children can let off some steam. Children's portions available. No smoking Profits go towards the upkeep of St Michael's Mount. ***Seats*** *88 (+40 outside).* ***Open*** *10.30-5 (Jul & Aug to 5.30).* ***Closed*** *Nov-Mar. Amex, MasterCard,* ***VISA***

Chequers Inn

16 Map 15 E1 **P**

ıesbury St Neots Cambridgeshire PE19 2TA

ountry pub, where you can sit in the main bar with its roaring -polished dark furniture or at tables with green tablecloths for ng area for more substantial meals. The changing blackboard ...-cooking by landlord David Taylor: hearty ploughman's, liver ...on, chicken and mushroom pie, fricasee of chicken, home-made quiche and vegetarian choices like pasta and courgette provençale. Puddings include chocolate orange mousse cake, crème brulée and fresh raspberry pavlova. Set family Sunday lunch £13. Children are welcome indoors and are kept amused on sunny days in the outdoor play area in the fenced-off garden. *Open 10.30-3, 7-11 (Sun 12-2, 7-10.30).* ***Bar Food*** *12-2, 7-9.45 (till 9 Sun). Free House.* ***Beer*** *Boddingtons, Bass. Garden, outdoor eating, children's play area. Amex, Diners, MasterCard,* ***VISA***

St Neots — Eaton Oak

Tel 01480 219555 **Fax 01480 407520** Map 15 E1 **P**

Crosshall Road Eaton Ford St Neots Cambridgeshire PE19 4AG

The Eaton Oak is located at the junction of the A1 and A45 but the bedrooms are happily undisturbed by traffic – you can expect a comfortable overnight stay. The rooms in the motel extension are large and warm, with fitted units, colour TVs, tea-makers, direct-dial telephones and well-fitted bath/shower rooms. In the main building (once a farmhouse) the bar has been extended along with the restaurant and a conservatory added which leads on to the garden. Families are well looked after (even a free kiddies menu) and an outdoor play area is provided. Disabled WC. *Open 11-11 (Sat 11-2.30, 6-11, Sun 12-10.30).* ***Beer*** *Charles Wells, guest beer. Garden, children's play area. Family room.* ***Accommodation*** *9 bedrooms, all en suite, £50 (single £40). Children welcome overnight, additional bed (£12) available. Amex, MasterCard,* ***VISA***

Salcombe — Soar Mill Cove — 66% — £140

Tel 01548 561566 **Fax 01548 561223** Map 13 D3 **HR**

Soar Mill Cove nr Salcombe Devon TQ7 3DS

A spectacular sea view is one of the rewards of following the narrow winding country lane (follow signs to Soar from Marlborough just before you get to Salcombe) that ends at the hotel, which stands alone above a sandy beach. It's a purpose-built single-storey building with all its immaculate bedrooms boasting their own patios, and several their own private garden. Six rooms, including the two full suites, are suitable for families (rates start at 20% for under-6s), who also appreciate the special youngsters' high tea served from 5pm. The genteel atmosphere – reproduction antiques, glass drop and gilt chandeliers and velour upholstery – also attracts older guests, many of whom return year after year to a warm welcome from Keith and Norma Makepeace and their family. Overall, there's a clever mix of adult facilities and family-friendliness; a second children's playroom has recently been added along with the addition of a 'superior wing' of three new bedrooms. Not a conference delegate or tour group in sight at any time! ***Rooms*** *19. Garden, indoor & outdoor swimming pools, tennis, playroom & play area, games room, laundry room. Closed Nov-Jan. MasterCard,* ***VISA***

Restaurant — £85

After an energetic day, or even a lazy one, the ritual of dinner is the highlight here. It begins with a tempting array of canapés offered with pre-dinner drinks and ends with an equally impressive selection of petits fours – all home-made, as is the bread. Dinner itself is a daily-changing, four-course affair (with a choice of four main dishes) that makes good use of local produce like lobsters, Devon beef and lamb and organically grown vegetables from the hotel's extensive kitchen garden. Bacon-wrapped scallops on a pea purée with sweet pepper coulis, hot soufflé of Cornish Yarg ('timed to rise to prefection' – inspiring confidence), fresh-from-the-sea poached turbot with a Sauvignon and parsley butter sauce, and veal schnitzel with a sweet and sour pineapple and honey sauce are typical of the dishes that emerge from son-of-the-house Keith Makepeace's kitchen. Vegetables are notably well of ten or so good desserts might include gateau pithiviers, pral crème brulée; British cheeses are served with either biscuits or bread. Lunch is an informal affair from an individually priced a bowl of soup or Soar Bay chowder via sandwiches and salad dishes like steak and grilled local sole. Every wine on the list No children under 3 in the dining-room. No smoking. ***Seats*** *L 12.30-2.30 D 7.30-9.30. Set D £34.*

SALCOMBE South Sands 60% £110

Tel 01548 843741 **Fax 01548 842112** Map 13 D3 H

Salcombe Devon TQ8 8LL

Salcombe is one of the most southerly towns in England, and South Sands is well placed to get the best of the sunshine, with great views across the estuary. In the same ownership (the Edwards family, with John and Bridget in charge here) as the *Tides Reach* but even closer to the shore with the sandy beach reaching right up to the terrace walk, the South Sands caters more for younger children with ten family suites – double- and twin-bedded rooms – and a special high tea served in the pubby terrace bar/coffee shop from 5pm for youngsters aged 2-11 (no under-7s in the restaurant for dinner). Generally good-sized bedrooms, half with freestanding pine and half with white melamine fitted furniture, are uncluttered, with carpeted, fully-tiled bathrooms and views either of the valley or the estuary. Guests may use the leisure facilities of the sister hotel; next door, the boathouse provides dinghy sailing tuition and hire, windsurfing and canoeing. Friendly staff. Half-board terms are preferred and only a £10 reduction per head is made in high season for B&B terms. Special value breaks at the beginning and end of the season offer particularly good value for money - the beach is right there on the doorstep (and the summer ferry to town), so all you need is good weather. ***Rooms*** *30. Terrace, indoor swimming pool, spa bath, steam room, solarium, moorings (boats up to 20ft), dinghy park, playroom, coffee shop (10.30-8.30). Closed Nov-Feb. MasterCard,* ***VISA***

JaB is short for 'Just a Bite'. The majority of these establishments are also recommended in our *Bistros, Bars & Cafés* Guide which features establishments where one may eat well for less than £15 per head.

SALISBURY Bernières

Tel 01722 414536 Map 14 C3 JaB

58 The Close Salisbury Wiltshire SP1 2EX

Bernières is within the museum of The Royal Gloucester, Berkshire and Wiltshire Regiments, in the north-west corner of the Cathedral close. It's run by the same team that previously ran Redcoats, and the style has changed little. Sandwiches (from £1.70), baked potatoes with various fillings (from £2.30) and salads, including tuna and mayonnaise (£4), Cheddar and pineapple and turkey breast, are the mainstay. There is a daily special, perhaps smoked salmon and prawn mousse with new potatoes and salad (£4.25) or poached chicken breast with broccoli and mayonnaise. A cream tea special (£4.75) includes a scone, jam and cream, a slice of cake and tea. Lack of space, and a flight of stairs, rather than lack of goodwill means that this is not ideally suited to push-chairs and buggies (which will have to be left at the bottom of the stairs). They do have two high-chairs however, and as far as food for the little ones goes 'if we've got it, they can have it'. In summer, eat out on the charming walled patio or picnic (with food purchased from the tea room only) on the extensive lawns that reach down to the river. No smoking inside. ***Seats*** *32 (+ 30 outside).* ***Open*** *10-4.15.* ***Closed*** *Jan, also Sun Dec-Feb. No credit cards.*

Seaview Hotel 64% £70

.983 612711 **Fax 01983 613729** Map 15 D4 

Street Seaview Isle of Wight PO34 5EX

delightful, well-kept, family-run seaside hotel that has recently benefited from ıbstantial re-investment including expanded dining facilities, new south-facing balconies for some of the smaller bedrooms, new shower cubicles in several bathrooms, and a total revamp of four bedrooms. Owners Nicholas and Nicola Hayward are now set to take their charming little hotel-cum-local inn up a gear or two. The hotel is set just back from the seafront and a small patio with white iron tables and chairs is a delightful sun trap from which you can watch the world go by. Within, a narrow hallway separates a busy bar and the dining-room; to the rear are two snug lounges (one for non-smokers) and another nautically-themed, pubby bar with bare boards. Pretty bedrooms – blues and yellows are the favoured colours – are most appealing, with lots of pictures, books and objets d'art. The best, and largest, rooms feature antique furniture; others have simple white-painted built-in units, and most en suite facilities feature baths and power showers. Two of the rooms have small patios (unfortunately overlooking the small rear car park), while the three smallest rooms now boast south-facing balconies. On the top floor there's also a family suite, its two bedrooms separated by a sitting-room. The cosy lounge on the first floor is non-smoking. ***Rooms** 16. Terrace. Closed 25 Dec. Amex, Diners, MasterCard,* ***VISA***

Restaurant £55

Chef Charles Bartlett now has a brand new kitchen to celebrate his ten years here, and diners can choose between a new conservatory or the intimacy of the original dining-room, candle-lit at night; both are air-conditioned. There's a reasonable choice on the à la carte which effectively doubles as a set-price menu (£14.90 for two courses, £18.85 for three, plus £5 for more involved main courses like roasted monkfish with moules marinière or chargrilled medallions of venison with sour cream and shredded beetroot). Popular Sunday lunch. Snacks are served in the adjacent bar or out on the terrace. Sensibly priced wines. Booking advised. ***Seats** 60. L 12-2 D 7.30-9.30. Closed D Sun (except Bank Holiday weekends).*

Sennen Cove — Old Success Inn

Tel 01736 871232 **Fax 01736 871457** Map 12 A4 P

Sennen Cove Penzance Cornwall TR19 7DG

Located off the A30, next to the huge expanse of Whitesands Bay and only a mile north of Land's End, this 17th-century inn has been well refurbished to provide accommodation in twelve comfortable bedrooms that have impressive sea views. Especially popular are the rooms that capture the famous sunset sinking into the sea, the most attractive being the spacious honeymoon suite with its four-poster bed. All rooms have pretty floral curtains and print wallpaper, solid modern pine furnishings and good clean en suite facilities. Added comforts include satellite TV and tea-makers and residents have use of a stylish lounge complete with picture window and sea view. The pubby 'Charlies Bar' is modern and open-plan in layout with a mix of pub furniture, stools and high-backed benches and various local seafaring photographs of bygone days decorate the walls. Children welcome. *Open 11-11 (Sun 12-10.30). Free House.* ***Beer** Bass, St Austell Trelawney's Ale, Sharp's Doom Bar, guest beer. Terrace,* ***Accommodation** 12 bedrooms, 10 en suite, £32-£73 (single from £19). Children welcome overnight (under-2s stay free in parents' room, 2-15s half-price), additional bed & cot available. MasterCard,* ***VISA***

Shaftesbury — Royal Chase Hotel 60% £87

Tel 01747 853355 **Fax 01747 851969** Map 14 B3 H

Shaftesbury Dorset SP7 8DB

A friendly, family-run hotel south of the town centre on a roundabout where the A30 and A350 intersect. Until 1922 the building was used as a monastery and the present bar was once the chapel. Much has changed since those days and now the hotel offers among its facilities a cosy library lounge and a popular indoor leisure area. Best of the bedrooms are the Crown rooms. Bathrooms in the older parts of the building are quite compact. Families are well catered for, particularly in holiday periods, and children up to 15 stay free in their parents' room. ***Rooms** 32. Garden, croquet, indoor swimming pool, steam room, sun beds, playground. Amex, Diners, MasterCard,* **VISA**

SHALDON — Ness House Hotel

Tel 01626 873480 **Fax 01626 873486** Map 13 D3 P

Marine Drive Shaldon Devon TQ14 0HP

Originally built as a summer residence by Lord Clifford in 1810, the Regency looking Ness House Hotel is set in 22 acres of parkland and overlooks the Teign estuary and across to the town of Teignmouth. The twelve rooms (1 bridal suite, five apartments, 2 family suites, 3 doubles and 1 single) all have en suite facilities and are equipped with modern facilities. There is a spacious open-plan bar with a no-smoking area and, at the back, a small, simple lounge. Room service is available. *Open 11-11 (Sun 12-10.30). Free House.* ***Beer** Eldridge Pope Royal Oak, Palmers IPA, Tetley, Fergusons Dartmoor Legend, guest beer. Garden.* ***Accommodation** 14 bedrooms, all en suite, £65-£80 (family room £95, single from £39). Children welcome overnight (under-14s stay free in parents' room), additional bed (£15) & cot available. No dogs. Amex, MasterCard,* **VISA**

SHANKLIN — Cliff Tops Hotel — 64% — £60

Tel 01983 863262 **Fax 01983 867139** Map 15 D4 

Park Road Shanklin Isle of Wight PO37 6BB

A modern hotel, one of the Isle of Wight's largest, with fine sea views and bright, spacious day rooms. It stands high above Sandown Bay, and a public lift leads down to the seafront. There's a choice of bars, a leisure club and conference rooms for up to 240 delegates. Most of the bedrooms have balconies. ***Rooms** 88. Garden, indoor swimming pool & splash pool, gym, sauna, spa bath, steam room, solarium, beauty & hair salon, snooker, playground. Amex, Diners, MasterCard,* **VISA**

> We endeavour to be as up-to-date as possible, but inevitably some changes to data and key personnel may occur at restaurants and hotels after the Guide goes to press. Prices should also be taken as indications rather than firm quotes.

SHANKLIN — Hambledon Hotel

Tel 01983 862403 **Fax 01983 867894** Map 15 D4 

Queens Road Shanklin Isle of Wight PO37 6AW

A home-from-home is what Beryl and Norman Birch aim to provide at their comfortable family hotel, which is 175 yards from the lift that goes down to the esplanade and beach. Guests can use the leisure facilities (indoor swimming pool, water slide, sauna, spa bath, steam room and gym) at the nearby (50yds) Cliff Tops Hotel. Two suites and five large rooms offer modest comfort (all en suite) but have ample space for the cots (with linen) provided, and amenities include high-chairs, booster seats, toys and children's books. Nappies and baby clothes placed in a special bucket in the bedroom will be washed, dried and returned the same day and by night there is a baby-listening service and patrol by 'Aunty' Beryl, a qualified nursery nurse. All bedrooms have en-suite showers but a bathroom is provided for children who prefer something in which they can sail a rubber duck. Children may eat with parents or take early tea at 5pm. Special diets are catered for and food will be puréed for babies. Outside is a safe garden, with slide. £199 half-board per person per 7 day, high-season rate; £146 in January, lowest-season rate. First child under 1 free, next under-1 £3 per day ("twins and even triplets can be big business here"); 1-2s £55, 3-5s £83, 6-10s £103, 11-14s £135 per week. B&B terms are offered if there's room, however the majority of the business is repeat holiday business. The hotel is open all year. ***Rooms** 11. MasterCard,* **VISA**

SHEFFIELD Just Cooking

Tel 0114 272 7869 Map 6 C2 JaB
16-18 Carver Street Sheffield S1 4FS

A simply furnished, 'L'-shaped self-service restaurant offering well-executed home-made produce. The day begins with teas, coffees, cakes, quiche (£4.25) and salads, the choice widening at lunchtime to include hot blackboard specials such as lamb pasanda, chicken with leeks and tarragon (£5.25) and pork provençale (£5-50). There is always at least one vegetarian choice (garlic vegetable crumble, angel broccoli bake – both £4.80). Delicious sweets include black cherry and walnut roulade, French apple flan and bread-and-butter pudding (all £1.95). The Carver Street car park is almost opposite. No smoking. ***Seats*** *72.* ***Open*** *10-3.30 (Wed 10.30-7.30, Sat 10-4).* ***Closed*** *Sun & Bank Holidays. No credit cards.*

SHEFFIELD Novotel 63% £73

Tel 0114 278 1781 **Fax 0114 278 7744** Map 6 C2 H
Arundel Gate Sheffield S1 2PR

Central location opposite City Hall and close to both the Crucible and Lyceum Theatres. Cheerful, open-plan public areas are matched by practical, well-planned bedrooms that all come with extra sofa-beds (ideal for families) and WCs separate from the bathroom. Children up to 16 stay free in parents' room. Parking for 45 cars. ***Rooms*** *144. Indoor swimming pool, keep-fit equipment. Amex, Diners, MasterCard,* ***VISA***

SHEPPERTON Blubeckers Eating House

Tel 01932 243377 **Fax 01932 241147** Map 15 E2 JaB
Church Square Shepperton TW17 9JY

Not quite matching the stylish country mill setting of its sister outlet in Odiham, Hants (our 1992 Family Restaurant of the Year), this well-established restaurant is right on a bend in the road opposite Shepperton's pretty church square. The old building contains a warren of rooms filled with red and check tablecloths and high-chairs with balloons tied to them. Almost as soon as you sit down the helpful, efficient staff produce a jokey children's menu, along with a cup of wax crayons. Children's favourites include fish sticks, junior burgers, cheesey potato skins, rooster's chicken, ribs, chicken on a stick and scampi (£2.75-£3.75), all served with fries or baked potato, baked beans or fresh vegetables. There's a long list of tempting puddings (£3.45) for adults, and for children there's Smartie smacker (£1.45), bananas and shark-infested custard (£1.25), chocolate dipper and pancakes with soft ice cream; some rather dubious-sounding children's cocktails (humdinger, slime juice, Dracula's dribble, from £1.25) should also raise a laugh (or a shriek!). Sunday lunch (£9.95 for three courses) offers good value, with a choice of any starter or pudding from the normal dinner menu. Good ribs, burgers, haddock and spinach potato-topped pie plus desserts that should test even the finest of trenchermen! A monthly-changing blackboard set menu (£9.95/£12.95) offers good value. There is no room in the Ladies to change a baby, but otherwise it's a fine destination for a family outing, albeit a little cramped. After lunch a short stroll past the Warren Lodge Hotel will take you to the edge of the Thames where younger children will be delighted by the ducks and river birds. See also entry under Odiham. Branches in Chobham and Hampton Court. ***Seats*** *85. Open L Sun only (also every day during December 12-3) 12.30-9.30, D 6-11. Closed 3 days Christmas. Set menu £9.95/£12.95. Amex, Diners, MasterCard,* ***VISA***

SHERBORNE Eastbury Hotel 67% £70

Tel 01935 813131 **Fax 01935 817296** Map 13 F2 H
Long Street Sherborne Dorset DT9 3BY

An elegant Georgian town house which dates, in part, as far back as the 16th century; new owners John and Alison Pickford have taken care to retain as many original features as possible. The beautifully-proportioned older rooms stick to period-style furnishings, with comfortable sofas and armchairs in the drawing-room. An elegantly decorated modern conservatory is used as the dining-room. All ground-floor public lounge areas have recently been redecorated. Bedrooms, named after flowers, have en suite bathrooms with tubs and showers and all the usual mod cons. The well-kept walled garden is a special attraction. Ask for directions on how to negotiate the town's one-way system to find the hotel's small car park! Families are welcome (changing facilities are promised this year). Conference facilities for up to 100; parking for 20 cars. No dogs. ***Rooms*** *15. Garden. Amex, MasterCard,* ***VISA***

SHERBORNE Oliver's

Tel 01935 815005 Map 13 F2 JaB

19 Cheap Street Sherborne Dorset DT9 3PU

A former delicatessen, with original tiled walls, is the setting for this welcoming café-restaurant. Everything on the self-service counter is home-made: croissants (from 90p), cakes (from 80p) and Danish pastries (£1.20). Sandwiches (from £1.90) are freshly made, as is 'Oliver's Bulging Baguette' (£3.90), which contains a delicious combination of salad and cold meat. Hot dishes are also offered, such as filled baked potatoes, a daily casserole or perhaps chicken, ham and vegetable pie (£3.90). Hearty soups are available in the winter. Clotted cream tea is £2.50. There's a choice of teas, espresso and iced coffee. Children's portions. One of the three eating rooms (there is also a small courtyard garden) is reserved for non-smokers. ***Seats*** *55 (+ 12 outside).* ***Open*** *9-5 (Sun from 10).* ***Closed*** *25, 26 Dec & 1 Jan. No credit cards.*

SHREWSBURY Poppy's Tea Room

Tel 01743 232307 Map 6 A3 JaB

8 Milk Street Shrewsbury Shropshire

Part of a handsome 17th-century building, the well-spaced ground floor and walled courtyard are easily accessible to the most laden of families and also has excellent facilities for disabled visitors (with ramps and specially adapted toilets), while the oak-floored upper room, particularly popular in winter, contains the finest example of cross-timbered construction remaining in Shrewsbury. Throughout the day there is something for everyone with sandwiches (from £1.60), several varieties of home-baked scones, plenty of excellent home baking and a fine choice of teas and coffees. Lunchtime selections (11-3) run from home-made soup of the day (£2) and ciabatta topped with pesto, tomato and mozzarella (£3.50) to stuffed baked potatoes (from £3) with tasty fillings such as Szechuan beef (£3.75). Other dishes could include poached salmon (£4.50) and roast breast of chicken with stuffing (£4.25) both served with salad or a baked potato. An all-day breakfast (£2.10) is very popular, as is afternoon tea (£3.75) served between 2 and 4. There is one small room for smokers. ***Seats*** *66 (+ 20 outside).* ***Open*** *9.30-4.* ***Closed*** *Sun & 25 Dec. No credit cards.*

SIBFORD GOWER Wykham Arms

Tel 01295 780351 Map 14 C1 

Sibford Gower Banbury Oxfordshire OX15 5RX

Yellow stone, mature thatch and a blaze of flowers and hanging baskets are picture-postcard material here in summer at this attractive 17th-century village pub. In winter the interior is warmed by real fires and the tiny dining-room with low beams and exposed stone walls takes on an altogether more cosy air. The renovated bars are fully carpeted and quite sedate, their best feature being an old stone well, now glass-covered to form an unusual bay-window table. Well-kept Hook Norton Best and local micro-brewery Merivales Edgecutter. Children are made very welcome and there are swings under the trees and a play area in a pretty back garden. New owners are sprucing the Wykham up and intoducing home-cooked fresh food (not yet inspected). *Open 12-3, 6.30-11 (Sun 12-10.30). Free House.* ***Beer*** *Hook Norton Best, Wadworth 6X, Bass, Fuller's London Pride, Merrivales Edgecutter. Garden. Patio. MasterCard,* ***VISA***

A jug of fresh water!

SIDMOUTH Victoria Hotel 72% £146

Tel 01395 512651 **Fax 01395 579154** Map 13 E2 **H**
The Esplanade Sidmouth Devon EX10 8RY

Built in 1903, this impressive hotel stands in its own grounds at one end of the promenade looking out across Lyme Bay. Beyond the grand, porticoed entrance the lobby boasts a fine moulded barrel ceiling and the first of the numerous fresh flower displays to be found throughout the hotel. Public areas are grand and spacious, with various lounges and a bar off a fine, oak-panelled inner hall. Furnishings are tasteful and stylish with lots of deep sofas and comfortable armchairs in which to while away an hour or two while notably smart staff tend to every need. There is entertainment every night with a pianist alternating with a quartet from day to day and a dinner dance each Saturday. Generally spacious bedrooms feature either cream or darkwood units, Victorian-style light fittings and matching floral bedcovers and curtains. Only the poly-cotton bedding does not quite live up to the style of the hotel. Fresh flowers in the rooms are a nice touch and Deluxe rooms also get fruit and bathrobes. Many rooms have furnished balconies. Beds are turned down at night and there is 24hr room service. Families are well catered for. No dogs. Ample free parking. ***Rooms*** *65. Garden, tennis, putting, indoor & outdoor swimming pools, sauna, spa bath, sun bed, hairdressing, snooker & games room, lock-up garages. Amex, Diners, MasterCard,* ***VISA***

SINGLETON Weald & Downland Open Air Museum Café

Tel 01243 811348 (Museum) / 811333 (Café) Map 11 A6 **JaB**
Singleton nr Chichester West Sussex PO18 0EU

An educational visit to the fascinating 40-acre site displaying over 35 historic buildings rescued from destruction can be rounded off with a good light lunch or afternoon tea collected from a counter set in a 16th-century cart shed and eaten either in a timber-framed medieval hall or at picnic benches on a lakeside lawn. Their home-baked bread, made using flour ground at an old water mill on the site, accompanies a ham platter (£3.50) and ploughman's (£3.25) and the same flour is used to make dough for the pizzas (£1.55) and pastry for the savoury flans (£1.75) but not bread for the sandwiches (from £1.20). Other offerings include sausage rolls (£1.10) and hot specials like picnic pie (made with corned beef – £2.10) and home-made vegetable and pasta bake (£3.50). Home-made cakes (65p-95p) include lemon, date and walnut, and ginger. Children's portions and small pizzas are available, and they are happy to heat bottles and baby food. One high-chair. Vast lawned area for letting off steam on brighter days. The café is only accessible to museum visitors; the entrance fee is £4.50 for adults and £2.25 for children. No smoking. ***Seats*** *45 (+ 50 outside).* ***Open*** *11-5.30.* ***Closed*** *Nov-Feb. No credit cards.*

SISSINGHURST Granary Restaurant

Tel 01580 713097 **Fax 01580 713911** Map 11 C5 **JaB**
Sissinghurst Castle Sissinghurst Kent

Part of the National Trust-run Sissinghurst Gardens, the restaurant attracts no entrance fee and no parking fee (though it would be a pity to miss Vita Sackville-West's garden with its famous 'outdoor rooms'). Formerly a cattle shed, the self-service restaurant is full of exposed beams, and picture windows look out across neighbouring farmland. Almost everything on a fairly extensive menu is made on site and includes regional specialities and things like steak, ale & mushroom pie (£5.95) and spiced aubergine bake (£5.85). Also jacket potatoes (prawn mayonnaise topping £3.50), pork and chicken paté (£4.50), cakes, pastries and afternoon teas. About six English and organic wines are served by the glass (with meals only). A timed ticket system is in operation for visitors to the gardens (but not for access to the restaurant, although this does get very busy at peak times) so you are likely to have to queue for entrance. No smoking. ***Seats*** *200.* ***Open*** *12-5.30 (Sat & Sun from 10).* ***Closed*** *all Mon, also mid-Oct-Good Friday (except Oct 27-Dec 24 when open Wed-Sun 11-4). MasterCard,* ***VISA***

Skelwith Bridge — Chesters Coffee Shop

Tel 01539 432553 Map 4 C3 JaB
Kirkstone Galleries Skelwith Bridge nr Ambleside Cumbria

Sharing space with a showroom and shop in a restored slate works, Chesters enjoys a pretty riverside setting. An impressive array of home baking (65p-£1.95) includes chocolate fudge cake, John Peel pie, tiffins, carrot cake with fudge topping, Westmorland crunchie (£1.35), orange and coconut cake, date slices, flapjacks (£1.10) and several puddings (banana toffee or apple and passion fruit flan £1.95). Given the popularity of Karen Lawrence's cakes, the savoury menu is kept small – home-made soup (maybe curried pea and apple or pepper and courgette £1.95), quiches (perhaps ham and asparagus or three-cheese £3.25), a selection of rolls (from £1.95) or walnut and Stilton paté (£2.50). After lunch savoury items are more limited. Terrace in front for summer days. Soups, sandwiches and cold fare are all suitable for children; no portions or special menu. One high-chair, and there is now a changing table for babies in the Ladies toilet. Ample own parking. No smoking. ***Seats*** *50 (+ 30outside).* ***Open*** *10-5.30 (winter till 4.45).* ***Closed*** *24-26 Dec & 1 week Jan. No credit cards.*

Skidby — Half Moon Inn

Tel 01482 843403 Map 7 E1 
16 Main Street Skidby East Riding of Yorkshire HU16 5TG

Chips with everything is not the stuff of the Half Moon; its speciality is home-made Yorkshire puddings – eight different combinations including lamb chops or curry! They are almost big enough to obscure the waitress. The half-acre garden has its own 'Sproggies Bar' for children, together with the only huge, suspended spiral climbing frame in the country. The welcome to children of all ages extends to the provision of baby-changing facilities in the Ladies. The pub itself is not without idiosyncrasies, having four little bars and wooden pillar supports. Alongside snacks like ploughman's lunches and sandwiches are home-made pies, soups, chilis, curries and burgers. *Open 11-11 (Sun 12-10.30).* ***Bar Food*** *12-9.30.* ***Beer*** *John Smith's, Marston's Pedigree. Garden, outdoor eating, children's play area. MasterCard,* ***VISA***

Skipton — Bizzie Lizzies

Tel 01756 793189 **Fax 01756 701131** Map 6 C1 
36 Swadford Street Skipton North Yorkshire BD23 1QY

A bright and cheerful chippie by a canal bridge on the fringe of town (head for the Cavendish or Coach Street car park), looking down on a basin where the barges moor. In addition to the freshest fish around, there are alternatives of Southern Fried chicken (£4.75), and Yorkshire puddings filled with steak and kidney (£4.99). Ginger sponge and apple crumble to follow. Upstairs there is waitress service (cod and chips £3.99 at lunchtime, £4.35 at night) while on the ground floor there is a further seating area where you can eat your 'take-away'. The take-away is open till 11.30pm (Fri & Sat till midnight). Reduced prices for senior citizens; lots of treats for kids, including goodie bags with crayons. ***Seats*** *70 (+ 50 in 'take-away').* ***Open*** *11.30-10 (Sun from 12, winter till 9).* ***Closed*** *25 & 26 Dec. No credit cards.*

Skipton — Randell's Hotel — 65% — £86

Tel 01756 700100 **Fax 01756 700107** Map 6 C1 H
Keighley Road Snaygill Skipton North Yorkshire BD23 2T

Purpose-built hotel just a mile outside the town centre on the A629, with the Trans-Pennine Waterway passing to the rear and the Dales close at hand. Spacious bedrooms are light and contemporary with fully-tiled private facilities; one room has facilities for disabled guests. Day rooms include an open-plan lobby and a first-floor bar. There's also a well-equipped leisure centre. A new purpose-built conference centre caters for up to 80 theatre-style; the Malham Suite seats 300 for sit-down banqueting. Splendid facilities for youngsters, including the state-registered Playzone supervised nursery (for under-7s: Mon-Fri 8-6, weekends 10-3; two hours' free use per day for hotel guests) with outdoor play area. 24hr room service. Children up to 16 stay free in parents' room. Parking for 150 cars. ***Rooms*** *76. Terrace, indoor swimming pool, gym, squash, sauna, spa bath, steam room, solarium, hair & beauty salons. Amex, Diners, MasterCard,* ***VISA***

SLOUGH Courtyard by Marriott 60% £93

Tel 01753 551551 **Fax 01753 553333** Map 15 E2 **H**
Church Street Chalvey nr Slough Berkshire SL1 2NH

At the first roundabout towards Slough from J6 of the M4, this was the first Marriott hotel in this country aimed primarily at the weekday business traveller, although the weekend B&B tariff (£58) is also very attractive to families on the move. Some rooms have two double beds and children up to 12 may stay free in their parents' room. There's no porterage or room service but food and drink may be taken to rooms from the cheerful Number One all-day bar/brasserie or 24hr vending machines. Uncluttered bedrooms are well equipped and good bathrooms have both under-floor heating and heated mirrors. Meeting rooms for up to 40. ***Rooms** 148. Mini-gym, brasserie (7am-11pm). Amex, Diners, MasterCard,* **VISA**

SLOUGH Spaggo's

Tel 01753 790303 **Fax 01753 790173** Map 15 E2 **JaB**
30 Bath Road Slough Berkshire SL1 3SR

Joint winner (with *Tummies*, see below) of our 1996 Family Restaurants of the Year Award, this converted pub has a curving, open-plan, two-level interior and a catering concept that manages cleverly to cater for both the Slough trading estate midweek business market (there's a separate bar area with sofas) and for families at weekends. Almost every chair within the dining area is different and supporting internal columns are painted an eclectic mix of colours – examples of the rather quirkiness of the operation whose success cannot be sneezed at (turning what was a run-down pub business into a bustling pizza and pasta restaurant has been an enormous challenge for Claude and Tammy Mariaux). The regular menu features a variety of starters, from home-made tomato soup (£2.50) or deep-fried Cajun calamari (£3.50) to starter-size pasta dishes, good salads, bruschetta and garlic focaccia. Ten or so pasta dishes, served in steaming bowlfuls – along with the doggy bags provided, a nice touch – are a highlight of the menu, encompassing spaghetti carbonara, fettuccine, rigatoni, tortellini, ravioli and lasagne; nine varieties of pizzas (a definite speciality) are cooked in a special multi-layered pizza oven (from all-day breakfast to 'flaming fire-meater' and 'vegged out'). Rather run-of-the-mill burgers, Cajun chicken, salmon fillet, ribs and peppered sirloin steak complete the main courses. Special deals include children's meals for £2.95 with a choice of pizza, ribs, burger or 'spag bol'; there are also good-value two-course weekday Tic-Toc lunches (£5.95 – guaranteed service within 15 minutes or there's no charge). During Saturday and Sunday lunchtimes (12-4pm) cartoon videos enliven the TV screens along with Spag's and Canneloni the clowns on hand to help children roll their sleeves up and make do-it-yourself pizzas – they seem to love getting stuck into the bowls of tomato sauce base, diced cheese, mushrooms, sweetcorn, pineapple and mild pepperoni sausage; the clowns also help with face-painting, collage- and charm bracelet-making with dried pasta and story-telling (if it's not too chaotic). One-cup tiramisu is an adult delight (along with dark chocolate chip mousse for chocoholics, blackcurrant crème brulée and apple and cinnamon cheesecake) and ice creams and sorbets always seem to hit the spot for junior palates. High-chairs are provided, along with a large Duplo table in a lounge/bar area with sofas; baby-changing (and disposal) facilities are in the Ladies. There is room in the safe garden for 50-odd seats at patio tables and full table service is provided in good weather; swings for younger children are at the end of the garden, further enhancing the family-friendliness of Spaggo's. Children's birthday parties (Mon-Fri 4-5.30pm) by arrangement. Spaggo's is 20 minutes' drive from London; Legoland in Windsor is 10 minutes away; walks in nearby Burnham Beeches can also be a sheer delight. From the M4, take Junction 6, go under the motorway heading north into Slough, go over the first roundabout (by the two hotels that we also recommend here) then turn right at the next major junction with traffic lights – you can't miss it on the left (almost opposite the Slough ice arena – Tel 01753 820900 – on the other side of the dual carriagweay). ***Seats** 90 (50 outside). Open 11.30-3 & 5.30-12, Sat 12-12, Sun 12-10. MasterCard, Amex,* **VISA**

Slough — Tummies Bistro

Tel 01628 668486 **Fax 01628 663106** Map 15 E2 JaB
5 Station Road Cippenham Slough Berkshire SL1 6JJ

Claude and Tammy Mariaux's popular pine-clad bistro is to be found just off the A4 on the outskirts of Slough (leave the M4 via the Slough West Junction 7 turn-off). Smart, smiling staff encourage customers of all ages with a variety of gimmicks, such as coloured pencils to sketch or fill in the place mats (best examples are immortalised on the restaurant ceiling!) and free Sunday lunch (always including a traditional roast) for two if you bring a party of 10 or more. The kitchen team produce such delights as smoked chicken and wild mushroom tagliatelle, moules marinière (£3.75/£5.95), salmon fishcakes with tomato, pesto and new potatoes (£7.50) and fillets of pork in a cream and mustard sauce (£9.25). Vegetarians are well catered for with offerings like tomato and goat's cheese salad (£3.75), spinach and ricotta strudel with new potatoes (£7.95) and wild mushroom and saffron risotto (£7.50). Desserts (all £3.25) could include blackcurrant and lemon syllabub, raspberry brulée and treacle tart. Children under 12 are offered their own menu. ***Seats*** *55.* ***Open*** *11.30-3 (Sun 12-6) & 5.30-12.* ***Closed*** *L Sat & Bank Holidays, D Sun, all 25, 26 Dec & 1 Jan. Amex, MasterCard,* ***VISA***

Smarden — The Bell

Tel 01233 770283 Map 11 C5 P
Bell Lane Smarden Kent TN26 8PW

Tiled and rose-covered medieval Kentish inn in peaceful countryside (take the road between the church and Chequers pub, then left at the junction). Rambling and rustic interior full of character with low, hop-festooned oak beams, inglenook fireplaces and a motley mix of old wooden furnishings in three flagstoned bars that are candelit in the evenings. Adjacent games/family room with pool table. Bar food is reliable, especially the hearty range of home-made daily specials such as chicken in tarragon, beef in beer casserole and pork with Dijon mustard sauce. Ploughman's platters and sandwiches available lunch and evening. Well-stocked bar dispensing eight real ales on handpump, the heady Biddenden scrumpy cider and eight wines by the glass. No under-14s in the Cellar Bar or Monk's Bar. Good summer garden. New owners as we went to press. *Open 11.30-2.30 (till 3 Sat), 6-11 (Sun 12-3, 6.30-10.30).* ***Bar Food*** *12-2 (till 2.30 Sun), 6.30-10 (till 10.30 Fri & Sat). Free House.* ***Beer*** *Fremlins, Flowers Original, Fuller's London Pride, Shepherd Neame Master Brew, Goacher's Best, Ringwood Old Thumper, guest beers. Garden, outdoor eating. Family room. Closed 25 Dec. Amex, MasterCard,* ***VISA***

Snettisham — Rose & Crown

Tel 01485 541382 **Fax 01485 543172** Map 10 B1 P
Old Church Road Snettisham King's Lynn Norfolk PE31 7LX

Tucked away just off the main road that runs through the village centre, Anthony and Jeanette Goodrich's splendid, white-painted 14th-century inn was originally built to house the craftsmen who built the beautiful local church just up the road. Beyond the attractive flower-decked facade lie a warren of three bars linked by a narrow, twisting corridor, off which are much-improved (and now rather smart) loos. Heavy oak beams, uneven red-tiled floors, inglenook fireplaces and comfortable settles characterise the two small front bar rooms; to one side of the front entrance is a small dining-room where breakfast is also served. Best bets on the food front are the blackboard menus: look for home-made soup, good pork and herb sausages, crab salad, pork stir-fry, supreme of chicken with wild mushrooms, and homely puds. A varied selection of five real ales usually includes two changing guest ales (try a pint of Wolf), plus there are good wines from Adnams, all available by the glass (but not all whites are served cool enough). To the rear is another bar, which leads through to a modern, poorly-ventilated extension that houses a third drinks servery area and (up a few steps or with direct access from the car park) a large, high-ceilinged dining-room with its own grill area (everything-with-chips and help-yourself salad). The pub can become very crowded when busy and the big rear extension helps cater for the families that flock here in season. After feasting on the under-12s' menu youngsters can escape into the safe, walled garden and clamber around the large play area that boasts a slide, play house, two wooden forts, monkey bars and a connecting walkway, all under a pretty willow tree. Less active children may find the guinea pig cage at one end of the lawned garden more entertaining. There is a mother's baby-changing unit in the Grill Room's Ladies and high-chairs are provided. Regular live music (mainly jazz). Upstairs, via a very steep, short staircase, are three airy, prettily decorated bedrooms (all with TV and tea-maker) – en suite, delightful and comfortable. Beware of the head-cracking low doorways! A tiny cottage 30 yards down the road is also available for B&B – fine for young families (as long as they don't mind poor TV reception). Plans are afoot to add further bedrooms above the rear extension. *Open 11-11, Sun 12-10.30. Free House.* ***Beer*** *Bass, Adnams Bitter, Greene King Abbot Ale, two guest beers.* ***Bar Food*** *12-2.30, 6-9.30. Garden, outdoor eating, children's play area.* ***Accommodation*** *3 rooms, all en suite, £55 (single £35). Children welcome overnight, additional bed & cot available (£10). Closed 25 Dec. No dogs. MasterCard,* ***VISA***

SOUTH HARTING White Hart

Tel 01730 825355 Map 15 D3 **P**

High Street South Harting West Sussex GU31 5QB

Pleasant village pub with three beamed bars, wooden tables, polished wood floors, log fires and a decent choice of good, fresh food. Known for their traditional country recipes, the licensees display their menu on a blackboard where specials appear daily – seafood mornay, spicy Mexican chicken and steak and kidney pie are typical choices. Separate simple bar snack menu includes sandwiches, salads and ploughman's platters. On Thursday, Friday and Saturday evenings the restaurant, formerly an old scullery, with flagstone floors and open inglenook fireplace, serves an à la carte menu. Vegetarians may wish to try the broccoli and cream cheese bake or vegetarian lasagne. Desserts may include pear and ginger gateau and various fruit pies. In fine weather, families may wish to venture into the beautiful garden overlooking the South Downs where children can safely play around the pond and waterfall. *Open 11-3, 6-11 (Sun 12-3, 7-10.30).* ***Bar Food*** *11-2 (from 12 Sun), 7-10 (no food Mon eve). Free House.* ***Beer*** *Ind Coope Burton Ale, Friary Meux Best, Tetley, guest beer. Garden, outdoor eating, children's play area. Family room (with toy box). No credit cards.*

A jug of fresh water!

SOUTH HOLMWOOD Gourmet Pizza Company

Tel 01306 889712 Map 15 E3 **JaB**

Horsham Road South Holmwood nr Dorking Surrey

Part of a small chain, this particularly family-friendly outlet is about two miles south of Dorking on the A24 (see entry under London for further adult menu details). Six high-chairs, and crayons provided at the table for colouring and completing the games on the children's menu (plain, pepperoni or chicken pizza and pasta ribbons or twirls plus ice cream sundaes and lollipops for those who finish all their food); separate Mother & Baby room. Children's parties catered for and children's entertainment on Sundays from 12.30 to 3.30pm. There's a purpose-built adventure playground and a lawned, fenced garden outside. Ample parking. ***Seats*** *110 (plus 30 outside). Open noon-10.45pm. Closed 25 & 26 Dec. MasterCard, Amex,* ***VISA***

Pubs – note that food is only recommended in those pubs with ***Bar Food*** times in the statistics at the end of an entry. Restaurant food in pubs is *never* recommended unless specifically mentioned. Some pubs are recommended for B&B or Atmosphere only – each entry's statistics indicate our recommendation.

South Molton — Whitechapel Manor — 76% — £130

Tel 01769 573377 **Fax 01769 573797** Map 13 D2 **HR**
South Molton Devon EX36 3EG

Follow the Whitechapel sign from a roundabout on the A361 near South Molton to find this delightfully peaceful (saving only the RAF on occasion) Elizabethan manor house fronted by terraced lawns and enjoying a fine view across the Yeo Valley. A fine Jacobean carved oak screen separates the entrance from the Great Hall, where comfortable chairs are set around the fireplace under a time-bowed William and Mary ceiling. The other day room is a blue leather-furnished bar, also with a real fire on chilly days. There's a scattering of antiques both downstairs and in the bedrooms, which range from small to large – some with separate sitting/dressing-rooms that are also ideal for a child's bed – with soft colour schemes and extras like a games compendium and a jug of iced water from their own spring. Bathrooms, decorated to match the rooms, all have panelled tubs with showers above, generously sized bottles of bath oil and towelling robes. The hotel is run by the mother-and-son team of Patricia Shapland and Steve Evans. ***Rooms** 10. Garden, croquet. Amex, Diners, MasterCard,* ***VISA***

Restaurant — £90

A pleasing, understated dining-room; each table is decorated with a miniature potted 'tree' made of dried flowers to match the large display filling the fireplace. David Alexander is now in charge in the kitchen and making a good job of the fixed-price menu that might include dishes like foie gras and chicken liver terrine with toasted home-made brioche; seared scallops with a saffron, spring onion and herb risotto; steamed cod with marinated courgettes and a sweet red pepper sauce and fillet of Devon beef on a crispy polenta crouton with lardons, braised shallots and red wine sauce. For afters there are desserts like chilled rice pudding with orange and cardamom syrup, lemon cheesecake with raspberry compote, a good hot chocolate and orange tartlet with raspberry sorbet and chocolate sauce and/or a selection of particularly good British cheeses. No children under 5. No smoking. ***Seats** 24. L 12-1.45 D 7-8.45. Set menu £34 (£40 with cheese course).*

Southsea — Barnaby's Bistro

Tel 01705 821089 Map 15 D4 **JaB**
Osbourne Road Southsea Hampshire PO5 3LU

Prompt, attentive service and interesting cooking in a strikingly pink and mauve restaurant. Diners have a choice of fixed-price or à la carte menus. Lunch offers the best value, as prices increase in the evening. Start with soup – broccoli and blue cheese with garlic bread (£1.95 lunch/£2.95 evening), or deep-fried camembert with mango coulis (£2.60/£3.25); follow with breast of chicken with apricots and cinnamon (£4.50/£7.50), pork with apple, cider and cream (£4.50/£7.50) or one of their enormous selection of vegetarian dishes – pasta with roasted pine nuts, broccoli and Provençal sauce (£3.95/£5.95). There is an Early Bird menu between 5 and 7 (three courses £4.95), and a four-course dinner menu for £11.95. ***Seats** 52. **Open** 11.30-2 & 6-11. **Closed** 25 & 26 Dec, 1 Jan. Amex, Diners, MasterCard,* ***VISA***

JaB is short for 'Just a Bite'. The majority of these establishments are also recommended in our *Bistros, Bars & Cafés* Guide which features establishments where one may eat well for less than £15 per head.

SOUTHWOLD The Crown £72

Tel 01502 722275 **Fax 01502 727263** Map 10 D2 **IR**
High Street Southwold Suffolk IP18 6DP

Next-door brewers, Adnams, take the credit for the stylish restoration of Southwold's central Georgian inn. While not without fault in attempting to be most things to all comers, the Crown is to be applauded for its success in bringing straightforward food, prime-condition beers and excellent wines to the average spender. The nautically themed rear bar is complete with binnacle and navigation lamps; the bar's curved and glassed-in rear panel gives the entirely fitting impression of being the flagship's bridge. To the front, facing the High Street, the Parlour serves as lounge and coffee shop; the front bar and attendant restaurant, decked out with green-grained panelling and Georgian-style brass lamps, has a refined air, yet is totally without pretension or stuffiness. New head chef Gary Marsland offers a daily-changing bar menu highlighting excellent local fish such as steamed fillet of cod with asparagus, kumquat and dill cream, grilled whole herrings on mixed leaves with a lime and leek syrup, and Thai-style shell and seafish chowder. Other options range from cream of onion soup and escalope of pork with Stilton and walnut glaze to venison sausage and black pudding casserole. Most meals are served in both starter and main-course sizes at good-value prices. Finish off with date and almond cheesecake, iced rhubarb parfait with stem ginger or a selection of Neal's Yard cheeses. In addition to the fine wine list chosen by Simon Loftus there's a splendid supplementary, monthly-changing list of 18 or so wines, available by both glass and bottle. The non-smoking restaurant has interesting fixed-price menus. Traditional roast beef and Yorkshire pudding is served in the restaurant on Sundays. Bedrooms are well equipped, with antique or decent reproduction pieces and bright fabrics and furnishings: all have private bathrooms though three are not strictly en suite (the bathroom is across a corridor); one family room has a double and two single beds. Pleasant staff offer a warm welcome and good but informal service. A light breakfast is served promptly in the bedroom along with the morning paper. *Open 10.30-3, 6-11 (from 7 Oct-Apr), Sun 12-3, 7-10.30.* ***Bar Food*** *12.15-1.45, 7.15-9.45.* ***Beer*** *Adnams. Patio, outdoor eating.* ***Accommodation*** *12 bedrooms, 9 en suite, £72 (family room £87, single £41). Children welcome overnight, additional bed (£10) & cot (£5) available. Check-in from 2pm onwards. No dogs. Pub & accommodation closed 1 week Jan. Amex, Diners, MasterCard,* ***VISA***

SOWERBY BRIDGE The Hobbit

Tel 01422 832202 **Fax 01422 835381** Map 6 C1 **P**
Hob Lane Sowerby Bridge Calderdale HX6 3QL

Standing on the very lip of the moor (follow directions, below, carefully), the Hobbit enjoys panoramic views over the Pennines and Sowerby Bridge far below. A relaxed and welcoming place, it's a haven for families, with Bilbo's bistro open all day, every day: youngsters receive a fun pad on arrival. Connecting bedrooms are available for families, with special weekend rates, while a thoughtful array of accessories appeals equally to the mid-week business traveller. Satellite TVs, for instance, include a video channel and fresh milk is conveniently kept in a corridor fridge. A cottage annexe across the road contains a pair of splendidly-furnished executive bedrooms which also benefit from the finest views down the valley. No-smoking areas in bistro and restaurant. Watch out for the many and varied theme nights, notably the murder and mystery evenings, and special children's events. Take the A58 to Sowerby Bridge by the Railway Viaduct, turn onto Station Road, then right at the police station, left at the T-Junction, continue up the hill and then right at the crossroads. *Open 12-11 (up to 2am with meals), Sun 12-10. Free House.* ***Beer*** *Theakston Best, Ruddles Best, guest beer. Garden, two patios.* ***Accommodation*** *22 bedrooms, all en suite (14 with shower only), £63-£73 (single £42/£49), weekend reductions. Children welcome overnight (under-6s stay free in parents' room, 6-12s £11), cot available. No dogs. Amex, Diners, MasterCard,* ***VISA***

SPARKFORD Sparkford Inn

Tel 01963 440218 **Fax 01963 440358** Map 13 F2 
Sparkford Yeovil Somerset BA22 7JH

Families driving west along the A303 with restless children should take note of this former 15th-century coaching inn, which is situated a minute's drive away in the centre of Sparkford village, 6 miles west of Wincanton. Youngsters can expend some energy in the well equipped and safe outdoor play area or, especially when the weather is inclement, amuse themselves in the supervised 'Snakes and Ladders' indoor play room (open weekends and school holiday lunchtimes). Here they will find a 25ft bouncy castle, punch bag and balls, trampoline and large soft play area with see-saws, animal shapes and slide. Facilities for children extend to their own menu, high-chairs and a baby-changing shelf in the Ladies. With children happily entertained, parents can relax with a drink in the beamed and comfortably furnished bars that retain many original features. Menus, especially the blackboard specials, looked promising on a recent visit; upstairs, there are three homely and simply furnished en suite bedrooms (£32 double). Owners Nigel and Suzanne Tucker also run the *Star Inn* at Stanton St John, Oxfordshire (see entry). *Open 11-2.30 (till 3 Sat), 6.30-11 (Sun 12-3, 7-10.30). Free House.* ***Beer*** *Bass, Wadworth 6X, Worthington Best, Fuller's London Pride, guest beer. Garden, children's play area. Family room. Amex, MasterCard,* ***VISA***

SPARSHOLT The Plough

Tel 01962 776353 Map 15 D3 
Sparsholt Winchester Hampshire SO21 2NW

A delightful flower- and shrub-filled garden complete with children's playhouses, wooden garden chalet, chickens and donkeys is a popular summer feature at this much-extended 200-year-old cottage, located on the edge of the village. The smartly refurbished bar area, incorporating the original cottage front rooms, feature pine tables, a dresser and comfortable cushioned chairs, with plenty of attractive prints brightening up the walls and an open fireplace for cooler days. New tenants have settled in well and have maintained the high standard of cooking that earned the Plough our recommendation for food under the previous landlords. Two sensibly short blackboards list the varied range of decent pub food on offer, from hearty, home-cooked snacks served with fresh crusty bread (broccoli and almond soup, cauliflower cheese, salmon tagliatelle, bourride of fish, moules marinière) to steak, ale and mushroom pie with vegetables and more imaginative, sauced dishes such as rack of lamb with wild mushrooms and brandy cream, and shark steak with mixed peppercorn sauce. A handwritten menu on the bar lists 'doorstep' sandwiches (salmon and cucumber, beef and horseradish, fresh crab) that require a knife and fork to eat. Short list of home-made puddings. Well-kept Wadworth ales and at least eight wines are served by the glass. *Open 11-3, 6.30-11 (Sun 12-3, 7-10.30).* ***Bar Food*** *12-2, 7-9 (Fri & Sat to 9.30).* ***Beer*** *Wadworth 6X & Henry's IPA, guest beer. Garden, children's play area. No credit cards.*

STAFFORD De Vere Tillington Hall 63% £95

Tel 01785 253531 **Fax 01785 259223** Map 6 B3 
Eccleshall Road Stafford Staffordshire ST16 1JJ

Half a mile from the M6 (J14), this modern De Vere hotel adds good leisure and conference facilities (200 maximum, ample parking) to bedrooms that include four-poster rooms and two specially adapted for disabled guests. The hotel's main attraction for families is obviously the proximity of Alton Towers and American Adventure theme parks; packed lunches can be provided. A fun pack is given to children on arrival and entertainment is put on during holiday periods; children's channels are included on the satellite TV. Children's splash pool and outdoor playground; indoor play room and Tillington Ted Club activities (perhaps a tea party, Punch & Judy or magic show on selected dates) for younger guests during school holidays. Informal eating in the leisure club dining area and bar. Children up to 14 share adult accommodation free, paying for meals as taken. Very family-friendly at selected weekends and during school holidays due to its proximity to Alton Towers. ***Rooms*** *90. Garden, indoor swimming pool, gym, sauna, spa bath, sun beds, beauty salon, tennis, snooker. Closed 28 & 29 Dec. Amex, Diners, MasterCard,* ***VISA***

STAFFORD Soup Kitchen

Tel 01785 254775 Map 6 B3 JaB
Church Lane Stafford Staffordshire ST16 2AW

A very busy tea shop, which has recently expanded into the next door cottage, in a pedestrian-only lane just off the town centre. It's waitress- or self-service but even at the latter one of the exceptionally friendly staff is liable to offer to carry your tray. Egg mayonnaise (£1.20), chili con carne (£2.95), cottage pie, pizzas (from £2.15), jacket potatoes (from £2.15), toasted sandwiches (from £2.95), cheesecake (£2), fresh cream slice and scones (60p) are just a small sample from the all-day menu. Until noon there are also a couple of breakfast options – bacon roll (£1.75, £2.10 with a poached egg), cheese on toast (£2.10) and an all-day breakfast at £3.25. Children, who are most welcome, have their own fish finger/burger menu. There are high-chairs and 'baby dinners' for the tinies. Bibs, toys and feeder cups are provided along with a changing shelf in the Ladies. An enlarged kitchen has been built, so there are great plans in hand for the food. ***Seats*** *220.* ***Open*** *9.30-4.45.* ***Closed*** *Sun & Bank Holidays. No credit cards.*

STAMFORD George of Stamford 72% £105

Tel 01780 755171 **Fax 01780 757070** Map 7 E3 HR
71 St Martins Stamford Lincolnshire PE9 2LB

Arguably the finest and grandest of England's old coaching inns, the George is a fully modernised hotel (recommended in our *1997 Hotels & Restaurants Guide*) that retains some wonderful period atmosphere. It's believed that there's been a hostelry of sorts here since the Norman period, originally as a stopping place for pilgrims on their way to the Holy Land, and a crypt under what is now the cocktail bar is certainly medieval, while much of the present building, which dates from 1597, remains in the veritable warren of rooms that make up the public areas. Facing the High Street, the oak-panelled London Suite and York Bar were once waiting rooms for the "twenty up and twenty down" stages which passed this way, but for the modern pub-goer this bar is probably the least attractive, being solidly masculine in its appearance. The Garden Lounge, however, which is exotically bedecked in orchids, palms and orange trees, provides a fine setting for informal eating throughout the day (7am-11pm): dishes range from open sandwiches and pasta meals to sizzling beef with ginger and mushrooms and noisettes of lamb with green peppercorn and brandy sauce. Lunch includes a fine cold buffet, with which, incidentally, up to 13 wines are offered by the glass. Next door, and by far the most picturesque spot, is the enclosed courtyard. Surrounded by the ivy-covered hotel buildings, hung with vast flowering baskets and illuminated by old street lamps, it makes an ideal venue for morning coffee and afternoon tea, as well as barbecues on mid-summer evenings. Restaurant dining, in an elegant, chandeliered hall sporting silver urns, duck presses, and domed carving wagons (daily roast joints) and serving trolleys (smoked salmon, cheese, desserts) still in daily use, runs along traditional (and comparatively pricey) lines with adventurous touches; gentlemen are 'respectfully' requested to wear a jacket and tie. The super wine list is keenly priced, expertly compiled and simple to use. Accommodation at the George is strictly hotel, which is fine if you're prepared to pay. A liveried porter shows you to the room and there's a full, cosseting night service. The comfort of plushly-draped bedrooms, close-carpeted through to the bathrooms fitted out with bespoke toiletries, generous towels and rather wonky telephone showers is all wonderfully 'British'. A morning tray of tea (with folded daily paper – no, it's not ironed!) appears at the appointed time, and a traditional English breakfast is served down in the Garden Lounge. *Open 11-11 (Sun 12-10.30).* ***Bar Food*** *12-11 (till 10.30 Sun). Free House.* ***Beer*** *Adnams Broadside, Ruddles Best. Cobbled courtyard, outdoor eating, beautician, hair salon. Family room.* ***Accommodation*** *47 bedrooms, all en suite (3 single rooms with shower only), £105-£160 (single £78/£88). Children welcome overnight, additional bed (£20) & cot available. Amex, Diners, MasterCard,* ***VISA***

Stanstead Abbots Briggens House 70% £120

H

Tel 01279 829955 **Fax 01279 793685** Map 15 F2
Stanstead Road Stanstead Abbots nr Ware Hertfordshire SG12 8LD

A grand former stately home, a few miles off the M11, set in 80 acres of grounds and splendid gardens with its own arboretum, 9-hole golf course and fishing on the River Stott. High standards of service are typified by the smart, uniformed doormen. A magnificent carved wood staircase leads up from the entrance hall with its glass chandelier to 22 bedrooms in the main house; 32 more are in the converted coach house and have lower ceilings, but all are equally tastefully decorated with a good range of extras included as standard; 40 bedrooms were refurbished last year. Swagged drapes and stylish reproduction antiques give an elegant air; top of the range are Executive doubles (£139), suites and two rooms with four-posters (£169). 24hr room service. In summer, tables are set on the expansive lawns outside the French windows leading off the lounge. Function facilities for 100 in eight meeting rooms. Children under 16 free in parents' room. QMH County Hotels. ***Rooms*** *54. Garden, croquet, boules, outdoor swimming pool, tennis, golf (9), pitch & putt, putting, fishing. Closed 27-29 Dec. Amex, Diners, MasterCard,* ***VISA***

Stanton St John Star Inn

P

Tel & Fax 01865 351277 Map 15 D2
Stanton St John Oxford Oxfordshire OX9 1EX

A former 18th-century butcher's shop and abattoir (now owned by Wadworth) with lots of period feel in two bars on two levels, both low-beamed, one brick-floored, the other carpeted and furniture-crammed. Families can eat in a separate no-smoking room. Beyond a straightforward printed menu listing ploughman's, sandwiches, grills and children's dishes, daily specials may feature pork and cider casserole, game pie and sea trout and turbot pie, with banana and ginger cheesecake or treacle and walnut tart to finish. A separate vegetarian menu offers a choice of six dishes. £1 charge for paying by credit card. Landlords the Tuckers also own the *Sparkford Inn* in Somerset (see entry). *Open 11-2.30, 6.30-11 (Sun 12-3, 7-10.30).* ***Bar Food*** *12-2, 7-10 (till 9.30 Sun).* ***Beer*** *Wadworth Henry's IPA, 6X, Old Timer (in winter) & Farmer's Glory, Hall & Woodhouse Tanglefoot, guest beer. Garden, outdoor eating, children's play area. Family room. Closed 25 Dec. Amex, MasterCard,* ***VISA***

Staple Fitzpaine Greyhound Inn

Tel 01823 480227 **Fax 01823 480773** Map 13 E2
Staple Fitzpaine Taunton Somerset TA3 5SP

Built as a hunting lodge by the local lord of the manor in 1640, the much extended creeper-clad Greyhound nestles in rolling landscape close to the Blackdown Hills. The rinterior comprises a series of rambling, connecting rooms, some with flagstone floors, some with old timbers or natural stone walls and stools made out of old barrels. The gravelled terrace garden has a play area with a splendid rustic climbing frame and slide and the welcome to youngsters extends indoors to their own menu, baby-changing facilities in the Ladies and an annual 'fun day'. The bar menu encompasses chargrills with a choice of sauces, baked jacket potatoes, ploughman's platters, sandwiches, Mexican tacos, home-made burgers, devilled whitebait, deep-fried Brie and vegetarian options (vegetable lasagne); a more exciting, daily-changing à la carte menu (home-made carrot and coriander soup, grilled sea bass with mushroom and white wine sauce, peppered pork, summer pudding, strawberry cheesecake) is also available in the bars. Live jazz and blues on Thursdays, a comedian performs once a month on a Saturday and an annual beer festival featuring 20 real ales. Four en suite letting bedrooms should be completed in late 1996. *Open 12-3, 5-11 (from 6 Sat), Sun 12-4, 7-10.30.* ***Bar Food*** *12-2 (till 2.30 Sat), 7-10 (till 9.30 Sun). Free House.* ***Beer*** *Exmoor Ale, Flowers Original, Cotleigh Tawny, Bass, guest beer. Terrace, outdoor eating, summer barbecue, children's play area. Family room. MasterCard,* ***VISA***

> Many hotels offer reduced rates for weekend or out-of-season bookings. Always ask about special deals and family rooms.

Stapleford — Stapleford Park — 87% — £165

Tel 01572 787522 **Fax 01572 787651** Map 7 E3 **HR**
Stapleford nr Melton Mowbray Leicestershire LE14 2EF

Set in 500 acres of parkland laid out by Capability Brown, this beautiful country house hotel is approached via the gatehouses and protected from hundreds of grazing sheep by a splendid stone ha-ha. The core of the house was built by the Sherard family in the 17th century and their family portraits dominate the public rooms; Victorian additions blend in perfectly. Drawing rooms have comfortable sofas, splendid carved and moulded ceilings and roaring winter fires. Upstairs, luxuriously-appointed bedrooms (the tariff rises to £300) have been designed by more than 25 famous names, based on their image of life in the country – not only recognised designers such as Nina Campbell and David Hicks but also more surprising names like Turnbull & Asser (a very masculine room with shirt fabric-inspired wall coverings), and Crabtree & Evelyn with a room full of over 200 floral pictures. Marble bathrooms are equally sumptuous, with heavy bathrobes, luxury toiletries and tubs practically deep enough for a swim. A four-bedroomed self-contained cottage has bedrooms by Coca Cola, MGM, Range Rover and IBM. Children up to 10 stay free in parents' room. The hotel was taken over by Peter de Savary's Carnegie Club early in 1996 and plans were already in place for nine more bedrooms, a swimming pool and a health and beauty centre as we went to press. ***Rooms*** *42. Garden, croquet, coarse fishing, tennis, clay pigeon shooting, putting, riding, basketball. Amex, Diners, MasterCard,* ***VISA***

Restaurant — £90

The Grinling Gibbons dining-room lives up to the standard of the rest of the hotel, filled with his splendid swags and carvings. This room is generally only used in the evenings, when chef Malcolm Jessop offers an à la carte menu rooted in the French tradition. However, this is not a place to stand on ceremony and you are invited to cut your own bread at table and pour your own wine (this informality stops short of encouraging the wearing of jeans). Jessop uses a broad brush to paint a worldwide picture, but the finesse is not lost. Typical dishes might include a flower of grilled aubergine and Parma ham served with a pear, fennel and red pepper salad garnished with mache and truffle oil; smoked Scottish salmon baskets filled with *orzo* pasta salad and served with fresh asparagus on a lemon and chive dressing; spicy crab cake with sautéed scallops on a tequila and grapefruit sauce, garnished with tortilla strips and citrus fruit confit; grilled swordfish with a jalapeno, mango and pineapple relish on a cashew and lemon grass pilaf with grilled red and green onions; grilled medallions of Scottish beef with a black and white bean ragout, forest mushrooms, haricot verts and tobacco onions. Desserts are equally tempting: The Stapleford Wave is a sampler plate for those not calorie-counting, while fruit nachos (sweet tortillas topped with a mixed-fruit salsa, two ice creams and a fruit coulis) and white chocolate piano (filled with fresh berries under a bitter chocolate lid) show that the eclectic, witty style continues right to the end. Lunch is a lighter table d'hote affair (rigatoni tricolori, salmon and haddock fishcakes) and there's an all-day menu with everything from pasta and salads to hamburgers and satisfying sandwiches; on Sundays in winter a traditional lunch is served in the vaulted Old Kitchen, while a comprehensive barbecue perfectly captures the modern country-house mood in the summer. Outdoor eating for 40 on the terrace. No smoking. No children at dinner (high tea is provided). Disabled toilets. ***Seats*** *70. Parties 8. Private Room 40. L 12-2.30 D 7-9.30 (Fri & Sat to 10). Set L £12.50/£15 (Mon-Fri) £22.50 (Sun).*

Stiffkey — Red Lion

Tel & Fax 01328 830552 Map 10 C1 **P**
44 Wells Road Stiffkey Wells-next-the-Sea Norfolk NR23 1AJ

Nestling in the Stiffkey valley amid rolling Norfolk countryside, this peaceful village once boasted three pubs, but all became victims of the Watney revolution in the 1960s. After 28 years as a private house the Red Lion, a fine 16th-century white-painted brick and flint cottage on the main coast road, was resurrected in 1990 as a free house and has been thriving ever since, attracting a loyal local clientele. Inside, three charming rooms have bare board or quarry-tiled floors, three warming logs fires – one in a splendid inglenook – and a simple rustic mix of wooden settles, pews and scrubbed tables. Apart from the ambience, it is the good home-cooked food, which focuses on fresh local produce, that draws people here. A blackboard menu lists the daily-changing choice of dishes which may include Cromer crab, Stiffkey mussels marinière, Thai spring rolls and soft herring roes on toast for starters, followed by fish pie, game pie, pan-fried rump steak, wild mushroom and broccoli lasagne and grilled fresh fish from King's Lynn. Lunchtime snacks include ploughman's lunches, filled French sticks and bread and cheese. For pudding try the deep-pan apple pie, summer pudding or treacle and nut tart. Good range of East Anglian beers and a short list of Adnams wines (several served by the glass in summer). After a day on the beach or strolling the Peddars Way this is a good stop for families, who have use of a large and airy rear conservatory with access to the terraced garden. *Open 12-3, 7-11 (from 6 Bank Holidays & school holidays), Sun 12-3, 7-10.30.* ***Bar Food*** *12-2, 7-9. Free House.* ***Beer*** *Greene King Abbot Ale & IPA, Woodforde's Wherry, Nelson's Revenge & Great Eastern Ale, guest beer. Garden, outdoor eating. Family room. MasterCard,* ***VISA***

STILTON — Bell Inn — £74

Tel 01733 241066 **Fax 01733 245173** Map 7 E4 IR

Great North Road Stilton Peterborough Cambridgeshire PE7 3RA

Reputedly the oldest coaching inn on the Great North Road, the Bell boasts a Roman well in its courtyard and an impressive 15th-century stone frontage. Discreetly concealed from the road are two wings of en suite bedrooms whose 20th-century trappings include telephones, satellite television and whirlpool baths, while tokens of the past are confined to the odd four-poster bed. This is a pity, as the rest of the building is simply splendid. The village bar retains its stone-flagged floor and cosy alcoves huddled round the great log fire; this is where the original Stilton cheese was sold to travellers in the 1720s. Today it's served on its own with plum bread, or in a celery soup, or in a lamb casserole with Stilton dumplings. For the less single-minded, there's steak, ale and mushroom pie or coriander lamb, followed by home-made traditional desserts like sticky toffee pudding and crème brulée. More serious food on a weekly-changing table d'hote and set four-course dinner (£22.50) menus is on offer in the galleried restaurant, where linen-covered tables are widely spaced in two sections under gnarled oak beams and a vaulted ceiling with original exposed rafters. Recommended in our *1997 Hotels and Restaurants Guide. Open 12-2.30, 6-11 (Sun 12-3, 7-10.30).* ***Bar Food*** *12-2, 6.30-9.30 (Sun 7-9). Free House.* ***Beer*** *Marston's Pedigree, Ruddles Best, Tetley, guest beer. Garden, terrace, outdoor eating.* ***Accommodation*** *19 bedrooms, all en suite, £74-£94 (single £59-£64). Children welcome overnight (under-3s stay free if sharing parents' room), additional bed (£5-£10) & cot available. No dogs. Closed 1 week Christmas. Amex, MasterCard,* ***VISA***

STOCKPORT — Boutinot's Bistro

Tel 0161-477 0434 Map 6 B2 JaB

8 Vernon Street Stockport SK1 1TY

Sisters Micheline Kershaw and Jeanne Pegg run this friendly bistro, where an all-day breakfast (à la carte items or £3.25 for 'the works') heads the menu. Also on offer are sandwiches plain or toasted (£2.35 to £2.75), jacket potatoes, salads, vegetarian dishes and main dishes such as coq au vin with vegetables (£4.30), lasagne, poached salmon with herb mayonnaise and crusty bread (£4.50) or sauté of lamb's kidneys with mustard, served on a mushroom pilaf. Also scones, cakes, teacakes and puddings. Families are welcome, with a children's section for the under-8s and children's portions offered (except between 12 and 2pm, unless 3 years old or under). Three high-chairs, and a quiet area upstairs for nursing mothers. ***Seats*** *78 (+ 12 outside).* ***Open*** *8.30-5.* ***Closed*** *Sun & most Bank Holidays. No credit cards.*

Stoke-on-Trent Stoke-on-Trent Moat House 70% £114

Tel 01782 609988 **Fax 01782 284500** Map 6 B3 **H**
Etruria Hall Festival Way Etruria Stoke-on-Trent Staffordshire ST1 5BQ

Ten minutes' drive from the M6, and equidistant from J15 and J16, the hotel stands by the A53 at the heart of the 1986 Garden Festival park (the hotel opened in 1991). Day rooms, leisure club and smart up-to-date bedrooms are in a sympathetically designed stone-clad complex which reflects within it many of the original hall's features. Two rooms are equipped for disabled guests. Good children's facilities include a supervised sports club; under-16s stay free in parents' room. No dogs. ***Rooms*** *143. Garden, indoor swimming pool, gym, sauna, spa bath, steam room, solarium, beauty salon, snooker, games room, table tennis, coffee shop (9am-10pm). Amex, Diners, MasterCard,* ***VISA***

Stourton Spread Eagle Inn

Tel 01747 840587 **Fax 01747 841552** Map 14 B3 **P**
Stourhead Stourton Warminster Wiltshire BA12 6QE

Fine 18th-century brick inn owned by the National Trust and peacefully located within a neat complex of buildings – tea room and National Trust shop – close to the tiny parish church and Stourhead House with its magnificent landscaped gardens, enchanting lakes and woodland walks. As one would expect, the interior of the inn has been tastefully refurbished, the bars sporting sturdy wooden furnishings, good prints and paintings and warming open fires. High standards extend to the five charming, recently refurbished en suite bedrooms which retain architectural details, including Georgian and Regency fireplaces, and boast quality co-ordinating fabrics, antique and older-style furniture, easy chairs and various ornaments, clocks and pieces of china adding a homely touch. Each room has a TV, telephone, beverage-making kit and spotless bathroom with both a bath and overhead shower. The inn can get busy in the summer months with Stourhead visitors, but out-of-season this is an idyllic rural retreat. *Open 11-11, (Sun 12-10.30). Free House.* ***Beer*** *Ash Vine, Stourhead 50, Eldridge Pope Hardy Ale & Pope's Traditional. Courtyard. Family room.* ***Accommodation*** *5 bedrooms, all en suite, £69 (single £45). Children welcome overnight, additional bed (£12.50) & cot available (£5). No dogs. Amex, Diners, MasterCard,* ***VISA***

Stow-on-the-Wold Fosse Manor 60% £106

Tel 01451 830354 **Fax 01451 832486** Map 14 C1 **H**
Fosse Way Stow-on-the-Wold Gloucestershire GL54 1JX

Resident proprietors Bob and Yvonne Johnston and their loyal staff run a family haven that attracts many repeat visitors. Built in the style of a Cotswold manor house, it stands in its ivy coat in grounds set back from the A429 (originally the Fosse Way) about a mile south of Stow-on-the-Wold. Bedrooms (including several suitable for family occupation) overlook colourful gardens and the bright look of the day rooms is enhanced throughout by potted plants, fresh flowers and spotless housekeeping. Children up to 16 stay free in their parents' room. Ask the proprietors about the indoor swimming pool, sauna, spa bath and solarium (which were previously hotel facilities). Conference/banqueting facilities for 44/72. Parking for 60 cars. ***Rooms*** *20. Garden, putting, playground. Closed 1 week Christmas. Amex, Diners, MasterCard,* ***VISA***

Stratfield Turgis Wellington Arms £70

Tel 01256 882214 **Fax 01256 882934** Map 15 D3 **I**
Stratfield Turgis Basingstoke Hampshire RG27 OAS

Hard by the A33, a charming old inn with a handsome white Georgian facade and a mix of the old and the new inside. The cosy, pubby L-shaped bar features a polished flagstone floor, a characterful mish-mash of wooden tables and chairs laid for bar snacks; it leads directly round into a friendly drawing room in country-house style with open fire, sunken-cushioned sofas, gilt-framed oil portraits and French windows which open on to a small lawned area where bench picnic tables are set. Light meals and snacks include sandwiches and ploughman's platters, tomato and sweet pepper quiche, mussels in white wine and garlic, stir-fry chicken and tagliatelle carbonara and daily blackboard specials (perhaps grilled supreme of coley and whole baked plaice) complete the picture. Fifteen bedrooms in the original building include two 'luxury doubles' (one a suite with a heavily-carved four-poster and spa bath); 20 further rooms are in a two-storey modern extension to the rear, uniformly decorated with Laura Ashley pastel blues and yellows plus modern light oak furniture suites; hotel room facilities like a comfortable armchair, remote-controlled TV, powerful showers and tea/coffee making facilities are standard. A couple of modern suites serve as both small meeting rooms and family rooms with pull-down additional beds. Next door to the Duke of Wellington's estate (Stratfield Saye House, where river fishing can be arranged) and close to Wellington Country Park (ideal for family outings). Badger Inns. *Open 11-11 (Sun 12-10.30).* ***Bar Food*** *12-2.30, 6-10 (Sun 7-9.30).* ***Beer*** *Hall & Woodhouse. Garden, outdoor eating.* ***Accommodation*** *35 bedrooms, all en suite, £70/£85/£95/£110 (single £60/£75), weekend £50/£75 (single £40), family room £120. Children welcome overnight, additional bed & cot (both £10) available. Amex, Diners, MasterCard,* ***VISA***

STRATFORD-UPON-AVON Stratford Manor 64% £100

Tel 01789 731173 **Fax 01789 731131** Map 14 C1 H

Warwick Road Stratford-upon-Avon Warwickshire CV37 0PY

Four linked blocks provide practical accommodation in a modern redbrick hotel on the A439 (leave the M40 at J15); the hotel was built in 1990 and is set in 21 acres. Fully-equipped leisure centre; conference facilities in eight rooms catering for up to 380 plus six syndicate rooms and parking for 220 cars. Many large family and eight interconnecting bedrooms, with under-16s staying free in parents' room. Shire rooms have four-posters and an extra seating area. Now owned and run by Marston Hotels; previously trading as the Windmill Park. ***Rooms*** *104. Indoor swimming pool, tennis, gym, sauna, spa bath, steam room, solarium, aerobic/dance studio, pool table, games room, children's play area. Amex, Diners, MasterCard,* ***VISA***

STREATLEY-ON-THAMES Swan Diplomat 68% £139

Tel 01491 873737 **Fax 01491 872554** Map 15 D2

High Street Streatley-on-Thames Berkshire RG8 9HR

This charming hotel (the welcome is friendly and professional) spreads itself along the south bank of the River Thames, enabling the public rooms, including the pine-clad bar and the comfortable lounges, to have extensive views of the river, the boats and the ducks. Likewise, over half the bedrooms overlook the water, many of these with their own balconies. The attractively decorated bedrooms are furnished with traditional-style mahogany pieces combining comfort with all mod cons. For the energetic, the well-equipped Reflexions fitness centre, incorporated in the building, is available free for guests. Moored alongside is the Magdalen College Barge, which, as well as looking picturesque, provides an unusual setting for meetings and cocktail parties. Spacious car park. 24hr room service. An ideal spot for afternoon tea, especially on the river terrace, with its picturesque view. Watch the ducks swim past while enjoying your Berkshire Cream Tea (£5.95), including scones, clotted cream, jam, salmon and cucumber sandwiches and apple and carrot cake. ***Rooms*** *46. Garden, croquet, indoor 'fitness' swimming pool, sauna, solarium, gym, bicycles, rowing boats, moorings. Amex, Diners, MasterCard,* ***VISA***

Riverside Restaurant £85

Attractive, summery dining-room with trelliswork ceiling, rattan-effect chairs, crisp napery and Royal Doulton china, but it's the river views that steal the show. New 25-year-old head chef Darren Vaughan took over just as we went to press; another major change is that the riverside terrace was now being made available for sheltered alfresco dining under huge African sunshades. Both à la carte and a limited-choice prix-fixe chef's menu are offered at night. Sunday lunch brings a fixed-price traditional menu with a choice of roasts; on other days lunch is in the Duck Room Brasserie, a small area between the bar and the restaurant proper. Staff are notably polite and pleasant. ***Seats*** *75. Parties 12. L (Sun only, except brasserie) 12-2 D 7.30-9.30 (Sat from 7 in summer). Closed D Sun & Mon. Set Sun L £22.50 Set D £29.50.*

STRETTON Ram Jam Inn £60

Tel 01780 410776 Fax 01780 410361 Map 7 E3 **IR**
Great North Road Stretton nr Oakham Leicestershire LE15 7QX

Hard by a service station nine miles north of Stamford on the northbound lane of the A1 (southbound drivers take the B668 exit to Oakham and follow signs), the Ram Jam Inn, named after a special brew produced in its early days, makes a very welcome break. Public rooms are primarily devoted to informal eating areas. All-day snacks and meals are available in the three interconecting dining-rooms, one of which is set up as a restaurant; the two other informal rooms overlook the orchard; outdoor eating with 20 seats on a terrace. One menu is served throughout, with granary baps and open sandwiches for quick snacks. Typical dishes include an ever-popular chargrilled chopped steak burger piled high with deep-fried shaved vegetables, half a pint of shell-on prawns, home-made gravad lax, daily-changing soup, fish and pasta dishes, Rutland sausages with onion marmalade and mash, a quartet of marinated herrings with sour cream and crusty fresh bread, and good desserts like lemon tart or chocolate mousse terrine with black cherry coulis and praline ice cream. A roast is added to the menu for Sunday lunchtimes. New 'instant lunch' menu (£6.25/£7.95), served 12-2, offers particularly good value. Good children's options and pleasantly informal service; high-chairs and changing facilities provided. All the bedrooms overlook the garden and orchard and are individually and tastefully decorated with limed-pine furniture; they are surprisingly quiet, considering the proximity to the road. To one side of the entrance is an air-conditioned conference room seating up to 30. If only every roadside inn was as good as this! *Open 7am-10pm.* ***Meals*** *7am-10pm.* ***Beer*** *Ruddles Best & County, Tetley – all under pressure.* ***Accommodation*** *7 bedrooms, all en suite, £60 (family room sleeping 4 £68, single £50). Children welcome overnight, cot provided (£10, free in family room). Garden, terrace, outdoor eating. Closed 25 Dec. Amex, Diners, MasterCard,* ***VISA***

STRINESDALE Roebuck Inn

Tel & Fax 0161 624 7819 Map 6 B2 **P**
Brighton Road Strinesdale Stockport OL4 3RB

A family welcome from Sue, Mark, Mary and Peter, and a prodigious choice from the menu await those who venture up the moor to the Howarth and Walters families' imposing hillside pub; the pub's not easy to find on a map – it's about a mile off the A672, taking Turfpitt Lane south of Denshaw. While the little ones can choose from fish fingers, beefburgers or sausages, a monthly-changing specials board can help buck the otherwise chips-and-peas mentality. Go, perhaps, for pot-roast leg of lamb with red wine, chicken tikka masala or poached halibut with mushroom sauce. Sandwiches and ploughman's platters are readily available lunch and evening for those in need of a lighter bite. Value-for-money mid-week 3- and 4-course set menus. From bookable tables by the picture windows views down the moor's edge end in an urban skyline; in the foreground a paved yard beckons animal-loving youngsters whose parents don't mind them getting mucky. *Open 12-3, 6-11 (Sun 12-10.30).* ***Bar Food*** *12-2.30, 6-10 (Sun 12-10). Free House.* ***Beer*** *Oldham Bitter, Boddingtons. Garden, outdoor eating, children's play area. Amex, MasterCard,* ***VISA***

STROUD Mother Nature

Tel 01453 758202 Fax 01453 752595 Map 14 B2 **JaB**
2 Bedford Street Stroud Gloucestershire GL5 1AY

Walk through the wholefood shop and down some steps to this lively, unpretentious wholefood and vegetarian café. Lynne Searby believes in free expression in the kitchen, hence an ever-changing choice of dishes: quiches, pizzas (both £1.65), spinach and courgette soup (£1.50), Caribbean cauliflower cheese, broccoli crunch, spinach and mushroom lasagne and 'Priest has Fainted' (aubergine and nut) – all £2.85. Home-made cakes and puddings include three different kinds of carrot cake, apricot or date slice (70p-£1), banana pudding, Spotted Dick and bread-and-butter pudding (all £1.25). Husband Trevor runs the shop and a 'baguette take-away'. £1.75 minimum charge at lunchtime, when smoking is not allowed. Children's portions available. Wide choice of teas. Unlicensed. ***Seats*** *40.* ***Open*** *9-4.30.* ***Closed*** *Sun & Bank Holidays (except Good Friday). No credit cards.*

STROUD — The Old Lady Tea Shop

Tel 01453 762441 Map 14 B2 **JaB**
1 Threadneedle Street Stroud Gloucestershire GL5 1AF

Run by Penny Grimes and Sally Burford, this first-floor tea shop is over Walkers Bakery, which supplies most of the impressive choice of cakes, flapjacks and patisseries. There's also a small menu of light snacks: toasted sandwiches (from £1.75), pizza (from £2), ploughman's (£2), bacon sandwiches (£1.50), stuffed jacket potatoes (from £2) and daily specials such as cheese, potato and onion pie (£2.50 including a salad). All-day breakfast £2.50. Cream teas £1.60. A sign in the window states that smokers are welcome. Unlicensed. ***Seats** 32. **Open** 9.30-4. **Closed** Sun & Bank Holidays. No credit cards.*

STUDLAND BAY — Knoll House — 63% — £164*

Tel 01929 450450 **Fax 01929 450423** Map 14 C4 **H**
Studland Bay nr Swanage Dorset BH19 3AH

Knoll House succeeds because there is a balance between the constituencies and t heir competing interests' - that is to say the tried and tested rules have evolved over the years and work to all guests' advantage. The Ferguson family have been here since 1959 and they have greatly extended the original country house set in 100 acres, creating a popular summertime retreat for families, particularly those with younger children. There is a well-organised children's dining-room serving 'real' food, and a host of amenities including a splendid outdoor adventure playground complete with a large pirate ship, climbing frame, nets, towers, aerial and tube slides and more. The clean (NT) beach and dunes are a few hundred yards away across the road and can be glimpsed through the trees from the front bedrooms; beach huts can be hired. All rooms are comfortably homely and possess clean, simple bathrooms, though some are not en suite. For adults there's a child-free lounge as well as a spacious bar and restaurant with much-sought-after window tables. The leisure centre is compact but comprehensively equipped and does not have an outside membership. No televisions are provided, though they can be hired and there is a separate television lounge. *A somewhat complicated tariff here. The price we quote is the daily rate in early July (the second highest of seven tariff periods) for two people on half-board sharing an en suite room. In fact most people stay long enough (3+ nights, 4 if Fri or Sat included) to qualify for full board at the same rate; weekly rates (which are the only option in mid-July to end Aug) are at a discount to the daily rate. ***Rooms** 70. Garden, tennis, golf (par 3), pitch & putt, indoor & outdoor swimming pool, splash pool, mini-gym, sauna, steam room, spa bath, solarium, playroom & play area, games rooms, gift shop, self-service launderette, writing/bridge room. Closed Nov-Easter. MasterCard, **VISA***

SUDBURY — Mabey's Brasserie — £55

Tel & Fax 01787 374298 Map 10 C3 **R**
47 Gainsborough Street Sudbury Suffolk CO10 7SS

Robert Mabey's eponymous flagship restaurant is more bistro than brasserie as it's only open at usual meal times. The decor is pine and pews with a blue colour scheme; and the menu, written on blackboards above the open kitchen, is varied. Prawn tempura with Oriental dipping sauce, Caesar salad with shaved parmesan, grilled calf's liver with creamy mash and bacon, poached salmon with ginger and lime butter sauce, and Provençal pork cassoulet with garlic sausage and chips are typical of the style. Desserts range from lemon and coconut sponge and classic vanilla crème brulée to chilled poached nectarine with passion fruit syrup. Coffee is served with hand-made fudge. Regular monthly themed menu events. Air-conditioned. Separate dining-room for smokers and a new function room for parties. ***Seats** 60. Parties 8. Private Room 35. L 12-2 D 7-10. Closed Sun, Mon & 5 days at Christmas. Amex, MasterCard, **VISA***

Swanton Morley Darby's

Tel & Fax 01362 637647 Map 10 C1
Swanton Morley Dereham Norfolk NR20 4JT

A "family" free house converted from two brick cottages in 1986 by the licensee – John Carrick – a local farmer, after the local mega-brewery closed the village's last traditional pub. A rustic ambience has been created in the main bar with beams, exposed brick walls and open brick fireplace with log fire. Both here and in the neatly laid-out dining area visitors can enjoy reliable, home-cooked meals, as well as filled baguettes and ploughman's platters. Main menu choices include popular favourite plus garlic and Stilton mushrooms, venison and turkey pie and vegetable bake. Daily blackboard specials may feature Brancaster mussels with white wine and cream, beef and vegetable casserole and tagliatelle carbonara. Puddings may include blackberry and apple crumble and chocolate cheesecake. Sunday roasts are a popular attraction. Younger diners have their own menu (Peter Rabbit – small ham salad) which is served in the dining area or in the small children's room, complete with a box of toys for impatient toddlers. Those seeking overnight accommodation will be surprised when directed 3/4 mile along the narrow lane to Park Farm, a fine farmhouse peacefully located in open countryside. Six fresh, airy and spotless en suite bedrooms (four with showers only) are housed in a splendid cattleyard conversion offering exposed ceiling timbers, freestanding pine furnishings, TVs, clock-radios and beverage-making facilities. One room is geared to accept wheelchair visitors. Overflow accommodation in the farmhouse is more modest; four bedrooms, including two character attic rooms share two bathrooms. Guests wishing to venture to the pub have use of a free taxi service and sleeping children will be well looked after if parents want a night out. The welcome attributed to visiting children extends beyond the menu, children's room and toy box into the garden, where an enclosed play area on a soft wood-chip floor boasts a climbing net and frame. Down on the farm there is a connecting family room, provision of a further bed and cot (£2), high-chair at breakfast, a kitchen area for mums to prepare food and numerous animals to keep youngsters amused. 3- to 13-year olds are charged £1 per year old per night. *Open 11-2.30, 6-11 (Sat 11-11, Sun 12-3, 7-10.30).* ***Bar Food*** *12-2, 7-9.45 (Sat 12-9.45, Sun 12-2.30, 7-9.30). Free House.* ***Beer*** *Adnams Southwold, Mild & Broadside, Woodforde's Wherry, Hall & Woodhouse Tanglefoot, four guest ales. Garden, outside eating, children's play area. Family room.* ***Accommodation*** *9 bedrooms, 5 en suite £40 (family room £60, single £20-£24). Children welcome overnight. MasterCard,* ***VISA***

A jug of fresh water!

Swindon Blunsdon House 69% £97

Tel 01793 721701 **Fax 01793 721056** Map 14 C2
Blunsdon Swindon Wiltshire SN2 4AD

H

From J15 of the M4 take the A419 Cirencester road. After about 7 miles turn right to Broad Blunsdon. The well-kept driveway and frontage make a good first impression as you approach the hotel, which was a farm guest house in 1958, a country club in 1960, and a fully licensed hotel since 1962 – and the Clifford family have been here from the beginning. It's now a popular conference rendezvous (up to 300 delegates in seven rooms and eight syndicate rooms; ample parking) with extensive leisure club facilities. There are ample lounges and bars, while all the bedrooms are reasonably roomy and many have pleasant views. Decoration and appointments are of smart modern business standard, and bathrooms all have shower attachments; some have spa baths. 24hr room service. Families are well catered for; children up to 16 stay free in parents' room. No dogs. ***Rooms*** *88. Garden, tennis, golf (9), indoor swimming pool, splash pool, gym, squash, sauna, steam room, spa bath, sun beds, beauty salon, putting, games room, indoor & outdoor play areas. Amex, Diners, MasterCard,* ***VISA***

SWINDON — Chinese Experience — £45

Tel 01793 877888 **Fax 01793 873883** Map 14 C2 R
Peatmoor Swindon Wiltshire SN5 5YZ

Way out on the western edge of town, where the new housing estates meet open countryside, is this extraordinary, lakeside restaurant built by Lawrence Lee in 1990. Drive under an ornate Chinese arch to be confronted by a large two-storey building that could have been lifted straight off a 'willow pattern' plate. A pair of imperial lions guard the ornamental pond-flanked entrance and there is even a little pagoda on an island in the lake. The menu includes all the popular dishes, from paper-wrapped prawns and wun tun soup to Peking duck, sweet and sour pork, shredded chili beef and bang bang chicken, although Lawrence's personal preference is for the Cantonese dishes. Dishes that come with mushrooms generally use the Western, cultivated kind but if you ask they will use Chinese varieties. High-chairs and baby-changing facilities provided. ***Seats** 300. L 12-2 D 6-11. Set menus £17 & £20 per head (both min 2). Closed 25-27 Dec. Amex, Diners, MasterCard,* **VISA**

TAPLOW — Cliveden — 92% — £252

Tel 01628 668561 **Fax 01628 661837** Map 15 E2 
Taplow nr Maidenhead Berkshire SL6 0JF

Our 1996 Hotel of the Year is a remarkable and majestic hotel with a fascinating history: over the years it has been home to a Prince of Wales, several dukes and the Astor family and has been at the centre of Britain's social and political life for over three centuries. Now a Stately Home and gardens owned by The National Trust, it is open to visitors at certain times and set in 350 acres of parkland and gardens overlooking the River Thames; there's a series of estate walks (electronic commentary is available from Robert Hardy), some winding down to the river where the hotel's boats are moored – in summer guests can join a champagne cruise along the river before dinner on *Suzy Ann*, a 1911 launch; the electric canoe, *Liddesdale*, can be hired by the hour. Riding can also be arranged on the 376-acre estate and along the banks of the river. The mansion was built in 1666 and the dominant feature of the south facade is a terrace that looks down on the breathtaking 17th-century parterre. Inside, the magnificent Great Hall has a lavish, carved-wood interior and a stone fireplace, works of art, tapestries and armour. Also admire the main staircase, panelled library, the Adam-style boudoir (once Nancy Astor's sitting-room), the panelled French Rococo dining-room – where a traditional English breakfast is served by staff wearing long white gloves – the redbrick and vaulted cellar private dining-room, the Mountbatten boardroom and the east and west wing corridors; wonderful portraits and paintings are hung throughout. Even the porte-cochère houses something interesting: George Bernard Shaw's silver-topped cane. Each air-conditioned bedroom and suite (including 'full' and 'junior' – all around £400) is sumptuously and stylishly furnished and decorated, offering every conceivable need and luxury, including fresh fruit, bathrobes and guest slippers. De Luxe rooms have a separate dressing-room. Bathrooms (most with his and hers washbasins) are simply stunning. Honeymooners even receive monogrammed bedside mats! In the suites (where afternoon tea and pre-supper Bucks Fizz are served) you'll also find a music centre and a video recorder (the hotel provides a very comprehensive video and compact disc collection with plenty for children, too). The recently-added Clutton wing offers additional bedrooms. The Garden wing houses the state-of-the-art Churchill boardroom with its own terrace that overlooks the luxurious Pavilion Spa. Here you will now find separate steam rooms for ladies and gentlemen and two Canadian hot tubs; an attractive Conservatory dining-room is in the original walled garden. Children under two are barred from the facilities at all times, while those up to the age of 12 can use them until noon; however, there is an unsupervised creche room and an entertainment programme (from boat trips to picnics) can be organised for children. Impeccably dressed staff provide outstanding service and housekeeping is of the highest order. Banqueting for up to 160, conferences for 42. Children up to five stay free in parents' room. ***Rooms** 37. Garden, croquet, indoor and outdoor tennis, riding, coarse fishing, boating, indoor and outdoor swimming pools, hot tubs, spa pool, saunas, plunge pool, spa bath, steam room, gym, squash, badminton, beauty treatment rooms, hairdressing, snooker & billiards, valeting, Daimler Sovereign limousine. Amex, Diners, MasterCard,* **VISA**

See over

Terrace Dining Room £140

Once the main drawing-room of the house, the room is incomparably grand, with stunning views across the parterre, down to the river and for many miles beyond. Table settings are immaculate, and service is polished and professional. Cooking is a mixture of modern and traditional British and classical French, with dishes ranging from kedgeree with a curry sauce and crisp chorizo sausage to smoked foie gras with a turnip and potato purée, wild mushrooms and grilled leeks on a truffle sauce, chateaubriand with tapénade-rolled potatoes, and Oriental-flavoured duck breast on a pearl barley and foie gras risotto. Interesting vegetarian options, impeccably-sourced mixed cheeses and tempting puddings. A manageable wine list has the odd tasting note – ask about half bottles and what else lurks in the cellar! No smoking. 'A donation of £2.50 to The National Trust is charged to each guest. Service is neither included nor anticipated'. ***Seats*** *65. Parties 12. Private Room 54. L 12.30-2.30 D 7-10.30. Set Club L £26 (Sun £38.50) Set D (residents) £36.*

Waldo's £120

Of the hotel's two main restaurants, this is perhaps chef Ron Maxfield's showcase, with genuinely talented cooking that is more modern (British for the most part) and innovative than upstairs, relying, of course, on the finest ingredients. Access is down a flight of stairs, past a wall of old servants' bells, and through a lobby adorned with photos of the rich and famous who stayed at the house during the Astor period. History continues in the Gents cloakroom where there are drawings of Christine Keeler and Mandy Rice-Davies by Dr Stephen Ward – the main protagonists in the Profumo affair that led to the downfall of the Macmillan government in 1964. A pianist plays in the pine-panelled bar, and the small restaurant itself resembles a private club with suitably formal service. The menu is fixed-price (choice of three or four courses, or a special truffle menu). No smoking. The restaurant is named after Thomas Waldo Story, from whom the Fountain of Love in the grounds was commissioned by William Waldorf Astor in 1897. ***Seats*** *26. Parties 4. D only 7-9.30. Closed Sun & Mon. Set D £45/£49 & £75 (6-course truffle menu).*

TARRANT MONKTON Langton Arms

Tel 01258 830225 **Fax 01258 830053** Map 14 B4 
Tarrant Monkton Blandford Forum Dorset DT11 8RX

Thatched, rose- and creeper-clad, this mellow 17th-century brick pub, picturesquely situated opposite the parish church, is surely everybody's idea of a traditional village inn. A splendid 'local' atmosphere pervades the beamed bars where drinkers can sample well-kept small brewery beers and diners can tuck into reliable home-cooked bar meals. Favourite dishes – cod and chips, chicken curry, lasagne and filled baguettes – are listed on a printed menu, while daily specials such as chicken and leek pie, Somerset Brie and bacon filo, Langton marinated chicken, mixed fish kedgeree, carrot cake and treacle tart are highlighted on two boards. Evenings bring speciality themes for different nights of the week – fish 'n' chips on Monday, steaks on Thursdays. Extra evening dishes and a Sunday lunch menu are served in the adjacent Langton's Bistro. In general, food prices are exceptionally keen. Summer barbecues are a regular and popular feature. At least 12 wines are offered by the glass from a short list supplied by Christopher Piper wine merchants. Three single-storey blocks built around the rear courtyard house six spacious and well-maintained en suite bedrooms, all with bath and shower, furnished in pine and sporting pretty duvets and curtains. TV, tea-maker, telephone and hairdryer are standard extras. A warm welcome awaits children, who not only have their own room filled with toys but also a separate menu, food bar and excellent play areas, including a bouncy castle, in the spacious and safe rear garden. *Open 11.30-2.30, 6-11 (Sat 11-11, Sun 12-3, 7-10.30).* ***Bar Food*** *11.30-2.30, 6-10 (Sun 12-2.45, 7-10). Free House.* ***Beer*** *Smiles Best, Wadworth 6X, four guest beers. Garden, outdoor eating, children's play area.* ***Accommodation*** *6 bedrooms, all en suite, £54 (single £35). Children welcome overnight, additional bed (£5) & cot available. MasterCard,* ***VISA***

TEALBY Tealby Tearooms

Tel 01673 838261 Map 7 E2 **JaB**
Front Street Tealby Lincolnshire LN8 3XU

Originally the village store, Richard Glover's tearooms are situated in one of Lincolnshire's most picturesque villages. The light and sunny front room is neatly furnished in modern pine, with clothed tables and walls adorned with pictures and prints, many of which are for sale. Good home-made scones (£1.10 with butter and jam), excellent cakes: sponge, carrot cake, chocolate fudge cake, meringues filled with raspberries and cream and Lincolnshire plum loaf to go with your pot of tea. Set teas include a good-value cream tea (scones, jam and cream £2.10) and full afternoon tea (sandwiches, scones, cake £4.05). Light snacks include home-made soup – maybe game or mushroom (£1.85), filled jacket potatoes (from £2.10), freshly made sandwiches (cheese and tuna £1.50, ham salad £1.65), and salads – quiche lorraine £3.90 – which are available all day. The small rear room is ideal for families and children will be made a fuss of by the friendly owners. Here they keep a high-chair, juice cups, plastic bowls and children's cutlery and offer smaller slices of cake or child-size portions of the hot snacks available. A large toilet area designed for the disabled also suffices as a baby-changing area. A welcoming refreshment spot for weary walkers on the Viking Way. Access and facilities for disabled visitors. ***Seats*** *55.* ***Open*** *10.30-5.30.* ***Closed*** *Mon (except Bank Holidays) also Tue-Fri Oct-Mar. No credit cards.*

TELFORD Holiday Inn Telford/Ironbridge 68% £112

Tel 01952 292500 **Fax 01952 291949** Map 6 B3 **H**
St Quentin Gate Telford Shropshire TF3 4EH

With easy access to the M54 (J4) and town centre, this modern low-riser is adjacent to the 450-acre town park and the Telford Racquet and Exhibition Centre. Children up to 19 can stay free in parents' room; two rooms have facilities for disabled guests. Ample free parking. ***Rooms*** *100. Patio, indoor swimming pool & splash pool, mini-gym, sauna, spa bath, steam room, sun beds, beauty salon. Amex, Diners, MasterCard,* ***VISA***

TELFORD Telford Golf & Country Moat House 64% £119

Tel 01952 429977 **Fax 01952 586602** Map 6 B3 **H**
Great Hay Sutton Hill Telford Shropshire TF7 4DT

Standing south of the town centre above Ironbridge Gorge, the hotel combines comfortable modern accommodation with golf and country club facilities and a state-of-the-art conference centre. Children under 16 stay free in parents' room; good family facilities at weekends (the hotel is convenient for the seven Ironbridge museums), plus a children's menu and small play area in the coffee shop. The hotel was likely to undergo a change of ownership as we went to press. ***Rooms*** *86. Garden, golf (18), pitch & putt, golf driving range, indoor swimming pool, gym, spa bath, sauna, solarium, steam room, playroom, snooker, coffee shop (8am-8pm, till 6pm Mon & Tue). Amex, Diners, MasterCard,* ***VISA***

TETBURY Calcot Manor 77% £125

Tel 01666 890391 **Fax 01666 890394** Map 14 B2 **HR**
Tetbury Gloucestershire GL8 8YJ

This delightful manor house complex continues to develop in all the nicest ways, without spoiling the feel of its medieval origins; it makes a concerted effort to attract families without destroying the calm country-house atmosphere. A newly-built pub, "The Gumstool", has a local following and is ideal for informal eating, particularly for families who do not want the formality of restaurant dining; the comfortable hotel sitting-rooms remain for those who prefer more tranquil surroundings. Bedrooms vary in size from very adequate to expansive; most are in the main house with additions housed in attractive stable and barn buildings overlooking a courtyard.

All bedrooms have recently been refurbished and those wishing for a little luxury can opt for a De Luxe room with whirlpool bath and corona draped bed for only a small supplement. Four family cottage suites – with bunk beds discreetly hidden behind curtains in the lounge of the suite – offer a mini-library of Beatrix Potter books, sophisticated baby-listening/talking devices, piped children's videos and bathroom toys. An enclosed garden adjacent to the family block has a wooden play train and outdoor toys. Children's high tea is served from 5pm, with high-chairs, small cutlery, beakers and bibs all provided. Banqueting and conferences for up to 70; ample parking. Three miles west of Tetbury on A4135. ***Rooms** 20. Garden, croquet, tennis, outdoor swimming pool, playroom & play area, bicycles. Amex, Diners, MasterCard,* ***VISA***

Restaurant £65

Yet another change of chef, but this time Michael Croft (previously at the *Mirabelle* in London and at the *Royal Crescent* in Bath) is in charge of the kitchen and things are sailing along on a more even keel. Plans are afoot to refurbish and extend the restaurant in 1997 but meanwhile the menu style is still modern English on both the table d'hote and carte. A simple but satisfying lunch might comprise terrine of duck and foie gras with a sauce gribiche, pot-roasted guinea fowl with rösti potatoes and creamed mushrooms, and a chocolate tart with espresso coffee sauce. Pushing the boat out at dinner you might be tempted by minestrone risotto with roasted scallops, potted crab, seared mullet with cabbage and bacon on a warm tomato vinaigrette, whole pan-fried lemon sole – this is about as far from the pretentiously-described, prissily-presented, so-called country-house-style of cooking as you could imagine – but none the worse for it. Desserts (or should we call them puddings?) might include steamed Viennese chocolate pudding with chocolate sauce and toffee and banana tart with banana ice cream (or farmhouse cheeses). The wine list is immaculately presented with the house selection matching various wines with dishes. The dining-room is romantically candle-lit at night. A terrace provides four tables for outdoor eating, when weather permits. No smoking in the dining-room itself. Disabled toilets. ***Seats** 50. Private Room 35. L 12.30-2 D 7.30-9.30. Set L £17 (Sun £16) Set D £17 & £22.*

Tewkesbury — Tewkesbury Park — 62% — £98

Tel 01684 295405 **Fax 01684 292386** Map 14 B1 **H**
Lincoln Green Lane Tewkesbury Gloucestershire GL20 7DN

Just 5 minutes from J9 of the M5, Tewkesbury Park is more country club than country house, and conferences (up to 150 people; ample parking) are big business. Well-appointed bedrooms afford views of the 176 acres of parkland and of the Malvern Hills. 24hr room service. Children up to 14 free in parents' room. No dogs. Whitbread Hotels. ***Rooms** 78. Garden, tennis, golf (18), putting green, indoor swimming pool, gym, squash, sauna, steam room, spa bath, solarium, beauty salon, snooker, playroom & play area, coffee shop (10am-10pm). Amex, Diners, MasterCard,* ***VISA***

Thame — Abingdon Arms

Tel 01844 260116 **Fax 01844 260338** Map 15 D2 **P**
21 Cornmarket Thame Oxfordshire OX9 2BL

Known locally as 'The Abo', this 18th-century, former coaching inn offers a fairly modest face to the main street of town but inside several rooms have been opened up to create a long bar with rug-strewn, bare board floors, some exposed brickwork, magazines and newspapers to read and a lively, friendly atmosphere. To the rear, an old barn, is used for functions in the evening and offers an additional lunch menu in summer; beyond this a beer garden comes with rustic tables (some with rustic baby seats attached), slide, swing and climbing frame. Features of the menu are hugely thick 'doorstep' sandwiches and bowls of home-made tagliatelle with various toppings. Other items range from ploughman's platters and burgers to steak and kidney pudding, bangers and mash, Exeter stew with parsley dumplings and an all-day breakfast. All main menu items are available in children's portions at half price. Disabled WC. *Open 11-11 (Sun 12-10.30).* ***Bar Food** 12-2.30, 6-9 (till 8.30 Fri, Sat & Sun). Free House.* ***Beer** Hook Norton Best, Boddingtons, Marston's Pedigree, Wychert Ale, guest beers. Garden, outdoor eating, children's play area. Closed 25 Dec. MasterCard,* ***VISA***

THATCHAM Regency Park Hotel 68% £111

Tel 01635 871555 **Fax 01635 871571** Map 15 D2 H
Bowling Green Road Thatcham nr Newbury Berkshire RG18 3RP

Peacefully located in five acres of grounds on the northern edge of Thatcham, the Regency Park is based on an Edwardian house that is now rather overshadowed by a modern, redbrick extension. Large, comfortable bedrooms come with either blue or peach watered-silk effect wall coverings, sofas, mini-bars and all the usual facilities. Executive rooms, with two king-sized beds, are even more spacious and ten have their own balconies. There is one full suite. Public areas are air-conditioned and include a pleasant bar and small lounge. 24hr room service. Children up to 11 stay free in parents' room. ***Rooms*** *50. Garden, all-weather tennis, news kiosk. Amex, Diners, MasterCard,* ***VISA***

THELBRIDGE Thelbridge Cross Inn

Tel 01884 860316 **Fax 01884 860316** Map 13 D2 P
Thelbridge Witheridge Devon EX17 4SQ

Two miles west of Witheridge on the B3042 this attractive, white-painted inn is isolated high up in a very rural part of Devon with views across to Dartmoor. The much modernised interior is carpeted and open-plan in layout with some comfortable settees, a couple of log fires and is delightfully free of live music, juke box or pool table. The bar offers some good local cider, country wines and some sixty whiskies including twenty malts. The adjacent barns have been well converted to provide a comfortable block of seven bedrooms and a large self-catering apartment. Bedrooms are rather compact with pretty matching fabrics and modern units, but room is found for a telephone, TV, tea-maker and a small fully-tiled private shower room in each. An occasional attraction is the original 'Lorna Doone' stagecoach which brings extra Sunday lunch trade. *Open 11.30-3 (from 12 Sun), 6.30-11. Free House.* ***Beer*** *Bass, Butcombe Bitter, Wadworth 6X (summer). Garden, children's play area. Family room.* ***Accommodation*** *8 bedrooms, all en suite, £60 (family room sleeping four £70, single £35). Children welcome overnight (under-10s stay free in parents' room, 10-14s 75% adult tariff), additional bed & cot available. No dogs. Amex, Diners, MasterCard,* ***VISA***

THOMPSON Chequers Inn

Tel 01953 483360 Map 10 C2 P
Griston Road Thompson Thetford Norfolk IP24 1PX

Well off the beaten track, this splendid, long and low, thatched 14th-century inn is worth finding – 1 mile off the A1075 Watton to Thetford road along a tiny lane on the edge of the village – for its peaceful location and unspoilt charm. Beneath the steep-raked thatch of this ancient ale house, once a row of several cottages, lies a series of low-ceilinged inter-connecting rooms served by a long bar. Wonky wall timbers, low doorways, open log fires, a rustic mix of old furniture and collections of farming implements, brass and copper characterise the well-maintained and atmospheric interior. Good rear garden with rural views and children's play area. Handy for excellent local woodland walks. *Open 11-3, 6-11 (Sun 12-3, 7-10.30). Free House.* ***Beer*** *Adnams Southwold, Bass, Tetley, Fuller's London Pride, guest beers. Family room. Diners, MasterCard,* ***VISA***

THRESHFIELD Old Hall Inn

Tel 01756 752441 Map 6 C1 
Threshfield Skipton North Yorkshire BD23 5HB

A lovely stone-built Dales inn, based on a Tudor hall from which its name comes, the Taylors' pub gains further character from its idiosyncratic individuality. An eccentric mix of flagstone floors, classical music and chamber pots suspended from the ceiling is accentuated by the 'Brat Board' at ankle height by the fireplace: chicken nuggets and chips followed by two scoops of multi-flavoured ice creams seem fairly brat-proof. One daily-changing blackboard menu offers up to 15 starters and main courses; perhaps Dales sausage with onion gravy, tortellini with tomato sauce, crepe Alfredo (chicken, spinach and garlic), Wensleydale ploughman's and wild boar and pheasant pie with a Cumberland sauce, with fresh market seafood specials.

More elaborate evening dishes might include pan-fried venison with garlic mash and caramelised onions, medallions of monkfish with bacon, mushrooms and garlic and pan-fried chicken breast with mozzarella and Madeira and mushroom sauce. Finish off with lemon tart or pecan and maple cheesecake. A perennially hectic place; ordering and paying at the bar can be a little chaotic, though for a little peace and quiet the garden is a delightful alternative. *Open 11.30-3, 6-11 (Sun 12-3, 6-10.30). Closed Mon lunch.* ***Bar Food*** *12-2, 6.15-9.30 (no food all day Mon & Sun eve in winter). Free House.* ***Beer*** *Timothy Taylor's Best & Landlord, Theakston Best, guest beers. Garden, outdoor eating. Family rooms. No credit cards.*

THUNDRIDGE — Marriott Hanbury Manor 85% — £189

Tel 01920 487722 **Fax 01920 487692** Map 15 F1 **HR**
Thundridge nr Ware Hertfordshire SG12 0SD

A handsome and substantial Jacobean-style mansion surrounded by 200 acres of golf course and mature parkland. Its history includes a period as a convent during which additional wings and a cloister were added. A long, sweeping drive leads directly from the A10 to the front entrance, where a valet is on hand to park your car. A genuinely warm greeting is extended in the entrance hall, to the right of which is the magnificent galleried oak hall with its huge tapestries, open fireplace, panelled walls and lofty ceiling from whose beams are suspended immense crystal chandeliers. The library serves as a peaceful retreat during the day but in the evening it is often used as an overflow for the splendidly elegant bar with its pale cream walls and richly-coloured upholstery. Bedrooms are decorated with impeccable taste and furnished with traditional polished-wood freestanding pieces. All enjoy good views over the grounds and come with every modern convenience plus extra comforts like towelling robes in the superb marble bathrooms. The range covers Executive, Superior, Junior Suites and King Suites; 27 rooms are in the Garden Court, a short walk away from the main house. The hotel's leisure complex is most luxurious and includes a palatial indoor swimming pool and a creche (9.30-12.30 Mon-Fri, 10-4 Sat & Sun) among its facilities. Very friendly, obliging staff. Children up to 16 share parents' room free and a children's menu is offered as part of the 24hr room service. Poles Hall, a former chapel with a barrel-vaulted ceiling, is a most unusual function venue; conference/banqueting facilties for up to 140/100; ample parking. Small dogs only. ***Rooms*** *96. Garden, croquet, golf (18), tennis, putting, indoor swimming pool, spa bath, sauna, steam room, sun beds, gym, snooker, beauty & hair salons, news kiosk. Amex, Diners, MasterCard,* ***VISA***

Zodiac Restaurant and Conservatory — £130

Taking its name from the signs of the zodiac discreetly incorporated into the fine plasterwork of its barrel-vaulted ceiling, this is an extremely elegant dining-room with caryatids and atlantes supporting the mantle above a large fireplace, cream panelled walls with fluted pilasters and high-quality table settings and appointments, all illuminated by three glittering chandeliers. Albert Roux of *Le Gavroche* is retained as a consultant but it is executive chef Rory Kennedy who runs the show with an à la carte menu that promises that 'our gourmet creations will delight the eye and tempt the palate'. Prices are rather laboriously spelt out and '5% service' is included. Nevertheless, a typical dish of warm oysters with champagne bouillon infused with sorrel ('twelve pounds fifty') is likely to get a meal off to a good start; follow this with sautéed sea scallops and steamed crayfish, a 'wigwam' of English lamb or saddle of rabbit with root vegetables, baby onions and prunes. Weekday lunches (plus dinner on Friday and Saturday) are served in the Conservatory (and out on the patio in fine weather, with views over the golf course), bring a weekly-changing à la carte (main dishes £13-£17.50) with a choice of six dishes at each stage. The air-conditioned Vardon's brasserie (open 7 days) is on the first floor of the golf clubhouse, above the Health Club; here you will find all-day snacks and a children's menu; in addition, a £19.50 buffet lunch is served from Monday to Friday, with a normal brasserie menu and bar menus on Saturday. No smoking. No children under eight in Zodiac room; jacket and tie for gentlemen at dinner. ***Seats*** *48. Parties 8. Private Room 8. L (Mon-Fri in Conservatory, Sun in Zodiac) 12.30-2.30 D (in Zodiac, plus Conservatory Fri & Sat) 7-10. Closed D Sun. Set L £23 (Sun £26.50) D £30.*

THURLESTONE Thurlestone Hotel 69% £140

Tel 01548 560382 **Fax 01548 561069** Map 13 D3 H
Thurlestone Kingsbridge Devon TQ7 3NN

The elegance of the 20s combines with the amenities of the 90s in a handsome hotel in a lovely setting with spectacular sea views. The Gorse family have been here from the start, and they are now into their second century, having survived their first centenary celebrations last year! The hotel is splendidly geared to family holidays (particularly at half-term breaks, when dancing, competitions, film shows and parties are all laid on), with an excellent leisure club; there's also has an off-peak trade in conferences (for up to 120). Day rooms include The Village Inn (a pubby brasserie with informal eating), whose timbers are said to have come from the *San Pedro*, part of the Spanish Armada. Accommodation is graded as 'de luxe' (sea view, video player, private bar, undercover parking, no dogs allowed, most with balconies), 'sea view' and 'country view'. 26 of the bedrooms were completely refurbished last year. 24hr room service. Children up to 16 can stay free of charge in their parents' room, but a minimum charge of £15 is made for breakfast and children's supper. Ample parking (100 open, 20 covered spaces). Children's facilities include entertainment during school holidays, changing facilities in the pool complex, high-chairs, cots, linen and children's supper from 5.15-6pm; a family bedroom is available with bunk beds. ***Rooms** 68. Garden, tennis, golf (9), putting, indoor & outdoor swimming pools, splash pool, gym, squash, sauna, spa bath, solarium, beauty & hair salon, badminton, games room, snooker, playroom & play area. MasterCard,* **VISA**

TICKTON Tickton Grange 62% £75

Tel 01964 543666 **Fax 01964 542556** Map 7 E1 H
Tickton nr Beverley East Riding of Yorkshire HU17 9SH

A family-owned Georgian house standing just off the A1035 east of Beverley in 3½ acres of rose gardens, where afternoon teas are served in the summer. Day rooms retain a traditional appeal, and bedrooms are decorated in a fresh, light style. There are two suites (£90), one with a Georgian four-poster bed. Tickton truffles are offered as a welcome. The Whymant family run the hotel along friendly and informal lines. ***Rooms** 18. Garden, croquet. Amex, Diners, MasterCard,* **VISA**

If we recommend meals in a hotel a *separate* entry is usually made for its restaurant. Pub and inn entries include bar food details where recommended.

TIDESWELL Poppies

Tel 01298 871083 Map 6 C2 JaB
Bank Square Tideswell Derbyshire SK17 8LA

An informal little town-centre restaurant decorated with poppies. Light snacks are featured throughout the day: soup (£1.60), stir-fry vegetables (£3.25, or £3.75 with meat), various things on toast – tuna, mushrooms (each £1.80), salads (from £3.75), sandwiches (from £1.45) and scones, cakes and set teas (Cream Tea £2.70, Fruit Cake Tea with Derbyshire white Stilton cheese – £2.90). In the evening (you can have just a single dish, although most people have a full meal) choices run from *spanakopitta* (spinach, feta cheese, eggs and herbs in filo pastry £2.95) or home-made paté flavoured with juniper berries (£3.10) to main courses such as halibut stroganoff (£8.50), boozy black pudding (in whisky and mustard sauce – £6.25), and red pepper stuffed with pine nuts, onions and rice (£6.10). A plate of Derbyshire farmhouse cheeses is £3.85. No smoking in main dining-area. Children are welcome but there are no special facilities. Children's portions on request and an extra plate can be provided for the smallest appetites; one high-chair is available. There are several local family attractions, including a farm in the village which is open to the public and has a children's play area. ***Seats** 36. **Open** 10-4.30 (Sat till 5) & 7-9.30 (Fri & Sat only), Sun 12-7.30 (winter till 5). **Closed** D Sun, all Mon & Tue in winter, Wed & Thu all year, 25 Dec & all Jan. Amex, Diners, MasterCard,* **VISA**

TIVERTON Four & Twenty Blackbirds Tea Shoppe

Tel 01884 257055 Map 13 D2 JaB
43 Gold Street Tiverton Devon EX16 6QB

An old-world tea shop whose several rooms are replete with beams, antique tables and chairs, objets d'art and fresh flowers. Something good to eat is available all day long, from home-made biscuits, cakes and quiches (£4.95) to sandwiches, salads, omelettes, jacket potatoes with various fillings (from £2.50) and, till noon, a full English breakfast (£5.50). Three set teas: Queen's, with boiled egg (£4), Blackbird, with sandwich and cake (£5.25), King's, with Cheddar, chutney and cake (£5.50). Unlicensed, but you can bring your own wine (no corkage). Vegetarian dishes could include bean bake or parsnip and cashew loaf with sherry sauce. They will happily cater for little ones, offering whatever parents know their children require (jacket potatoes, baked beans, boiled egg with soldiers). Children's mugs and plates are also provided. High-chairs available. ***Seats** 40 (+ 4 outside). **Open** 8.30-5.30. **Closed** Sun, 25 & 26 Dec. No credit cards.*

TIVETSHALL ST MARY Old Ram

Tel 01379 676794 **Fax 01379 608399** Map 10 C2 P
Ipswich Road Tivetshall St Mary Norfolk NR15 2DE

Conveniently situated beside the A140 between Norwich and Ipswich, this old 17th-century inn positively bustles with people all day with travellers and locals seeking refreshment within the rambling and carefully refurbished series of rooms. Road-weary visitors in need of overnight accommodation will not be disappointed with the five "luxury" en suite bedrooms built into the eaves with sloping roofs and exposed timbers. Tastefully decorated with Laura Ashley wallpaper and co-ordinating fabrics and kitted out with quality modern lightwood, each boasts satellite TV, direct-dial telephone, tea-maker, trouser press and hairdryer. Two are mini-suites with comfortable easy chairs and all gain top marks for their spotless bathrooms with gleaming tiles, fluffy towels and robust, powerful showers over tubs. Room prices are also quoted without breakfast. Staff are particularly friendly and efficient. No under-7s after 8pn. Disabled WC and baby-changing facilities. *Open 7.30-11 (till 10.30 Sun). Free House. **Beer** Ruddles County, Adnams Southwold, Boddingtons, Ram Bitter (brewed by Woodforde's). Garden. **Accommodation** 5 bedrooms, all en suite £55-£61.90 (single £37.50-£42.50). Children welcome overnight (under-2s stay free in parents' room, 2-10s £10). Check-in after noon. No dogs. Closed 25 & 26 Dec. MasterCard, **VISA***

TOLVERNE Smugglers Cottage

Tel 01872 580309 **Fax 01872 580216** Map 12 B3 
Tolverne Philleigh nr Truro Cornwall TR2 5NG

Located beside an enchanting reach of the River Fal, and close to the King Harry ferry, this thatched cottage tea room has been run by the Newman family for over 60 years. It is open daily during the summer months for coffee and cakes (10.30-12), good buffet lunches (12-2) – perhaps home-made soup (£2.60), roasted Mediterranean vegetable quiche (£4.25) or Smugglers fish pie (£4.50) both served with freshly prepared salads, Cornish cheese ploughman's (£3.95) – and afternoon teas: Cream Tea (£3), chocolate fudge cake, carrot cake (both £1.65). Splendid terraced gardens afford serene river views. Scenic trips along the river can be taken in a boat skippered by Peter Newman. No-smoking room. ***Seats** 50 (+ 80 outside). **Open** 10.30-5.30. **Closed** Nov-Apr. MasterCard, **VISA***

TOLWORTH Superfish

Tel 0181-390 2868 Map 15 E2 JaB
59 The Broadway Tolworth Surrey KT6 7DW

Part of the excellent Surrey-based chain serving traditional British fish and chips fried, the Yorkshire way, in beef dripping. See Morden entry for more details. Licensed. ***Seats** 36. **Open** 11.30-2 (Sat till 2.30) & 5-10.30 (Thu-Sat till 11). **Closed** Sun, 25, 26 Dec & 1 Jan. Amex, MasterCard, **VISA***

TOPCLIFFE Angel Inn

Tel 01845 577237 **Fax 01845 578000** Map 5 E4 P
Long Street Topcliffe Thirsk North Yorkshire YO7 3RW

At the junction of the A167 and A168, the pre-Norman village of Topcliffe is convenient for, and equidistant from, both the A19 and A1 (3 miles). The 17th-century Angel, once a coaching inn, has been sympathetically remodelled and extended by its present owners. Three bar areas, games room, residents' lounge and a large garden complete with rockery and ornamental fish pond allow a multiplicity of choices for guests' relaxation. The purpose-built wing of bedrooms (above a self-contained function suite) is tastefully furnished in varnished pine, and facilities in all rooms include satellite TVs and mini-bars as well as dial-out phones, hairdryers and trouser presses. Residents have their own entrance, allowing them free access and security 24 hours per day, and effective double-glazing ensures a completely restful night. *Open 11-11 (Sun 12-10.30). Free House.* ***Beer*** *John Smith's, Theakston Best. Garden. Family room.* ***Accommodation*** *15 bedrooms, all en suite, £50 (family room £60-£70, single £35-£40). Children welcome overnight (additional cot available). No dogs. MasterCard,* ***VISA***

TOPSHAM Georgian Tea Room

Tel 01392 873465 Map 13 E2 JaB
Broadway House 35 High Street Topsham Devon EX3 0ED

Only the bread is not home-made at this tea room in a large Georgian house that you can't miss as you enter town. Pretty embroidered cloths, fresh flowers and bone china add a certain charm. Cakes and cookies – Victoria sponge, fruit cake (80p-£1), flapjacks (70p) – are joined at lunchtime by a good selection of savoury items ranging from a hot meat dish of the day (steak and kidney pie, cottage pie, beef lasagne £3.90/£4.50), various platters (gammon, cheese, slimmers – all £4.50) and quiches (from £3.10) to jacket potatoes, sandwiches and beans on toast. Some dishes, including the cream tea with its home-made jam and clotted cream to go with excellent scones still warm from the oven, come in smaller portions at a reduced price not only for children but also for the elderly – a nice touch. You'll need to book for lunch on Tuesdays and Thursdays when, in addition to the regular menu, there is a special roast lunch. No smoking. High-chairs and bibs for the tiny tots, and for the not-so-tiny ones there's a box of toys to keep them busy when they get the wriggles. Private lounge for feeding babies. Within walking distance of a swimming pool, and children's recreation ground. ***Seats*** *28 (+ 24 outside).* ***Open*** *9.30-5.* ***Closed*** *6 days Christmas. No credit cards.*

TORCROSS Start Bay Inn

Tel 01548 580553 **Fax 01548 580513** Map 13 D3 P
Torcross Kingsbridge Devon TQ7 2TQ

Arguably the 'best pub fish and chips in Devon' can be found at this 14th-century thatched inn, which is superbly situated between the beach at Slapton Sands and the freshwater lagoon and nature reserve of Slapton Ley. Landlord Paul Stubbs is a keen diver and fisherman and his catch of fresh seafood contributes to the vast amount of fresh fish that is delivered daily to this extremely popular seaside inn. The modest bar and dining areas are simply furnished with a mix of tables and chairs and various old photographs of the storm-ravaged pub adorn the walls. Every available seat is taken soon after opening, especially in the summer. Fish and chip connoisseurs come eager to sample the delicious battered cod, haddock and plaice, available in three sizes, the jumbo size served on a huge plate accompanied by good, plump chips. Blackboards outside inform you that only polyunsaturated oils are used for frying. Also on the menu are daily fish specials such as whole lemon sole, monkfish tails, skate wings and scallops in garlic butter or batter. The freshest of crab is cooked and dressed on the premises and used in their platters and sandwiches. The rest of the menu lists standard pub fare that will not disappoint meat eaters; vegetarians might now be offered the likes of spinach and mushroom lasagne or mushroom balti. Although the service is fast and efficient, be prepared to wait a little while as the fish is cooked to order. *Open 11.30-2.30, 6-11 (Sun 12-2.30, 7-10.30), end July-Sept 11.30-11, (Sun 12-10.30).* ***Bar Food*** *11.30-2 & 6-9 (till 10 Fri & Sat), Sun 12-2, 7-9.* ***Beer*** *Flowers IPA & Original, Bass. Beachside patio, outdoor eating. Family room. No credit cards.*

N Compass Inn

218242 **Fax 01454 218741** Map 13 F1 **P**

adminton South Gloucestershire GL9 1JB

n summer, the oldest part of the inn dates back to the late 17th century tirely unspoilt bars boast some old timbers and exposed stonework. The Orangery, a sort of glass-roofed courtyard, is a good spot in summer and has new garden-type furniture this year. Most of the generally good-sized bedrooms are in a newer wing. Darkwood fitted furniture is the norm with wing armchairs and the usual amenities – beverage tray, trouser press (some with iron and ironing board attached), hairdryer etc. Most of the well-kept bathrooms have tubs (just two have shower only), many with shower above. There are also several meeting rooms. Less than half a mile from M4 Junction 18. Secure car parking for overnight residents. *Open 11-11 (Sun 12-10.30). Free House.* ***Beer*** *Bass, Smiles Best, Archers Village. Garden, terrace. Family room.* ***Accommodation*** *28 bedrooms, all en suite, £79.95-£99.50 (single £59.95). Children welcome overnight (under-14s stay free in parents' room – breakfast charge), additional bed & cot (£3) available. Dogs by arrangement. Accommodation closed 24-26 Dec, pub closed 26 Dec eve. Amex, Diners, MasterCard,* ***VISA***

Torquay Grand Hotel 68% £125

Tel 01803 296677 **Fax 01803 213462** Map 13 D3 **H**

Sea Front Torquay Devon TQ2 6NT

Large, white-painted Edwardian hotel where Agatha Christie honeymooned, on the seafront just 100 yards from Torquay railway station. Bedrooms have a variety of pleasant colour schemes, good easy chairs and darkwood furniture. There are sea views from about half the rooms (attracting a higher tariff), of which those designated 'Riviera' are the most spacious. Beds are turned down at night and 24hr room service is offered. The main day room is Boaters Bar with a sun lounge beyond; the more pubby Pullman Bar is reached from outside the hotel and serves real ale. Children under 3 sharing parents' room stay free. Excellent facilities for families. Conference facilities for up to 300. ***Rooms*** *110. Garden, tennis, indoor & outdoor swimming pools, mini-gym, solarium, spa bath, hair salon, children's play room, games room, snooker. Amex, Diners, MasterCard,* ***VISA***

Torquay Imperial Hotel 83% £189

Tel 01803 294301 **Fax 01803 298293** Map 13 D3 **H**

Park Hill Road Torquay Devon TQ1 2DG

The Imperial is a grand hotel dating from the mid-19th century and looking very smart after a major refurbishment programme. An imposing marble-floored lobby with fluted Corinthian pilasters and glittering chandeliers sets the tone for extensive public areas that boast many fine period features: the colonnade with painted panels, luxurious Palm Court lounge with Lloyd Loom-furnished Sun Deck beyond, bar with deeply comfortable leather armchairs and Regency Lounge with dancing to a live band every Friday and Saturday night. Outside, ranks of sunloungers surround the pool and, from the hotel's elevated position high above the bay, terraced gardens reach right down to the shore. Most of the bedrooms have their own entrance lobbies and more than half have good-sized, furnished balconies overlooking the bay. Traditionally furnished either with reproduction antique or freestanding darkwood pieces, they come in a variety of bright, tasteful colour schemes and all have good bathrooms, with generous towels and bathrobes. High levels of service include a proper concierge, evening turn-down and extensive 24hr room service. For younger guests there is the Scallywags Club and all sorts of activities during the summer and other holiday periods. Children under 16 may share their parents' room free of charge. Banquets/conferences for 350/400 in the Torbay Suite. Full business support services. ***Rooms*** *167. Garden, croquet, tennis, indoor & outdoor swimming pools, gym, squash, sauna, spa bath, solarium, beauty salon, snooker, playroom. Amex, Diners, MasterCard,* ***VISA***

A jug of fresh water!

Torquay — Livermead Cliff Hotel — 60% — £78

Tel 01803 299666 **Fax 01803 294496** Map 13 D3 **H**
Sea Front Torquay Devon TQ2 6RQ

Right by the sea, with 20 steps leading to a sheltered cove, the Perry family's hotel is a popular holiday spot and a good place for families (children up to 15 stay free in their parents' room). It's also geared up to the conference trade (for up to 80 delegates), so it's quite a busy place all year round. Picture windows in the lounge look out to sea and the outdoor pool also has commanding views. Good housekeeping and friendly staff. 24hr room service. ***Rooms*** *64. Garden, outdoor swimming pool, mini-gym, solarium, games room. Amex, Diners, MasterCard,* **VISA**

Torquay — The Mulberry Room

Tel 01803 213639 Map 13 D3 **JaB**
1 Scarborough Road Torquay Devon TQ2 5UJ

Lesley Cooper started The Mulberry Room ten years ago as a tea room plus restaurant with rooms, but now concentrates on the latter role, opening for lunch and dinner from Wednesday to Sunday. Local fish, vegetables and farm produce play an important part in her catering as shown in braised shoulder of lamb with cranberry jelly, brochette of cod with olives and sweet peppers (both £6.50) and fresh Brixham crab with salad (£7.50). Chicken liver paté is a popular starter, as are home-made soups and bread (£2.50) and caponata – a Sicilian sweet-and-sour aubergine dish (£3.50). To finish you might choose a plate of cheeses or walnut and carrot cake with coffee sauce (£2.50). There are always suitable items on the menu for little people, and an early evening children's meal can be provided on request. Baby-changing facilities provided. No smoking. ***Seats*** *24.* ***Open*** *12-2 & 7.30-9.30.* ***Closed*** *Mon & Tue. No credit cards.*

Torquay — Osborne Hotel — 65% — £108

Tel 01803 213311 **Fax 01803 296788** Map 13 D3 **H**
Hesketh Crescent Meadfoot Beach Torquay Devon TQ1 2LL

The Osborne describes itself as a country house hotel by the sea, and its location within a well-maintained Regency crescent on the hillside ensures good views over the bay. Bedrooms and apartments offer a high level of comfort, and there are good business facilities (conference/banqueting for 80/100; ample parking) and leisure pursuits. No dogs. The Raffles bar/brasserie, with its polished mahogany, ceiling fans and shining brasswork, evokes memories of its Singapore namesake An all-day sandwich list (starting at £2.50) is joined at lunchtime by a wide-ranging menu including light snacks such as marinated chicken wings in a spicy tikka sauce (£3.45), deep-fried potato skins with garlic dip (£3.25) and baked potatoes with various interesting fillings (from £3.25). The choice expands still further in the evening when starters might include prawn and brie salad (£3.75) or fried banana, wrapped in bacon, with salad and curry and mango mayonnaise (£3.50). Then come main courses like fillet of local trout with ginger and pepper sauce (£6.75), Barnsley lamb chop grilled with honey and mustard (£6.75) or breast of chicken stuffed with Stilton in a white wine sauce (£6.95). Children's portions and menu. Four high-chairs are available, and there's a baby-changing area in the Ladies. There's a safe garden and an indoor games room. Close by are the Babbacombe model village and Kent's cavern. ***Rooms*** *23. Garden, indoor & outdoor swimming pools, tennis, putting, gym, sauna, solarium, snooker, brasserie. Amex, Diners, MasterCard,* **VISA**

JaB is short for 'Just a Bite'. The majority of these establishments are also recommended in our *Bistros, Bars & Cafés* Guide which features establishments where one may eat well for less than £15 per head.

TORQUAY — Palace Hotel — 68% — £110

Tel 01803 200200 **Fax 01803 299899** Map 13 D3 **H**
Babbacombe Road Torquay Devon TQ1 3TG

The Palace is set in 25 acres of gardens and woodland stretching to the sea. It opened in 1921 as a hotel offering some of the finest sporting facilities in the land and still admirably provides the active guest with some of the best (golf, swimming, tennis and squash professionals on hand). Music or entertainment is provided nightly, and families are very well catered for. Out of season the hotel is often busy with conferences (handling up to 1000 delegates theatre-style). Six large bedroom suites have splendid views, individual decor and good-quality furniture; other rooms are simpler but comfortable with handsome period bathrooms. 24hr room service. Children up to three stay free in parents' room. Parking for 150 cars. No dogs (kenneling nearby). ***Rooms*** *141. Garden, croquet, indoor & outdoor swimming pools, squash, sauna, indoor & outdoor tennis, 9-hole golf course, snooker, nanny, indoor & outdoor play areas, hair salon. Amex, Diners, MasterCard,* **VISA**

TOTNES — Willow

Tel 01803 862605 Map 13 D3 **JaB**
87 High Street Totnes Devon

In the Narrows of Totnes, Willow is a vegetarian and vegan restaurant whose chefs (half-a-dozen of them!) use organic ingredients as much as possible. Cakes and pastries, available throughout the day, range from the 'healthy' to the 'naughty but nice'. Lunch and dinner menus change daily, offering the likes of carrot and celery soup (£1.35), Pennsylvanian chowder (£1.45), cashew paella, broccoli soufflé (both £3.10), mushroom and parsley flan (£1.85, with salad £2.95) and filled baked potatoes (£2.45). The evening style is similar but more ambitious, maybe spinach filo pie (£5.55) with a green salad or Ghanaian vegetable casserole (£5.15). Wednesday is Indian night, bringing thalis (from £5.50) and individual curries (£3.20). Live music every Friday. Organic wines. One high-chair; family room. A children's table and chairs with toys and books provided will ensure that mum and dad get a few moments' peace in which to let their meal go down. Close to the castle, boat-trips and steam-train rides. ***Seats*** *55 (+ 30 outside).* ***Open*** *10-5 (Fri from 9), also 6.30-9.30 (varies with the seasons).* ***Closed*** *Sun & 25 Dec. No credit cards.*

TREGADILLET — Eliot Arms (Square & Compass)

Tel 01566 772051 **Fax 01566 773010** Map 12 C3 **P**
Tregadillet Launceston Cornwall PL15 7EU

The pretty, creeper-covered Eliot Arms was built in the 14th century as a coaching inn. Once inside, it's like being in the 'Old Curiosity Shop', as every inch of wall space is littered with a host of memorabilia. Pride of place goes to the splendid collection of over 70 clocks, including six grandfather clocks, as well as paintings, plates, books, ornaments and a collection of 400 snuff boxes. Unspoilt layout with lots of rambling little rooms with rug-strewn slate floors and nice old furniture freely and successfully mixing with modern seating. Overnight accommodation is offered in two bedrooms (not en suite). Sheltered garden. *Open 11-2.30 (till 3 Sat), 6-11 (Sun 12-2.30, 7-10.30). Family room. Free House.* ***Beer*** *Marston's Pedigree, Flowers Original, Wadworth 6X, Morland Old Speckled Hen. Garden, children's play area. Family room. Closed 25 Dec. No credit cards.*

TRENT — Rose & Crown

Tel 01935 850776 Map 13 F2 **P**
Trent Sherborne Dorset DT9 4SL

Nestling insleepy village deep in rural Dorset, Charles & Nancy Marion-Crawford's thatched pub is refreshingly unpretentious within with its rug-strewn stone floors, roaring winter log fires and simple furnishings. No pub games, fruit machines or music to disturb the peace, but children's play things can be found in the garden, which enjoys open country views. The emphasis is on good, fresh food, making excellent use of local garden vegetables, game (in winter) and beef. A sensibly-short, weekly-changing blackboard menu is served throughout the pub and the attractive and airy 40-seat conservatory makes a pleasant dining-room. Interesting main courses may include herb-crusted mignons of beef with wild mushroom sauce, home-made crab cakes with roasted pepper mayonnaise and hot and sour pork medallions on a bed of Singapore noodles, with chocolate and banana roulade or a decent West Country cheeseboard to finish. Good fresh fish highlight the board in summer (herb-crusted fillet of hake with a fruit sabayon, whole West Bay plaice with lemon and prawn butter). Sandwiches and ploughman's platters are available lunchtime and evening. Vegetarians can sample vegetable biriyani with naan bread and pickles or tagliatelle with mixed vegetables and Cajun spices. Families are well catered for – it's an ideal venue for a family outing on a summer's evening. *Open 12-2.30, 7-11 (Sun 12-3, 7-10.30). Closed Sun eve winter & all 25 Dec.* ***Bar Food*** *12-1.45, 7-9 (till 9.30 Fri & Sat). Free House.* ***Beer*** *Shepherd Neame Spitfire, Butcombe Bitter, two guest beers. Garden, outdoor eating, children's play area. Family room (no smoking). Amex, MasterCard,* ***VISA***

TRESCO Island Hotel 67% £190*

Tel 01720 422883 **Fax 01720 423008** Map 12 A2 HR
Tresco Isles of Scilly TR24 0PU

Tresco, England's 'Island of Flowers', is privately owned and maintained, its lanes free of traffic. Guests arriving at the quay or heliport are transported by tractor-drawn charabanc to the island's only hotel, set in beautifully tended gardens by the shore. Picture windows make the most of the spectacular location and the panoramic sea views: should the mists close in there's a Terrace Bar (with a wide range of snacks that includes children's favourites and cream teas) and a Quiet Room stacked with books, magazines and games. Some bedrooms enjoy sea views, while others overlook the gardens; rooms with a sea view start attract a higher tariff at the height of the season (less at other times). Special holiday packages for gardeners, bird-watchers and others. Bicycle hire locally. *Half-board terms only. Eight high-chairs, eight booster seats, and an abundance of cots (no charge for under-2s), baby-listening/sitting and child-minding during the day are all available, and children's high-tea is served from 5.30 to 7pm. There's an indoor play area plus a safe garden - and it's close to the beach, so if you forget the buckets and spades, just ask and they're sure to find you some. No dogs. The direct helicopter flight from Penzance (20 minutes' flying time; no Sunday service either by sea or air) is the recommended way to reach Tresco. ***Rooms*** *40. Garden, croquet, bowling green, tennis, outdoor swimming pool, fishing, boat hire and sailing tuition, games room. Closed Nov-end Feb. Amex, MasterCard,* ***VISA***

Restaurant £95

Bar snacks are available from an extensive menu at lunchtime, while in the evening there's an imaginative table d'hote and extras that attract a supplement like Devonshire beef and local Tresco shellfish and lobster. For those who want to push the boat out there is a cold seafood platter with crab, lobsters and Scottish gravad lax. Typical dishes might include local fillet of lemon sole grilled with calvados, a cold meat platter, chilled water melon and ginger soup, chargrilled pork loin steak with garlic and thyme, and butterscotch cheesecake with sautéed pineapple in dark rum and cane sugar. West Country cheeses, a catch of the day and a Sunday buffet complete the picture. Plenty of half bottles on a decent, fairly priced wine list. No smoking. ***Seats*** *110. Private Room 10. L 12-2.15 D 6.45-9.30. Set D £22-£30.*

TRURO The Royal 62% £65

Tel 01872 70345 **Fax 01872 42453** Map 12 B3 H
Lemon Street Truro Cornwall DTR1 2QB

Well-run, privately-owned, handsome granite hotel in the city centre. Rooms are on three floors (no lift) and higher-priced (£90) Executive rooms offer more work space, CD players and fax machines. A family bedroom sleeps three, with room for an additional bed. 24hr room service. No dogs. Secure parking for 40 cars. ***Rooms*** *37. Keep-fit equipment, snooker. Closed 3 days Christmas. Amex, MasterCard,* ***VISA***

Tunbridge Wells — Spa Hotel — 72% — £101

Tel 01892 520331 **Fax 01892 510575** Map 11 B5 **HR**
Mount Ephraim Tunbridge Wells Kent TN4 8XJ

The Spa was built in 1766 as a country mansion for Sir George Kelly and remained a private home for its first century. It became a hotel in 1880 and has been in the same family ever since. Sister hotel to *The Goring* in London, it stands in 14 acres of gardens and parkland that include two lakes. The foyer opens on to a spacious lounge with Corinthian columns, darkwood panelling and a gas log fire at each end; half is reserved for non-smokers. The Equestrian Bar is a favourite place for a drink or bar food. Bedrooms vary in size, decor and price, but all feature freestanding furniture. Although conferences form most of the weekday business, there is an atmosphere of a moderately grand hotel run along traditional lines, with excellent leisure facilities in the Sparkling Health club. Children up to 14 may stay free in their parents' room (or there are interconnecting family rooms). One room is adapted for disabled guests. No dogs. ***Rooms** 74. Garden, tennis, croquet, indoor swimming pool, gym, sauna, steam room, sun beds, beauty & hair salon. Amex, Diners, MasterCard,* **VISA**

Chandelier Restaurant — £60

In the large, high-ceilinged Regency dining-room, good-quality produce is best enjoyed in the simpler dishes. Both table d'hote and à la carte menus are offered, with a two-course price option at lunchtime only when you might find spinach and prawn roulade with tomato and basil coulis followed by sautéed lamb's kidneys in a grain mustard sauce and then iced vanilla terrine with toffee pieces and a caramel sauce. The evening table d'hote sees similar fare and is priced according to your selection from nine main courses - from an omelette to paupiette of sole stuffed with crab on duxelles with a light ginger butter sauce. Excellent wine recommendation deal (a half bottle each of white and red plus two glasses of dessert wine: £17.50). ***Seats** 90. Parties 24. L 12.30-2 D 7-9.30. Closed L Sat. Set L £12/£14.50. Set D £14.50-£21.*

Tushingham — Blue Bell Inn

Tel 01948 662172 Map 6 B3 **P**
Bell O' Th' Hill Tushingham Whitchurch Cheshire SY13 4QS

'Bell O' Th' Hill' is the sign to look for by a new stretch of the A41, four miles north of Whitchurch. Standing in extensive grounds on a bend in the old road is this remarkable building of 17th-century origins with a black and white, timbered frame, massive oak doors and a wealth of original timbers, oak panelling and memorabilia within. There's a single bar, the pub's focal point, where the ales are real and the welcome's a mite unusual. Landlord Patrick Gage hails from California, while his wife Lydia is from Moscow. This somehow matches the mild eccentricity of an establishment which lists amongst its claims to fame the presence of a ghost duck and the more physical presence of a Great Dane and a miniature poodle. Wooden benches in front for an alfresco drink look suitably ancient, while 'paddock' rather than garden would describe the safe outdoor area allocated to youngsters who are particularly welcome to play with the Gage children (and the dogs). *Open 12-3, 6-11 (Sun 12-3, 7-10.30). Free House. **Beer** Hanby Drawwell, Treacleminer & Black Magic Mild, occasional guest beer. Garden. Family room. No credit cards.*

Ullswater — Old Church Hotel — 67% — £105

Tel 01768 486204 **Fax 01768 486368** Map 4 C3 **HR**
Watermillock Ullswater Cumbria CA11 0JN

Kevin and Maureen Whitemore provide a warm welcome for guests at their pleasant lakeside hotel, which was built in 1754 on the site of a 12th-century church. Both lounges are built for relaxation and are packed with board games and periodicals. Maureen's bold colour schemes brighten the bedrooms (priced according to the view: £85 for fell views, £125 for luxury rooms with lake views), with crown canopies and half-testers framing really comfortable beds. Excellent breakfasts. Seven miles from the M6 (J40). No dogs. ***Rooms** 9. Garden. Closed Nov-Mar. Amex, MasterCard,* **VISA**

Restaurant **£60**

The smaller lounge doubles as an aperitif bar where guests gather prior to dinner (availability is limited for outside diners and booking is essential). Kevin's menu offers a short, straightforward selection with dishes like mushrooms and crispy bacon in garlic butter, grilled goat's cheese with a walnut dressing, fillet of cod with leeks and a cheese crumble topping, pork fillet with a horseradish cream sauce, sticky toffee pudding, and warm Swiss honey and walnut tart with vanilla ice. Just three excellent British cheeses. No smoking. No children under 7 – other arrangements are made for youngsters. ***Seats*** *24. Parties 6. D only 7.30-8.30 (order by 7). Closed Sun. Set D £23.50.*

Upper Benefield — Wheatsheaf Hotel

Tel 01832 205254 **Fax 01832 205245** Map 7 E4

Upper Benefield Oundle Northamptonshire PE8 5AN

Situated beside the A427 Corby to Oundle road, this stone inn was originally built as a farmhouse in 1659 and subsequently became a coaching inn with the addition of stables to the rear. These have been neatly converted to house eight functional en suite bedrooms, featuring modern pine furnishings, built-in wardrobes and good writing space for visiting businessmen. TVs, tea-makers, telephones and radios are standard throughout. Food on offer here ranges from a new cosmopolitan menu (pizzas, Cajun steak, club sandwiches, German potato soup, steak and kidney pie) served in the Garden Bistro to an à la carte menu in the small restaurant. Specials may include Dover sole with fennel butter sauce, John Dory or ostrich steaks! Children's facilities include high-chairs, board games and toys and a swing in the garden. *Open 11-11 (Sun 12-3, 7-10.30).* ***Bar Food*** *12-2, 6-10 (Sun 7-9). Free House.* ***Beer*** *Courage Directors, guest beer. Garden, outdoor eating.* ***Accommodation*** *9 bedrooms, all en suite, £55-£65 (single £45); weekend reductions (£48/£38). Children welcome overnight (under-2s free), additional bed (£15) & cot (£10) available. Dogs by arrangement. Amex, Diners, MasterCard,* **VISA**

Ventnor — Royal Hotel — 60% — £90

Tel 01983 852186 **Fax 01983 855395** Map 15 D4

Belgrave Road Ventnor Isle of Wight PO38 1JJ

Neat gardens front a Victorian sandstone hotel. Bedrooms are well maintained; six are suitable for families. Small banquets/conferences for up to 80. ***Rooms*** *55. Garden, outdoor swimming pool, playground. Amex, Diners, MasterCard,* **VISA**

Ventnor — Spyglass Inn

Tel & Fax 01983 855338 Map 15 D4

The Esplanade Ventnor Isle of Wight PO38 1JX

After totally rebuilding the distinctively pink-painted Spyglass Inn, Stephanie and Neil Gibbs (both native Islanders) reopened it in 1988. Wandering around the several interconnecting rooms, which include two reserved for non-smokers and several where children are welcome, it is difficult to believe that the pub is not hundreds of years old. The bar counter is built of old pews and the whole place is full of old seafaring prints and photographs, as well as numerous nautical antiques ranging from a brass binnacle and ship's wheel to old oars and model ships in glass cases. The setting could not be better, at one end of the seafront with a front terraced area stretching right to the edge of the sea wall. In winter, the waves break right over the wall and more than one customer has been known to get a soaking by mistiming their exit from the pub. Inside, you might try ham and mushroom tagliatelle, chicken and ham pie, chili or pork spare ribs, but the thing to look out for is the local seafood: crab served out of its shell in generous bowlfuls with salad, and locally-caught lobsters. In winter, there are home-made soups from a blackboard menu, and on Saturday nights a candle-lit dinner, for which booking is advisable, complete with pianist. There is live music nightly (not Mon in winter) from a small group who might play country, folk or jazz. Three neat little flatlets with upholstered rattan furniture and a sea-facing balcony offer accommodation for up to two adults and two children; DIY breakfasts in the kitchenettes. A public car park is just 50 yards away, but check your brakes before venturing down here – the road to the seafront has hairpin bends and a gradient of 1 in 4. 'Children, well-behaved dogs and muddy boots welcome.' *Open 10.30-11 (closed 3-7 Sept-May), Sun 12-10.30.* ***Bar Food*** *12-2.15, 7-9.30 (summer school holidays 12-9.30, till 9 Sun). Free House.* ***Beer*** *Hall & Woodhouse Badger Best & Tanglefoot, Wadworth 6X, guest beers. Patio/terrace, outdoor eating. Family room.* ***Accommodation*** *3 en-suite flatlets, sleeps 4, from £40. Children welcome overnight (under-8s stay free). Closed 25 Dec eve. MasterCard,* ***VISA***

Waddesdon Five Arrows Hotel

Tel 01296 651727 **Fax 01296 658596** Map 15 D2 **P**
High Street Waddesdon Buckinghamshire HP18 0JE

A delightful Victorian confection built by the Rothschilds to house the architects and artisans working in nearby Waddesdon Manor (NT) – itself worth a visit. The name comes from the family crest with its arrows representing the five sons sent out by the dynasty's founder to set up banking houses in the financial capitals of Europe. Restored in 1993 from top to toe and often bedecked with flowers (there's a fine garden to the rear) the hotel/inn is in the capable hands of Robert Selbie and chef Julian Alexander-Worster. One enters straight into the bar, from which open several rooms with antique tables, colourful upholstered chairs plus the odd settee and armchair; pictures from Lord Rothschild's own collection grace the walls along with numerous photos of old Waddesdon – charmingly un-pub-like. A short, modern blackboard menu might offer smoked marinaded venison with an orange confit and rich mushroom soup to start, followed by Cajun blackened salmon with a rémoulade sauce or baked cod with a herb crust, with home-made puddings like treacle tart and chocolate liqueur terrine for dessert. The good wine list majors on the various Rothschild wine interests that extend to Portugal and Chile as well as the famous Chateau Lafite. Six good-sized bedrooms are individually decorated with matching en suite bathrooms (two with shower and WC only) and boast extra large beds (with pure Egyptian cotton sheets) and antique Victorian washstands along with modern comforts: remote-control TV, direct-dial phones and tea/coffee-making facilities. No smoking in the bedrooms. *Open 11.30-3 & 6-11, (Sun 12-3 & 7-10.30).* ***Bar Food*** *12-2.30 (till 2 Sun), 7-9.30 (till 9 Sun). Free House.* ***Beer*** *Fuller's London Pride & ESB, Chiltern Brewery Beechwood Bitter, Theakston Old Peculier. Garden, outdoor eating.* ***Accommodation*** *6 bedrooms, all en suite, £65 (single £50). Children welcome overnight (stay free in parents' room), additional bed available. No dogs. MasterCard,* ***VISA***

A jug of fresh water!

Walberswick Mary's Restaurant

Tel 01502 723243 Map 10 D2 **JaB**
Manor House Walberswick Suffolk IP18 6UG

The Jelliffs' neat restaurant and tea shop is in a small coastal village across the River Blyth from Southwold. Things like toasted tea cakes (£1), freshly-made sandwiches (from £2) and cream teas (£3.25) are available all day. Lunch is between 12 and 2, the menu specialising in local fish (though there is something for everyone): grilled or deep-fried plaice (£5.50), seafood thermidor (£8.25) and sausages with potatoes and onions (£5.25) plus blackboard specials. Starters include home-made soup with croutons (£2.50), prawn cocktail (£3.75) and grilled banana with Stilton and cream. In the afternoon high teas could include scrambled eggs on toast (£3.95), cold meat salad with potatoes (£6.25) and grilled kippers (£5.75). Dinner is more ambitious, but still relies strongly on local products: maybe fresh asparagus (£3.25), prawns in filo pastry with a soy dip (£3.75) or brandied liver paté (£3.25) to begin; lamb's kidneys with a sherry and mustard sauce (£8.50), grilled slip sole (£8.25) or a platter of deep-fried seafood (£6.50) to follow. Simple desserts are all home-made. No smoking in the twin eating rooms but it's allowed in the small bar or outside in the secluded garden, where tables are set around the Union Jack flagpole. Large car park at the rear. ***Seats*** *45.* ***Open*** *10-6, also (Fri/Sat only) 7.15-9.* ***Closed*** *Mon (except during school summer holidays), also Tue, Wed & Thu Nov-Easter. No credit cards.*

WALLINGFORD Annie's Tea Rooms

Tel 01491 836308 Map 15 D2 JaB
79 High Street Wallingford Oxfordshire OX10 OBX

At Jean Rowlands' cosy tea room in the High Street six different set teas (£2.20-£2.60) are served from 2.30 and scones, toast and teacakes are available all day. Between 12 and 2.30 lunch takes centre stage, bringing soup – maybe carrot and coriander or watercress (£1.95), open sandwiches (£1.95-£2.50), ploughman's (from £2.95), main-course salads (from £3.20) and a hot dish of the day – perhaps pork, apple and cranberry hotpot (£3.85). Desserts include ice creams, fruit pie and Annie's banana boat. Filled baked potatoes in winter. One high-chair; small walled garden. No smoking. ***Seats*** *31 (+ 4 outside).* ***Open*** *10-5 (summer till 5.30).* ***Closed*** *Sun (except teatime Jul-Sep), Wed & Bank Holidays. No credit cards.*

WANSFORD-IN-ENGLAND The Haycock 70% £99

Tel 01780 782223 **Fax 01780 783031** Map 7 E4 HR
Wansford-in-England Peterborough Cambridgeshire PE8 6JA

A lovely 17th-century honey-coloured stone coaching inn located next to the junction of A1 and A47 and set in 6 acres of grounds that include lovely gardens stretching along the banks of the river Nene and the village cricket pitch. It has been much extended in sympathetic style, the most recent additions being a large conference/ballroom (a lovely setting for functions with its soaring oak beams, enormous fireplace and private garden, catering for up to 200) and the stone-walled Orchard Room with all-day bar and coffee-shop menu (7am-11pm, with a fine lunchtime buffet). Other day rooms include a pubby bar and two traditional lounges. Bedrooms in the older parts of the building are full of character, but all have been decorated with great style and flair using high-quality fabrics and furnishings; one ground-floor twin room has a wide door and handrails for disabled guests. Bathrooms are equally luxurious. The variety of food on offer in both bar (excellent bar snacks – fish and chips, spicy ribs of pork, smoked chicken salad, linguine with prawns and olive oil, open mushrooms with cream cheese and garlic, Montgomery Cheddar or Colston Bassett Stilton, home-baked cheesecake, tiramisu), Orchard Room (one room is non-smoking) and restaurant caters for all tastes and pockets; an outdoor barbecue takes place daily in summer, with seating for 100 in a courtyard. Candelabras and highly polished silver add to the mellow, traditional atmosphere of the twin dining-rooms. The restaurant menu is pretty traditional, too, with a daily roast sirloin of prime English beef always featuring on the silver trolley. Outstanding, carefully compiled and sensibly-priced list of wines with helpful notes; twelve available by the glass. Arcadian Hotels; hotel, inn and pub all rolled into one. *Open 7am-10pm.* ***Bar Food*** *12-10.30.* ***Beer*** *Ruddles Best & County, Bass, Batemans XB, John Smith's, guest beer. Garden, croquet, fishing, pétanque, helipad.* ***Accommodation*** *50 bedrooms, all en suite, from £99-£125 (four-poster from £140, suite from £175, single £78-£90). Children welcome overnight (under-5s stay free in parents' room, 5-14s half price), additional bed & cot available. Amex, Diners, MasterCard,* ***VISA***

WANTAGE Vale & Downland Museum

Tel 01235 771447 Map 14 C2 JaB
19 Church Street Wantage Oxfordshire OX12 8BL

A museum of past and present local life set in a 17th-century cloth-merchant's house and converted farm buildings. It's also an art gallery and a tourist information centre. In the coffee shop good home baking is the showpiece, from biscuits (10p-15p), flapjacks and shortbread (both 30p) to cakes like coconut (60p), coffee, chocolate and iced walnut (all 75p). The lunchtime menu runs from soup – vegetable (£1.20) to filled jacket potatoes (from £1.95), quiche (£2.10) and salads. The winter months might produce macaroni cheese, lasagne or tuna and pasta bake (£2.50). Beakers, bibs and baby food can all provided on request; there's also a children's playhouse with toys, and hopscotch in the garden. Five high-chairs and booster seats and a pull-down shelf in the Ladies. Unlicensed. No smoking. ***Seats*** *40 (+ 20 outside).* ***Open*** *10.30-4.30 (Sun 2.30-5).* ***Closed*** *Mon, Good Friday, 25, 26 Dec & 1 Jan. No credit cards.*

WARE Sunflowers

Tel 01920 463358 Map 15 F2 **JaB**
7 Amwell End Ware Hertfordshire SG12 9HP

Simply decorated little vegetarian restaurant over a wholefood shop. The food is fresh and healthy, with organic produce to the fore. Pizza or quiche with salad (£2.25), filled jacket potatoes and nut roast (all with salads £1.95-£2.50) and sandwiches (from £1). Daily blackboard specials might include moussaka or vegetable crumble (£2.50). Home-made cakes (from 50p) are available all day. No smoking. Unlicensed. ***Seats*** *28.* ***Open*** *9-5.* ***Closed*** *Sun & Bank Holidays (except Good Friday). No credit cards.*

WAREHAM Springfield Country Hotel 60% £100

Tel 01929 552177 **Fax 01929 551862** Map 14 B4 **H**
Grange Road Stoborough nr Wareham Dorset BH20 5AL

Set in six acres of stylishly landscaped gardens off the A351, a pleasant redbrick hotel with an appealing modern exterior. The spacious foyer is dominated by a splendid stag's head and there are two cosy bars. Bedrooms are agreeable and neatly maintained, all featuring a uniform pink decor, and includes family rooms sleeping up to four; compact bathrooms. Good family facilities, including high teas and Saturday morning activities. A new building was being added as we went to press; this will join the main hotel building to the function suite (catering for up to 200, theatre-style, and 160 banqueting) and leisure club and provide 16 new Executive bedrooms, a new dining-room and five further conference rooms. ***Rooms*** *48. Garden, tennis, indoor & outdoor swimming pool, gym, squash, sauna, steam room, spa bath, solarium, beauty salon, badminton, games room. Amex, MasterCard,* ***VISA***

WARMINGTON The Wobbly Wheel

Tel 01295 690214 **Fax 01295 690354** Map 14 C1 **P**
Warwick Road Warmington Banbury Warwickshire OX17 1JJ

Premier House (part of the Greenalls brewery group) have converted and extended the old Wobbly Wheel (on the B4100, between Junction 10 & 11 of the M40) into the grand prix version of a family entertainment pub. Set in its own garden and play area, the 'Captain Coconut's Adventure Island' is a self-contained fun-house (admission £1, £2 at weekends and Bank Holidays) for all who can pass beneath the gorilla's outstretched palm (under 4ft 9in); more funds will be required for pop and candy. Pub food from the next-door, chain-themed 'Millers Kitchen' is ground out by the barrow-load – hardly a gourmet destination. Fifteen lodge-style bedrooms look out over open country, promising a restful night once the fun factory's finished. One family bedroom (£57.25) has two interconnecting rooms with one double bed, two singles and no charge for an extra Z-bed: excellent value – booking recommended. There are dozens of other outlets in the Premier Lodge chain, particularly around the Manchester area, but not all offer accommodation – ask for a brochure.
Pub open 12-11, Sun 12-10.30. Garden, outdoor playing area. Family room. ***Accommodation*** *15 bedrooms, all en suite, £42.25. Children welcome overnight, additional bed and cot available. Amex, Diners, MasterCard,* ***VISA***

WARMINSTER Bishopstrow House 81% £141

Tel 01985 212312 **Fax 01985 216769** Map 14 B3 **HR**
Boreham Road Warminster Wiltshire BA12 9HH

New owners have brought a new, less formal style (both children and pets are welcome and there is no longer a dress code in the restaurant) and much refurbishment to this late-Georgian house set in 28 acres of grounds on the B3414 about a mile south-east of town. In place of chintz and frills has come a more sophisticated decor based largely on fabrics from Ralph Lauren and Mulberry (a local firm). To the elegant day rooms – library, drawing-room – has been added a bar in the inner hall with its rug-strewn, stone-flagged floor, and there is also an appealing conservatory. Fresh flowers abound, especially orchids, which are something of a house signature. Individually decorated bedrooms, which include three 'full' and four 'junior' suites, all have antique pieces among their furnishings and also get fresh flowers plus fruit, biscuits and magazines, while the bathrooms, many of which have been upgraded (ten now have separate showers) and often sport marble features, come with towelling robes and quality toiletries. Room service operates 24 hours a day and in the evenings beds are turned down, curtains drawn and bedside lights lit. The Ragdale Spa offers a complete range of health and beauty treatments; both swimming pools are delightful. Sister hotel to the Feathers Hotel in Woodstock. ***Rooms*** *30. Garden, croquet, indoor & outdoor tennis, indoor & outdoor swimming pools, splash pool, game fishing, sauna, gym, sun beds, beauty salon. Amex, Diners, MasterCard,* ***VISA***

Mulberry Restaurant £75

The refurbishment has extended to the restaurant, which is now lighter and brighter, with Russian impressionist prints around the walls and wooden slatted shutters at windows that look out over the gardens. Chris Suter is still in charge of the kitchens, however, with his inventive modern cooking straightforwardly described in English on menus that might include crispy duck confit with shallot and cassis dressing, rocket salad with parmesan, grilled vegetables with leek risotto and truffle oil (a vegetarian main dish choice), polenta-crusted fish cakes with tomato and tarragon sauce, and braised shank of lamb with mashed potato. To finish, farmhouse cheeses, banoffi pie with butterscotch sauce, rhubarb and apple crumble or lemon-glazed fruits with lemon parfait. On Friday and Saturday nights the menu, which is at other times priced à la carte, comes only at the fixed price of £26.50. There's an interesting and well-conceived wine list. No smoking. ***Seats*** *65. Private Room 22. L 12.30-2 D 7.30-9.30. Set L £12.50/£14.50 (Sun £18) Set D (Fri & Sat) £26.50.*

WARWICK The Brethren's Kitchen

Tel 01926 492797 Map 14 C1 JaB
Lord Leycester Hospital Warwick Warwickshire CV34 4BH

The brethren's former dining room is home to this little restaurant, whose short menu is available all day. Sandwiches (cheese and pickle £1.55, salmon and cucumber £1.95), toasted snacks, filled jacket potatoes (from £2.65) and salads form the regular savoury choice, and a blackboard announces daily specials such as egg mayonnaise with prawns (£3.15) or chicken topped with ham and cheese served with parsley potatoes (£4.50). On the home baking front there's a display of cakes, slices and sponges (from 85p). Cream tea £1.95. A children's menu (£2.25) offers beans or spaghetti shapes on toast, ice cream and a glass of squash or lemonade. One high-chair and changing facilities in the Ladies. Ramps for wheelchair access. No smoking. Parking at rear of building. ***Seats*** *40.* ***Open*** *10-5.* ***Closed*** *Mon (but open Bank Holidays) & end Oct-Tue before Easter. No credit cards.*

Our inspectors *never* book in the name of Egon Ronay's Guides. They disclose their identity only if they are considering an establishment for inclusion in the next edition of the Guide.

WARWICK Piccolino's Pizzeria

Tel 01926 491020 Map 14 C1 JaB
31 Smith Street Warwick Warwickshire CV34 4JA

A dependable alternative to the larger high-street chains (there's a branch also in Leamington Spa – see entry), Piccolino's is family-owned and family-friendly too. Cooked-to-order pizzas (*napoletana* £4.95, *quattro formaggi* £5.70) are notably good, pasta alternatives (*tortellini ricotta* £5.20, *tagliatelle alla marinara* £5.90) richly sauced, and there are steaks (sirloin £9.25) for those willing to splash out more. Speciality ice creams. Service is typically relaxed and informal. ***Seats*** *75.* ***Open*** *12-2.30 & 5.30-11 (Fri till 11.30, Sun till 10.30, Sat 12-11.30).* ***Closed*** *25, 26 Dec & Easter Sun. MasterCard,* ***VISA***

WATERPERRY The Pear Tree

Tel 01844 338087 **Fax 01844 339833** Map 15 D2 JaB
Waterperry Gardens nr Wheatley Oxfordshire OX33 1JZ

Counter-service tea shop in a horticultural centre where the counter holds a tempting display of home baking – even the dozen or so different sandwiches (maybe tuna mayonnaise £2.15, or brie and cranberry £2.25) are made with home-baked bread. Other savoury items include cauliflower cheese and vegetable lasagne (both £3.95); various salads accompany. At lunchtime there are hot specials like stuffed aubergines with ham and cheese (£5.25), flaky fish pie or mushroom stroganoff (£3.40). Set cream tea £3. Eat outside and admire the gardens in fine weather. A friendly place, with a nice big green space outside for young ones to run about in, and plenty of room inside too for the odd buggy or push-chair; two high-chairs and lidded beakers are provided for tiny tots; although there's no special menu for children, with careful choosing you should be able to select a suitable meal for your child without having to rely on the obvious attraction of cakes and pastries. A table for baby-changing is available both in and outside the Ladies toilets. ***Seats** 80 (+ 80 outside). **Open** 10-5 (Oct-end Mar till 4.30). **Closed** 1 week Christmas. MasterCard, **VISA***

WEEDON The Crossroads 55% £51

Tel 01327 340354 **Fax 01327 340849** Map 15 D1 H
High Street Weedon Northamptonshire NN7 4PX

A well-run Premier Lodge (Greenalls) located on the busy intersection of the A5 and A45, with efficient triple-glazing for the rooms where it matters. Most of the public areas are in the original building and comprise a large, characterful bar with a small, south-facing balcony. Bedrooms are all in a U-shaped motel-style block (except for 10 in the main building). Two are adapted for guests in wheelchairs. Excellent value for families as some rooms have two double beds, others with two sofa beds, all at the same price. ***Rooms** 48. Garden, tennis. Amex, Diners, MasterCard, **VISA***

WELBECK Dukeries Garden Centre, Coffee Shop

Tel 01909 476506 **Fax 01909 48047** Map 7 D2 JaB
Welbeck Estate nr Worksop Nottinghamshire S80 3LP

Situated in the walled gardens of historic Welbeck Abbey, the coffee shop is housed in restored Victorian greenhouses with exposed beams and bare brick walls. All the food is made on the premises; lunchtime brings daily specials such as steak casserole, mince patties, chicken korma, vegetable lasagne and cheese and onion pie (£3.99-£4.60). Available all day are freshly made rolls (from £1.40), filled jacket potatoes (from £1.75), hot sausage rolls, soup and various cakes and gateaux (50p-£1.75). On Sundays there is a traditional roast lunch (£5.35) in addition to the regular menu. Four high-chairs are provided along with a changing shelf in the disabled toilet. An adventure playground and toddler's village is 100 yards away in the garden centre. Close to Wookey Hole and Cheddar Gorge. No smoking. ***Seats** 140 (+ 36 outside). **Open** 10-5.30 (winter till 4.30). **Closed** 4 days Christmas. MasterCard, **VISA***

We welcome bona fide complaints and recommendations on the tear-out pages at the back of the Guide for Readers' Comments. They are followed up by our professional team.

WELLS Cloister Restaurant

Tel 01749 676543 Map 13 F1 JaB
Wells Cathedral Wells Somerset BA5 2PA

Self-service restaurant in the cloisters of the Cathedral. A daily choice of savoury specials, all prepared on the premises, could include vegetable risotto, cauliflower cheese (£3.50) or Somerset chicken casserole. For dessert, perhaps baked lemon sponge and cream or Somerset apple and cider dessert (£1.50). Scones with cream and jam, tea and coffee served all day. Children's portions. Profits go towards the upkeep of the Cathedral. No smoking. ***Seats** 100. **Open** 10-5 (Sun from 12.30). **Closed** Good Friday & 2 weeks Christmas. No credit cards.*

Wells Good Earth

Tel 01749 678600 Map 13 F1 JaB
4 Priory Road Wells Somerset BA5 1SY

Aptly named, this restaurant has a wholefood shop alongside. Daily-changing lunchtime savouries (some priced for either large or small portions) include home-made soup (cream of carrot and coconut, watercress and lemon £1.07/£1.75), vegetable lasagne, Mexican pasta casserole (both £2.55), filled baked potatoes (from £2.15), salads (£1.65/£2.30) and pizza with a light bread base and a choice of tasty toppings (from £1.75). Fruit cake, carrot cake, flapjack and a vegan cake (from 78p). Children are well catered for, with baby-changing facilities, high-chairs and, in the leafy courtyard, a play area. No smoking. Park in the adjacent Palace Courtyard car park and if you spend more than £5 the Good Earth will pay the 25p charge. ***Seats*** *80 (+ 20 outside).* ***Open*** *9.30-5.30.* ***Closed*** *Sun & Bank Holidays. MasterCard,* **VISA**

West Bexington Manor Hotel 59%

Tel 01308 897616 **Fax 01308 897035** Map 13 F2 H
Beach Road West Bexington Bridport Dorset DT2 9DF

Richard and Jayne Childs' old manor house is just a short walk from Chesil Bank and has a stone-walled cellar bar, leafy conservatory and residents' lounge. Reliable bar food encompasses good fish dishes (perhaps fish soup, whole plaice, Dover Sole), lobster thermidor, oysters, rabbit in mustard, venison in red wine and juniper, and Thai chicken curry. Hearty snacks are available in the form of sandwiches, ploughman's platters, lasagne and steak and kidney pie. Good choice at Sunday lunchtimes and at least 20 wines by the glass to chose from. For pudding, try the chocolate roulade or summer pudding. Books, magazines and dried flower arrangements add a homely, welcoming touch to simply furnished but well-equipped bedrooms that come complete with tea and coffee kits, TVs, direct-dial phones, sherry, elderflower water and goodnight chocolates. A couple of larger, family bedrooms will sleep up to four (two additional beds are supplied). Children's high-teas can be provided between 5.30 and 6.30pm and there are four high-chairs. A safe garden offers swing, slide, climbing frame, while indoor activities can be catered for with crayons, colouring sheets and toys. *Open 11-11 (Sun 12-10.30).* ***Bar Food*** *12-2, 6.30-10 (from 7 Sun). Free House.* ***Beer*** *Furgusons Dartmoor Bitter, Wadworth 6X, Manor Bitter. Garden, outdoor eating, children's play area. Family room.* ***Accommodation*** *13 bedrooms, all en suite, £78 £84 (single £45-£49). Children welcome overnight, additional bed (£7.50) & cot (£4) available. No dogs. Accommodation closed 25 Dec. Amex, Diners, MasterCard,* **VISA**

West Byfleet Superfish

Tel 01932 340366 Map 15 E3 JaB
51 Old Woking Road West Byfleet Surrey KT14 6LG

Part of the excellent Surrey-based chain serving traditional British fish and chips fried in beef dripping, the Yorkshire way. See Morden entry for more details. Above is Jane's Upstairs restaurant which offers a wider choice of dishes and wines plus home-made sweets in more stylish surroundings. Booking at Jane's is essential: Tel 01932 345789. ***Seats*** *30.* ***Open*** *11.30-2 (Sat till 2.30) & 5-10.30 (Thu-Sat till 11).* ***Closed*** *Sun, 25, 26 Dec & 1 Jan. Jane's is closed also on Monday. Amex, MasterCard,* **VISA**

West Runton Links Country Park Hotel 62% £120

Tel 01263 838383 **Fax 01263 838264** Map 10 C1 H
Sandy Lane West Runton nr Cromer Norfolk NR27 9QH

Set in 35 acres of coastal parkland, midway between Sheringham and Cromer on the A149, the privately-owned Links is a large, distinctive mock-Tudor building from the Edwardian era. Guests are well looked after in comfortable day rooms and decently-equipped bedrooms (satellite TV, 24hr room service); some rooms have a private sitting-room (Executive rooms £140, four-poster £150). The Garden Rooms are larger; an adjoining room for children can be provided on request; facilities for disabled guests. Suitable for sports-orientated families (all facilities free to residents); children under 16 free in parents' room. The Runton Suite caters for up to 200 (weddings are popular). There's a splendid scenic view of the coastline from the 7th green of the par 33 golf course. The railway station is 200yds away. ***Rooms*** *40. Garden, indoor swimming pool & splash pool, tennis, 9-hole golf course, sauna, sun beds. Amex, MasterCard,* **VISA**

WESTCLIFF-ON-SEA Oldham's

Tel 01702 346736 Map 11 C4 P
13 West Road Westcliff-on-Sea Essex SS10 9AU

This licensed fish restaurant opposite the Palace Theatre has been in the same family for over 30 years. The standard-sounding fish and chip menu offering cod (£4.75/£5.25), plaice (£4.50/£5) and haddock (£5), all served with chips and garnish, is much enlarged by house specials: deep-fried king prawns in breadcrumbs with a hint of garlic (£5.50), fresh salmon (either fried or poached £7.25) plus a few meat and vegetarian offerings: barbecued spare ribs (£5.75), hot or cold chicken with salad (£4.50) and vegetarian pasty with chips and salad (£2.95). Children's menu £2.50. ***Seats** 80. **Open** 11-9.30 (Sun till 9). **Closed** 25, 26 Dec & 1 Jan. No credit cards.*

WESTON Otter Inn

Tel & Fax 01404 42594 Map 13 E2 P
Weston Honiton Devon EX14 0NZ

Situated 400 yards off the busy A30 and beside the River Otter, this much-extended 14th-century cottage is a popular refreshment stop en route to and from the West Country, and a particular favourite with families. The original old cottage interior is delightfully unspoilt, with a vast inglenook fronted by comfortable armchairs and old tables. Plenty of prints, books and various bric-a-brac make this a cosy and relaxing spot in which to sit. The main bar extension is very much in keeping, with heavy beams, a real assortment of old sturdy tables and chairs, an unusual chamber pot collection hanging from the beams and the added touch of fresh flowers on each table. Beyond some double doors is a skittle alley and games room. A hand-scripted bar menu highlights many of the usual snacks such as sandwiches, salads, ploughman's lunches, filled jacket potatoes and steaks; main-course specialities include smoked fish platter, steak and kidney pie, chicken Gloria, home-made pasta stuffed with cheese with a garlic, basil and wine sauce, and locally-made sausages with mash. Lunchtime salad buffet as well as daily dishes chalked up on boards offering more variety and greater interest, such as baked sea bass, duck with fresh cherry and orange sauce, lamb and fillet steak platter with spinach and Stilton sauce and a vegetarian dish of the day (asparagus and nut mousse). Winter spit-roasts over the open fire on Thursday evenings. Children who have been cooped up in the car for long periods will relish their own 'ducklings' menu ("ask for crayons and paper to keep you happy") and the space in the splendid riverside garden, which offers youngsters the chance to paddle in a very safe shallow section of the river; they may also be entertained by the resident rabbits, guinea pigs, ducks and chickens. Babes in arms are extremely well catered for, with free baby food offered and changing facilities provided in the Ladies. *Open 11-3, 6-11, (Sun 12-3, 7-10.30). **Bar Food** 12-2, 7-10 (till 9.30 Sun). Free House. **Beer** Eldridge Pope Hardy Country, Bass, Boddingtons, Worthingtons, guest beer. Garden, outdoor eating, summer barbecue, indoor and outdoor play area. Family room. MasterCard,* ***VISA***

WESTON-UNDER-REDCASTLE Hawkstone Park Hotel 62% £73

Tel 01939 200611 **Fax 01939 200311** Map 6 B3

Weston-under-Redcastle Shrewsbury Shropshire SY4 5UY

Parent hotel to the historic park and follies created in the 18th Century by Sir Rowland Hill (some five minutes' drive away and with separate admission charges), Hawkstone Park is rather better known as a golfing venue; indeed Sandy Lyle learnt his game on these fairways and greens. Away from this Golf Society haven, hotel guests have their own cocktail bar (evenings only) within the U-shaped old coaching inn which houses comfortable, well-equipped bedrooms in various extensions and additions. While a major redevelopment programme, including 100 new bedrooms and extra conference and banqueting facilities, remains currently at the artist's impression stage, plans were well ahead as we went to press for restaurant extensions to be completed by spring 1997. ***Rooms** 65. Garden, croquet, golf (2 x 18-hole & Academy practice courses), putting, driving range, room, snooker, coffee shop (8.30am-11pm). Amex, Diners, MasterCard,* ***VISA***

WHITBY Elizabeth Botham & Sons

Tel 01947 602823 Map 5 F3 JaB
35/39 Skinner Street Whitby North Yorkshire

Established in 1865 by Elizabeth Botham and still owned by the same family, now in its fourth generation, this traditional tea shop is situated up a steep flight of stairs, above a bakery that provides much of its produce. Snacks include sandwiches (from £1.60), scones, teacakes and their own Bothams biscuits (35p); also filled jacket potatoes (from £2.10). Lunchtime brings a set menu (£5.50 for two courses) based on a traditional English dish like steak & kidney pie, braised beef or a roast; fish and chips in either breadcrumbs or batter (£4.95), a salad buffet including Cheddar ploughman's (£3.30), Dales lunch – blue and white Wensleydale with home-made chutney (£3.55) and their own pork pie with crusty bread (£3.10). All-day breakfast £3.75. Two set teas (Cream Tea £1.70, Afternoon Tea with sandwiches instead of scones and cream £3.60). Children's meals (sausages or fish fingers and chips, spaghetti on toast, and ice cream). Two high-chairs, a Lego table for youngsters and baby-changing facilities. No smoking. ***Seats** 100. **Open** 9-5. **Closed** Sun, also Mon Oct-May. MasterCard,* ***VISA***

Also at:
30 Baxtergate Whitby North Yorkshire
Contrastingly modern branch with a smaller menu but the same food. Unlicensed. No smoking. *Open from 8.30.*

WHITBY Magpie Café

Tel 01947 602058 Map 5 F3 JaB
14 Pier Road Whitby North Yorkshire YO21 3PU

This marvellous seafood restaurant was originally a merchant's house in the 18th century; it's now run by the third generation of the Mackenzie family, who have brought the menu up to date. Traditional fish and chips are still the mainstay of the lengthy menu, and there's generally a wide choice that includes cod, haddock, plaice, lemon sole, woof and halibut, all of it landed locally; grilling and poaching are alternatives to deep-frying. Prices (salad garnish included) range from £5.45 to £8.95. There are also daily specials, salads (crab is very popular), meat and vegetarian options (such as mushroom and butter bean stroganoff with rice £4.45), a special menu for weight-watchers, children's dishes and plenty of hot and cold desserts. Cream Tea £2.95, Afternoon Tea £3.75. Children are welcomed, with eight high-chairs, toy boxes and baby-changing room all provided. Customers may purchase bibs and disposable nappies. Street parking out of season, otherwise use Cliff Street car park. ***Seats** 100. **Open** 11.30-9 (earlier closing Sun-Thu Oct-Dec). **Closed** Dec-Feb. MasterCard,* ***VISA***

WHITBY Shepherd's Purse Wholefood Restaurant

Tel & Fax 01947 820228 Map 5 F3 JaB
95 Church Street Whitby North Yorkshire YO22 4BH

Close to the harbour and beach, down a cobbled alley in old Whitby, is this vegetarian restaurant with rooms, stocking locally produced cheeses, bread and several organic wines and providing a good range of speciality coffees and teas to accompany the day's food offerings: soup with garlic bread (£2.50), a generous meze for two people including houmus, tsatsiki, crudités, salsa and corn chips (£4.50), cider, celery and apple loaf (£4.95), pizzas and pasta dishes, ginger and mango crumble (£2.50). There are also three special lunchtime platters, Shepherd's (ploughman's), Eastern (onion bhajis, samosas, mango chutney, poppadum) and Mediterranean (feta cheese, olives, fresh basil, salad, French stick) all at £3.50. Scones and cakes are available all day (95p-£2.50). Children's menu; high-chairs and a sitting room available for nursing mothers. Toys, colouring books, and jigsaws are provided to keep little ones amused. Waitress service in the evenings makes for more expensive dishes, though the choice remains much the same. Breakfast available for those staying overnight (9 rooms). No smoking. ***Seats** 40 (+ 40 outside). **Open** 10-5 (also 7-10 on fine evenings – please enquire). **Closed** 25 & 26 Dec. MasterCard,* ***VISA***

WHITBY Trenchers

Tel 01947 603212 **Fax 01947 821025** Map 5 F3 **JaB**
New Quay Road Whitby North Yorkshire Y021 1DH

Down by the harbour, this large, bright, bustling eatery is immaculately kept – the marble loos are particularly impressive – and well run by a family team with the help of numerous smartly kitted-out staff who combine friendliness and efficiency to a high degree. It's close to the harbour, so it's not surprising that seafood is a speciality: Whitby cod or haddock with chips (£5.95, large £8.25), plaice, skate, halibut, fisherman's casserole (£5.95), seafood salad (£8.25), fresh-dressed Whitby lobster (£12.95). Also steak pie, cottage pie, lasagne and a couple of vegetarian main courses. Freshly cut sandwiches from £1.95. Serious wine list. Children and babies are welcome at any time and are well-catered for, with their own Junior's Choice of seven meals (all at £3.55), 20 high-chairs and eight booster seats, and a purpose-built baby-changing area, with mat, nappies, wipes and a chair for nursing mothers. ***Seats** 200. **Open** 11-9. **Closed** mid Nov-mid Mar. No credit cards.*

WHITEWELL Inn at Whitewell

Tel 01200 448222 **Fax 01200 448298** Map 6 B1 **IR**
Whitewell Forest of Bowland Clitheroe Lancashire BB7 3AT

Our 1997 Pub of the Year Award winner is set amid the wild beauty of North Lancashire, well away from the hurly burly, standing next to the village church; it overlooks the River Hodder (on which the inn has eight miles of fishing rights) at the head of the Trough of Bowland, one of the least-known areas of outstanding natural beauty in the country. Back in the 14th century, the inn was home to the keeper of the King's deer, and the Queen still owns the building as part of the Duchy of Lancaster. Inside, it's wonderfully relaxed, laid-back, even mildly eccentric, with a haphazard arrangement of furnishings and bric-a-brac. In the main bar there are wooden tables, old settles, roundback chairs, a stone fireplace, log fire in cold weather, and heavy ceiling beams. An entrance hall has colourful rugs, more settles, even a piano, and a selection of magazines, papers and books for some serious loitering. A wide variety of pictures, dotted about the building, comes from the Inn's own art gallery; there's also a small wine merchant business. Head chef Breda Murphy was enticed over from the *Ballymaloe* cookery school in Ireland. Her food is served in both the bar and restaurant, which overlooks the river; the interesting bar meal selection offers the likes of a daily home-made soup (onion and thyme), chicken liver paté, seafood pancake, fishcakes, leek, potato and mushroom gratin, Cumberland bangers with champ (Irish mashed potatoes with spring onions), salads, substantial sandwiches, cheeses from London's Neal's Yard Dairy and home-made puddings (chocolate mousse, lemon meringue pie). The bar supper menu is similar but varies slightly, perhaps offering goujons of fresh fish, chicken breast stuffed with banana and mango and specials like plaice stuffed with salmon mousse. Good Arabica coffee is served in a cafetière and ground coffee is also packed for taking home – typical of the kind of thought that goes into Richard Bowman's running of the inn. A good wine list completes the picture. There are eleven bedrooms, all furbished with antique furniture, peat fires and Victorian baths. Unusual extras include video recorders and superb stereo systems, as well as books, magazines, and a set of binoculars; the best and largest rooms overlook the river and the country beyond (and attract the higher tariff). Everything is usually immaculately clean. On sunny days the attractive rear lawn – furnished with simple benches – is an ideal spot to relax and soak in the view. Children are made most welcome. All-in-all, the Inn at Whitewell comes up trumps in everything it sets out to do – satisfaction for overnight guests is almost guaranteed, and it's not often that we say that! *Open 11-3, 6-11 (Sun 12-3, 7-10.30).* ***Bar Food** 12-2, 7.30-9.30. Free House. **Beer** Marston's Pedigree, Boddingtons. Riverside garden, outdoor eating. **Accommodation** 11 bedrooms, all en suite, £69/£78 (suite £98, single £49.50-£79). Children welcome overnight (under-12s £12, over-12s £15), additional bed & cot available. Amex, Diners, MasterCard,* **VISA**

WHITNEY-ON-WYE Rhydspence Inn

Tel 01497 831262 Map 9 D4 P
Whitney-on-Wye Hay-on-Wye Hereford & Worcester HR3 6EU

Set in the heart of Kilvert country, on the A438 about a mile out of Whitney-on-Wye, this is a well-loved, reliably entertaining inn with a delightful timbered interior, two attractive bars with real fires, old furniture and beams aplenty. Nice touches include magazines and newspapers, creating an atmosphere in keeping with the old library chairs. The charming dining-room and restaurant overlook the garden. Five comfortable bedrooms have beams, sloping floors, plus an armchair at the least; some rooms are more romantic; one has a four-poster; all have TVs and hot beverage facilities but no phones. Bar food suggestions include seafood pie, lasagne, beef curry, sizzling Cajun chicken and vegetable stir-fry. Separate restaurant menu (not recommended here) including popular Sunday lunches. Summer lunchers can enjoy the view over the Wye Valley from the terraced garden. *Open 11-2.30, 7-11 (Sun 12-2.30, 7-10.30).* ***Bar Food** 11-2 (from 12 Sun), 7-9.30.* ***Beer** Bass, Robinson Best, guest beer. Garden, outdoor eating. Family room.* ***Accommodation** 7 bedrooms, all en suite, £55-£65 according to season (4-poster £75, single £27.50-£32.50,). Children welcome overnight (under-2s stay free in parents' room), additional bed & cot (£12) available. No dogs. Amex, MasterCard,* ***VISA***

WIGGLESWORTH Plough Inn

Tel 01729 840243 Map 6 B1 P
Wigglesworth Skipton North Yorkshire BD23 4RJ

For over sixteen years now the Goodall family have operated, enlarged and improved their 18th-century country inn which was once the farm buildings and ale house of a vast Dales estate. The busy food operation features the output of a wood-burning pit barbecue whose contents can be hot- or cold-smoked over hickory, mesquite or oak chippings. Around the resultant rack of ribs, hickory chicken and smoked halibut steak is a menu full of Yankeeisms, from potato skins with sour cream and corn on the cob 'thro' Caesar salad with smoked chicken to 'steak and prawn combo'. More traditionally, there are still bistro-style bar snacks served in the original village bar and evening meals in a bright conservatory restaurant. Accommodation offered is either Standard (over the original pub) or Superior in a carefull-conceived extension which blends in immaculately with the original timbered black-and-white frontage. Within are all the trappings of modern-day comfort from TV and radio to direct-dial phones and tea and coffee trays: all the rooms are of a decent size with well-kept en suite bathrooms and effective double glazing. While the front rooms look across a village street where practically nothing happens from day to day, those to the rear soak in the ever-changing moods of the twin Dales peaks of Ingleborough and Pen-Y-Ghent. *Open 11.30-3, 7-11 (Sun 12-3, 7-10.30).* ***Bar Food** 12-2, 7-9.30. Free House.* ***Beer** Tetley Best, Boddingtons. Garden, outdoor eating. Family room.* ***Accommodation** 12 bedrooms, all en suite £55 (single £32.45). Children welcome overnight (under-2s stay free, 2-12s £5 in parents' room), additional bed & cot available. No dogs. Amex, Diners, MasterCard,* ***VISA***

WILLERBY Grange Park 67% £92

Tel 01482 656488 **Fax 01482 655848** Map 7 E1 H
Main Street Willerby nr Hull East Riding of Yorkshire HU10 6EA

Adjacent to the A164 and Willerby Shopping Park, Grange Park is a much-extended Victorian house standing in 12 acres of grounds four miles from the centre of Hull. Besides comfortable modern accommodation it offers extensive purpose-built conference facilities (up to 550 in 4 suites and 10 syndicate rooms; ample parking), 24hr room service and informal bar meals with an Italian slant in the Cedars pubby bar in the grounds. Club Tamarisk includes a gymnasium, pool and baby-changing facilities. ***Rooms** 101. Garden, indoor swimming pool, gym, sauna, beauty & hair salons, children's playground. Amex, Diners, MasterCard,* ***VISA***

WILMINGTON Home Farm 58% £56

Tel 01404 831246 **Fax 01404 831411** Map 13 E2 **H**
Wilmington nr Honiton Devon EX14 9JR

A thatched former farmhouse (a working farm until 1950) with a five-acre garden, cobbled courtyard, flagstoned bar and homely lounge with piano, books and board games. Bedrooms are divided between the main house and the Garden and Courtyard wings. Children welcome: under-5s free if sharing their parents' room. ***Rooms*** *13. Garden. Closed 4 days Christmas. Amex, Diners, MasterCard,* ***VISA***

WINCHESTER The Cathedral Refectory

Tel 01962 853224 **Fax 01962 841684** Map 15 D3 **JaB**
The Visitors Centre Inner Close Winchester Hampshire SO23 6LF

In a part of the visitors centre near the Cathedral's west entrance, a team of volunteers led by chef-manager Nigel Rogers produces excellent food in a counter-service eaterie. The Dean rightly claims that in the refectory 'you can enjoy a tradition of hospitality which goes back to the days of the Benedictine monastery'! Everything, even the bread (and sandwiches – from £1.60 – come with a choice of granary, farmhouse, walnut and soda bread) is made in-house and is uniformly excellent: soup simply bursting with flavour (£2.10); filled baked potatoes (from £2.90), quiche of the day served with baked potato and salad (£4.95); trenchers (£3.45) – a modern version of a medieval concept in which thick slices of bread (the trencher) come with a variety of toppings – tomato, pesto and sheep's cheese with green salad or Eldon pork sausages and mashed potato. More filling dishes might include mutton hot pot – chump chops, braised with kidneys and black pudding, served with red cabbage (£5.95) or excellent baked ham with Cumberland sauce (£5.95). There is also a splendid array of home-baked biscuits and cakes – the moist-iced passion cake is delicious. The Cathedral Cream Tea (£2.95) is served from 2.30. Children's portions and children's menu; plenty of high-chairs; baby-changing facilities. Walled patio garden for summer eating. All profits go to the upkeep of the Catherdral. No smoking. ***Seats*** *90.* ***Open*** *9.30-5 (Sun from 10). No credit cards.*

WINCHESTER Lainston House 75% £147

Tel 01962 863588 **Fax 01962 776672** Map 15 D3 **H**
Sparsholt Winchester Hampshire SO21 2LJ

Well signposted off the A272 Winchester-Stockbridge road, this fine William and Mary house glories in 63 acres of classic English parkland that include the remains of a 12th-century chapel. The entrance hall/reception is particularly welcoming in winter, when a log fire smoulders in a large Delft-tiled fireplace; those in the comfortable lounge with its floral fabrics and brass chandeliers sport flowers. The remaining public room is the library lounge displaying some fine carved cedar panelling. Main-house bedrooms have high ceilings and elegant proportions; the 14 in the Chudleigh Court extension have more uniformity but perhaps the best are six rooms created out of the former stable block. These are very sumptuous with some fine antiques and luxurious bathrooms that even boast TVs. All rooms have quality furnishings and stylish decor. Friendly staff and good cooked breakfasts. 24hr room service. Various conference and function rooms (catering for up to 50 theatre-style) include a restored half-timbered barn; ample parking. ***Rooms*** *37. Garden, croquet, tennis, putting green, fishing, snooker. Amex, Diners, MasterCard,* ***VISA***

WINDERMERE Holbeck Ghyll

Tel 015394 32375 **Fax 015394 34743** Map 4 C3 **JaB**
Holbeck Lane Windermere Cumbria LA23 1LU

This 19th-century hotel with its splendid location overlooking Lake Windermere is just the spot for afternoon tea, out on the lawns in summer or by log fires in the traditionally furnished, country-house-style lounges in winter. The set tea (£8.50) offers a choice of smoked salmon or prawn sandwiches (oatcakes topped with cottage cheese, walnuts and fresh pineapple for vegetarians) followed by home-made fruit scones, Lakeland fruit cake and home-made chocolate chip and pecan cookies or shortbread. Most things are also available individually. Dishes on the lunch menu could include BLT with chicken and garlic mayonnaise (£5.95), goujons of lemon sole with salad and fries (£7.95), smoked fish or roast ham in a salad, sandwiches and omelettes, with Cumbrian warm sticky toffee pudding and home-made ice cream to finish. A new Terrace restaurant has been opened this year with the lighter eater in mind (omelette and salad £4.25, mushroom, vegetable and prawn risotto, club sandwich £5.95, Sunday lunch roast £7.95). No smoking. ***Seats** 40. **Open** 12-5 (also more formal evening menu). Amex, Diners, MasterCard,* ***VISA***

WINDERMERE Miller Howe Café

Tel 015394 46732 Map 4 C3 **JaB**

Alexandra Buildings Station Precinct Windermere Cumbria LA23 1BQ

Within Lakeland Plastics (a large kitchenware store near the railway station) the recently refurbished café offers scones (80p) and shortbread (85p), soup, jacket potatoes, the day's quiche (£4.95), sugar-baked ham with mustard, Cumberland sausage with apple sauce and date chutney, and bobotie (an African dish of spiced minced lamb with apricots, almonds and an egg custard topping). Specials could include mushroom stroganoff (£4.95), or salmon with soy sauce, ginger and orange on a bed of crispy bean sprouts (£6.50). Sticky toffee pudding and tipsy trifle are popular desserts. Everything is available all day and there's no minimum charge but there is often a queue as space is limited. There are small portions for children and free baby food for their very youngest customers. Two high-chairs, crayons, colouring sheets, cartoon videos and toys are all provided. Within the store there are baby-changing facilities and a play area. No smoking. ***Seats** 56 (+ 15 outside). **Open** 9-5 (Sat till 6, Sun 10-4) **Closed** 25 Dec. MasterCard,* ***VISA***

WINDSOR Oakley Court 78% £188

Tel 01753 609988 **Fax 01628 37011** Map 15 E2 **HR**

Windsor Road Water Oakley nr Windsor Berkshire SL4 5UR

Set in 35 acres of landscaped grounds that slope gently down to the banks of the Thames (about halfway between Windsor and Maidenhead), Oakley Court – a grand Victorian manor – is only about half an hour from central London. The spacious lounges have open log fires, chandeliers and original, ornate plasterwork ceilings. The panelled library has over 500 volumes with which to while away the hours. Bedrooms are most appealing, with almost all rooms in separate extensions (the Riverside and Garden Wings) close to the main house; many are particularly spacious and boast splendid red granite bathrooms; the six luxurious suites in the original house have a more traditional, period feel. In the 60s and 70s the Court was used as the atmospheric setting for many films, including the *St Trinians* series, the *Rocky Horror Picture Show* and several Hammer horror productions. Boats for hire from the hotel's private jetty. Ample parking. No dogs. Queens Moat Houses. ***Rooms** 92. Garden, croquet, golf (9), boating, fishing, gym, sauna, solarium, snooker. Amex, Diners, MasterCard,* ***VISA***

Le Boulestin £100

All change here with Boaters Brasserie having moved into the space formerly occupied by the Oak Leaf Restaurant which has itself been replaced by this restaurant (where Boaters used to be) as the hotel's more formal eating option. If the name sounds familiar (Boulestin was a famous Covent Garden restaurant) you may also recognise the monogrammed china, which has been acquired along with the name. The restaurant occupies three interconnecting rooms, of which the first, with its dado panelling, marble fireplace and fine plasterwork ceiling, is much to be preferred. A more important change is that Murdo MacSween has returned to take over as executive chef (he had a most successful stint here in the past) with his appealingly inventive style: sautéed scallops with black pudding; smoked salmon as a salad with baby capers; salad of chargrilled leeks, shaved parmesan, warm poached egg and langoustines; saltimbocca of red mullet with ratatouille provençale and a saffron and black olive butter sauce; breast of chicken with Chinese noodles and spring onions. There are also some simpler dishes like grilled Dover sole, Scotch fillet of beef béarnaise and the roast joint of the day. Among desserts like caramelised banana tart with coconut ice cream and apricot coulis, and crisp almond and orange feuilletines, a pear ravioli on kirsch sabayon with lavender ice cream proved most successful.

See over

A fine wine list (do we detect Anthony Byrne's hand at work?) has much from France and a fair smattering from the New World. No smoking. ***Seats*** *75. Parties 12. Private Room 18. L 12.30-2 D 7.30-10. Set L £22 (Sun £23.50) Set L & D £45 Set D £33.*

Boaters Brasserie £55

A skiff hanging from the ceiling and some straw boaters on the walls reflect the name but there is not really the informal feel one expects to find in a brasserie. The menu is nicely varied, however, with plenty of choice ranging from an all-day breakfast to vegetable tempura with a red onion chili and tomato salsa, grilled fresh tuna niçoise with soft-boiled eggs, Cumberland sausage with mash and onion gravy, goujons of sole with tartare sauce and chips, stir-fry chicken and several pasta dishes. Finish with sticky toffee pudding, lemon tart with clotted cream, apple charlotte with sauce anglaise and ice cream or a selection of cheeses with grapes and celery. Good choice of wines by the glass. Air-conditioned. No smoking. ***Seats*** *70 (+ 40 outside). L 12.30-2.30 D 7-10.*

WINSLOW Bell Hotel

Tel 01296 714091 **Fax 01296 714805** Map 15 D1 P
Market Square Winslow Buckinghamshire MK18 3AB

Handsome Georgian coaching inn that proudly overlooks the market square in this pleasant small town. Good pubby bar with heavy beams and inglenook fireplace, and comfortable lounge areas with oak and leather furniture, easy chairs, attractive prints and plates. At present there are seventeen bedrooms, two designed for the disabled, all spacious with floral fabrics, reproduction darkwood furniture – one with a four-poster – clean, tiled bathrooms and added extras like TVs, telephones, tea-makers, hairdryers and trouser presses. A further twenty two bedrooms are currently being built. *Open 10am-11pm (Sun 12-10.30).* ***Beer*** *Greene King. Courtyard.* ***Accommodation*** *17 bedrooms, all en suite, £44.50-£49.50 (family room sleeping three £49.50, single £39.50-£47). Children welcome overnight, additional bed (£5) & cot available. Amex, MasterCard,* ***VISA***

WINTERTON-ON-SEA Fisherman's Return

Tel 01493 393305 Map 10 D1 
The Lane Winterton-on-Sea Norfolk NR29 4BN

Small it maybe, but this prettily-kept row of former fishermen's cottages is an ideal hang-out for locals and visitors alike, be they fishermen or not. Built in traditional brick and flint, the buildings are probably 16th-century, and unaltered over the last quarter century or more. The cheery public bar, complete with warming wood-burner, is lined in varnished tongue-and-groove panelling and hung with sepia photographs and prints of Lowestoft harbour, the Norfolk Broads and the pub itself. A smaller and possibly older lounge, low-ceilinged, with a copper-hooded fireplace and oak mantel, is carpeted these days and ideal for a quick, if cramped, snack. Families will more likely head to the 'Tinho', a timbered rear extension with pool table and games machines which leads mercifully quickly to a lovely enclosed garden with a pets' corner and an adventure playground. The printed menu offers standard pub fare, but look to the blackboard for interesting daily specials like spicy aubergine soup, salmon and mussel lasagne, baked lamb in gooseberry sauce, and plum and apple crumble. Toasted sandwiches and ploughman's platters are served all day. A tiny flint-lined spiral staircase leads up under the eaves to three cosy bedrooms, which share the house television (propped up on a seaman's trunk) and two bathrooms (one with shower only). The largest room, a family room, also has a sitting area with its own television. Modest comforts, maybe, but entirely adequate for a brief stay, a stone's throw from the beach and long walks over the dunes. Visitors are made truly welcome by John and Kate Findlay, and seen on their way with the heartiest of seafarer's breakfasts. *Open 11-2.30, 6-11 (from 7 in winter), Sat 11-11, Sun 12-3, 6.30-10.30.* ***Bar Food*** *12-2, 6-9.30 (from 6.30 Sun, from 7 in winter). Free House.* ***Beer*** *John Smith's, Adnams Best, Wolf Bitter, guest beers. Garden, outdoor eating, children's play area. Family room.* ***Accommodation*** *3 bedrooms, £45 (single £30). Children welcome overnight (babies free if in own cot), additional bed (£5) available. Check-in by arrangement. No credit cards.*

WIRKSWORTH Crown Yard Kitchen Restaurant

Tel 01629 822020 Map 6 C3 **JaB**
Crown Yard Market Place Wirksworth Derbyshire DE4 4ET

Look for the Heritage Museum sign, walk through the arch and up the winding slope and you will find this bright, airy restaurant. Home baking includes biscuits and tea cakes; there are rolls and sandwiches (from 95p), jacket potatoes (£1.30-£2), all-day breakfasts (£2), salads, lasagne, steak & kidney pie (with a mixed salad or jacket potato – £3.75) and cod mornay, plus daily vegetarian specials. Roast lamb or beef for Sunday lunch. A children's menu offers a waffle and three fish fingers served with baked beans, a fruit drink, and ice cream; children's portions are always available. Two high-chairs and a toy box with books are provided. Seating on a terrace in summer. Smoking is not allowed between 12 and 2. Ladies and gents toilets have ramps for wheelchair access. ***Seats*** *34 (+ 12 outside).* ***Open*** *9-5 (Sun 10-8).* ***Closed*** *25 Dec, 1 Jan & 2 weeks Jan. MasterCard,* ***VISA***

WISLEY Conservatory Café & Terrace Restaurant

Tel 01483 225329 **Fax 01438 211270** Map 15 E3 **JaB**
The Royal Horticultural Society's Garden Wisley Surrey GU23 6QA

Everything in the garden is lovely, and that includes the Conservatory Café (run by Cadogan Caterers) which manages to maintain creditably high standards despite serving upwards of 4,000 customers on a busy day. Virtually everything for the light, airy café, with its large terrace, is made on site – light sponges oozing fresh cream (from £1.70), Eccles cakes, Chelsea buns (both 80p), almond florentines (70p), lemon meringue pie (£2.10), salads, sandwiches (from £1.65), well-filled Cadogan pasties (£1.70), quiches (£1.95 or £4.50 with a choice from the salad buffet), filled jacket potatoes (from £3.20) and, at lunchtime, various hot vegetarian dishes at £3.95. The table-service Terrace restaurant offers traditional English breakfasts (£6.50) until 11.30 then, from noon, an à la carte menu (minimum charge £8 11.30-2.15) including a traditional roast and, in the afternoon, a choice of set teas (from £3.15). Children's Boxes (£1.95) contain a sandwich, mini-Cheddar, Kit-Kat, piece of fruit and a Kinder Surprise egg. Within The Royal Horticultural Society's Garden (entrance fee), the café and restaurant are open from 9am on Sundays, but only to RHS members. Twelve high-chairs and baby-changing facilities. No smoking. ***Seats*** *350 (+ 200 outside).* ***Open*** *10-5.30 (winter till 4).* ***Closed*** *Sun (except to RHS members) & 1 week Christmas. MasterCard,* ***VISA***

WITNEY Witney Four Pillars Hotel 62% £100

Tel 01993 779777 **Fax 01993 703467** Map 14 C2 **H**
Ducklington Lane Witney Oxfordshire OX8 7TJ

Just outside Witney at the junction of the A40 and A415, a modern hotel with an attractive stone frontage. Bright, practical accommodation, rustic-style bar-lounge, purpose-built Blakes leisure centre with a decent-size indoor pool. Popular for conferences (up to 140) and banquets (130); ample parking. Family facilities include a splash pool for toddlers alongside the bright, daylight pool; children up to 16 stay free in parents' room. Disabled toilets include baby-changing facilities. ***Rooms*** *74. Gym, indoor swimming pool, sauna, spa bath, sun beds, snooker. Amex, Diners, MasterCard,* ***VISA***

WIVELISCOMBE Langley House 66% £86

Tel 01984 623318 **Fax 01984 624573** Map 13 E2 **HR**
Langley Marsh Wiveliscombe nr Taunton Somerset TA4 2UF

Peter and Anne Wilson's pale-peach Georgian house (with 16th-century origins) nestles in lovely countryside at the foot of the Brendon Hills; drive half a mile north of Wiveliscombe on the road to Langley Marsh. It's a pretty place with four acres of landscaped gardens, a cobbled courtyard and attractive, homely drawing-rooms. Bedrooms are particularly stylish and appealing with well-planned colour schemes and lots of little extras, from a sewing kit to a hot water bottle; the majority of rooms overlook the garden. Two bedrooms were refurbished last year and king-size beds installed. The Wilsons' personal care and attention are of a high order and breakfasts are super. Families are welcome – a drying room is provided and considerations are made for youngsters. ***Rooms*** *8. Garden, croquet, playground. Amex, MasterCard,* ***VISA***

See over

Restaurant £75

The beamed, candle-lit restaurant with its silver and crystal table settings enhances the air of well-being to which Peter's three-course (weekday) and four-course (weekend) modern English dinner menus do full justice. There is no choice until the dessert course. Two-tone bavarois of sweet peppers with a chilled tomato coulis could get things under way, followed perhaps by fillet of sea bass with Provençal breadcrumbs on a bed of leeks with beurre blanc. The main dish might be mignons of lamb (cut from the saddle) with a port wine sauce, young spinach and baby new potatoes. Small choice of good West Country cheeses like long Clawson unpasteurised Stilton and Capricorn goat's cheese, served with home-made walnut and banana bread. Half a dozen desserts (strawberry galette, icky sticky toffee pudding or elderflower and elderberry syllabub) round things off nicely. A fine wine list, albeit with no introductory or tasting notes at all; wines are listed by price. No smoking. No children under 7. ***Seats** 20. Parties 8. Private Room 20. L by arrangement D 7.30-8.30 Set D from £28.50.*

Wolverhampton Healthy Way

Tel 01902 772226 Map 6 B4 JaB
87a Dartington Street Wolverhampton WV1 4EX

A small, informal counter-service wholefood restaurant in the town centre serving hearty, healthy dishes such as vegetable lasagne and spinach roulade with salads (both £3), quiches, pizzas and freshly prepared sandwiches (from £1.40). Hot spinach soufflé is a speciality (£3) and savoury pancakes and tuna pasta bake are popular main courses (both £3.40). Carrot cake and fruit flan (95p & £1.35) are a couple of the home-made sweets. No smoking between 12 and 2. ***Seats** 30. **Open** 9-5. **Closed** Sun & Bank Holidays. No credit cards.*

Woodbridge Seckford Hall 68% £105

Tel 01394 385678 **Fax 01394 380610** Map 10 D3 H
Woodbridge Suffolk IP13 6NU

Family-owned and run since 1950, this imposing Elizabethan manor house is reached by following the A12 Woodbridge by-pass (don't turn off into the town) until a distinctive sign announces the hotel on the left. The house is surrounded by 34 acres of gardens and woodlands which include a willow-fringed lake. Its interior is characterised by period features such as linenfold panelling, heavily beamed ceilings, huge fireplaces and the carved wooden doors of the Great Hall (lounge). These are offset by plush velvet furnishings and richly-coloured carpets. Bedrooms are comfortably furnished more in private-house than hotel style, four have four-poster beds and some studios and suites (one with facilities for disabled guests) are in a courtyard leisure complex that includes an inspired conversion of an old tithe barn into a delightful heated swimming pool. Banqueting/conference facilities for 100. Adjacent 18-hole golf course. ***Rooms** 32. Garden, indoor swimming pool, gym, solarium, spa bath, fishing, coffee shop (10am-10pm). Closed 25 Dec. Amex, Diners, MasterCard, **VISA***

Woodstock Brothertons Brasserie

Tel 01993 811114 Map 15 D2 JaB
1 High Street Woodstock Oxfordshire OX20 1TE

The informal, relaxed atmosphere of this popular town-centre brasserie is perfect for enjoying a morning coffee, lunch, tea or evening meal. The printed menu keeps regular favourites like Brothertons smokies (£4.05), deep-fried brie with cranberry sauce (£3.60), large Mediterranean prawns with garlic (£4.95) and crepes (chicken with mushrooms and parsley £6.95), supplemented by daily-changing specials like spaghetti carbonara (£3.30/£5.30 with salad), half a roast duck with almonds and honey (£11.50), monkfish thermidor (£9.95) and best end of lamb in red wine (£9.85). Traditional English puddings to finish. Scones and jam for tea (£1.80) and a roast dish on Sundays (£6.50-£7.50). ***Seats** 65. **Open** 10.30am-10.30pm. **Closed** 25, 26 Dec & 1 Jan. Amex, Diners, MasterCard, **VISA***

WOOLACOMBE Woolacombe Bay Hotel 65% £170*

Tel 01271 870388 **Fax 01271 870613** Map 12 C1 
South Street Woolacombe Devon EX34 7BN

Family summer holidays, winter breaks and conferences (for up to 200 delegates) are the main business at this imposing Edwardian hotel, whose lawns and gardens reach down to three miles of golden sands. The attractions extend outside the immediate vicinity, as guests enjoy preferential rates at both Saunton Sands Golf Club and Eastacott Meadows riding stables. Public rooms are fairly grand, bedrooms (including a new twin and a new family room) bright and roomy, with mostly modern furnishings. There are self-catering suites, apartments and flats. Families are extremely well catered for, with a children's club in high season, baby-changing facilities in the Ladies powder room, rooms with bunk beds, high tea served from 5.15 and high-chairs galore. 'The Hot House' features a new gym and health suite. No dogs. *Half-board terms only. ***Rooms*** *64. Garden, croquet, tennis, pitch & putt, indoor & outdoor swimming pools, gym, squash, sauna, spa bath, steam room, solarium, beauty & hair salon, indoor bowls, billiards room, playroom, play area & organiser in high season, snooker. Closed 2 Jan-10 Feb. Amex, Diners, MasterCard,* ***VISA***

> Always ring ahead and inform establishments of your exact requirements when travelling with children. Unannounced can, sadly, still mean unwelcome.

WOOLLEY MOOR White Horse

Tel 01246 590319 Map 6 C3 
White Horse Lane Woolley Moor Derbyshire DE5 6FG

Bill and Jill Taylor are the landlords of the smart, friendly and very popular White Horse. Approached from the A61 at Stretton, Woolley Moor is a tiny hilltop hamlet above the river Amber at the point where it flows into Ogston reservoir. The large paddock and garden have a sandpit, swings, and small adventure playground to help keep the youngsters happy and there's both a boules pitch and a football pitch. There are at least two dozen trestle tables outside; bag one for a summer lunch, but remember the number before going inside to order. Within, there's restaurant seating for around 60 people, and it fills up quickly, so booking is recommended. On the printed menu, dishes such as steak and kidney pie, creamy chicken pie and seafood quiche are offered alongside filled jacket potatoes, ploughman's and sandwiches. Gooey desserts could include chocolate and brandy mousse and butterscotch and walnut fudge cake. Blackboard specials may feature venison sausage bake, pork chop with orange and cranberry sauce and wild mushroom ragout. It's substantial stuff, nicely cooked and presented and, above all, tasty. The Smoke Room still remains the village local, with is quarry-tiled floor, red leather banquettes, Britannia tables and prominent dartboard; Monday night dominoes are played in a seriously competitive spirit. This is where a good drop of ale comes in. In addition to draught Bass, a healthy rotation of guest beers is publicised well in advance, a good proportion of them from independent breweries. Piped music, when playing, is of the classical kind. This is a smart and impressive pub, professionally managed, and it runs like clockwork. No under-14s in the bar areas. *Open 11.30-2.30, 6-11 (Sat 11.30-3.30, 6-11, Sun 12-3.30, 5-10.30).* ***Bar Food*** *11.30-2 (till 2.15 Sat), 6.30-9 (Sat 6-9.15, Sun 12-2.15, 5.30-8.30). Free House.* ***Beer*** *Bass, Jennings Dark Mild, three guest beers. Garden, outdoor eating, children's play area. No credit cards.*

> Pubs – note that food is only recommended in those pubs with ***Bar Food*** times in the statistics at the end of an entry. Restaurant food in pubs is *never* recommended unless specifically mentioned. Some pubs are recommended for B&B or Atmosphere only – each entry's statistics indicate our recommendation.

WORCESTER Heroes

Tel 01905 25451 **Fax 01905 619509** Map 14 B1 JaB
26-32 Friar Street Worcester Hereford & Worcester WR5 2LZ

Housed in a two-storey timbered Tudor building, Heroes offers, in contrast to its surroundings, a fashionably varied menu, with plenty of international flavour. The range is typified by burgers (from £4.75), grills (8oz rump steak at £8.95), pizzas (from £3.85) and pasta dishes (tagliatelle carbonara – with bacon, mushrooms, cream and garlic – £6.95). Starters and light snacks include garlic bread with cheese (£1.80) and taramasalata with pitta bread (£3.45), and main dishes incorporate Mexican specialities such as burritos or chimichangas (from £7.95) and some vegetarian dishes (mushroom stroganoff £6.25). Daily specials offer a choice of dishes between £7 and £8, and a selection of cakes and pastries is available during the day, with cappuccino coffee or a choice of teas. Traditional roast lunch with all the trimmings on Sundays (two courses £7.75) in addition to the regular menu. Pavement tables in summer. Children's portions. During the day park in the Friar Street NCP, street parking at night. ***Seats** 60 (+ 12 outside). **Open** 11-10.30 (Fri & Sat till 11). **Closed** 25 Dec. Amex, Diners, MasterCard,* ***VISA***

WORFIELD Old Vicarage 67% £95

Tel 01746 716497 **Fax 01746 716552** Map 6 B4 HR
Worfield Bridgnorth Shropshire WV15 5JZ

Set in two acres of grounds overlooking fields and farmland, Peter and Christine Iles's redbrick Edwardian parsonage reflects the peace and quiet of its village setting. Twin conservatories jutting out into the garden house a relaxing lounge. Individually designed bedrooms, each named after a local village, sport reproduction furniture, pretty soft furnishings and copious extras. Four rooms in the Coach House have superior fittings (larger showers, jacuzzis, safes) and open on to a private garden with unspoilt views across the valley to the River Worfe; two rooms are adapted for the use of wheelchair-bound guests. Staff are particularly friendly and families with children are welcome – no charge for extra bed or a cot for under-10s in parents' room; high tea at 6pm. The Wenlock family suite has a separate lounge area and sleeps two adults and two children on sofa-beds. 24hr room service. ***Rooms** 14. Garden, croquet. Closed around Christmas/New Year. Amex, Diners, MasterCard,* ***VISA***

Restaurant £85

Soft lighting, polished tables and a parquet floor set the scene for reliably good cooking from chef John Williams. Typical starters might be a pressing of duckling, ham hock and mushy peas with balsamic dressing, melon with iced grapes and warm apple and jasmine tea dressing or bresaola with marinated broccoli, olive oil and lemon. Follow this with main dishes like medallion of Ludlow venison with sweet and sour red cabbage and a watercress and ginger butter, or fillet of Cornish red mullet with a soup of lobster scented with mussels and basil. Excellent artisanal British cheeses and/or desserts like fine apple tart cooked to order and served with vanilla ice cream or a contrast of chocolate desserts. The super wine list points you in the direction you want to go, with brief annotations on each wine; fair prices, a wide selection from around the world plus a good selection of half bottles. No children under 8 - other arrangements are made for youngsters. No smoking. Disabled toilet facilities. ***Seats** 50. Private Room 16. L Sun 12-2 other days by arrangement D 7-9 (Sun at 7). Set Sun L £15.50 Set D £24 (Mon-Thu), £29.50 (Fri/Sat), £24.50 (Sun).*

WORTHING Fogarty's

Tel 01903 212984 Map 11 A6 JaB
10 Prospect Place off Montague Street Worthing West Sussex BN11 3BL

Housed in one of Worthing's oldest buildings, once a fisherman's cottage, this charming tea room continues to provide its customers with good home baking, both sweet and savoury, for morning coffees and afternoon teas (cream tea £2.90), and tasty lunch dishes that could include steak and kidney pie (£4.90), salmon and prawn pancake (£5.50), half a fresh lobster, grilled or cold with salad (£7.50) and freshly made salads. A selection of fresh cream cakes including meringues (£1.95), and pastries such as strawberry tartlets, baked cheesecake and the ever-popular banoffi pie never fail to please. No smoking. ***Seats** 36 (+ 12 outside). **Open** 9-5. **Closed** Sun, Mon, 2 weeks Feb & 2 weeks Sep. No credit cards.*

WORTHING Seasons

Tel 01903 236011 Map 11 A6 JaB
15 Crescent Road Worthing West Sussex BN11 1RL

Located in the old part of the town, Seasons is a bright, clean, self-service vegetarian and vegan restaurant with pine furniture and several prints hanging on the pale green walls. A variety of dishes is available, including a full vegetarian cooked breakfast at £2.50, or £2.95 for their 'maxi' version. Home-made cakes and scones (from 60p) are served throughout the day, while lunchtime specials (from £3) could include cheese-sauced pancakes, buckwheat slice with a red cabbage ragout and brazil nut cannelloni with a fresh basil and tomato sauce. There's also a large selection of salads, plus jacket potatoes and quiches (from £1.50). Children's portions. Unlicensed, but they generally serve 3 or 4 non-alcoholic wines. No smoking. ***Seats** 40. **Open** 9-4. **Closed** Sun & Bank Holidays. No credit cards.*

WRIGHTINGTON High Moor Inn £55

Tel 01257 252364 **Fax 01257 255120** Map 6 B1 R
High Moor Lane Wrightington nr Wigan Lancashire WN6 9QA

The restaurant's interior features lots of oak, stone flagging, iron fireplaces and exposed beams, all adding up to an appealing rustic charm. The cooking, under the direction of chef-partner Jim Sines, is also appealing, with nice little touches like oysters priced individually, asterisked 'house speciality' menu items (hot chicken confit with tomato relish, fish and shellfish rendezvous with a butter sauce, braised boneless oxtail with bubble & squeak, sticky toffee pudding with toffee ice cream) and 'Early Doors' budget menu available from 5.30 to 7pm. Desserts might include knickerbocker glory and a terrine of dark chocolate wrapped in vanilla sponge with hot cherries, while the splendid cheeseboard features several English farmhouse cheeses. Straightforward snack lunch menu covers a range from fresh baguette sandwiches to beef and Guinness casserole. Cheerful service and the 'Early Doors'/Sunday fixed-price meals encourage families; a traditional Sunday lunch is served until 4pm; on Sunday evenings only the early evening menu (extended to 8.30pm) is available, not à la carte. Fairly-priced wine list with many (chalked up on the board) available by the glass. Master McGrath's at Scarisbrick (qv) is in the same ownership. ***Seats** 95. Parties 14. L 12-2 D 5.30-10 (Sun meals 12-8.30). Set L £9/£11 Set D (5.30-7 only) £9.50/£11.50. Amex, Diners, MasterCard,* **VISA**

WYE New Flying Horse Inn

Tel 01233 812297 Map 11 C5 P
Upper Bridge Street Wye Kent TN25 5AN

With a 400-year-old history, this well maintained village centre inn is characterised by low ceilings, black beams, open brickwork and a large open fireplace. The spick and span main bar has gleaming, copper-topped tables and simple chairs while the neat lounge bar boasts some comfortable armchairs and access to the splendid sun-trap patio and extensive lawned garden. Reliable bar food is listed on a changing chalk board; dishes may include watercress soup, avocado and smoked chicken, spicy roast poussin and halibut with tomato and rosemary. For pudding, try the pear and almond flan or the double chocolate mousse. Ploughman's and sandwiches are available at lunchtime only. Evening restaurant menu. Six main-building bedrooms – including one four-poster and one spacious family room – have been smartly refurbished with attractive pastel colours, quality fabrics and some decent individual pieces of furniture. Good bathrooms with showers over tubs. In addition, there are four uniform, en suite rooms in a converted stable block. Invicta Country Inns. *Open 11-3, 6-11 (Sun 12-3, 7-10.30) **Bar Food** 12-2.15, 6.30-9.15. **Beer** Shepherd Neame. Garden, patio, outdoor eating, summer barbecue. Family room. **Accommodation** 9 bedrooms, all en suite, £47.50 (single £37.50). Children welcome overnight (under-5s stay free in parents' room). MasterCard,* **VISA**

WYMONDHAM Number Twenty Four £45

Tel & Fax 01953 607750 Map 10 C2 R
24 Middleton Street Wymondham Norfolk NR18 0BH

A homely town-centre restaurant where reservations need to be made well in advance for Saturday nights. Chef-proprietor Richard Hughes offers a lunchtime blackboard menu (casserole of mussels with celery, grapes and Pernod cream, particularly good local sausages with buttery mash and a jammy onion marmalade, warm Japanese-style chicken salad) with individually priced dishes; a few more choices are added to the evening three-course menu. The style is typified by dishes like black pudding slice with apple and juniper sauce, Puy lentils and balsamic vinegar, terrine of local pork, chicken and apricot with fresh fig chutney, dried fruits and zests, pan-fried Lowestoft cod with crispy potato scales, red wine, shallots and bacon, treacle and almond tart with orange syrup and caramel-roasted fresh pineapple with coconut milk ice cream. The Grand Dessert is 'a monster selection of all things sweet' – highly recommended if you've got room! Alternatively, interesting cheeses (Cashel Blue, Applewood smoked) are served with biscuits, salad and grapes. Good vegetarian options. Sound, reliable, cooking without pretensions in friendly, informal surroundings. Wines are very sensibly priced. No smoking before 9.30. ***Seats*** *65. Parties 40. Private Room 50. L 11-2.30 D 7.30-9.30. Closed D Tue, all Sun, Mon & 24-31 Dec. Set D £13.50. MasterCard,* ***VISA***

A jug of fresh water!

WYRE PIDDLE Anchor Inn

Tel 01386 552799 Map 14 C1 P
Main Street Wyre Piddle Pershore Hereford & Worcester WR10 2JB

Standing low and white-painted at the roadside, bedecked with fairy lights and flower baskets, the Anchor reveals its wealth of talents on further investigation. This is one of the region's premier summer pubs with its grassy terraces and rolling lawn graduating down to the Avon river bank where holidaymakers may moor their narrowboats. Views across the river take in the verdant Vale of Evesham whence come the asparagus and strawberries that enrich the summer menus. Seasonal printed menus – garlic mushrooms, steak and kidney pie, salads and scampi – are supplemented by blackboard specials such as artichoke and crab bake, chicken livers with mushroom and Burgundy sauce, grilled sardines and duck breast with apple and calvados. Round off your meal with apple and raspberry pie or a chocolate choux bun. No sandwiches, but open baps and ploughman's platters are available all day. An elevated dining-room has possibly the best view (although it's the food in the bar that we specifically recommend here). Family Sunday lunch. Watch out for the theme nights, live music and ten real fruit wines. ***Open*** *11-2.30 (till 3 Sat), 6-11 (Sun 12-3, 7-10.30).* ***Bar Food*** *12-2.15 (till 2.30 Sat & Sun), 7-9.15 (till 9.30 Sat, 9 Sun).* ***Beer*** *Marston's Pedigree, Flowers IPA, Boddingtons, two guest beers. Garden. Closed 25 Dec eve & all 26 Dec. Amex, MasterCard,* ***VISA***

YARM The Coffee Shop

Tel 01642 791234 **Fax 01642 788235** Map 5 E3 JaB
Strickland & Holt 44 High Street Yarm Stockton-on-Tees TS15 9AE

A haven of wholesome, home-prepared food on the first floor of a small, family-run department store. Heading the menu is a full English breakfast (£6.25 – served until 11.30); other choices include sandwiches (closed, open or toasted – from £3), jacket potatoes (served with a small salad, from £3.05), Yarm rarebit (£3.15), broccoli bake (£4.15) and prawn and mushroom tartlet served with potatoes and green salad (£5.09). Among the sweet things are ginger grundy, carrot cake (£1.99), apple pie and home-made ice creams. Two high-chairs, early evening children's meals from 4pm, and Lego to play with. There's a terrace for fine weather. ***Seats*** *70 (+ 20 outside).* ***Open*** *9-5.* ***Closed*** *Sun & some Bank Holidays. MasterCard,* ***VISA***

YARMOUTH Jireh House

Tel 01983 760513 Map 14 C4 **JaB**
St James's Square Yarmouth Isle of Wight PO41 0NP

Cosy, comfortable tea rooms in a 17th-century guest house. The atmosphere is homely and relaxing, making it a popular spot for enjoying a range of straightforward snacks and meals that are all available all day. Coconut and cherry slice, carrot cake, gateaux and crumbles are priced from 55p, and there are two afternoon teas, one with scones, jam and clotted cream (£2.85), the other adding sandwiches and cake (£4.95). Also on the menu are egg mayonnaise, ploughman's (from £3.35), jacket potatoes, salads (from £3.50) and hot specials such as macaroni cheese (£2.65), vegetable bake and a selection from the local catch – maybe sea bass, halibut and brill. Three set menus (£8.95–£13.50), include soup and sweet with one of grilled salmon, fillet steak or half a lobster. Cooked breakfast (£3.50-£4.50) is served at any time. In summer head for the garden; there is also a conservatory. No smoking. ***Seats*** *72 (+ 12 outside).* ***Open*** *9am-9.30pm.* ***Closed*** *Nov-Mar. No credit cards.*

We endeavour to be as up-to-date as possible, but inevitably some changes to data and key personnel may occur at restaurants and hotels after the Guide goes to press. Prices should also be taken as indications rather than firm quotes.

YORK Bettys

Tel 01904 659142 Map 7 D1 **JaB**
6 St Helens Square York YO1 2QP

See Harrogate for details.
Seats *174.* ***Open*** *9-9.* ***Closed*** *25 & 26 Dec. MasterCard,* ***VISA***

YORK Grange Hotel 74% £105

Tel 01904 644744 **Fax 01904 612453** Map 7 D1 **HR**
1 Clifton York North Yorkshire YO3 6AA

A fine Regency town house, carefully restored from a group of flats, just 400 yards north of the city walls on the A19 road to Thirsk. The relaxed, homely atmosphere is exemplified by the elegant morning room – plump cushions on the couches, a fine open fire, oil paintings hanging on the walls and fresh flowers. The bedrooms (including a four-poster room) may not be large but are individually furnished with fine-quality fabrics, antique furniture and English chintz; two rooms have facilities for disabled guests. The young management and friendly staff have high hotel-keeping standards and help make this a good alternative to uniform, commercial rivals. Meeting rooms for up to 60. ***Rooms*** *30. Amex, Diners, MasterCard,* ***VISA***

Ivy Restaurant £60

Head chef Christopher Falcus produces both table d'hote and à la carte. The first might offer smoked salmon and pickled wild mushroom salad, chargrilled sirloin of beef and orange and pink grapefruit terrine studded with basil. On the carte you might find braised venison dumpling with port and smoked bacon, chargrilled scallops with cucumber and sweet pepper vinaigrette, roast turbot with spring cabbage, steak and kidney pudding or a fish and shellfish pot with red wine and root vegetables. Vegetarian options, too. Simpler but equally inviting fare is offered in the 45-seat, brick-vaulted Brasserie converted from the old cellars. A new seafood bar recently opened. Disabled toilet facilities. ***Seats*** *55. Parties 14. Private Room 50. L 12.30-2.30 D 7-10 (Brasserie 12-3 & 6.30-10.30, closed Sun). Closed L Sat & D Sun. Set L £14 (Sun £15) Set D £23.*

Any person using our name to obtain free hospitality is a fraud. Proprietors, please inform the police and us.

YORK National Trust Tea Rooms

Tel 01904 659282
30 Goodramgate York YO1 2LG

Map 7 D1 JaB

Round the corner from the National Trust shop and very near the Minster, the tea rooms are well kept and efficiently run. The menu covers morning coffee and afternoon tea (cheese scone 95p, cakes from 95p), all-day breakfasts (£4.75), sandwiches (from £2.40), salads, savoury snacks, and lunchtime dishes of the day (consult the blackboard) such as salmon and prawn crumble or mushroom, nut and tomato bake (both £5.25). For pudding, perhaps banana cheesecake with sticky toffee sauce or Yorkshire lemon tart. Plenty of children's choices. Note the selection of Yorkshire fruit wines (to be consumed with meals only). No smoking. St John's car park. ***Seats*** *50.* ***Open*** *10-5.* ***Closed*** *Sun, 25 & 26 Dec. MasterCard,* ***VISA***

Any person using our name to obtain free hospitality is a fraud.
Proprietors, please inform the police and us.

YORK Spurriergate Centre

Tel 01904 629393
St Michael's Church Spurriergate York YO1 1QR

Map 7 D1 JaB

Spiritual food in a carefully renovated and converted redundant church by one of York's most historic crossroads. Paved stone and notable 15th-century stained glass lend bags of atmosphere, and there's plenty of wholesome food to feed the body: scones and tea cakes (85p), quiche (£2), sandwiches (from £2), jacket potatoes and luncheon specials such as potato and cashew curry (£3.50), tomato and lentil bake, chicken and mushroom pie (£4.50) and moussaka. 'Kid's specials' (£1.65). Six high-chairs, crayons and colouring menus are all provided. Spurriergate of the early 15th century was the street of the spur-makers. No smoking. ***Seats*** *106.* ***Open*** *10-4.30 (Sat till 5).* ***Closed*** *Sun, also second Tue of each month. No credit cards.*

We do not accept free meals or hospitality
– our inspectors pay their own bills.

YORK Taylors

Tel 01904 622 865
46 Stonegate York

Map 7 D1 JaB

Situated in a beautiful grade two listed building, this coffee house has been home to York gossip since it opened in 1886. There's a selection of some 20 different extra-fine teas and 15 coffees, all of which are specially selected, imported and blended. The foods on offer are as in the various branches of Bettys (in the same ownership), though the choice is a fraction more limited. Hot dishes are typified by Swiss Alpine macaroni (£5.95), Spanish omelette (£5.55) and some Yorkshire specialities such as rarebits (from £5.98) prepared with Theakston's Yorkshire ale and locally made sausages with fresh vegetables (£6.15). There are also salads, sandwiches (poached fresh salmon and watercress £4.15), toasts, tea breads and scones. The cake trolley includes such delights as coffee or chocolate cream eclairs (£1.72), hazelnut meringue (£2.15) and apple strudel (£2.15). Cream tea £4.15. Traditional Yorkshire afternoon tea £8.30. Unlicensed. Children welcome; six high-chairs and a baby-changing area with shelf, table and chair is provided on the ground floor next to the Ladies. Nappies, bibs, wipes, children's toys, comics, beakers and baby dishes are all available. A children's menu for the under-12s offers a good selection of hot dishes, sandwiches and ice creams, and half portions of all their normal menu dishes can be ordered. A range of preservative- and additive-free foods can be supplied for small babies and they are happy to heat up customers' own milk or baby food. No smoking. ***Seats*** *65.* ***Open*** *9-5.30.* ***Closed*** *25, 26 Dec & 1 Jan. MasterCard,* ***VISA***

York — Treasurer's House

Tel 01904 646757 Map 7 D1 JaB
Minster Yard York YO1 2JD

Originally home to the medieval treasurers of York Minster, this splendid house is now a National Trust property and its cellars have been converted into a tea room. Friendly, helpful staff dispense good-quality home baking such as Yorkshire lemon tart (a favourite from the NT recipe book), plus excellent cakes (from 85p). There's a good choice of savoury dishes with quiche (£3.95) and filled jacket potatoes (£3.50) in addition to smoky bacon, cheese and tomato sandwich (£2.50), Yorkshire cheese platter (£3.95) and home-made soup (£1.95). Round things off with a delicious sticky toffee or bread-and-butter pudding. Three Yorkshire fruit wines available by the glass. No smoking. ***Seats** 60. **Open** 10.30-4.30. **Closed** Nov-third week Mar. No credit cards.*

York — Viking Moat House 69% £139

Tel 01904 459988 **Fax 01904 641793** Map 7 D1 H
North Street York North Yorkshire YO1 1JF

Tall, modern Queens Moat Houses hotel and conference centre standing in a convenient central location on the south bank of the River Ouse, within the ancient city walls. Style and comfort are not lacking in the brick-walled reception, the lounge and the bar, the last two with river views. Bedrooms are well lit and amply furnished. 24hr room service. A choice of conference suites can handle up to 300 delegates. Limited underground garaging but there is an NCP car park nearby. Bodyclub health and fitness centre. No dogs. ***Rooms** 187. Gym, sauna, spa bath, solarium, golf practice net, brasserie (10am-10pm). Amex, Diners, MasterCard, **VISA***

Scotland

The addresses of establishments in the following former **Counties** now include their new Unitary Authorities:

Borders
Scottish Borders

Central
Stirling, Falkirk

Fife
Fife, Clackmannanshire

Grampian
Aberdeen City, Aberdeenshire, Moray

Lothian
East Lothian, City of Edinburgh, Midlothian, West Lothian

Strathclyde
Argyll & Bute, East Ayrshire, West Dunbartonshire, East Dunbartonshire, City of Glasgow, Inverclyde, East Renfrewshire, North Ayrshire, (inc Isle of Arran), North Lanarkshire, Renfrewshire, South Ayrshire, South Lanarkshire

Tayside
Angus, Dundee City, Perth & Kinross

Dumfries & Galloway, Highland (+ Orkney, Shetland & Western Isles) remain essentially the same

ABERDEEN **Stakis Aberdeen** 63% £128

Tel 01224 313377 **Fax 01224 312028** Map 3 D4 **H**
161 Springfield Road Aberdeen City AB9 2QH

In a residential area on the western edge of the city, a hotel offering a variety of bedrooms, including Executive and family rooms, all complete with the expected up-to-date accessories. Extensive refurbishment has recently been carried out in both day rooms and bedrooms. There's a well-equipped leisure club and large, comprehensive conference facilities catering for up to 1000 delegates. Children up to 15 stay free in parents' room. ***Rooms*** *112. Tennis, indoor swimming pool, gym, spa bath, sauna, steam room, sun beds. Amex, Diners, MasterCard,* ***VISA***

ABERFELDY **Farleyer House**

Tel 01887 820332 Map 3 C4 **JaB**
Weem by Aberfeldy Perth & Kinross PH15 2JE

In a fine position overlooking the Tay valley to the west of town on the B846, Farleyer House started life as a croft in the 16th century. Two centuries later, enlarged and transformed, it became the dower house to Menzies Castle. Snackers will make for the Scottish Bistro, open for lunch and supper, with a menu that makes very good use of Scottish produce. Home-cured gravad lax and quail's eggs or hot potato and goat's cheese terrine (£3.50) could start a meal, followed perhaps by sauté of guinea fowl, candied grapefruit and cherry brandy sauce or roast haunch of Highland venison with cinnamon sauce (£7.95). To round things off, perhaps chocolate marquise with oranges, hot apple galette or the Scottish cheeseboard (£3.95). Children welcome, separate children's menu and smaller portions on request; one high-chair (more can be supplied with notice). Crayons and paper can be provided and an outdoor play area has swings and a cubby-house (unsupervised). ***Seats*** *52.* ***Open*** *(Scottish Bistro) 12-2 & 6-9.30. Amex, Diners, MasterCard,* ***VISA***

AIRTH **Airth Castle** 68% £100

Tel 01324 831411 **Fax 01324 831419** Map 3 C5 **H**
Airth by Falkirk Falkirk FK2 8JF

There are lovely views over the Forth Valley from this carefully restored castle, whose oldest parts date from the 14th century. Some bedrooms and two of the conference rooms (up to 400 delegates) are in a recent extension. Public areas are splendid, with fine proportions, ornate ceilings and elegant traditional furniture. Modern-day facilities are provided in bedrooms that range from spacious Executive-style to romantic four-poster. 36 rooms are suitable for family use. Leisure amenities are in the country club at the end of the drive. The hotel is on the A905 (leave the M876 at J3 or the M9 at J7). No dogs. ***Rooms*** *75. Garden, tennis, indoor swimming pool, mini-gym, sauna, steam room, spa bath, sun beds. Amex, Diners, MasterCard,* ***VISA***

ALEXANDRIA **Cameron House** 81% £165

Tel 01389 755565 **Fax 01389 759522** Map 3 B5 **HR**
Loch Lomond Alexandria West Dunbartonshire G83 8QZ

Cameron House has a wonderful setting, right on the shores of Loch Lomond, in 100 acres of lawns, gardens and woodland. The majestic Georgian building offers a mixture of traditional luxury and elegance (in the day rooms and bedrooms) and state-of-the-art technology (in the splendidly equipped Leisure Club and the bar). Bedrooms and bathrooms are generously laid out and provide all the expected comforts. Families are well catered for, with a daily crèche (normally to 5pm, but extended to 9pm Thursday and Friday), early suppers at 6 and baby-sitting available. No dogs. Now owned by De Vere Hotels. ***Rooms*** *68. Garden, croquet, tennis, golf (9), fishing, indoor swimming pools, watersports centre, gym, squash, badminton, sauna, steam room, spa bath, solarium, beauty & hair salon, snooker, mountain bikes. Amex, Diners, MasterCard,* ***VISA***

Georgian Room £80

The main hotel dining-room (there's also a brasserie for lighter meals) is sumptuous and graceful, an ideal backdrop for Jeff Bland's sophisticated Scottish cooking with a modern touch. Typical of his style are ravioli of wild Scottish salmon filled with caviar and garnished with cabbage and scallops, or roast loin of venison with tomato noodles and elderflower wine jus; for dessert, you can indulge in a fig and plum tart, with almond and apricot sauce and a nutmeg ice cream, or a chocolate millefeuille with caramelised pear. There are fixed-price and à la carte menus, including an evening Celebration Menu of six courses (£40, except Saturday). No children under 14. No smoking in the restaurant. ***Seats*** *42. Parties 10. Private Room 42. L 12-1.45 D 7-10. Closed L Sat & Sun. Set L £14.95/£17.50 Set D £35 & (Sat only) £37.50.*

APPLECROSS Applecross Inn

Tel 01520 744262 Map 2 A3 

Shore Street Applecross Highland IV54 8LR

This most unpretentious of pubs has a spectacular setting looking out across Raasay to the Isle of Skye beyond, and is run by expatriate Yorkshire folk Berni and Judith Fish, with Berni looking after the bar while Judith makes good use of excellent seafood in the kitchen. From the blackboard menu the things to go for are the queen scallops cooked in wine and cream with mushrooms, squat lobster cocktail, dressed crab salad perhaps, or a half-pint of shell-on-prawn tails with dip. There are steak and chicken main courses, too, and a variety of snacks from speciality home-made soup and garlic mushrooms to venison- and veggie-burgers. Homely puds like rhubarb crumble and raspberry cranachan and a good cheeseboard follow. Five modest bedrooms are clean and cosy and share a shower room, a pine bathroom and memorable sea views. A peat fire warms the small lounge that is also used by the owners, and the large garden is right on the shore. No smoking in the bedrooms. Fifty malt whiskies on offer. *Open 11am-12pm (Sat till 11.30, Sun from 12.30), closed 2.30-5 Tue-Fri, Sun eve and Mon lunch in winter.* ***Bar Food*** *12-9.* ***Beer*** *McEwan's 80/-, Theakston's. Seashore garden.* ***Accommodation*** *5 bedrooms (none en suite), £45 (single £22.50). Children welcome overnight (under-5s stay free in parents' room, 5-14s £10). Accommodation closed 25 Dec and 1 Jan. MasterCard,* **VISA**

ARDENTINNY Ardentinny Hotel 62% £86

Tel 01369 810209 **Fax 01369 810241** Map 3 B5 

Ardentinny Loch Long nr Dunoon Argyll & Bute PA23 8TR

On the very edge of Loch Long, within the Argyll Forest park (where there are 50 miles of traffic-free walks), with views over the Loch to the moody 2,000ft Creachan Mor, plus an interesting, rambling garden – these are the hotel's main attraction. Hearty bar food is served in both pubby Viking and Harry Lauder bars and the Buttery; Clyde yachtsmen, who can tie up at the hotel's own jetty or free moorings, are regular visitors. A good choice of food might include salmon and broccoli fishcakes with dill mustard sauce as a snack or main meal and Musselburgh pie (big, chunky pieces of steak braised with ale and mussels). Smoked haddock rarebit, cod fillet and mash with piquant spinach sauce, and haggis with Drambuie en croute are other regular favourites, and Sunday brunch is a popular affair. The best bedrooms (all up a narrow, winding staircase) are designated 'Fyne' and attract a considerable supplement for their fine views, larger bathroom and remote-controlled television; accommodation is generally modest but comfortable, neat and bright; some rooms have showers only and others are large enough for families (further supplements are payable). A few steps lead directly down from the hotel to the pebbly shoreline; ask the way to the nearby sandy beach with its lovely rhododendron-lined setting. The hotel can arrange boat trips for pleasure or fishing, and mountain bikes can also be hired. *Bar open 11-11 (often later on Fri & Sat eve).* ***Bar Food*** *12-2.30, 6-9.30 (Sat 12-3.30, 6-9.30, Sun noon-9). Children's menu, children allowed in bar to eat. No real ale. Lochside garden, outdoor eating.* ***Accommodation*** *11 bedrooms, all en suite, £86 (single from £45), reductions Mar-mid May & Oct. Children welcome overnight, additional beds (£10) & cots supplied (£3); dogs £3. Hotel closed 1 Nov-15 Mar. Amex, Diners, MasterCard,* **VISA**

AUCHMITHIE But'n'Ben

Tel 01241 877223 Map 3 D4 JaB
Auchmithie by Arbroath Angus DD11 5SQ

Margaret and Iain Horn's simple, friendly cottage restaurant, 3 miles north-east of Arbroath, offers good local produce with a distinct Scottish flavour from midday, with home-made soup and a selection of main courses (from £4.95) encompassing local haddock fried in oatmeal, kedgeree and crab and salmon salads, with home-made cream gateaux and apple pie to follow (£1.50). A hearty Scottish high tea from 4 to 5.30pm brings a choice between perhaps Arbroath smokie pancakes and minced meat or game pie, with wholemeal bread, home-made scones, cake and tea for £7.50. The choice widens in the evenings when more substantial main courses such as pan-fried scallops, fruits de mer and Aberdeen Angus steaks are offered. No smoking in the dining-room. ***Seats*** *40.* ***Open*** *12-9 (Sun till 5.30).* ***Closed*** *Tue. MasterCard,* ***VISA***

AUCHTERARDER Gleneagles Hotel 86% £240

Tel 01764 662231 **Fax 01764 662022** Map 3 C5 H
Auchterarder Perth & Kinross PH3 1NF

A grand hotel in a fabulous setting of some 830 acres - to appreciate it at its best, approach from the south on the A823 through Glen Devon and Glen Eagles. It's a mecca for golf, tennis, riding, shooting, fishing, even falconry, a sporting dream in fact. No shortage of famous names either: Jack Nicklaus, Virginia Wade, Mark Phillips, Jackie Stewart, Champneys and illustrious high street retailers in the shopping arcade such as Harvey Nichols, Mappin & Webb and Burberry's. You'll need a map (provided) to get around; it's easy to lose your bearings, even in the public areas, which include the bar, a dramatic new and theatrical room reflecting the original 1920s design of Gleneagles, a new reading-room and a fine drawing-room, where afternoon tea is laid out enticingly. Bedrooms range from the standard without views to luxurious suites whose prices could include a chauffeur transfer from nearby Glasgow or Edinburgh airport or a round of golf on the Monarch's course. All are decorated and furnished to a high standard with smart bathrooms. Popular with conferences (up to 360) and residents can freely use the country club, though other activities, say, off-road driving, command a price. ***Rooms*** *234. Garden, croquet, tennis, golf, pitch & putt, putting green, riding, fishing, mountain bikes, indoor swimming pool, gym, squash, sauna, steam room, spa bath, beauty & hair salon, playground, snooker, shopping arcade, bank, post office. Amex, Diners, MasterCard,* ***VISA***

AUCHTERHOUSE Old Mansion House 68% £100

Tel 01382 320366 **Fax 01382 320466** Map 3 C5 HR
Auchterhouse by Dundee Angus DD3 0QN

A 16th-century whitewashed Scottish Baronial house skilfully converted by Nigel and Eva Bell to a charming and relaxed hotel. Some nice architectural features include the vaulted entrance hall, an open Jacobean fireplace and a splendidly ornate 17th-century plasterwork ceiling in the original drawing-room. Pleasantly furnished bedrooms – two are family suites with separate children's bedrooms – have good bathrooms well stocked with toiletries. The house is on the B954 seven miles from Dundee. ***Rooms*** *6. Garden, tennis, croquet, outdoor swimming pool, squash. Closed 25 & 26 Dec, 1st week Jan. Amex, Diners, MasterCard,* ***VISA***

Restaurant £75

Much local produce is used for a varied carte that is supplemented by a separate vegetarian menu. Cullen skink (smoked haddock and potato soup), East Coast seafood pancake with a Chablis cream sauce, collops in the pan with sherry and pickled walnuts, and apple pancake with an apricot and calvados sauce show the style. Set-price lunch and bar menus are also available. No under-10s at night. No smoking. ***Seats*** *50. Parties 10. Private Room 22. L 12.30-1.45 D 7-9.30 (Sun till 8.30). Set L £16.95.*

AVIEMORE — Stakis Coylumbridge — 62% — £104

Tel 01479 810661 **Fax 01479 811309** Map 3 C4 H

Aviemore Highland PH22 1QN

Skiing is the main amenity at Aviemore, but this sprawling modern hotel caters admirably for all sorts of activities for both adults and children. There's a sports hall for children, a fun house and an outdoor play area. It's also geared up for large conferences (maximum 750 delegates). Most of the bedrooms are big enough for family use. A couple of rooms are suitable for disabled guests. The hotel incorporates a shopping area (9am-6pm) including clothing, gifts and books. ***Rooms*** *175. Tennis, indoor swimming pools, hydrotherapy pool, sauna, solarium, hair salon, archery, target shooting. Amex, Diners, MasterCard,* ***VISA***

A jug of fresh water!

AYR — Fouters Bistro — £50

Tel 01292 261391 Map 4 A1 R

2a Academy Street Ayr South Ayrshire KA7 1HS

Visitors from all over are so pleased to find Fouters, originally owned by the British Linen Bank, by the Town Hall steeple in the centre of town. It's been run as a cheerful bistro since 1973 by Laurie and Fran Black and the Scottish produce of which they are champions is cooked in French style with consistently enjoyable results. Lunchtime starters may include home-made lobster bisque (£1.85), followed by moules marinière, warm smoked chicken salad with woodland mushrooms (£5.25) or haddock fillets in crispy batter with home-made chips perennially favoured by young and old alike; there's no obligation to partake of more than a single course. More ambitious diners, however, still go for the fillet of hot-smoked salmon with salad and new potatoes (£6.95) and the all-time summer favourite half-lobster lunch (including soup and a pud, £13.95). Home-made ice creams feature on the dessert menu along with the popular bread-and-butter pudding made with egg custard, sherry and brandy, and up to a dozen cheeses are offered as a sampler (£2.25) or full platter (£4.50). More robust Provençal fare is served in the evenings, and similarly 'real food' is adapted for children's enjoyment on request. Two high-chairs, beakers, bottle-warming and a changing shelf in the Ladies. ***Seats*** *38.* ***Open*** *12-2 & 6.30-10.30 (Sun 7-10).* ***Closed*** *L Sun, all Mon, 25 & 27 Dec, 31 Dec-3 Jan. Amex, Diners, MasterCard,* ***VISA***

AYR — The Hunny Pot

Tel 01292 263239 Map 4 A1 JaB

37 Beresford Terrace Ayr South Ayrshire KA7 2EU

Sun-yellow walls, old pine tables, lots of bears and plenty of honey celebrate Winnie the Pooh at this informal coffee shop and take-away on the edge of the town centre. Everything on the premises is home-made and available all day, taking in various baked potatoes (from £2.36), savoury and sweet sandwiches (baked ham, banana delight, sweet mincemeat), omelettes and all sorts of home-baked goodies – hazelnut meringue, carrot cake and sticky toffee pudding (£2.10). Daily blackboard specials might be quiche lorraine, tuna and new potato niçoise (£4.78) or vegetarian lasagne (£5.24), with rhubarb and ginger crumble to round things off. Pooh's Old Fashioned Afternoon Tea comes at £5, for smaller appetites there's Piglet's Cream Tea at £3, while the famous Tigger's Treat of hot chocolate and marshmallows, whipped cream and Swiss chocolate shavings, served with hot chocolate fudge cake and cream, is virtually guaranteed to stop them bouncing! There's a good range of teas and fresh-ground and flavoured coffees, but sandwiches, soups and cakes only to go with them on Sundays. Children's portions and one high-chair. The window seat is best for families. Use of disabled toilet for baby-changing. ***Seats*** *46.* ***Open*** *10-10 (Sun 10.45-5.30).* ***Closed*** *25, 26 Dec & 1, 2 Jan. No credit cards.*

AYR The Stables £30

Tel 01292 283 704 Map 4 A1 **R**
Queen's Court 41 Sandgate Ayr South Ayrshire KA7 1BD

In a shopping area of restored Georgian and Victorian buildings within which The Stables is housed, Edward J.T. Baines's characterful coffee shop-cum-wine bar demonstrates the art of ethnic Scottish cooking, and specialities include salmon, eel, duck and venison from the family smokehouse in Auchterarder. The all-day menu offers everything from scones (freshly-baked each morning 80p) or a clootie dumpling (£1.90) to a full meal, perhaps their ham and haddie (£5.40) or 'Tweed kettle'(£6.05), a casserole of salmon, mushroom, celery, spring onions and mace popular in 18th-century Edinburgh. In between come snacks such as haggis (£3.60), rumbledethumps (a traditional dish of mashed potatoes, cabbage, syboes and cream £1.45), chicken stovies (£3.60) and Crofters (from £2.85 – granary cottage loaves or baked potatoes with various fillings). There is always a small but select choice of Scottish farmhouse cheeses. The wine list includes a selection of traditional country wines (silver birch, meadowsweet, raspberry), along with mead, sloe liqueur, damson gin and a good range of single malt whiskies, including a malt of the month. Healthy options and children's portions are clearly marked on the 12-page, printed menu booklet; there's garden seating also in summer and no smoking in the main dining area. A couple of high-chairs cope with the really young ones (for whom they will liquidise something in the kitchen or heat up customers' own baby food and bottles) and there is a little menagerie of toy animals and a few picture books to keep the little ones amused. ***Seats*** *50 (+20 outside).* ***Open*** *10-5 (Sun 12.30-4.45 in season).* ***Closed*** *Sun out of season, 25, 26 Dec & 1, 2 Jan. No credit cards.*

Pubs – note that food is only recommended in those pubs with ***Bar Food*** times in the statistics at the end of an entry. Restaurant food in pubs is *never* recommended unless specifically mentioned. Some pubs are recommended for B&B or Atmosphere only – each entry's statistics indicate our recommendation.

BALLACHULISH Ballachulish Hotel 60% £90

Tel 01855 811606 **Fax 01855 821463** Map 3 B4 **H**
Ballachulish Highland PA39 4JY

On the A828 three miles north of Glencoe, the hotel enjoys panoramic views from its position on Loch Linnhe. The original Baronial building has been considerably extended, most recently with 22 bedrooms and a library. Guests have free use of the leisure centre at the sister hotel the *Isles of Glencoe* (*qv*) about two miles away, and the Highland Mysteryworld is another family attraction. There's also a supervised creche (arrangements need to be made a little in advance) open from 9am-3pm (except during school summer holidays). Children under 2 share their parents' room free of charge; 2-7s are charged £12, 8-16s £18.95 B&B per child when sharing. Informal eating in the bar; high-tea is offered at 5.30; six high-chairs are provided. The garden's farm area (with a donkey and sheep) is an added attraction. ***Rooms*** *54. Garden. Closed 5-31 Jan. Mastercard,* ***VISA***

BALLACHULISH Isles of Glencoe Hotel 60% £98

Tel 01855 811602 **Fax 01855 811770** Map 3 B4 **H**
Ballachulish nr Fort William Highland PA39 4HL

A practical, modern hotel and leisure centre next to the A82 just south of the bridge on a peninsula that juts into Loch Leven. Bedrooms are comfortable and uncluttered, and some ground-floor rooms are adapted for disabled guests. The hotel caters well for families, and its leisure amenities have been increased with the opening of the Highland Mysteryworld next door (reduced admission for hotel guests). Friendly staff. ***Rooms*** *39. Garden, indoor swimming pool, splash pool, mini-gym, sauna, steam room, spa bath, sun beds, solarium, adventure playground. Mastercard,* ***VISA***

BANCHORY Raemoir House 71% £95

Tel 01330 824884 **Fax 01330 822171** Map 3 D4

Raemoir Banchory Aberdeenshire AB31 4ED

Sixteen miles south west of Aberdeen and 2½ miles north of Banchory on the A980 is Raemoir House, an 18th-century mansion set in a 3500-acre estate which has been in the Sabin family since 1943. Mrs Kit Sabin, who started the hotel, has recently retired, but the next two generations are keeping up the good work. Rich red brocade chairs, panelled walls and valuable antiques enhance the traditional look of the morning room, and the counter in the billiard room bar is fashioned from a Tudor four-poster. Bedrooms are all different in size and character; one is the Old English room featuring a 400-year-old four-poster. Six rooms are in the historic 16th-century Ha'Hoose immediately behind the mansion. There are five self-catering apartments converted from the original coachhouse and stables. Good bar and picnic lunches are available, with informal family eating in the Music Room, Morning Room or private sitting-room (but not after 6.30pm and not in the bar itself); a high-tea is served from 5-7pm. High-chairs are provided and the children's menu includes 'Henry Duck in the Pond' (cold meat decorated with raw vegetables) alongside the ubiquitous favourites (boiled egg with soldiers, fish fingers, chicken nuggets); vegetarian options and half portions of some dishes from the bar menu are also on offer. Raemoir is very much a family-run hotel, and nearly all mother's and baby's requirements (from potties and baby baths to baby-listening facilities and laundry facilities) are both understood and provided on request. It's a delightful, rather special hotel – staying here is rather like spending time in a country house as a personal guest of the owners; one of those special places to which one always promises to return (and many do). One bedroom has more than two beds and three rooms are interconnecting. ***Rooms** 25. Garden, croquet, tennis, keep-fit equipment, sauna, sun beds. Closed 1st 2 weeks Jan. Amex, Diners, MasterCard,* **VISA**

The Macintyre Room £75

A lengthy international menu with a good smattering of Scottish food is on offer in this relaxed and very traditional dining-room. Smoked fish always features in the à la carte menu with Scottish specialities such as creamed Arbroath smokies and locally smoked salmon. Lobster Newburg is a favourite, and meat dishes are also available, with the famous 12oz Aberdeen Angus steak, poultry and game in season. Home-made sweets and a variety of cheeses (both Scottish and imported) will provide a nice finish. Bar lunches, with a traditional Sunday lunch. Some quite reasonable prices on a good all-round wine list. ***Seats** 70 (+ 20 outside). Private Room 80. L 12.30-2 D 7.30-9. Set Sun L £15.50 Set D £25.*

> **JaB** is short for 'Just a Bite'. The majority of these establishments are also recommended in our *Bistros, Bars & Cafés* Guide which features establishments where one may eat well for less than £15 per head.

BANCHORY Tor-na-Coille Hotel 66% £76

Tel 01330 822242 **Fax 01330 824012** Map 3 D4 **H**

Inchmarlo Road Banchory Aberdeenshire AB31 4AB

Built as a private house in 1873 and run as a hotel since the turn of the century, Tor-na-Coille retains much of its Victorian character. The function room can accommodate 90 people for a banquet or conference. Bedrooms are furnished with antiques. Room prices range from £76 to £96. Children under 12 stay free in parents' room. The hotel copes very well with children; a cot, baby bath, potty, changing mat, baby-sitting and baby-listening are all available by prior arrangement. Baby food, children's menu and cutlery are also provided. Further facilities are offered during Summer school holidays (ring for details). Laundry service on site. Indoor playroom and outdoor playground. ***Rooms** 22. Garden, croquet, squash. Closed 25-27 Dec. Amex, Diners, MasterCard,* **VISA**

BEARSDEN — Fifty Five BC

Tel 0141-942 7272
128 Drymen Road Bearsden East Dunbartonshire G61 3RB
Map 3 B6 **JaB**

The style is modern Scottish/French at this informal restaurant and bar with considerable family appeal. The bar menu offers sandwiches and croissants served with home-made crisps (BLT £4.25), Italian, ploughman's, and melon, apple and Cheddar salads (£4.25), 55BC quiche (£3.95), beef or chicken burgers (4oz £4.95, 8oz £5.95) and quite accomplished main dishes such as red roast chicken (£4.95), chicken and bacon crepe and the day's pasta special served with garlic bread (£4.50). Desserts include hot apple strudel and a brandy-snap basket of ice cream with strawberry coulis (both £2.50). ***Seats*** *50.* ***Open*** *(bar food) 12-3 & 5-6.30 (Sat till 3.30, Sun 12.30-4).* ***Closed*** *D Sun & 1 Jan. Amex, Diners, MasterCard,* **VISA**

BEATTOCK — Auchen Castle — 64% — £78

Tel 01683 300407 **Fax 01683 300667**
Beattock nr Moffat Dumfries & Galloway DG10 9SH
Map 4 C2 **H**

Built in 1849, the Castle enjoys panoramic views across Annandale to the Moffat Hills from its elevated position in 50 acres of immaculately-kept grounds. The baronial-style mansion houses the best bedrooms, with the best views, while the spacious but more functional rooms are in the Cedar Lodge. The hotel is signposted on the A74, a mile north of Beattock. ***Rooms*** *25. Garden, fishing. Closed 3 weeks Christmas/New Year. Amex, Diners, MasterCard,* **VISA**

BURRELTON — Burrelton Park Hotel

Tel 01828 670206 **Fax 01828 670676**
High Street Burrelton by Cooper Perth & Kinross PH13 9NX
Map 3 C5 **P**

Nine miles north of Perth on the A94 this is a long, low roadside inn in typical Scottish vernacular style. It is as neat outside in its brown and cream livery as it is well-kept within. On completion of extensive renovations to the public areas (due as we went to press), the increased capacity of the lounge and bar has given rise to an all-new, all-day menu encompassing choices from haddock and chips to sirloin steak baguettes, with added vegetarian options and a section for children. While the restaurant retains its à la carte format, a daily menu-of-the-moment bridges the gap with fresh seafood dishes being a house speciality. Six spotless, low-ceilinged bedrooms have TV but no phones, and good en suite bathrooms, each with a thermostatically-controlled shower over the tub. Efficient double-glazing effectively cuts out the traffic noise. Note that credit cards are not accepted for bills of less than £20. New owners. *Open 11-11 (Fri & Sat till 12).* ***Bar Food*** *12-10.30 (Restaurant 6.30-10). Free House.* ***Beer*** *Theakston's, guest beer. Family room.* ***Accommodation*** *6 bedrooms, all en suite, £45 (single £30). Children welcome overnight, additional bed & cot available. Pub closed 1 Jan. MasterCard,* **VISA**

BUSTA — Busta House Hotel

Tel 01806 522506 **Fax 01806 522588**
Busta Brae Shetland Islands ZE2 9QN
Map 2 D1 **P**

This 16th century former laird's home overlooking the sea is a tremendously civilised hotel in a wild place, simply furnished in Scottish rural style with four acres of walled garden and a private harbour too. Open to non-residents for good home-cooked bar lunches and suppers recent specials have included crabmeat, mushroom and coriander tagliatelle; turkey, spring onion and cranberry quiche and nut roast with spicy tomato sauce, followed by whisky and marmalade trifle and home-made orange and Cointreau ice cream. Raven Ale from 'nearby' Orkney and 136 malt whiskies on offer guarantee a loyal drinking fraternity. P&O ferries sail to the Shetland Islands from Aberdeen and holidays of the fly/sail and drive kind are readily arranged. *Open 12-2.30 (Sun from 12.30), 6-11 (Sun from 6.30).* ***Bar Food*** *12-2.30 (Sun from 12.30),6.30-9.30 (6.30-9 winter, except Fri & Sat).* ***Beer*** *Orkney Raven Ale. Garden, outdoor eating.* ***Accommodation*** *20 bedrooms, all en suite, £84 (single £63). Children welcome overnight (if sharing parents' room £10), additional bed and cot available. Bar and accommodation closed 22 Dec-3 Jan. Amex, Diners, MasterCard,* **VISA**.

CAIRNDOW Loch Fyne Oyster Bar £50

Tel 01499 600236 Map 3 B5 

Clachan Farm by Cairndow Argyll & Bute PA26 8BH

Hard by the road that sweeps round the head of Loch Fyne in a fine location stands this informal restaurant in converted farm buildings. Freshwater fish and shellfish, both smoked and cured, are the main attraction here, plentifully supplied from the loch right outside the door and on sale in the shop through which diners pass to and from the long, L-shaped dining-room. Waitress-served at pine or larch wood chairs and tables are the bradhan rost (hot-smoked salmon with a whisky sauce £8.50), kippers (£4.95), and the oysters (natural £4.90 for 6, baked with spinach and breadcrumbs or spicy pork sausages – £6.95) for which the Bar is justifiably famous. There's usually a vegetarian option and a daily fresh fish dish such as deep-fried haddock (£5.95), or you can push the boat out with a shellfish platter of langoustines (£14.95) or crab (£16.95), while the pound-and-a-half lobster platter at £29.50 is easily enough for two. A few picnic tables outside have glorious views of the surrounding steep hills; stick to straightforward dishes and you can Rest And Be Thankful after an exhilarating drive over the pass and down through the glens. See also entry under Elton (near Peterborough, England). Baby-changing facilities. ***Seats*** *80.* ***Open*** *9-9 (Nov to end-Feb, Mon-Thu 9-6, Fri-Sun till 9).* ***Closed*** *25, 26 Dec & 1 Jan. Amex, MasterCard,* **VISA**

We endeavour to be as up-to-date as possible, but inevitably some changes to data and key personnel may occur at restaurants and hotels after the Guide goes to press. Prices should also be taken as indications rather than firm quotes.

CARBOST Old Inn

Tel & Fax 01478 640205 Map 2 A3 

Carbost Isle of Skye Highland IV47 8SR

On the shores of Loch Harport, and near the Talisker distillery, a charming chatty little island cottage, popular as a walkers' base. Accommodation is offered in six rooms, all en suite, although all but one have shower only. One family room has a connecting bunk room for children, and all have colour TV but no phones. *Open 11-2.30 (Sun from 12.30), 5-12 (Sat to 11.30, Sun 6.30-11) and all day in summer. No real ales. Family Room. Lochside patio/terrace, children's play area.* ***Accommodation*** *6 rooms £47, (single £23.50). Children welcome overnight (under-4s stay free in parents' room, 5-9s £7.50, 10-15s £12.50). MasterCard,* **VISA**

CASTLECARY Castlecary House Hotel

Tel 01324 840233 **Fax 01324 841608** Map 3 C5 

Castlecary Village by Cumbernauld North Lanarkshire G68 OHD

The original private house has been extended to incorporate a large lively bar with fruit machines, a large selection of draught beers and a more peaceful, partitioned-off 'snug' with plush seating. Good modern bedrooms are mostly in a couple of 'cottage' blocks set motel-style around the car park; comfortable beds have crisp cotton sheets and feather pillows and all rooms have direct-dial phones, remote-control TV, beverage tray, trouser press and fully-tiled bathroom (about half with tub and half with shower). Four single rooms in the main building share a shower room and come at a considerably reduced rate. Two flats have a double and a twin room each (£66 plus £10 per extra adult). Four more rooms have recently been converted from an old outbuilding. *Bar open 11-11 (Fri/Sat till 11.30, Sun 12.30-11). Free House.* ***Beer*** *Belhaven, Bass, Caledonian Deuchars IPA, three guest beers.* ***Accommodation*** *48 bedrooms, 44 en suite, £45 (Club £55, single £15). Children welcome overnight (0-12 yrs free if sharing parents' room), additional bed (£10) & cot available. Diners, MasterCard,* **VISA**

Colbost — Three Chimneys Restaurant

Tel 01475 11258 Map 2 A3 
Colbost by Dunvegan Isle of Skye Highland IV55 8ZT

Eddie and Shirley Spear's charming restaurant, housed in a remote former crofter's cottage several miles west of Dunvegan (B884), is open from mid-morning through to 4.30 daily for the service of light meals. Following morning coffee and shortbread, at lunchtime you can choose just a single dish – moules marinière (£4.95), hot kipper tart with lemon butter sauce (£5.75), potted wild duck paté or herring in oatmeal (£5.95) – or construct a full meal with main courses like fillet of Highland lamb or beef hot-pot with mustard dumplings (£9.30) and cream crowdie (soft cheese) in hazelnuts for vegetarians. Local seafood, though, is the house speciality – it's delivered to the kitchen door direct from the fishing boats. There's soup such as leek and salmon as well as prawn and lobster bisque and fresh Skye oysters (£7.95 for 6), then warm salad of pan-fried scallops and monkfish with prawns and bacon (£14.95); round things off with an old-fashioned fruity bread pudding, chocolate roulade with coffee bean sauce or dairy ices. There's a £3.50 minimum charge between 12.30 and 2, but service of snacks and tea with scones and cakes then continues well into the afternoon. Set dinners at night start from £27.50. A genuinely caring attitude towards families makes this a good place to visit if on holiday with the kids. ***Seats** 30 (+8 outside). **Open** 10.30-4.30. **Closed** Sun (except Easter and Whitsun) & Nov-Easter. MasterCard, **VISA***

Comrie — Tullybannocher Farm Food Bar

Tel 01764 670827 Map 3 C5 JaB
Comrie Perth & Kinross PH6 2JY

Peter Davenport's counter-service restaurant started life twenty five years ago as an adjunct to his farm but is now the main business here; it's in a small cluster of log cabin-style buildings that include a bric-a-brac shop, artists' gallery and garden shop, just a mile or so out of town. A good selection of salads accompanies the likes of fresh salmon or trout (from £5.50), steak pie with Guinness and venison casserole (£5.50); lighter options for starters or snacking include Orkney sweet-pickled herrings (£3), smoked salmon, garlic mushrooms and moules marinière (£5.25). Daughter Leslie is in charge of the good home baking – carrot cake, millionaire shortbread, apricot and apple pie and fresh fruit tarts (made with locally grown strawberries and something of a speciality); other snack items include filled jacket potatoes, bacon rolls, and home-made soup. Tables outside on the grass provide for summer eating and children are most welcome; there is a table for baby-changing in the ladies. A la carte evening meals from 6pm encompass duck, salmon and venison dishes and steaks. ***Seats** 90 (+ outside).**Open** 10-9. **Closed** Mid Oct-Easter. Amex, MasterCard, **VISA***

Craigellachie — Craigellachie Hotel — 68% — £99

Tel 01340 881204 **Fax 01340 881253** Map 2 C3 H
Craigellachie Moray AB38 9SS

Built in 1893, the hotel stands by the A95, in the village where the Rivers Spey and Fiddich meet. Public areas include a spacious drawing-room with antiques and grand piano, plus a small library and snug green bar with a good choice of local malt whiskies. Bedrooms have modern facilities (including direct-dial telephone) and are furnished in traditional style with quality fabrics. ***Rooms** 30. Garden, gym, sauna, beauty salon, outdoor playground, games room, snooker. Amex, Diners, MasterCard, **VISA***

Crieff — Crieff Hydro — 64% — £108

Tel 01764 655555 **Fax 01764 653087** Map 3 C5 H
Crieff Perth & Kinross PH7 3LQ

A short drive from JA9 of the M80, the Crieff Hydro stands in 800 acres of grounds and offers an impressive range of leisure activities and services including live entertainment, theatre, watersports, riding tuition and and off-road Land Rover driving. Families are well catered for, and there are plenty of activities for children, too. Most of the bedrooms are of a decent size, furnished with either lightwood units or more traditional pieces; nine two-storey family chalets are in the woods behind. A new wing incorporating 36 Executive bedrooms, a conference suite and a theatre for up to 260 has recently been completed and a guest bar opened. Disabled guests can be accommodated in a bedroom en suite and can use the specially adapted changing-room in the swimming pool. The Victorian garden also has a small section for wheelchair access and the visually impaired. Conference facilities for up to 300 include a wide range of services, from secretarial to marquee hire and exhibition staging. Dogs are allowed only in the chalets; alternatively, kennels are available with prior booking. ***Rooms** 222. Garden, croquet, tennis, golf (18-hole), pitch & putt, putting green, bowling, football pitch, riding school, indoor swimming pools, gym, squash, badminton, whirlpool, sauna, steam room, spa bath, sun beds, hair & beauty salon, snooker, playroom, playground, gift shop. Amex, Diners, MasterCard,* ***VISA***

CRINAN — Crinan Coffee Shop

Tel 01546 830261 Map 3 B5 **JaB**
Crinan by Lochgilphead Argyll & Bute PA31 8SR

Here's an idyllic setting for a characterful coffee shop, standing at the end of the 200-year-old Crinan Canal just a stone's throw from its parent hotel and perched right on the wall of the lock basin. Run with great enterprise and a no-nonsense approach it produces king-size sausage rolls (£1.65), quiche and salad (£3.20) and an array of filled rolls; scones, doughnuts, honey and oat slice, date and walnut loaf (45p-£1.20), fresh cream gateau, lemon tart and the speciality cloutie dumpling (£1.45). A cold buffet supper is also served in high season. Children's portions; three high-chairs. ***Seats** 50. **Open** 8.30-5 (Jul & Aug till 9). **Closed** end Oct-Easter. No credit cards.*

CRINAN — Crinan Hotel — 69% — £190*

Tel 01546 830261 **Fax 01546 830292** Map 3 B5 **HR**
Crinan by Lochgilphead Argyll & Bute PA31 8SR

Situated in a tiny fishing village at the northern end of the canal connecting Loch Fyne with the Atlantic, the hotel offers beautiful views either westwards up the Jura sound or down over the canal's 15th and final lock. Nick and Frances Ryan have been here since 1970, and Frances (as Frances McDonald) designed the hotel's interior. The light and airy bar incorporates an art gallery. Bedrooms are individually furnished, and the best have private balconies to make even more of the stunning views. Local attractions include the famous Argyll Gardens and seal colonies (boat trips arranged). *Half-board terms. ***Rooms** 22. Garden. Amex, MasterCard,* ***VISA***

Westward Restaurant — £70

The hotel's main restaurant, decorated in soft, gentle colours, makes use of the finest seafood, prime Aberdeen Angus beef and Kintyre lamb. The dinner menu consists mainly of fish dishes, typically River Add salmon with hollandaise, or the high-quality meat alternatives. Amusing and authoritative tasting notes accompany each wine on a sensibly priced list that's obviously been assembled with great relish. ***Seats** 45. D only 7-9. Closed 1 week Christmas.*

Lock 16 Restaurant — £95

On the hotel's top floor, this specialist seafood restaurant depends very much on the local fishing fleet which comes in to unload at the quayside below. A bad catch and the restaurant might not open, so it's always best to check. On a good day the fishermen will land jumbo prawns from Corryvreckan, lobsters from the Sound of Jura, Princess clams from Loch Fyne and mussels from Loch Craignish, so you can reasonably expect dishes such as Crinan seafood stew, moules marinière and wild salmon. Nick Ryan cooks in a traditional, simple way, to preserve all the freshness and flavour. To round off the meal, try the fresh strawberry millefeuille and either Stilton or mature Scottish farmhouse cheddar, served with oatcakes. Booking and smart clothes are required. ***Seats** 20. D only at 8. Closed Sun & Mon, also Oct-1 May. Set D £30 & £40.*

DIRLETON Open Arms Hotel 67% £115

Tel 01620 850241 **Fax 01620 850570** Map 3 D5 **H**
Dirleton nr North Berwick East Lothian EH39 5EG

The new owners have created two new bedrooms at their cosy little hotel near the North Berwick coast. It's a popular spot with holidaymakers and also regularly hosts functions and conferences. Children up to 12 can stay free in parents' room. ***Rooms*** *9. Garden. MasterCard,* ***VISA***

DRUMNADROCHIT Polmaily House 66% £112

Tel 01456 450343 **Fax 01456 450813** Map 2 B3 **HR**
Drumnadrochit Highland IV3 6XT

Set back from the A831 about 1½ miles north-west of Loch Ness, Polmaily House stands in 18 acres of its own gardens and woodland. Constant refurbishment by John and Sonia Whittington-Davis has made it a very comfortable hotel, attractively decorated and furnished in traditional style, including some antiques. All bedrooms have en suite bathrooms and modern facilities, including a video recorder. One bedroom is specially adapted for disabled guests. Families are well catered and children are charged a percentage of the adult tariff, according to their age. The price quoted above is for an 'A Grade' room. The standard room rate is £90. There are now fitness machines for adults, a tree house for children in the top meadow and both indoor and outdoor play areas. ***Rooms*** *12. Garden, croquet, tennis, riding, indoor swimming pool, playroom, playground, games room. Closed mid Nov-mid Dec. MasterCard,* ***VISA***

Urquhart Restaurant £55

Sonia does the cooking, using mostly local produce and always offering a choice of fresh fish, poultry, game or Aberdeen Angus fillet. The à la carte selection includes patés, mixed grill, some pasta and one vegerarian dish, plus a special 'slimmers choice'. Desserts (made in the hotel bakery) are followed by coffee and mints at table or in the drawing-room. In the latter smokers can pause to have a cigarette during their meal, as the restaurant is no-smoking. Light lunches are served in the pool-side garden, or in less clement weather in the conservatory and bar. Sandwiches (£2.25-£3.25), variations on the traditional ploughman's lunch (from £4.25) and a hot dish of the day such as lasagne (£5.75) served with French bread and salad are the stock-in-trade, and there are also lots of choices for the youngsters; they're more likely, though, to be playing by the pool, or the rabbit pen, or taking a pony ride while the grown-ups unwind. Morning coffee and afternoon teas are also served with the various gateaux, cheesecakes and scones all coming from their own bakery. ***Seats*** *40. Parties 20. L by arrangement D 7.30-9.30. Set D £20.*

DULNAIN BRIDGE Auchendean Lodge 62% £70

Tel 01479 851347 Map 2 C3 **HR**
Dulnain Bridge Grantown-on-Spey Highland PH26 3LU

Built at the beginning of the century as a hunting and fishing lodge, Auchendean Lodge (in Gaelic 'the field of shelter') enjoys a spectacularly beautiful location with views of the Dulnain and Spey rivers, ancient pine forests and the Cairngorm Mountains. Ian Kirk and Eric Hart, owners since 1988, maintain a traditional style of furnishings while providing modern facilities (but no phones in bedrooms). Plenty of outdoor activities (including fishing and skiing) are available locally. Other attractions include a ride on a steam train from Boat of Garten station. 24hr room service. ***Rooms*** *8. Garden, pitch & putt. Closed 4 weeks Nov or Jan. Amex, Diners, MasterCard,* ***VISA***

Restaurant £55

The four-course menu changes daily, making good use of local game, fish, vegetables and wild mushrooms in a variety of applications: roasts, soups, casseroles, sauces, etc. Choices might include poached sea trout with sorrel sauce or wild venison casserole with red wine, juniper and herbs. To finish, try apple and hazelnut crumble or omelette soufflé with Amaretto and almonds, or indulge in the good selection of Scottish cheeses. Picnics and vegetarian meals can be provided with prior notice. There's a wide-ranging and fairly-priced wine list. The menu states that 'credit card commission is charged extra'. No smoking. ***Seats*** *18. D only 7.30-9. Set D £23.50.*

Dulnain Bridge — Muckrach Lodge — 59% — £90

Tel 01479 851257 **Fax 01479 851325** Map 2 C3 H
Dulnain Bridge Grantown-on-Spey Highland PH26 3LY

A Victorian hunting lodge set in ten acres of grounds with fine views of the Dulnain valley. It's a fine base for touring the beautiful Speyside country, and a most pleasant place for just sitting back and relaxing. The feel is friendly and informal in both lounge and bar, and there are fine views from most of the bedrooms, which include a four-poster room. The former steading (stables) houses two full suites, one especially adapted for wheelchair-bound guests. Children up to 12 years stay free in parents' room. No dogs. ***Rooms*** *14. Garden, fishing. Amex, Diners, MasterCard,* **VISA**

We do not accept free meals or hospitality – our inspectors pay their own bills.

Dumfries — Opus Salad Bar

Tel 01387 255752 Map 4 B2 JaB
95 Queensberry Street Dumfries Dumfries & Galloway DG1 1BH

Some 28 years now in the same hands, Mrs Halliday's first-floor salad bar still offers thoroughly consistent hot and cold fare from the self-service counter. It's all made on the premises and covers a range of wholesome dishes from cream of mushroom or lentil soup made with ham stock (£1), to lasagne or vegetable crumble (both £2.50) and a large selection of salads (75p per portion). Assorted cheesecakes, lemon and carrot cake, banoffi pie (from £1), scones and biscuits accompany a delectable cup of tea or coffee at any time through the day. Children's portions; one high-chair. Nursing mums and babies are made welcome, and there is room for changing in the Ladies. ***Seats*** *44.* ***Open*** *9-4.30.* ***Closed*** *Sun. MasterCard,* **VISA**

Dunvegan — Harlosh House — £65

Tel & Fax 01470 521367 Map 2 A3 RR
by Dunvegan Isle of Skye Highland IV55 8ZG

Built in 1750, Harlosh House has a wonderful setting, about four miles south of Dunvegan, on the shore of Loch Bracadale looking across to the Cuillin Hills. Pre-dinner drinks and coffee are taken in a cosily-comfortable lounge where a real fire burns on chilly nights. Peter Elford is the self-taught chef-patron whose simple but interesting way with the local fish and shellfish (the four-course menu almost always features seafood, the main exception being Sunday, when the main dish is generally venison) is a real winner. A recent dinner began with langoustine tails and scallops in the lightest of *tempura* batters with an *aïoli* dip and salad of rocket and *mizuna* followed by lovage soup (Peter is very keen on fresh herbs) before a perfectly cooked piece of halibut resting on a bed of plum tomato with basil and baby capers. Desserts, the only course where there is a choice, were cappuccino chocolate mousse, a trio of home-made sorbets, tangy *tarte au citron* and a selection of Scottish cheeses with oatcakes. Good coffee came with a selection of home-made chocolates. No smoking. Booking advisable. ***Seats*** *18. D only 7-8.30. Closed Nov-Easter. Set D £24.50. MasterCard,* **VISA**

See over

Rooms £90

Lindsay Elford is the charming hostess and also looks after six pleasing, pine-furnished bedrooms that are bright and comfortable. There are no telephones to disturb the peace but all come with plenty of books plus a bowl of fresh fruit and a beverage tray (with fresh milk). Bathrooms (just one room is not en suite but has a private bathroom on the floor below) boast large bath sheets and quality toiletries. Families are welcome (the Elfords have their own youngsters) with babies in cots free and reductions for children up to 12 sharing their parents' room. Younger guests are served their own high tea before dinner. Excellent cooked breakfasts include free-range eggs and local bacon. No smoking in bedrooms.

East Kilbride Stakis Westpoint Hotel 74% £123

Tel 01355 236300 **Fax 01355 233552** Map 3 C6 **H**
Stewartfield Way East Kilbride South Lanarkshire G74 5LA

Major developments at this striking modern hotel on an industrial estate include 24 additional bedrooms and 10 more conference rooms. It's a place of versatile appeal, with a fine leisure centre and the ability to handle conferences of up to 400 delegates. Bedrooms have all the expected modern conveniences, and the Executive rooms boast spacious sitting areas; some rooms are adapted for disabled guests. 24hr room service. ***Rooms** 99. Indoor swimming pool, splash pool, gym, sauna, steam room, spa bath, sun beds, beauty salon, playroom, snooker. Amex, Diners, MasterCard,* ***VISA***

Edinburgh Caledonian Hotel 79% £285

Tel 0131-459 9988 **Fax 0131-225 6632** Map 3 C6 **HR**
Princes Street City of Edinburgh EH1 2AB

Built at the turn of the century by the Caledonian Railway Company, the 'Caley' is virtually a national monument. Traditional standards of hospitality and service have been maintained while moving with the times in terms of comfort and amenities. The bar and lounge have recently been refurbished and a new American-style eating outlet added. Bedrooms, including 22 full suites, are individually styled, featuring traditional freestanding furniture and well-chosen fabrics. 43 Superior business bedrooms have large work stations, fax and computer points and a voicemail facility. De luxe rooms and those with a view of the Castle attract a supplement. Towelling robes are provided in all the bathrooms, some of which boast elegant antique-style fittings. Two rooms are specially adapted for disabled guests. Families are particularly well catered for with children up to 16 staying free in parents' room. No dogs, but kennels are available with a week's notice. 24hr room service. A mini-gym and solarium were added mid-1996, with a full leisure club due for completion by the end of 1996. Families will also enjoy the American-themed franchise restaurant, *Henry J Bean's Bar & Grill.* ***Rooms** 236. Amex, Diners, MasterCard,* ***VISA***

La Pompadour £105

Opened in 1925 and named after Louis XV's mistress, the Pompadour is elegant and formal, with ornate plasterwork framing large wall-paintings of delicate flowers. A pianist plays soothing music and excellent staff provide impeccable service. Executive chef Tony Binks has been here since 1980 and, together with his young team, continues to use the best of Scottish produce to good effect. Besides the à la carte, a wide selection of menus for parties and individuals is available for both lunch and dinner. A typical dinner menu might include salmon ravioli with a celeriac salad or foie gras salad seasoned with ginger and layered with crisp bacon rashers and Muscat grapes. Mains feature the likes of fillet of turbot served with an orange Jacqueline sauce and loin of wild venison sweet-cured with lime and juniper. ***Seats** 60. L 12.30-2 D 7.30-10.30. Closed L Sat & Sun & D Sun in winter, also all Jan. Set L from £15 Set D from £25.*

Carriages Restaurant £60

The hotel's informal eaterie, recently refurbished, with the addition of a central buffet with a daily hot special (£8.50 per visit). Fairly straightforward dishes are à la carte only on weekdays. Parsnip and Stilton soup, chargrilled steaks and poultry, and pan-fried fish show the style. To finish, Scottish cheeses or a selection of desserts from the trolley. ***Seats** 130. L 12-2.30 D 6.30-10. Set Sun L £14.95.*

EDINBURGH Carlton Highland 68% £166

Tel 0131-556 7277 **Fax 0131-556 2691** Map 3 C6 H

North Bridge City of Edinburgh EH1 1SD

Besides well-equipped bedrooms and comfortable day rooms the Carlton Highland (located between Princes Street and the Royal Mile) has a fine leisure club, conference facilities for up to 300 and a night club with dancing and live entertainment several nights a week. One room is equipped for disabled guests. Children up to 15 stay free in their parents' room. ***Rooms*** *197. Indoor swimming pool, gym, squash, sauna, steam room, solarium, beauty & hair salon, playroom, snooker, coffee shop (10am-6pm). Amex, Diners, MasterCard,* ***VISA***

EDINBURGH The Engine Shed Café

Tel 0131-662 0040 Map 3 C6 JaB

19 St Leonard's Lane City of Edinburgh EH8 9SD

As the name would suggest, this vegetarian café is in an old stone building that was formerly an engine shed (for a standing engine that pulled other engines up the hill). On the ground floor there's a bakery (wholesale) which interestingly makes its own tofu. The first-floor café is run by Garvald Community Enterprises, a charity employing people with special needs. The bright, airy room has stone walls displaying up-and-coming artists' works and there's a large public noticeboard. There's always home-made soup served with a fresh roll (£1) and the hot dishes of the day include vegetarian lasagne, pizza and a vegan tofu and bean casserole, served with a choice of two salads (from £2.75). Otherwise home baking dominates with carrot cake, chocolate brownies, scones, millionaire shortbread (from 70p) or filled rolls; Wednesday is the popular baked potato day. Children are made particularly welcome since access is easy, the café is spacious and they love the tofu whips (yoghurt-style dessert)! High-chairs, beakers, good changing facilities and a lift for buggies indicate a caring attitude towards parents and their wee ones. Unlicensed. No smoking. ***Seats*** *55.* ***Open*** *10.30-3.30 (Fri till 2.30, Sat 10.30-4, Sun 11-4).* ***Closed*** *1 week Christmas, 1 week Easter & 1st 2 weeks July. No credit cards.*

EDINBURGH Fishers

Tel 0131-554 5666 Map 3 C6 P

1 The Shore Leith City of Edinburgh EH6 6QW

Fishers is an outstanding seafood speciality bar which serves full meals all day, noon till 10.30pm. It's located in a renovated corner building at the end of The Shore, at the foot of what looks like an ancient bell-tower or lighthouse. The bar area, in which you can also eat, groups high stools around higher-still tables; up a short flight of steps the main eating area features light-wood panelling with night-sky blue tables and chairs, windows half of frosted glass, half giving a view of the harbour and beyond, and all presided over from a great height by a bejewelled mermaid figure. The pricing structure and the variety of food on offer are admirably suited to most appetites and pockets, whether for serious eating or quick snacking. In addition to the photocopied/hand-written menu, a blackboard of daily specials offers a host of starters and main courses which should appeal to more than fish fans alone. Tomato and basil soup and game terrine provide alternative starters to the ubiquitous sardines, smokies and calamari, and there's the odd meat alternative (lamb's liver with onion gravy, say) to the turbot with pesto, prawns and capers, and sea trout with a strawberry and basil sauce that are star turns on the daily specials board. The Fishers' dedication to the very best seafood makes it a worthy 1997 Scotland Regional Winner of our Seafood Pub of the Year award. Salads are fresh and in plenty; choose your dressing from a piquant selection of different vinaigrettes (eg onion, hazelnut or raspberry) thoughtfully provided on each table. If any room remains, there are simple home-made fruit flans, pies and crumbles. Altogether excellent quality and value-for-money; booking essential. *Open 11am-1am.* ***Bar Food*** *12-10.30. Free House.* ***Beer*** *regularly changing guest beers. Riverside, outdoor eating. Family room. Pub closed 25 Dec & 1 Jan. MasterCard,* ***VISA***

EDINBURGH Helios Fountain

Tel 0131-229 7884 Map 3 C6 JaB
7 Grassmarket City of Edinburgh EH1 2HY

Jos Bastiaensen's vegetarian and vegan coffee house at the rear of a crafts and book shop continues to draw the crowds, particularly students and academics, who appreciate the relaxed, unpretentious surroundings and very keen prices; ever-popular year round is the student special of hot soup with a choice of two salads and bread for £2.25. From 10am cheese scones and savouries such as spicy lentil pie (£1.95) are gradually joined by a selection of cakes as they're ready: spicy Indian carrot cake, banana yoghurt and the gooey vegan chocolate and coconut cake (95p); biscuits, too, like tollhouse cookies and date slice from 70p. Lunch brings hot mushroom and onion quiche and perhaps a cheese wheat berry casserole (from £2.50) and six salads (full house £2.60) such as red cabbage and tomato or raisin and toasted coconut to accompany. One high-chair; half portions for children. A toy box is provided and a changing area with table and changing mat outside the toilets. No smoking. ***Seats** 40. **Open** 10-6, Sun 12-4 (till 8 during Festival, Sun 11-6). **Closed** 25, 26 Dec & 1, 2 Jan. MasterCard, **VISA***

EDINBURGH Henderson's Salad Table

Tel 0131-225 2131 Map 3 C6 JaB
94 Hanover Street City of Edinburgh EH2 1DR

Here for more than 30 years, the Henderson family continue to preside over their hugely popular counter-service vegetarian restaurant in a large basement below the family fruit shop. The day starts at 8am with organic fruit juices, yoghurt and wholemeal croissants while the counter display gradually fills up with cold savouries and salads till the lunchtime explosion. Hot dishes such as spinach tian, aubergine and tomato layer and potato and wild mushroom goulash (from £2.95), chalked on a blackboard which also highlights vegan options, are available from 11.30 to 2.30 and again from 4.30 to 10.30. Two soups, vegetable or yellow split pea perhaps (£1.40), a platter of four salads (£3.75) from the multitudinous selection, and to finish, Scottish cheese platter with oatcakes (£3.95) and desserts such as fresh fruit fool or meringue and ginger vacherin (from £1.80) are indicative of the wide and ever-evolving selection available; to drink there's also organic grape juice, some 30 wines (12 by the glass) and Caledonian ale, not to mention coffees, teas and infusions by the score. An informal atmosphere where toddlers and babies are more than welcome. Children's portions on request; four high-chairs and changing facilities in both Gents and Ladies. Bottles and baby-food can be warmed if required. ***Seats** 180. **Open** 8am-10.30pm. **Closed** Sun (except during Festival – open 9am-10pm), 25, 26 Dec & 1 Jan. Amex, MasterCard, **VISA***

EDINBURGH Kalpna £35

Tel 0131-667 9890 Map 3 C6 R
2 St Patrick Square City of Edinburgh EH8 9EZ

Gujerati and South Indian vegetarian food has few finer homes than Kalpna, whose elephant logo was designed to show that you can be big, strong and intelligent without eating meat. Here you will feast on stuffed lentil pasties, rice pancakes, mixed vegetables with nuts in a piquant sauce, roasted almonds with peas, and aubergines with spinach, tomatoes and fenugreek leaves. The lunchtime buffet costs just £4.50, and there are various price options in the evening with a choice of thali set meals. The wine list includes Veena, a light Riesling blended with Indian spices. No smoking. ***Seats** 60. Parties 30. Private Room 70. L 12-2 D 5.30-11. Closed L Sat, all Sun, 25 & 26 Dec, 1 Jan. Set L from £4.50 Set D £8.50. MasterCard, **VISA***

Many hotels offer reduced rates for weekend or out-of-season bookings. Always ask about special deals and family rooms.

EDINBURGH Lazio

Tel 0131-229 7788 Map 3 C6 JaB
95 Lothian Road City of Edinburgh EH3 9AW

Run by the Crolla family since 1981, this long, narrow restaurant with a mural of the owners' home village on the end wall is newly air-conditioned following a smart-looking refurbishment. Authentic pasta and pizzas are their stock-in-trade from around £5, but those in the know say there's better quality and value in the new line of thin-crust pizzas (Lazio and quattro stagioni – £6.20) and calzone (£6.70). Roast peppers, aubergines and artichokes, and seafood salads (from £4.40) start the main meals, with plenty of veal, steak and chicken dishes and classic Italian sauces to follow (from £8), and a multitude of ice creams if you can't make room for the gigantic home-made cheesecake (£2.80). Look for some unusual Italian wines on the new list. It's Italian, so 'it's no problem !' as far as families are concerned. They have one high-chair and will provide small portions; but you can't go far wrong with pizza and ice cream. ***Seats*** *65.* ***Open*** *noon-1.30am.* ***Closed*** *25, 26 Dec & 1 Jan. Amex, Diners, MasterCard,* **VISA**

EDINBURGH Lune Town

Tel 0131-220 1688 Map 3 C6 JaB
38 William Street City of Edinburgh EH3 7LJ

A long-standing family-run restaurant with cosy ground floor and basement rooms and sound Cantonese cooking which brings the crowds flocking back. Dim sum and soups remain around £2, and you can enjoy a 4-course set lunch for a mere £6.90. Try the wun tun soup, arguably one of the best around, and for main course Cantonese aromatic duck (half £11.50), chicken with cashew nuts (£6.50) and wun tun oyster sauce noodles (£5.20). A discretionary minimum charge of £15 can apply in the evenings, when booking is advised; there's also a small no-smoking room downstairs. ***Seats*** *75.* ***Open*** *12-2.30 & 6-12 (Sat 3-12, Sun 4-11).* ***Closed*** *L Sat & Sun, 25 Dec, 1 Jan & 4 days Chinese New Year. Amex, Diners, MasterCard,* **VISA**

EDINBURGH Scottish National Gallery of Modern Art

Tel 0131-332 8600 Map 3 C6 JaB
Belford Road City of Edinburgh EH4 3DR

Located in the museum basement, this is a popular café with a bright and airy dining area but whose most attractive attribute is the outdoor terrace where the metallic tables and chairs match the style of the modern sculptures exhibited on the lawn. The self-service café has a limited but nonetheless inventive menu. Always on the go are baked potatoes with cheese or coleslaw (£2.50) and savoury croissants with such fillings as ham and gruyère or egg mayonnaise (from £3 including salad). At lunchtime (12-2.30) soups could be tomato and basil or chilled vichyssoise (£1.50), hot dishes might include vegetable chili and creamy mushroom and turkey casserole (from £4), and alternative salad platters such as tuna and rice or honey-baked ham are always available. Puddings might be rhubarb fool or raspberry pavlova (both £2). The usual array of home-baking accompanies the teas, coffees and cold drinks served through the afternoon. ***Seats*** *70 (+100 outside).* ***Open*** *10-4.30 (Sun from 2, but 10-4.30 during the Festival).* ***Closed*** *25, 26 Dec, 1-3 Jan & May Day. No credit cards.*

EDINBURGH Verandah £40

Tel 0131-337 5828 **Fax 0131-313 3853** Map 3 C6 R
17 Dalry Road City of Edinburgh EH11 2BQ

The decor matches the name, with wooden, slatted blinds covering the walls of this very presentable and friendly establishment south west of the city centre. At lunchtime there's a good value thali with a choice of main dish – between chicken (murgh bhuna) or lamb (makhani gosht) – plus a piece of chicken tikka, pakora, a vegetable dish, rice and chapati all served at the same time. On Sundays, when the dishes vary, this menu is half-price for children. The à la carte covers the full range of dishes from kebabs and biryani to lamb pasanda, rogan josh, a selection for vegetarians and a couple of fish (flown in from Bangladesh) dishes. Tandoori items and the nan bread come from a clay oven that is fired by charcoal in the traditional manner. Children are offered Uncle Wally's Special - free to smaller children - based around un-spiced chicken cooked in the tandoor oven, with ice cream to follow. There are also several thalis (complete meals where small portions of a number of different dishes are served together, £10.15-£16.95). ***Seats** 44. L 12-2.30 D 5-12 (3-9pm on 25 Dec). Set menus £12.95, £16.95 & £19.95 per person (all min 2). Amex, Diners, MasterCard,* ***VISA***

ELIE Ship Inn

Tel 01333 330246 Map 3 C5 **P**
The Toft Elie Fife KY9 1DT

Part of a terrace of old cottages down by the harbour, the Ship has been a hostelry since 1838. The original bar still has wooden benches around the dark-painted, boarded walls, beamed ceiling and a back room with booth seating. There are two restaurant rooms with old dining tables, sturdy kitchen chairs and, on the first floor, a small balcony with coin-operated binoculars for scanning the harbour. The single menu, available throughout, features traditional home-made dishes such as garlic mushrooms and sweet herring salad to start, and seafood crepes, spicy fried chicken and steaks with haggis whisky sauce for main course. There are some fairly standard desserts, blackboard specials, Sunday roast and a children's menu. Cakes and biscuits are served with tea and coffee throughout the day. In July and August, tables on the sea wall opposite the Ship are served by an open-air barbecue. When the tide is out a vast expanse of sand is revealed where the Ship's own cricket team plays regular Sunday fixtures. *Open 11am-midnight (Fri & Sat till 1), Sun 12.30-11.* ***Bar Food** 12-2.30 (Sun 12.30-3), 6-9.30 (Sun till 9). Free House.* ***Beer** Belhaven 80/- Ale, Boddingtons, Theakston Best. Family Room. Pub closed 25 Dec. MasterCard,* ***VISA***

ERISKA Isle of Eriska 80% £175

Tel 01631 720371 **Fax 01631 720531** Map 3 B5 **HR**
Eriska Ledaig by Oban Argyll & Bute PA37 1SD

Here for well over twenty years, the Buchanan-Smiths are always making improvements to their lovely baronial-style mansion, situated on a magical and idyllic island, accessible by private bridge, off the A828 Fort William road, a few miles north of Connel. If young Beppo is now the driving force, dad Robin is usually around, whether to carry your bags or greet you for dinner, while mum Sheena oversees the leisure centre for part of the day, making sure you either swim enough lengths in the indoor pool or don't overdo the weights, not to mention tending the immaculately-kept gardens and collecting the herbs for supper. The island itself, which can justly be described as a paradise, offers nature trails, bracing walks, a golf course and water sports at the pier, yet is just over two hours' scenic drive from Glasgow or Edinburgh. The house's oak-panelled central hall with its huge fireplace and imposing staircase is the hub of the hotel; afternoon tea with home-made goodies or a glass of champagne before dinner is served here; next to it are a drawing-room with grand piano and a library with a fine array of malt whiskies. Everywhere there are antiques, pictures, books, family mementoes and stunning flower arrangements that spill over into the bedrooms, each individually furnished in fine style, all with stunning views. Bathrooms are immaculate; several have separate walk-in shower, all are beautifully tiled, offering a heated towel rail, bathrobes, quality toiletries and good lighting. Naturally, an evening turn-down service is provided, along with a hot water bottle, and other pluses include real bed linen, the provision of candles (in case of power failure), a Thermos of iced water, bowl of fruit and separate radio alongside the remote-control TV. Breakfast is, of course, a hearty affair and will set you up for the day ahead. Service from all the staff is perfectly in tune with the surroundings - unfailingly courteous with just the right degree of friendliness. Watch out for the badgers, who come sniffing up to the library steps just before dinner - they know they're on to a good thing, as do 70% of guests, who return year after year. ***Rooms** 17. Garden, croquet, tennis, golf (9-hole), pitch & putt, putting, fishing, indoor swimming pool, gym, sauna, steam room, spa bath, games room, windsurfing, water-skiing, clay-pigeon shooting, observation lounge. Closed Jan & Feb. Amex, MasterCard,* ***VISA***

Restaurant **£85**

For many years Sheena presided over the kitchen, and though she still keeps an eye on things, the mantle of chef has passed to talented Euan Clark. There's a distinct Scottish flavour to the dishes on the nightly-changing menu that offers several courses with choice of starter, second, main and dessert course. In addition, there's a savoury (virtually extinct from most British menus) and cheeses after dessert. Loch Creran salmon usually features to start with, perhaps marinated with crème fraiche and chives, or else try a warm terrine of Highland game served with baby onions and wild mushrooms. Warm yourself with a cock-a-leekie soup or sautéed king scallops in a lemon grass-scented nage, and follow with a fillet of turbot with a herb crust, served with a tomato fondue and red wine sauce or roast rib of Angus beef, carved at the table, with all the trimmings. Desserts include a steamed syrup pudding with banana custard, iced apricot mousse and raspberry bavarois; thereafter Scotch woodcock, Ham Darby or Whitley goose - a glass of port for those who can determine the ingredients of the last two! Depart the candle-lit dining-room with its polished wooden tables and settle back on a sofa with coffee and petits fours. You will sleep soundly! The wine list offers tremendous value; plenty of half bottles. ***Seats*** *40. D only 8-9. Set D £35.*

FALKIRK — Coffee Cabin

Tel 01324 625757 Map 3 C5 **JaB**

23 Cockburn Street Falkirk FK1 1DJ

In her tiny coffee shop tucked away behind the main shopping area, Fiona Marshall has been cooking and baking for her happy band of regulars for over ten years. Cream scones, sponges with butter icing and fruit slices (from 50p) are typical items, with peach melba, fruit meringues and spicy fruit crumble (£1) among the sweets. For savoury palates there are hot Hawaiian and toasted sandwiches (£1.20), macaroni cheese with toast (£1.35) and jacket potatoes with fillings ranging in price up from £1.75 for a generous cheese and coleslaw filling; half-portions of virtually anything are available for the wee ones and those on the tightest of budgets. Soup such as lentil or Scotch broth (90p) comes with crusty wholemeal bread and butter, breakfast costs £2.20 and consists of bacon, eggs, sausages, beans and tomatoes plus toast and tea or coffee. Space here is not conducive to high-chairs, and there are no special facilities, but children's portions are always available and they're happy to heat up bottles and baby-food. Unlicensed. ***Seats*** *30.* ***Open*** *9.30-5.* ***Closed*** *Sun, 25, 26 Dec & 1 Jan. No credit cards.*

FOCHABERS — Gordon Arms

Tel o1343 820508 Fax 01343 820300 Map 2 C3 **P**

High Street Fochabers Moray IV32 7DH

Antlers decorate the exterior of a former coaching inn standing alongside the A96 and a short walk away from the River Spey, while the public bar sports a variety of fishing bric-a-brac, including stuffed prize catches. Simple overnight accommodation is provided by 13 well-equipped bedrooms with Tvs, tea-makers, hair dryers and direct dialled telephones; these include both older rooms with large carpeted bathrooms and a number of smaller but quieter ones in the extension. *Open 11-11 (Fri & Sat till 12.30, Sun from 12). Free House.* ***Beer*** *Theakston's, guest beer. Garden. Family room.* ***Accommodation*** *13 bedrooms, all en suite, £65 (single £45). Children welcome overnight (from £10), cot available. Amex, MasterCard,* ***VISA***

FORFAR — Royal Hotel — 57% — £70

Tel & Fax 01307 462691 Map 3 C4 **H**

Castle Street Forfar Angus DD8 3AE

A modest entrance conceals a thriving, compact, well-kept hotel complete with leisure centre, ballroom and roof garden. Accommodation includes some family rooms. ***Rooms*** *19. Indoor swimming pool, mini-gym, sauna, spa bath, sun beds. Amex, Diners, MasterCard,* ***VISA***

FORT WILLIAM — Crannog Seafood Restaurant

Tel 01397 705589 Map 3 B4 **JaB**
Town Pier Fort William Highland PS33 7NG

Finlay Finlayson's own fishing boat continues to bring much of the produce for his quayside restaurant, originally a ticket office and bait store and converted in 1989. Pride of place goes to the fresh langoustines he lands and no less to the smokehouse which provides first-rate smoked salmon (£5.50), gravad lax (£5.95) and smoked mussels and aïoli (£3.95). Other starters include potted crab and squat lobster tails (both £3.50), the langoustines with mayonnaise (£5.95/£11.95) and the hearty Crannog Muckle Stew (£8/£13.50), the latter prices being for main-course portions. A blackboard lists daily specials such as salmon fishcakes or grilled salmon with herb hollandaise (£7.25) and includes a vegetarian option; to finish, Scottish cheeses (£3.95) or perhaps the delicious cranachan of whipped cream, raspberries, toasted oats and whisky. No children's menu or portions offered, but waitresses will discuss children's requirements with customers and will accommodate any reasonable requests. High-chairs available; chair in Ladies for baby-changing. ***Seats** 70. **Open** 12-2.30 & 6-10 (winter to 9.30). **Closed** 25 Dec & 1 Jan. MasterCard,* **VISA**

Pubs – note that food is only recommended in those pubs with ***Bar Food*** times in the statistics at the end of an entry. Restaurant food in pubs is *never* recommended unless specifically mentioned. Some pubs are recommended for B&B or Atmosphere only – each entry's statistics indicate our recommendation.

GARVE — Inchbae Lodge — 57% — £64

Tel 01997 455269 **Fax 01997 455207** Map 2 B3 **HR**
Inchbae by Garve Ross-shire Highland IV23 2PH

A few miles north of Garve on the A835 by the Blackwater river (on which the hotel has a mile of fishing rights), Inchbae is a former private hunting lodge with a very pubby bar that is popular with locals. The bar menu which can cope with most appetites, ranges from a good soup with home-baked bread and a large platter of West Coast mussels to Brie and broccoli filo bake, breaded pink trout with flaked almonds, champion haggis with neeps and tatties and scottish steaks with a choice of sauces. There's always a selection of home-made puds and children get their own special menu. Bedrooms, half in the original lodge and half in an adjacent red cedar chalet, have no TVs, radios or telephones to disturb the peace, and all but four have shower and WC only. Those in the main building are prettiest, with plum and pale green colour scheme, pine and country antique furniture; three rooms have an extra bed or more for family use; smokers are restricted to the chalet rooms. Two lounges, warmed by real fires in winter, are filled with a motley collection of sofas and easy chairs. Children are welcome, and a high-tea of children's favourites is served at 5pm in the bar before the grown-ups' dinner *Open 11-2.30, 5-10.30 (Sun 12.30-2.30, 6.30-10.30. **Bar Food** 12-2, 5-8.30, (Sun 12.30-2, 6.30-8.30). No real ales. **Accommodation** 12 rooms, all en suite, £64 (single £37). Children welcome overnight (under-18s stay free in parents' room). Garden, children's play area. Pub & Accommodation closed 25-30 Dec. MasterCard,* **VISA**

The Dining-Room — £60

Pat Price, chef and owner, offers a three-course dinner that might traditionally begin with haggis and neeps or a seafood platter with oak-smoked trout, rum-cured salmon and Orkney herring marinated in sherry, and continue with grilled salmon served with a vermouth, Dijon mustard and lemon sauce, or with an 8oz fillet steak with whisky, grain mustard and cream sauce. It is also wise to leave room for desserts such as chocolate pots with orange and Cointreau. A la carte choice is available in the bar with a low-priced selection including soups, salads, fish and meat plus a vegetarian choice of three mains. Smoking only in bar and lounge. ***Seats** 30. Parties 8. L (bar) 12-2, Sun from 12.30 D 7-8 (dining-room) 5-8.30 (bar). Set D £21.*

Gatehouse of Fleet — Murray Arms Inn — £85

Tel 01557 814207 **Fax 01557 814370** Map 4 B2 I
Anne Street Gatehouse of Fleet Dumfries & Galloway DG7 2HY

A warm, friendly old posting inn (established over 300 years) whose hospitable day rooms include the Burns Room, where the poet reputedly wrote *Scots Wha Hae*. There's also a little cocktail bar. Bedrooms, all centrally heated, have all that is necessary to provide a good night's rest. These, and the bathrooms, are kept in very good order. A cottage in the garden is very suitable for families. Children up to 16 free in parents' room. The inn stands on the A75 Dumfries to Stranraer road. ***Rooms** 13. Garden, croquet. Amex, Diners, MasterCard,* ***VISA***

Gifford — Tweeddale Arms

Tel 01620 810240 **Fax 01620 810488** Map 3 D6 P
High Street Gifford East Lothian EH41 4QU

Probably the oldest building in the village, the black-and-white Tweedale Arms stands alongside a peaceful village green. The comfortable, mellow lounge features some old oil paintings while the bar has tapestry-style upholstery and baskets of dried flowers hanging from the old beams. The bar menu offers a good selection of carefully cooked dishes ranging from pickled herrings and crab with avocado among a dozen starters and main dishes such as Aberdeen Angus steaks, tagliatelle with mushroom stroganoff, curried lamb and smoked haddock with broccoli and cheese sauce. Good clean bedrooms have either light or darkwood freestanding furniture and modern en suite bathrooms; all have TV, direct-dial phone, trouser press and a tea/coffee making kit. Family-run in friendly fashion, the inn also has three family rooms. *Open 11-11 (Fri & Sat till 12).* ***Bar Food** 12-2, 7-9. Free House.* ***Beer** Burton Ale, Morland Old Speckled Hen, Greenmantle, two guest beers. Garden, children's play area. Family room.* ***Accommodation** 17 bedrooms, all en suite, £65 (single £47.50). Children welcome overnight (under-12s stay free n parents' room), additional bed & cot available. MasterCard,* ***VISA***

Glasgow — Beardmore Hotel — 78% — £121

Tel 0141-951 6000 **Fax 0141-951 6018** Map 3 B6 HR
Beardmore Street Clydebank G81 4SA

Sharing a site with the HCI International Medical Centre on the north bank of the River Clyde, eight miles from the city centre and airport, the hotel boasts a major feature in its purpose-built 170-seat auditorium. This stretch of the river was previously one of the centres of Glasgow's shipbuilding industry, and many of the commissioned paintings in the conference rooms are of paddle steamships built at the Beardmore shipyard. The public areas are light and spacious, similarly the air-conditioned bedrooms (six specially adapted for disabled guests) and suites, all contemporarily furnished, which offer all the usual amenities including satellite TV and mini-bar. Smart bathrooms have good-sized tubs and power showers. ***Rooms** 168. Patio. Indoor swimming pool, gym, sauna, spa bath, sun beds, aerobics & step class, news kiosk. Amex, Diners, MasterCard,* ***VISA***

Symphony Room — £80

Open only on Friday and Saturday evenings, the art-deco-style restaurant, as the name suggests, has a musical theme with pictures of (dead) composers. Chef James Murphy trained at *The Dorchester* under Anton Mosimann, so has a good pedigree, which is evident in his cooking. A four-course performance has choices in each section, except for the soup, usually of the seafood variety, perhaps a consommé of smoked salmon with langoustine dumplings. Start with fresh pasta, seared salmon and mussels or breast of squab pigeon served with woodland mushrooms and barley risotto, and for a main course try the saddle of venison with roasted shallots and smoked bacon. Desserts include the house brulée and toasted brioche with warm fruits and peach sabayon. Good cheeses, fine selection of breads, and staff that are perfectly in tune with the kitchen. The Brasserie (open seven days) offers an excellent buffet, both at lunchtime and in the evening. ***Seats** 60. Parties 6. Private Room 60. D only 7-9.30. Closed Sun-Thu. Set D £27.50.*

GLASGOW Café Gandolfi

Tel 0141-552 6813 Map 3 B6 JaB
64 Albion Street City of Glasgow G1 1NY

Rustic wooden floors and walls and designer furniture are distinguishing features of Seumas McInnes's bustling café in the old Merchant district. Following breakfast from 9am and mid-morning snacks of croissants and fruit scones (from £1.25) and eggs en cocotte (£2.60), the choice widens at lunch on a seasonal menu which might include feta cheese with roast garlic (£4), roast rack of lamb with mint couscous and Savoy cabbage pizza (from £7.80), alongside regular favourites such as Cullen Skink, Arbroath smokies, Caesar salad, boiled haggis and smoked venison open sandwiches (£3.60-£7.50). There is always a wide choice of sandwiches, a good cheese selection, and puddings include summer fruits pudding, chocolate and rum hearts (£3.20), walnut tart and home-made ice creams (from £3). No under-14s after 8pm. Children's portions and high-chairs available. ***Seats*** *70.* ***Open*** *9am-11.30pm (Sun from 12).* ***Closed*** *25, 26 Dec & 1 Jan. MasterCard,* ***VISA***

GLASGOW Café India £45

Tel 0141-248 4074 Map 3 B6 R
171 North Street Charing Cross City of Glasgow G3 7DH

Next door to Mitchells Library, this is a light, airy (and air-conditioned) restaurant with friendly, helpful staff. It is furnished with Charles Rennie Mackintosh chairs and decorated with some verdant panels in the style of 'Le Douanier' Rousseau. The emphasis in the kitchen is on the cooking of the Punjab – masalas, karahi bhoonas and balti dishes – that often features ginger, cumin and garlic among the spices used. There are also offerings from the tandoor oven, a small selection of Western dishes and a children's section on the menu. Own parking. ***Seats*** *250. Meals 12-12 (till 12.30am Fri & Sat). Set L £4.95 (business), £6.95 (buffet) & £8.95 (all till 2.30) Set D £9.95 (pre-theatre, 5.30-7.30) & £12.50. Amex, Diners, MasterCard,* ***VISA***

GLASGOW Chapter House

Tel 0141-221 8913 Map 3 B6 JaB
26 Bothwell Street City of Glasgow G2 6PA

Make for the Christian bookshop Pickering & Inglis in the heart of the business district to find this light, airy café and its new offshoot, a highly successful sandwich shop called Pickerings. Up-market take-aways at the latter include the likes of turkey, mozzarella and cranberry, and brie, pear and strawberry (both £1.60) while over the café's 'we-serve-you' counter a simple but consistently good selection of healthy, home-made products includes tray-baked nutty florentines, shortbread and Empire biscuits (75p-£1.10), while at lunch the choice expands to include soup, lentil broth say, with roll and butter (£1.60), salads, quiche and daily hot dishes like chicken and herb casserole, leek and potato pie or courgette and vegetable gratin (£3.10). Finish with trifle, fresh fruit salad or perhaps bramble and apple tart (£1.30). The various combination prices (soup and sandwich – £3.10, soup, roll and dessert are particularly popular, and it's a haven for families on Saturdays with its rocking horse and even a toy box for the kids, and tables outdoors during fine weather. Unlicensed. ***Seats*** *60.* ***Open*** *8.30-4.30 (Sat from 9).* ***Closed*** *Sun, Bank Holidays, 25, 26 Dec & 1, 2 Jan. Acccess,* ***VISA***

GLASGOW D'Arcy's £40

Tel 0141-226 4309 Map 3 B6 
Basement Courtyard, Princes Square Buchanan Street City of Glasgow G1 3JN

Set in a basement of the trendy Princes Square shopping centre, D'Arcy's is a model of versatility with scones and pastries, sandwiches and breakfast items opening proceedings before the full menu comes on stream at 11.30am with a long list standard fare such as creamy chicken curry, hot tossed salad of bacon and avocado or mushroom and mangetout stroganoff (from £6.25) supplemented by specialities of the day like pan-fried apples in Drambuie sauce (£3.95) and stir-fry of lamb fillets with mangetout and oyster sauce (£9.95); pastry-cook Gunna's sweet delights follow (from £3.65), offering nutty Swiss carrot cake, individual strawberry pavlovas and caramel shortcake with hot chocolate sauce and ice cream. Fixed-price meals after 3pm (with complimentary wine before 7pm) are a popular draw from £8.95 for two courses, as is Sunday brunch, served between 12 and 4.30, a bargain at £6.60. The children's menu offers half-price meals and small portions of main dishes. Three high-chairs are provided and there's a surface in the disabled toilet for baby-changing. ***Seats*** *80.* ***Open*** *9am-midnight (Sun 11.30-4.30).* ***Closed*** *25 Dec & 1, 2 Jan. Amex, Diners, MasterCard,* ***VISA***

GLASGOW Glasgow Hilton 78% £160

Tel 0141-204 5555 **Fax 0141-204 5004** Map 3 B6 **HR**

1 William Street City of Glasgow G3 8HT

A modern 20-storey city-centre landmark situated close to the M8 (J18). The glass and granite exterior is complemented by an eyecatching and stylish interior with public rooms arranged off a well-lit and spacious central atrium. Air-conditioned standard bedrooms (with sealed windows) are not large and have a uniform up-to-date decor and furnishings, but Executive rooms have extras like bathrobe and slippers, and use of the top-floor Executive lounge with complimentary Continental breakfast, afternoon tea and evening drink. One floor caters specifically to Japanese guests, with green tea added to the beverage tray and a yukata (Japanese pyjamas) provided as standard. A traditional Japanese breakfast is also available. Extensive 24hr room service and conference/banqueting facilities for up to 1100. Valet parking. No dogs (kennels available nearby). ***Rooms*** *319. Indoor swimming pool, gym, sauna, steam room, spa bath, sun beds, beauty & hair salons, news kiosk. Amex, Diners, MasterCard,* ***VISA***

Camerons Restaurant £95

The inspiration for the interconnecting rooms is a grand Scottish hunting lodge, and the result is one of the most appealing of any modern hotel restaurants. The menu combines a light, modern style with the best of Scottish produce in dishes like Loch Fyne oysters glazed with a champagne sabayon, roast supreme of maize-fed chicken over a mixed tomato and avocado fondue and fillet of veal topped with a cep mousse on a confit of shallots and balsamic jus. To finish, try a pistachio crème brulée and chocolate tart with vanilla cream or a cherry and white chocolate mousse on praline sauce. Fine wine list. Informal eating in Minsky's New York Deli & Restaurant. ***Seats*** *55. Parties 22. Private Room 14. L 12-2.30 D 7-10.30. Closed L Sat, all Sun. Set L £16.95.*

GLASGOW Holiday Inn Garden Court 65% £75

Tel 0141-353 2595 **Fax 0141-332 7447** Map 3 B6 **HR**

Theatreland 161 West Nile Street City of Glasgow G1 2RL

Opened in December 1995, the hotel is in the heart of theatreland next to the new concert hall. Tartan decor in the compact bedrooms that offer, apart from the usual facilities, in-house movies, an ironing board and iron (though not in the family rooms, some of which are interconnecting). Rooms for disabled guests are available, and also rooms designated non-smoking. The £45 weekend rate (Fri-Sun incl) includes two full Scottish breakfasts. The hotel operates a one price per room policy; children under 12 eat free from the children's menu. Parking opposite the hotel. ***Rooms*** *80. Patio. Amex, Diners, MasterCard,* ***VISA***

La Bonne Auberge £55

A French-style brasserie that owner Maurice Taylor first established over twenty years ago in the city's Park Circus area. There's a selection of Continental dishes from a cream of langoustines or lightly steamed mussels to supreme of chicken with spring onion mash and tomato salsa and pan-fried salmon fillet. Steaks from the grill; desserts include warm sticky toffee pudding and baked lemon tart. The pre-theatre special menu (£7.95/£9.95), served until 7.30pm, allows you to choose a soup, light meal and dessert. Very modestly-priced wine list includes a dozen by the glass. ***Seats*** *72. Parties 8. Private Room 60. L 12-2.30 D 6-10.15 (Sun till 9). Closed L Sun, all 25, 26 Dec & 1 Jan. Set D £16.95.*

GLASGOW Janssen's Café/Restaurant

Tel 0141-334 9682 Map 3 B6 JaB
1355 Argyle Street City of Glasgow G3 8AD

Dutchman Jan Leenhouts and his Glaswegian wife cheerfully supervise production of a formula that allows most items to be taken as full meals or in smaller tapas-style portions. Chargrilled chicken satay, pescado fritto, and tortillas (from £5/£7.50), houmus, taramasalata and *moules à la marseillaise* indicate the variety, which is supplemented by interesting specials like pan-fried chicken with Japanese red curry sauce and Mediterranean-style stuffed courgettes with rice (£7.50). Appelbol (apple baked in puff pastry – £3.60) is a speciality dessert, American-style cakes, profiteroles and crunchy toffee cake are toothsome alternatives. Half-portions for children (and high-chairs) are readily available. Close to Kelvin Grove Art Galleries and the Transport Museum. *Seats 50. Open 12-10.30 (Fri & Sat till 11, Sun till 9). Closed 25, 26 Dec & 1, 2 Jan. MasterCard,* ***VISA***

GLASGOW The Jenny

Tel 0141-204 4988 Map 3 B6 JaB
18 Royal Exchange Square City of Glasgow G1 3AB

Standing in a newly-pedestrianised square, The Jenny is an authentic re-creation of one of the Victorian tea rooms for which Glasgow was once famous; cottagey decor and waitresses in floral print dresses help to create the charming atmosphere. Set prices include cooked breakfast before 11am (£6.45) and a set afternoon tea (£5.85), though all day there are savoury brioche buns, croissants and toasted sandwiches (from £2) with various toppings, and through the lunch hours popular staples like haggis with neeps and tatties (£4.25), rumbledethumps (£6.25), smoked salmon royale and various ever-changing meat, fish and vegetable pies accompanied by either cauliflower cheese or sauté potatoes. A sideboard (from which one helps oneself) is laden with all sorts of home baking: brandy snaps, sticky toffee pudding, banoffi pie and orange and brandy pudding. Four high-chairs and a children's menu provided. A bistro menu of tradional Scottish food takes over on weekend evenings. No smoking downstairs. ***Seats** 110. **Open** 8-7 (Thu/Fri/Sat till 12, Sun 11-6). **Closed** 25 Dec & 1 Jan. Amex, Diners, MasterCard,* ***VISA***

GLASGOW Jurys Glasgow 59% £96

Tel 0141-334 8161 **Fax 0141-334 3846** Map 3 B6 H
2 Shelly Road Great Western Road City of Glasgow G12 0XP

Overlooking a boating pond, this first Scottish outlet for the Irish-based Jurys group has good leisure and conference facilities, and caters well for families. The hotel stands on the Great Western Road three miles west of the city centre (leave the M8 at Junction 17 and follow the A82 for 2½ miles). Free parking for 400 cars. ***Rooms** 133. Indoor swimming pool, splash pool, mini-gym, sauna, spa bath, sun beds, beauty salon. Closed 24-29 Dec. Amex, Diners, MasterCard,* ***VISA***

A jug of fresh water!

GLASGOW Loon Fung £45

Tel 0141-332 1240 **Fax 0141-332 3705** Map 3 B6 R
417 Sauchiehall Street City of Glasgow G2 3JD

Colourful carvings of the dragon and phoenix (Loon Fung) decorate one end of this smart restaurant, which takes pride in its authentic Cantonese cooking. It's open all day, with a business lunch served from 12 to 2 Mon-Fri, and dim sum (30 varieties) available until 7. Scallops with bamboo shoots, crunchy stuffed duck, chicken with sweet ginger and pineapple, a dozen ways with prawns and sizzling lamb or steak are among the many popular choices. ***Seats** 190. Parties 30. Meals 12-11.30. Set L £5.90 (not Sat or Sun) Set D from £13. Amex, MasterCard,* ***VISA***

GLASGOW Sannino

Tel 0141-332 8025 Map 3 B6 JaB
61 Bath Street City of Glasgow G2 2DD

The decor is traditional darkwood panelling, Tiffany-style lamps and heavy brass rails, and the menu lists conventional lines in pizzas (from £5.50) and large or small portions of pasta (£3.85-£7.50); the full 16-inch pizza (£8.95-£14) nominally serves two, with different toppings on each half if you like, though with a generous side salad (£2) there's probably quite enough for four. A good-value business lunch is £5.50 and the early evening menu (Sun-Thu 5-7pm) offers 3 courses and coffee for £7.95. ***Seats*** *150.* ***Open*** *12-12.* ***Closed*** *25 Dec & 1 Jan. Amex, Diners, MasterCard,* ***VISA***

Check different opening hours before visiting Sannino's other outlet at:
61 Elmbank Street Tel 0141-332 3565 Map 3 B6

GLASGOW Upstairs at the Chip

Tel 0141-334 5007 Map 3 B6 JaB
12 Ashton Lane City of Glasgow G12 8SJ

This popular bar above the more formal and celebrated *Ubiquitous Chip* restaurant remains trendy and Bohemian, and eating here is largely a vehicle for some serious people-watching while supping from the fine wine list. Daytime and evening (from 5 o'clock onwards) try some resolutely simple bar food offering a nice balance of traditional and modern dishes, with a slight emphasis on salads and casseroles in the daytime. From the early-evening selection come vegetarian haggis with neeps and tatties (£3.45/£5.95), egg and red onion mayonnaise (£2.25) and roasted olive bread with chargrilled vegetables (£2.65); Ayr-landed skate with apricot butter (£8.25), chargrilled red snapper with creole sauce (£5.95) and cream cheese and leek bridie (£5.95) to satisfy a larger appetite and Scotch rib-eye steak and rack of lamb (from £10.45) for ravenous carnivores. Lunchtime dishes are generally priced slightly lower, with a larger selection of salads and cold food; Saturdays are particularly popular with families and on Sundays breakfast runs from 12.30pm. Excellent Scottish cheeses and some 15 wines by the glass. ***Seats*** *52.* ***Open*** *12-11 (Sun from 12.30).* ***Closed*** *25, 31 Dec & 1, 2 Jan. Amex, Diners, MasterCard,* ***VISA***

GLASGOW Willow Tea Room

Tel 0141-332 0521 Map 3 B6 JaB
217 Sauchiehall Street City of Glasgow G2 3EX

Immaculately restored from the 1904 original, this is a glorious example of Charles Rennie Mackintosh art deco design and the old-fashioned cream teas (£6.95) served all day are entirely in keeping. Locally-baked cakes – Empire biscuit, apple pie, carrot cake, meringues and cloutie dumpling (£1.25-£1.85) – and savoury items such as filled baked potatoes and hot filled croissants and bagels (from £3.75) supplement the platters of hot roast beef and ham, the cold St Andrews salad platter of smoked salmon, trout and prawns (£5.50) and the muffins, scones, crumpets and pancakes that keep the regulars coming back for more. Specials, which change daily often include a hearty portion of haggis (£3.95). Extensions incorporating the downstairs Gallery tea room have virtually doubled capacity this year. ***Seats*** *100.* ***Open*** *9.30-4.30.* ***Closed*** *Sun & Bank Holidays. No credit cards.*

GLENELG Glenelg Inn £80

Tel & Fax 01599 522273 Map 3 B4 
Glenelg by Kyle of Lochalsh Highland IV40 8JR

With a fine location on the shore of Glenelg Bay, Christopher Main's sympathetically refurbished inn combines a rustic bar with civilised restaurant and, created out of the old stable block, six spacious bedrooms which have been individually decorated and furnished with antiques. The bar menu, for residents only on Sunday, offers dishes as varied as venison liver pate, local seafood pie, hill-bred lamb cutlets and sticky toffee pudding, with the addition of soups, sandwiches and pastries at lunchtime only. In the non-smoking restaurant, the fixed-price dinner menu (served from 7.30 to 9pm) is recommended in our *1997 Hotels & Restaurants Guide*. After dinner (Set D £19), residents repair to the "Morning Room" where the atmosphere lends itself to conviviality; Victorian paintings and photos. a green leather Chesterfield, stag's head and various antiques and objects d'art make a comfortable setting. A large walled and fenced in garden overlooks the sea and is safe for children. *Open 12-2.30, 5-11.* ***Bar Food*** *(no food Nov-Mar) 12-2.30, 7-9. Garden. No real ales.* ***Accommodation*** *6 bedrooms, all en suite, £80. Children welcome overnight (under-3s stay free in parents' room), additional bed & cot available. No dogs. Check-in by arrangement. Pub closed Sun & lunchtimes Nov-Mar, Accommodation closed Nov-Mar. No credit cards.*

GLENROTHES Balgeddie House 65% £96

Tel 01592 742511 **Fax 01592 621702** Map 3 C5 **H**
Balgeddie Way Glenrothes Fife KY6 3ET

An 18th-century Georgian house converted to a hotel eight years ago and located in a suburb of Glenrothes new town (though it still retains some country house character). Bedrooms on the first floor are superior and spacious, with fine modern bathrooms, those on the second floor are twins, with sloping ceilings. There's a choice of bars – cocktail for pre-dinner drinks, the Paddock serving bar lunches and suppers and the Lodge with machines and pool table – and a lounge. Outside there's a lawn the size of a football pitch and eight acres of landscaped gardens complete with palm trees. Children stay free in their parents' room. Functions/conferences for up to 70. ***Rooms*** *18. Garden. Closed 1 Jan. Amex, Diners, MasterCard,* ***VISA***

GOLLANFIELD Culloden Pottery Restaurant

Tel 01667 462749 Map 2 C3 **JaB**
Gollanfield nr Inverness Highland IV1 2QT

By the A96 halfway between Inverness and Nairn, the restaurant is above a craft and gift shop; more wholefood than vegetarian (there is also some fish on the menu), everything is made on the premises using organic produce wherever possible. Soup (£1.70), nut paté and houmus (both £2.25) all come with crusty wholemeal bread and there is a good selection of composite salads to go with the day's hot lunch dishes like mushroom stroganoff, Mediterranean crumble (from £4.95) and the ever-popular mushroom burgers (£4.55), all offered with chips, baked potato or salad. Sandwiches and filled jacket potatoes cope with lesser appetites; for the sweet-toothed there are fruit pies with cream, gateau or cheesecake (from £1.30) and cakes such as delicious, moist fruit slice (£1). Children have their own section on the menu and a play area outside with swings, a slide, scramble net and rustic play house. Baby-changing facilities are provided in the Ladies. For disabled visitors there's a special loo on the ground floor and a stair lift up to the restaurant. No-smoking area. ***Seats*** *42.* ***Open*** *9.30-8 (closes earlier mid-week out of season).* ***Closed*** *25, 26 Dec & 1, 2 Jan. MasterCard,* ***VISA***

GREENLAW Castle Inn

Tel 01361 810217 **Fax 01361 810500** Map 3 D6 **P**
Greenlaw Scottish Borders TD10 6UR

The handsome Georgian Castle Inn is the sort of place you could take a variety of people to and feel confident that they would find something to their taste. The Mirror Room, where drinking and dining take place, has a large mirror above a marble fireplace transforming what would otherwise be a hall into a splendid room, with a comfortable sitting area by the fireplace and elegant Georgian windows through which there's a view to well-kept gardens. Family facilities are excellent, with high-chairs, baby foods, a children's menu served throughout the day, books in the library and cheerful, tolerant staff. Of the bedrooms, including two with plenty of family accommodation, only two have en suite bathrooms, the other four sharing two baths and a shower room. *Open 11-11 (Fri & Sat till 11.30, Sun from 12). Free House.* ***Beer*** *Caledonian 80/- Ale, guest beer. Garden. Family Room.* ***Accommodation*** *6 bedrooms, 2 en suite, £50 (single £27.50). Children welcome overnight (free in parents' room, family room £60), additional bed and cot available. Amex, Diners, MasterCard,* ***VISA***

INGLISTON — Norton House — 66% — £125

Tel 0131-333 1275 Fax 0131-333 5305 Map 3 C6 H

Ingliston nr Edinburgh Midlothian EH28 8LX

Norton House stands in parkland on the western outskirts of the city, handily placed for the airport. Its Victorian origins are clear from the outside and confirmed within by handsome wood panelling and marblework. The Oak Room bar is in the main building while in the grounds the Norton Tavern features a walled garden, a barbecue area and a children's play area. Comfortable, well-equipped bedrooms include suites and mini-suites, superior and standard rooms. Families are well catered for, and children under 12 can stay free in their parents' room. Banqueting/ conference facility for 160/250. 24hr room service. Part of the Virgin Hotels group. ***Rooms*** *47. Garden, croquet, outdoor play area. Amex, Diners, MasterCard,* ***VISA***

INNERLEITHEN — Traquair Arms

Tel 01896 830229 Fax 01896 830260 Map 4 F3 

Traquair Road Innerleithen Scottish Borders EH44 6PD

Five minutes' walk from the River Tweed, the Traquair Arms is a handsome stone building on the road leading to St. Mary's Loch; incidentally, it's a delightful journey across country roads to one of the most picturesque parts of the Borders. A well-stocked bar features the Traquair's own Bear Ale on tap with a teddy bear-clad pump. The choice of dining areas including the garden, weather permitting, and a wide choice of freshly prepared meals served all day, is typical of the Traquair Arms' admirable flexibility, which also runs to breakfast for non-residents, morning coffee, afternoon tea and high tea. A variety of omelettes and salads is served in the bar and hot dishes include Finnan Savoury (smoked haddock in cheese, onion and cream sauce), Traquair steak pie (cooked in home-brewed ale), and at least three vegetarian dishes. One benefit of dining in the bar is that the glass doors lead off into the garden, which is enclosed and safe for youngsters to let off steam. Service is genuine and informal, the atmosphere convivial and children are positively welcomed. The smart, well-kept bedrooms (three are singles) have en suite facilities, colour TVs and phones; particularly recommended is the handsome Scottish breakfast complete with superb kippers. Traquair House next door is well worth a visit – it's a romantic old house with pretty grounds and contains an old brewhouse; the front gates of Traquair are firmly shut and will remain so until a Stuart returns to the throne of Scotland. *Open 11- 12.* ***Bar Food*** *12-9. Free House.* ***Beer*** *Traquair Bear Ale, Broughton Greenmantle Ale, occasional guest beers. Garden, outdoor eating.* ***Accommodation*** *10 bedrooms, all en suite, £64 (single £42). Children welcome overnight (0-5s free, 6-12s 50% adult rate in parents' room), additional bed & cot available. Pub closed 2 days Christmas. Amex, MasterCard,* ***VISA***

> We endeavour to be as up-to-date as possible, but inevitably some changes to data and key personnel may occur at restaurants and hotels after the Guide goes to press. Prices should also be taken as indications rather than firm quotes.

INVERNESS — Bunchrew House — 67% — £105

Tel 01463 234917 Fax 01463 710620 Map 2 C3 

Bunchrew Inverness Highland IV3 6TA

A couple of miles out of town on the A682, Bunchrew House is a fine-looking Scottish baronial mansion set alongside the Beauly Firth in 20 acres of woodland. The bar and restful lounge both feature dark brown painted panelling and open fires in winter. About half the comfortable bedrooms have reproduction antique furniture while more recent rooms have good-quality darkwood pieces. All have mini-bars and there is room service throughout the day and evening. Banqueting/conference facilities for up to 90. ***Rooms*** *11. Garden, croquet, fishing. Closed 2 weeks Jan. Amex, MasterCard,* ***VISA***

JOHNSTONEBRIDGE Annandale Lodge £47

Tel 0800 741174 **Fax 01576 470644** Map 4 C2 **B**
Annandale Water Service Area nr Lockerbie Dumfries & Galloway DG11 1HD

Arguably the prettiest setting for a lodge in the UK with many of the spacious bedrooms having their own balconies overlooking the lake and surrounding hills. Just 30 miles north of Carlisle (M74, J16), Annandale Water is unlike any other service area with the buildings blending in with the landscape. Bedrooms (most non-smoking, three specifically designed for disabled guests) provide a double bed and sofa bed, Sky TV, credit card telephone, trouser press, hairdryer, tea & coffee making facilities and a decent bathroom. ***Rooms** 42. Terrace, shop. Amex, Diners, MasterCard, **VISA***

KENMORE Kenmore Hotel 62% £97

Tel 01887 830205 **Fax 01887 830262** Map 3 C5 **H**
Kenmore by Aberfeldy Perth & Kinross PH15 2NU

The Kenmore, dating from 1572, claims to be Scotland's oldest inn and stands in a lovely Perthshire village at the east end of Loch Tay on the A827. The Poet's Parlour bar, devoted to Burns, is cosy with its green tartan seats; Archie's Bar is simpler, with glorious views of the river. Bedrooms, 14 in a Victorian gatehouse opposite, vary considerably in decor and furnishings with everything from melamine to antiques. Guests have concessionary use of the swimming pool and leisure facilities at the nearby Kenmore Club; Kenmore itself attracts both golf enthusiasts and fishermen; they have 3 miles of private beats on the River Tay. *Open 11-11. Riverside garden. Family room. No real ales. **Accommodation** 39 bedrooms, all en suite, £97 (single £60). Children welcome overnight. Amex, MasterCard, **VISA***

KENTALLEN OF APPIN Holly Tree 65% £55

Tel 01631 740292 **Fax 01631 740345** Map 3 B4 **H**
Kentallen of Appin Highland PA38 4BY

The Holly Tree has evolved from a former railway station, and retains some of the more interesting features of that original incarnation. Nowdays, its level of comfort and hospitality makes it a delightful spot from which to enjoy the splendid views of Loch Linnhe and the hillside behind. Families are well catered for and children under 5 are charged £3.50 when staying in their parents' room. ***Rooms** 10. MasterCard, **VISA***

KILBERRY Kilberry Inn

Tel & Fax 01880 770223 Map 3 A6 **P**
Kilberry by Tarbert Argyll & Bute PA29 6YD

An invigorating 16 mile drive down a winding, single-track road with superb views will bring you to this single storey white cottage located half a mile from the glorious coastline. John and Kath Leadbeater, English chef-proprietors, are vigorously interested in good food and justifiably proud of their achievements here, in an out of the way spot where the vegetables come via van and taxi, and fresh fish is strangely hard to get. It's very much a dining pub, though locals and others are equally welcome to drop in for a drink; the building was originally a crofting house, and the snugly comfortable little bar, with a peat fire at one end, a wood-burning stove at the other, still has and unpretentious rural style. Leading off at the left, the brighter, plainer dining and family room has good sized pine dining tables. The daily blackboard-listed short menu (perhaps only four or five main courses at lunchtime) is cheerfully annotated. Typical dishes might include fresh tomatoes stuffed with "locally caught haggis", a hearty country sausage pie with fresh salad or a fish pie of local salmon; at night a few fancier dishes are also added, perhaps chunks of rump steak cooked in Theakston's Old Peculier Ale or prime pork fillet cooked in cider with apples. Kath has a famously light hand and the pastry is superb; she also makes the bread as well as a selection of over 25 pickles, jams and chutneys on sale at the bar. Whatever you do, make sure you leave room for one of Kath's delicious fruit pies, which are laid out on the counter as soon as they come out of the oven. Equally scrumptious are the bread-and-butter pudding, fresh lemon cream, grapefruit cheesecake and chocolate fudge.

Accommodation is offered in two smart en suite bedrooms (one double, one twin (£55 double, £34.50 single), no smoking, breakfast served 8-9am, no food Sundays apart from breakfast. Note that the pub never opens on Sundays. *Open 11-2.30, 5-11.* ***Bar Food*** *12.15-2, 6.30-9. No real ales. Family room (no smoking). Inn closed Sun.* ***Accommodation*** *closed mid Oct-Easter. MasterCard,* **VISA**

KILLIECRANKIE Killiecrankie Hotel 64% £152*

Tel 01796 473220 **Fax 01796 472451** Map 3 C4 H

Killiecrankie by Pitlochry Perth & Kinross PH16 5LG

Four acres of landscaped gardens overlook the River Garry and the Pass of Killiecrankie (turn off the A9 north of Pitlochry). There's something of the feeling of an inn about the little hotel, which was built as a manse in 1840. The small panelled bar has a suntrap extension and an upstairs lounge offers various board games plus a variety of books as distractions. Pine-furnished bedrooms are fresh and bright. Bar menu for informal lunches and suppers. *Half-board terms. ***Rooms*** *10. Garden, croquet. Closed Jan & Feb. MasterCard,* **VISA**

KINCRAIG Boathouse Restaurant

Tel 01540 651272 Map 3 C4

Insh Hall Kincraig Highland PH21 1NU

Just off the B5192, six miles south of Aviemore, the balcony of this log-cabin restaurant is a a splendid spot for watching all the activities at the adjacent Loch Insh watersports centre while enjoying the home-made fare on offer. During the day you can choose from toasted sandwiches and jacket potatoes (from £2.25), burgers (from £3.75), lasagne (£4.75) and venison pie (£5.75) plus a vegetarian section including vegetable spring rolls and veggieburgers (£3.75) and a children's menu of dinosaurs, pizza and fishy fries (£4.75 inclusive of ice cream and pop); in high season there's a barbecue for burgers, chicken and rump steaks from 12.30 to 2.30. After 6.30pm it becomes waitress service with some dishes such as Kingussie haggis with neeps and tatties in a whisky and onion sauce (£3.50/£6.95) and smoked salmon salad with lime and capers (£5/£9.50) available for hearty snacking, and a vegetarian filo strudel with curried korma cream (£9.50); main courses otherwise offer little or no choice below £12. High-chairs, bottle-warming and a children's menu are all available. No special facilities, but there's space in both Ladies and Gents for changing baby. The restaurant overlooks the beach and a small grassy area. No smoking, except in the bar. Construction is currently under way on an adventure park, fun trail and a children's lagoon on the lakeside. ***Seats*** *45 (+25 on balcony).* ***Open*** *10-10. (11-9, Oct-Feb).* ***Closed*** *Mon-Wed in Nov & Jan, 1st 2 wks Dec. MasterCard,* **VISA**

> Pubs – note that food is only recommended in those pubs with ***Bar Food*** times in the statistics at the end of an entry. Restaurant food in pubs is *never* recommended unless specifically mentioned. Some pubs are recommended for B&B or Atmosphere only – each entry's statistics indicate our recommendation.

KINLOCHBERVIE Kinlochbervie Hotel 64% £90

Tel 01971 521275 **Fax 01971 521438** Map 2 B2

Kinlochbervie by Lairg Highland IV27 4RP

Almost at the northernmost tip of mainland Scotland, 47 miles from Lairg, Kinlochbervie is a modern hotel high up on a hill overlooking a fishing harbour. Six bedrooms (and a first-floor residents' lounge crammed with literature for walkers and fishermen) also benefit from the setting. All rooms have showers as well as baths. A convivial bar and bistro adjacent are popular with locals. Any third person sharing a room is free of charge; for more than one child sharing a charge is made for breakfast. Cots can be provided and a children's menu is available in the bistro. A small sitting-room on the third floor has puzzles, games and children's books. ***Rooms*** *14. Sea and loch fishing. Closed Nov-Feb. MasterCard,* **VISA**

KIPPEN Cross Keys

Tel 01786 870293 Map 3 C5 P
Main Street Kippen Stirling FK8 3DN

A simple welcoming Scottish pub with rooms, set in a pleasant rural village not far from Stirling. The locals' public bar is large and basic, a smaller, long and narrow lounge is where most of the food is served, and an adjoining family room has high-chairs primed and ready for use. Bar food, chosen from a standard printed menu, enhanced by daily specials, includes the ever-popular "humble haddie" pancakes (as a starter or main course) and the likes of sweetcorn fritters with chilli dip, Kashmiri chicken Korma, poached salmon with lime and ginger sauce and a home-made Clootie Dumpling to finish. Most of the produce is from local suppliers and Kippen's bakery supplies the bread. The best bedrooms under the eaves have sloping ceilings and fine views, with the usual tea and coffee kits, wash handbasins and good quality towels. Breakfasts served on linen-laid tables in the restaurant are hearty, traditional fry-ups (but not too greasy) and service is pleasant and helpful. There's a beer garden, with a children's play area, at the rear with access from both the public and lounge bars. *Open 12-2.30 (Sun from 12.30), 5.30-11 (Fri & Sat till 12).* ***Bar Food*** *12-2 (Sun from 12.30), 5.30-9.30. Free House.* ***Beer*** *Broughton Greenmantle Ale, Younger's No. 3. Garden, play area, outdoor eating. Family room.* ***Accommodation*** *3 bedrooms (2 twins, 1 single), sharing a bathroom, £39 (single £19.50). Children welcome overnight (under-5s stay free in parents' room). Pub closed 1 Jan. MasterCard,* ***VISA***

KIRKCALDY Hoffmans

Tel 01592 204584 Map 3 C5 P
435 High Street Kirkcaldy Fife KY1 2SG

Situated to the east of the town centre (don't be fooled by the High Street address), this is an unlikely-looking venue for a pub serving imaginative food, but first impressions can deceive. Converted by owners Paul and Vince Hoffinan with subtly toned wall-coverings, brown-upholstered bench seating, polished tables, a large central ceiling fan, angled mirrors and fake greenery, it's smart and sophisticated within, and so popular that booking is advised for lunch as well as dinner. Local suppliers are listed at the front of the menu which is handwritten and changes daily; often it's not even decided on until just before opening-time, when suppliers and fishmongers have been visited and produce assessed. Fish is a particular interest of Vince's, from traditional deep-fried haddock to seafood and mushroom ragout; alongside such dishes as pan-fried liver and bacon and Chinese-style pork with noodles, the under-£5 lunchtime price remains remarkable value. In the evening the room is partitioned, half the space reserved for drinkers, the other run as an à la carte bistro, where tables are laid, candles lit and waitresses serve. Dishes are slightly more elaborate but no less value for money; spicy vegetable filo parcels, fresh halibut glazed with chili and lime and Dundee Bonnet – home-made by Vince's wife, Jan. Capable service is also genuinely friendly thanks to the Hoffman teamwork. It's not a drinkers' pub and children are encouraged – the idea being to "try to wean them into using pubs for the right reasons". High-chairs and "portions of proper food" are available. *Open 11am-midnight.* ***Bar Food*** *12-2, 7-10. Free House.* ***Beer*** *McEwan's 80/-, guest beer. Pub closed all Sun. No credit cards.*

KIRKTON OF GLANISLA Glenisla Hotel

Tel & Fax 01575 582223 Map 3 C4 P
Kirkton of Glenisla nr Alyth Angus PH11 8PH

Simon and Lyndy Blake extend a traditional warm welcome to their 300-year-old coaching inn set high up in Glenisla, one of the "Angus Glens", and dating back to the days before the Jacobite rebellion; even in summer, on chilly days a real fire smoulders in the bar. At lunchtime the daily-changing menu offers favourites like haddock and chips, ploughman's platters, Aberdeen Angus steaks, macaroni cheese and Cumberland sausage. King Orkney scallops are an ever-popular starter at dinner, with main courses such as Glenisla venison and apricot casserole, grilled Esk salmon and mushroom and artichoke crepes, and sticky toffee pudding to follow. Afternoons bring cream teas – scones from the oven with home-made jam, and children's high tea at 5.30. *Open 11-2.30, 6-11 (Sat 11-11, Sun 12-10.30).* ***Bar Food*** *12.30-2.30, 6.30-8.45 (Sat till 9, Sun till 8).* ***Beer*** *Theakston's Best, McEwan's 80/-, Boddingtons. Garden, outdoor eating. Family room. The hotel has 6 en suite bedrooms (Double £65, single £32.50) and under-2s are accommodated free. Pub closed 25 & 26 Dec. MasterCard,* ***VISA***

KYLE OF LOCHALSH Seagreen

Tel 01599 534388 Map 2 B3 JaB
Plockton Road Kyle of Lochalsh Highland IV40 8DA

Sharing premises with a bookshop in Kyle's old village school, Seagreen specialises, naturally, in seafood, as well as other natural organic produce and free-range eggs used in the baking. Counter service and blackboard menus throughout the day offer soup such as smoked haddock and sweetcorn chowder (£2.45), baked local oysters (70p each), mixed smoked seafood platter (£5.95), and wholesome 'lunch' specials, served till 5pm, of which wild mushroom and peanut rissoles (£4.75) and spinach, broccoli and feta cheese pie (£5.25) are typical examples. Consistently good home baking includes orange datie, coffee and walnut cake, egg- and sugar-free rich fruit cake and home-baked oatcakes served with the plate of local farmhouse cheeses (£3.50), while the truly sweet-toothed can go for the sticky toffee and hot chocolate fuge cakes (£3.50). Suppers from 6.30pm bring a short à la carte, with waitress-service, that includes cauliflower and almond soup and goat's cheese soufflé preceding locally-caught seafood like porbeagle shark steaks from Mallaig, marinated monkfish kebabs and Kyle of Lochalsh king scallops (£14.95). The café is especially busy between 5.30 and 6.30pm when children (and parents) can try breaking the burger habit. There are two high-chairs and nursing mums have a shelf and chair in the Ladies. A toy box is provided and there's plenty of space. Safe garden. Out of high season the hours may be curtailed, so booking in advance is essential. No smoking. ***Seats*** *50 (+15 outside).* ***Open*** *10-9.* ***Closed*** *25, 26 Dec & 1 Jan. MasterCard,* ***VISA***

LARGS Nardini's

Tel 01475 674555 Map 3 B6 JaB
The Esplanade Largs North Ayrshire KA30 8NF

To enter Nardini's seafront 'Continental lounge café' is to step back in time – a huge room with gold-painted wicker chairs and glass-topped tables, parlour plants and numerous waiters and waitresses in smart red waistcoats providing swift, friendly service. It's still run by the Nardini family, who first set up in Largs in 1890. Their own real dairy ice cream range of some 48 different flavours is unparalleled in the UK, and the speciality sundaes with names like Amaretto special (£4.30), misto coppa (£3) and Brasilia special (£4.50) are simply irresistible! Their own bakery provides not only bread for the sandwiches (Parma ham £2.70, fresh salmon £2.50) but bases for the dozens of pizzas (from £3) and a wide range of patisserie from a simple scone to Gateau St Honoré and fresh double cream torte (from £1.50). Breakfasts are served until 11am, the adjacent 250-seat restaurant offers a wide range of Italian and Scottish dishes – the locally landed fish is a speciality – and a confectionery shop in the foyer boasts an impressive range of luxury chocolates. The children's menus for lunch and high-tea in the restaurant are usually extensive - not just burgers and fish fingers (although they are also on the menu). There's a special Junior Choice section on the café menu 'for discerning under-12s' and among their special fixed-price menus are the Saturday Shopper's lunch (subtitled 'Dad's Reward') and the Sunday family lunch ('Rest Day For Mums'), served noon to 3pm (adults £7.50, children 5-12 £3.80, under-5s free!). Plenty of room for buggies, numerous high-chairs, and baby-changing facilities (including nappies) are provided in the Ladies. In a word, Nardini's is a veritable institution; you should not leave Largs without a visit. ***Seats*** *260 (+80 outside).* ***Open*** *8am-10.30pm (Oct-Mar Mon-Fri till 9, Sat & Sun till 10).* ***Closed*** *25 Dec. Amex, Diners, MasterCard,* ***VISA***

Also at:
Nardini at Regatta's Yacht Haven Marina Largs Tel 01475 686684
Moorings Tea Parlour The Pier Head Largs Tel 01475 689313

LINLITHGOW — Champany Inn Chop & Ale House — £50

Tel 01506 834532 **Fax 01506 834302** Map 3 C5 **R**
Champany Linlithgow West Lothian EH49 7LU

Adjacent to the main Champany Inn restaurant, this is a much less formal place to eat Aberdeen Angus steaks (smaller but considerably less expensive), along with burgers, sausages or deep-fried fish. A cold buffet is also available, including ham, chicken and salad. To finish, two home-made sweets (waffles and cheesecake) also feature on the menu. ***Seats*** *38 (+ 24 outside). L 12-2 (Sun 12.30-2.30) D 6.30-10 (Sat from 6). Closed 25, 26 Dec & 1, 2 Jan. Amex, Diners, MasterCard,* ***VISA***

LOCH ECK — Coylet Inn

Tel & Fax 01369 840426 Map 3 B5 **P**
Loch Eck nr Kilmun Argyll & Bute PA23 8SG

Owner Richard Addis has been here 25 years now, and thankfully little has changed in that time least of all the really special setting – just the west coast road to Dunoon, shrouded in trees, separates the pretty white building from the glorious beauty of Loch Eck and the hills beyond. Not another house can be seen in any direction; be early for a window seat in the bar or dining-room. Inside the public bar is handsome and cosy, the hall is an attractively simple little dining bar, where families (even tiny babies) are welcome, and in the dining-room proper are half a dozen tables (one large group size, in the prize window spot), wheelback chairs and a piano. The food is a mix of standard bar menu stuff, sandwiches (even in the evening) and ploughman's platters to vast, well-cooked platefuls of haddock and chips, or sizzling steaks; but it's worth choosing from the specials board – a twice-daily changing short blackboard list. It might typically feature home-made liver pate and Scotch broth, local game in season, steak and kidney pie, salmon fishcakes, grilled local salmon or trout at lunchtime. In the evening, the board may feature mushrooms au gratin, venison collops in port and red wine sauce and langoustine risotto of tender, fresh Loch Eck langoustines in garlic, cream wine and herb sauce. Vegetables are also exceptional – crisp mangetout, perfect new potatoes and tender carrots all included in the main-course price. Puddings (all home-made) come in hefty portions; chocolate roulade, pineapple cheesecake or a real apple pie are typical of the choice. Upstairs are three tiny bedrooms which offer simple comfort; all have sash windows with views over the Loch and pretty cottagey print paper and fabrics. The twin is a bit bigger than the two doubles, while the shared bathroom, a very attractive, immaculately clean, carpeted and pine-panelled room, is bigger than any of them. Breakfasts are ungreasy and commendably accommodating of personal preference, and the service is genuine and friendly from both the resident owners and their few, able staff. Lochside garden. *Open 11-2.30 (Sun from 12.30), 5-11 (Fri & Sat till 12, Sun from 6.30).* ***Bar Food*** *12-2, (Sun from 12.30), 5.30-9.30 (Sun 7-9). Free House.* ***Beer*** *Younger's No.3, McEwan's 80/-, Caledonian Deuchar's IPA. Garden, outdoor eating. Family room.* ***Accommodation*** *3 bedrooms, sharing facilities, £35 (single £17.50). Children welcome overnight. Check-in by arrangement. No dogs. MasterCard,* ***VISA***

MOFFAT — Black Bull

Tel 01683 220206 **Fax 01683 220483** Map 4 C2 
Churchgate Moffat Dumfries & Galloway DG10 8EG

Though much-modernised these days, this 16th century street-side local was a favourite haunt of Robert Burns who is duly commemorated by a newly-unveiled replica of his hand-etched window of c1790. Of the eight bedrooms, four look onto the courtyard and four onto the churchyard opposite; each has a different colour scheme and is fully equipped with TV, telephone and tea/coffee making facilities. The family room, children's menu, beer garden and nearby duck pond make this a popular summer haunt for holidaymakers. *Open 11-11 (Fri & Sat till 12, Sun 12.30-11).* ***Beer*** *Theakston Best, McEwan's 80/-, two weekly-changing guest beers, Garden. Family room.* ***Accommodation*** *8 bedrooms, 6 en suite, from £45 (single £29, family room £60). Children welcome overnight (under-14s stay free in parents' room), additional bed & cot available. No dogs. MasterCard,* ***VISA***

MONYMUSK — Grant Arms Hotel

Tel 01467 651226 **Fax 01467 651494** Map 3 D4 P

The Square Monymusk nr Inverurie Aberdeenshire AB51 7HJ

With 6,000 acres of rough and driven shooting and 10 miles of salmon and trout fishing on the river Don, this is very much a sporting inn as the decor of the panelled bar – antlers, stag's head, stuffed birds and odd fishing rods – confirms. A typically solid, unspectacular 18th-century Scottish inn on the village green, the bedrooms are clean and bright if not luxurious. All have radio alarms, telephones and tea/coffee making facilities but no televisions (there is one in the residents' lounge). The bar menu offers something for most tastes – fresh oysters, lobster bisque, noisettes of spring lamb with rosemary and Arran mustard, chargrilled rainbow trout and a choice of steaks. *Open 11-2.30, 5-11, (Sat 11-11.30, Sun 12-11.30). **Bar Food** 12-2 (Sun from 12.30), 6.30-8.45 (Fri & Sat till 9.45, Sun from 6). Free House. **Beer** Scottish & Newcastle 80/-, two guest beers. Garden, outdoor eating, children's play area. Family room. **Accommodation** 16 bedrooms, 8 en suite, £62 (single £43). Children welcome overnight (0-2s stay free). Amex, MasterCard,* **VISA**

NAIRN — Golf View Hotel — 67% — £120

Tel 01667 452301 **Fax 01667 455267** Map 2 C3 H

Seabank Road Nairn Highland IV12 4HD

A late-Victorian hotel whose grounds extend down to a sandy beach on the Firth of Forth opposite the Black Isle. You can also enjoy the view from the glass-walled swimming pool, part of a well-equipped leisure centre. Public areas feature elaborate floral drapes, brass chandeliers and co-ordinated furniture, and all bedrooms have comfortable armchairs and/or sofas. Banqueting and conference facilities for up to 120. ***Rooms** 47. Garden, tennis, putting, indoor swimming pool, gym, sauna, steam room, spa bath, sun beds. Amex, Diners, MasterCard,* **VISA**

NETHERLEY — Lairhillock Inn

Tel 01569 730001 **Fax 01569 731175** Map 3 D4 

Netherley Stonehaven Aberdeenshire AB3 2QS

Standing alone surrounded by fields, the Lairhillock is easily spotted from the B979; the closest major village is Peterculter, some four miles to the north and Netherley's a mile to the south. Formerly a farmhouse, the original building is 17th century and the interior is full of old rustic atmosphere. The public bar, in the oldest part, is by far the most characterful room, with its exposed stone, panelling, open fire, old settles and bench seating, every kind of horse tack, polished brasses and numerous other bits and pieces. The menu, changing daily, can be pretty polyglot with items such as gambas creole, crispinelli de spinato and crepes fruits de mer offered as starters, and as main courses chicken écossais or pork viennoise as alternatives to the venison escalopes, mixed grills and Aberdeen Angus steaks. The hugely popular sticky toffee pudding and Clootie Dumpling form the foundations of the dessert menu, with daily variations displayed on a blackboard. Across from the main building, in the old stables, is the evening restaurant which also serves traditional roasts on a Sunday. A conservatory with panoramic views, furnished with Lloyd Loom tables and chairs, provides an ideal room for families to eat in, with friendly, informal service. *Open 11-2.30, 5-11, (Fri & Sat till 12). **Bar Food** 12-2, 6-9.30 (Fri & Sat till 10). Free House. **Beer** Courage Directors, Thwaites Craftsman, McEwan's 80/-, Boddingtons, Flowers, guest beers. Patio & terrace, outdoor eating. Amex, Diners, MasterCard,* **VISA**

NEW ABBEY — Abbey Cottage

Tel 01387 850377 Map 4 B2 JaB

26 Main Street New Abbey by Dumfries Dumfries & Galloway DG2 8BX

Next to the ruined abbey, from which the town takes its name, the original part of this charming Victorian cottage is given over to the sale of local arts and crafts; the tea room is in an extension to the rear, which includes a special loo for the disabled. Mrs McKie's home baking runs from fruit scones (£1.10 with home-made jam and cream), fruit loaves, shortbread and carrot cake (from 70p) to savoury items like soup (tomato and vegetable, cauliflower and mushroom – £1.40), macaroni cheese (£2.95), salads (roast beef £4.15), baked jacket potatoes (tuna, cheese, chilli from £2.65) and a ploughman's lunch (£3.95) which features a vegetarian Cheddar from the nearby Loch Arthur Creamery (a Camphill Village Trust). Fresh fruit tart with cream and hot chocolate fudge cake (£1.45) will round things off nicely. The neat little brick-paved patio garden comes into its own in fine weather. Children are always welcome and there are two high-chairs, books to read and toys to play with; toddlers can have their food heated up. Mother's changing area. Children will love the duckpond at the abbey mill. ***Seats*** *52 (+16 outside).* ***Open*** *10-5.30.* ***Closed*** *Weekdays Nov & Dec, all Jan-mid Mar. MasterCard,* ***VISA***

New Abbey — Criffel Inn

Tel 01387 850305 Map 4 B2 P
The Square New Abbey Dumfries & Galloway DG2 8BX

Jim and Ann McAlister now run the Criffel; it's a solid Victorian place where things don't change much from year to year, and the basic philosophy remains unaltered. Upstairs, the residents' lounge has a domestic feel, and bedrooms with wood-effect melamine fitted furniture go in for a medley of floral patterns; only three currently have en suite showers but are being updated. Two bedrooms are of family size and there's one well-kept shared bathroom. *Open 12-2.30, 5.30-11 (Fri & Sat till 12). No real ales.* ***Accommodation*** *5 bedrooms, 3 en suite, £44 (single £19). Children welcome overnight (under-3s stay free in parents' room, 6-12s half price), additional bed & cot available. MasterCard,* ***VISA***

Newcastleton — Copshaw Kitchen

Tel 01387 375250 Map 4 C2 JaB
4 North Hermitage Street Newcastleton Scottish Borders TD9 0RB

Uniquely combined with a stylish antique shop, Jean Elliot's tiny tea room and restaurant still contains some of the original fittings from its days as a grocer's shop. Savoury items available all day include paté with oatcakes, pancakes filled with smoked haddock, prawns and mushrooms in a gruyère cheese sauce (£4.50), lasagne, curry and home-made beefburgers (from £4.25) and fresh baked trout (£5.50). Sweets and cakes on offer could be millionaire shortbread, almond slice and mint cake (from 50p) or for something heavier, sticky toffee pudding (£1.75) or Copshaw Calypso (made with bananas, chocolate and vanilla ice cream, meringue, banana liqueur and fresh cream £2.75). Full afternoon tea (£3.50) includes sandwiches, scones and cream sponge, while the high tea (£6.95) adds a hot main course of choice. The restaurant stays open on summer evenings (7-9), with main courses such as Italian chicken, pork with Stilton and Scottish salmon (from £7.75) and grilled steaks from £9. A reception area provides a convenient space for nursing mothers when it's quiet. One high-chair, children's menu and half-portions available. ***Seats*** *18.* ***Open*** *9.30-5, till 9 in summer (weekends only in winter, phone for opening times).* ***Closed*** *Tue. MasterCard,* ***VISA***

Newton Stewart — Creebridge House Hotel

Tel 01671 402121 **Fax 01671 403258** Map 4 A2 P
Minnigaff Newton Stewart Dumfries & Galloway DG8 6NP.

Formerly home to the Earls of Galloway, the 18th century, stone-built Creebridge House is set in very pretty gardens. It's more hotel than inn, but the bar with low ceilings, reclaimed pitch pine timber furniture, old oak beams and horse brasses has a comfortable country feel about it. There's a good range of bar meals from a snacky lunchtime-only menu (including sandwiches and filled croissants) to some accomplished fish specials such as paupiettes of salmon and halibut with a crayfish sauce, equally substantial Galloway venison, fillet of beef with mushroom sauce and "posh fish and chips" (local haddock fillet in real ale batter) served in newspaper on your plate. Bedrooms which include four family suites are all very well-kept and equipped with TVs, telephones, hairdryers and tea/coffee making kits, and good modern en suite bathrooms, all with shower over the tub. *Open 12-2.30, 6-11 (Fri, Sat & Sun till 11.30).* ***Bar Food*** *12-2 (Sun from 12.30), 6-9 (Sat till 10, Sun from 7). Free House.* ***Beer*** *Tetley Burton Ale, Orkney Dark Island, guest beer. Garden, outdoor eating. Family room.* ***Accommodation*** *20 bedrooms, all en suite, £75 (single £40). Children welcome overnight (under-12s free if sharing parents' room), additional bed & cot available. Accommodation closed 24-26 Dec. Amex, MasterCard,* ***VISA***

North Berwick — Marine Hotel — 64% — £98

Tel 01620 892406 **Fax 01620 894480** Map 3 D5 **H**

Cromwell Road North Berwick East Lothian EH39 4LZ

This imposing Victorian hotel offers delightful views of the Firth of Forth and has a long golfing tradition (it overlooks the 16th green of the North Berwick Championship Westlinks Course and there are dozens of courses nearby). ***Rooms*** *83. Garden, tennis, putting, outdoor swimming pool, sauna, sun beds, snooker. Amex, Diners, MasterCard,* ***VISA***

Onich — Onich Hotel — 61% — £88

Tel 01855 821214 **Fax 01855 821484** Map 3 B4 **H**

Onich nr Fort William Highland PH33 6RY

Ian and Grace Young run this hospitable hotel, set in beautiful scenery at the head of Loch Linnhe and ideal for outdoor activities such as fishing and climbing. Mountain bikes can be hired, and yacht moorings are available. For indoor amenity satellite TVs have recently been added to the bedrooms. ***Rooms*** *25. Closed 1 week Christmas, 1 week Jan. Garden, spa bath, solarium, games room, playground, brasserie (11am-10pm). Amex, Diners, MasterCard,* ***VISA***

Peebles — Cringletie House — 66% — £104

Tel 01721 730233 **Fax 01721 730244** Map 4 C1 **H**

Peebles Scottish Borders EH45 8PL

A red-stone, Scottish baronial-style mansion built in 1861 above and well-back from the A703 a mile or two to the north of town. The house is surrounded by gardens and looks across to the distant Meldon and Moorfoot Hills. The most impressive day-room is the first-floor, panelled drawing-room with fine original painted ceiling, lots of velour sofas and armchairs and, for most of the year, a real log fire burning in the marble fireplace. There is also a non-smoking lounge and, on the ground floor, a fine new conservatory now leads off the comfortable bar. Well-kept bedrooms are individually decorated, and furnished in traditional style with a scattering of antiques and homely touches like fresh flowers and bowls of sweets. Beds are turned down at night. Children are welcome and get their own high tea served around 5.30pm. Good cooked breakfasts and freshly-squeezed orange juice. Run in friendly fashion by the Maguire family for more than 20 years. ***Rooms*** *13. Garden, croquet, tennis, putting. Closed early Jan-early Mar. Amex, MasterCard,* ***VISA***

> **JaB** is short for 'Just a Bite'. The majority of these establishments are also recommended in our *Bistros, Bars & Cafés* Guide which features establishments where one may eat well for less than £15 per head.

Peebles — Kailzie Gardens

Tel 01721 722807 Map 4 C1 **JaB**

Kailzie Gardens Peebles Scottish Borders EH45 9HT

In the courtyard of privately-owned Kailzie Gardens beside the River Tweed (admission £2), Grace Innes's cottagey restaurant is housed in the converted stables. The widest choice from her all-embracing menu comes at lunchtime: two soups with home-baked bread might be cream of spinach or celery and leek (£1.50), there's a daily roast such as leg of lamb, or beef on Sundays (£5.10), and plenty of fresh fish – salmon, baked halibut, lemon sole and smoked haddock (never fried!) from £4.90. To follow there are always nutty meringues, apple cake and Ecclefechan tart (£2) and coffee or chocolate cream gateau (£2.50). Afternoon tea (£3.50) features home-baked scones and lovely fresh flans when the local fruits are in season. Children's portions available; two high-chairs and a changing room with shelf and chair for nursing mothers. Children's play area and a duck pond in the gardens. ***Seats*** *50.* ***Open*** *11-5 (Sat & Sun till 5.30).* ***Closed*** *Nov-mid Mar. No credit cards.*

PEEBLES — Peebles Hotel Hydro — 70% — £81

Tel 01721 720602 **Fax 01721 722999** Map 4 C1 **H**

Innerleithen Road Peebles Scottish Borders EH45 8LX

In Scottish border country, Peebles Hydro is a large Edwardian resort hotel offering a wide range of facilities and beautiful scenery all around. Period elegance survives in the grand public rooms, but Pieter Van Dijk, in charge since 1972, makes sure that his hotel keeps up with the times. This combination of tradition and modernity even shows in the weekend dancing options – ballroom or disco. Families are well catered for, and there are banqueting/conference facilities for 350/450. 24 hr room service. ***Rooms** 137. Garden, croquet, tennis, pitch & putt, putting, riding, indoor swimming pool, gym (no children), squash, sauna, steam room, spa bath, sun beds, solarium, hair salon, children's playroom and playground, games room, snooker, coffee shop (11am-11pm). Amex, Diners, MasterCard,* **VISA**

PETERHEAD — Waterside Inn — 67% — £99

Tel 01779 471121 **Fax 01779 470670** Map 2 D3 **H**

Fraserburgh Road Peterhead Aberdeenshire AB42 7BN

Approaching Peterhead from Aberdeen (A92) turn left and follow signs to St Fergus to find this modern hotel set on the unspoilt north-eastern coast of Scotland and offering a very well-equipped leisure centre and special breaks at various times of the year. Several areas (including restaurant, ballroom and foyer) have recently been refurbished and a creche was being built as we went to press. 40 studio bedrooms in a separate block are compact and functional, while those in the main building are more spacious and luxurious. Banqueting/conferences for 245/200. ***Rooms** 109. Garden, indoor swimming pool, gym, sauna, steam room, spa bath, sun beds, snooker, indoor and outdoor children's play areas. Amex, Diners, MasterCard,* **VISA**

PITLOCHRY — Luggie Restaurant

Tel 01796 472085 Map 3 C4 **JaB**

Rie-Achen Road Pitlochry Perth & Kinross PH16 5AM

For 'Luggie' read milking-pail; the old stone barn in the middle of town, which probably was once a dairy, is now a roomy self-service restaurant with rough-hewn walls and a beamed ceiling. The day starts, naturally, with a hearty Scottish breakfast (£5.50) and all day there are snacks, sandwiches and baked potatoes, variously filled (from £2.95). The lunch selection of main courses (served with potatoes and vegetables £5.50) includes omelettes, breaded haddock and steak pie, and there's a strong vegetarian showing: gypsy hot pot, mushroom stroganoff and vegetable and pasta bake. Home baking includes the usual array of scones, cakes and shortbread, and there's a good selection of children's meals. Book for high tea from 4pm (£6.95) and the evening carvery, Mar-Oct (main dishes from £7.50). Three high-chairs are available and a changing table with nappy dispenser is provided in the disabled toilet. Good area for woodland walks with the family. ***Seats** 80 (+ 80 outside). Open 9-5 (Mar-Oct till 9). Closed last 2 wks Nov & 1st 2 wks Dec. MasterCard,* **VISA**

> Any person using our name to obtain free hospitality is a fraud.
> Proprietors, please inform the police and us.

PORT WILLIAM — Corsemalzie House — 61% — £90

Tel 01988 860254 **Fax 01988 860213** Map 4 A3 **H**

Port William by Newton Stewart Dumfries & Galloway DG8 9RL

The McDougalls have been at Corsemalzie since 1981 but the stone mansion has been in its secluded forty acres of woodland for over a century. The main attraction is fishing, with rights on the renowned Rivers Bladnoch and Tarff as well as the nearby lochs. The comfortable lounges make it an ideal place to relax. Bedrooms are generally of a decent size; all have private bath or shower. ***Rooms** 15. Garden, croquet, putting, fishing, shooting, playground. Closed Feb. Amex, MasterCard,* **VISA**

PORTPATRICK Crown Hotel

Tel 01776 810261 **Fax 01776 810551** Map 4 A2 **P**
North Crescent Portpatrick Stranraer Dumfries & Galloway DG9 8SX

Right down by the harbour, the blue-and-white painted Crown is a bustling, friendly place with a real fire burning even in summer on chilly days and a lively mixture of locals and visiting yachtspeople. Restaurant and bar share the same menu (except for basket meals and sandwiches available in the bar only) and the thing to go for is the seafood. Chef Robert Campbell knows that the lobster and crabs are fresh because he's out in his boat at 6am every morning to collect them; much of the other fish is bought direct from the Fleetwood trawlers that call in at Portpatrick to unload their catches. There are herring aplenty, trout, crab and lobster for a summer salad, and main dishes ranging from cod and chips to "surf with turf", a Crown speciality; for meat-eaters beef hot-pot and savoury pancakes supplement a range of steaks. Smart, appealing bedrooms have loose rugs over polished parquet floors, a variety of good freestanding furniture and attractive floral fabrics, along with pristine bathrooms and the standard modern necessities of direct-dial phone and TV; there is one family suite. *Open 11-11.30.* ***Bar Food*** *12-2 (Sat & Sun till 2.30), 6-10. Free House.* ***Beer*** *S&N 70/- & 80/-, Theakston's. Garden, outdoor eating.* ***Accommodation*** *12 bedrooms, all en suite, £70 (Single £35). Children welcome overnight (under-4s stay free in parents' room, 4-10s £10), additional bed & cot available. MasterCard,* ***VISA***

Our inspectors *never* book in the name of Egon Ronay's Guides. They disclose their identity only if they are considering an establishment for inclusion in the next edition of the Guide.

RATHO Bridge Inn

Tel 0131-333 1320 **Fax 0131-333 3480** Map 3 C6 **P**
27 Baird Road Ratho City of Edinburgh EH28 8RA

Staring life as a farmhouse, and only becoming a hostelry when the Union Canal was built alongside, the Bridge Inn fell into decline along with the canal and was almost derelict when taken over by the irrepressible Ronnie Rusack 25 years ago. Not content with just reviving the Inn, Ronnie has been instrumental in making some seven miles of canal navigable again and runs two restaurant barges (one with a marriage licence!) and numerous pleasure craft including one for the disabled run by a charity Ronnie himself founded. Inside, the original Inn features boarded walls and a collection of the many old bottles found when clearing the canal; a family-orientated extension (the 'Pop Inn') features wheelback chairs and views over the water. The latter's informal menu delivers home-made broth and burgers, roasts and grills throughout the day and decent, locally made puds. From the à la carte menu served lunch and evening in the bar, steaks are a particularly good bet, with Scottish meat cooked in full view on an open grill and a good choice of sauces for the more adventurous. Children have their own special menu of favourites (with the likes of fish fingers, chicken drumsticks and fruit jelly and ice cream), as do the over-60s (with the "Golden Years" menu) should they wish it. There's an adult-powered carousel on the patio, a "pirate boat" play area in the grounds, proper baby-changing and nursing facilities (that come complete with complimentary nappies and baby powder) and plenty of high-chairs and booster seats. There is hardly room to list everything that goes on here but don't miss the "Pumpathon" of classic fire engines that gathers here annually on the first weekend in May. *Open noon-11 (Fri & Sat 11am-12pm, Sun 12.30-11).* ***Bar Food*** *12-8 (Sun from 12.30). Free House.* ***Beer*** *Belhaven 80/- Ale, guest beers. Garden, outdoor eating, children's play area. Amex, Diners, MasterCard,* ***VISA***

We do not accept free meals or hospitality – our inspectors pay their own bills.

RINGFORD Old School Tea Room

Tel 01557 820250 Map 4 B2 JaB
Ringford Dumfries & Galloway DG7 2AL

Home baking comes top of the class at this former school house, right on the A75, run true to form by Isabel Pitcairn. Her scones, cakes and tea cakes make up the 'staffroom specials' on a menu that features both afternoon tea (£1.95) and cream teas (from £2.20). The School Club sandwiches are triple-deckers layered with sliced chicken and ham, or lentil and mushroom paté with tomato and onion (£3.60). There are also some interesting soups like parsnip and potato and yellow split pea and ham served with crusty bread (£1.75), a popular open French Toastie topped with ham, gruyère and a fried egg (£2.85) and baked tatties whose most popular filling is currently haggis and neeps (£3.30). Ask for children's portions; three high-chairs available, and a mother's changing area in Ladies. Easy access for pushchairs and wheelchairs. ***Seats*** *48 (+10 outside).* ***Open*** *10-6.* ***Closed*** *Mon Oct-Mar. No credit cards.*

ST ANDREWS Brambles

Tel 01334 475380 Map 3 D5 JaB
5 College Street St Andrews Fife KY16 9AA

Paul Rowe continues to provide the inspiration at his splendid little eating house that appeals equally to townsfolk, students and tourists. A blackboard lists the daily fare, all fresh and tasty and mainly with a traditional ring: smoked sausage and salami pizza and grilled chicken breast with garlic butter (£5.95) vie for attention alongside the numerous vegetarian options like cashew nut roast and spinach pie served in standard or large portions (£4.25/£4.95). Fish-lovers will go for the kippers, poached salmon and monkfish and halibut with wild mushrooms (£6.25), while for just a snack there are still filled baked tatties (from £1.50) and omelettes; good baking, too, includes up to a daily dozen sponge cakes (from 70p), summer pudding, chocolate mousse and banoffi pie (£1.50-£1.75). There are tables outside in the garden; no smoking within. One booster seat and two clip-on baby seats. Children's portions; bottles and food can be warmed for the littlest ones. ***Seats*** *30 (+ outside).* ***Open*** *9-5, Sun from 12 (Fri & Sat 7.30-9 for 5-course dinner).* ***Closed*** *Sun in Jan/Feb & 2 weeks Christmas. MasterCard,* ***VISA***

ST FILLANS Four Seasons Hotel 60% £80

Tel & Fax 01764 685333 Map 3 C5 HR
St Fillans nr Crieff Perth & Kinross PH6 2N6

This long, low, white hotel, run by the Scott family, stands among beautiful scenery at the head of Loch Earn. Day rooms include a cosy little bar with Oregon pine and natural stone, a mansard-roofed lounge and a tiny library on the first floor. Bedrooms are simple but quite spacious and bright, and most enjoy views over the loch. There are six chalets on the wooded hillside behind the hotel, suitable for couples and small families. Children up to 5 can stay free in parents' room. ***Rooms*** *18. Terrace, fishing, gift shop. Closed mid Dec-Feb. Amex, Diners, MasterCard,* ***VISA***

Restaurant £60

In the dining-room, with fabulous views over the loch, you can enjoy Andrew Scott's good cooking, with lunch and supper from two small but varied à la carte lists, and dinner from a fixed-price menu. Typical choices from his Scottish cuisine include grilled salmon or Loch Earn trout, pink-cooked wood pigeon with mushrooms and whisky, venison sausages with onion gravy, pastry case of monkfish with basil and tomato, fillet of lamb and the classic roast sirloin of beef served with Yorkshire pudding. There are also a couple of vegetarian dishes and a good selection of cheese served with home-made bread and oatcakes. The sweet trolley features traditional British desserts such as lemon tart and apple and cinnamon pie. Light lunches and snacks are served in the bar. ***Seats*** *55. Parties 20. Private Room 16. L 12.15-2.15 D 7-9.30. Set Sun L £13.95 Set D £23.50.*

St Mary's Loch Tibbie Shiels Inn

Tel 01759 42231 Map 4 C1 
St Mary's Loch Scottish Borders TD7 5NE

The Inn itself is a lovely whitewashed cottage with later additions in the glorious Yarrow valley; Tibbie Shiels was the first licensee from 1803 to 1878 and her famously unforgettable name lives on still. It can be recommended for three main things: first, the atmospheric bar, busy with friendly locals and fishing and sailing types, second the quality of the meat dishes (Scottish lamb and Aberdeen Angus beef), and third the situation of the Inn itself on the shores of St. Mary's Loch. The large dining-room overlooks the loch and surrounding hills in this utterly remote and enchanting place. Dishes include chicken liver with port and brandy paté, poached salmon and poacher's venison(!) with seasonal apple and blackberry pie and year-round the Christmassy Cloutie Dumpling to follow. The Tibbie is an excellent place to stop after a sojourn of the Southern Upland Way, with high tea served from 4-6pm and a miniature menu for the minors. Five en suite rooms are available for bed and breakfast (£46). *Open 11-11 (Fri & Sat till midnight, Sun from 12.30).* ***Bar Food*** *12.30-2.30, 6.30-8.30. Free House.* ***Beer*** *Belhaven 80/- Ale, Broughton Greenmantle Ale. Patio & terrace, outdoor eating. Family room. Pub closed Mon & Tue Nov-Mar. MasterCard,* **VISA**

We welcome bona fide complaints and recommendations on the tear-out pages at the back of the Guide for Readers' Comments. They are followed up by our professional team.

Selkirk Philipburn House Hotel

Tel 01750 20747 Map 4 C1 JaB
Linglie Road Selkirk Scottish Borders TD7 5LS

The Hills family's characterful, friendly hotel was due to reopen in January 1997 following major refurbishment which will see some extension to the popular bar with its open fire, garden outlook and outdoor seating in fine weather. Here, Jim Hill's Quick Bite menu includes many old favourites from down the years such as croque monsieur or madame (the latter with prawns) and a 'Tiroler Grostle' of fried potatoes, onions, ham and herbs. Among the desserts could be old-fashioned walnut tart and (not recommended if driving) The Seducer – tiny babas soaked in Italian liqueur with ice creams and sorbets, brandied cherries, whipped cream and praline. They also serve Scottish breakfast and afternoon tea. No smoking. ***Seats*** *50 (+ outside).* ***Open*** *7.30-9.30, 12-2, 3-5 & 7.30-9.30. Amex, MasterCard,* **VISA**

Sheriffmuir Sheriffmuir Inn

Tel 01786 823285 **Fax 01786 823969** Map 3 C5 
Sheriffmuir Dunblane Clackmannanshire FK15 0LN

Built just 6 months before the battle of Sheriffmuir was fought almost literally on its doorstep between the Jacobites and the Hanoverians, the Inn has a wild and lovely location high up in the Ochil Hills, yet it's easy to reach and well-signposted from the main A9. Inside, all is neat and comfortable with and open fire and equally warm welcome from Roger Lee. Opt for the home-made items on brother Peter's daily specials board – Greek lamb casserole, chicken satay and trout with lemon butter sauce. There are always home-made soups, steak and Guinness pie, and chips with haddock for those of more catholic persuasion, with children's portions and vegetarian options always readily available. *Open 11.30-2.30, 5.30-11 (Sat 11.30-11 & Sun 12-11).* ***Bar Food*** *11.30-2.30, 5.30-9 (Sat & Sun 11.30-9). Free House.* ***Beer*** *Marston's Pedigree, Tetley Burton Ale, Arrols 80/- , guest beer. Garden, outdoor eating, children's play area. Family room. MasterCard,* **VISA**

A jug of fresh water!

SKEABOST BRIDGE Skeabost House 60% £94

Tel 01470 532202 **Fax 01470 532454** Map 2 A3 H
Skeabost Bridge by Portree Isle of Skye Highland IV51 9NP

Twelve acres of woodland and gardens surround a former hunting lodge on Loch Snizort. The name Skeabost dates from Viking times, when it meant 'The Sheltered House'. It's a comfortable place, with the same family owners since 1970, and relaxation is easy in the lounges, the flagstoned sun lounge, the 60-seat conservatory, the cosy bar and the billiard room. Pretty bedrooms include one with a four-poster and a few in the nearby Garden House. One is a large family room. The hotel owns eight miles of the River Snizort, which runs through the grounds, and has a boat on a nearby loch. ***Rooms** 26. Garden, golf (9-hole), pitch & putt, fishing, snooker, craft shop. Closed Nov-Mar. MasterCard,* ***VISA***

STONEHAVEN Marine Hotel

Tel 01569 762155 **Fax 01569 766691** Map 3 D4 P
9 The Shorehead Stonehaven Aberdeenshire AB3 2JY

Down by the harbour, the Marine is very pubby with a regularly-changing selection of real ales and the same menu is served in the lounge/bar as in the more family-oriented, first-floor dining-room with its blue nautical decor and waitress service. It carries standard pub fare such as golden fried haddock steaks and salads but it's the exotic blackboard that people come back for: Cajun-blackened halibut, chicken Indienne, Thai curries, baltis and a range of Tex-Mex derivations. Equally popular in summer is the fresh fish and seafood, much of it landed just across from the pub. Six modest but clean bedrooms (the two largest are family rooms with cots available) all have harbour views and are furnished with fitted white melamine units and matching duvets and curtains; they have shower cabinets in the rooms but share two loos. All have phones, televisions and beverage kits. *Open 11-11.45 (Sun from 12).* ***Bar Food** 5-9.30 (in winter till 9). Children welcome overnight (under-3s stay free in parents' room, 3-12s £5). Free House.* ***Beer** Dunnottar Ale (the house brew), Bass, Timothy Taylor Landlord and guest beers. Family room.* ***Accommodation** 6 bedrooms £35 (single £25). MasterCard,* ***VISA***

STORNOWAY Cabarfeidh Hotel 64% £88

Tel 01851 702604 **Fax 01851 705572** Map 2 A2 
Manor Park Stornoway Isle of Lewis Western Isles HSI 2EU

Set amid attractive and peaceful scenery, this early-70s hotel (the name means stag's head) is just a short walk from the Ullapool ferry terminal on the largest of the Outer Hebrides islands. The Viking Bar (with a longship for a counter), a cocktail bar and a restaurant divided into three differently-styled areas comprise the public rooms. Cheerful bedrooms, all en suite (children up to 14 stay free in parents' room). 24hr room service. ***Rooms** 47. Garden, croquet, pitch & putt, putting green, splash pool, gym, sauna, steam room, spa bath, sun beds, beauty & hair salon, playroom, games room, snooker. Amex, Diners, MasterCard,* ***VISA***

STRANRAER North West Castle Hotel 68% £70

Tel 01776 704413 **Fax 01776 702646** Map 4 A2 
Stranraer Dumfries & Galloway DG9 8EH

Tastefully extended since being built in 1820, the hotel stands opposite the ferry port. It was once the home of the Arctic explorer Sir John Ross, whose name is commemorated in the panelled bar, and was the first hotel in the world to have its own indoor curling rink, which now is a major attraction here, with international competitions each year. Bedrooms include six suites, and many rooms have enough space for an extra bed or cots. Conference and banqueting facilities for 100/180; enquire about special arrangements at two local golf courses and nearby squash courts. Children under 14 stay free in their parents' room. Sister establishment to the *Cally Palace Hotel* in Gatehouse of Fleet and *Kirroughtree Hotel*, Newton Stewart. No dogs. ***Rooms** 71. Garden, indoor swimming pool, mini-gym, sauna, spa bath, sun beds, playroom, games room, snooker. MasterCard,* ***VISA***

STRATHBLANE Kirkhouse Inn £65

Tel 01360 770621 **Fax 01360 770896** Map 3 B5
Glasgow Road Strathblane Stirlingshire G63 9AA

At the foot of Campsie Fell on the A81 just south of town this is decidedly more hotel than pub. Choose between the cocktail bar with its plush banquette seating or the large public bar which, despite the usual paraphernalia of amusements, is nonetheless quite civilised. Bedrooms are done out in a variety of pleasant colour schemes and either light or darkwood units; hotel-style en suite facilities run to remote-control TVs, trousers presses and 24 hour room service. Staff are notably friendly. *Bar open 11-11 (Fri & Sat till midnight, Sun from 12.30). Free House.* ***Beer*** *Maclay's 80/-. Garden, beauty salon.* ***Accommodation*** *15 rooms, all en suite, £65 (single £45). Children welcome overnight (under-12s free if sharing parents' room), additional bed & cot available. Amex, Diners, Mastercard,* ***VISA***

STRATHCARRON Carron Restaurant JaB

Tel 01520 722488 Map 2 B3
Cam-Allt Strathcarron Highland IV54 8XY

Standing right by the A890, Seamus and Sarah Doyle's agreeable modern restaurant has spectacular west-facing views out over Loch Carron, and on fine evenings the sunsets alone are well worth the trip. Open in season for 11 hours a day, they serve tea, coffees, snacks and sandwiches (tuna, smoked salmon or prawn, and toasted sandwiches from £1.95), grilled sausages home-cooked ham or roast beef salad (from £4.75). Seafood from the loch is the house speciality, as often as not chargrilled on the barbecue; queenie scallops in garlic butter (£4.95) and whole langoustines (£5.95/£11.95) are supplied by the local fishermen, plus there's a selection of Scottish steaks, salmon, pork chops and venison, vege-kebabs, beef kebab and jiggered chops (£5.75-£7.95) all cooked to order in front of you. All the desserts are £2.95 and could include strawberry pavlova, apple pie, crème caramel and sherry trifle. Other delectable home baking includes scones, carrot cake, gingerbread, shortbread and Scotch pancakes with local honey (from 85p), and there's an excellent selection of cheeses, all produced locally. Children's portions and children's meals available all day; one high-chair, two booster seats and the combined Ladies and disabled toilet has a chair for baby-changing. Safe, large grassed area for letting off steam. No smoking. ***Seats*** *45.* ***Open*** *10.30-9.15.* ***Closed*** *Sun & end Oct-Easter. Amex, MasterCard,* ***VISA***

> If we recommend meals in a hotel a *separate* entry is usually made for its restaurant. Pub and inn entries include bar food details where recommended.

STROMNESS Hamnavoe Restaurant JaB

Tel 01856 850606 Map 2 C1
35 Graham Place Stromness Orkney KW16 3BY

Chris Thomas's attractive little restaurant, in an alley off the High Street, specialises in fish and seafood purchased fresh from the fishing boats at Stromness harbour. There's a good choice ranging from creamy fish soup, queen scallops with prawns in puff pastry, and Orkney crab in whisky sauce wrapped in smoked salmon (£2.50-£4.25) to start, followed by baked monkfish wrapped in smoked bacon and fillet of salmon steamed with Oriental herbs (from £7.50); non-fish alternatives include pork fillet with tapenade in creamy tomato and pepper sauce and vegetable strudel pancake baked in puff pastry, topping out with grilled Orkney fillet steak (£11). Good home-made bread and desserts like dark and white chocolate terrine, Irish cream cheesecake and cloutie dumpling (from £2.50) are indicative of the excellent value for money, an object lesson to many in far more accessible locales. Families are welcomed and children's portions are available, but there are no special facilities. ***Seats*** *36.* ***Open*** *D only 7-11.* ***Closed*** *Mon & mid Oct-mid Apr (except 25 Dec). No credit cards.*

SWINTON Wheatsheaf Hotel

Tel & Fax 01890 860257 Map 3 D6 **P**

Main Street Swinton Berwickshire Scottish Borders TD11 3JJ

The Wheatsheaf, dominating this simple Scots farming hamlet six miles north of Coldstream, overlooks the plain little village green and has very limited parking; at busy periods the main street is full up with cars. This is very much a dining pub with a very well-regarded restaurant, the Four Seasons, and it's wise to book even for bar meals. The emphasis is on fresh produce with a menu reproduced on one blackboard, daily specials listed on another and lots of seafood. Scallops on a saffron-scented salad followed by whole sea bass with fennel and prawns typify the style; alternatives might include quail in Thai dressing, egg Florentine, pork and apricot stroganoff and courgette and aubergine provençale. Freshly baked wheaten rolls are presented as a matter of course, and butter comes in a slab on a saucer; salads are imaginative and fresh. There are four tidy bedrooms fitted with TVs; one has an en suite bathroom, and two more have showers. ***Bar Food*** *12-2, 6-9.30 (Sun 12.30-2.15, 6.30-8.30). Free House.* ***Beer*** *Broughton Greenmantle Ale, guest beer. Garden, outdoor eating, children's play area.* ***Accommodation*** *4 bedrooms, 3 en suite, £64 (single £42). Children welcome overnight (under-5s stay free in parents' room, 5-10s £7), additional bed & cot available. Pub closed all day Mon, Sun night in winter, two weeks Feb and last week Oct. MasterCard,* ***VISA***

TAYVALLICH Tayvallich Inn

Tel 01546 870282 Map 3 A5 **P**

Tayvallich by Lochgilphead Argyll & Bute PA31 8PR

This simple, white-painted dining pub is in a marvellously pretty location at the centre of a scattered village stretching round a natural harbour at the top of Loch Sween. Sit outside, on the front terrace, at one of the five parasolled picnic tables, and enjoy the view of a dozen little boats, and low wooded hills fringing the lochside; the word Tayvallich means "the house in the pass". Inside the bar is tile-floored with raffia-back chairs and little wood tables, the dining-room similar, but spacious and relaxing, with a woodburning stove, attractive dresser, and bentwood chairs around scrubbed pine dining tables. The freshest local seafood is so local that oysters come from just yards away in Loch Sween itself, and 'hand-dived' scallops from the Sound of Jura just round the coast. Their seafood platter must surely be among the very best in the whole of the British Isles, well worth the long, seemingly endless descent down the one-track, bluebell-lined road (B8025) from Crinan. There are plenty of non-fish alternatives and half-portions in abundance for the kids; puddings such as chocolate nut slab and banoffi pie are all made by tireless landlady Patricia Grafton. The whole atmosphere is very informal and relaxed; holidaymakers turn up in shorts and babies are commendably tolerantly treated, with clip-on chairs and specially rustled-up toddler food and chips. *Open 11-2.30, 5-11 (Fri & Sat till 1am, Sun till 12, and all day July & August).* ***Bar Food*** *12-2, 6-8 (restaurant meals till 9, weekends only in winter). Free House.* ***Beer*** *Tetley. Patio/grassy foreshore, outdoor eating. Inn closed all Mon Nov-Easter. MasterCard,* ***VISA***

> We endeavour to be as up-to-date as possible, but inevitably some changes to data and key personnel may occur at restaurants and hotels after the Guide goes to press. Prices should also be taken as indications rather than firm quotes.

TROON Marine Highland Hotel 67% £146

Tel 01292 314444 **Fax 01292 316922** Map 4 A1 **H**

Crosbie Road Troon South Ayrshire KA10 6HE

This handsome Victorian sandstone structure overlooks the 18th fairway of Royal Troon championship golf course. Accommodation options are standard, de luxe or top-of-the-range Ambassador suites. Children up to 18 share parents' room free. Leave the A77 and follow the B789 to Troon. Scottish Highland Hotels. ***Rooms*** *72. Indoor swimming pool, gym, squash, sauna, steam room, spa bath, sun beds, beauty salon. Amex, Diners, MasterCard,* ***VISA***

TURRIFF — Towie Tavern

P

Tel 01888 511201 **Fax 01651 872464** Map 2 D3
Auchterless nr Turriff Aberdeenshire AB53 8EP

A favourite for its satisfying, wholesome food, this is a roadside pebbledash pub on the A497, some four miles south of Turriff and a short distance from the National Trust's 13th century Fyvie Castle. Seafood is featured at the Towie and the menu changes monthly, with daily blackboard specials; the 'Fisherman's choice' offers whatever is available that day with first-class goujons of lemon sole, coquilles of scallops and monkfish Mornay, and smoked chicken and Waldorf salad for the less fishy-minded. Spinach and vegetable crepes and home-made sticky toffee pudding complete the altogether rosy picture. Facilities for children include an outdoor play area. *Open 11-2.30, 6-12 (Sat 11-12, Sun 12-11).* ***Bar Food*** *12-2, 6-9.30 (Sun till 9). Free House.* ***Beer*** *Theakston's, guest beer. Terrace, outdoor eating. MasterCard,* ***VISA***

TWEEDSMUIR — Crook Inn — 59% — £52

H

Tel 01899 880272 **Fax 01899 880294** Map 4 C1
Tweedsmuir nr Biggar Peeblesshire Scottish Borders ML12 6QN

This famous old drovers' inn stands on the A710 Moffat to Edinburgh road in glorious Tweed valley countryside with a strange but winning amalgam of old stone-flagged farmers' bar and 1930s' ocean liner-style lounges. Burns wrote *Willie Wastle's Wife* in what is now the bar, and locally-born John Buchan set many of his novels in the area. Neat bedrooms are simple in their appointments, with no TVs or telephones to interrupt splendid solitude. A craft centre (glass-making a speciality) has recently been created from the old stable block, enforcing the Crook's claim to be Scotland's oldest licensed inn. New owners as we went to press. *Open 11-12 (Sun 11-11). Free House.* ***Beer*** *Broughton Greenmantle Ale. Garden. Family room.* ***Accommodation*** *8 rooms, all en suite, £52 (single £36). Children welcome overnight, under-12s stay free in parents' room), additional bed & cot available. Amex, Diners, MasterCard,* ***VISA***

ULLAPOOL — Ceilidh Place — £110

Tel 01854 612103 **Fax 01854 612886** Map 2 B2
West Argyle Street Ullapool Wester Ross Highland IV26 2TY

This row of whitewashed cottages does not really have the atmosphere of a pub or an inn and is impossible to classify, being a glorious mixture of arts centre, hotel, coffee shop and restaurant. In the coffee shop by day there's counter service of a range of home-made goodies like soup, filled rolls and baked potatoes, nut roast, haddock and chips, chicken and ham pie, Bakewell tart, scones and carrot cake. From early evening there's table service and a printed menu from which you can have just a single dish or a more formal meal in the conservatory area with its white-clothed tables. Peppered mackerel fillets, Loch Broom mussels and Arbroath smokies are typically fishy dishes, with local venison, lemon chicken and prize-winning haggis for carnivores and half a dozen vegetarian alternatives. Thirteen spotless bedroom (three not en suite) are simply but appealingly appointed, some with dark-stained fitted units, some with the odd antique and most with beamed ceilings; all the bathrooms have tubs with hand-held shower attachments. The first-floor residents' lounge with large windows on two sides is quite delightful; a separate Club House offers budget accommodation with bunk beds and communal showers, and live entertainment in the summer months. Their other establishment called John Maclean's General Merchants, on Shore Street down by the harbour, is a delicatessen, bakery and general store with a first-floor coffee shop run on much the same lines. *Open 11-11 (Sun from 12.30). Food 10-9.30. Free House.* ***Beer*** *McEwan's 80/-, Orkney Dark Island, Belhaven Light. Outdoor eating.* ***Accommodation*** *13 bedrooms, 10 en suite, £110 (single £55). Children welcome overnight, additional bed (from £6) & cot available free. Amex, Diners, MasterCard,* ***VISA***

WEEM Ailean Chraggan Hotel

Tel 01887 820346 **Fax 01887 820327** Map 3 C4 **P**
Weem by Aberfeldy Perth & Kinross PH15 2LD

Beautifully set against a steep woodland backdrop and with two acres of gardens overlooking the Tay this is a delightful little cottage inn. For over thirty years now Alastair Gillespie and family have produced simple, well-cooked meals highlighted by superb local seafood; try the Loch Etive mussels, served in huge steaming portions with garlic bread, or the Sound of Jura prawn platter. Bedrooms are equally commendable: spacious and light with nice pieces of old furniture, armchairs and, in two rooms, small dressing areas. All are equipped with TVs, hairdryers and tea/coffee making facilities. Ask for one of the front bedrooms, which have inspiring views looking south across the river. Patio and lawned garden. *Open 11-11.* ***Bar Food*** *12-2, 6.30-9 (Sat till 9.30). No real ales. Garden, outdoor eating, children's play area.* ***Accommodation*** *3 bedrooms, all en suite, £56 (single £28). Children welcome overnight (half price), additional bed & cot available. Closed 1 & 2 Jan, 25 & 26 Dec. MasterCard,* ***VISA***

WHITEHOUSE Old School Tea Room

Tel 01880 730215 Map 3 B6 **JaB**
Whitehouse nr Tarbert Argyll & Bute PA29 6XR

Five miles south of Tarbert on the A83, Jan Mylet's neat little tea room has a well-established reputation for good baking. Savoury choices throughout the day include sandwiches and rolls, filled croissants and jacket potatoes (£2.50), a vegetarian soup (such as minestrone – £1.30), quiche and salad, and light lunch dishes such as mushroom lattice (£4.50) and poached salmon steak (£6) both served with rolls and gewnerous salads. There's rich butterscotch fudge or spicy prune cake for pudding or just a snack, as well as dainty meringues and 'creamy things' from 70p. Children's portions are available and tables out on the lawn in summer. Unlicensed. ***Seats*** *30.* ***Open*** *11-7.30.* ***Closed*** *Tue & Nov-Easter. No credit cards.*

Wales

The addresses of establishments in the following former **Counties** now include their new Unitary Authorities:

Clwyd
Conwy, Denbighshire, Flintshire, Wrexham

Dyfed
Ceredigion, Carmarthenshire, Pembrokeshire

Gwent
Monmouthshire, Torfaen, Newport, Caerphilly, Blaenau Gwent

Gwynedd
the new Gwynedd, Isle of Anglesey

Mid Glamorgan
Bridgend, Rhondda Cynon Taff, Merthyr Tydfil

South Glamorgan
Vale of Glamorgan, Cardiff

West Glamorgan
Swansea, Neath & Port Talbot

Powys remains the same

ABERAERON Hive On The Quay

Tel 01545 570445 Map 9 B4 JaB
Cadwgan Place Aberaeron Ceredigion SA46 0BT

Everything is home-made at the Holegate family's absolutely delightful café-restaurant, which opens on to the courtyard of an old harbour wharf where their own boat lands the catch of the day. Well into its third decade, this is a dedicated family enterprise comprising also a honey-bee exhibition and shop, a kiosk selling the renowned honey ice cream and a fresh fish shop. The eating possibilities here are equally varied, from cakes and sandwiches to grilled local mackerel (£3.50), Cardigan Bay shell-on prawns (£2.75) and freshly-landed lobster and crab, all with an array of salads, self-served from the counter at lunchtime. All day there are bara brith and honey spice cake, banana sandwiches and boiled egg and soldiers for the children at tea-time. Organic flour is used in the baking, cheeses selected from local farmhouse sources, and puddings like chocolate truffle pie and raspberry and almond tart (from £2.75) as well as the honey and hazelnut ice cream and specialist sundaes are home-made and quite delicious. Suppers, waitress-served from 6pm in summer, offer such delights as Provençal fish soup with rouille (£3.95), chicken and spinach terrine (£3.25), caramelised onion tart (£6.50) and Welsh paella (£9.50). A children's hot menu is served from 6pm (in season) and children's portions are available. Four high-chairs are provided and there's a safe walled courtyard in which children can feel free of any restrictions. Children may also be fascinated by the exhibition (admission fee charged, open 11-1 & 2-5 from Spring Bank Holiday-mid Sept) with its observation hives and instructional video. ***Seats*** *60 (+10 outside).* ***Open*** *10.30-5 (Jul & Aug 10-9).* ***Closed*** *mid Sep-spring Bank Holiday. MasterCard,* ***VISA***

ABERDOVEY Penhelig Arms Hotel £68

Tel 01654 767215 **Fax 01654 767690** Map 8 C3 
Aberdovey Gwynedd LL35 0LT

Built in the early 1700s as Y Dafarn Fach (The Little Inn) and for generations an integral part of the village's history. The black-and-white painted inn stands right on the main road (A493) with unrivalled views across the Dyfi estuary to Ynyslas. In front, now the tiny car park and sun terrace, was a shipbuilder's yard at the turn of the century, while behind, the Towyn to Machynlleth train rumbles out of a tunnel to the request stop at Penhelig Halt. For such a narrow site the Penhelig Arms utilises every square inch of available space and packs in a wealth of charm under the ever-present guidance of proprietors Robert and Sally Hughes. Its popularity at lunchtime ensures a regular overflow from bar to dining-room. Menus are updated daily, offering the likes of freshly-cut sandwiches, leek, bacon and broccoli soup, lamb curry and steak and mushroom pie; plus creamy fish and prawn pie, monkfish and salmon with hollandaise, treacle tart and chocolate roulade. Quality and price move up a gear at dinner. Sunday lunchtime sees a reduced bar menu as the fixed-price menu (£11.50) is always popular. In addition to real ales there's a range of house wines from an enthusiast's cellar; champagne at £3 a glass isn't offered everywhere! Care and attention to detail has gone into ensuring residents' every comfort in a relaxed atmosphere that contrives to make one feel immediately at home. What the smaller bedrooms lack in space they make up for in appealing interior design, careful addition of up-to-date comforts (TV, telephone to hairdryers and quality toiletries) and immaculately-kept en suite bathrooms. All but one have a share of the view, one of the finest of any hotel in Wales, and three superior rooms have a little extra space with easy chairs and super little front-facing balconies. It goes almost without saying that a splendid Welsh breakfast will set you up for the day's touring, sightseeing or just lazing around which lies ahead. *Open 11-3, 6-11 (Sun 12-3, 7-10.30).* ***Bar Food*** *12-2, 7-9. Free House.* ***Beer*** *Tetley Bitter, Burton, guest beer. Garden, outdoor eating.* ***Accommodation*** *10 bedrooms, all en suite, £68-£78 (single £39). Children welcome overnight (free if sharing parents' room), additional bed & cot available. Closed 25 & 26 Dec. MasterCard,* ***VISA***

A jug of fresh water!

ABERDOVEY Trefeddian Hotel 60% £90

Tel 01654 767213 **Fax 01654 767777** Map 8 C3 H
Aberdovey Gwynedd LL35 0SB

Standing in splendid isolation above the A493 half a mile north of Aberdovey, Trefeddian has been the home of the Cave-Brown-Cave family for over 70 years. Guests return year after year to enjoy both the tranquillity of the location and the abundance of outdoor activities in the area. Best of the neat, practical bedrooms are those newly upgraded at the front, several with balconies from which to enjoy south-facing views over the Aberdovey links course to the sweep of Cardigan Bay beyond. Self-catering accommodation is also available in a house, flat and bungalow. Family facilities include three family rooms, children's playroom and playground, and high teas in the dining-room at 5.30pm. ***Rooms*** *46. Garden, indoor swimming pool, splash pool, tennis, pitch & putt, solarium, snooker. Closed 2 Jan-6 Mar. MasterCard,* ***VISA***

ABERGAVENNY Llanwenarth Arms Hotel £59

Tel 01873 810550 **Fax 01873 811880** Map 9 D5 I
Brecon Road Abergavenny Monmouthshire NP8 1EP

A refined roadside inn (on the A40) between Abergavenny and Crickhowell, standing on an escarpment above the Usk valley. Chef/landlord D'Arcy McGregor's creative cooking leaves little to chance, his bar menus making full use of the best local produce available. The seasonally-changed main menu is served throughout the two bars, family conservatory dining area and splendid summer terrace set some 70 feet above the river with views across to Sugar Loaf Mountain. Smoked trout salad, fresh pasta, poached salmon, king prawns in a Chinese-style sauce, goujons of hake, chicken wrapped in Parma ham, steaks and pan-fried venison with a port and redcurrant sauce give the style; home-made puds range from profiteroles to waffles and bread-and-butter pudding (served with brown-bread ice cream for the indulgent). Cauliflower and ham soup, smoked salmon and fresh asparagus, baked sea bass with spring onions and ginger might feature as daily specials. Residents enjoy the use of their own lounge, and a Victorian-style conservatory furnished with comfortable cane furniture. Bedrooms, approached by way of a sheltered courtyard, are attractively furnished and immaculately kept, each one enjoying its fair share of the view. TVs, telephones, trouser presses, tea/coffee making facilities and hairdryers are all standard; bathrooms also have over-bath showers and ample supplies of toiletries. Salmon and trout fishing for residents. *Open 11-3, 6-11 (Sun 12-2, 7-10.30).* ***Bar Food*** *12-2 (till 1.30 Sun), 7-10 (Sun 7-8.15). Free House.* ***Beer*** *Bass, Ruddles County. Patio, outdoor eating. Family room.* ***Accommodation*** *18 bedrooms, all en suite, £59 (single £39). Children welcome overnight (under-16s half-price), additional bed & cot available (£5). No dogs. Amex, Diners, MasterCard,* ***VISA***

Any person using our name to obtain free hospitality is a fraud.
Proprietors, please inform the police and us.

ABERGORLECH Black Lion

Tel 01558 685271 Map 9 B5 
Abergorlech nr Carmarthen Carmarthenshire SA32 7SN

At the heart of one of Wales's best-kept villages, the white-painted Black Lion stands between a tiny stone chapel and the Cothi River bridge; private fishing beats are nearby. The single bar with flagstone floors and high settles leads to a flat-roofed dining extension. On the main menu, pink trout, fillet steaks, boeuf bourguignon and generous salads satisfy the heartiest appetites, while blackboard daily specials might feature lasagne, butterfly king prawns or vegetable lasagne. Opposite the pub, a scenic riverside garden with picnic tables features regular summer barbecues. Children welcome. *Open 11.30-3.30, 7-11 (from 6.30 in summer), Sun 12-3, 7-10.30.* ***Bar Food*** *12-2, 7-9 (snacks only Mon lunch, no food Mon Eve, except Bank Holidays). Free House.* ***Beer*** *Worthington, guest beer. Riverside garden, outdoor eating. Amex, MasterCard,* ***VISA***

ABERSOCH — Porth Tocyn Hotel — 69% — £90

Tel 01758 713303 **Fax 01758 713538** Map 8 B3 HR
Bwlchtocyn Abersoch Gwynedd LL53 7BU

Run in commendable style since 1948 by the Fletcher Brewer family, the hotel has gained a reputation for attentive hospitality. Once a row of lead-miners' cottages, it stands high above Cardigan Bay; it's about 2½ miles south of Abersoch, through the hamlets of Sarn Bach and Bwlchtocyn. The chintzy interlinked lounges contribute just the right degree of homeliness. Bedrooms, though generally small, are individually furnished in a similar style, many with restful sea views (these rooms attract a small supplement), all with private bathrooms and showers. Families with children are well catered for (children stay free in parents' room) – their 'useful information for families' info sheet is particularly user-friendly in setting out the aims and expectations of 'a sophisticated hotel geared to the needs of adults with children in tow'. Flexibility is the key here: breakfast, available '8.30am to 12-ish', may also be served in the room. ***Rooms** 17. Garden, tennis, children's playroom. Closed mid Nov-week before Easter. MasterCard,* **VISA**

Restaurant — £60

The focal point of Louise Fletcher Brewer's self-styled 'dinner party cooking' is her short-choice two- or five-course dinner menu that is changed completely each day. In practice, the style is less 'cordon bleu' than you might expect, with baked mushroom strudel on a chili coriander sauce, asparagus mousse with warm salad, balsamic vinegar and toasted pine nuts, roast pork fillet in Calvados with purées of apple and strawberry, and steamed plaice on a lobster bisque with sautéed mussels all typical dishes. There's always an inter-course fresh soup (perhaps celery and Stilton or tomato and basil) and the nursery puddings are a popular dessert, especially at the all-you-can-eat hot and cold buffet on Sundays. Welsh and other cheeses and coffee with home-made petits fours. There's a fair wine list, though only the house selections have tasting notes; £21 for a decent house champagne is excellent value. Lunch is casual, maybe alfresco by the pool. High tea for youngsters is 5-6pm. ***Seats** 50. Parties 20. L 12.30-2 D 7.30-9.30. Set L (Sun) £15.50 Set D £19/£25.50.*

ABERSOCH — Riverside Hotel — 59% — £70

Tel 01758 712419 **Fax 01758 712671** Map 8 B3 
Abersoch Gwynedd LL53 7HW

John and Wendy Bakewell, here since 1967, say that like monks they took a solemn vow of hospitality when they made the move from farming all that time ago. Family-friendly in every respect, they have remained true to their word, as their many returning visitors will attest. An acre of garden stretches out along the bank of the River Soch which is a haven for all manner of marine life. Bedrooms are neat, modern and functional. Reduced rates for children, with many facilities supplied including cots, high-chairs, a laundry room and high tea served at 5.30pm. No dogs. ***Rooms** 12. Garden, indoor swimming pool (open Apr-end of Sept). Closed mid Nov-Apr. Amex, Diners, MasterCard,* **VISA**

AFON-WEN — Pwll Gwyn Hotel

Tel 01352 720227 Map 8 C2 
Afon-wen nr Mold Flintshire CH7 5UB

Formerly a 17th-century coaching inn of some renown with an unusual remodelled Victorian frontage (on the A541), Pwll Gwyn's fortunes are being revived today by enthusiastic and energetic tenants Andrew and Karen Davies. Andrew provides the brains (and the brawn) behind an intelligently run kitchen whose output is much dictated by his shopping from Liverpool's markets. Best bets for the bar food, therefore, come from the daily blackboard: avocado, chicken and curry mayonnaise, liver and smoked bacon with gravy and potato cake or fillet of cod with lemon pepper coating. Desserts, too, are impressive: cappuccino cake and toffee crunch cheesecake feature on a long list of home-made delights. More substantial cooking with a classical base comes in the form of weekly-changing specials available in the two separate dining-rooms (one for non-smokers); special event evenings (Italian, Chinese, Indian). *Open 12-3, 7-11, Sun 12-3, 5-10.30 (from 7 in winter).* ***Bar Food*** *12-2.30, 7-9.30.* ***Beer*** *Greenalls. Garden, outdoor eating. Family room. MasterCard,* ***VISA***

Barry — Mount Sorrel Hotel — 59% — £70

Tel 01446 740069 **Fax 01446 746600** Map 9 C6 **H**
Porthkerry Road Barry Vale of Glamorgan CF62 7XY

Converted from two Victorian houses some 30 years ago, with more recent additions for extra accommodation, meeting rooms and leisure facilities. Comfortable day rooms (named after Welsh castles), very acceptable bedrooms (children up to 16 stay free when sharing with parents); two suites have interconnecting rooms and six other rooms are suitable for families, three with bunk beds. ***Rooms*** *43. Indoor swimming pool, keep-fit equipment, sauna. Amex, Diners, MasterCard,* ***VISA***

Beaumaris — Bulkeley Hotel — 59% — £85

Tel 01248 810415 **Fax 01248 810146** Map 8 B1 **H**
Castle Street Beaumaris Isle of Anglesey LL58 8AW

A sturdy Georgian building opposite the pier with splendid views across the Menai Straits to Snowdonia. Bedrooms generally have a somewhat faded elegance, though several have lately been modernised; included are studios, some suites and two large family rooms. Children up to 12 stay free in parents' room. Plenty of parking. ***Rooms*** *42. Garden, sauna, steam room, spa bath, solarium, beauty salon, news kiosk, night club. Amex, MasterCard,* ***VISA***

Bodfari — Dinorben Arms

Tel 01745 710309 **Fax 01745 710580** Map 8 C2 **P**
Bodfari nr Denbigh Denbighshire LL16 4DA

The 17th-century Dinorben Arms is off the A541 (taking the B5429 and sign to Tremeirchion). David Rowlands has injected a new lease of life to this well-known old pub with much refurbishment undertaken and a variety of menus on offer. The emphasis is still very much on home-cooking and the standard is unlikely to change as long as Irene and Mary are in the kitchen (they've been there for 34 years between them!). Lunchtimes concentrate on the self-served smörgåsbord and in the evenings both cold starters and sweets are mostly served buffet-style in the Well Bar. The 'Chicken Rough', originally presented to be eaten with fingers, lives on since being introduced in 1961; the Farmhouse Buffet (Wed/Thu) and Carverboard (Fri/Sat) are more recent and very popular evening additions. Special dishes nightly may include rack of Welsh lamb or grilled halibut, however there are plenty more snacky items, children's and vegetarian choices (perhaps aubergine moussaka). Families are well catered for in their own room and on the smart, flower-decked, tiered patios, and at the top of the extensive hillside gardens is a children's adventure play area; changing unit in Ladies. For dedicated drinkers there are four real ales, eight wines by the glass, 25 cognacs and over 120 whiskies. *Open 12-3.30, 6-11 (Sun 12-10.30).* ***Bar Food*** *12-3, 6-10.30 (Sun 12-10.30). Free House.* ***Beer*** *John Smith's, Webster's Yorkshire Bitter, Ruddles County, guest beer. Garden, outdoor eating, children's play area. Family room. MasterCard,* ***VISA***

Burton Green — Golden Grove Inn

Tel 01244 570445 Map 8 D2 **P**
Llyndir Lane Burton Green Rossett Wrexham LL12 0AS

Best found by turning off the B5445 at Rossett, by the signs to Llyndyr Hall; at the end of a lane seemingly leading nowhere stands a group of black and white timber-framed buildings which comprise the pub and its many outhouses. Within is a treasure trove of antiquity with some splendid 14th-century oak beams and magical old inglenooks and fireplaces. A modern extension housing a carvery dining-room leads to drinking patios and a large, safe garden replete with swings and wooden play equipment, justifiably popular in the summer months; regular barbecues. Live jazz Thursday and weekend evenings. *Open 12-3, 6-11, (Sat 12-11, Sun 12-4, 7-10.30).* ***Beer*** *Marston's. Garden, children's play area. MasterCard,* ***VISA***

CARDIFF — Chapter Kitchen

Tel 01222 372756 Map 9 D6 JaB
Chapter Arts Centre Market Road Canton Cardiff CF5 1QE

The Chapter Arts Centre comprises an art gallery, theatre, two cinemas and this minimalist all-day café, whose metal chairs and hardwood tables set up constant echoes. The mainly wholefood-oriented menu is about 60% vegetarian with hearty soups such as spinach and butter bean (£1.20), hefty salads, Glamorgan sausages (£3.20) and carrot and walnut burgers alongside the likes of aubergine pie, chick pea and courgette bake and chicken tandoori (all under £3.50 with salad included). There are also filled baps and baked potatoes, flapjacks and cheesecake. On weekends you could stop in for tapas (prices from £1.20) which have recently proved highly popular: patatas bravas, meatballs, kidneys in sherry, gambas and cured ham. Espresso coffee, herb teas, cans of Spanish beer and wine by the glass are among beverage alternatives. Half portions for children. One high-chair and one booster seat, and a separate mother and baby room are provided, and there's a spacious, safe garden to run about in. ***Seats*** *80.* ***Open*** *9am-10pm.* ***Closed*** *Bank Holidays & 10 days Christmas. No credit cards.*

CARDIFF — Harry Ramsden's

Tel 01222 463334 Map 9 D6 JaB
Landsea House Stuart Street Cardiff CF1 6BW

Facing the inner harbour of the new Cardiff Bay development, Harry's first Welsh outlet is in a prime spot (Techniquest hands-on science museum is right next door) and has already scored a notable, family-size hit. The prime fish fillets are exemplary and the chips pass muster; adults meeting Harry's Challenge (a whole haddock fillet with chips and all the trimmings – £10.95) receive a signed certificate – and a free sweet! A Postman Pat menu delivers speedily to the youngest diners, while 8-12s receive an Investigator pack to help them sort out who's been nicking the chips. Mealtimes run at a high decibel count from the voluble kids and less-than-background music; excursion leaders can expect to wait their turn in the bar for a summons to an available table and to queue again at the cash desk when the juniors have had their fill. ***Seats*** *200. Open 11.30am-11pm (Sun & Bank Holidays till 9.30). Closed 25 & 26 Dec. Amex, MasterCard,* ***VISA***

CARDIFF — Quality Friendly Hotel 60% £76

Tel 01222 529988 **Fax 01222 529977** Map 9 D6 H
Merthyr Road Tongwynlais Cardiff CF4 7LD

The first hotel in the group to be opened in Wales lives up to its friendly image. Decent airy bedrooms are well stocked with practical facilities and extras such as satellite TV and mini-bars. Premier rooms, with more space for families, have sitting areas, extra work space and fax points. Adjacent to the vast A470 interchange; follow signs to Tongwynlais and business park from the M4 at J32. Children up to 14 stay free in parents' room. ***Rooms*** *95. Indoor swimming pool, gym, sauna, steam room, spa bath, solarium, playroom. Amex, Diners, MasterCard,* ***VISA***

CHEPSTOW — Castle View Hotel

Tel 01291 620349 **Fax 01291 627397** Map 9 D6 P
16 Bridge Street Chepstow Monmouthshire NP6 5EZ

Four miles from the M4 Junction 22, this 300-year-old house was constructed mostly using stone from Chepstow Castle which commands the huge riverbank opposite. Ivy-covered and genuinely welcoming, it's immaculately kept by Martin and Vicky Cardale. The original stone walls and timbers enhance the setting for a snack. Through both light and 'bigger bites', the bar menu encompasses omelettes and steak sandwiches, vegetable crêpes and hazelnut and mushroom fettuccine, with turkey, ham and sweetcorn or steak, kidney and Tetley pie as carnivorous alternatives. In the dining-room, an evening table d'hote is supplemented by a short à la carte on which the local Wye salmon is a regular feature. Up-to-date bedrooms with mahogany furniture and en suite bathrooms (one with shower only); radio and TV (with use of videos), mini-bars, direct-dial phones and beverage trays are standard throughout. The cottage suite (sleeping up to four) incorporates a quiet residents' lounge;

overlooking the garden – a restful spot – are two spacious family rooms sleeping up to 4. *Open 12-2.30, 6-11 (Sun 12-2.30, 7-10.30).* ***Bar Food*** *12-2.30, 6.30-9.30 (no food Sun eve). Free House.* ***Beer*** *Tetley, guest beer. Garden, outdoor eating.* ***Accommodation*** *13 bedrooms, all en suite, £49.50-£57.50 (single £37.50). Children welcome overnight (under-12s stay free in parents' room, 12-16s half-price) additional bed & cot available. Amex, MasterCard,* ***VISA***

CHEPSTOW Marriott St Pierre Hotel 70% £138

Tel 01291 625261 **Fax 01291 629975** Map 9 D6 **H**
St Pierre Park Chepstow Monmouthshire NP6 6YA

St Pierre Country Club enjoys an enviable reputation for its golfing (two 18-hole courses) and extensive recreational facilities set in 400 acres of mature parkland just two miles from the first Severn Bridge (leave the M4 at J21 following the M48 to J2, then take the A48 towards Newport). The 14th-century mansion at the hotel's heart includes a spacious and well-lit foyer and reception lounge, beyond which you can relax in a fine oak-panelled bar and lounge over-looking the final greens. Access for banqueting, conferences (for up to 220) and ever-present golf societies is kept sensibly apart, through the Trophy Bar. Poolside grill and sports bar and the self-contained leisure centre are interconnected. A varied choice of bedrooms ranges from ground-floor courtyard suites and mansion bedrooms overlooking the park to a dozen detached lodges, with from three to six bedrooms, in St Pierre's Lakeland Village, which is much favoured for golf or house parties and family get-togethers. Public areas and bedrooms have both benefited from a recent refurbishment programme. Children up to 16 years are accommodated free in parents' room. ***Rooms*** *143. Garden, croquet, tennis, golf (2x18), indoor swimming pool, gym, squash, sauna, steam room, spa bath, solarium, bowls, play area, snooker, beauty salon, kiosk. Amex, Diners, MasterCard,* ***VISA***

CILGERRAN Castle Kitchen

Tel 01239 615055 Map 9 B4 **JaB**
High Street Cilgerran nr Cardigan Pembrokeshire SA43 2SG

A pretty, white-painted corner café at the top of the lane leading to Cilgerran Castle, a listed monument. Home baking includes Welsh cakes, bara brith, cream horns, extra-large éclairs, carrot cake, fruit cake and hot chocolate fudge cake. Choose these individually, or go for the cream tea with scones for £2. Toasted snacks and crumpets accompany morning coffee, and the £7.75 luncheon menu, which always includes a roast (not just Sundays), is an alternative to the short selection of salads, home-baked quiche and omelettes such as cheese and tomato (£3.85) served with sauté potatoes. A set-price supper menu provides three courses for £13.75 with alternative dishes à la carte. Children's favourites are readily available (as are children's portions). One high-chair. ***Seats*** *25.* ***Open*** *10-4 (Sat till 3, Sun 12-2.30) & 7.30-9 (Tue-Sat, advance bookings only).* ***Closed*** *Mon, 1 week Jun & Christmas week. No credit cards.*

CLYTHA Clytha Arms

Tel & Fax 01873 840206 Map 9 D5 **P**
Clytha nr Abergavenny Monmouthshire NP7 9BW

Andrew and Beverley Canning's converted dower house successfully bridges the gap between local pub and residential inn. Their informal approach and innate sense of fun (check the mural cartoons in both loos) contribute greatly to the Clytha's burgeoning success. In the bar a varied range of real ales is the perfect accompaniment to super-value snacks such as salmon burger with tarragon mayonnaise, faggots and peas with beer and onion gravy, and leek and laverbread rissoles. Beyond a comfortable lounge bar with sofas is the no-smoking dining-room, an appropriate setting for some more classy cooking with rather more than a nod to Andrew's own Welsh roots. Bacon, laverbread and cockles, scallops with leeks and Caerphilly and chicken supreme with Carmarthen ham and parmesan all make the best use of locally-available produce. There are good home-made puds and interesting Welsh cheeses to follow. The Clytha Arms is the 1997 Wales Regional Winner of our Seafood Pub of the Year award. No bar snacks Sat or Sun (only restaurant menu). The three en suite bedrooms are decorated in individual styles; plum and cream roses in the Victorian twin room, a blue and yellow standard double and the rather special four-poster room, thoughtfully furnished and, for all but the truly unromantic, well worth a modest supplement. *Open 11.30-3 (not Mon), 6-11 (Sat 11.30-11, Sun 12-3.30,*

See over

*7-10.30). **Bar Food** 12.30-2.15 (Tue-Fri only), 7.30-9.30 (Mon-Fri). Restaurant 12.30-2.15 (Sun till 2.30), 7.30-9.30 (not Sun). Free House. **Beer** Hook Norton Best, Brains Bitter, Bass, three guest beers. **Accommodation** 3 bedrooms, all en suite, £45 (4-poster £65, single £40). Children welcome overnight (under-5s stay free in parents' room), additional bed & cot supplied. Garden, outdoor eating, children's play area. Family room. Accommodation & restaurant closed Sun eve, all pub closed Mon lunchtime. MasterCard,* **VISA**

COWBRIDGE Off The Beeton Track

Tel 01446 773599 Map 9 C6 JaB
1 Town Hall Square Cowbridge Vale of Glamorgan CF71 7ED

Alison and David Richardson's little town-centre restaurant with courtyard provides much to tempt all tastes and pockets. The day starts at 10am for coffee and home baking then from midday choose from either the quick snack menu – soup and open sandwiches (from £2), filled jacket potatoes (from £2.65) and omelettes – or hot daily specials such as lamb with mint and onion sauce, pork with garlic and mustard and plaice with prawn and mushroom sauce (all £5.75), and always a vegetarian dish of the day. Additionally there is a weekday set lunch menu (£8.25). Afternoon teas (£1.85) and Welsh teas with bara brith (£2.35) are served from 3 to 5, followed by an early dinner three-course menu from 6.45-8 (£11.75 Tue to Fri only) and a more elaborate à la carte served until 9.30. Traditional Sunday lunch and good Welsh cheeses. Children's portions are offered and there is one high-chair. The Garden is a safe place for children and the restaurant is close to St Fagons Welsh Folk Museum, beaches and a local park with swings and a play area. Changing shelf in Ladies. A free public car park is at the back. ***Seats** 30. **Open** 10-5 & 6.45-9.30. **Closed** D Sun & Mon (all Mon in winter) & 10 days Jan. Diners, MasterCard,* **VISA**

Pubs – note that food is only recommended in those pubs with ***Bar Food*** times in the statistics at the end of an entry. Restaurant food in pubs is *never* recommended unless specifically mentioned. Some pubs are recommended for B&B or Atmosphere only – each entry's statistics indicate our recommendation.

CRICKHOWELL Bear Hotel £56

Tel 01873 810408 **Fax 01873 811696** Map 9 D5
Brecon Road (A40) Crickhowell Powys NP8 1BW

One of the original coaching inns on the London to Aberystwyth route, the Bear today bristles with personality and honest endeavour. Front bars, a hive of activity, are resplendent with oak panelling, ornamental sideboards and welcoming log fires. Refurbishment of three of the inn's oldest bedrooms has revealed open stone fireplaces which date it back to 1432. Further top-grade bedroom accommodation is housed in a modern Tudor-style courtyard extension, and in a garden cottage containing two bedrooms and a suite with its own spa bath. A furter extension houses five new bedrooms, all of which are well appointed and boast jacuzzi baths Four-poster beds and antique furniture abound throughout. Reliable bar food encompasses gratin of cockles, mussels and laverbread, local hot smoked salmon and goat's cheese with honey and pine kernel dressing for starters, followed by baked mackerel with sage and lemon sauce, salmon fishcakes and Welsh lamb cutlets. Round off a meal with rich Belgian chocolate mousse cake or spiced fruit compote. Plenty of standards (paté, filled pancakes and pork pie) in small portions for little people; aubergine, tomato and parmesan charlotte for vegetarians. ***Open** 11-3, 6-11 (Sun 12-3, 7-10.300. **Bar Food** 12-2, 6-10 (Sun 7.30-9.30). Free House. **Beer** Bass, Ruddles Best & County, Webster's Yorkshire Bitter. Garden, outdoor eating. Family room. **Accommodation** 34 bedrooms, all en suite, £56-£90 (single £42-£70). Children welcome overnight (under-5s £5, 5-14s £10), additional bed & cot available. Amex, MasterCard,* **VISA**

DINAS MAWDDWY Dolbrodmaeth Inn

Tel 01650 531333 **Fax 01650 531339** Map 8 C3 P
Dinas Mawddwy nr Machynlleth Powys SY20 9LP

A former farmhouse tucked off the A470 with gardens sloping down to the River Dovey, this is a little gem. Engineer Graham Williams, once with the BBC, and wife Jean, a former cookery teacher, run this rebuilt inn (almost destroyed by fire in 1982), which now houses two cosy bars and an airy dining lounge. From the latter there are picturesque views of grounds that include a paddock, river walk and private fishing. The eight bedrooms are floored with carpet tiles and sport bright home-spun curtains and duvets, designed and made by an artistic daughter and direct-dial telephones. Though small, the bathrooms are brightly tiled with over-bath showers and multifarious energy-conscious features – even the beer cooling system boasts hot water output. Families are welcome: two rooms interconnect as a suite and one room boasts a double and single bed (plus room for a cot); children's games (and badminton) can be played on the large lawn. *Open 11-11 (Sun 12-10.30). Free House.* ***Beer*** *Tetley Bitter, Burton Ale. Garden, outdoor eating,* ***Accommodation*** *8 bedrooms, all en suite, £52 (family room £84, single £38.50). Children welcome overnight, (under-10s free if stay in parents' room), additional bed and cot available. Dogs by arrangement. Closed 2 weeks Feb. Amex, Diners, MasterCard,* ***VISA***

> Always ring ahead and inform establishments of your exact requirements when travelling with children. Unannounced can, sadly, still mean unwelcome.

FELINDRE FARCHOG Salutation Inn

Tel 01239 820564 Map 9 B5 P
A487 Felindre Farchog nr Crymych Pembrokeshire SA41 3UY

Felindre, a dot on the map where the A487 road bridge crosses the Nyfer, *is* the Salutation. Well-tended lawns slope down to the river, and there are gardens and terraces for a peaceful drink. The single-storey bedroom wing is neat and well-appointed. Bright duvets set the tone, with satellite TV, radio alarms, tea-makers and hairdryers providing up-to-date refinements. Three family rooms have bunk beds, and cots are also provided free of charge. Bar snacks and restaurant. *Open 12-2, 5.30-11, Sun 12-3, 7-10.30. Free House.* ***Beer*** *Burton Ale. Riverside garden, outdoor eating. Family room.* ***Accommodation*** *9 bedrooms, all en suite, £48 (family room £58, single £30). Children welcome overnight, (under-2s stay free in parents' room, 2-14s £5) additional bed & cot available. Check-in by arrangement. MasterCard,* ***VISA***

HANMER Hanmer Arms

Tel 01948 830532 **Fax 01948 830740** Map 6 A3 
Hanmer nr Whitchurch Wrexham SY13 3DE

Standing in the shadow of St Chad's church at the heart of a quiet hamlet now mercifully by-passed by the A539. The mellow brick Hanmer Arms is certainly of 16th-century origin, with a history closely linked to the old communities of the Shropshire Lake District. In a newly hollowed-out interior of this self-styled 'village hotel' are contained two bars, reception lounge and restaurant, with further dining and function rooms on the upper level. The strong point here lies in the apartment-style bedrooms laid out in the reconstructed barn and outhouses which stand around a central cobbled courtyard full of old farming artefacts. Decorated in country style with full en suite bathrooms, they are well equipped with phones, radio alarms and satellite TV. The most spacious have plenty of room to accommodate families overnight, while for the businessman there's also plenty of work space. Boardroom and conferences for up to 90 delegates. Five-acre woodland trail. *Open 11.30-11 (Sun 12-3, 6-10.30). Free House.* ***Beer*** *Tetley Traditional, Burton Ale. Garden.* ***Accommodation*** *26 bedrooms, all en suite, from £48 (suites £58, single from £38). Children welcome overnight (under-9s stay free in parents' room, 9-16s £8), additional bed & cot supplied. Amex, Diners, MasterCard,* ***VISA***

Hay-on-Wye — Kilverts

Tel 01497 821042 **Fax 01497 821580** Map 9 D5 **P**

Bull Ring Hay-on-Wye Powys HR3 5AG

An inimitable collection of hats and Victorian Spy cartoons imbue the bar of Colin Thomson's hotel/pub/bar with great character; the atmosphere is also enhanced nightly by the playing of an upright piano and live jazz on alternate Thursdays. Food is a further attraction, with the likes of seafood pie and home-made spicy beefburger alongside daily specials ranging from chicken livers with Marsala sauce (plus sandwiches and ploughman's platters at lunchtime) to spinach and mushroom roulade; fresh fish (baked cod gratin with lemon and tarragon sauce, grilled lemon sole) is best from Thursdays to Sundays; other dishes might include roast poussin with chestnut stuffing and beef lasagne. Home-made desserts like crème brulée and summer pudding. Residents' accommodation is both comfortable and stylish with brass bedsteads, smoked-glass tables and attractive floral bed linen. In addition to tea trays, direct-dial phones, TVs and radios, accoutrements include hairdryers and trouser presses. Bathrooms are a little utilitarian, nonetheless incorporating powerful showers and copious amounts of hot water. A marquee is erected for functions in summer – it's also a venue for Hay Jazz at the end of July. *Open 11-11 (till 11.30 Bank Holidays), Sun 12-10.30.* ***Bar Food*** *12-2, 7-9.30. Free House.* ***Beer*** *Boddingtons, Whitbread Castle Eden Ale, Bass. Patio, garden, outdoor eating.* ***Accommodation*** *11 bedrooms, all en suite (6 with shower only), £48-£60 (single £24). Children welcome overnight (under-6s stay free in parents' room, 6-12s £6), additional bed & cot available. Accommodation closed 24 Dec, pub & accommodation closed 25 Dec. Amex, MasterCard,* ***VISA***

Holyhead — Trearddur Bay Hotel — 65% — £98

Tel 01407 860301 **Fax 01407 861181** Map 8 B1 **H**

Holyhead Isle of Anglesey LL65 2UN

A family-friendly coastal hotel on the western tip of Anglesey, just two miles from Holyhead and the Irish ferry terminal. Best of the smart public areas are the cocktail bar and lounge overlooking the bay, while for relaxation in more informal surroundings there's a choice between a pubby locals' bar (adults only) and the new Inn at the Bay, suitable for families. A self-contained indoor swimming pool is in the garden, while for hardier types the real thing, and a safe, sandy beach, are just across the road. The majority of bedrooms, including nine studio suites, share views of the sand dunes and rocky coastline; those facing west with new private balconies are certainly the pick. Friendly, cheerful staff; children welcome, charged according to age from £6, cots and bunk beds available. ***Rooms*** *30. Garden, indoor swimming pool, games room. Amex, Diners, MasterCard,* ***VISA***

Letterston — Something's Cooking

Tel 01348 840621 Map 9 A5 **JaB**

The Square Letterston Pembrokeshire SA62 5SB

Trevor Rand's superior fish and chip restaurant with its newly-added conservatory stands by the A40 at its junction with the B4331. Cod fillet with chips, mushy peas, granary roll and butter, and a pot of tea (all for £4.25) is an excellent-value lunchtime special. Additional firm favourites include a wide choice of lightly-battered fresh fish, potted shrimps, local dressed crab salad (£5.95) and the ever-popular shellfish platter which includes cod, shell-on prawns, coleslaw and chips for £5.75. Non-fishy alternatives such as Southern fried chicken, barbecue spare ribs and vegetarian spring rolls boost the regular menu and children have their own selection. With its quality sea fish, good wheelchair access (including to the toilets) and 'loads' of high-chairs, this is a well-run, family-friendly outfit. For aficionados, the 1957 Wurlitzer juke box is a bit special, too. Ask for children's portions. Three high-chairs provided. No smoking. ***Seats*** *70.* ***Open*** *11-10.30 (Sun 6-10 summer & Bank Holidays only).* ***Closed*** *L Sun (all Sun in winter), 2 weeks Christmas. MasterCard,* ***VISA***

Llanarmon Dyffryn Ceiriog West Arms Hotel £100

Tel 01691 600665 **Fax 01691 600622** Map 8 D2
Llanarmon Dyffryn Ceiriog nr Llangollen Wrexham LL20 7LD

In a picturesque hamlet at the head of the Ceiriog valley, this 16th-century former farmhouse stands to the front of well-manicured gardens which run down to the river bridge. Black and white painted outside and bedecked with creeper and summer flowers, it's a haven of cosy comfort within, the tone set by open log fires, flagstone floors, blackened beams and rustic furniture. Tucked round the back, the Wayfarers' Bar serves a modest selection of well-prepared snacks in chintzy surroundings with an adjacent family lounge and patio. Following soup and tuna and mixed bean salad, local Ceiriog trout heads a list of main meals which might include steak, kidney and mushroom pie, chicken kebabs with spicy sauce and various daily specials featuring fresh fish and local game in season. Jam roly-poly and bread-and-butter pudding are typical of the traditional puddings. Bedrooms retain the period comfort afforded by handsome antique furnishings alongside modern fitted bathrooms: homely extras include pot pourri and quality toiletries. Five rooms are reserved for non-smokers and the two suites have plenty of space for family use (sleeping up to 5). Room service 8am-11pm. Disabled facilities. *Open 11-11 (Sun 12-10.30).* ***Bar Food*** *12-2.30, 7-9.30. Free House.* ***Beer*** *Boddingtons. Garden, outdoor eating.* ***Accommodation*** *13 bedrooms, all en suite, £100-£110 (single £55). Children welcome overnight, additional bed (£25) & cot (£6.50) are available. Hotel closed 2 weeks Jan/Feb. Amex, Diners, MasterCard,* ***VISA***

> **JaB** is short for 'Just a Bite'. The majority of these establishments are also recommended in our *Bistros, Bars & Cafés* Guide which features establishments where one may eat well for less than £15 per head.

Llanddarog Butcher's Arms

Tel 01267 275330 Map 9 B5 **P**
Llanddarog nr Carmarthen Ceredigion SA32 8NS

Well into a second decade at the Butcher's, self-taught butcher, proprietor and accomplished chef David James still runs his kitchen with unbridled enthusiasm. There have been changes aplenty over the years, of which the by-passing of Llanddarog by the A40 is not the least significant; hidden up a side road by the church, the Butcher's Arms is now a serene spot. As fads have come and gone, however, the kitchen here has remained constant and the food consistent. Familiar lunch dishes include avocado and bacon salad, cheese, ham and potato pie and seasonal tagliatelle with prawns and asparagus. Home-made pies – chicken and leek and seafood – are as popular today as a decade ago. In the evenings, generously-priced specials which supplement the menu are even more substantial. Fresh fish may be plaice fillets stuffed with asparagus and prawns with a white wine sauce. There may be Welsh lamb with mint and cider sauce, pork fillet with garlic and mushroom sauce and perhaps King Henry's feast, a single beef rib roast. Mavis James looks after the bookings (advised at weekends) and ordering with the same care that she applies to polishing the ubiquitous brass and miners' lamps, tending a roaring winter fireor arranging the floral displays which fill the fireplace in the tiny main bar in summer. Recent conversion of the old beer cellar and bottle store has created a further bar which, in turn, leads out to the rear garden. The Butcher's remains a village local, with a robust pint of Felinfoel a firm favourite among the loyal band of Welsh-speaking regulars. *Open 11-3 (not Sun), 5.30-11 (from 6.30 Sun).* ***Bar Food*** *11-2.30 (not Sun), 6-9.45 (Sat 5.30-9.45, Sun 7-9.30). Free House.* ***Beer*** *Felinfoel Bitter, Dark & Double Dragon, guest beers. Front patio, garden, outdoor eating. Closed Sun lunch. MasterCard,* ***VISA***

LLANDUDNO — St Tudno Hotel — 70% — £110

Tel 01492 874411 **Fax 01492 860407** Map 8 C1 **HR**

The Promenade Llandudno Conwy LL30 2LP

This year marks Martin and Janette Bland's quarter century at St Tudno. Their original conversion from retirement home to Victorian-style town house was years ahead of its time, and both its abiding quality and understated sophistication today are a tribute to their dedicated professionalism. Parlour plants, original fireplaces and deep armchairs set the tone in both the bar/lounge and sitting-room (reserved for non-smokers), while in contrast a bright coffee lounge beyond the reception desk sports fresh flowers, cane furniture and floral decor. It's very family-friendly, and high tea is served from 5 to 6pm. A small bottle of sparkling wine greets guests in bedrooms that, though generally not large, are individually decorated in pretty co-ordinating fabrics and wall coverings with a good eye for detail. Rooms are properly serviced in the evenings as are the bathrooms with their generous towelling and good toiletries. Some smart, bright bathroom refurbishments were carried out in the spring of 1996 and conversion of two smaller front-facing bedrooms into a spacious suite was on line as we went to press; as with all front rooms this will attract a surcharge. The Bland tradition of good service is enduring: guests' feelings of well-being are certainly enhanced by the friendliness and attention to detail of a young and well-motivated team to whom nothing appears to be too much trouble. ***Rooms** 21. Patio, indoor swimming pool. Amex, Diners, MasterCard,* ***VISA***

Garden Room Restaurant — £70

Murals of trellises and trees, potted plants, conservatory-style furniture and air-conditioning all combine to good effect here, where joint-head chefs David Harding and Ian Watson present seasonal menus with additional daily specials. Dinner offers up to six courses with five or six choices of starters and main courses separated by soup (tomato, ginger and orange, perhaps) or a sorbet if desired. Tortellini of lobster with cabbage and vermouth sauce, salad of smoked chicken, pink grapefruit and walnut oil vinaigrette, and grilled goat's cheese with hot crispy bacon and salad; followed by Trelough duckling with tomatoes and olives, loin of venison with chocolate and red wine sauce and a butterfly of wild salmon with a vegetable medley well illustrate the variety of choice. A vegetarian alternative such as aubergine pattie with a tomato compote is always available. Organically-produced Welsh cheeses and Stilton come after, or before, some nicely varied desserts including warm pear tart with Can-y-delyn ice cream and bread-and-butter pudding with an apricot glaze and rhubarb. Lunch is a shorter, three-course affair and a good range of lighter dishes is served in the coffee lounge and bar. Much work goes into the compilation of the wine list, which is clearly laid out and easy to use. No smoking. ***Seats** 66. L 12.30-1.45 D 7-9.30 (Sun till 9). Set L £15.50 Set D £22/£29.50.*

LLANGAMMARCH WELLS — Lake Country House — 72% — £115

Tel 01591 620202 **Fax 01591 620457** Map 9 C4 

Llangammarch Wells Powys LD4 4BS

Clearly signposted a country mile from the A438 at Garth, this mainly Edwardian mansion nestles in 50 acres of mature parkland along the banks of the River Irfon. At its heart an elegantly proportioned drawing-room (a perfect setting for light lunches and afternoon teas) with dimmed chandeliers and well-tended fire befits the laden afternoon tea trolley. Bedrooms have fine views and are individually styled with a fair smattering of antiques; incorporated sitting areas are now the norm and one self-contained suite on the ground is now being let; bathrooms are smartly tiled, with luxury items including bespoke toiletries and bathrobes. Smart, efficient staff mirror the owners' enthusiasm, helping to arrange horse riding locally and fishing on three rivers and the hotel's lake. Children up to ten years old may stay free if sharing with their parents. Under-7s not allowed in the dining-room in the evenings; one cot, one high-chair and a family room available. ***Rooms** 19. Garden, pitch & putt, tennis, fishing, snooker. Amex, Diners, MasterCard,* ***VISA***

Restaurant **£80**

Richard Arnold's fixed-price dinners are invariably imaginative and sometimes quite intricate, starting invariably with a choice of soups, for instance courgette and rosemary or gazpacho, before entrées such as ravioli of wild mushrooms, roquette and shallots and grilled codling and hake fillets with tomato, herb and garlic sauce in olive oil. Fillet of beef on celeriac purée with an onion confit, and turbot on a saffron sauce with a smoked salmon and lovage lattice are typical main dishes, and there are some well-crafted desserts, an alternative selection of home-made ice cream or both Welsh and English cheeses to follow. Generally quite favourable prices on a comprehensive wine list with a collector's fondness for Bordeaux; the rest of the world is well represented and also has sensible tasting notes. ***Seats*** *50. L 12.15-2 D 7-8.45. Set L £15.50 Set D £27.50.*

LLANGORSE Red Lion

Tel 01874 658238 **Fax 01874 658595** Map 9 D5 
Llangorse nr Brecon Powys LD3 7TY

Just a mile from Llangorse Lake, at the heart of the village by St. Paulinus Church, stands the Rosiers' welcoming local. Picnic tables in front by the village stream make it a picturesque spot. Riding, fishing and water-skiing (mid-week only), all available locally, draw many regulars to the Red Lion. Accommodation in neat pastel-shade bedrooms with attractive duvets is practical rather than luxurious, though TV, radio-alarms and tea-makers ensure an acceptable level of comfort. Five have well-kept bathrooms en suite, the remainder (with showers and washbasins only) share a couple of adjacent toilets. Built into the hillside, all rooms have level access to a rear garden reserved for residents. Good selection of twenty malt whiskies. *Open 11.30-3, 6.30-11, (Sun 12-3, 7-10.30). Closed Mon-Fri lunch Nov-Feb. Free House.* ***Beer*** *Flowers Original, Boddingtons, guest beer. Streamside terrace/patio, outdoor eating.* ***Accommodation*** *10 bedrooms, 5 en suite, £40-£50 (family room £50, single £25-£30). Children welcome overnight (under-12s stay free in parents' room), additional bed & cot available. No dogs. No credit cards.*

LLANGYBI Cwrt Bleddyn Hotel 71% £115

Tel 01633 450521 **Fax 01633 450220** Map 9 D6 
Tredunnock nr Usk Monmouthshire NP5 1PG

A large house standing in 17 acres of mature grounds some three miles from Caerleon, between Llangybi and Tredunnock, Cwrt Bleddyn can trace its heritage back to the 14th century. Some original features date back just to the 17th century but the interior is modernised to a great extent, including 25 spacious bedrooms, several designated for family use, and 11 suites. Children up to 16 can stay free in their parents' room. The lounge and private meeting rooms feature carved panelling and fireplaces and the sun lounge/cocktail bar has a spectacular, high-domed glass ceiling. Good family facilities; coffee shop in leisure club 11am-11pm. Ample parking. Ask about the wine appreciation and murder weekends. Virgin Hotels. ***Rooms*** *36. Garden, croquet, tennis, indoor swimming pool, gym, sauna, squash, steam room, solarium, spa bath, beauty salon, hair salon, snooker, play area. Amex, Diners, MasterCard,* ***VISA***

LLANRWST Ty-Hwnt-i'r-Bont

Tel 01492 640138 Map 8 C2 
Llanrwst Conwy LL26 0PL

Look out for a big celebration this year of the Holt family's Silver Jubilee at their characterful little 500-year-old listed cottage down by the bridge. The best of Welsh bakery is truly home-made, and the mixer and ovens make an early start in the Holt household. Try the scones with jam and cream or the full tea (£4.50) which also includes white and brown bread and a piece of bara brith, or, for savoury palates, fresh-filled baps (from £1.80 to £2.25), ploughman's (£4.30) or perhaps a ham salad (£5.25), with Derek Holt's own Welsh wholegrain mustard. No bookings are taken, and the telephone number shown has no extension in the café proper. Unlicensed. Three high-chairs; children's portions on request. There's a large, completely enclosed play area adjoining the tea room. No smoking. ***Seats*** *50.* ***Open*** *10-5.30.* ***Closed*** *Mon (except Bank Holidays) & end Oct-Tue before Easter. No credit cards.*

LLANTRISANT Greyhound Inn

Tel 01291 672505 **Fax 01291 673255** Map 9 D6 **P**
Llantrisant nr Usk Monmouthshire NP5 1LE

Just 2½ miles from Usk, the Greyhound occupies a hillside, with fine views of the Lowes River valley which flows to the sea at Newport some 9 miles downstream. The low stone 17th-century farm house is much extended now with split-level bar and succession of drinking and eating rooms stepped into the hill. Conversion of the former barn has produced a dozen en suite bedrooms with blackened roof trusses and decorated in a cottage style becoming both the building's nature and its rural location. Up-to-the-minute equipment includes remote-control TV and direct-dial phones; two larger family rooms have an extra bed; all have both bath and showers. French windows in the best, ground-floor rooms open on to private patios in a garden setting with lily pond and ornamented fountain. There is no direct access from the nearby A449 dual carriageway, so be sure to obtain exact directions on booking. Hundreds of trees have been planted and all rooms are double-glazed to prevent any intrusive road noise. *Open 11-3, 6-11, (Sun 12-3, 7-10.30). Free House.* ***Beer*** *Wadworth 6X, Flowers Original, Marston's Pedigree, Boddingtons, Morland Old Speckled Hen, guest beer. Garden, patio. Family room.* ***Accommodation*** *10 bedrooms, all en suite, £55-£60 (single £40-£47). Children welcome overnight (under-5s stay free in parents' room), additional bed (£5) & cot available. No dogs. Accommodation closed 24 & 25 Dec. MasterCard,* ***VISA***

LLANWRTYD WELLS Drover's Rest

Tel 01591 610264 Map 9 C4 **JaB**
The Square Llanwrtyd Wells Powys LD5 4RS

Nestling by the Irfon River bridge at the heart of Wales's smallest town (population 600), Peter James's delectable café and restaurant is a business on the move. A tireless champion of local Welsh produce, he and his fresh young team use it to good effect in a string of traditional and innovative dishes. Start the day with a substantial Welsh breakfast or a vegetarian version which includes baked beans and a vegetable rösti (£4.60). At lunchtime, in addition to fresh-filled sandwiches and baked potatoes, go for the Welsh and buck rabbits (with two poached eggs), traditional bara brith and Caerphilly cheese salad plate (£3.80), plump Welsh river trout with fresh organic vegetables (£8.50) or the daily-changing specials such as carrot and orange soup, goat's cheese soufflé, stuffed peaches with honey-baked ham and mayonnaise and cod steak baked in white wine with asparagus (£6.95). Savoury flans and pasta dishes or perhaps Moravian mushrooms with mixed herbs, garlic and breadcrumbs (£6.95) keep vegetarians more than happy, while sister Paula's succulent patisserie simply demands you leave room for her profiteroles, crème brulée or Paris-Brest. The popular Welsh Afternoon Tea (£4.50) includes buttered bara brith, Welsh cakes and Caerphilly cheese, while the English Tea comes with scones, jam and cream, and home-made cake. Book for more elaborate evening fare Monday to Thursday from 7.30pm and family Sunday lunches (£7.95); from Friday to Sunday the gourmet dinners continue in popularity. Two high-chairs, a children's menu and children's portions are all on offer. ***Seats*** *45 (+12 outside).* ***Open*** *9.30-5 (Sun from 10), also Fri-Sun 7.30-10.30.* ***Closed*** *25 Dec. MasterCard,* ***VISA***

LLANWDDYN Lake Vyrnwy Hotel 67% £77

Tel 01691 870692 **Fax 01691 870259** Map 8 C3 **HR**
Lake Vyrnwy Llanwddyn Montgomery Powys SY10 0LY

The magnificent, if austere, stone mansion high on a wooded hillside looks across 1100 acres of man-made lake set amid the vast Vyrnwy Estate. Built at the same time as the dam in 1890 (drinking water from here is still supplied to Liverpool 68 miles away), this is indeed a magical spot and, now as then, a retreat for all country-lovers. True to their Victorian origins, the generously proportioned public rooms have an ageless feel, with chintz sofas, Bechstein piano, tapestries and oil paintings gracing the lounge, while a clubby atmosphere in the bar is enhanced by pitch pine, leather armchairs and sporting prints. For an informal drink, the spectacular views can be enjoyed from the balcony of the adjacent Tavern. The majority of bedrooms share this aspect; each is individually designed with much antique and period furniture in evidence and many special features of unique appeal, from private sitting areas and balconies to four-poster beds and jacuzzi baths. Conference and banqueting facilities accommodate up to 120. ***Rooms** 35. Garden, tennis, shooting, fishing, boat hire, sailing, bicycles. Amex, Diners, MasterCard,* ***VISA***

Restaurant £65

The kitchen's home production knows no bounds here, with the estate and gardens providing their fair share of seasonal produce. Numerous canapés and home-made breads are listed nightly on the dinner menu which offers five or more choices at each course. Mousseline of Carmarthen Bay crab, Barbary duck roulade, roast black Welsh beef with Yorkshire pudding, French corn-fed guinea fowl with cabbage and lentils, Swiss dark chocolate terrine and traditional Welsh farmhouse cheeses all typify both the range of choice and the meticulous care which goes into Andrew Woods' menu-planning. The set dinner price is fully inclusive, right down to coffee served with petits fours - home-made, of course. No smoking. ***Seats** 80. Private Room 70. L 12.30-1.45 D 7.30-9.15. Set L £13.95 (Sun £14.95) Set D £22.50.*

LLWYNDAFYDD Crown Inn

Tel & Fax 01545 560396 Map 9 B4

Llwyndafydd nr New Quay Ceredigion SA44 6FH

A handsome, white-painted 18th-century inn at the head of the hidden romantic valley of Cwm. This highly popular spot with families in summer has a large patio and play area for the children (who are offered regular favourites on their own menu). In addition to a standard range of adult bar food (the evening restaurant menu is pricier) there are well-made curries and daily specials on a board like local fish (baked cod in cheese and prawn sauce, pan-fried local plaice, Teifi sewin and salmon), wild rabbit casserole, chicken pie and braised pigeon breast with tomato and mushrooms. Home-made pizzas, from children's-size to family-size, are made to order. Ice cream features on the dessert choice alongside home-made gateau and lemon soufflé. Popular for Sunday lunch (half price for children). *Open 12-3, 6-11 (till 10.30 Sun).* ***Bar Food** 12-2, 6-9.30 (Sun 12-3, 6-9). Free House.* ***Beer** Flowers IPA & Original, guest beers. Garden, outdoor eating area, tiered patios. Family room. Closed Sun eve Oct-Easter (except Christmas period). MasterCard,* ***VISA***

LLYSWEN Griffin Inn

Tel 01874 754241 **Fax 01874 754592** Map 9 D5

Llyswen Brecon Powys LD3 0UR

Mythically speaking, the griffin is a creature of vast proportions, half lion, half dragon, its whole being considerably less awesome than its constituent parts. No such problems exist for Richard and Di Stockton, for their Griffin is nothing short of splendid in all departments and conspicuously well run. That locally-caught salmon and brook trout feature so regularly on the menu is scarcely surprising as the Griffin employs its own ghillie, and fishing stories abound in the bar, which is the centre of village life. It's hung with framed displays of fishing flies and maps of the upper and lower reaches of the Wye valley, and dominated by a splendid inglenook fire. In the adjacent lounge, low tables, high-backed Windsor chairs and window seats make a comfortable setting in which to sample their 'Tiffin' menu (dishes for two people served Monday to Friday evenings); this might offer sweet and sour pork with rice or lentil, pepper and pasta gratin followed by a long choice of home-made sweets (apple strudel, banana and caramel flan) and Welsh cheeses. Evening meals provide a wider choice of more substantial fare, either in the no-smoking restaurant or the bars, as space allows. Here you might order Cornish mussels in white wine and garlic, ragout of wild rabbit, pan-fried breast of wood pigeon with bubble and squeak in wine jus or chicken chasseur. Tip-top Sunday lunch is only served in the dining-room (no bar food) and booking is suggested at least a week ahead. The ten recently-refurbished, en suite bedrooms revert to the fishing theme. They are cottagey in style, wonderfully tranquil, and though there are telephones, television is considered superfluous. Two rooms are in an annexe across the road. A family suite has its own lounge, shares a bathroom and sleeps four. The splendid residents' lounge on the upper floor of the inn's oldest part is dramatically set under original rafters dating, it is thought, back to its origins as a 15th-century sporting inn. There is no garden but children may eat in the bar and small portions are served; two high-chairs provided. *Open 12-3, 7-11, (Sun 12-3, 7-10.30). **Bar Food** 12-2 (no bar food Sun), 7-9 (Sun cold supper for residents only); Sun lunch at 1pm in dining-room only. Free House. **Beer** Boddingtons, Flowers IPA, guest beers. Outdoor eating. **Accommodation** 8 bedrooms all en suite, £60 (family room £90, single £34.50). Children welcome overnight (under-10s stay free in parents' room), additional bed & cot available. Accommodation closed 25 & 26 Dec. Amex, Diners, MasterCard,* ***VISA***

MACHYNLLETH — Centre for Alternative Technology

Tel 01654 702400 Map 8 C3 JaB
Pantperthog Machynlleth Powys SY20 9AZ

At this unique eco-centre on a seven-acre site three miles north of Machynlleth (signposted from the A487), the many attractions include lakes, ponds, organic gardens and an adventure playground. A water-powered funicular leads up from the car park, providing stunning views down the wooded Dyfi valley. Organically produced fresh ingredients are used whenever possible in the wholly vegetarian all-day café where on a daily-changing blackboard menu popular snacks include 'sausage' rolls, cheese and onion pasties and pizza slices, flapjacks, fruit custards and many other pastries. More substantial meals come in the shape of homity pie, lasagne, bean casserole, cashew nut loaf, mushroom and courgette provençale and the ever-popular meatless spaghetti bolognese; all the main dishes still cost no more than £3.75. Of the kitchen's electric power, 90% is generated by water, wind and solar panels. The self-service counter and widely-spaced pine tables within are supplemented by picnic tables in a courtyard with adjacent playgrounds, one for toddlers, the other for bigger little people. Well geared-up for family outings. One high-chair, six booster seats and changing facilities in both Gents and Ladies. Note: there is an admission charge for the Centre. No smoking. ***Seats** 80 (+50 outside). **Open** 10-5. **Closed** 25 Dec. MasterCard,* ***VISA***

Any person using our name to obtain free hospitality is a fraud.
Proprietors, please inform the police and us.

MACHYNLLETH — Quarry Shop

Tel 01654 702624 Map 8 C3 JaB
13 Maengwyn Street Machynlleth Powys SY20 8EB

Part of the same co-operative that runs the Centre for Alternative Technology (see above), this friendly, counter-service wholefood shop and café has pine furniture within and pavement tables outside in fine weather. From 9 to 11 breakfast includes muesli, toast, yoghurt and fruit, while at lunchtime the vegetable soup (£1.50) comes with a home-made roll and the daily main dish might be aubergine tofu with fruity couscous (£3.80), with fresh fruit trifle and home-made cakes, bara brith and apricot slice for the sweeter-toothed. Salads come in two sizes (£1/£1.50); there are plenty of ices, fruit drinks and teas and good facilities for children. One high-chair; feeder cups, and half-portions on request. Baby-changing facilities in both Gents and Ladies; changing mat and potty provided. No smoking. ***Seats** 35. **Open** 9-5 (winter till 4.30, Thu in winter till 2). **Closed** Sun (except Jul/Aug). No credit cards.*

MACHYNLLETH — Wynnstay Arms — 60% — £55

Tel 01654 702941 **Fax 01654 703884** Map 8 C3
Maengwyn Street Machynlleth Powys SY20 8AE

Machynlleth is well placed in the valley of the River Dyfi as a base from which to visit Snowdonia and the Alternative Technology Centre. Many of the town's buildings date back to the 17th century and the Wynnstay (formerly the Unicorn) was a Royal Mail staging post. The comfortable lounges have a supply of books and board games and there's a convivial bar with a log fire in winter. Bedrooms are on the functional side, with half designated as non-smoking. Children up to 16 stay free in parents' room. ***Rooms** 20. Amex, Diners, MasterCard,* ***VISA***

MARFORD Trevor Arms

Tel 01244 570436 **Fax 01244 571244** Map 8 D2 
Marford Wrexham LL12 8TA

Quaint 17th-century architecture is a feature of Marford's original buildings, which all incorporate a cross to ward off evil spirits. The Trevor Arms, built later as a coaching inn, echoes these features and also plays its full part in village life centred on a very busy locals' bar which occupies the pub's oldest part. The original and somewhat modest bedrooms are also housed here. Though not lacking in modern appointments such as TV, radio and direct-dial phones most offer only shower/WC en suite bathrooms. Six rooms, including one with a four-poster and a family room sleeping up to three, have en suite baths. Large garden, covered barbeque patio and children's play area. *Open 11-11.30 (Sun 12-10.30).* ***Beer*** *Thomas Greenalls Original, Greenalls Draught, Tetley Bitter, guest beers. Garden, barbecue, children's play area. Family room.* ***Accommodation*** *20 bedrooms, all en suite, £41-£47 (single £28), cooked breakfast £3.50 pp extra. Children welcome overnight (under-5s stay free in parents' room, 5-14s £10)), additional bed & cot available. MasterCard,* ***VISA***

We welcome bona fide complaints and recommendations on the tear-out pages at the back of the Guide for Readers' Comments. They are followed up by our professional team.

MISKIN Miskin Manor 70% £100

Tel 01443 224204 **Fax 01443 237606** Map 9 C6 
Pendoylan Road Groes Faen Pontyclun Cardiff CF72 8ND

Built of mellow grey Welsh stone, the present manor dates from the 1850s. Overlooking its own lake and the River Ely, the hotel stands in 20 acres of mature gardens and woodland. Oak linenfold panelling is a dominant feature of the elegantly proportioned day rooms, which are brightly decorated to reflect their pastoral aspect. Individually furnished bedrooms, notable for their size and luxurious appointments, have their share each of the view. Crown-canopied beds, two four-posters and a suite occupied in the 1920s by the future Edward VIII imbue this fine house with a tangible legacy of its own history. A short walk from the hotel, the self-contained Health and Leisure club with playroom and creche (9am-3pm Mon-Fri) is shared by guests (free use) and local members. The hotel is prominently signposted from the M4 at J34. ***Rooms*** *32. Garden, croquet, indoor swimming pool, gym, squash, spa bath, steam room, sauna, solarium, beauty salon, badminton, coffee shop (11am-9.30pm), play area. Amex, Diners, MasterCard,* ***VISA***

NEVERN Trewern Arms Hotel

Tel 01239 820395 Map 9 A5 
Nevern nr Newport Pembrokeshire SA42 0NB

This hidden hamlet in a valley on the B4582 is a world all on its own with historic pilgrims' church and Celtic cross, nurseries, cheese dairy and cake shop. Across the stone bridge over the Nyfer (or Nevern), the Trewern Arms is creeper-clad with sparkling fairy lights, exuding a magical air. Bedrooms, carefully added to the original 18th-century stone building, are furnished in cane and pine with floral curtains and matching duvets. The bathrooms are all en suite (7 with shower/WCs only); TVs and tea-makers are standard. There are three spacious family rooms (one sleeping up to four). A foyer lounge upstairs has plenty of literature for walkers and fishermen, and the lounge bar below sports comfortable armchairs and sofas. Children are welcome until 9pm. *Open 11-3, 6-11, (Sun 12-3, 7-10.30). Free House.* ***Beer*** *Whitbread Castle Eden Ale, Flowers Original, guest beers. Garden, children's play area.* ***Accommodation*** *9 bedrooms, all en suite, £45 double (family room sleeping three £55, single £30). Children welcome overnight, additional bed available. Check-in by arrangement. No dogs. MasterCard,* ***VISA***

Newport — Celtic Manor — 77% — £120

Tel 01633 413000 **Fax 01633 412910** Map 9 D6 **HR**
The Coldra Newport NP6 2YA

Just one minute from J24 of M4, this 19th-century manor house is set in a 300-acre estate. Well set up for both business and pleasure, the hotel maintains high standards of decor, maintenance and service. An elegant reception lounge, clubby bar and drawing-room have benefited greatly from a recent re-styling and the large patio conservatory which is used for breakfast is a boon to families looking for a snack at any time of the day. Bedrooms are of a good size and feature triple glazing, freestanding darkwood furniture with ample writing space, attractive window seating and smartly tiled, well-lit bathrooms. The Ian Woosnam Golfing Academy alongside two 18-hole golf courses and a spectacular new clubhouse have now opened as part of the hotel, and is just a short hike away (preferably by golf buggy) uphill through Coldra Woods. The tennis club, with squash to follow, was nearing completion as we went to press, and extension of the hotel itself to nearly twice its current size is planned over the next two years. ***Rooms** 73. Garden, indoor swimming pool, gym, sauna, solarium, golf (2x18), tennis, beauty & hair salons, playroom. Amex, Diners, MasterCard,* ***VISA***

Hedley's Restaurant — £75

An L-shaped dining-room of oak panelling and stained-glass generally avoids the funereal, leaving imaginative menus and the unashamedly slick service to bring dining here to life. There's plenty to enjoy in dishes such as pan-fried scallops with a velouté of chives and smoked salmon, persillade of Breconshire venison with red cabbage and chestnut confit, and tiramisu with coffee ice cream. At weekends Trefor Jones's five-course 'Concept of the Chef' gives rein to more elaborate creations like nage of Dover sole and mussels scented with vanilla and ballotine of squab pigeon served with leek and wild mushroom suet pudding. Desserts such as poached pear in red wine on a fruit chutney are similarly elaborate and the list of Welsh cheeses is exemplary. Sunday lunch is served in the Patio Brasserie, where there is also dinner with dancing on Friday evenings. ***Seats** 80. Parties 16. Private Room 100. L 12-2 D 7-10. Set L £19.50/£23 Set D £26/£32. Set Sun L in Patio Brasserie £12.95. Closed L Sat.*

Newport — Cnapan

Tel 01239 820575 Map 9 D6 **JaB**
East Street Newport SA42 0SY

Part guest-house (with five letting bedrooms) and part restaurant, this friendly country house on the village main street is run by the Lloyd and Cooper families. The light lunch menu, served from 12 to 2, starts with a good nourishing vegetable soup and continues with the likes of Welsh cheese platters, oat-based flans – perhaps salmon, tuna, sardine and tomato or broccoli, orange, fried onion and cheese – and the celebrated local fresh crab salad (£6). There's one daily hot dish, a 'children's hamper' menu and good puds such as treacle tart with custard or cream (£2.35) or layered chocolate sponge in a boozy orange marinade. Evening meals, for which booking is required, are rather more elaborate and priced accordingly and there's a full roast lunch on Sunday. Booster-seats provided along with a baby-changing area. Safe garden. A popular place for a family lunch on Sundays. ***Seats** 36. **Open** 12-2. **Closed** Tue, Feb, 25 & 26 Dec. MasterCard,* ***VISA***

Nottage — Rose & Crown

Tel 01656 784850 **Fax 01656 772345** Map 9 C6 **P**
Nottage Heol-y-Capel nr Porthcawl Bridgend CF36 5ST

Just a mile from Royal Porthcawl Golf Club and the town's West Bay stands this white-painted row of stone-built former cottages at the heart of a tiny hamlet. In an area short of good pub accommodation, its friendly, refurbished village bar and neat cottage bedrooms are justly popular. Pastel-shaded decor with fitted-pine furniture, practical bathrooms and room comforts including phone, TV and trouser press promise a restful and comfortable stay. Scottish & Newcastle. *Open 11.30-11, (Sun 12-3, 7-10.30). **Beer** John Smith's, Ruddles County & Best, Webster's Yorkshire Bitter, Theakston Best. Garden, children's play area. **Accommodation** 8 bedrooms, all en suite, £34.95, breakfast £2.95-£5.50pp extra. Children welcome overnight (under-2s stay free in parents' room, 2-11s £2.95), additional bed & cot available. Guide dogs only. Amex, MasterCard, Diners,* ***VISA***

Penmaenpool George III Hotel £88

Tel 01341 422525 **Fax 01341 423565** Map 8 C3 I
Penmaenpool nr Dolgellau Gwynedd LL40 1YD

Squeezed in between the A493 (which is at roof level) and the head of the Mawddach Estuary, the 17th-century George III Hotel is run by five members of the Cartwright family. It enjoys magnificent views – shared by all but two of the bedrooms – across the water to wooded hills beyond. The unpretentious Dresser Bar – so named because the bar counter is made out of the bottom half of an old Welsh dresser – is a place where wooden tables are polished, brass ornaments gleam and a welcoming fire burns in the grate. The refurbished Cellar Bar (actually at ground level) is open only in the summer when there are also tables outside, on what was a railway line, next to the water. Residents have their own cosy lounge with beamed ceiling and inglenook fireplace. The bedrooms, half of which are in the adjacent, former Victorian railway station, have traditional freestanding furniture and pretty floral fabrics – William Morris in the old station rooms – plus smart modern bathrooms. All have direct-dial phones, TV, trouser press and beverage kit. Families should head for the Cellar Bar; the children's menu offers popular favourites; baby-changing facilities are provided. Free fishing permits for residents and mountain bike hire. Disabled WC. *Open 11-11, (Sun 12.30-3, 7-10.30). Free House.* ***Beer*** *Ruddles Best, John Smith's, Cambrian Premium, guest beer. Garden, patio. Family room.* ***Accommodation*** *11 bedrooms, all en suite, £70-£88 (single £45). Children welcome overnight, additional bed (under-12s £12.50) & cot supplied. MasterCard,* ***VISA***

Our inspectors *never* book in the name of Egon Ronay's Guides. They disclose their identity only if they are considering an establishment for inclusion in the next edition of the Guide.

Penybont Severn Arms Hotel

Tel 01597 851224 **Fax 01597 851693** Map 9 C4 P
Penybont nr Llandrindod Wells Powys LD1 5UA

A white-painted former coaching inn by the junction of the A488 and A44, at the heart of the Ithon Valley. Loved by JB Priestley for its creaky floors, old oak beams and sloping ceiling, it has some of the best family rooms around, tucked under the eaves of the pub's top storey, with pastoral views down the garden to a wooden bridge over the river. Caring management by Geoff and Tessa Lloyd has extended over twelve years and the bedrooms are both immaculately kept and well equipped; all en suite, most have trouser presses and all have TV, radio, direct-dial phones. hairdryers and tea-making facilities. From the flagstoned entrance there's access to the village bar festooned with local football trophies, a more sedate lounge bar and extensive dining-room. Residents enjoy use of their own quiet TV lounge on the first floor. *Open 11-2.30, 6-11, (Sun 12-3, 7-10.30). Free House.* ***Beer*** *Tetley, Worthington Best, Bass, John Smiths. Garden. Family room.* ***Accommodation*** *10 bedrooms, all en suite, £50 (single £28). Children welcome overnight (under-5s 33%, 5-12s 50% adult tariff), additional bed (£5) and cot (£2) available. Accommodation closed one week Christmas-New Year. Amex, Diners, MasterCard,* ***VISA***

Pisgah Halfway Inn

Tel 01970 880631 Map 9 C4 P
Devil's Bridge Road Pisgah nr Aberystwyth Ceredigion SY23 4NE

650 feet up, overlooking the Rheidol Valley below, Sally Roger's marvellous country pub is in a lovely setting with magnificent views. It's well known as a beer-lovers' favourite, with its choice of up to four real ales. Never modernised or extended, this 250-year-old Inn retains a traditional feel – candle-lit in the evenings and log fire in winter. Families use the Stone Room bar (walls made of stone). The grassy upper car park offers free overnight pitching for campers and pony-trekkers can leave their mounts in a paddock. *Open 11.30-2.30, 6.30-11 (may be open all day in summer), Sun 12-3, 7-10.30. Free House.* ***Beer*** *Felinfoel Double Dragon, Flowers Original, guest beers. Garden. Family room. No credit cards.*

Red Wharf Bay Old Boathouse Café

Tel 01248 852731 Map 8 B1 JaB
Red Wharf Bay Isle of Anglesey LL75 8RS

Set just back from the shoreline behind its newly-extended patio and looking out across the Menai Straits, Mrs Griffiths' super summer café, in the family for 26 years, is a perennial favourite. The day starts with Welsh breakfast until mid-day when light lunch specials take over in the shape of Greek salad, deep-fried whitebait and Creole prawns (from £3), though the simpler sandwiches and baked potatoes are not overlooked. Home baking of scones (£1.25 with jam and cream) is equally dependable, and the luscious desserts include banoffi pie, coffee choux and caramel apple cheesecake (£2.85). Neatly-spaced pine tables within are now supplemented by an eye-catching conservatory, twinkling by candle-light in the evenings, when salmon and broccoli mornay, lemon pepper chicken and Welsh lamb in honey and mustard sauce (from £5.50) are typical of the expanded supper menu. Children's menu and portions available; two high-chairs and a room available for nursing mothers on request. Indoor toys and crayons can be provided. No smoking. ***Seats** 45. **Open** 10-10. **Closed** Nov-Easter. Credit card facilities are planned for 1997.*

Red Wharf Bay Ship Inn

Tel 01248 852568 **Fax 01248 853568** Map 8 B1 P
Red Wharf Bay nr Benllech Isle of Anglesey LL75 4RJ

Landlord Andrew Kenneally has now been at the low, white-painted Ship for 26 years. The inn is fronted by hanging baskets and stands right on the bay shore. Quarry-tiled floors plus genuine exposed beams and stonework make for an interesting interior where the ship's wheels and chiming clocks, Tom Browne cartoons and Toby Jug collection give it great character. With food as the main draw, there's a steady stream of early arrivals and local regulars to sample from a selection of bar food which is sensibly varied daily between cold and hot choices and never overly long. Typical dishes might include deep-fried cockles, moussaka, vegetable chili, duck in orange sauce, braised beef in Guinness and baked half-shoulder of lamb with redcurrant and rosemary sauce; finish with dark and white chocolate gateau or pecan pie. The Cellar Room is no-smoking. There's a separate children's menu served in a smaller rear family room or out in the shoreside garden. A no-smoking restaurant opens upstairs for diners at weekends. *Open 12-3.30, 7-11 (11-11 summer), Sun 12-3, 7-10.30 (12-10.30 on summer). **Bar Food** 12-2.30, 6-9.30 (from 7 in winter), Sun 12-2, 7-9. Free House. **Beer** Friary Meux, Tetley Bitter, Ind Coope Burton Ale, guest beers. Garden, front patio, outdoor eating area. Family room. MasterCard,* **VISA**

Ruthin Ruthin Castle 62% £88

Tel 01824 702664 **Fax 01824 705978** Map 8 C2 H
Corwen Road Ruthin Denbighshire LL15 2NU

Extensive gardens and parkland surround ancient Ruthin Castle, where relics of the past include a drowning pool, whipping pit and dungeons. The castle has known attack, siege and virtual destruction, but more peaceful diversions today centre around the cocktail bar, splendid lounge and comfortable en suite bedrooms appointed in traditional style. The Great Hall is the scene of regular medieval banquets, which hotel guests may attend. No dogs. ***Rooms** 60. Garden, fishing, snooker. Amex, Diners, MasterCard,* **VISA**

St David's St Non's Hotel 60% £70

Tel 01437 720239 **Fax 01437 721839** Map 9 A5 H
St David's Pembrokeshire SA6 6RJ

At the centre of Britain's only coastal National Park, St Non's is named after the mother of St David and stands half a mile from the city centre overlooking the Cathedral and historic Bishop's Palace. The hotel passed into the same ownership as *Warpool Court* only last year (see next entry) and has undergone a most welcome face-lift. Terms in the family rooms are particularly user-friendly with children accommodated free and breakfast and high tea charged on a graduated scale (£8-£15) according to their age. Other bonuses include five ground-floor bedrooms for the less mobile. ***Rooms** 21. Garden. Closed 2 Dec-1 Jan. Amex, Diners, MasterCard,* **VISA**

ST DAVID'S Warpool Court 66% £110

Tel 01437 720300 **Fax 01437 720676** Map 9 A5 H
St David's Pembrokeshire SA62 6BN

Bordering the National Trust parkland, Warpool Court was built in the 1860s as St David's Cathedral School and stands amid spectacular scenery with panoramic views over St Brides Bay to the offshore islands beyond. Equally eye-catching within is the Ada Williams collection of unique armorial and ornamental hand-painted tiles which bedeck the public areas and a number of the bedrooms. Commendable refurbishment of all the bathrooms with marble tiling, brass fittings and bright, recessed lighting greatly enhances guests' overall feeling of well-being. Children under 14 stay free in parents' room. ***Rooms** 25. Garden, croquet, tennis, covered outdoor swimming pool (Easter-Oct), keep-fit equipment, sauna, games room, play area. Closed Jan. Amex, Diners, MasterCard,* ***VISA***

If we recommend meals in a hotel a *separate* entry is usually made for its restaurant. Pub and inn entries include bar food details where recommended.

TINTERN Royal George 59% £75

Tel 01291 689205 **Fax 01291 689448** Map 9 D5 H
Tintern Chepstow Monmouthshire NP6 6SF

This 'most romantic valley in Wales' (William Wordsworth) is the setting for Tony and Maureen Pearce's hotel in the village centre at the foot of a wooded hillside. Across the main road (A466) is the Wye, and the ruins of Tintern Abbey are just a short walk away. The hotel began life in 1598 as the Irons Master's cottage for the nearby mines and was converted into a coaching inn in the 17th century. There are hints of the building's previous lives in its present appearance and versatility; there's ample space for residents, with exclusive use of one of the bars and two lounges, one stocked with books and board games. All the well-kept bedrooms (all sporting bright, upgraded bathrooms) overlook the gardens, and the best have private balconies. One child under 14 free in parents' room. ***Rooms** 19. Garden. Amex, Diners, MasterCard,* ***VISA***

TRECASTLE Castle Coaching Inn

Tel 01874 636354 **Fax 01874 636457** Map 9 C5 
Brecon Road Trecastle Brecon Powys LO3 84H

A famous inn on the old coaching route through the Brecons. The opened-out bar and dining areas make good use of natural daylight and retain sufficient of the pub's original features such as the flagstone floors and vast open fireplace to preserve the Castle's unique character. All the bedrooms are en suite, with smartly-tiled bathrooms and up-to-date amenities that include direct-dial phones, TVs, radio alarm clocks and hairdryers. There are two good-sized family rooms, one with bunk beds. To the pub's rear there's a safe, enclosed garden in which to enjoy panoramic views down the Gwyddor valley. Children are made very welcome; baby-changing facilities in the Ladies. *Open 11-3, 6-11 (11-11 Easter-Sep), Sun 11-3, 7-10.30 (12-10.30 Easter-Sep). Closed Mon Jan-Mar. Free House.* ***Beer** Courage Directors, Marston's Pedigree, guest beer. Garden. Family room.* ***Accommodation** 10 bedrooms, all en suite, £40-£45 (single £35). Children welcome overnight (under-10s stay free in parents' room, 10-16s £5), additional bed & cot available. Check-in bar hours only. No dogs. MasterCard,* ***VISA***

Pubs – note that food is only recommended in those pubs with ***Bar Food*** times in the statistics at the end of an entry. Restaurant food in pubs is *never* recommended unless specifically mentioned. Some pubs are recommended for B&B or Atmosphere only – each entry's statistics indicate our recommendation.

TRELLECH Village Green

Tel 01600 860119 Map 9 D5 

Trellech nr Monmouth Monmouthshire NP5 4PA

Bob and Jane Evans's 450-year-old village local combines bistro-style food with the more traditional concept of pub-with-restaurant. Thus we find here a combination of all three with an à la carte restaurant (recommended in our *1997 Hotels and Restaurants Guide*) and a brace of pubby bars that offer traditional pub snacks like ploughman's platters, sandwiches and baked potatoes. Between the two bars a stone-walled bistro, festooned with dried flowers hanging from its rafters, offers an inviting menu: home-made soup, smoked halibut with pickled samphire, bresaola with walnut oil and toasted pine kernels, spicy lamb sausage with mango sauce and breaded king prawns with lime mayonnaise – and these are just starters! Main courses are displayed on daily-changing blackboards and might include Tuscan fish stew, ostrich sausages, Indonesian pork and duck breast with winberries. It's back to the menu for sweets such as sticky coffee and ginger pudding, pecan and caramel tart, apple and shortbread pie and baked banana calypso with toffee ice cream. This is all inventive stuff and well worth a detour. A large Ladies room upstairs provides sufficient space for baby-changing. Alongside the pub two small bedroom suites with kitchenettes are let on a bed-and-breakfast or self-catering basis. There is room for a small family (children accommodated free) and TV is provided, but no phones; the en suite facilities have WC and showers only. *Open 11-2.30, 6.30-12 (not Sun & Mon), Sun 12-3 only.* ***Bar Food*** *12-2, 7-9.45 (not Sun & Mon eve).* ***Beer*** *Bass, Worthington Best.* ***Accommodation*** *2 bedrooms, both en suite, from £45 (single £35). Children welcome overnight (under-8s free in parents' room), additional bed available. Check-in by arrangement. No dogs. Closed Sun eve, all Mon (except Bank Holiday Mon eves) & 1 week Jan. MasterCard,* ***VISA***

JaB is short for 'Just a Bite'. These majority of these establishments are also recommended in our *Bistros, Bars & Cafés* Guide which features establishments where one may eat well for less than £15 per head.

TREMEIRCHION Salusbury Arms

Tel 01745 710262 Map 8 C1 

Tremeirchion St Asaph Conwy LL17 0HN

A former estate coaching house with origins dating back to the 14th-century. The Grade II listed pub takes its name from Tremeirchion's ancestral owners. Jim and Heulwen O'Boyle have carefully restored the building which is spick-and-span within, with a cosy feel to its interlinked village bar, lounges and dining-room. Jim's regularly-changing real ales are a serious attraction, as is Heulwen's bubbling welcome. The Salusbury Grill, home-made steak and ale pie (or chicken and mushroom) are regular favourites and there's usually a range of specials like Lancashire hotpot in Yorkshire pudding, steamed mussels and garlic bread and fresh cod in batter, alongside regular bar snacks like sandwiches, baked potatoes, vegetarian burgers, scampi and breaded plaice; brunch fry-ups are also offered at lunchtime. A cheery welcome for children (who'll find a lovely garden to play in), a burgeoning trade in family Sunday lunches (booking advised), and a Welsh songstress entertaining on weekend evenings completes the picture. *Open 11-11 (Sun 12-3, 7-10.30).* ***Bar Food*** *12-2.30, 7-9.30, (no food Sun eve). Free House.* ***Beer*** *Boddingtons, Morland Old Speckled Hen, Flowers Original guest beers. Garden, outdoor eating, Family room. No credit cards.*

We endeavour to be as up-to-date as possible, but inevitably some changes to data and key personnel may occur at restaurants and hotels after the Guide goes to press. Prices should also be taken as indications rather than firm quotes.

WELSH HOOK Stone Hall £65

Tel 01348 840212 **Fax 01348 840815** Map 9 A5 **RR**
Welsh Hook Wolfscastle nr Haverfordwest Pembrokeshire SA62 5NS

Hidden down country lanes 1½ miles off the A40 (signed from Wolfscastle), the restaurant's interior is as Welsh as one would hope to find at such an address as this: stone alcoves, exposed roof timbers, flagged floors, metre-thick walls and, by the huge hooded range, bread ovens built into the original inglenook. The setting may be Welsh but Martine Watson's cooking is uncompromisingly French. A la carte starters might include king prawns sautéed with lovage butter and cucumber slices, and a warm salad of duck confit before half a pheasant cooked in tea with sultanas and walnuts, beef fillet with Bordelaise sauce and halibut with a stuffing of prawns and fennel on a mixed spice sauce. Finish with crème brulée, a nougat glacé with mixed fruit or a traditional tarte tatin. The no-choice, four-course table d'hote offers particularly good value. Not a half bottle in sight on the wine list, but prices are so reasonable that it hardly matters. No children under 10 after 7pm. ***Seats** 34. Private Room 20. L by arrangement D 7-9.30. Closed 2 weeks Jan. Set D £16. Amex, Diners, MasterCard,* ***VISA***

Rooms £65

Residents enjoy the use of their own lounge and five en suite bedrooms (three doubles and two singles), which are all immaculately kept. Children, made welcome overnight, are offered their own supper at 5.30pm. The resident cats are great favourites, so no dogs admitted! Garden and patio.

WELSHPOOL Powis Castle Tea Rooms

Tel 01938 555499 Map 8 D3 **JaB**
Powis Castle Welshpool Powys SY21 8RF

You needn't pay admission to the famous gardens to enjoy a snack at this National Trust restaurant, reached by way of a long drive winding past ponds and peacocks. A spacious hall, refectory-style, adjoins the castle keep; from morning coffee through light lunches to afternoon teas it's a bustling place. Notable among the dishes on offer are their own-recipe apple and cheese soup (£1.95), 'Clive's Petit-Pate' – a sweet lamb pie commemorating Clive of India (£2.95) and Welsh onion cake served with a lunchtime salad; assorted Welsh cheeses, too, are the highlight of the Coachman's Choice (£4.95). Powis Welsh Cream Tea (£2.85) and Welsh Garden tea including scones and bara brith run through the afternoon when for children there are sausage rolls with baked beans and Marmite sandwiches. It's licensed with main meals and there's now a selection of flavoured traditional Welsh meads. There is a mother and baby room downstairs (just off the museum); four high-chairs are provided. No smoking. ***Seats** 80. **Open** 11-5.30. **Closed** Mon (except Bank Holidays), Tue (Apr-Jun & Sep, Oct) & all Nov-Mar (except days up to Christmas when the NT shop is open). MasterCard,* ***VISA***

WREXHAM Bumble

Tel 01978 355023 Map 8 D2 **JaB**
2 Charles Street Wrexham LL13 8BT

All-day snacks are the stock-in-trade of this popular spot above a cluttered little gift shop of the same name. Following morning specials of biscuits, teacakes and scones the choice goes more savoury with home-made soup, jacket potatoes, salads, rarebits, and a hot special of the day such as chicken and mushroom pie with jacket potato and salad (£3.75). Other popular home-produced options include pizza with various fillings (from £3.50), ploughman's platters and fresh fruit flans such as cherry or apple with cream or ice cream (£1.55). Bumble blend tea remains a favourite afternoon choice with assorted cakes, meringues and pies from the tempting cabinet display. Unlicensed, but you can bring your own, no corkage. Two high-chairs provided; ask for children's portions. ***Seats** 60. **Open** 9-5. **Closed** Sun. Diners, MasterCard,* ***VISA***

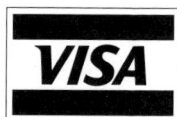

Channel Islands & Isle of Man

Alderney

Braye — First & Last — £45

Tel 01481 823162 Map 13 F4 R

Braye Alderney

The only restaurant on the island to benefit from the sea view has a panoramic dining-room on the first floor. The blue decor is strongly marine and as you would expect in this location, fish is the order of the day. Bouillabaisse is something of a speciality and (as available) lobster, crab, scallops and mussels with half portions on request; there are also plenty of steaks and omelettes, and a concise wine list. In the evening, red lanterns are lit for a more romantic atmosphere. No children after 9.30. ***Seats** 75. Parties 24. L 12-1.45 D 6.45-11. Closed Oct-Mar, also Mon exc Bank Holidays. Set Sun L £9.50. Amex, Diners, MasterCard,* ***VISA***

St Anne — Georgian House

Tel & Fax 01481 822471 Map 13 F4

Victoria Street St Anne Alderney

There are numerous nice touches which make the Georgian House stand out; one is a courtesy car between the house and the harbour (book it when you make your reservation); another is the Garden Beyond, the peaceful, fragrant garden area complete with open air bar and grill, designed to take full advantage of the kind climate in summer, and a third is the friendly welcome from owners Elizabeth and Stephen Hope. Food here is of the highest standard and locally-caught fish and crustaceans feature strongly. The lunch menu is kept simple with the likes of wonderful moules à la crème, whole fresh Alderney crab (price depends on weight), and fish cakes with prawn and parsley sauce. In addition, the chalkboard announces daily specials like home-made leek and potato soup, bargain Herm oysters, fresh sea bass with thyme, hot salt beef with dumplings and pasta bolognese. The dinner menu is more elaborate, with a platter of fruits de mer (24hrs' notice recommended in winter) and 12oz sirloin flambéed in brandy typical of the offerings. Home-made desserts are a must – summer pudding in the form of a layered terrine is made with local berries and the raspberry flan with fruit from the owners' garden. Special 3-course Sunday lunch menu. Bedroom accommodation with colour TV, direct-dial telephones and en suite bathrooms is offered in a suite with its own sitting-room and balcony (highly suitable for family use) plus two single rooms; ask about package deals including air fares. *Open 10.30-3, 6.30-12.* ***Bar Food** 12-2.30, 7.30-9.30. Children allowed in bar to eat, children's menu. Free House.* ***Beer** Ringwood Best & Fortyniner, Guernsey Summer/Winter Ale. Garden, outdoor eating.* ***Accommodation** 1 suite (£55 – family of 4 £70), 2 singles (£27.50), all en suite. Accommodation closed Christmas & New Year. Pub closed Tue evenings. Amex, Diners, MasterCard,* ***VISA***

St Anne — Inchalla Hotel — 64% — £80

Tel 01481 823220 **Fax 01481 824045** Map 13 F4

The Val St Anne Alderney

Set in its own secluded grounds with lovely views across the English Channel and to the bird sanctuary island of Burbou, Inchalla has been in the capable and attentive hands of Valerie Willis since 1982. A lounge with its own conservatory is the main day room, and a new bar was built in 1996. Bedrooms are smart and well equipped, with adjoining family rooms charged on a graduating scale according to children's age. No dogs. ***Rooms** 9. Garden, sauna, spa bath. Closed 2 weeks Christmas. Amex, MasterCard,* ***VISA***

We welcome bona fide complaints and recommendations on the tear-out pages at the back of the Guide for Readers' Comments. They are followed up by our professional team.

Guernsey

CASTEL La Grande Mare 72% £113

Tel 01481 56576 **Fax 01481 56532** Map 13 E4 H
Vazon Bay Castel Guernsey GY5 7BD

Situated on Guernsey's west coast with seaward aspects over the broad sandy sweep of Vazon Bay and the English Channel beyond, La Grande Mare enjoys its own 100 acres of land, complete with a private golf course. The pastel-washed building, in a style appealingly somewhere between a traditional Guernsey farmhouse and a Mediterranean villa and bedecked with balconies, is set around an outdoor pool and patio. Inside, public rooms are relaxed and welcoming: arched windows, limed oak furniture and exposed brickwork enhance the Continental feel created by rugs and soft upholstery. However, it is in the bedroom accommodation that La Grande Mare is particularly unusual and innovative, in that it ranges from luxury suites (some with four-posters) to self-contained studios, one- or two-bed apartments and a villa for eight. Bathrooms, all with exotic Italian tiles, are spacious, extensively equipped and meticulously maintained; all suites have facilities for fixing light snacks and all ten apartments have a fully-fitted kitchen. ***Rooms** 34. Garden, croquet, outdoor swimming pool, splash pool, spa bath, golf (18), fishing. Amex, Diners, MasterCard,* ***VISA***

CASTEL Hotel Hougue du Pommier £78

Tel 01481 56531 **Fax 01481 56260** Map 13 E4 I
Castel Guernsey GY5 7FQ

A lovely inn dating back to 1712, 'Hougue du Pommier' means 'apple-tree hill' and the apples from the ten acres of orchards surrounding this fine old Guernsey farmhouse were once used to make local cider. The Tudor Bar exudes a traditional atmosphere, with beams and an inglenook fireplace. By the solar-heated swimming pool is a sunny Tea Garden in a secluded spot surrounded by trees where bar meals are served all day; nearby are a sauna, sunbed room and a games room wih ping-pong table and video games. There's also a 10-hole pitch-and-putt golf course and a putting green, and the sandy beaches of Grandes Rocques and Cobo are just ten minutes' walk away. Quiet bedrooms with a good range of family accommodation overlook the particularly well-kept hotel gardens; all have remote-control TVs, telephones and beverage trays. Children's High Tea served from 5.30pm. *Bar open 11-2, 6-11.30, Sun 12-3.30, 6-11.30 (Sunday open to diners and residents only).* ***Beer** Guernsey Brewery. Garden. **Accommodation** 43 bedrooms, all en suite, £52-£78 according to season (4-poster £72-£98, single £26-£50). Children welcome overnight (0-5 yrs stay free, 5-12 yrs 50% of tariff), additional bed & cot available. No dogs. Amex, Diners, MasterCard,* ***VISA***

A jug of fresh water!

FOREST Mallard Hotel 67% £70

Tel 01481 64164 **Fax 01481 65732** Map 13 E4 H
Forest Guernsey

Conveniently located near the airport, this family-friendly hotel is virtually a resort in itself. Public rooms are particularly large and the big attraction is of course the outdoor solar-heated swimming pool with plenty of outdoor tables. A children's soft play area has a Disney theme, and the hotel has its own 4-screen cinema (used also by non-residents) as well as a state-of-the-art golf simulator. Bedrooms are comfortable, with trouser press, hairdryer, colour TV and tea/coffee facilities. Rooms overlooking the swimming pool have south-facing balconies, while those rooms facing the back of the building are quieter. Self-contained apartments, sleeping four, are available for weekly rental. Parking for 120 cars. ***Rooms** 47. Garden, outdoor swimming pool, keep-fit equipment, sauna, spa bath, sun beds, tennis, mini-golf, pétanque, playground, playroom, games room, 4-screen cinema. Closed 1 Dec-mid Mar. Amex, Diners, MasterCard,* ***VISA***

KINGS MILLS Fleur du Jardin Hotel

Tel 01481 57996 **Fax 01481 56834** Map 13 E4 P

Kings Mills nr Castel Guernsey GY5 7JT

Named after a prize-winning herd of Guernsey cattle kept here when it was a working farm, this 16th-century inn is in the centre of Kings Mills village, close to Vazon Bay, and has a tastefully traditional country feel. Several low-ceilinged, beamed dining-rooms interconnect, creating a quiet atmosphere. The cooking is the highlight here with an extensive menu on which the daily specials – strong on fish and game – are probably the best bet: typically, grilled bream Provençal-style, medallions of monkfish in crushed black pepper, and braised rabbit in Pommery mustard sauce. Also, there are commendable vegetarian choices such as three bean chilli on a bed of brown rice, and a popular four-course family Sunday lunch served in both the bar and restaurant; eight or nine wines are available by the glass. The bedrooms are attractive and amenities include remote-control TVs, telephones and tea/coffee-making facilities; some rooms have trouser presses and small refrigerators. There's a beautiful view of the surrounding countryside from the heated outdoor swimming pool set in two acres of gardens and grounds, with plenty of free parking. *Open 11-2.30, 5-11.45 (Sun 12-2, 7-9.30 with food only).* ***Bar Food*** *12-2, 6-9.30 (Sun from 7). Children allowed in bar to eat, children's menu. Free House.* ***Beer*** *Guernsey Brewery Sunbeam & Summer/ Winter Ale. Garden, outdoor eating, children's play area.* ***Accommodation*** *17 bedrooms, all en suite, from £55 to £75 according to season. Children over 4 welcome overnight (under-12s stay at 50% adult rate if sharing parents' room, high-tea included), additional bed & cot available. No dogs. Amex, MasterCard,* ***VISA***

L'ERÉE Taste of India £35

Tel 01481 64516 Map 13 E4 

Sunset Cottage L'Erée Guernsey GY7 9LN

One of the very few Indian restaurants on the island, well located at the end of Rocquaine Bay near Lihou island right on the west coast. The menu is strong on tandoori and there's also a section called Exquisite Dishes, which are the specialities. Good-quality ingredients are used with a delicate mix of spices; seafood dishes include tandoori lobster and garlic salmon. There is also a branch in St Peter Port (Tel 01481 723730). ***Seats*** *40. L 12-2 D 6-11. Closed Tue (Nov-Apr), 25 Dec. Set Sun L £9.95 Set D £15 & £25. Amex, Diners, MasterCard,* ***VISA***

LE BOURG Deerhound Inn Hotel

Tel 01481 38585 **Fax 01481 39443** Map 13 E4 

Le Bourg Forest Road Forest Guernsey GY8 0AN

Per and Karon Bonthelius run this converted old Guernsey farmhouse situated above Petit Bot valley and beach, off the main road and not far from the airport. The welcome is warm and their approach is very much 'hands on', with Swedish chef Mats assisting Karon in the kitchen. The bar food menu is nonetheless full of local delights, particularly in the daily 'Fish Specials' such as the grilled turbot with garlic and lime butter, scallops Thermidor and sole bretonne we recently found on offer. A choice of dual-priced (starter/main) pasta dishes, large or double-decker sandwiches and firm favourites like beef stroganoff and chicken curry supplement the summer salads and usual favourites for 'the little people'. The bedrooms are generally modest (as is their price) and only four have en suite bathrooms; one is a family room with bunk beds. The TV lounge doubles as a children's playroom when needed; they've just built an outdoor swimming pool and there are swings, a see-saw and a slide in the garden. Baby-listening devices are provided and baby-sitting can be arranged. *Open 10.30-11.45, (Sun 12-2, 6-9.30 with meals only).* ***Bar Food*** *12-1.45, 7-9.30. Free House.* ***Beer*** *Tetley, Theakston Best, Ringwood, guest beers. Garden, outdoor eating, children's play area.* ***Accommodation*** *10 bedrooms, 4 with en suite showers, £30-£40 according to season (single £15-£20). Children welcome overnight (under-3s stay free in parents' room, 3-12s half-price), additional bed & cot available. Amex, MasterCard,* ***VISA***

Pleinmont Imperial Hotel £63

Tel 01481 64044 **Fax 01481 66139** Map 13 E4 I
Pleinmont Torteval Guernsey GY8 0PS

This attractive small hotel ideally located at the south end of sandy Rocquaine Bay, and overlooking the harbour at Portelet is personably run by Patrick and Dianna Lindley. Lounge bar, restaurant (restored to its all-wood design of 100 years ago) and most of the bedrooms benefit from a beautiful view of the bay; sea view rooms attract a supplement (up to £2.50 per person per day). Four rooms have attractive balconies with patio furniture; all have clean and bright accommodation with tea-coffee facilities, colour TV and direct-dial telephone. A self-catering apartment is also available. Children are welcome overnight; there's an all-day patio cafe and High Tea is served at 6pm. The hotel leads on to 20 miles of cliff walks, and is just a short walk from the beach. *Open 10.30-11.45 (Mon-Wed to 11 in winter, Sun 11-3).* ***Beer** Randalls. Safe garden, outdoor eating.* ***Accommodation** 17 bedrooms, all en suite, £45-£63 according to season (single £20-£42), £30-£45 room only; special Spring/Autumn tariffs include free car hire. Children welcome overnight, extra bed & cot provided (under-2s stay free). Lounge bar closed Sun eve Nov-Mar. Accommodation closed Dec-Feb. MasterCard,* ***VISA***

St Peter Port St Pierre Park 71% £145

Tel 01481 728282 **Fax 01481 712041** Map 13 E4 
Rohais St Peter Port Guernsey GY1 1FD

The St Pierre Park, built in 1983 on the edge of town in 45 acres of landscaped gardens, boasts impressive leisure facilities with its Tony Jacklin-designed 9-hole golf course, three outdoor tennis courts, a 25m indoor swimming pool and a fully-equipped health suite. Best of the elegant day rooms, the lounge and bar overlook the garden and ornamental lake. Bedrooms offer plenty of space and up-to-date facilities including satellite TV and baby listening; all have either a balcony or terrace and a couple of ground floor rooms have been adapted for use by those with physical disability. Children under 12 stay free in their parents' room; there are 51 family rooms with packages including high tea in the Cafe Renoir and creche facilities in high season. There is a children's playground within the grounds and the hotel's stated policy is: 'children are most welcome and not forgotten at the St Pierre Park'. At Easter, typically, there might be a an Easter egg hunt, a Sunday afternoon children's tea party and crazy golf. No dogs. ***Rooms** 135. Garden, croquet, golf course (9-hole), pitch & putt, putting, tennis, indoor swimming pool, gym, sauna, steam room, spa bath, solarium, beauty & hair salons, snooker, coffee shop (10am-10.30pm), gift & clothes shop, outdoor play area. Amex, Diners, MasterCard,* ***VISA***

St Peters Longfrie Inn

Tel 01481 63107 Map 13 E4 
Rue de Longfrie St Peters Guernsey GY7 9RX

Arguably Guernsey's most popular family pub is situated in its own grounds in a rural setting outside the village. Formerly a 16th-century farmhouse, it now contains an indoor 'fun factory' (supervised indoor bedlam might be a more apposite description) for children under 10, a large beer garden with swings and extensive playing area, ample car parking, and standard pub fare with a positively ghoulish selection for the little devils! Baby-changing facilities, high-chairs and helpful staff complete the family-friendly atmosphere; adults without children may find it all too much before 8.30pm. Under the same ownership as *Fleur du Jardin* (see entry under Kings Mills). Overnight accommodation is now available in five en suite double bedrooms with facilities for families (rates on application), and exclusive use of a private residents' lounge. *Open 11.30-2.30, 5.30-11.30 (Sun 12-2.30, 6.30-11.30 with food only).* ***Beer** Guernsey Brewery Sunbeam & Summer/Winter Ale. Garden, children's play area.* ***Accommodation** 5 bedrooms, all en suite, £38-£52. Children welcome overnight (under-4s stay free). Amex, Diners, MasterCard,* ***VISA***

Herm

Herm — White House — 64% — £110*

Tel 01481 722159 **Fax 01481 710066** Map 13 E4 **HR**

Herm

'Paradise is this close' say the White House's resident directors, who, as wards of Herm Island, also administer its 18 self-catering cottages and a camp site. The only hotel on the island, an escape from the hurly-burly of mainland life, the White House produces its own electricity and is self-contained with a succession of homely lounges, an elegant sea-view restaurant and a pub with a Carvery dining-room. In the bedrooms, the best of which have sea views and balconies, there are no televisions, phones or clocks, and a butane cooker is provided for boiling the tea kettle. *Half-board terms only. No dogs. ***Rooms** 38. Garden, croquet, tennis, outdoor swimming pool. Closed Oct-Mar. MasterCard,* ***VISA***

Restaurant — £40

The White House has its own oyster farm, so it will come as no surprise that the specialities on the set menu are largely seafood. Conservatory lunches, priced according to the main course, offer such dishes as grilled Guernsey plaice, chicken breast with tiger prawns and vegetable stroganoff. Dinner choices include Herm oysters and Guernsey scallops with crab vinaigrette, followed by rack of English lamb basted with honey and perhaps steamed sea bass on a bed of linguine and a saffron-scented sauce. To follow choose between orange pancakes with iced praline parfait, baked rhubarb and apple charlotte and a French cheese selection served with toasted brioche. No smoking. The Ship Inn pub (open 9am-9.30pm, Sun 9-2.30pm) has a carvery dining-room and is ideal for informal family dining; children are offered their own young sea dogs' menu. Morning coffee with pastries, afternoon teas and Sunday lunch are also offered. The 'sun-drenched' patio is an ideal place to sample on of their splendid ice cream sundaes, made with the highest buttermilk-content ice cream in the world. ***Seats** 118. Parties 12. L 12.30-2 D 7-9.30. Set L from £11.75 (Sun £9.95) Set D £14.95/£15.75.*

Jersey

Gorey — Jersey Pottery Restaurant

Tel 01534 851119 **Fax 01534 856403** Map 13 F4 JaB
Gorey Village Gorey Jersey JE3 9EP

One of Jersey's most popular and busiest tourist attractions, where the pottery-making process can be watched, from throwing to glazing. Next to the attractive conservatory restaurant is the self-service café, which fills up rapidly for cold luncheons and afternoon tea. Prawns and crab appears in salads (prawn £6.25/£8.95), in cocktails, in the shell (fresh crab £10.50) or in half melons. Filled rolls are priced from £2.45 for egg mayonnaise and cress to £3.95 for smoked salmon. A selection of cakes and pastries made on the premises includes scones (95p), Bakewell tarts (£1.25), gateaux and fruit tarts. There are tables set outside near the conservatory restaurant, which offers an extensive à la carte menu. Children's portions. No-smoking area. ***Seats** 200 (+100 outside). **Open** 9-5.30. **Closed** Sun & 10 days Christmas. Amex, Diners, MasterCard,* **VISA**

Grouville — Grouville Bay Hotel 62% £80

Tel 01534 851004 **Fax 01534 857416** Map 13 F4 H
Grouville Jersey JE3 9BB

Located right next to the Royal Jersey Golf course, the hotel enjoys attractive views over the greens and in the other direction looks out towards the 12th-century Mont Orgueil Castle; there's a footpath to the nearby beach. Bedrooms face either the golf course and the sea (with balconies), or the garden and the terrace and pool. There is plenty of family activity with nearly half the rooms having three or more beds; cots are provided and under-5s stay free in parents' room. Early suppers for children, plenty of high-chairs and baby-sitting are all available. Comfortable public rooms. ***Rooms** 56. Garden, croquet, outdoor swimming pool, children's swimming pool and playroom, games room. Closed mid Oct-Apr. Amex, Diners, MasterCard,* **VISA**

Always ring ahead and inform establishments of your exact requirements when travelling with children. Unannounced can, sadly, still mean unwelcome.

Havre des Pas — Hotel de la Plage 66% £70

Tel 01534 23474 **Fax 01534 68642** Map 13 F4 H
Havre des Pas St Helier Jersey JE2 4UQ

On the outskirts of St Helier right on the seafront, this is a well-run modern hotel with picture windows to enhance the views. Day rooms are in various styles: subdued and modern in the split-level lounge-bar, tropical in the Caribbean Bar, bamboo in the sun lounge. The rate quoted is for an inland-view bedroom; sea-facing rooms, some with balconies, carry supplements. All have en suite bathrooms with the usual electric gadgets and bathrobes. No dogs. ***Rooms** 78. Keep-fit facilities, sun beds, games room. Closed mid Oct-end Apr. Amex, Diners, MasterCard,* **VISA**

Havre des Pas — Ommaroo Hotel 59% £90

Tel 01534 23493 **Fax 01534 59912** Map 13 F4 H
Havre des Pas St Helier Jersey JE2 4UQ

This traditional town hotel overlooking the sea and pool at Havre des Pas has an attractive garden and sun terrace. With its relaxing lounges and bars, special children's menus, early high teas and nightly entertainment in season, it's justifiably popular with families. Facilities in standard bedrooms include bath, shower or both; de luxe rooms with bath and shower, sea views and balconies attract a supplementary charge. ***Rooms** 85. Garden. Amex, Diners, MasterCard,* **VISA**

PORTELET BAY Portelet Hotel 66% £104

Tel 01534 41204 **Fax 01534 46625** Map 13 F4
Portelet Bay St Brelade Jersey JE3 8AU

Now in the same group as *Hotel de la Plage* (*qv*), the Portelet was built in the 30s and retains some Art Deco features, notably at the entrance. Most popular of the public rooms is the sun lounge overlooking the pool and St Brelade's Bay beyond. Elsewhere there's a quiet residents' lounge and a 70s-style cocktail bar. Many of the bedrooms have private balconies. Early-morning tea or coffee and newspapers are complimentary and there's a courtesy mini-bus to town. High tea at 5.30pm, children's menu, baby foods and high-chairs are all provided. A family disco takes place each week. Guests may use the facilities of the Aquadome plus tennis and squash at the sister *Merton Hotel* (see below) for a small charge. Seymour Hotels. No dogs. ***Rooms*** *86. Garden, outdoor swimming pool, children's splash pool, tennis, putting, fishing, games room, snooker. Closed Oct-Apr. Amex, Diners, MasterCard,* ***VISA***

ST BRELADE Hotel La Place 67% £120

Tel 01534 44261 **Fax 01534 45164** Map 13 F4 H
Route du Coin La Haule St Brelade Jersey JE3 8BF

Just four miles from St Helier and seven minutes from the airport, La Place is nonetheless for those who like rural surroundings. It was once a farmhouse, but it's now much enlarged by modern extensions; the main public rooms, however, are part of the original 400-year-old building. There's a delightful open-air seating area in a south-facing courtyard, a bright bar with green bamboo furniture and two lounges, one of which has a black-beamed ceiling, a pink granite fireplace, antique furniture and polished brass ornaments. Bedrooms provide good, modern comforts for holidaymakers, and special attention to businesspeople's requirements in the executive study rooms complete with fax machines, desk-top accessories and reference books. Currently there are seven bedrooms set around the pool, with a further garden cottage suite planned for this year. Children up to 12 stay free in parents' room. ***Rooms*** *40. Garden, outdoor swimming pool, sauna, outdoor play area. Amex, Diners, MasterCard,* ***VISA***

ST BRELADE Old Smugglers Inn

Tel 01534 41510 Map 13 F4
Ouaisne Bay St Brelade Jersey

Two 13th-century fishermen's cottages were rebuilt from their ruins in 1721 by local fishermen and remained as such until the early 1900s when they were enlarged and developed into the Finisterre hotel retaining most of the original granitework, beams and fireplaces. After the German occupation the property underwent further changes and the Old Smugglers Inn emerged. Today a succession of small dining-rooms (including a 50-seater family room with a non-smoking area) serve food from an extensive menu supplemented by daily market fish such as Jersey plaice, crab and lobster. Hot grilled crab claws with piri-piri sauce are a popular starter, followed by salad selections, the 'Burger Box' and traditional goodies from chicken and leek pie to fillet steak with garlic mushrooms. Separately, the chidren's menu provides puzzles and crayoning in case of a wait for Pirate Pete's fish fingers or Captain Hook's scampi. No children under 14 in the bar; baby-changing facilities available. Folk nights on Sunday. *Open 11-11.* ***Bar Food*** *12-2, 6-8.45 (no food Sunday eve in winter). Free House.* ***Beer*** *Bass, two guest beers. Terrace. Family room. Amex, MasterCard,* ***VISA***

ST BRELADE Sea Crest 64% £94

Tel 01534 46353 **Fax 01534 47316** Map 13 F4
Petit Port St Brelade Jersey JE3 8HH

Owners Julian and Martha Bernstein run this relaxing white-painted modern hotel, which overlooks a rocky bay at the south-west end of the island, with attention to detail that is apparent in personal touches throughout; note their collection of modern art in the public rooms. Bedrooms, five with balconies, overlook the bay so that guests can watch the often spectacular sunsets. No dogs. ***Rooms*** *7. Garden, outdoor swimming pool, children's splash pool. Closed mid Jan-mid Feb. Amex, MasterCard,* ***VISA***

Restaurant £75

Set menus change every week, so that with the carte as well there's plenty of choice available in the picturesque seaward-looking dining-room. Good seafood is well handled in sensibly simple style – moules marinière, sea bass with crab and ginger, Dover sole either grilled or meunière, dressed local crab – or there is home-made tagliatelle, pan-fried calf's liver, rack of lamb and a section of dishes prepared at the table such as king prawns in spring onion and black bean sauce. An extensive, predominantly French, wine list has some very fair prices. Tables on the terrace for light meals in summer. ***Seats*** *60 (+ 20 outside). Parties 25. L 12.30-2 D 7.30-10. Closed L Sun (also D Sun in winter), all Mon. Set L £11.50 Set D £18.50.*

St Brelade's Bay — St Brelade's Bay Hotel — 70% — £140

Tel 01534 46141 **Fax 01534 47278** Map 13 F4 **H**

St Brelade's Bay Jersey JE3 8EF

Family owned and run for five generations and set in seven acres of award-winning gardens, St Brelade's Bay Hotel is a popular spot for family holidays, especially as there's a resident lifeguard at the two heated freshwater swimming pools. Although the exterior looks modern the interior has a timeless elegance with moulded ceilings and chandeliers, comfortable sofas and chairs and an abundance of fresh flowers. First- and second-floor rooms are traditional, while those on the third floor are more modern; all are attractively and tastefully decoratedand furnished. Sea-view rooms have a balcony, while on the other side bedrooms overlook the gardens. Children's tea is served from 5.15-6, then children's supper from 7-7.30 (for over-5s: no children under 5 permitted in the restaurant after 6pm). Active youngsters are encouraged to take advantage of the 'Dolphin Awards' programme of swimming lessons; swimming galas and competitions arranged during high season. There are also indoor (arcade games, table tennis, pool table) and outdoor play areas and a children's video and TV lounge. Twice-weekly discos (chidlren welcome until 10pm). Baby-sitting can be arranged. Push-chairs can be hired from the hall porter. Ask about the variety of communicating rooms: for example, there is a twin with garden views and communicating single room with bunk beds. ***Rooms*** *72. Garden, croquet, tennis, pitch & putt, outdoor swimming pool, children's swimming pool, playground and playroom, keep-fit equipment, sauna, sun beds, snooker. Closed mid Oct-end Apr. MasterCard,* **VISA**

St Helier — Apollo Hotel — 63% — £87

Tel 01534 25441 **Fax 01534 22120** Map 13 F4 **H**

9 St Saviour's Road St Helier Jersey JE2 4LA

A modern two-storey hotel built round a courtyard. Public areas provide plenty of space to relax; there are two bars (one in pub style), a coffee shop serving snacks throughout the day, an indoor leisure centre and a sun-trap terrace. Bedrooms, some with balconies, include many suitable for family occupation. Children up to 5 stay free in parents' room. No dogs. ***Rooms*** *85. Terrace, indoor swimming pool, gym, sauna, spa bath, solarium. Amex, Diners, MasterCard,* **VISA**

St Helier — De Vere Grand — 68% — £130

Tel 01534 22301 **Fax 01534 37815** Map 13 F4 **HR**

Esplanade St Helier Jersey JE4 8WD

With its long gabled frontage, the De Vere Grand is a distinctive feature on the St Helier seafront – and the entrance is appropriately impressive, with ornate coloured pillars and a marble floor. The smart period-style bar and lounge have fine views and so do balconied front bedrooms, which attract a hefty surcharge. It's a busy hotel catering for both holiday and business visitors (conference/banqueting facilities for 180/280). Families are well provided for with free accommodation for under-14s in their parents' room, plus baby-sitting and children's meals also available. Good leisure facilities. ***Rooms*** *115. Terrace, indoor swimming pool, keep-fit equipment, sauna, steam room, spa bath, sun bed, snooker. Amex, Diners, MasterCard,* **VISA**

See over

Regency Room £75

The elegant Regency Room, offering only a four-course table d'hote dinner, is the main hotel dining-room. Warm ballotine of chicken leg with a mushroom farce, a petit bouillabaisse, and honey-glazed loin of pork from the trolley typify the nightly choices. Separate vegetarian and vegan menu. ***Seats** 250. D only 7-9.30. Set D £19.50.*

Victoria's £75

The classical French à la carte menus here are a little more sophisticated than in the Regency Room; illustrative are scrambled egg millefeuille with goose foie gras and Madeira jus, grilled turbot on creamed leeks with a crayfish mousseline, a trio of pan-fried beef, venison and veal fillets with three complementary sauces, and several flambé dishes among both main courses and desserts. Dancing to live music each evening. Alongside France, only Italy is well represented on the wine list with scant offerings from elsewhere, and some hefty mark-ups. ***Seats** 160. L 12.30-2.15 D 7-10. Closed D Sun. Set L £11.50/£15.50 (Sun £16.50) Set D £23.50.*

St Helier Hotel de France 73% £120

Tel 01534 614000 **Fax 01534 614999** Map 13 F4 H
St Saviour's Road St Helier Jersey

With a smart new lay-out at the front of the hotel, the main drive being re-routed to make way for Mediterranean-style gardens and alfresco eating, the Hotel de France is staying well abreast of the times. The reception hall has also been enlarged and front-facing bedrooms redesigned to create an even more comfortable ambience for guests. The hotel boasts a multi-screen cinema, a nightclub, a splendid health and fitness centre, an all-day brasserie and a supervised Children's Club in the summer season. Extended conference facilities and syndicate rooms with an in-house management team and self-contained organisers' office has extended theatre-style capacity to 1,000, with banqueting for 850. Children under the age of 12 stay free in their parents' room. 4-11pm; starting with 'Splash Down' in the indoor pool followed by high tea; face-painting, T-shirt painting or even chocolate-making might follow in the hotel's own 'Chocolate Factory'. There are cots in the club room 'for those too young to stay the pace'! At the Hotel de France they recognise that 'a holiday is not a holiday if the children are not occupied'. Nineteen bedrooms are interconnecting family rooms. ***Rooms** 320. Garden, outdoor & indoor swimming pool, gym, squash, sauna, spa bath, solarium, beauty & hair salon, games room, snooker, news kiosk (8-12, 4-7). Amex, Diners, MasterCard,* ***VISA***

We do not accept free meals or hospitality – our inspectors pay their own bills.

St Helier Museum Café

Tel 01534 58060 Map 13 F4 JaB
The Weigh Bridge St Helier Jersey JE2 3NF

Now fully operational after the construction of a modern wing which hosts the Museum Café, an agreeable, bright place with white tiles and black modern furniture. Everything is freshly prepared in the open-plan kitchen. The small menu might offer roast beef with horseradish (£5.55), cod with salsa verde (£5.75 or pasta spirals with a wild mushroom sauce (£5.25). Salads are popular, all priced around £5 – the vegetarian salad – with avocado, nuts, egg, mozzarella and olives is particularly delicious. Children's portions and a children's colouring menu are provided. High-chairs available. Kids might enjoy seeing the Victorian nursery in the museum. Some tables are set outside, on the side of the museum entrance. ***Seats** 55 (+40 outside).* ***Open** 10-4.45 (Sun 1-4.45, winter till 4).* ***Closed** 4 days Christmas. Amex, Diners, MasterCard,* ***VISA***

St Lawrence — British Union Hotel

Tel 01534 861070 Map 13 F4 P

Main Road St Lawrence Jersey JE3 1NL

Owned by Guernsey's Ann Street Brewery, this pleasant pub with a good atmosphere and warm welcome stands across the road from St Lawrence Parish Church. A central bar divides two lounges, with an additional family/games room to the rear. Well-prepared daily specials will often include Jersey plaice alongside steak and ale pie and vegetarian options; there are the usual chicken, fishy and piggy dishes on the laminated menu as well as lots for the 'little angels' and ice cream, gateau and apple pie for dessert. *Open 10am-11.pm, (Sun 11-1, 4.30-11.30).* ***Bar Food*** *12-2, 6-8.30 (no food Sundays). Family room, children's menu.* ***Beer*** *Guernsey Sunbeam. Patio, outdoor eating. No credit cards.*

St Ouen — Lobster Pot, Coach House

Tel 01534 482888 **Fax 01534 481574** Map 13 F4 

L'Etacq St Ouen Jersey JE3 2FB

Housed in a modern hotel converted from an old granite farmhouse, the pubby bar in what was once the cow byre plays a contrasting role to the busy restaurant (recommended in our *1997 Hotels & Restaurants Guide*, especially for its first-class local seafood). A large open-air paved terrace is the main attraction at this very scenic spot overlooking sandy St Ouen's Bay. When we last visited a good mix of lunchtime bar food ranged from baked potatoes and omelettes to various steaks and fishy salads such as crab and lobster; some of the seafood is landed just 200 yards away, so it's as fresh and as local as you can get! As we went to press both the hotel and restaurant were due to close for a complete refurbishment over the winter months, so a new look Lobster Pot is eagerly awaited for the spring of 1997. It would be advisable to contact the hotel direct for further information on accommodation tariffs and opening hours. *No dogs allowed. Amex, Diners, MasterCard,* ***VISA***

St Peter — Mermaid Hotel — 64% — £92

Tel 01534 41255 **Fax 01534 45826** Map 13 F4 H

Airport Road St Peter Jersey JE3 7BN

A modern hotel near the airport, standing in 18 acres of grounds overlooking a small natural lake. Bedrooms have the expected facilities and though not large they benefit from south-facing balconies with a lake view. The hotel is self-contained with restaurants, bar, pub and impressive leisure facilities. No dogs. Children under 5 free in parents' room – early suppers provided. ***Rooms*** *68. Garden, croquet, tennis, golf (9-hole), outdoor & indoor swimming pools, keep-fit equipment, sauna, spa bath, solarium. Amex, Diners, MasterCard,* ***VISA***

St Peter's Village — Star & Tipsy Toad Brewery

Tel 01534 485556 **Fax 01534 485559** Map 13 F4 P

St Peter's Village Jersey JE3 7AA

Right on the A12, in St Peter's Village, the Star was Jersey's first brew pub back in 1992. The parlour, snug and conservatory all provide a view of early stages of the brewing process through a wall of windows, and guided tours and tastings are conducted daily. Indoor and outdoor play areas keep the 'Little Toadies' amused, while the family room with its children's menu (prices include ice cream!) and baby-changing facilities make this a perfect pub for families: no food, though, on Sundays or Monday nights in winter. A sister pub to St Helier's *Tipsy Toad Town House*, it has new proprietors since mid-1996 in Steve and Vicky Beer, and we're promised few changes – but how long before they start brewing Beers' Beers? There is live music Friday to Sunday nights and the Tipsy Toad folk festival is held annually during the 3rd week of September. *Open 10am-11pm, Sun 11-1, 4.30-11. Free House.* ***Beer*** *Tipsy Toad, Jimmy's Bitter and Horny Toad home-brews, Crazy Diamond, Cyril's Bitter and independent guest ales. Beer garden, children's play area. Disabled facilities. Family room, indoor play area. Amex, MasterCard,* ***VISA***

St Saviour — Merton Hotel — 60% — £80

Tel 01534 24231 **Fax 01534 68603** Map 13 F4 
Belvedere Hill St Saviour Jersey JE2 7RP

Our 1997 Family Hotel of the Year (see page 12 for further details of improvements made during winter 1996/7). Located right outside St Helier, on a sloped street off the A3, a spacious hotel whose main feature is the amazing, all-weather Aquadome water leisure centre with supervised indoor and vast outdoor swimming pools, spas, 80m water slide, cascade pools, water cannon, children's boats and slides plus a toddlers' pool. The Aquadome facilities are also made available (charged mid May-mid Sept, free at other times of year) to residents in other hotels in the Seymour Hotel group: see entries for the *Portelet Hotel* overlooking Ouaisne and St Brelade bays, *Hotel de la Plage* in Havre des Pas and the *Pomme d'Or Hotel* on the waterfront in St Helier. Good for children, with a new creche/playroom and entertainment for them in the evening. 21 new family suites and a further additional family rooms (now totalling 57, some with bunk beds) were created during a major renovation over the last couple of years. In addition, special arrangements have now been made for children's entertainment in the evening; the Neptune Club is open from 6.30-9.30pm (Easter-October) for 4- to 12-year-olds and creche facilities are provided for under-4s. Children's meal times (with special menus), dozens of high-chairs, playground facilities with proper protective flooring and a guests' launderette are typical of the arrangements made to ensure that every element of a successful family holiday is considered. Evening entertainment, including a disco, is also laid on for adults; baby-sitting can be arranged. Informal family eating in the hotel's bistro-style coffee shop and Cascades in the Aquadome. Lift to all floors of the hotel. 7-day half-board holiday prices range from around £375 to £425 (per person) according to season and include return flights from Southampton; alternatively, there is a high-speed catamaran (or more leisurely ferry) from Weymouth. Children under 2 sharing their parents' bedroom in a cot are accommodated free of charge; ask about price reductions (around 50% of adult tariff for B&B, plus special early and late season offers) for children under 12, and special car hire rates. B&B terms are offered but in high season the hotel mainly offers holiday packages. One of Jersey's most attractive parks – Howard Davis Park – is a short stroll from the hotel. Seymour Hotels. ***Rooms** 304. Garden, indoor and outdoor swimming pool, children's swimming pool, squash, tennis, coffee shop, games room. Closed Nov-end Mar. Amex, Diners, MasterCard,* ***VISA***

Sark

SARK — Aval du Creux Hotel — 57% — £80

Tel 01481 832036 **Fax 01481 832368** Map 13 E4 **HR**
Harbour Hill Sark GY9 0SE

Eight miles east of Guernsey is the island of Sark, a peaceful retreat with forty miles of coastline, bracing walks and no traffic. Peter and Cheryl Tonks' friendly little hotel, originally a farmhouse, is a good place for family holidays. There are two lounges and a small bar hung with local pictures. Half-board terms preferred – we quote the B&B rate here. ***Rooms*** *6. Garden, outdoor swimming pool, children's splash pool, boules. Closed Nov-May. Amex, Diners, MasterCard,* ***VISA***

Restaurant £55

As well as hotel residents and Sark visitors, folk from Guernsey have been known to make a day trip by boat to Sark, principally to have lunch in the oyster bar or lobster restaurant. Seafood in general plays the leading role here, with local crab served hot in a shell topped with melted brie, as well as fresh oysters from the local waters and a massive seafood mixed grill. Alternative house specialities include chef's classic paté de foie and supreme de volaille Aval, while on the lighter lunch menu you'll find omelettes, pancakes and baguettes filled with seafood not to mention the 'Aval bookmaker'- with steak, ham, tomato, lettuce and mayonnaise it's a meal in itself. No smoking. ***Seats*** *40 (+ 60 outside). L 12-2 D 7-9. Set L £9.95. Set D £17.95.*

SARK — Dixcart Hotel — 64% — £70

Tel 01481 832015 **Fax 01481 832164** Map 13 E4 **HR**
Sark GY9 OSD

Sark's longest-established hotel was originally a 16th-century longhouse, the main dwelling in one of the 40 feudal Tenements which still warrant a seat in Sark's parliament. There's a homely lounge and bar for the occasional rainy day and fifty acres of land with private access to the Dixcart Bay beach. Children welcome if well behaved. ***Rooms*** *15. Garden. MasterCard,* ***VISA***

Restaurant £45

The restaurant's beautiful view over the sloping gardens is peaceful and relaxing. The table d'hote menu features plenty of local seafood and alternatives like duck breast with fresh fruit chutney and Sark pork medallions with redcurrant jus. A wider choice of steak dishes, chicken and local lamb or veal supplements the à la carte selection of Dixcart favourites – plaice, sea bass, crab and lobster. Simpler snacks and seafood dishes in the public bar, children's snug and adjacent barbecue terrace are served both lunchtime and evenings. ***Seats*** *60. L 12-1.30 D 7-9. Set menu D £15 (Sun L £11.50).*

SARK — Stocks Hotel — 61% — £80

Tel 01481 832001 **Fax 01481 832130** Map 13 E4 **HR**
Sark GY9 0SD

The family-run, granite-built hotel lying in a quiet wooded valley overlooking Dixcart Bay and 20 minutes walk from the harbour has a homely atmosphere in the lounge, and comfortable, unfussy bedrooms decorated with darkwood furniture and floral fabrics. Lack of TVs in the rooms fails to deter youngsters from enjoying the wonderfully safe environment described by one as "like an Enid Blyton adventure". The hotel has a climbing frame and a safe garden for playing in. Baby-changing facilities are also provided, along with extra beds, cots and family rooms. Children's bicycles may be hired locally; there are beaches and horse-riding facilities close by. ***Rooms*** *24. Garden, outdoor swimming pool, Courtyard Bistro (10am-10pm). Closed Oct-Mar. Amex, Diners, MasterCard,* ***VISA***

See over

Cider Press Restaurant £50

Both the table d'hote menu (priced according to the number of courses taken) and a short à la carte are offered with local fish and shellfish always well represented, though often at a supplement. Waldorf salad and poached monkfish medallions typically precede grilled fillets of Guernsey plaice and pan-fried duck breast, with Aunty Wendy's desserts from the sideboard to follow. Refreshingly, there's a good and inexpensive wine list. No children under 8 in the restaurant (there's high tea for resident children from 5-7) but the Courtyard Bistro, which is open for coffee, lunch, cream teas and light evening meals, has a children's menu. ***Seats*** *60. Parties 12. Private Room 12. L (Sun only) 12-2.30 D 7-9. Set Sun L £13 Set D from £10.*

Isle of Man

DOUGLAS L'Expérience

Tel 01624 623103 Fax 01624 626214 Map 4 B4 JaB
Summerhill Douglas Isle of Man IM2 4PL

An informal seafront restaurant whose authentic onion soup (£2.85), served under a crust of melted cheese, is claimed to be a meal in itself. If this is not your choice there is a French Ploughman's lunch with brie (£3.75), various croques (including croque splendide with ham, cheese, mushrooms and an egg – £3.45), or various omelettes (£4.75-£5.50) served with baked potato or chips. From the specials menu you could have a half spring chicken stuffed with black-peppered cream cheese or pork provençale. Patio. In the evenings, only fixed-price French menus (from £15) are served – so it's best for families at lunchtime only. ***Seats*** *65.* ***Open*** *12-2 & 7-11.* ***Closed*** *L Good Fri & 5th July, all Sun & Tue in winter, last week Oct & first 3 weeks Nov, 4 days Christmas, 3 days New Year. Amex, Diners,* ***VISA***

PEEL Creek Inn

Tel 01624 842216 Fax 01624 843359 Map 4 A4 P
The Quayside Peel Isle of Man IM5 1AT

Slap bang on the harbour front, picnic tables abound in summer outside this bustling pub with its large, bright and recently-enlarged bars. Friendly proprietors Robert and Jean McAleer can always be found busily serving up fresh fish and seafood obtained from the nearby fish yards. Home-made kipper and smoked salmon paté, salmon and broccoli pie, 'queenies' served on the shell in a mornay sauce, and salmon and mushroom supreme might all feature on the menu or among the blackboard specials, with pride of place going nonetheless to their memorable Manx seafood platter. Other offerings range from open sandwiches to curries and steak and kidney pie, with several fruit tarts or home-made gateaux to follow. Junior diners are offered smaller portions. A full selection of Irish spirits – from Bushmills to Dry Cork Gin – and at least 10 wines by the glass supplement the four real ales on offer. As we went to press, completion of four en suite bedrooms was scheduled for April 1997, to coincide with the opening of a major new heritage centre opposite.
Pub open 10am-11pm (Fri & Sat to midnight, Sun 12-3, 7-10.30). Free House. ***Bar Food*** *11-10.45 (Sun 12-2, 7-10). Children's menu.* ***Beer*** *Okells Bitter & Mild, Tetley Bitter, Coachouse Bitter, guest beer. Outdoor eating on the quayside. Children welcome in bar 12-2.30 only if eating. Pub closed 25 Dec. MasterCard,* ***VISA***

Pubs – note that food is only recommended in those pubs with ***Bar Food*** times in the statistics at the end of an entry. Restaurant food in pubs is *never* recommended unless specifically mentioned. Some pubs are recommended for B&B or Atmosphere only – each entry's statistics indicate our recommendation.

RAMSEY Harbour Bistro £45

Tel 01624 814182 Map 4 B4 R

5 East Street Ramsey Isle of Man IM8 1DN

Ken and Patrick Devaney champion informal eating in their friendly bistro near the quay. Seafood is quite a feature on the menu, with fresh local supplies every day; the famous local queenie scallops cooked with Provençal sauce, with bacon, onion and black pepper, or with creamed garlic sauce on a bed of spinach, can be ordered as a starter or main course. Bistro oxtail soup and seafood chowder start things off, with a host of fish to follow and the alternative duck, Manx lamb and steak dishes, sauced or plain, for die-hard carnivores. Indulgent desserts – "to hell with the calorie count" – include banana pancakes with rum, honey and ice cream. ***Seats** 50. L 12-2 D 6.30-10.30. Closed D Sun, 2 weeks Jan & 1 week Oct. Set Sun L £11. MasterCard,* **VISA**

ST JOHN'S Shuttle Stop Café

Tel 01624 801600 **Fax 01624 801893** Map 4 A4 JaB

The Courtyard Tynwald Mills Craft Centre St John's Isle of Man IM4 3AD

The licensed, ground-floor café in this complex of craft shops near the seat of the Manx Parliament is a useful place to know about for families. Staff are helpful, serving an all-day menu with sandwiches (try a prawn hoagie £2.50), cakes and good home-made sweets like fudge, lemon meringue or banoffie pie. Lunchtime specials (available 11.45-2.30) offer a home-made soup, cheese-topped garlic bread, scampi, cod, shepherd's pie,home-made lasagne, salads and filled jacket potatoes. Children will find colouring books and crayons, high-chairs and regular favourites (home-made beefburger, fish fingers, chicken nuggets, sausage with chips and baked beans) on the menu. Traditional Sunday lunch is £4.99 (£2.75 for children). Outside, there is further seating for 30 people, a children's recreational area with swings, slides, a tunnel and a picnic area. The baby-changing facilities are now more easily accessible (and clearly signed) outside in the craft centre. ***Seats** 95. Open 10-6. Closed Good Friday, 25, 26 Dec & 1 Jan. MasterCard,* **VISA**

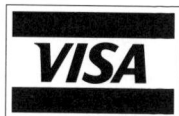

Maps

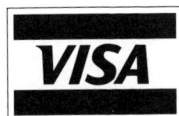

Maps

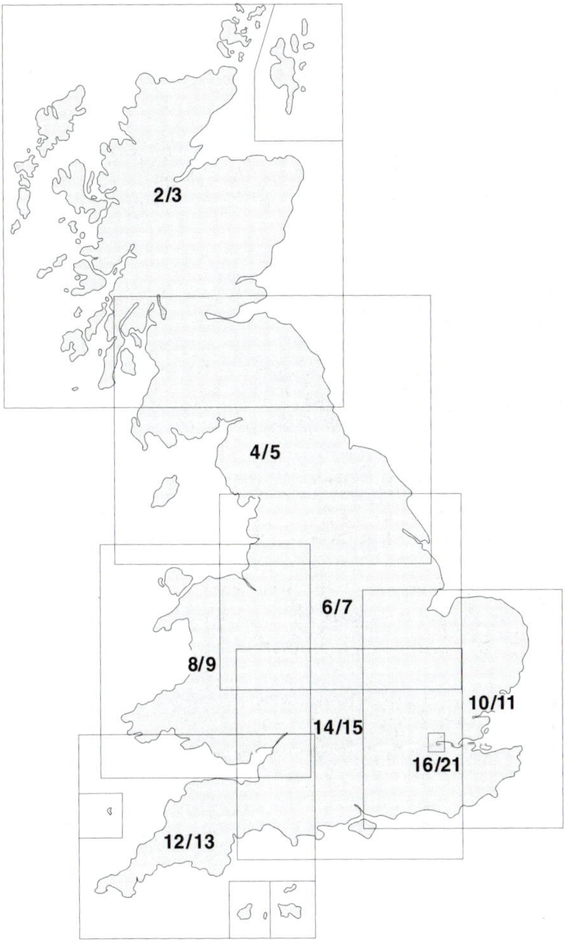

2/3

4/5

6/7

8/9

10/11

14/15

16/21

12/13

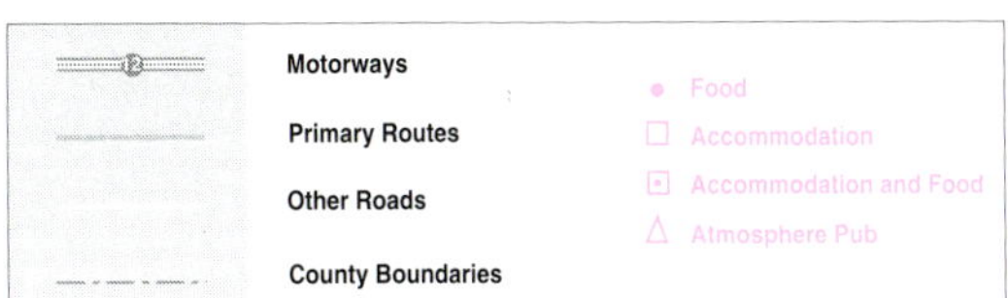

Designed and produced by
European Map Graphics Ltd. Finchampstead, Berks

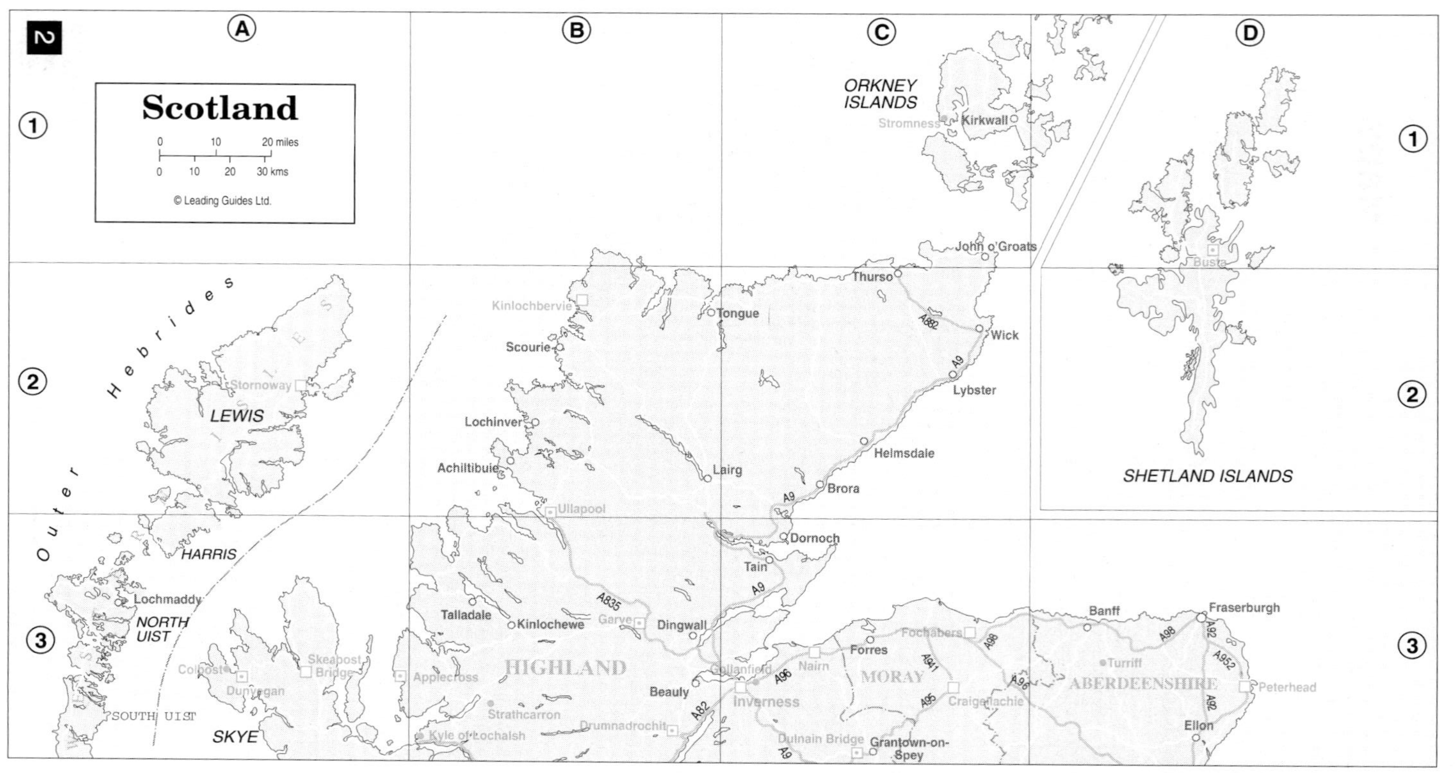
2
Scotland
0 10 20 miles
0 10 20 30 kms
© Leading Guides Ltd.
A
B
C
D
1
2
3
ORKNEY ISLANDS
Stromness
Kirkwall
SHETLAND ISLANDS
Busta
Outer Hebrides
LEWIS
Stornoway
HARRIS
NORTH UIST
Lochmaddy
SOUTH UIST
SKYE
Colbost
Dunvegan
Skeabost Bridge
John o' Groats
Thurso
Tongue
Wick
Lybster
Helmsdale
Brora
Dornoch
Tain
Kinlochbervie
Scourie
Lochinver
Achiltibuie
Lairg
Ullapool
Talladale
Kinlochewe
Garve
Dingwall
Applecross
HIGHLAND
Strathcarron
Kyle of Lochalsh
Drumnadrochit
Beauly
Inverness
Culloden
Nairn
Forres
MORAY
Fochabers
Craigellachie
Dulnain Bridge
Grantown-on-Spey
Banff
Turriff
ABERDEENSHIRE
Fraserburgh
Peterhead
Ellon
A9
A882
A835
A82
A96
A941
A95
A98
A92
A952

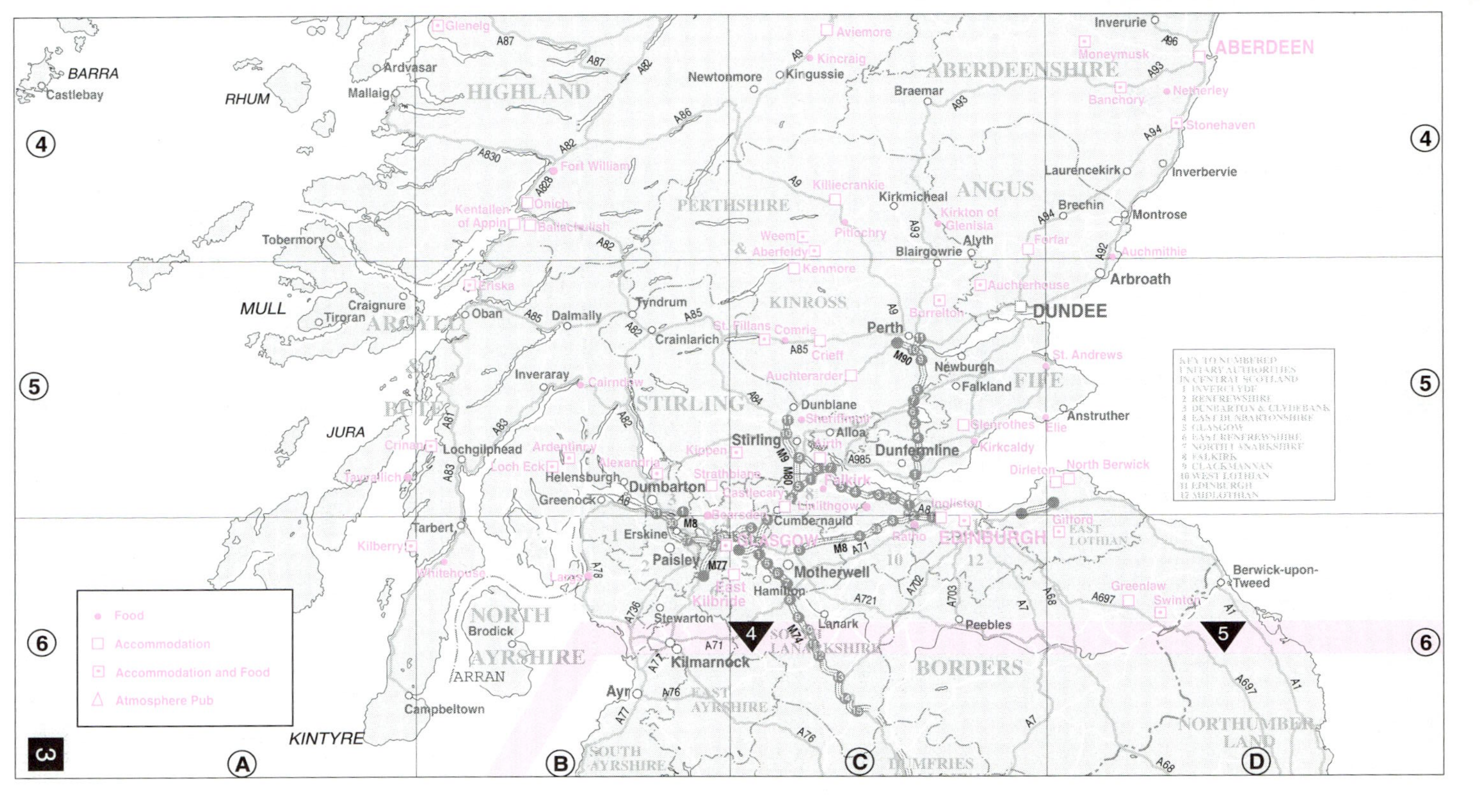

3
BARRA
Castlebay
RHUM
Mallaig
Ardvasar
Glenelg
HIGHLAND
Fort William
Onich
Kentallen of Appin
Ballachulish
Tobermory
MULL
Craignure
Tiroran
ARGYLL & BUTE
Eriska
Oban
Dalmally
Inveraray
Cairndow
JURA
Crinan
Tayvallich
Lochgilphead
Kilberry
Tarbert
Whitehouse
Campbeltown
KINTYRE
ARRAN
Brodick
NORTH AYRSHIRE
Largs
Newtonmore
Kingussie
Kincraig
Aviemore
PERTHSHIRE & KINROSS
Killiecrankie
Pitlochry
Weem
Aberfeldy
Kenmore
Tyndrum
Crainlarich
St. Fillans
Comrie
Crieff
Auchterarder
STIRLING
Dunblane
Sheriffmuir
Stirling
Kippen
Strathblane
Alloa
Airth
Falkirk
Linlithgow
Castlecary
Cumbernauld
Bearsden
Loch Eck
Ardentinny
Alexandria
Helensburgh
Dumbarton
Greenock
Erskine
Paisley
GLASGOW
East Kilbride
Motherwell
Hamilton
Stewarton
Kilmarnock
Ayr
EAST AYRSHIRE
SOUTH AYRSHIRE
SOUTH LANARKSHIRE
Lanark
DUMFRIES
Braemar
ABERDEENSHIRE
Inverurie
Moneymusk
Banchory
Netherley
ABERDEEN
Stonehaven
Laurencekirk
Inverbervie
ANGUS
Kirkmicheal
Kirkton of Glenisla
Blairgowrie
Alyth
Brechin
Montrose
Forfar
Auchmithie
Arbroath
Auchterhouse
Burrelton
DUNDEE
Perth
Newburgh
Falkland
FIFE
St. Andrews
Anstruther
Elie
Glenrothes
Kirkcaldy
Dunfermline
North Berwick
Dirleton
Ingliston
Ratho
EDINBURGH
Gifford
EAST LOTHIAN
Peebles
BORDERS
Greenlaw
Swinton
Berwick-upon-Tweed
NORTHUMBERLAND
KEY TO NUMBERED UNITARY AUTHORITIES IN CENTRAL SCOTLAND
1 INVERCLYDE
2 RENFREWSHIRE
3 DUNBARTON & CLYDEBANK
4 EAST DUNBARTONSHIRE
5 GLASGOW
6 EAST RENFREWSHIRE
7 NORTH LANARKSHIRE
8 FALKIRK
9 CLACKMANNAN
10 WEST LOTHIAN
11 EDINBURGH
12 MIDLOTHIAN
Food
Accommodation
Accommodation and Food
Atmosphere Pub
A B C D
4 5 6

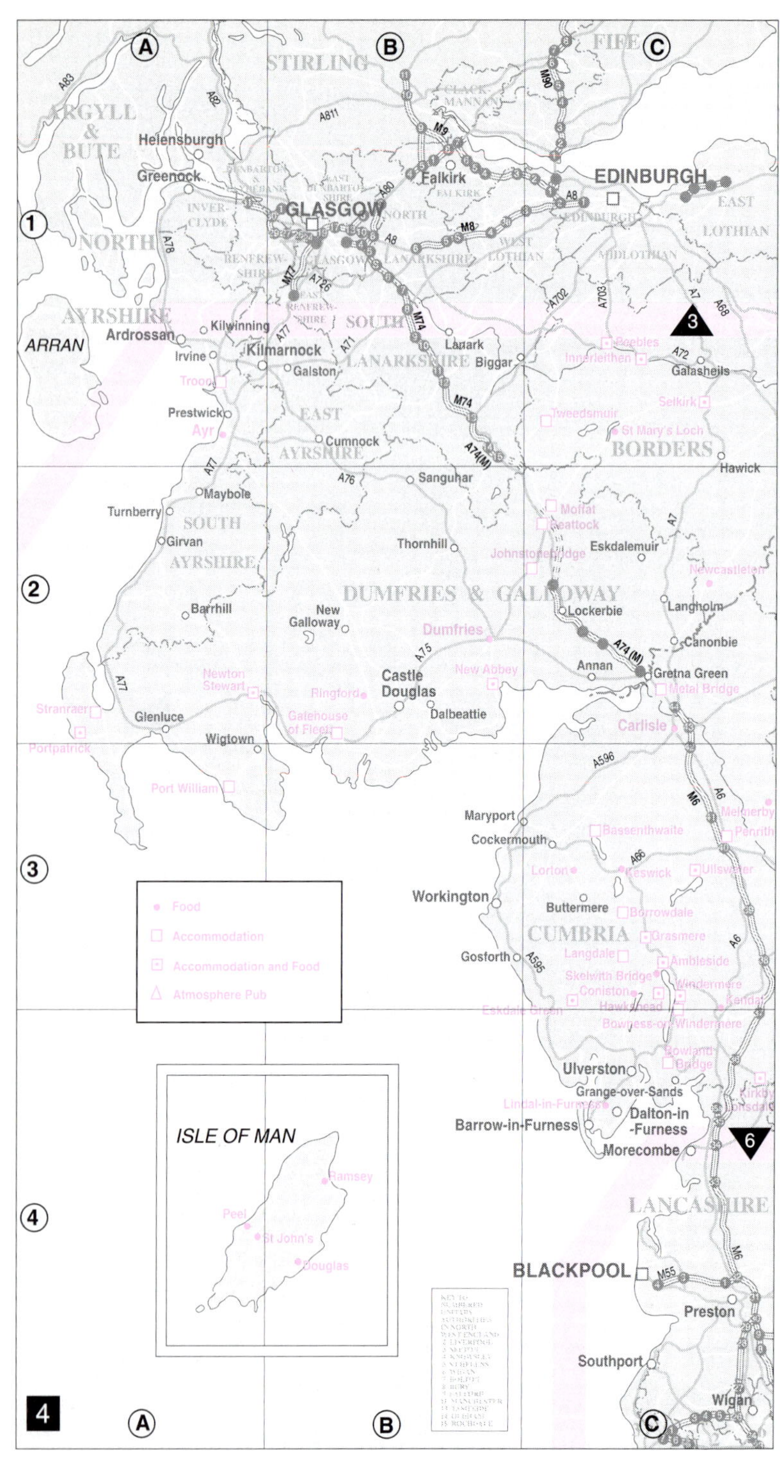

A
B
C
1
2
3
4
STIRLING
FIFE
ARGYLL & BUTE
CLACK-MANNAN
Helensburgh
Greenock
INVER-CLYDE
NORTH
AYRSHIRE
ARRAN
Ardrossan
Kilwinning
Irvine
Troon
Prestwick
Ayr
GLASGOW
Falkirk
FALKIRK
EDINBURGH
EAST LOTHIAN
MIDLOTHIAN
WEST LOTHIAN
NORTH LANARKSHIRE
RENFREW-SHIRE
EAST RENFREW-SHIRE
SOUTH LANARKSHIRE
Kilmarnock
Galston
Lanark
Biggar
EAST AYRSHIRE
Cumnock
Peebles
Innerleithen
Galashiels
Selkirk
Tweedsmuir
St Mary's Loch
BORDERS
Hawick
Sanquhar
Maybole
Turnberry
SOUTH AYRSHIRE
Girvan
Thornhill
Moffat
Beattock
Johnstonebridge
Eskdalemuir
Newcastleton
DUMFRIES & GALLOWAY
Barrhill
New Galloway
Dumfries
Lockerbie
Langholm
Canonbie
Annan
Gretna Green
Metal Bridge
Newton Stewart
Stranraer
Portpatrick
Glenluce
Wigtown
Ringford
Gatehouse of Fleet
Castle Douglas
Dalbeattie
New Abbey
Carlisle
Port William
Maryport
Cockermouth
Bassenthwaite
Melmerby
Penrith
Lorton
Keswick
Ullswater
Workington
Buttermere
Borrowdale
CUMBRIA
Grasmere
Gosforth
Langdale
Ambleside
Skelwith Bridge
Coniston
Windermere
Hawkshead
Kendal
Eskdale Green
Bowness-on-Windermere
Ulverston
Bowland Bridge
Grange-over-Sands
Lindal-in-Furness
Kirkby Lonsdale
Barrow-in-Furness
Dalton-in-Furness
Morecombe
LANCASHIRE
BLACKPOOL
Preston
Southport
Wigan
ISLE OF MAN
Ramsey
Peel
St John's
Douglas
Food
Accommodation
Accommodation and Food
Atmosphere Pub
A83
A82
A811
M9
M90
A80
A8
M8
A78
M77
A726
A77
A71
M74
A74(M)
A702
A703
A7
A68
A72
A76
A75
A596
M6
A6
A66
A595
M55
3
6
4

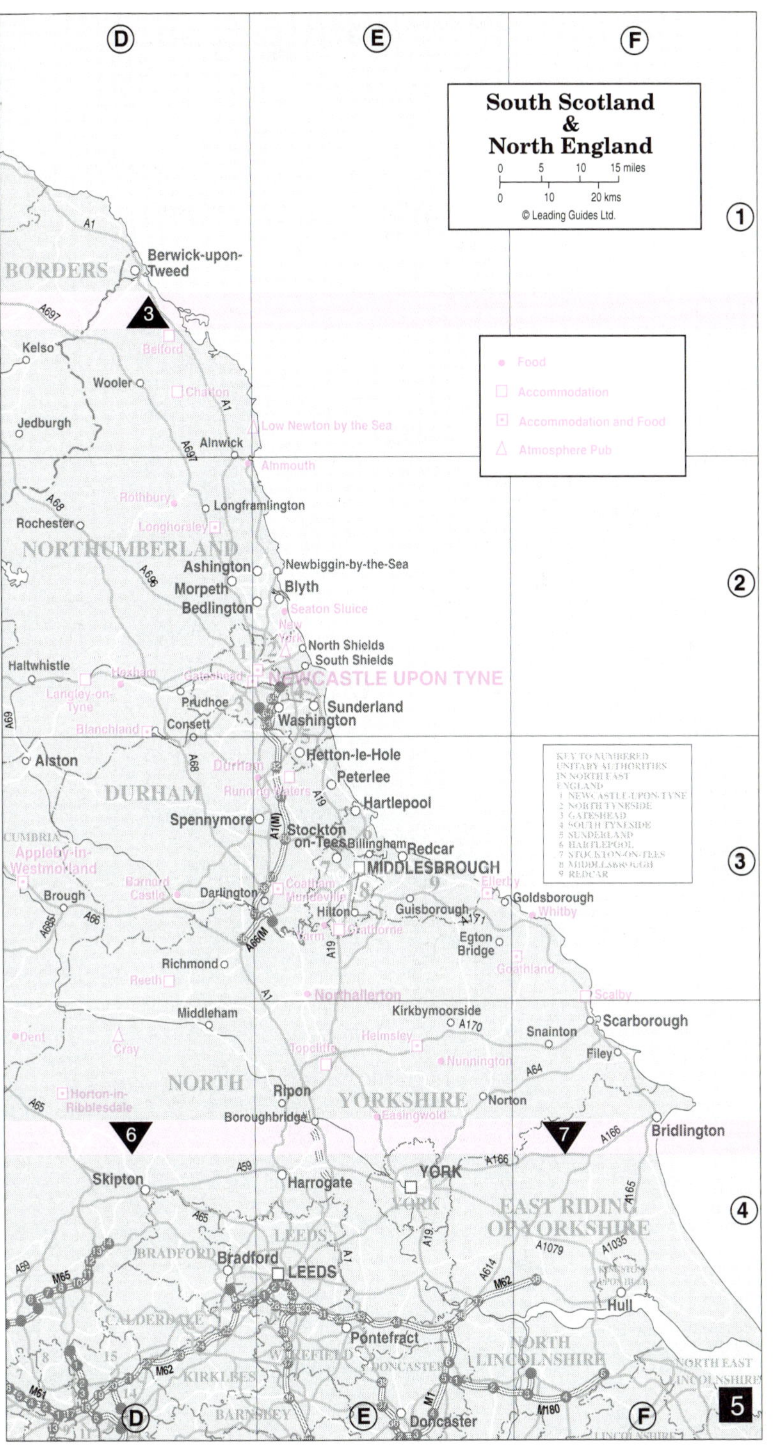

South Scotland & North England
0 5 10 15 miles
0 10 20 kms
© Leading Guides Ltd.
Food
Accommodation
Accommodation and Food
Atmosphere Pub
Berwick-upon-Tweed
BORDERS
Kelso
Belford
Wooler
Chatton
Jedburgh
Low Newton by the Sea
Alnwick
Alnmouth
Rothbury
Longframlington
Rochester
Longhorsley
NORTHUMBERLAND
Ashington
Newbiggin-by-the-Sea
Morpeth
Blyth
Bedlington
Seaton Sluice
North Shields
South Shields
Haltwhistle
Hexham
Gateshead
NEWCASTLE UPON TYNE
Langley-on-Tyne
Prudhoe
Sunderland
Washington
Blanchland
Consett
Alston
Hetton-le-Hole
Durham
Peterlee
DURHAM
Running Waters
Hartlepool
Spennymore
Stockton on-Tees
Billingham
Redcar
CUMBRIA
Appleby-in-Westmorland
MIDDLESBROUGH
Barnard Castle
Coatham Mundeville
Ellerby
Brough
Darlington
Goldsborough
Hilton
Guisborough
Whitby
Egton Bridge
Richmond
Goathland
Reeth
Northallerton
Scalby
Middleham
Kirkbymoorside
Scarborough
Dent
Cray
Helmsley
Snainton
Topcliffe
Nunnington
Filey
NORTH
YORKSHIRE
Ripon
Norton
Horton-in-Ribblesdale
Boroughbridge
Easingwold
Bridlington
Skipton
Harrogate
YORK
EAST RIDING OF YORKSHIRE
LEEDS
BRADFORD
Bradford
CALDERDALE
Hull
Pontefract
WAKEFIELD
NORTH LINCOLNSHIRE
KIRKLEES
NORTH EAST LINCOLNSHIRE
BARNSLEY
Doncaster
KEY TO NUMBERED UNITARY AUTHORITIES IN NORTH EAST ENGLAND
1 NEWCASTLE-UPON-TYNE
2 NORTH TYNESIDE
3 GATESHEAD
4 SOUTH TYNESIDE
5 SUNDERLAND
6 HARTLEPOOL
7 STOCKTON-ON-TEES
8 MIDDLESBROUGH
9 REDCAR

5

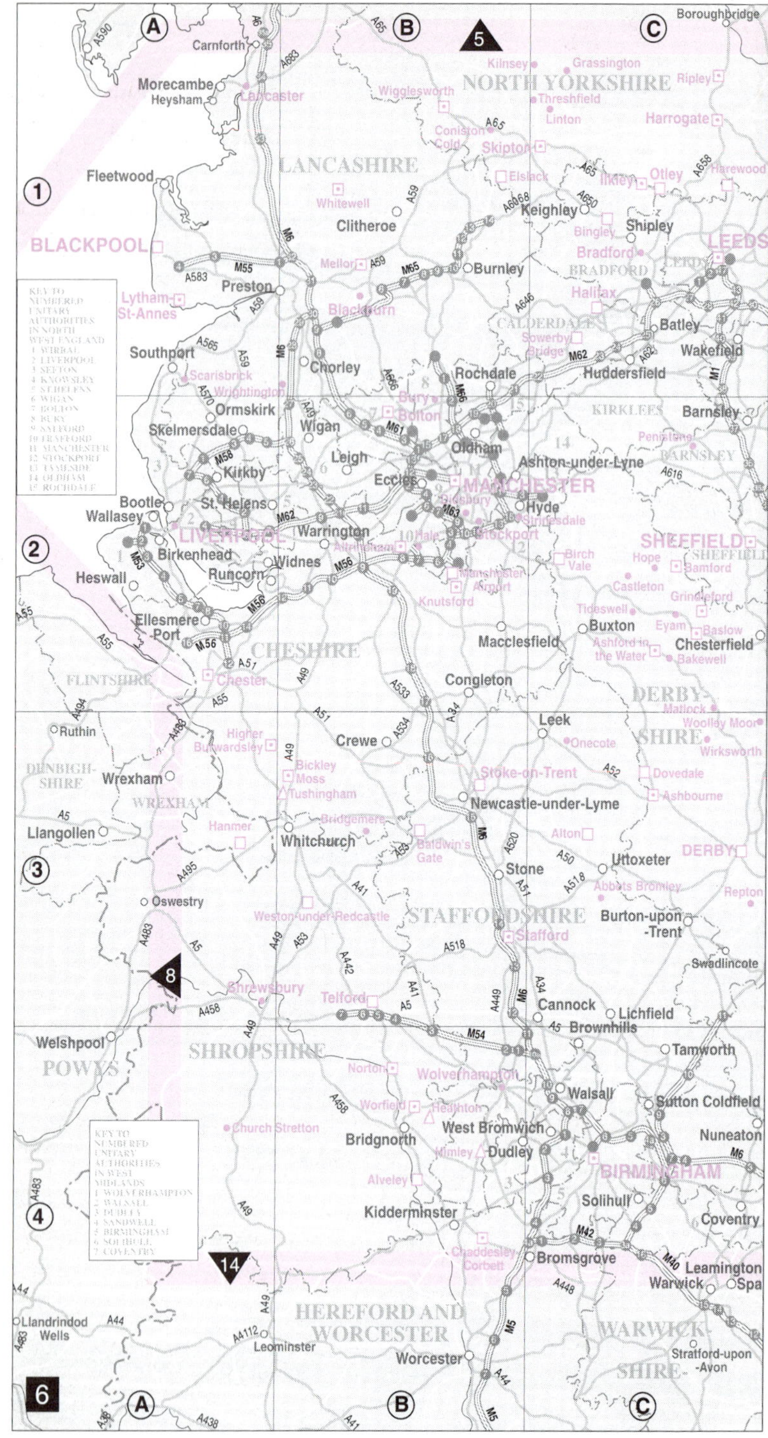

5
8
14
6
A
B
C
1
2
3
4
NORTH YORKSHIRE
LANCASHIRE
CHESHIRE
FLINTSHIRE
DENBIGH-SHIRE
WREXHAM
STAFFORDSHIRE
SHROPSHIRE
POWYS
HEREFORD AND WORCESTER
WARWICK-SHIRE
DERBY-SHIRE
CALDERDALE
KIRKLEES
BRADFORD
LEEDS
BARNSLEY
SHEFFIELD
KEY TO NUMBERED UNITARY AUTHORITIES IN NORTH WEST ENGLAND
1 WIRRAL
2 LIVERPOOL
3 SEFTON
4 KNOWSLEY
5 ST.HELENS
6 WIGAN
7 BOLTON
8 BURY
9 SALFORD
10 TRAFFORD
11 MANCHESTER
12 STOCKPORT
13 TAMESIDE
14 OLDHAM
15 ROCHDALE
KEY TO NUMBERED UNITARY AUTHORITIES IN WEST MIDLANDS
1 WOLVERHAMPTON
2 WALSALL
3 DUDLEY
4 SANDWELL
5 BIRMINGHAM
6 SOLIHULL
7 COVENTRY
Boroughbridge
Carnforth
Lancaster
Morecambe
Heysham
Kilnsey
Grassington
Ripley
Wigglesworth
Threshfield
Linton
Harrogate
Coniston Cold
Skipton
Elslack
Ilkley
Otley
Harewood
Fleetwood
Whitewell
Clitheroe
Keighley
Bingley
Shipley
BLACKPOOL
Bradford
Leeds
Mellor
Burnley
Preston
Lytham-St-Annes
Blackburn
Halifax
Sowerby Bridge
Batley
Wakefield
Southport
Chorley
Rochdale
Huddersfield
Scarisbrick
Wrightington
Bury
Bolton
Ormskirk
Wigan
Barnsley
Skelmersdale
Oldham
Penistone
Leigh
Ashton-under-Lyne
Kirkby
Eccles
MANCHESTER
Bootle
St. Helens
Hyde
Wallasey
LIVERPOOL
Warrington
Didsbury
Stalybridge
Stockport
Birkenhead
Widnes
Hale
Altrincham
Birch Vale
Hope
Bamford
Runcorn
Manchester Airport
Heswall
Knutsford
Castleton
Grindleford
Tideswell
Eyam
Baslow
Ellesmere Port
Buxton
Macclesfield
Ashford in the Water
Chesterfield
Bakewell
Chester
Congleton
Matlock
Woolley Moor
Wirksworth
Ruthin
Higher Burwardsley
Crewe
Leek
Onecote
Bickley Moss
Tushingham
Stoke-on-Trent
Dovedale
Wrexham
Ashbourne
Newcastle-under-Lyme
Llangollen
Hanmer
Bridgemere
Whitchurch
Baldwin's Gate
Alton
Derby
Stone
Uttoxeter
Oswestry
Abbots Bromley
Repton
Weston-under-Redcastle
Stafford
Burton-upon-Trent
Swadlincote
Shrewsbury
Telford
Cannock
Lichfield
Brownhills
Welshpool
Tamworth
Norton
Wolverhampton
Walsall
Worfield
Hednton
Sutton Coldfield
Church Stretton
Bridgnorth
West Bromwich
Nuneaton
Himley
Dudley
BIRMINGHAM
Alveley
Solihull
Kidderminster
Coventry
Chaddesley Corbett
Bromsgrove
Leamington Spa
Warwick
Llandrindod Wells
Leominster
Worcester
Stratford-upon-Avon
M6
M55
M65
M62
M1
M61
M66
M63
M58
M53
M56
M54
M42
M40
M5
A6
A65
A683
A590
A59
A6068
A650
A658
A646
A583
A565
A570
A49
A666
A62
A616
A55
A51
A533
A34
A494
A483
A534
A52
A5
A495
A520
A50
A53
A41
A518
A442
A449
A458
A448
A44
A4112
A438

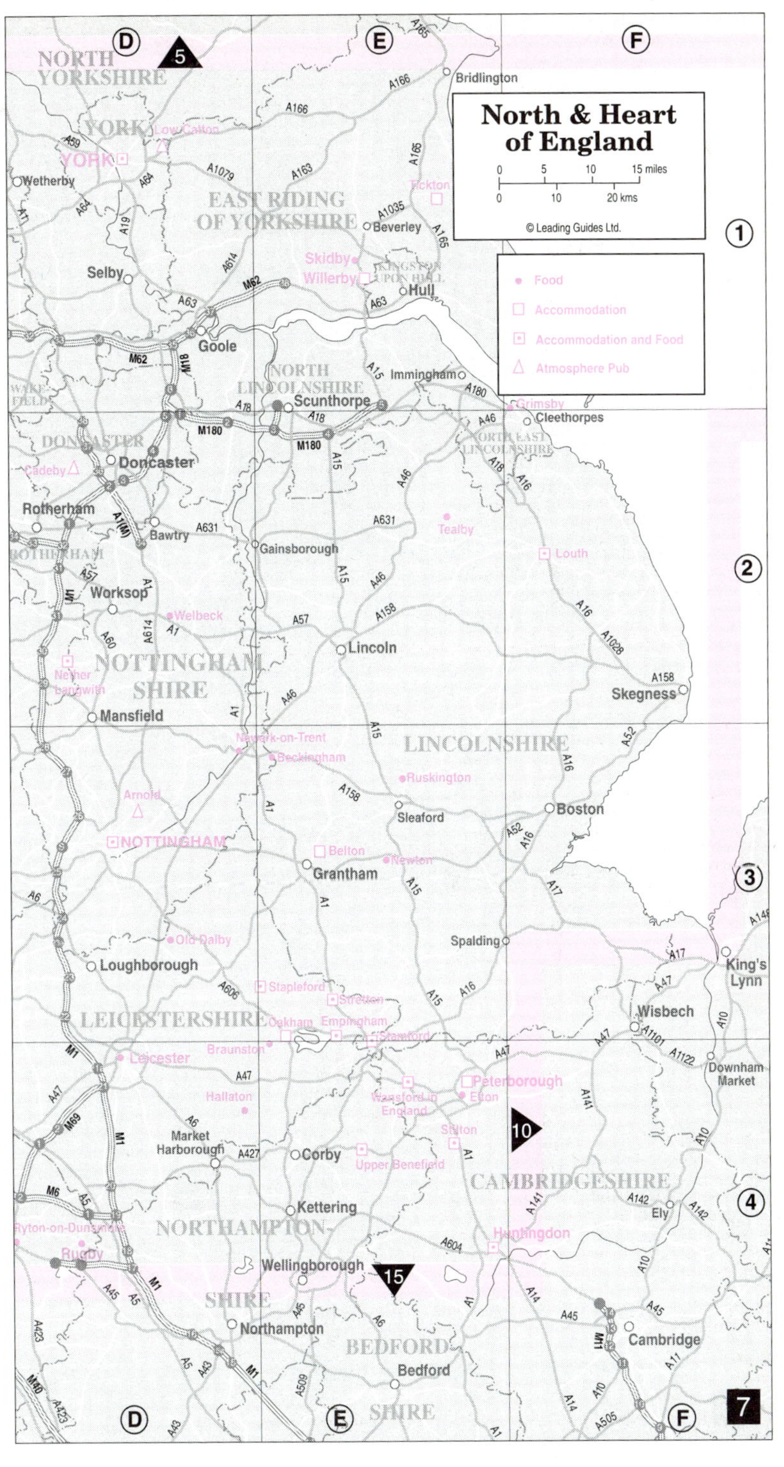
North & Heart of England
0 5 10 15 miles
0 10 20 kms
© Leading Guides Ltd.
Food
Accommodation
Accommodation and Food
Atmosphere Pub
NORTH YORKSHIRE
YORK
Low Catton
Wetherby
Bridlington
EAST RIDING OF YORKSHIRE
Tickton
Beverley
Skidby
Willerby
KINGSTON UPON HULL
Hull
Selby
Goole
NORTH LINCOLNSHIRE
Immingham
Scunthorpe
Grimsby
Cleethorpes
NORTH EAST LINCOLNSHIRE
DONCASTER
Cadeby
Doncaster
Rotherham
Bawtry
ROTHERHAM
Gainsborough
Tealby
Louth
Worksop
Welbeck
Lincoln
NOTTINGHAMSHIRE
Nether Langwith
Mansfield
Skegness
Newark-on-Trent
Beckingham
LINCOLNSHIRE
Ruskington
Arnold
Sleaford
Boston
NOTTINGHAM
Belton
Grantham
Newton
Old Dalby
Spalding
Loughborough
Stapleford
Stretton
King's Lynn
LEICESTERSHIRE
Oakham
Empingham
Stamford
Wisbech
Braunston
Leicester
Downham Market
Hallaton
Peterborough
Wansford in England
Elton
Stilton
Market Harborough
Corby
Upper Benefield
CAMBRIDGESHIRE
Kettering
Ely
NORTHAMPTONSHIRE
Ryton-on-Dunsmore
Rugby
Huntingdon
Wellingborough
Northampton
Cambridge
BEDFORDSHIRE
Bedford
D
E
F
1
2
3
4
5
10
15

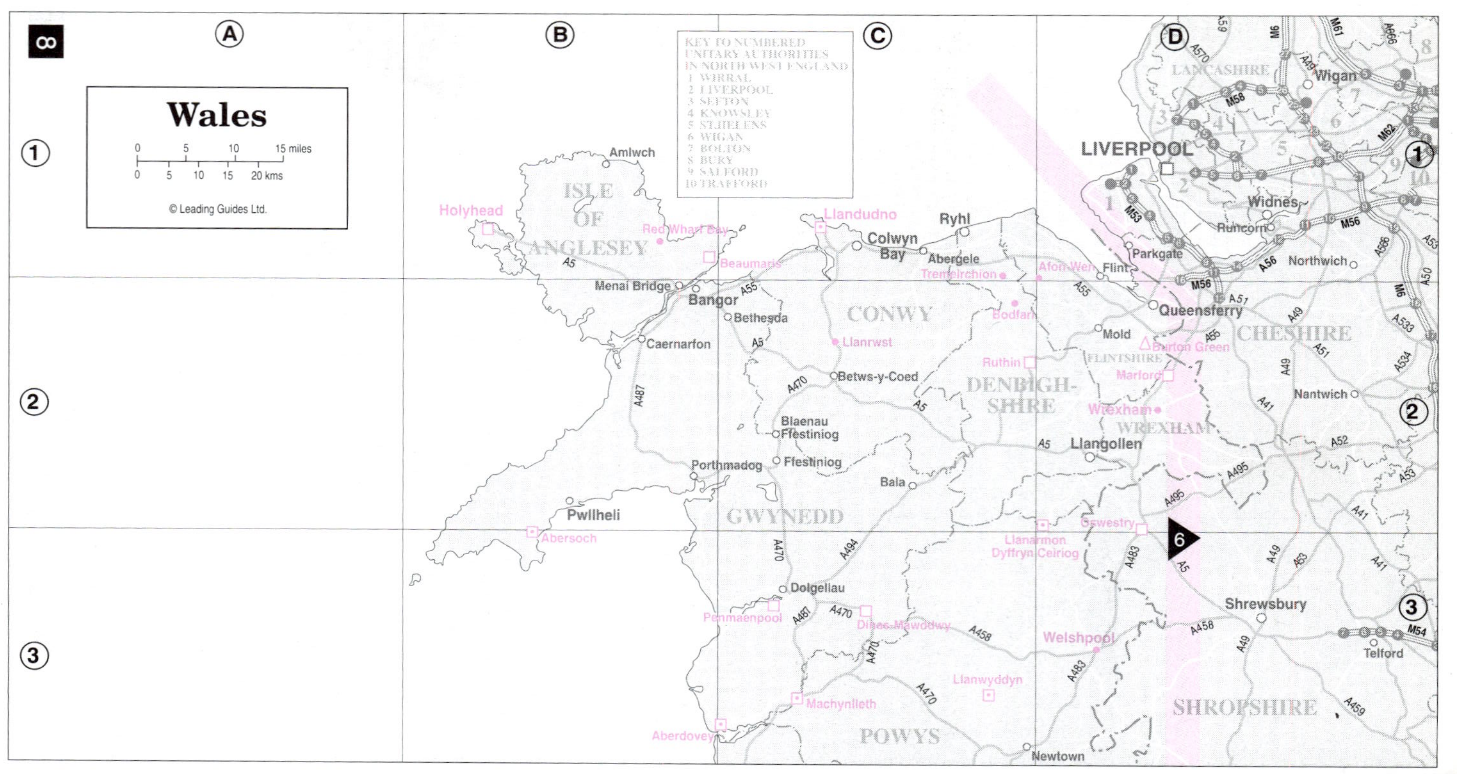
8
Wales
0 5 10 15 miles
0 5 10 15 20 kms
© Leading Guides Ltd.
KEY TO NUMBERED UNITARY AUTHORITIES IN NORTH WEST ENGLAND
1 WIRRAL
2 LIVERPOOL
3 SEFTON
4 KNOWSLEY
5 ST.HELENS
6 WIGAN
7 BOLTON
8 BURY
9 SALFORD
10 TRAFFORD
ISLE OF ANGLESEY
Holyhead
Amlwch
Red Wharf Bay
Beaumaris
Menai Bridge
Bangor
Bethesda
Caernarfon
Llandudno
Colwyn Bay
Ryhl
Abergele
Trefnant
Afon-Wen
Flint
Parkgate
LIVERPOOL
Widnes
Runcorn
Wigan
Northwich
Queensferry
Mold
Burton Green
Bodfari
CONWY
Llanrwst
Betws-y-Coed
Ruthin
DENBIGH-SHIRE
FLINTSHIRE
Marford
Wrexham
WREXHAM
CHESHIRE
Nantwich
LANCASHIRE
Blaenau Ffestiniog
Ffestiniog
Porthmadog
Pwllheli
Abersoch
Llangollen
Bala
GWYNEDD
Oswestry
Llanarmon Dyffryn Ceiriog
6
Shrewsbury
Telford
Dolgellau
Penmaenpool
Dinas-Mawddwy
Welshpool
Llanwyddyn
Machynlleth
Aberdovey
POWYS
Newtown
SHROPSHIRE

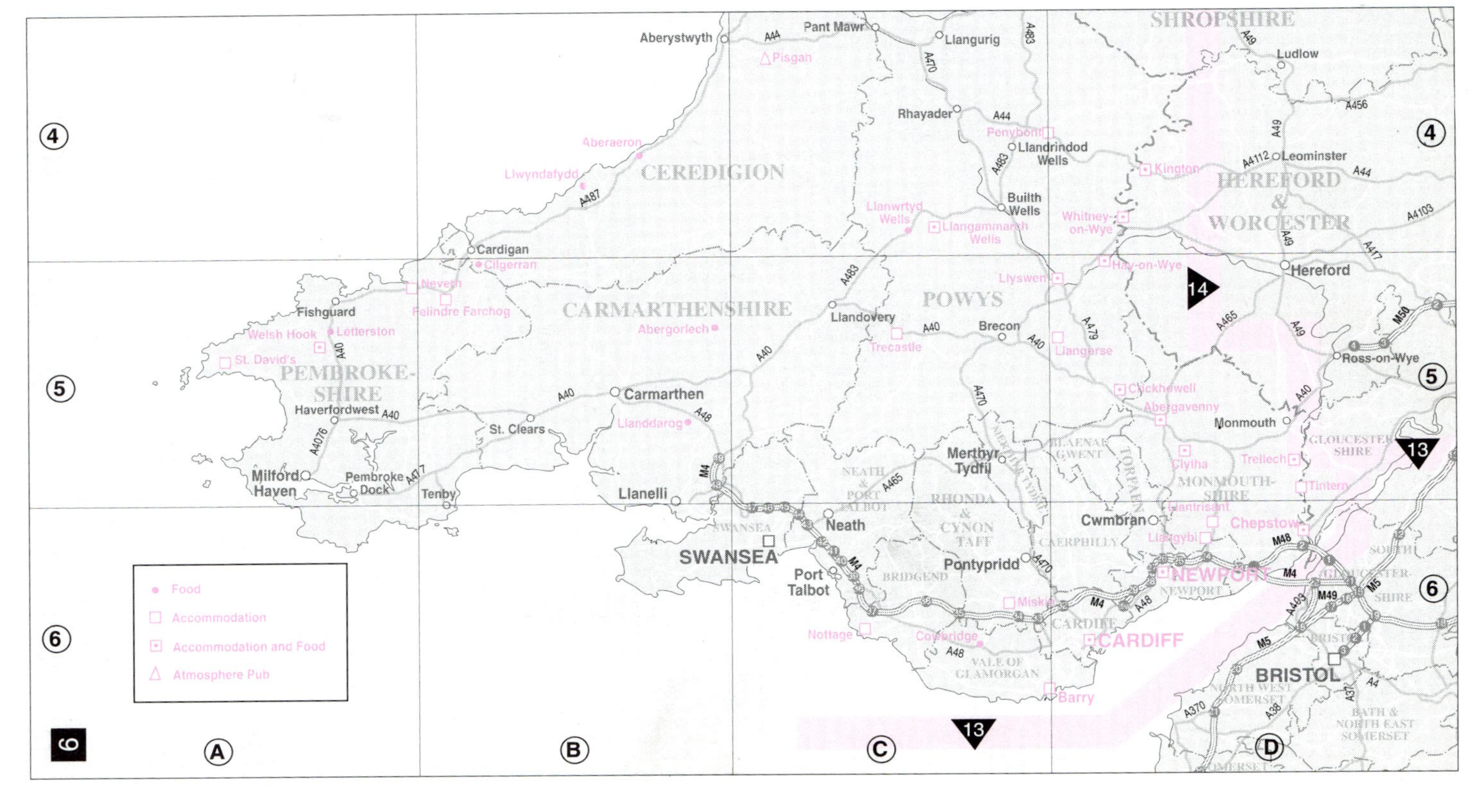

9
Food
Accommodation
Accommodation and Food
Atmosphere Pub
SHROPSHIRE
HEREFORD & WORCESTER
CEREDIGION
CARMARTHENSHIRE
POWYS
PEMBROKE-SHIRE
GLOUCESTERSHIRE
MONMOUTHSHIRE
TORFAEN
BLAENAU GWENT
MERTHYR TYDFIL
RHONDA CYNON TAFF
NEATH & PORT TALBOT
SWANSEA
BRIDGEND
CAERPHILLY
NEWPORT
CARDIFF
VALE OF GLAMORGAN
BATH & NORTH EAST SOMERSET
NORTH WEST SOMERSET
Aberystwyth
Pant Mawr
Llangurig
Pisgah
Ludlow
Rhayader
Penybont
Llandrindod Wells
Leominster
Kington
Aberaeron
Llwyndafydd
Llanwrtyd Wells
Llangammarch Wells
Builth Wells
Whitney-on-Wye
Cardigan
Cilgerran
Nevern
Felindre Farchog
Hay-on-Wye
Llyswen
Hereford
Fishguard
Welsh Hook
Letterston
St. David's
Abergorlech
Llandovery
Trecastle
Brecon
Llangorse
Ross-on-Wye
Crickhowell
Abergavenny
Monmouth
Haverfordwest
St. Clears
Carmarthen
Llanddarog
Milford Haven
Pembroke Dock
Tenby
Llanelli
Merthyr Tydfil
Clytha
Trellech
Tintern
Llantrisant
Cwmbran
Chepstow
Llangybi
Neath
SWANSEA
Port Talbot
Pontypridd
NEWPORT
Miskin
Nottage
Cowbridge
CARDIFF
Barry
BRISTOL
14
13
A
B
C
D
4
5
6
A44
A470
A483
A49
A456
A44
A4112
A487
A483
A4103
A417
A479
A465
A49
M50
A40
A48
A4076
A477
M4
A465
A470
M48
M49
A403
M5
A4
A37
A38
A370

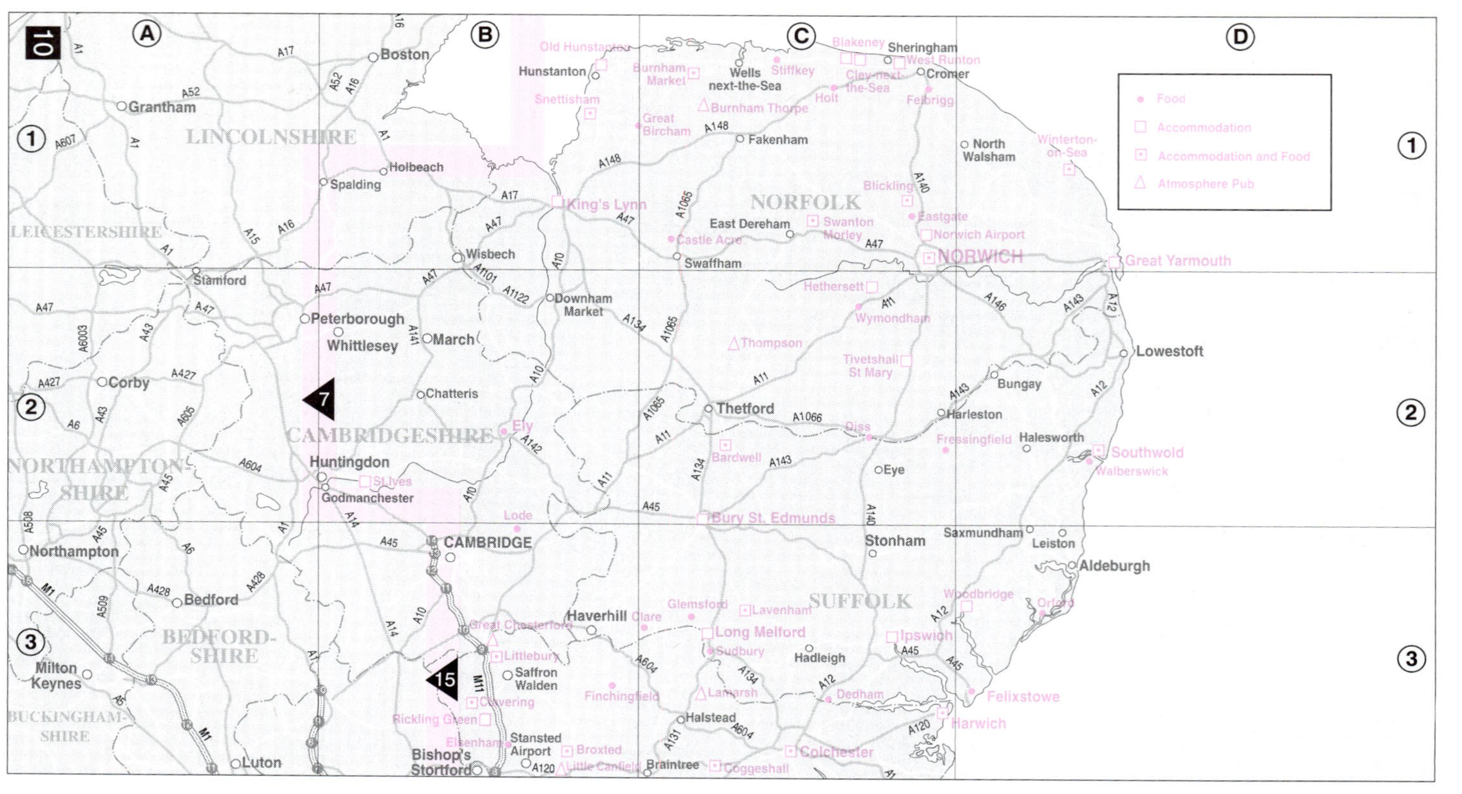

10
A
B
C
D
1
2
3
Food
Accommodation
Accommodation and Food
Atmosphere Pub
LINCOLNSHIRE
LEICESTERSHIRE
NORTHAMPTON-SHIRE
CAMBRIDGESHIRE
BEDFORD-SHIRE
BUCKINGHAM-SHIRE
NORFOLK
SUFFOLK
Boston
Grantham
Holbeach
Spalding
Stamford
Peterborough
Whittlesey
March
Wisbech
Corby
Chatteris
Huntingdon
St Ives
Godmanchester
Northampton
Bedford
Milton Keynes
Luton
CAMBRIDGE
Ely
Lode
Downham Market
King's Lynn
Hunstanton
Old Hunstanton
Snettisham
Burnham Market
Great Bircham
Burnham Thorpe
Wells next-the-Sea
Stiffkey
Fakenham
Blakeney
Sheringham
West Runton
Cley-next-the-Sea
Holt
Cromer
Felbrigg
North Walsham
Winterton-on-Sea
Blickling
East Dereham
Swanton Morley
Castle Acre
Swaffham
Eastgate
Norwich Airport
NORWICH
Great Yarmouth
Hethersett
Wymondham
Thompson
Tivetshall St Mary
Thetford
Diss
Bardwell
Eye
Bungay
Harleston
Fressingfield
Halesworth
Lowestoft
Southwold
Walberswick
Bury St. Edmunds
Stonham
Saxmundham
Leiston
Aldeburgh
Woodbridge
Orford
Ipswich
Felixstowe
Harwich
Hadleigh
Dedham
Colchester
Lavenham
Long Melford
Sudbury
Glemsford
Clare
Haverhill
Great Chesterford
Littlebury
Saffron Walden
Finchingfield
Lamarsh
Halstead
Coggeshall
Braintree
Clavering
Rickling Green
Elsenham
Stansted Airport
Broxted
Little Canfield
Bishop's Stortford
7
15
A1
A17
A52
A16
A607
A15
A47
A6003
A43
A427
A605
A6
A604
A45
A508
A509
A428
M1
A5
A14
A10
A11
M11
A120
A141
A1101
A1122
A134
A1065
A148
A140
A146
A143
A12
A1066
A142
A131

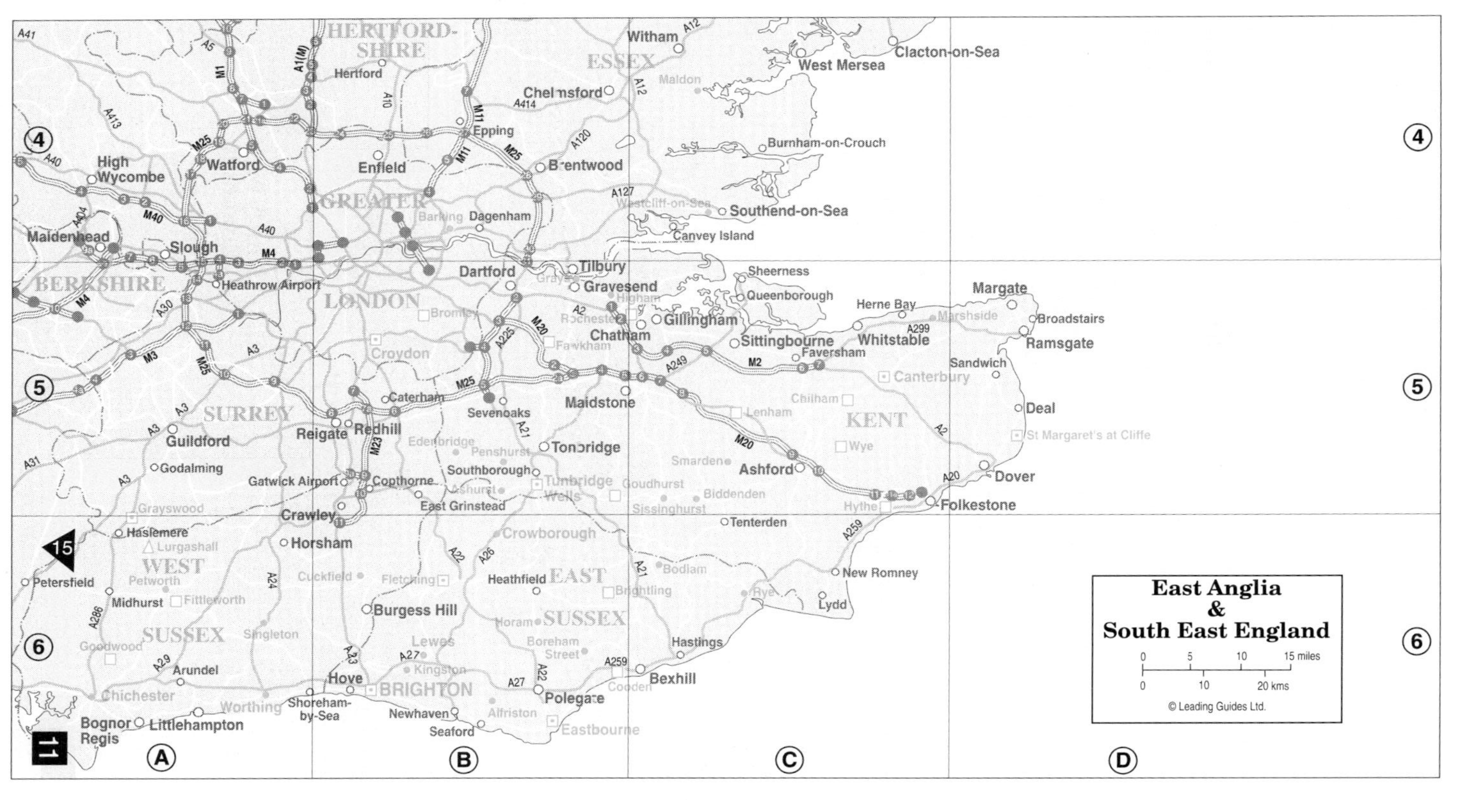
East Anglia
&
South East England
0 5 10 15 miles
0 10 20 kms
© Leading Guides Ltd.
11
15
HERTFORDSHIRE
ESSEX
GREATER LONDON
BERKSHIRE
SURREY
KENT
WEST SUSSEX
EAST SUSSEX
Witham
Clacton-on-Sea
West Mersea
Maldon
Hertford
Chelmsford
Epping
Burnham-on-Crouch
High Wycombe
Watford
Enfield
Brentwood
Southend-on-Sea
Westcliff-on-Sea
Canvey Island
Barking
Dagenham
Maidenhead
Slough
Heathrow Airport
Tilbury
Dartford
Grays
Gravesend
Higham
Rochester
Chatham
Gillingham
Sheerness
Queenborough
Sittingbourne
Faversham
Herne Bay
Whitstable
Marshside
Margate
Broadstairs
Ramsgate
Sandwich
Canterbury
Chilham
Lenham
Wye
Deal
St Margaret's at Cliffe
Dover
Folkestone
Hythe
Ashford
Smarden
Biddenden
Sissinghurst
Tenterden
New Romney
Lydd
Rye
Bodiam
Brightling
Hastings
Bexhill
Cooden
Eastbourne
Polegate
Alfriston
Seaford
Newhaven
Boreham Street
Horam
Heathfield
Crowborough
Lewes
Kingston
BRIGHTON
Hove
Shoreham-by-Sea
Worthing
Littlehampton
Bognor Regis
Chichester
Arundel
Goodwood
Singleton
Midhurst
Fittleworth
Petworth
Petersfield
Lurgashall
Haslemere
Grayswood
Godalming
Guildford
Reigate
Redhill
Caterham
Croydon
Bromley
Fawkham
Sevenoaks
Maidstone
Tonbridge
Tunbridge Wells
Goudhurst
Southborough
Penshurst
Edenbridge
Ashurst
East Grinstead
Copthorne
Gatwick Airport
Crawley
Horsham
Cuckfield
Fletching
Burgess Hill
A41
A5
M1
A1(M)
A10
M11
A414
A12
A120
A127
A413
A40
M25
M40
A404
M4
A30
M3
A3
A31
A286
A29
A24
M23
A23
A27
A22
A26
A21
A225
M20
M2
A249
A299
A2
A20
A259
A
B
C
D
4
5
6

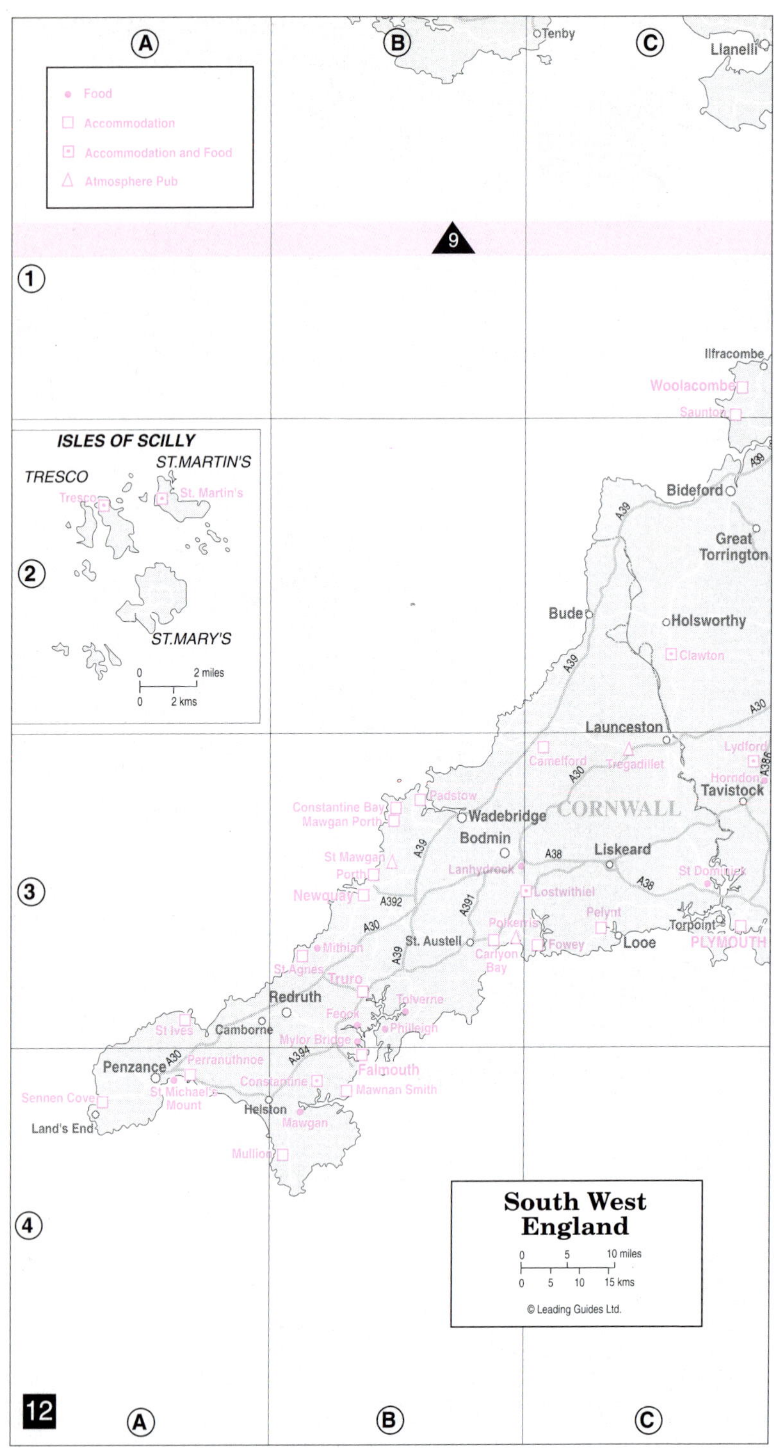

A
B
C
Tenby
Llanelli
Food
Accommodation
Accommodation and Food
Atmosphere Pub
9
1
2
3
4
ISLES OF SCILLY
ST.MARTIN'S
TRESCO
Tresco
St. Martin's
ST.MARY'S
0 2 miles
0 2 kms
Ilfracombe
Woolacombe
Saunton
A39
Bideford
Great Torrington
Bude
Holsworthy
Clawton
A30
Launceston
Camelford
Tregadillet
Lydford
Horndon
A386
Tavistock
Padstow
Constantine Bay
Mawgan Porth
Wadebridge
CORNWALL
Bodmin
A38
Liskeard
St Mawgan
Porth
Lanhydrock
St Dominick
Newquay
A392
Lostwithiel
A391
Pelynt
Polkerris
Torpoint
A30
St. Austell
Fowey
Looe
PLYMOUTH
Mithian
Carlyon Bay
St Agnes
Truro
Redruth
Tolverne
Feock
St Ives
Camborne
Philleigh
Mylor Bridge
A394
Penzance
Perranuthnoe
Falmouth
Constantine
Sennen Cove
St Michael's Mount
Mawnan Smith
Helston
Land's End
Mawgan
Mullion
South West England
0 5 10 miles
0 5 10 15 kms
© Leading Guides Ltd.

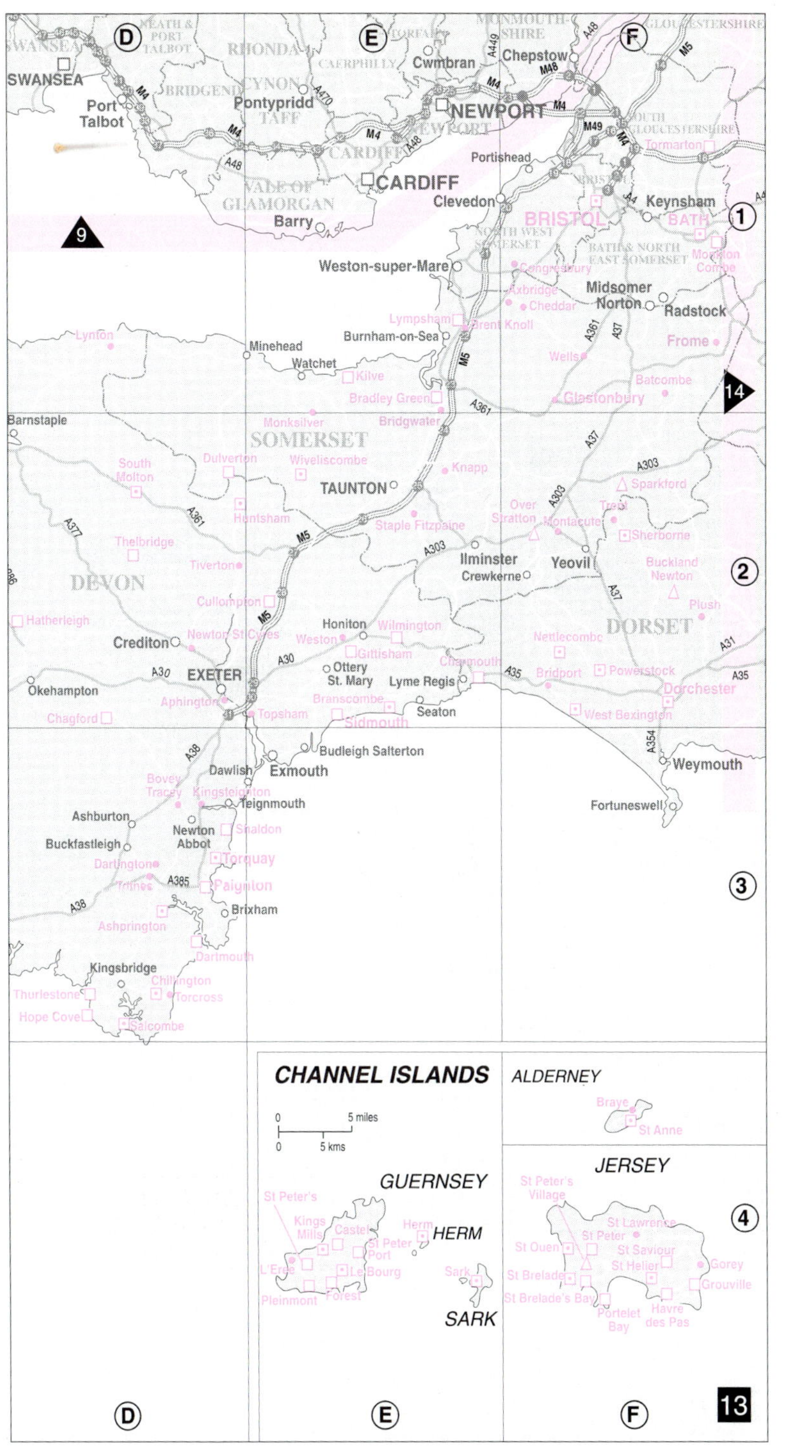
D
E
F
SWANSEA
Port Talbot
Pontypridd
Cwmbran
Chepstow
NEWPORT
CARDIFF
Barry
Portishead
Clevedon
Keynsham
BRISTOL
BATH
Weston-super-Mare
Midsomer Norton
Radstock
Frome
Wells
Glastonbury
Minehead
Watchet
Burnham-on-Sea
Lynton
Barnstaple
SOMERSET
TAUNTON
DEVON
Ilminster
Crewkerne
Yeovil
DORSET
Honiton
Crediton
EXETER
Okehampton
Ottery St. Mary
Lyme Regis
Seaton
Sidmouth
Budleigh Salterton
Exmouth
Dawlish
Teignmouth
Newton Abbot
Ashburton
Buckfastleigh
Torquay
Paignton
Brixham
Dartmouth
Kingsbridge
Salcombe
Weymouth
Fortuneswell
Dorchester
Bridport
Sherborne
CHANNEL ISLANDS
ALDERNEY
Braye
St Anne
GUERNSEY
St Peter's
Kings Mills
Castel
St Peter Port
L'Eree
Le Bourg
Pleinmont
Forest
HERM
Herm
SARK
Sark
JERSEY
St Peter's Village
St Lawrence
St Peter
St Ouen
St Saviour
St Helier
Gorey
St Brelade
Grouville
St Brelade's Bay
Portelet Bay
Havre des Pas
0 5 miles
0 5 kms
9
14
1
2
3
4

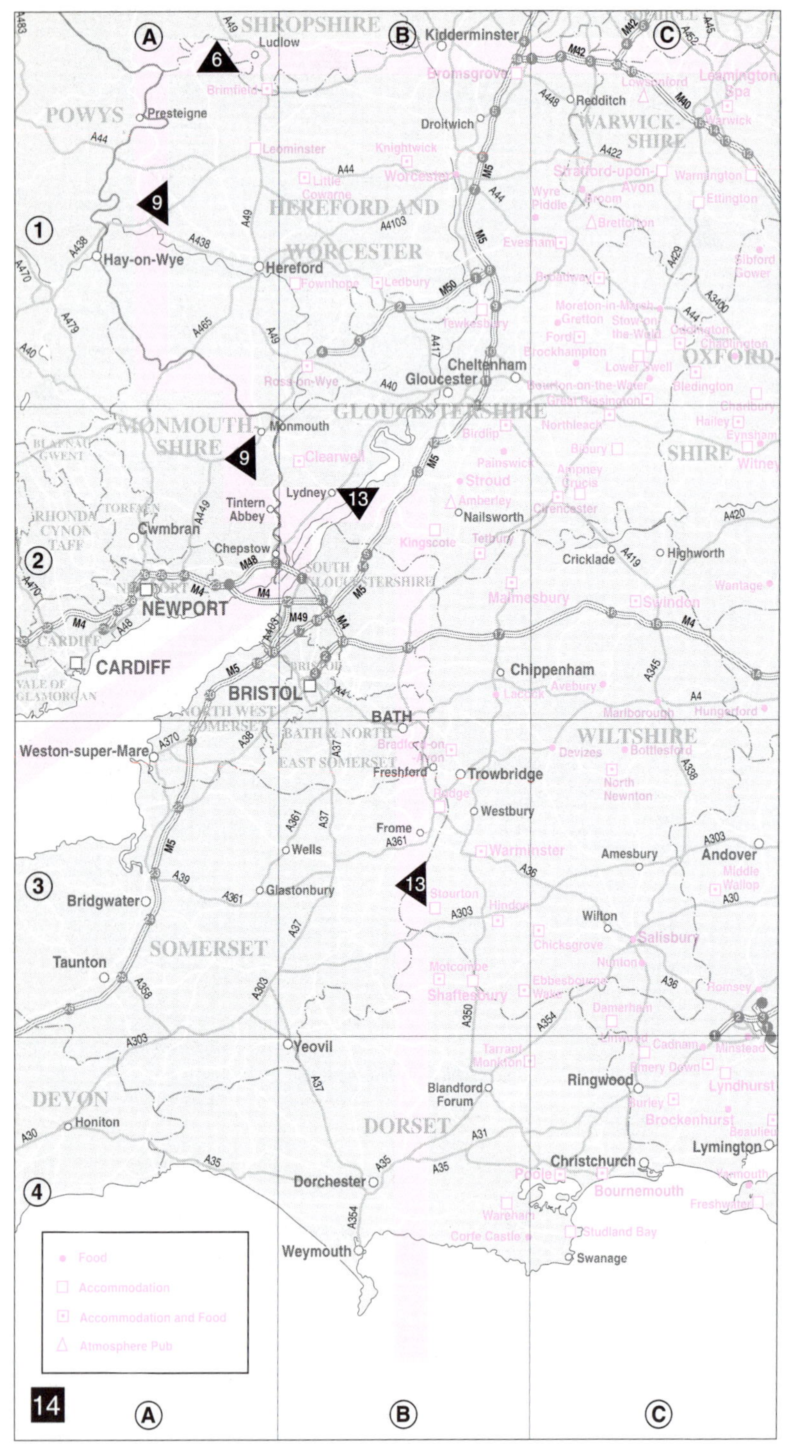

SHROPSHIRE
Ludlow
Kidderminster
Bromsgrove
Brimfield
Redditch
Lowsonford
Leamington Spa
Warwick
POWYS
Presteigne
Droitwich
WARWICK-SHIRE
Leominster
Knightwick
Worcester
Little Cowarne
Stratford-upon-Avon
Warmington
Wyre Piddle
Broom
Ettington
Bretforton
HEREFORD AND WORCESTER
Evesham
Hay-on-Wye
Hereford
Fownhope
Ledbury
Broadway
Sibford Gower
Moreton-in-Marsh
Gretton
Stow-on-the-Wold
Ford
Tewkesbury
Chadlington
Brockhampton
Lower Swell
OXFORD-SHIRE
Cheltenham
Gloucester
Ross-on-Wye
Bourton-on-the-Water
Great Rissington
Bledington
Charlbury
Hailey
Eynsham
Witney
GLOUCESTERSHIRE
MONMOUTH-SHIRE
Monmouth
BLAENAU GWENT
Clearwell
Birdlip
Northleach
Bibury
Painswick
Stroud
Ampney Crucis
Amberley
Nailsworth
Cirencester
Lydney
Tintern Abbey
RHONDDA CYNON TAFF
TORFAEN
Cwmbran
Chepstow
Kingscote
Tetbury
Cricklade
Highworth
SOUTH GLOUCESTERSHIRE
Malmesbury
Wantage
NEWPORT
Swindon
CARDIFF
Chippenham
Avebury
Lacock
BRISTOL
VALE OF GLAMORGAN
NORTH WEST SOMERSET
BATH
BATH & NORTH EAST SOMERSET
Marlborough
Hungerford
Weston-super-Mare
Bradford-on-Avon
WILTSHIRE
Devizes
Bottlesford
Freshford
Trowbridge
North Newnton
Westbury
Frome
Wells
Warminster
Amesbury
Andover
Middle Wallop
Glastonbury
Stourton
Hindon
Bridgwater
Wilton
Salisbury
Chicksgrove
SOMERSET
Nunton
Taunton
Motcombe
Shaftesbury
Ebbesbourne Wake
Romsey
Damerham
Yeovil
Tarrant Monkton
Cadnam
Minstead
Ringwood
Lyndhurst
Blandford Forum
DEVON
Honiton
Burley
Brockenhurst
DORSET
Lymington
Christchurch
Poole
Bournemouth
Dorchester
Wareham
Freshwater
Weymouth
Corfe Castle
Studland Bay
Swanage
Food
Accommodation
Accommodation and Food
Atmosphere Pub
14

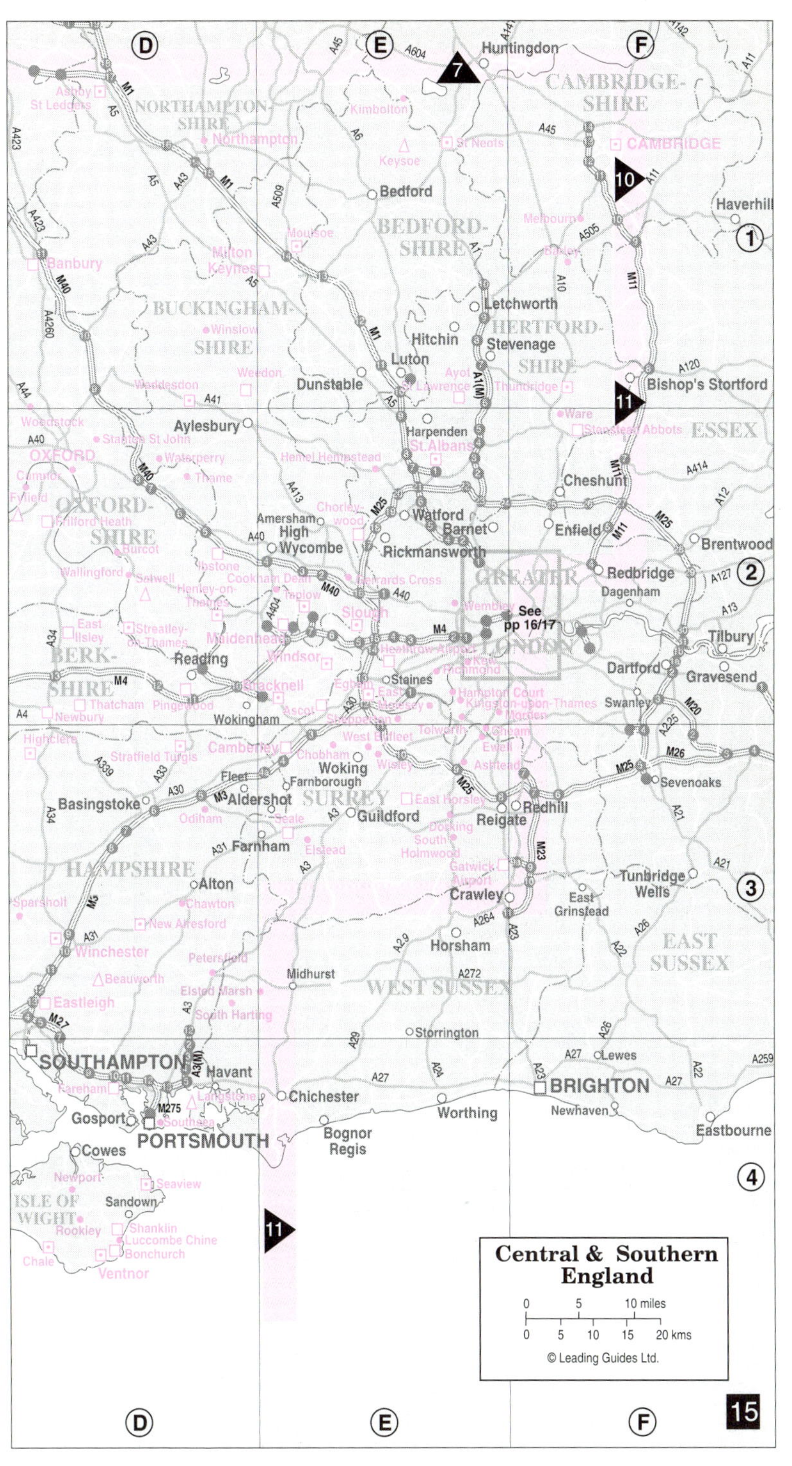

Central & Southern England
0 5 10 miles
0 5 10 15 20 kms
© Leading Guides Ltd.
D
E
F
1
2
3
4
7
10
11
11
15
Huntingdon
CAMBRIDGE-SHIRE
CAMBRIDGE
Haverhill
NORTHAMPTON-SHIRE
Northampton
Ashby St Ledgers
Kimbolton
St Neots
Keysoe
Bedford
BEDFORD-SHIRE
Moulsoe
Melbourn
Barley
Banbury
Milton Keynes
BUCKINGHAM-SHIRE
Winslow
Letchworth
Hitchin
HERTFORD-SHIRE
Stevenage
Luton
Dunstable
Weedon
Waddesdon
Ayot St Lawrence
Thundridge
Bishop's Stortford
Ware
Stansted Abbots
ESSEX
Woodstock
Aylesbury
Harpenden
St.Albans
Stanton St John
OXFORD
Waterperry
Thame
Hemel Hempstead
Cumnor
Fyfield
Cheshunt
OXFORD-SHIRE
Frilford Heath
Burcot
Amersham
Chorley-wood
Watford
Barnet
Enfield
High Wycombe
Rickmansworth
Brentwood
Ibstone
Wallingford
Satwell
Henley-on-Thames
Cookham Dean
Gerrards Cross
GREATER LONDON
Redbridge
Dagenham
Taplow
Slough
Wembley
See pp 16/17
East Ilsley
Streatley-on-Thames
Maidenhead
Tilbury
BERK-SHIRE
Reading
Windsor
Heathrow Airport
Kew
Richmond
Dartford
Gravesend
Staines
Egham
Bracknell
East Molesey
Hampton Court
Kingston-upon-Thames
Swanley
Newbury
Thatcham
Pingewood
Ascot
Shepperton
Morden
Wokingham
Highclere
Tolworth
Cheam
West Byfleet
Camberley
Ewell
Stratfield Turgis
Chobham
Wisley
Ashtead
Woking
Farnborough
Fleet
Sevenoaks
Basingstoke
Aldershot
SURREY
East Horsley
Redhill
Odiham
Seale
Guildford
Reigate
Dorking
Farnham
Elstead
South Holmwood
HAMPSHIRE
Gatwick Airport
Alton
Tunbridge Wells
Crawley
Sparsholt
Chawton
East Grinstead
New Alresford
Winchester
Horsham
EAST SUSSEX
Petersfield
Beauworth
Midhurst
WEST SUSSEX
Elsted Marsh
Eastleigh
South Harting
Storrington
SOUTHAMPTON
Havant
Lewes
Fareham
Langstone
Chichester
BRIGHTON
Worthing
Newhaven
Gosport
Southsea
Bognor Regis
Eastbourne
PORTSMOUTH
Cowes
Newport
Seaview
ISLE OF WIGHT
Sandown
Rookley
Shanklin
Luccombe Chine
Chale
Bonchurch
Ventnor
M1
M4
M11
M20
M23
M25
M26
M27
M275
M3
M40
A1(M)
A3(M)

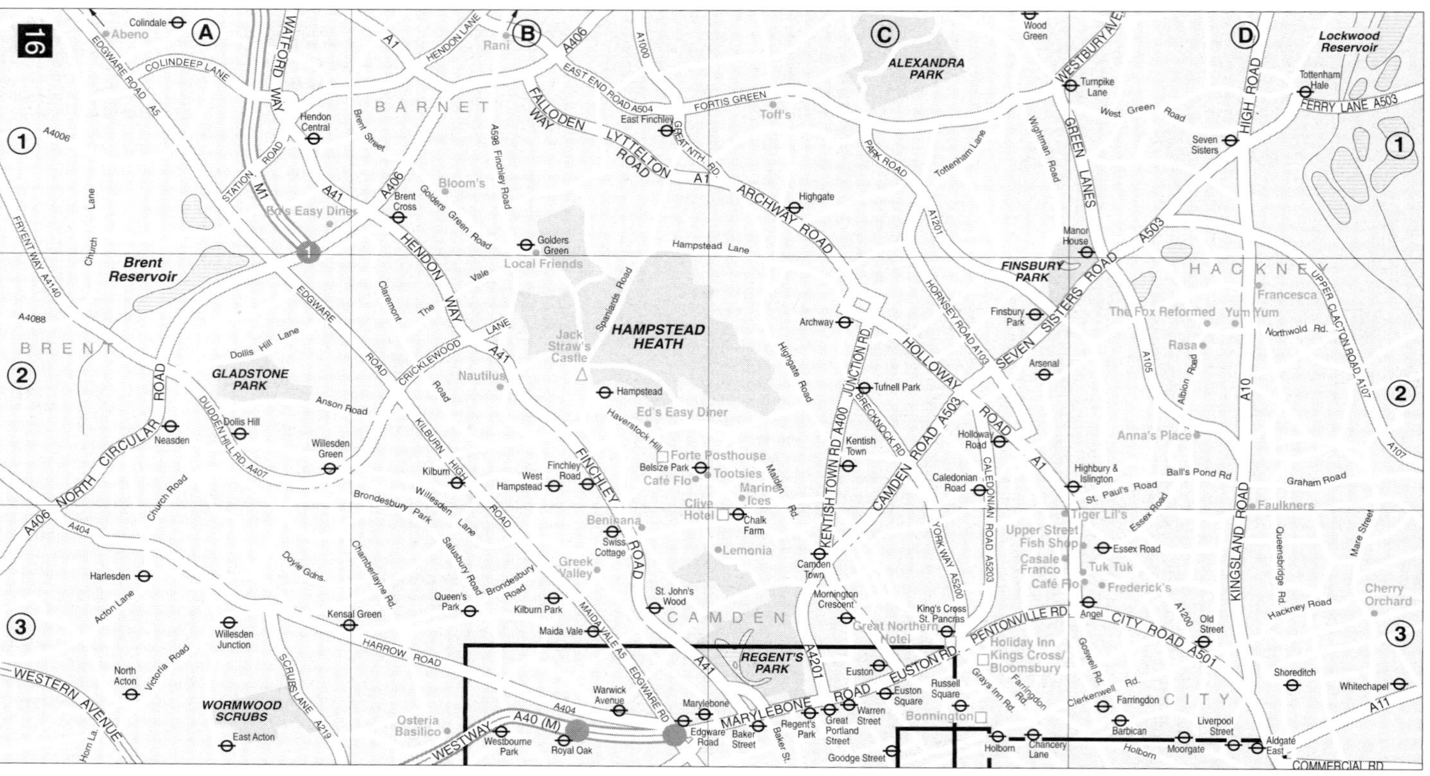
16
A
B
C
D
1
2
3
BARNET
BRENT
CAMDEN
HACKNEY
CITY
Brent Reservoir
GLADSTONE PARK
WORMWOOD SCRUBS
HAMPSTEAD HEATH
ALEXANDRA PARK
FINSBURY PARK
REGENT'S PARK
Lockwood Reservoir
Colindale
Abeno
Hendon Central
Brent Cross
Golders Green
Highgate
East Finchley
Archway
Tufnell Park
Kentish Town
Hampstead
Belsize Park
Chalk Farm
Camden Town
Mornington Crescent
Swiss Cottage
Finchley Road
West Hampstead
Kilburn
Kilburn Park
Queen's Park
Maida Vale
St. John's Wood
Neasden
Dollis Hill
Willesden Green
Kensal Green
Willesden Junction
Harlesden
North Acton
East Acton
Westbourne Park
Royal Oak
Warwick Avenue
Edgware Road
Marylebone
Baker Street
Regent's Park
Great Portland Street
Warren Street
Euston Square
Euston
Russell Square
King's Cross St. Pancras
Goodge Street
Holborn
Chancery Lane
Farringdon
Barbican
Moorgate
Liverpool Street
Aldgate East
Whitechapel
Shoreditch
Old Street
Angel
Essex Road
Highbury & Islington
Caledonian Road
Holloway Road
Arsenal
Finsbury Park
Manor House
Turnpike Lane
Wood Green
Seven Sisters
Tottenham Hale
Rani
Bloom's
Ed's Easy Diner
Local Friends
Toff's
Jack Straw's Castle
Nautilus
Forte Posthouse
Tootsies
Café Flo
Marine Ices
Clive Hotel
Benihana
Lemonia
Greek Valley
Osteria Basilico
Great Northern Hotel
Holiday Inn Kings Cross/ Bloomsbury
Bonnington
Upper Street Fish Shop
Casale Franco
Tiger Lil's
Tuk Tuk
Frederick's
Anna's Place
The Fox Reformed
Yum Yum
Rasa
Francesca
Faulkners
Cherry Orchard
EDGWARE ROAD A5
COLINDEEP LANE
WATFORD WAY
STATION ROAD
M1
A41
A406
A1
HENDON LANE
Brent Street
A598 Finchley Road
Golders Green Road
HENDON WAY
FALLODEN WAY
LYTTELTON ROAD
EAST END ROAD A504
GREAT NTH. RD
FORTIS GREEN
A1000
ARCHWAY ROAD
Hampstead Lane
Highgate Road
PARK ROAD
Tottenham Lane
A1201
Wightman Road
GREEN LANES
WESTBURY AVE
West Green Road
HIGH ROAD
FERRY LANE A503
SEVEN SISTERS ROAD
A503
A105
Albion Road
A10
UPPER CLACTON ROAD A107
Northwold Rd.
Graham Road
Ball's Pond Rd
KINGSLAND ROAD
Queensbridge Rd.
Mare Street
Hackney Road
HOLLOWAY ROAD
HORNSEY ROAD A103
JUNCTION RD.
KENTISH TOWN RD A400
BRECKNOCK RD
CAMDEN ROAD A503
CALEDONIAN ROAD A5203
YORK WAY A5200
St. Paul's Road
Essex Road
A1200
CITY ROAD A501
PENTONVILLE RD.
EUSTON RD.
MARYLEBONE ROAD
A4201
Goswell Rd.
Clerkenwell Rd.
Farringdon Rd.
Grays Inn Rd.
Holborn
A11
COMMERCIAL RD
Spaniards Road
Haverstock Hill
Malden Rd.
FINCHLEY ROAD
A41
The Vale
CRICKLEWOOD LANE
Claremont Road
EDGWARE ROAD
KILBURN HIGH ROAD
MAIDA VALE A5
EDGWARE RD
Willesden Lane
Brondesbury Park
Brondesbury Road
Salusbury Road
Chamberlayne Rd.
HARROW ROAD
Anson Road
Dollis Hill Lane
DUDDEN HILL RD. A407
NORTH CIRCULAR ROAD
Church Road
Church Lane
FRYENT WAY A4140
A4006
A4088
A406
A404
Doyle Gdns.
Acton Lane
Victoria Road
WESTERN AVENUE
Horn La.
SCRUBS LANE A219
A40 (M)
WESTWAY
A404
Baker St.

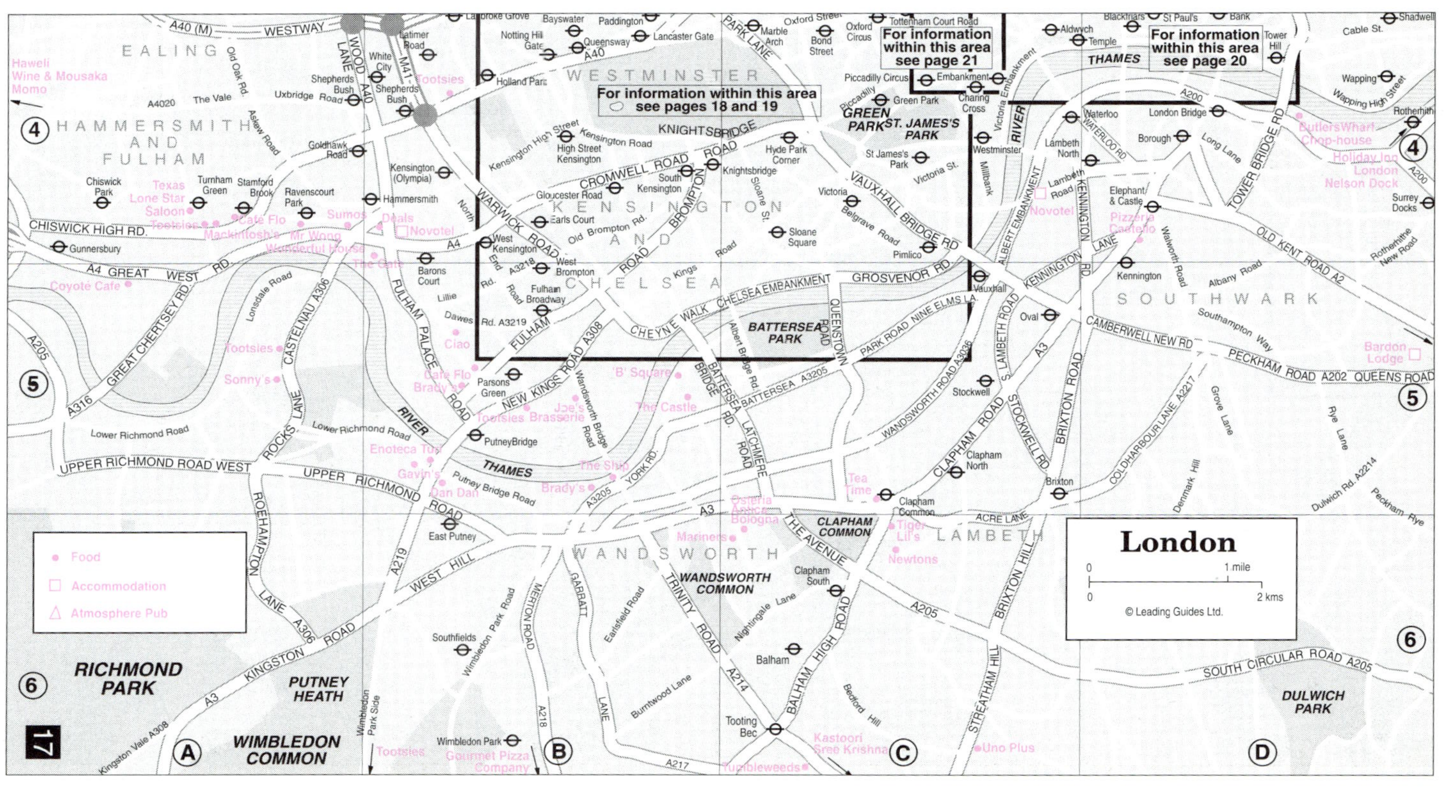
London
0
1 mile
0
2 kms
© Leading Guides Ltd.
Food
Accommodation
Atmosphere Pub
For information within this area see pages 18 and 19
For information within this area see page 21
For information within this area see page 20
EALING
HAMMERSMITH AND FULHAM
WESTMINSTER
KENSINGTON AND CHELSEA
SOUTHWARK
WANDSWORTH
LAMBETH
RICHMOND PARK
PUTNEY HEATH
WIMBLEDON COMMON
WANDSWORTH COMMON
CLAPHAM COMMON
BATTERSEA PARK
GREEN PARK
ST. JAMES'S PARK
DULWICH PARK
RIVER THAMES
Haweli
Wine & Mousaka
Momo
Texas Lone Star Saloon
Tootsies
Cafe Flo
Mackintosh's
Mr Wong
Wonderful House
Sumos
Deals
Novotel
The Cafe
Coyote Cafe
Sonny's
Ciao
Brady's
'B' Square
The Castle
Joe's Brasserie
Enoteca Turi
Gavin's
Dan Dan
The Ship
Tea Time
Osteria Antica Bologna
Mariners
Tiger Lil's
Newtons
Kastoori
Sree Krishna
Tumbleweeds
Uno Plus
Gourmet Pizza Company
Pizzeria Castello
Bardon Lodge
ButlersWharf Chop-house
Holiday Inn London Nelson Dock
A B C D
4 5 6
17

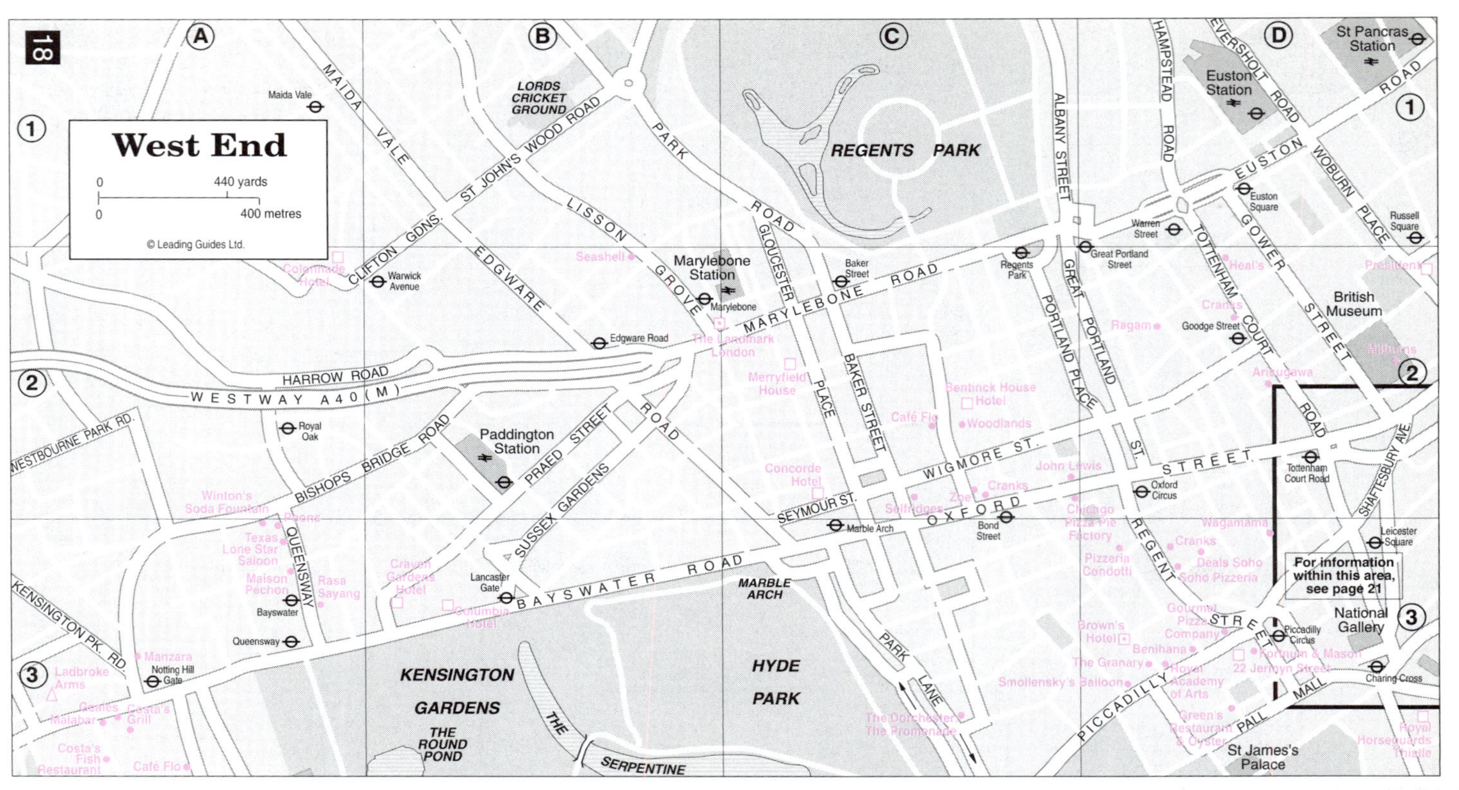

West End
0
440 yards
0
400 metres
© Leading Guides Ltd.
A
B
C
D
1
2
3
Maida Vale
MAIDA VALE
LORDS CRICKET GROUND
ST JOHN'S WOOD ROAD
PARK ROAD
REGENTS PARK
ALBANY STREET
HAMPSTEAD ROAD
Euston Station
EVERSHOLT ROAD
St Pancras Station
ROAD
EUSTON
Euston Square
WOBURN PLACE
Russell Square
Warren Street
Great Portland Street
TOTTENHAM COURT ROAD
GOWER STREET
Heal's
President
British Museum
Cranks
Goodge Street
Ragam
Arisugawa
CLIFTON GDNS.
Warwick Avenue
Colonnade Hotel
EDGWARE ROAD
LISSON GROVE
Seashell
Marylebone Station
Marylebone
GLOUCESTER PLACE
Baker Street
MARYLEBONE ROAD
Regents Park
GREAT PORTLAND STREET
PORTLAND PLACE
Edgware Road
The Landmark London
Merryfield House
BAKER STREET
Café Flo
Bentinck House Hotel
Woodlands
HARROW ROAD
WESTWAY A40(M)
WESTBOURNE PARK RD.
Royal Oak
BISHOPS BRIDGE ROAD
Paddington Station
PRAED STREET
SUSSEX GARDENS
Concorde Hotel
WIGMORE ST.
John Lewis
ST.
OXFORD STREET
Tottenham Court Road
SHAFTESBURY AVE.
Winton's Soda Fountain
Poons
Texas Lone Star Saloon
QUEENSWAY
Maison Pechon
Rasa Sayang
Bayswater
Queensway
Craven Gardens Hotel
Lancaster Gate
Columbia Hotel
BAYSWATER ROAD
SEYMOUR ST.
Marble Arch
Selfridges
Zoe
Cranks
Bond Street
Chicago Pizza Pie Factory
Oxford Circus
Wagamama
REGENT STREET
Cranks
Deals Soho
Soho Pizzeria
Pizzeria Condotti
Leicester Square
For information within this area, see page 21
MARBLE ARCH
KENSINGTON PK. RD.
Manzara
Notting Hill Gate
Ladbroke Arms
Geales
Malabar
Costa's Grill
Costa's Fish Restaurant
Café Flo
KENSINGTON GARDENS
THE ROUND POND
THE SERPENTINE
HYDE PARK
PARK LANE
The Dorchester
The Promenade
Brown's Hotel
The Granary
Smollensky's Balloon
Benihana
Gourmet Pizza Company
Royal Academy of Arts
Piccadilly Circus
Fortnum & Mason
22 Jermyn Street
National Gallery
Charing Cross
PICCADILLY
PALL MALL
Green's Restaurant & Oyster
St James's Palace
Royal Horseguards Thistle

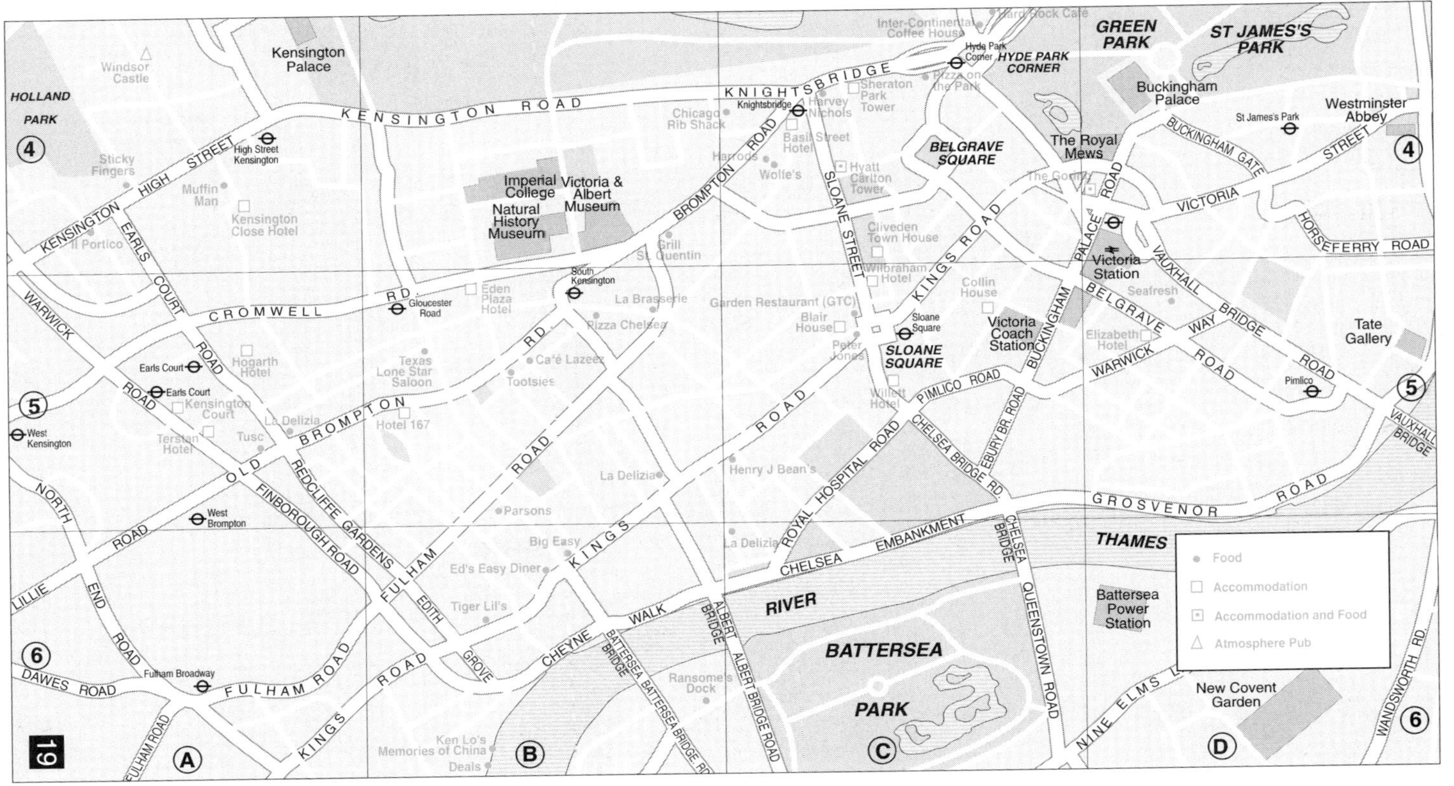
19
HOLLAND PARK
Windsor Castle
Kensington Palace
Sticky Fingers
Muffin Man
Kensington Close Hotel
Il Portico
High Street Kensington
KENSINGTON HIGH STREET
KENSINGTON ROAD
EARLS COURT ROAD
Earls Court
Kensington Court
Hogarth Hotel
Terstan Hotel
Tusc
La Delizia
West Kensington
WARWICK
NORTH END ROAD
LILLIE ROAD
DAWES ROAD
FULHAM ROAD
Fulham Broadway
West Brompton
OLD BROMPTON ROAD
FINBOROUGH ROAD
REDCLIFFE GARDENS
CROMWELL RD.
Gloucester Road
Imperial College
Victoria & Albert Museum
Natural History Museum
South Kensington
Eden Plaza Hotel
Texas Lone Star Saloon
Hotel 167
Tootsies
Café Lazeez
Pizza Chelsea
La Brasserie
Grill St Quentin
BROMPTON ROAD
FULHAM ROAD
Parsons
Big Easy
Ed's Easy Diner
Tiger Lil's
La Delizia
EDITH GROVE
CHEYNE WALK
KINGS ROAD
BATTERSEA BRIDGE
BATTERSEA BRIDGE RD
Ransome's Dock
Ken Lo's Memories of China
Deals
Chicago Rib Shack
Harrods
Wolfe's
Knightsbridge
KNIGHTSBRIDGE
Harvey Nichols
Basil Street Hotel
Hyatt Carlton Tower
Sheraton Park Tower
Inter-Continental Coffee House
Hard Rock Cafe
Hyde Park Corner
HYDE PARK CORNER
Pizza on the Park
SLOANE STREET
Cliveden Town House
Wilbraham Hotel
Garden Restaurant (GTC)
Blair House
Peter Jones
Sloane Square
SLOANE SQUARE
Willett Hotel
Henry J Bean's
La Delizia
ROYAL HOSPITAL ROAD
CHELSEA EMBANKMENT
ALBERT BRIDGE
ALBERT BRIDGE ROAD
RIVER
BATTERSEA PARK
CHELSEA BRIDGE
CHELSEA BRIDGE RD.
QUEENSTOWN ROAD
BELGRAVE SQUARE
Collin House
Victoria Coach Station
PIMLICO ROAD
EBURY BR. ROAD
BUCKINGHAM PALACE ROAD
The Royal Mews
The Goring
Victoria Station
Seafresh
Elizabeth Hotel
BELGRAVE ROAD
WARWICK WAY
VAUXHALL BRIDGE ROAD
GROSVENOR ROAD
THAMES
Battersea Power Station
NINE ELMS LANE
New Covent Garden
WANDSWORTH RD.
GREEN PARK
ST JAMES'S PARK
Buckingham Palace
BUCKINGHAM GATE
St James's Park
Westminster Abbey
VICTORIA STREET
HORSEFERRY ROAD
Tate Gallery
Pimlico
VAUXHALL BRIDGE
Food
Accommodation
Accommodation and Food
Atmosphere Pub
A
B
C
D
4
5
6

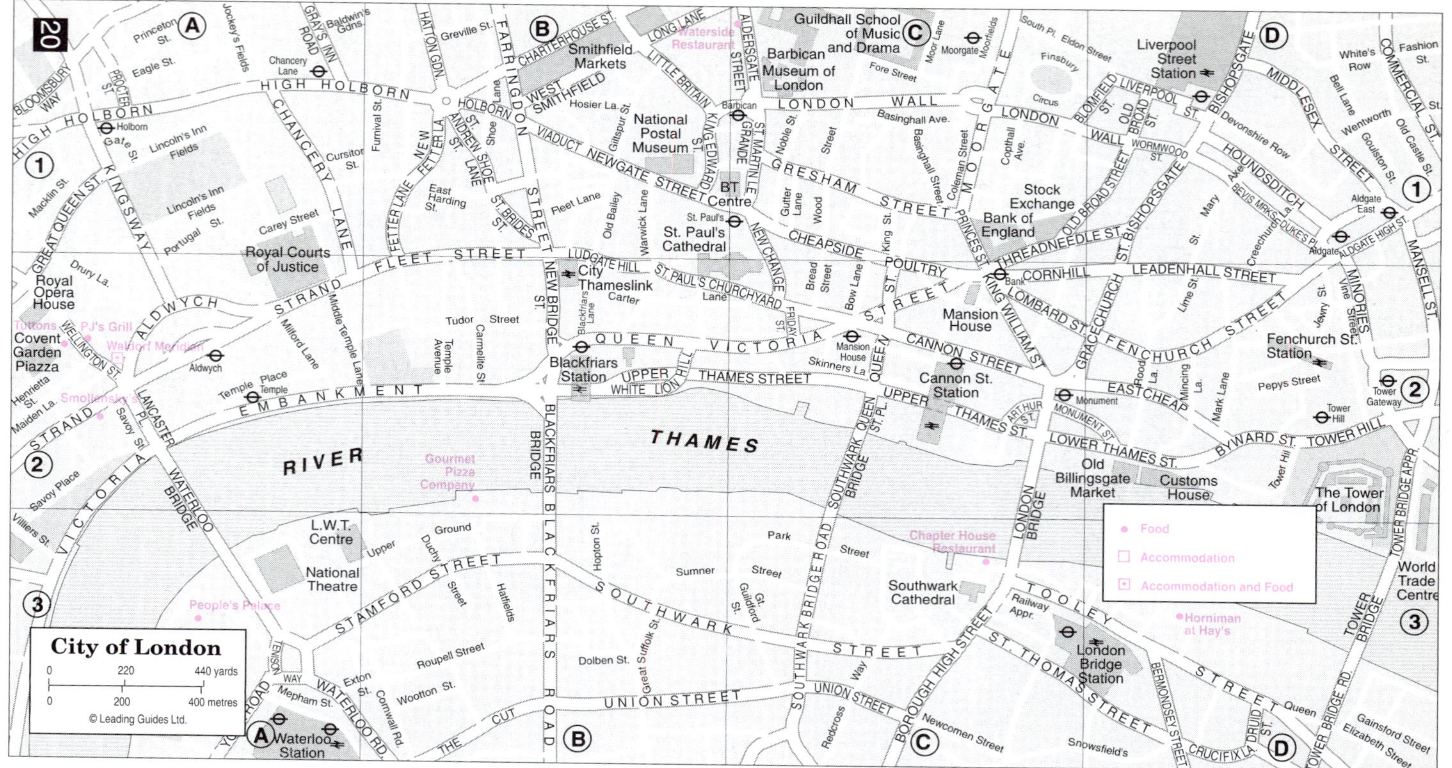

City of London
0 220 440 yards
0 200 400 metres
© Leading Guides Ltd.
Food
Accommodation
Accommodation and Food
Royal Opera House
Covent Garden Piazza
Tuttons
PJ's Grill
Waldorf Meridien
Smollensky's
Aldwych
Royal Courts of Justice
Lincoln's Inn Fields
Holborn
Chancery Lane
Smithfield Markets
Waterside Restaurant
National Postal Museum
St. Paul's Cathedral
City Thameslink
Blackfriars Station
Barbican
Museum of London
Guildhall School of Music and Drama
BT Centre
Mansion House
Bank of England
Stock Exchange
Cannon St. Station
Monument
Liverpool Street Station
Fenchurch St. Station
Aldgate
Aldgate East
Tower Hill
Tower Gateway
The Tower of London
World Trade Centre
Old Billingsgate Market
Customs House
London Bridge Station
Southwark Cathedral
Chapter House Restaurant
Horniman at Hay's
Gourmet Pizza Company
L.W.T. Centre
National Theatre
People's Palace
Waterloo Station
RIVER THAMES
FLEET STREET
STRAND
HIGH HOLBORN
KINGSWAY
LONDON WALL
QUEEN VICTORIA STREET
UPPER THAMES STREET
LONDON BRIDGE
BLACKFRIARS BRIDGE
WATERLOO BRIDGE
SOUTHWARK STREET
TOOLEY STREET
BOROUGH HIGH STREET

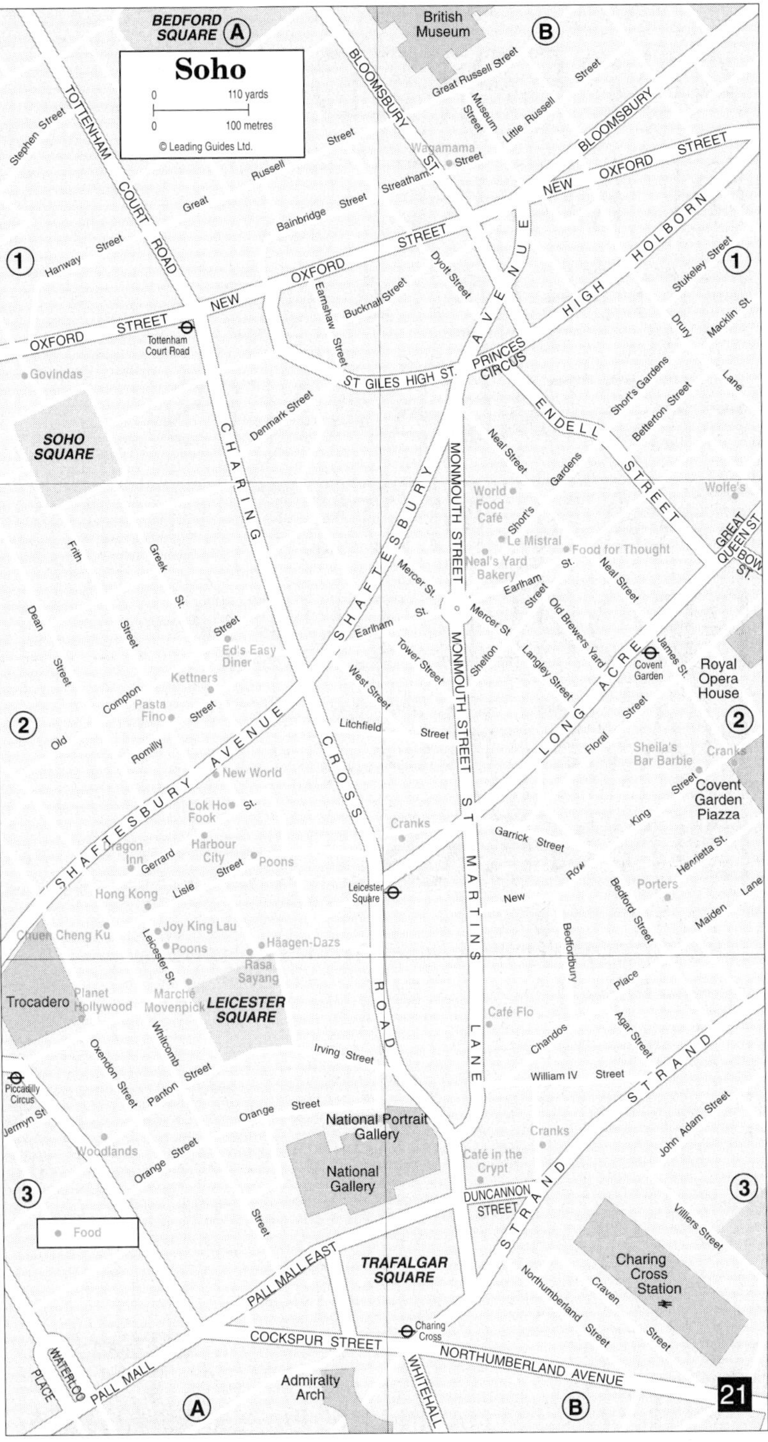
Soho
0 110 yards
0 100 metres
© Leading Guides Ltd.
BEDFORD SQUARE
British Museum
A
B
1
2
3
Stephen Street
TOTTENHAM COURT ROAD
Great Russell Street
Hanway Street
Bainbridge Street
Streatham Street
BLOOMSBURY ST.
Great Russell Street
Museum Street
Little Russell Street
BLOOMSBURY
Wagamama
NEW OXFORD STREET
OXFORD STREET
Tottenham Court Road
Earnshaw Street
Bucknall Street
Dyott Street
HIGH HOLBORN
Stukeley Street
Drury Lane
Macklin St.
ST GILES HIGH ST.
PRINCES CIRCUS
Govindas
SOHO SQUARE
Denmark Street
CHARING CROSS ROAD
SHAFTESBURY AVENUE
MONMOUTH STREET
Neal Street
ENDELL STREET
Short's Gardens
Betterton Street
World Food Café
Short's Gardens
Le Mistral
Food for Thought
Neal's Yard Bakery
Wolfe's
GREAT QUEEN ST.
BOW ST.
Frith Street
Greek St.
Dean Street
Mercer St.
Earlham St.
Earlham Street
Neal Street
Old Brewers Yard
Ed's Easy Diner
Kettners
Tower Street
West Street
Shelton Street
Langley Street
Covent Garden
James St.
Royal Opera House
Compton Street
Old Compton Street
Pasta Fino
Litchfield Street
LONG ACRE
Floral Street
Romilly Street
New World
Sheila's Bar Barbie
Cranks
Covent Garden Piazza
King Street
Lok Ho Fook
Dragon Inn
Harbour City
Cranks
Garrick Street
Gerrard Street
Poons
ST MARTINS LANE
Rose Street
Henrietta St.
Hong Kong
Lisle Street
Leicester Square
Bedford Street
Porters
Maiden Lane
New Row
Chuen Cheng Ku
Joy King Lau
Leicester St.
Poons
Häagen-Dazs
Bedfordbury
Rasa Sayang
Trocadero
Planet Hollywood
Marché Movenpick
LEICESTER SQUARE
Place
Café Flo
Agar Street
Oxendon Street
Whitcomb Street
Irving Street
Chandos
William IV Street
STRAND
Piccadilly Circus
Jermyn St
Panton Street
Orange Street
National Portrait Gallery
Cranks
John Adam Street
Woodlands
Orange Street
National Gallery
Café in the Crypt
DUNCANNON STREET
Food
Street
Villiers Street
Charing Cross Station
TRAFALGAR SQUARE
PALL MALL EAST
Northumberland Street
Craven Street
Charing Cross
COCKSPUR STREET
NORTHUMBERLAND AVENUE
WATERLOO PLACE
PALL MALL
Admiralty Arch
WHITEHALL

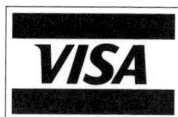

Index

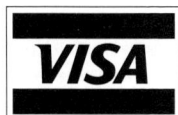

Readers' Comments

Please use this sheet, and the continuation overleaf, to recommend establishments of **really outstanding quality** and to comment on existing entries.
Complaints about any of the Guide's entries will be treated seriously and passed on to our inspectorate, but we would like to remind you always to take up your complaint with the management at the time. We regret that owing to the volume of readers' communications received each year we will be unable to acknowledge these forms, but your comments will certainly be seriously considered.

Please post to:
Egon Ronay's Guides, 77 St John Street, London EC1M 4AN

or contact our web site at:
http://www.egon-ronay.infocomint.com

Please use an up-to-date Guide. We publish annually. (...and Children Come Too 1997)

Name and address of establishment	**Your recommendation or complaint**

Name and address of establishment

Your recommendation or complaint

Your name and address *(BLOCK CAPITALS PLEASE)*

Readers' Comments

Please use this sheet, and the continuation overleaf, to recommend establishments of **really outstanding quality** and to comment on existing entries. Complaints about any of the Guide's entries will be treated seriously and passed on to our inspectorate, but we would like to remind you always to take up your complaint with the management at the time. We regret that owing to the volume of readers' communications received each year we will be unable to acknowledge these forms, but your comments will certainly be seriously considered.

Please post to:
Egon Ronay's Guides, 77 St John Street, London EC1M 4AN
or contact our web site at:
http://www.egon-ronay.infocomint.com

Please use an up-to-date Guide. We publish annually. (...and Children Come Too 1997)

Name and address of establishment	**Your recommendation or complaint**

Name and address of establishment | **Your recommendation or complaint**

Your name and address *(BLOCK CAPITALS PLEASE)*

Readers' Comments

Please use this sheet, and the continuation overleaf, to recommend establishments of **really outstanding quality** and to comment on existing entries.
Complaints about any of the Guide's entries will be treated seriously and passed on to our inspectorate, but we would like to remind you always to take up your complaint with the management at the time. We regret that owing to the volume of readers' communications received each year we will be unable to acknowledge these forms, but your comments will certainly be seriously considered.

Please post to:
Egon Ronay's Guides, 77 St John Street, London EC1M 4AN
or contact our web site at:
http://www.egon-ronay.infocomint.com

Please use an up-to-date Guide. We publish annually. (...and Children Come Too 1997)

Name and address of establishment | **Your recommendation or complaint**

Name and address of establishment	Your recommendation or complaint

Your name and address *(BLOCK CAPITALS PLEASE)*

READERS' COMMENTS

Please use this sheet, and the continuation overleaf, to recommend establishments of **really outstanding quality** and to comment on existing entries. Complaints about any of the Guide's entries will be treated seriously and passed on to our inspectorate, but we would like to remind you always to take up your complaint with the management at the time. We regret that owing to the volume of readers' communications received each year we will be unable to acknowledge these forms, but your comments will certainly be seriously considered.

Please post to:
Egon Ronay's Guides, 77 St John Street, London EC1M 4AN

or contact our web site at:
http://www.egon-ronay.infocomint.com

Please use an up-to-date Guide. We publish annually. (...and Children Come Too 1997)

Name and address of establishment	Your recommendation or complaint

Name and address of establishment	Your recommendation or complaint

Your name and address *(BLOCK CAPITALS PLEASE)*

Readers' Comments

Please use this sheet, and the continuation overleaf, to recommend establishments of **really outstanding quality** and to comment on existing entries. Complaints about any of the Guide's entries will be treated seriously and passed on to our inspectorate, but we would like to remind you always to take up your complaint with the management at the time. We regret that owing to the volume of readers' communications received each year we will be unable to acknowledge these forms, but your comments will certainly be seriously considered.

Please post to:
Egon Ronay's Guides, 77 St John Street, London EC1M 4AN

or contact our web site at:
http://www.egon-ronay.infocomint.com

Please use an up-to-date Guide. We publish annually. (...and Children Come Too 1997)

Name and address of establishment	**Your recommendation or complaint**

Name and address of establishment	Your recommendation or complaint

Your name and address *(BLOCK CAPITALS PLEASE)*

Readers' Comments

Please use this sheet, and the continuation overleaf, to recommend establishments of **really outstanding quality** and to comment on existing entries. Complaints about any of the Guide's entries will be treated seriously and passed on to our inspectorate, but we would like to remind you always to take up your complaint with the management at the time. We regret that owing to the volume of readers' communications received each year we will be unable to acknowledge these forms, but your comments will certainly be seriously considered.

Please post to:
Egon Ronay's Guides, 77 St John Street, London EC1M 4AN

or contact our web site at:
http://www.egon-ronay.infocomint.com

Please use an up-to-date Guide. We publish annually. (...and Children Come Too 1997)

Name and address of establishment	**Your recommendation or complaint**

Name and address of establishment

Your recommendation or complaint

Your name and address *(BLOCK CAPITALS PLEASE)*

Readers' Comments

Please use this sheet, and the continuation overleaf, to recommend establishments of **really outstanding quality** and to comment on existing entries. Complaints about any of the Guide's entries will be treated seriously and passed on to our inspectorate, but we would like to remind you always to take up your complaint with the management at the time. We regret that owing to the volume of readers' communications received each year we will be unable to acknowledge these forms, but your comments will certainly be seriously considered.

Please post to:

Egon Ronay's Guides, 77 St John Street, London EC1M 4AN

or contact our web site at:

http://www.egon-ronay.infocomint.com

Please use an up-to-date Guide. We publish annually. (...and Children Come Too 1997)

Name and address of establishment	**Your recommendation or complaint**

Name and address of establishment | **Your recommendation or complaint**

Your name and address *(BLOCK CAPITALS PLEASE)*

READERS' COMMENTS

Please use this sheet, and the continuation overleaf, to recommend establishments of **really outstanding quality** and to comment on existing entries. Complaints about any of the Guide's entries will be treated seriously and passed on to our inspectorate, but we would like to remind you always to take up your complaint with the management at the time. We regret that owing to the volume of readers' communications received each year we will be unable to acknowledge these forms, but your comments will certainly be seriously considered.

Please post to:
Egon Ronay's Guides, 77 St John Street, London EC1M 4AN
or contact our web site at:
http://www.egon-ronay.infocomint.com

Please use an up-to-date Guide. We publish annually. (...and Children Come Too 1997)

Name and address of establishment	**Your recommendation or complaint**

Name and address of establishment	Your recommendation or complaint

Your name and address *(BLOCK CAPITALS PLEASE)*

Readers' Comments

Please use this sheet, and the continuation overleaf, to recommend establishments of **really outstanding quality** and to comment on existing entries. Complaints about any of the Guide's entries will be treated seriously and passed on to our inspectorate, but we would like to remind you always to take up your complaint with the management at the time. We regret that owing to the volume of readers' communications received each year we will be unable to acknowledge these forms, but your comments will certainly be seriously considered.

Please post to:
Egon Ronay's Guides, 77 St John Street, London EC1M 4AN
or contact our web site at:
http://www.egon-ronay.infocomint.com

Please use an up-to-date Guide. We publish annually. (...and Children Come Too 1997)

Name and address of establishment	**Your recommendation or complaint**

Name and address of establishment

Your recommendation or complaint

Your name and address *(BLOCK CAPITALS PLEASE)*